Introduction to the Profession of Counseling

FOURTH EDITION

Frank A. Nugent
Professor Emeritus
Western Washington University

Karyn Dayle Jones
University of Central Florida

PEARSON

Merrill
Prentice Hall

Upper Saddle River, New Jersey
Columbus, Ohio

Library of Congress Cataloging-in-Publication Data

Nugent, Frank A.
  Introduction to the profession of counseling / Frank A. Nugent and Karyn Dayle Jones.—4th ed.
      p. cm.
  Includes bibliographical references and indexes.
  ISBN 0-13-098218-0
  1. Counseling—Textbooks. I. Jones, Karyn Dayle. II. Title.

  BF637.C6N83 2005
  158'.3—dc22

                                                        2004014014

Vice President and Executive Publisher: Jeffery W. Johnston
Publisher: Kevin M. Davis
Editorial Assistant: Amanda King
Production Editor: Mary Harlan
Production Coordinator: Peggy Hood, GTS
Design Coordinator: Diane C. Lorenzo
Text Design and Illustrations: GTS
Cover Designer: Jason Moore
Cover Image: SuperStock
Production Manager: Laura Messerly
Director of Marketing: Ann Castel Davis
Marketing Manager: Autumn Purdy
Marketing Coordinator: Tyra Poole

This book was set in Garamond by *The GTS Companies*/York, PA Campus. It was printed and bound by
R. R. Donnelley & Sons Company. The cover was printed by Coral Graphics Services, Inc.

Pearson Education Ltd.
Pearson Education Singapore Pte. Ltd.
Pearson Education Canada, Ltd.
Pearson Education—Japan

Pearson Education Australia Pty. Limited
Pearson Education North Asia Ltd.
Pearson Educación de Mexico, S.A. de C.V.
Pearson Education Malaysia Pte. Ltd.

10 9 8 7 6 5 4 3 2 1
ISBN: 0-13-098218-0

To Our Students

Preface

This book presents a comprehensive introduction to professional counseling, a profession that helps individuals, groups, and families work through troubles arising from situational conflicts experienced in everyday life. Professional counselors help people work through transitional periods, an emphasis especially significant during the shift into the new millennium. Counseling as we know it today developed after World War II largely as a result of the need to help veterans cope during their complex transition back into civilian life. Although the original focus was on assisting them with vocational exploration and training, their emotional and developmental needs soon became apparent. Up to that time, mental health treatment had been limited to a narrow range of techniques used either for managing persons who were chronically mentally ill or for exploring the neuroses of persons who were well-to-do. Neither approach was sufficient for working with normally functioning individuals, who, as a whole, have many varieties of complex and troublesome symptoms requiring a wide range of treatment options.

I first sensed the need for helping soldiers work through personal conflicts when I was serving in the U.S. Army during World War II as an educational reconditioning specialist at Stark General Hospital in Charleston, South Carolina, one of the army hospitals that received wounded soldiers returning from European battlefields. My task was to help prepare them, through a reeducation process, to return to civilian life. But these soldiers, who had physical disabilities, were suffering from profound anxieties about going home. None of us on the staff were prepared to cope with their mental anguish. Physicians, nurses, and physical therapists were helping them recover physically, but psychiatrists and psychologists were working elsewhere in the psychiatric wards. In those days it was thought that only people with mental illness needed psychological help. But times were changing. My work with the wounded soldiers prompted me, after the war, to obtain a master's degree in vocational counseling at Columbia University and, a few years later, a PhD in the newly formed program of counseling psychology at the University of California–Berkeley. Graduate programs such as these in the late 1940s and the 1950s were beginning to respond to the psychological needs of the general population.

The profession of counseling psychology, in its infancy after World War II, evolved from a mix of vocational, developmental, educational, and psychological theories and practices. These divergent roots pulled the fledgling profession in different directions over the years as it struggled to define and redefine itself. Throughout this period my own professional outlook and experience developed as well. The philosophy and content of this text are based on these experiences.

Training programs for counselors likewise have evolved, broadened, and deepened: Programs now include a wide variety of counseling approaches based on psychodynamic, humanistic, cognitive, cognitive-behavioral, and postmodern constructivist and social constructionist theories. Programs now attend to the developing self that evolves throughout one's adult life, a self in relation to others, to one's family, and to one's community. Training programs now attend to a person's holistic concerns—the need to nurture one's body, mind, spirit, and soul in a multicultural society. Feminist and ethnic counselors are influencing the profession significantly, particularly in their emphasis on the need to address client and family concerns in relation to the social-cultural context and the community. Increasing numbers of comprehensive neighborhood health care centers have emerged throughout the country to address the needs of individuals and families within the community.

Over the decades, as the counseling profession has adapted to the changing needs of society, it has developed approaches to theory and practice that give counselors the flexibility and depth necessary to work with people living in a multicultural society faced with a broad spectrum of concerns and conflicts. Counselors have thus developed a unique ability to help others work through transitions in a changing, pluralistic world, whether they be age-related developmental transitions; family, career, or spiritual transitions; or transitions related to social-cultural-political factors.

In the last decade changes in the mental health field again have been making new demands on counselors. Recent trends have challenged counselors to reexamine and clarify their role. Ongoing evaluation of the counselor role helps the profession understand how the counselor makes a special contribution to today's mental health field.

In light of societal changes, new postmodern, constructivist, and social constructionist approaches have been receiving increased attention, and there is an increased tendency for the profession to dialogue cross-culturally and with those in different academic disciplines and to work toward integrating diverse theoretical approaches. Training standards, licensing, and certification requirements continue to be raised; collaboration and teamwork continue to increase among counselors and other health care professionals and among the counseling settings in schools, colleges, and community.

OVERVIEW

As with previous editions, this text's philosophical and theoretical orientation to counseling is based on a phenomenological, psychosocial, life-span developmental approach. In this approach counselors help persons resolve or work through situational, developmental transitions and conflicts within a multicultural context. Following is a summary of the text:

- *Part 1: Foundations of Counseling:* The counselor role is defined and clarified, and the way the counselor functions in the various counselor work settings in schools, colleges, and community is described. A historical overview presents the formation of professional guidelines and tells how the profession incorporated new and more comprehensive theories, techniques, and practices to meet the needs of individuals in a changing multicultural society. The chapters on current professional, ethical, and legal issues and on the effective counselor emphasize the profession's responsibility to maintain, monitor, and improve effective counseling practice.

- *Part 2: Theories and Techniques:* Psychological and life-span developmental theories and techniques as they apply to counseling are given comprehensive coverage, including contemporary psychodynamic and Jungian theories, humanistic and cognitive-behavioral theories, constructivist and social constructionist theories, feminist perspectives, spiritual development, and brief counseling. The various ways assessment tools are used, depending on the counselor-client context, are described. Outreach prevention and intervention activities—psychoeducation, consultation, crisis intervention—are discussed as important adjuncts to counseling.

- *Part 3: The Counseling Process:* Here in the main section of the book is a description of individual counseling as a process in which an evolving, dynamic counselor-client relationship helps clients develop insights that lead to changes in attitudes and behavior. In separate chapters are descriptions of how the counseling process is adapted to families, groups, and older adults and to career counseling, multicultural counseling, and substance abuse counseling.

- *Part 4: Counseling Practice:* This last part features specific cases and actual counseling programs as examples of how counseling theories, techniques, and professional guidelines are applied in each of the various settings: schools, colleges, and communities.

New Features of the Fourth Edition

To address the burgeoning needs and trends of professional counseling, significant revisions and expansions have been made throughout the book. The issue of technology and online counseling has been addressed in several chapters throughout the text. The chapter on the effective counselor has been moved to the first section of the book and is now chapter 4. Other new features of the fourth edition include the following:

- *Part 1:* Expanded coverage of accreditation of training programs and updated licensing and certification requirements; expanded discussion of managed care and counselor use of the Internet and their ethical implications; also expanded sections on counselor collaboration, team counseling, and counselor burnout.

- *Part 2:* Expanded treatment of the dynamic, ongoing impact of Piaget's theory of cognitive development and Kohlberg's theory of moral development on the field of counseling and therapy. Expanded discussion of counselor use of diverse theoretical approaches in a multicultural, changing society and the concomitant counselor trend to integrate various theoretical, developmental approaches. New sections on postmodern constructivist and social constructionist approaches to counseling, including the use of narrative therapy. In the chapter on assessment, expanded the updated DSM-IV-TR and added alternative postmodern approaches to the diagnostic manual.

- *Part 3:* Added the newer alternative approaches to marriage and family therapy, including systemic cognitive-developmental therapy, postmodern family narrative therapy, new considerations of Adlerian therapy, and an alternative approach to couples counseling. Included a more in-depth coverage of the group counseling process; an expanded discussion of mixed-race individuals and their families; a discussion of newer approaches to substance abuse counseling; new sections on career counseling including training, credentialing, the use of the Internet, and postmodern approaches; and a new section on the counselor approach to aggression in women and intimacy problems with men.

- *Part 4:* Added information on comprehensive school counseling programs and the American School Counseling Association national standards for school counseling. Expanded information on developmental issues of children (including attachment and moral development), child maltreatment, and attention-deficit/hyperactivity disorder. Added and extended sections on play therapy, creative and expressive arts therapy, choice theory, and group guidance; added information on college student development. Updated information on the use of technology in college counseling.

This text is intended for undergraduate and graduate students in introductory courses in counseling. Because of its strong emphasis on applying theory to practice, it can also supplement counseling practicum or internship seminars for graduate students, as well as those courses designed for continuing professional education for practicing counselors. Students in health-related training programs, such as social work and psychiatric nursing, will also benefit from the kind of instructional material this text offers. For professionals who need to study for licensure or certification exams, this text is an excellent resource because it provides comprehensive coverage of all areas included in the exams.

I am pleased that Karyn Dayle Jones has joined me as the coauthor of this fourth edition. Her expertise as a mental health counselor specializing in working with children, adolescents and families greatly enhances the quality of the text. She was especially helpful with the chapters that cover career counseling and school and college counseling; in addition, she helped in expanding the coverage of Internet counseling throughout the text.

—Frank Nugent

ACKNOWLEDGMENTS

We very much appreciate those who reviewed the third edition and made comments and suggestions for improvement: Pamela E. Brott, Virginia Tech; Ken Coll, Boise State University; Aaron W. Hughey, Western Kentucky University; Richard Schmid, Henderson State University. Thanks again to the reviewers of previous editions: Sari Dworkin, California State University, Fresno; James Hillman, Thompson, Connecticut; Aaron W. Hughey, Western Kentucky University; Dana Jack, Fairhaven College, Western Washington University; Tracy L. Robinson, North Carolina State University; Gerald Spadafore, Idaho State University; David Sue, Western Washington University; and Candice Wiggum, Western Washington University. We also express our appreciation for the encouragement and support of Merrill/Prentice Hall publisher Kevin Davis and the ongoing help from editorial assistant Amanda King and production editor Mary Harlan. Thanks also for the support and guidance throughout the project from production coordinator Peggy Hood of The GTS Companies, and many thanks also go to Mary Benis for her hours of careful work in copyediting the manuscript.

I am also very grateful for the ongoing support from my wife, Ann, who helped research, edit, and rewrite this edition as well as the previous editions. Her professional contribution as well as her ongoing encouragement helped enrich the text immeasurably. And many thanks to Jackie Burley, who again cheerfully and efficiently typed the drafts of the manuscript.

F.A.N.

About the Authors

Frank A. Nugent

Frank A. Nugent, PhD, Professor Emeritus of Psychology, Western Washington University (WWU), Bellingham, has more than 50 years' experience in professional counseling. Over the years he has served as a counselor in schools and universities, as a counseling psychologist in private practice, and as a counselor educator, supervisor, and psychology professor. In 1993 the Washington State Counseling Association presented him with the Hank Bertness Award in recognition of his contributions to mental health and to the counseling profession during his long career.

Nugent received his MA in vocational counseling at Columbia University (1947), where he worked under Donald Super. Nugent worked, in turn, as a supervising counselor at the University of California–Berkeley and Stanford University Counseling Centers and as a counselor at Pleasant Hill High School in California. He completed his PhD in counseling psychology at the University of California–Berkeley (1959). Among Nugent's contributions is the creation of the student counseling center at Western Washington University, where he served as director from 1962 to 1973. He also initiated and coordinated for WWU's Psychology Department both the MEd program in school counseling in 1963 and the MS degree in mental health counseling in 1978. As president of the board for the Whatcom County Mental Health Clinic and, later, for the Lake Whatcom Residential Treatment Center, he helped spearhead the development of new facilities for both agencies.

At the state level Nugent was influential in gaining certification for school counselors and was recognized for promoting professional and ethical standards for both school and mental health counselors at the state and national levels. He served as president of the Washington State Psychological Association in 1968–69 and was initiator, cofounder, and first president of the Washington Mental Health Counselors Association in 1980. At that time he spearheaded the drive to obtain state licensing for mental health counselors.

Nugent received a Fulbright Senior Research Scholarship in 1982 to study counseling in Germany. After retirement he continued teaching part-time in WWU's psychology department; he also helped develop WWU's gerontology certificate program and taught courses in the extended-day program on the psychology of aging.

Karyn Dayle Jones

Karyn Dayle Jones, PhD, is an associate professor in counselor education at the University of Central Florida. She has 15 years of experience in the counseling profession.

Jones has authored or coauthored several book chapters and refereed publications. She has given many international, national, and regional professional presentations in the field of counseling and counselor education. She is the past president of the Counseling Association for Humanistic Counseling, Education and Development, a division of the American Counseling Association.

Jones is a Florida Licensed Mental Health Counselor, National Certified Counselor, and Certified Reality Therapist, and she has worked as a counselor in mental health agencies, schools, and private practice. Jones received her MA in mental health counseling at Rollins College (1991) and her PhD in counselor education from the University of South Carolina (1996). She has clinical experience providing individual, group, and family counseling to children, adolescents, and adults for such issues as child abuse, substance abuse, and various *DSM-IV-TR* disorders.

Research Navigator—
Research Made Simple!

www.ResearchNavigator.com

Merrill Education is pleased to introduce Research Navigator—a one-stop research solution for students that simplifies and streamlines the entire research process. At www.researchnavigator.com, students will find extensive resources to enhance their understanding of the research process so they can effectively complete research assignments. In addition, Research Navigator has three exclusive databases of credible and reliable source content to help students focus their research efforts and begin the research process.

HOW WILL RESEARCH NAVIGATOR ENHANCE YOUR COURSE?

- Extensive content on understanding the research process includes writing, conducting Internet research, and citing sources.
- Step-by-step tutorial guides students through the entire research process from selecting a topic to revising a rough draft.
- Research Writing in the Disciplines section details the differences in research across disciplines.
- Three exclusive databases—EBSCO's ContentSelect Academic Journal Database, *The New York Times* Search by Subject Archive, and "Best of the Web" Link Library—allow students to easily find journal articles and sources.

WHAT'S THE COST?

A subscription to Research Navigator is $7.50 but is **free** when ordered in conjunction with this textbook. To obtain free passcodes for your students, simply contact your local Merrill/Prentice Hall sales representative, and your representative will send you the Evaluating Online Resource Guide, which contains the code to access Research Navigator as well as tips on how to use Research Navigator and how to evaluate research. To preview the value of this website for your students, please go to www.educatorlearningcenter.com, and use the login name "Research" and the password "Demo."

Discover the Companion Website Accompanying This Book

THE PRENTICE HALL COMPANION WEBSITE: A VIRTUAL LEARNING ENVIRONMENT

Technology is a constantly growing and changing aspect of our field that is creating a need for content and resources. To address this emerging need, Prentice Hall has developed an online learning environment for students and professors alike—Companion Websites—to support our textbooks.

In creating a Companion Website, our goal is to build on and enhance what the textbook already offers. For this reason, the content for each user-friendly website is organized by topic and provides the professor and the student with a variety of meaningful resources. Common features of a Companion Website include the following:

FOR THE PROFESSOR—

Every Companion Website integrates **Syllabus Manager**™, an online syllabus creation and management utility.

- **Syllabus Manager**™ provides the instructor with an easy, step-by-step process to create and revise syllabi, with direct links into Companion Website and other online content without having to learn HTML.
- Students may log on to the syllabus during any study session. All they need to know is the web address for the Companion Website and the password assigned to the syllabus.
- After a syllabus is created using **Syllabus Manager**™, students may enter the syllabus for their course section from any point in the Companion Website.
- Clicking on a date, the student is shown the list of activities for the assignment. The activities for each assignment are linked directly to actual content, saving time for students.
- Adding assignments consists of clicking on the desired due date and then filling in the details of the assignment—name of the assignment, instructions, and whether it is a one-time or repeating assignment.

- In addition, links to other activities can be created easily. If the activity is online, a URL can be entered in the space provided, and it will be linked automatically in the final syllabus.
- The completed syllabus is hosted on our servers, allowing convenient updates from any computer on the Internet. Changes made to the syllabus are immediately available to students at their next log-on.

FOR THE STUDENT—

- **Counseling topics**—17 core counseling topics represent the diversity and scope of today's counseling field.
- **Annotated bibliography**—includes seminal foundational works and key current works.
- **Web destinations**—list significant and up-to-date practitioner and client sites.
- **Professional development**—provides helpful information regarding professional organizations and codes of ethics.
- **Electronic bluebook**—sends homework or essays directly to the instructor's e-mail with this paperless form.
- **Message board**—serves as a virtual bulletin board to post—or respond to—questions or comments to/from a national audience.
- **Chat**—real-time chat with anyone who is using the text anywhere in the country is ideal for discussion and study groups, class projects, and so on.

To take advantage of these and other resources, please visit the *Introduction to the Profession of Counseling,* Fourth Edition, Companion Website at

www.prenhall.com/nugent

Brief Contents

Contents

4   The Effective Counselor   79

Part 2   Theories and Techniques   95

5   Human Development Theories   95

8   Counseling Outreach: Prevention and Intervention   190

Part 3   The Counseling Process   205

9   Individual Counseling   205

Part 4   Counseling Practice   396

16   Counseling Programs in Elementary Schools   396

19   Counseling in the Community   475

Note: Every effort has been made to provide accurate and current Internet information in this book. However, the Internet and information posted on it are constantly changing, so it is inevitable that some of the Internet addresses listed in this textbook will change.

CHAPTER 1

The Current Scene

The demand for counseling services for people with normal developmental concerns continues to grow and spread in schools, colleges, and communities. Normal conflicts arise when individuals have difficulty fulfilling both their own needs and the expectations of others. Sometimes conflicts emerge because of contradictions or uncertainty regarding a person's motivations, attitudes, or feelings. Individuals may have mixed feelings about premarital sex or about attending college. Conflicts may result from discord between individuals and important persons in their lives. Parents and children or husband and wife may have contradictory values or different role expectations. Financial problems or the illness of a loved one may inhibit the pursuit of a person's life goals.

Counselors help individuals work through transitions and situational conflicts in a complex, multicultural society. Counselors help clients cope with changing family values, family breakups, shifting job markets, and the rising cost of education. Increasing numbers of people lack such essentials as food and shelter, creating pressures that frequently lead to depression, drug and alcohol addiction, and street crimes. Persons with feelings of loneliness or indifference may have difficulty coping effectively with their own needs or with society's demands.

Many families are unduly burdened by having to care for incapacitated older parents. The reverse problem occurs as well when young adults return to live with their parents and when grandparents must take on parenting roles for their grandchildren. Older adults struggle with conflicts of a different nature: Many are often thwarted in their search for new and meaningful roles in society by ageist stereotypes emphasizing deterioration during aging. Such conflicts may cause tension and anxiety that interfere with the ability to make decisions or the will to take action appropriate for the productive growth of self and society.

A dramatic increase in the need for counseling services has also occurred because of the growing numbers of reported cases of child neglect and abuse, domestic violence, and substance abuse. Many persons from dysfunctional families need both counseling and support services. Victims of abuse tend to perpetuate the abuse unless they and their families learn more constructive ways of relating to each other (Brown, 1991).

Developmental conflicts generally represent a healthy recognition that all is not well in one's interactions with others or in one's feelings about oneself. Recognition of the conflict is potentially constructive because it can motivate persons to attempt to change behavioral patterns that are stifling their personal, occupational, or social growth. Human developmental problems throughout neighborhoods and communities indicate social illnesses that require community involvement and social change.

WHAT IS PROFESSIONAL COUNSELING?

Professional counselors offer voluntary, confidential services that focus on the developmental, situational problems of persons of all ages and of various multicultural backgrounds. Regardless of where they work, counselors help individuals, families, and groups resolve conflicts, solve problems, or make decisions in a social, cultural context.

Counselors are prepared to engage in multiple roles to meet the variety of counseling services required by the public. Their primary role is counseling individuals, groups, or families regarding personal, interpersonal, social, cultural, or career concerns. Their other roles, which are distinct from actual counseling, involve them in outreach programs (including psychoeducational programs, consultation, and collaboration), assessment and diagnosis, and crisis intervention.

Counseling Is a Process

Professional counseling is a process during which counselor and client develop an effective relationship, one that enables the client to work through difficulties. Following a human development perspective, counselors perceive that individuals go through stages of development throughout their life span (see chap. 5). Client conflicts arise from normal developmental transitions, signaling an opportunity for clients to reassess and work through factors, attitudes, and feelings contributing to their disequilibrium. This developmental process emphasizes a client's strengths and potential for growth instead of focusing on a client's symptoms as pathologies or defects that must be eliminated or prevented.

Professional counseling and counseling psychology developed in the 1940s as a reaction to the overemphasis by psychiatrists, psychologists, and social workers on pathology and mental illness. At that time process-oriented relational therapy, developed by Otto Rank's followers Frederick Allen and Robert Taft in the 1920s and 1930s, was championed by Carl Rogers (1942), who in turn developed his theory of client-centered therapy. Furthermore, counseling psychologist Donald Super (1955) advocated the early developmental theories, urging counselors to attend to the developmental needs of normal people, particularly during transitional periods as they struggle with conflicts and anxieties of adjusting to new vocational tasks or roles.

Leading counselors continue to reaffirm the process-oriented nature of counseling, centering around the evolving counselor-client relationship (Ginter, 1989; Guterman, 1994).

According to Ginter (1989), "The single most distinguishing feature we possess that makes us unique is our theoretical grasp of the client-counselor relationship" (p. 83).

Counseling Involves Both Personal and Social Growth

Early counselors of the late 1940s and the 1950s were primarily concerned with client situational problems, problems that affect clients' optimal functioning in colleges, schools, and workplaces. In later decades, during the 1960s and the 1970s, personal problems and self-growth movements eclipsed situational concerns; many counselors, for example, ignored their clients' vocational concerns.

In recent decades counselors once more have been considering the person's well-being in the context of his or her environment. The client's relationship with others is now a primary consideration in the therapeutic process. Specially trained counselors are working with families, and career counseling has once again gained recognition as an important service to clients in both the educational setting and the workplace (Isaacson & Brown, 1997).

Increasing numbers of counselors have been attending to client concerns in a broader social-cultural context. In some cases counselors from schools, colleges, and community agencies are joining forces to offer family clinics or programs for at-risk schoolchildren and their families. Also emerging are comprehensive neighborhood health care centers that offer counseling, social, and medical services primarily for the uninsured and the poor. Counselors at these centers serve normally functioning individuals with the full range of developmental and situational problems (see chap. 19).

Counseling Includes Outreach Services

In addition to offering direct counseling, counselors are involved in prevention and intervention activities designed to improve the overall mental health environment in schools and communities. These activities, called outreach, include consultation, assessment and diagnosis, psychoeducation, and crisis intervention.

Consultation

Counselors in schools and colleges offer consultation to parents, faculty, and administrators who may be having difficulty in their interactions with students, parents, or staff. Counselors use their expertise to assess the difficulty and to make suggestions. Community counselors may consult with social agency staff who need professional advice on how to relate to or communicate with the public (Hershenson, Power, & Waldo, 1996).

Assessment and Diagnosis

Some counselors in private practice provide diagnostic evaluations of individuals for community agencies such as the Social Security Administration, the Division of Vocational Rehabilitation, or the courts. In such cases they provide psychological information to help the agency determine whether an individual's emotional stability or personal abilities qualify him or her for vocational training, Social Security benefits, or parole. Special training in diagnosis and evaluation is needed to carry out this service.

Psychoeducation

In all work settings counselors carry out psychological education intended to improve the overall mental health environment in schools, agencies, or communities. Workshops, classes, or seminars may be offered in parenting skills, assertiveness training, personal growth, career exploration, grief work, or drug and alcohol education (Baker & Shaw, 1987). Counselors in private practice offer psychological education through continuing education programs at universities, community colleges, and professional association conferences.

School counselors' involvement in guidance activities is a form of psychological education specific to the needs of schools. Counselors offer workshops or assemble and disseminate information about scholarships, college admissions, vocational training, school-related work placements, and personal and interpersonal growth.

Crisis Intervention

All counselors, regardless of setting, are involved in intervention when crises arise in the school or community agency in which they work. Should a crisis occur, counselors must be prepared to deal with severe depression, suicide threats, acute shock or trauma, alcohol or drug reactions, psychotic episodes, and even broken love affairs. Counselors must be prepared to decide whether the client needs to be referred to a medical professional or whether to notify the client's designated emergency contact person and/or whether to send the client to the local hospital ER.

WHO DOES PROFESSIONAL COUNSELING?

Professional Counselors and Counseling Psychologists

Professional counselors are similar to counseling psychologists in that both are uniquely trained to attend to the normal developmental conflicts of clients. They differ in their professional identification and level of training. Professional counselors have master's degrees or doctorates in counseling; those in private practice are credentialed, licensed, or certified by state legislatures or certified as counselors by national professional counseling associations. Professional counselors are usually trained in one or more of the following types of counseling specialties:

school	college and university
mental health	corrections
community	group
marriage and family	pastoral
rehabilitation	substance abuse
gerontology	cross-cultural
career	creative or expressive arts

Counseling psychologists have doctorates in psychology with a specialty in counseling. Those in private practice are licensed psychologists through state licensing boards.

Graduate work in counseling psychology includes more extensive internships and more emphasis on research methodology. Largely because of this emphasis on research, many counseling psychologists have become faculty members at universities and colleges, where they are engaged in training and supervising counselors and conducting research.

Comparison of Counselors and Psychotherapists

As counselors have expanded from working in educational settings to working in the community, and as large numbers of psychotherapists have moved from clinics and hospitals into private practice, considerable overlap has occurred in the services that counselors and psychotherapists offer. In some circumstances the terms *counseling* and *psychotherapy* are used interchangeably (Brammer, Abrego, & Shostrom, 1993; Gelso & Fretz, 2001; Thompson & Rudolph, 1992).

Counseling and psychotherapy generally differ in terms of the severity of the client's problems. Counseling emphasizes short-term counseling processes and focuses more on situational problems of everyday life, particularly during troublesome transitional periods. Psychotherapy specializes in more serious inner emotional problems that require a longer process which often involves reconstructing the client's personality.

Psychotherapists have been criticized for being preoccupied with the client's inner problems without regard for the impact the environment might have on the client's well-being, particularly such adverse conditions as poverty, pollution, violence, and prejudice (Hillman & Ventura, 1992). Ironically, early in the 20th century, health professionals were aware that adverse environmental conditions affected the individual's well-being. In child guidance clinics of the 1920s, a major treatment method for child behavioral problems was to change the child's environment (Levy, 1971; Rogers, 1939; see also chap. 2). In addition, the psychosocial approaches of Alfred Adler (1927) and Karen Horney (1939) emphasized the importance of the interrelationship between individuals and their environment. However, after the Rogerian client-centered approach became popular, followed by the development of psychotherapy and the rise of the personal growth movement of the 1960s and 1970s, for several decades therapists generally lost sight of the importance of considering the environmental impact on the welfare of the individual (see chap. 2).

Other Mental Health Specialists

Other licensed or certified mental health specialists offering counseling or therapy services include clinical or psychiatric social workers, clinical psychologists, psychiatrists, psychoanalysts, psychiatric nurses, and school psychologists. They generally are trained to assess and diagnose behavior disorders according to the *Diagnostic and Statistical Manual of Mental Disorders (DSM-IV-TR)* and treat symptoms according to a prescribed therapeutic plan.

Clinical or *psychiatric social workers* receive master's degrees in social work with an emphasis in family therapy. They are licensed in most states by state legislation; their training emphasizes social-cultural factors contributing to client and family problems. Generally serving as case workers, these specialists coordinate therapy services with other assistance needed by clients, such as health and home-care necessities. Their professional organization is the National Association of Social Workers (NASW). Historically, social workers have been in the forefront in recognizing the importance of family dynamics when working with dysfunctional persons. They have developed and applied a family system approach in various treatment programs for recovering alcoholics, drug addicts, and people in addictive relationships.

Clinical psychologists have PhD's or PsyD's in psychology. They are trained primarily in the assessment, diagnosis, and treatment of individuals with emotional disorders or mental dysfunctions. In training they are usually required to complete supervised internships in mental health clinics or mental hospitals. They are generally noted for the development and use of cognitive-behavioral therapeutic approaches, although psychodynamic-based clinical psychologists have been emerging throughout the country. Clinical psychologists are licensed in all states for private practice. Their major association is Division 12 of the American Psychological Association (APA).

Psychiatrists are medical doctors with advanced training in psychiatry. They are the only mental health specialists who can prescribe psychotropic drugs. They generally diagnose persons with psychological disorders and treat them with psychotropic medications. Only some psychiatrists undergo special training as *psychoanalysts*—a program that requires them to undergo psychoanalysis. Those who decide to become psychoanalysts generally are trained either in neo-Freudian approaches, such as object relations or ego-analytic techniques, or in Jungian analytical psychology.

Jungian psychoanalysts receive Diplomas of Analytical Psychology from the C. J. Jung Institute in Zurich, Switzerland, or from similar Jungian institutes elsewhere in Europe or the United States. Training involves many years of work and includes intensive personal analysis.

Psychiatric nurses take advanced nurses' training that includes counseling and therapeutic skills appropriate for individuals with health problems. Psychiatric nurses are particularly informed about the relationship between physiological symptoms and emotional disorders. They are especially involved in psychological problems of the frail elderly. They also specialize in grief work, which involves counseling those who are dying and those who are suffering from the loss of loved ones. In addition, they work with family members who are caretakers of older persons.

School psychologists generally have master's degrees. Their training emphasizes assessment and diagnosis of students with learning or behavioral disabilities; they assess the intelligence or mental functioning of children having academic or emotional difficulties in school. Although they are sometimes involved in treatment, school psychologists generally refer students and families to school counselors or other community mental health professionals for counseling or therapy. They also serve as consultants to school administrators, counselors, parents, and families.

WHERE DO PROFESSIONAL COUNSELORS WORK?

In the 1970s and 1980s counseling programs began expanding beyond schools and colleges into the community at large. New options and more jobs became available to counselors in community agencies and in business and industry (Baxter, 1990; Hollis & Wantz, 1993), a trend that is expected to continue. According to the 2002–2003 *Occupational*

Outlook Handbook, "Overall employment of counselors is expected to grow faster than the average for all occupations through 2010. In addition, numerous job openings will occur as many counselors reach retirement age" (Bureau of Labor Statistics, U.S. Department of Labor, 2002–2003, p. 155).

By being aware of the similarities of counselors' roles and duties in various work settings, counselors can acquire a feeling of professional unity. In this way they will be more likely to consult with one another regarding treatment options for clients and more apt to engage in joint psychoeducational workshops. Moreover, when counselors are aware of the many specialists among their peers in different work settings, they are more likely to refer clients needing specialized help to other counselors trained to work with such cases.

The way counselors apply their training in their various employment settings depends on their area of interest and specialization, the type of counseling or therapeutic services offered in their work settings, and mandates from legislative bodies or other funding agencies about who receives priority in services.

Local or state institutions or agencies that employ counselors are restricted by legislative bodies, budget agencies, or boards of directors—restrictions that tend to influence the types or range of services that are offered. Legislative bodies, for example, have increasingly been cutting funds for community mental health clinics, so such clinics, for the most part, have now limited their treatment to chronically disturbed persons (Hershenson et al., 1996).

The following descriptions of various work settings cover first the traditional counseling services—those found in schools; colleges; the various public and private community agencies, including mental health clinics and inpatient residential facilities; and federal and state counseling agencies, such as Veterans Administration (VA) hospitals, employment offices, and correctional facilities.

The second section features current trends in community counseling—the newer community counseling services that have emerged more recently, particularly those offered by business and industry, community career centers, religious organizations, and various types of comprehensive neighborhood health care clinics.

School Settings

Elementary Schools

When counselors are hired to work in elementary schools, they have good opportunities to counsel students both individually and in groups and to present extracurricular psychoeducational activities and classes. Because elementary teachers generally have the same children in class all day, the teachers are more likely than those in high schools or colleges to spot potential problems and to refer children to the counselor. Moreover, parents tend to be more involved with their young child's progress in elementary school and to be more available for consultation with counselors than they are later on, when their son or daughter enters middle school and, later, high school.

A survey of 96 outstanding elementary school counselor programs shows how counselors spend their counseling time (Gibson & Mitchell, 1999). Individual counseling was emphasized in 98% of programs, and group guidance and counseling was emphasized in 81%. In 75% of programs, counselors consulted with teachers and parents.

Secondary Schools

According to the standards set by both the American School Counselor Association (ASCA) and the American Counseling Association (ACA), secondary school counselors are trained to offer individual and group counseling, consultation, classroom guidance, and career planning activities. Nevertheless, they have generally found themselves bogged down in clerical and crisis intervention duties that leave insufficient time for counseling.

Increasing numbers of secondary school counselors and administrators have shown concern about inappropriate assignment of counselors to clerical or administrative duties and have recommended changes more in line with professional standards. In a national survey of secondary school counseling programs, state guidance directors indicated considerable concern that approximately 85% of school counselors were spending too much time in nonprofessional duties. The directors agreed that high school counselors should spend more time in counseling, group guidance, and career guidance (Peer, 1985).

In another study, reported by Wiggins and Moody (1987), a four-person team (one counselor educator and three experienced counselors) evaluated the effectiveness of counseling programs in seven junior high and four senior high schools in four Mid-Atlantic states. The evaluators found that administrators generally considered clerical duties a minor part of the counselors' workload and felt uncomfortable about counselor preoccupation with clerical duties. The evaluators concluded that counselors who agreed to take on heavy loads of clerical work tended to be those who lacked counseling skills or the ability to object to an excessive amount of noncounseling duties. These findings indicate that well-trained counselors who insist that they should spend the majority of their time in counseling can expect positive responses from reasonable and flexible administrators.

Advantages and Disadvantages of Working in Schools

Counselors in schools obviously have more opportunities than counselors in other work settings to work directly with children and adolescents with normal concerns and conflicts. Counselors are readily available, at no cost, to students and their families when problems or crises arise. Follow-up counseling is also possible. In fact, ongoing, intermittent brief counseling can be available throughout the school year and throughout the years that students are in school. Because parents are familiar with the school environment, they tend to be comfortable with school personnel who are offering help or guidance. School counselors are also in a good position to make referrals to and consult with mental health counselors in the community and in private practice.

On the other hand, many schools throughout the country are insufficiently staffed with school counselors, especially at the elementary level. In addition, secondary school counselors tend to do too much clerical and personnel work at the expense of counseling. Moreover, school counselors in both elementary and secondary schools are being called on to deal with an inordinate number of students with emotional crises, depression, and drug abuse (Kendrick, Chander, & Hatcher, 1994). This demand leaves little time for counseling students with normal developmental concerns. Furthermore, because of students' class schedules, it is difficult, especially in secondary schools, to arrange ongoing individual and group counseling or to consult with parents. Maintaining confidentiality in counseling, in accordance with the ACA Code of Ethics, can also be a problem for some counselors. Parents, teachers, and administrators may expect or demand feedback from counseling sessions without the permission of the child or adolescent. Another difficulty is that 21 states mandate teaching experience for counselors (Gibson & Mitchell, 1999).

Special Training for School Counselors

Elementary school counselors should understand family dynamics and the developmental needs of young children. They should have training in counseling techniques such as play and art therapy, sociodrama, and storytelling. These counselors should also be prepared to work with a wide variety of multicultural children, many of whom are bilingual. In addition, they should be aware of special problems, such as the effects of divorce and child abuse on young children. Knowledge of psychoeducational techniques is also important. And familiarity with parenting skills is valuable because parents often seek help from elementary counselors about how to communicate with or discipline their children more effectively.

Middle school and secondary school counselors should be familiar with multicultural developmental needs of adolescents, such as concerns about identity, sexuality, and dependence/independence. These counselors should also be prepared to work with substance abuse, teenage depression, career or job exploration, parent-adolescent conflicts, and intimate relationships with others.

Elementary, middle, and secondary school counselors all need skills in brief, intermittent counseling to be prepared to work with students at different times throughout the years that the students are in school.

College and University Settings

Four-Year Colleges and Universities

Compared with counselors in other settings, counselors in university and college counseling centers are in the best position to apply their training to counseling clients with normal developmental conflicts and concerns. On most campuses individual and group counseling services are offered with an expected guarantee of confidentiality. More outreach programs—workshops, groups, and other psychoeducational activities—are offered in these than in other counseling settings. As a former college counselor during the late 1940s and the 1950s and director of a university counseling center in the 1960s and early 1970s, Frank Nugent, one of the authors of this text, has long believed, and other professionals concur (Steenbarger, 1990), that university counseling centers best represent the model of developmental counseling recommended by ACA and APA Division 17.

Budget crunches have led most university counseling staffs to work on short-term counseling approaches that limit each student to about 10 counseling sessions. Students are screened to determine which of them can profit from brief counseling and which require referral to other agencies for more intensive help.

Advantages and Disadvantages of Working in Colleges and Universities.   In college and university counseling centers, counselors are able to carry out the majority of counseling tasks for which they are trained. Compared with clients in other settings, university students generally live on or near campus, close to the counseling center, and have schedules with enough flexibility that appointments can be arranged fairly easily. In addition, college mental health clinics, health centers, career placement bureaus, foreign-student offices, and other resources are generally nearby for referrals. Furthermore, counselors often have the opportunity to teach and supervise a variety of interns. In large universities many counselors are able to conduct research.

On the other hand, college and university counselors are generally limited in the range of clients they serve: Their clients generally have come from white middle-class backgrounds, although college campuses have become increasingly multicultural, particularly at urban universities; college counselors rarely see families or work with children; and most don't generally see individuals over the age of 30 or 40. At some universities counselors have difficulties with their professional identity. When they are not given faculty rank, they are often classified as student-personnel administrators—a classification contrary to their nonadministrative counseling relationship with students.

Special Training for College and University Counselors.   College counselors must be prepared to work with client problems peculiar to university settings, such as uncertainties about choice of major, blocking on exams, homesickness, problems with roommates, and fears of flunking out of school. Counselors also need multicultural training to work with clients from various ethnic backgrounds. In addition, they must be conscious of gender issues, and they must be prepared to work with gay and lesbian clients. Counselors also work with clients who are troubled about AIDS, substance abuse, eating disorders, and sexual harassment.

Most college counselors have either doctorates in counseling psychology or clinical psychology or master's degrees or doctorates in counseling. Professional associations representing college counselors are APA Division 17 and the American College Counseling Association (ACCA), the most recent division of ACA. Psychologists or counselors working in university settings are not required to be licensed or certified, but many of them are licensed through state licensing laws or are certified by national boards for counselors.

Community Colleges

Community college counselors serve a wider range of clients than do counselors at colleges and universities. Many community college students take nondegree technical training, and others take academic courses with the intention of transferring to 4-year colleges. Many of these students are older adults. Because many community colleges are located in inner cities and are especially geared to meeting the needs of students from various ethnic backgrounds, community college counselors especially need training in multicultural counseling. These counselors must also be sensitive to the needs of students who have nonacademic aptitudes and interests and students who may doubt their academic abilities.

Counseling in the Community: Traditional Services

Although services similar to those offered in schools and colleges are needed in the community, most government-funded mental health agencies limit services to dealing with crisis cases or to diagnosing, assessing, and treating the chronically mentally ill and their families. For those who need counseling, help is generally available only if they are affluent enough to pay private practitioners or if they have health insurance that covers services. Escalating costs of treatment, reduction of funding, and limited services since the early 1980s have brought about the development of alternative services in mental health care offered by employee assistance programs, career centers, and religious organizations. New community counseling services—managed health care programs and Internet counseling—have become prominent and have raised many issues. Descriptions of these more recent services follow later in this chapter. However, many counselors still work in the more traditional community mental health settings, each of which tends to influence and limit the type and degree of counseling services offered in that particular setting.

Community-Based Mental Health Services

The term *community-based services* is used here to describe services for which funding is dependent on state and/or local resources and for which administrative policies are determined locally. Agencies administered under state and/or federal jurisdiction with local branches are described later. The innumerable locally based community agencies usually fall into four types: (a) public clinics and agencies; (b) private, nonprofit clinics and agencies; (c) private, for-profit clinics and agencies; and (d) inpatient residential facilities. Local public agencies and private, nonprofit clinics that depend on some county and local funding usually have boards of directors selected from members of the community to help set administrative policies, raise funds, and monitor quality of services. Private services or clinics run by individual counselors or groups of therapists on a fee basis operate like any other profit-making business.

Public Clinics and Agencies.   Two types of outpatient public clinics most common in communities are county-based, government-funded comprehensive community mental health clinics and county youth agencies. *Comprehensive community mental health clinics* (CMHCs) offer the major local mental health services in a particular region or county in a state. As indicated earlier, largely because of budget mandates, the staffs of CMHCs work predominantly with individuals who are chronically mentally ill. Consequently, community mental health counselors who work in these settings are often frustrated. However, because of their training to work with normally functioning people, these counselors tend to look for strengths and potentialities in the individual or family that can be used to help resolve problems and may thus bring a fresh approach to those having severe emotional problems.

County youth agencies serve youths who are referred by state child protective agencies or who are wards of the state or are in foster homes. Clients may have substance abuse problems, be in trouble with the law for minor violations, or be chronic runaways.

Counseling services include individual, group, or family counseling; assessment of behavior for juvenile courts; intake interviews; and educational guidance (Collison & Garfield, 1990).

Private, Nonprofit Clinics and Agencies.   Nonprofit, locally based agencies are dependent primarily on funds or grants from such diverse sources as United Way, corporate foundations, fund-raising events, or contributions from private donors. They generally have boards whose members, drawn from the community, help the administrators raise funds, set policy, and monitor services. Private, for-profit agencies generally do not have such boards.

Counselors in private, nonprofit agencies work with individuals, couples, and families. They may offer specialized programs such as those geared for single parents or for adults coping with aging parents. In the past they have served primarily those in crises, but more recently, as discussed later in the chapter, comprehensive neighborhood health clinics have been emerging in some communities to serve those with situational, developmental problems.

For many years nonprofit crisis and emergency centers have been available in most communities for individuals who are experiencing acute emotional distress that requires immediate intervention. Counselors in these agencies help such individuals cope with feelings of disorientation and panic accompanying the crises. After clients gain equilibrium, short-term counseling is available in some instances, or a referral is made to other professionals or agencies for follow-up counseling.

In addition, crisis hot lines may be available 24 hours a day so that individuals experiencing trauma can call paraprofessionals or volunteers trained and supervised by counselors with master's degrees. Suicide prevention is a major activity of these telephone services. Other emergency centers offer help in specific types of trauma. Rape relief centers provide intervention, offer individual and group counseling, and maintain support groups to help heal trauma and feelings of violation. Centers for victims of domestic violence provide shelter, legal assistance, career counseling, and workshops to build self-esteem. Similarly, centers for juvenile runaways provide shelter, counseling, and consultation. These centers are usually staffed with professionally trained counselors supported by volunteers (see chap. 19).

Private, For-Profit Clinics and Agencies.   Private, for-profit agencies exist entirely on fees from clients or from clients' insurance. Likewise, counselors in private practice, either independently or in clinics, receive fees from their clients or their clients' health insurance. These providers offer counseling services for a wide range of problems; their clients may be individuals and families with normal concerns and stresses or those with more severe emotional trauma requiring longer-term treatment. Some private practitioners limit their practice to clients with specific concerns, such as substance abuse, aging, eating disorders, sexual dysfunctions, or vocational rehabilitation.

Currently, 47 states require that counselors be licensed before they can set up private practice. All states require that a person have a doctorate in counseling or clinical psychology to be a licensed psychologist. Those who are licensed to do private practice are generally the ones who provide psychological evaluation of individuals for government agencies, courts, and other judicial systems.

Inpatient Residential Facilities.   Patients who are chronically mentally ill and require long-term care generally reside in state mental hospitals. Local hospital staffs work with individuals with acute emotional flare-ups that require temporary hospitalization. These professionals offer crisis intervention, emergency treatment, and medication.

Residential treatment centers are available to individuals who are chronically emotionally disturbed but do not need to be committed to a state mental hospital. These centers offer supervised housing, care and management, and the opportunity to live as independently as possible. Unlike those committed involuntarily to state mental hospitals, people in residential treatment centers may choose to leave at any time. They receive counseling, learn social skills to increase their independence and feelings of self-worth, and get help in monitoring psychotropic medications.

Halfway houses, one type of residential treatment facility, are designed to help individuals make transitions to the community after they have been discharged from a state mental hospital. Counselors help residents gradually assume responsibility for independent living. They monitor the individuals' psychotropic drugs, help them rejoin their families, and assist them in finding jobs or appropriate training.

In all types of residential facilities, counselors and therapists with special training in expressive arts therapy apply therapeutic skills through music, art, dance, or drama. Such creative outlets as dancing, playing music, painting, enacting dramas, and role-playing are beneficial ways of stimulating depressed patients, relaxing agitated patients, or encouraging withdrawn patients to socialize (Collison & Garfield, 1990).

Advantages and Disadvantages of Working in Community-Based Counseling Settings. Working in a local community mental health clinic exposes counselors to a wide variety of counseling, consultation, and assessment techniques. Counselors have opportunities to work with families and with various age-groups, from children to the elderly. Unless counselors are in private practice, however, they are often unable to use their expertise in working with the concerns of normal individuals. Recently, though, that has been changing as comprehensive neighborhood health clinics for the general population have emerged in some communities, as discussed later in the chapter.

Private practice allows counselors the freedom to set up their practices the way they want. But establishing a practice can be slow and difficult; one must keep up with all the changing and confusing insurance, taxation, and licensing requirements. And licensed counselors with master's degrees have difficulty in many states being approved by health insurance companies for services rendered to clients (third-party payments). Once launched, however, private practice can be more lucrative than work in an agency or institution. In the past, private practice also tended to be isolating, but most practitioners now have joined a group of partners because managed care organizations require that mental health care providers combine services under one facility. Although client cultural backgrounds have generally been limited to the white upper-middle class, that trend, too, has been changing as increasing numbers of ethnic counselors have set up practice in culturally diverse communities.

Special Training for Community-Based Counselors.   To supplement basic counselor training, community agency counselors need more training in diagnostic and evaluative skills, must be knowledgeable about psychotropic medications, and must be familiar with the

DSM-IV-TR. They must have strategies for working with clients who experience acute emergencies, such as psychotic breakdowns, attempted suicides, or drug reactions. They also need to be familiar with entitlement programs and resources for the poor and the indigent.

In most states counselors in private practice not only must be licensed but also must take continuing course work to maintain their licenses. In addition, they need forensic skills if they wish to testify in court as expert witnesses. And they must be able to handle details of running a business, such as record keeping, billing, and public relations.

Federal and State Counseling Agencies

Federal and state agencies provide counseling services in vocational rehabilitation, employment offices, and correctional facilities.

Federal and State Vocational Rehabilitation Services.   VA hospitals offer vocational rehabilitation counseling to veterans who are disabled to help them find appropriate careers. VA hospitals typically hire counseling psychologists.

State vocational-rehabilitation centers offer services not only for veterans but for all individuals with disabilities. Counselors with master's degrees in rehabilitation counseling help clients find suitable training programs and employment and help them develop and maintain as independent a lifestyle as possible (Herr & Cramer, 1996). In some cities private comprehensive rehabilitation centers have emerged in which rehabilitation counseling, social, and medical services are coordinated under one facility or a cluster of facilities (see chap. 19).

Rehabilitation counseling is the only profession established and mandated by a legislative act of the U.S. Congress. Legislative guidelines impose certain expectations on counselors that are different from those of professional counseling associations. These include recruitment of cases, evaluation of a client's eligibility for services, and coordination and case management duties, in addition to the usual counseling functions (see chap. 12).

Employment Offices.   Employment counselors (placement counselors) work in state employment offices to help place individuals in jobs. These counselors generally do not have a master's degree in counseling but are expected to be well-informed about local and state labor market information, occupational trends, and job openings (Collison & Garfield, 1990). Employment counselors may offer workshops or training in searching for jobs, writing résumés, or going on job interviews (see chap. 12). State employment agencies differ from privately run career centers, discussed later in this chapter, which usually hire trained professional counselors and charge fees for services.

Correctional Facilities.   Correctional counselors work with criminal offenders in state and federal penal institutions, juvenile halls, judicial courts, and parole offices. They use counseling and casework methods to help inmates adjust to living in an institution. Counselors often are the only connection between inmates and the outside world and may be the only individuals who can help them deal with emotional, economic, and legal concerns (Collison & Garfield, 1990). Counselors working with individuals on parole help them find job training and placement; they also help parolees reunite with their families and other members of the community.

Correctional counselors are often confronted with a conflict between the role of counselor as a confidential and helping person and the role of law-enforcing disciplinarian (Collison & Garfield, 1990). In some agencies the counselor role is separated from the disciplinarian role, as is consistent with the ethical code of ACA (see chap. 3), which indicates that counselors should not have dual responsibilities with clients.

Advantages and Disadvantages of Working in Federal and State Agencies. Counseling jobs in government agencies are generally stable and provide more job benefits than those in locally run agencies. Counselors may find themselves restricted, however, to services determined by government policies and may be hampered in carrying out counseling duties by administrative red tape.

Counseling in the Community: Current Trends

Counseling services in business and industry, career centers, religious organizations, and local neighborhood comprehensive health care centers have been gaining prominence in the community.

Business and Industry

Since the early 1980s, counseling employees in business and industry has become one of the most rapidly growing specialties in counseling and in counseling psychology (Lewis & Lewis, 1986; May, 1992). Four programs have been developed for employees: (a) employee assistance programs (EAPs), (b) employment enhancement programs (EEPs), (c) career development counseling within the company, and (d) outplacement counseling. EAPs originally focused on alcohol problems of employees but have since expanded to serve those with personal, interpersonal, and family problems that interfere with their job performance. EEPs are preventive programs offered by companies to keep workers fit and healthy through exercise, diet, and relaxation techniques. Career development counseling helps employees develop their careers within the company system. Outplacement counselors serve employees who are terminated because their jobs are obsolete or because a company department is shutting down; these counselors help employees find new jobs and, if necessary, provide ways for them to develop new skills (see chap. 12).

In 1982 over half of the companies in *Fortune* magazine's top 500 companies offered EAPs. Since then, increasing numbers of smaller companies have developed EAPs through contracts with mental health clinics, social service agencies, or private practitioners. In a survey of staffing patterns of 275 EAP organizations in the United States, Hosie, West, and Mackey (1993) found that persons with master's degrees in counseling or in social work "were the most frequently employed and constitute the greatest percentage of the professional mental health staff in EAPs" (p. 355).

Advantages and Disadvantages of Working in Business and Industry. In EAPs counselors can work with the kinds of people they are best trained to serve—those who have situational concerns. Some counselors, however, serve only as intake interviewers who refer clients to other services offered in the community. Moreover, counselors employed by a company are often faced with the problem of being pressured by supervisors to release information about their clients (Dickman, Emener, & Hutchinson, 1985).

Special Training for Business and Industry Counselors.   Besides the usual training required of all counselors, EAP counselors need additional training not only in career counseling but also in business, personnel, and management. Because alcoholism is still a major cause of employee problems, training and experience in this area are also important. In addition, training in family counseling is needed to help clients whose problems on the job may be related to family troubles.

Community Career Centers

Career counseling centers emerged during the 1990s, especially in metropolitan areas. They offer individuals opportunities to explore career options, engage in career planning, and develop strategies to find the right job. These centers offer such educational workshops as how to write résumés, organize a job search, and prepare for job interviews. Workshops are also available for individuals who have lost their jobs, who are having interpersonal conflicts with managers or supervisors on the job, or who want to upgrade themselves in their current jobs. Activities include overcoming anxiety about job loss, managing stress, asserting oneself, and managing conflict with challenging colleagues. Career centers generally require yearly membership dues, with additional fees for special workshops or retreats. The centers are generally open evenings, which is a big advantage for clients. Counselors who work in these agencies generally have a master's degree in counseling or career counseling.

Pastoral Counseling Centers and Institutes

To meet the increasing needs of those desiring a comprehensive health care model that combines spiritual needs with mental and psychological concerns, pastoral counseling centers and institutes have emerged throughout the country. According to the AAPC (2003a), there are 100 pastoral counseling centers in the United States, and more than 3,000 pastoral counselors (see also chap. 19).

Accredited pastoral counseling centers and institutes are accountable to the American Association of Pastoral Counselors (AAPC). The AAPC "certifies Pastoral Counselors, accredits pastoral counseling centers, and approves training programs" (AAPC, 2003a, p. 1). An interfaith organization that includes Protestant, Catholic, and Jewish faiths, AAPC "is non-sectarian and respects the spiritual commitments and religious traditions of those who seek assistance without imposing counselor beliefs onto the client" (AAPC, 2003a, p. 1). The AAPC's comprehensive code of ethics, including such topics as confidentiality and dual relationships, is similar to ACA standards. AAPC's multitrack certification system for pastoral counselors, however, allows for varying levels of training and experience.

Pastoral counseling centers and institutes vary widely throughout the country. In some states they have well-established networks, as for example, the Pastoral Counseling Centers of Tennessee, Inc., with centers in several cities, training programs affiliated with Vanderbilt University, and well-developed community networking services (AAPC, 2003d).

Pastoral counseling centers offer individual, family, and couple counseling, as well as group and workshop activities. Fees accrue on a sliding scale and are generally affordable for most people. In larger cities various religious groups sponsor pastoral counseling services; some have networks of services throughout a city, as in Houston. Accredited pastoral counseling centers generally employ counselors who have a master's of divinity from a theological seminary and most of whom have also completed graduate training in counseling. Growing numbers are licensed counselors or licensed marriage and family therapists.

Pastoral counseling is available to all individuals in the community who are experiencing normal, everyday problems. Spiritual counseling is a special feature. Counselors attracted to these settings are open to and encourage the exploration of spiritual questions with their clients, many of whom indicate they would not have used traditional counseling services if the pastoral counseling center had not been available (AAPC, 2003a).

Many pastoral counseling centers are sponsored by the Samaritan Institute, a national network underwritten by the Martin Foundation to promote professional counseling that "integrates theology and psychology" (Samaritan Institute, 2003). There are 95 incorporated Samaritan Centers with 480 offices in 350 cities, in 33 states and in Tokyo, Japan. Samaritan counseling centers are ecumenical Christian and broadly diverse. Affiliated centers "are independently incorporated with a local governing board drawn from sponsoring congregations as well as the larger community" (Samaritan Institute, 2003).

Advantages and Disadvantages of Working at Religious-Sponsored Counseling Centers. Pastoral counseling centers have made impressive efforts to provide services for which the counselor is uniquely trained—helping a wide range of clients with normal developmental concerns. Unlike most other counseling models, however, these services, which include spiritual considerations, emulate a basic goal of professional counseling—working with the whole person.

In contrast with most other community mental health agencies, counseling services sponsored by religious groups are generally designed to help normally functioning individuals from all socioeconomic backgrounds. Figure 1.1 describes four agencies in Seattle, Washington—two traditional mental health clinics and two religious-sponsored counseling centers. The figure reveals the emphasis of mental health agencies on the chronically ill and on the use of psychotropic drugs, as compared with the two examples of religious-sponsored counseling centers. The figure also indicates that the Presbyterian Counseling Service has multiple locations throughout the city and that the Jewish Family Service's comprehensive health care program integrates all aspects of care—counseling, social services, career guidance, and medical care.

Although such counseling programs seem close to an ideal model of comprehensive community counseling services, there is always the risk that overzealous counselors may try to impose their own religious beliefs on their clients. This risk is held in check by the ethical code of the AAPC, which states that pastoral counselors should avoid any possible imposition of their own theology on clients: "We show sensitive regard for the moral, social, and religious standards of clients and communities. We avoid imposing our beliefs on others, although we may express them when appropriate in the pastoral counseling process" (AAPC, 2003b, III.C.).

Publicly Funded Centers:
Emphasis on Chronically Mentally Ill

HIGHLINE-WEST SEATTLE MENTAL HEALTH CENTER
....Intake for all sites: (206) 248-8226
....TTY: (206) 248-8235
      C 2600 SW Holden, Seattle 98126 ....(206) 933-7100
      C 1010 S 146th, Seattle 98168 ....(206) 241-0990
Special services for enrolled clients: Crisis intervention and aftercare services for clients with acute or chronic mental illness. 24-hour case management service provides psychiatric evaluation, medication monitoring, and a variety of support and referral services. Emergency response team after-hours, weekends, and holidays through Crisis Clinic. *Other services:* Comprehensive outpatient counseling for adults, children, youth, and their families; intake fee $20–125; sessions $20–$85; medical coupons and private insurance accepted. Supervised living services at residential care facilities for severely dysfunctional clients. Chemical dependency treatment for all ages. Parenting and child abuse prevention program and employment assistance. Individual, group, and family case management services for adult clients who are both mentally ill and developmentally disabled. Anger management and shoplifting groups. Community training and consultation.
Partial Hospitalization Program.........................(206) 248-8226
Intensive ambulatory treatment program for individuals who have acute or chronic mental illness with acute exacerbation of symptoms.

COMMUNITY PSYCHIATRIC CLINIC ....V/TTY: (206) 461-3614
4319 Stone Way N, Seattle 98103
C 10501 Meridian Ave N #D, Seattle 98133   (206) 461-4544
NOTE: Services vary at each site.
Crisis intervention and outreach for enrolled clients with acute or chronic mental illness. 24-hour case management teams provide psychiatric evaluation, medication monitoring, and a variety of other support and referral services. Emergency response team after-hours, weekends, and holidays reached through Crisis Clinic.
General services: Individual, group, and family counseling: Intake fee: $45–$120, regular sessions: $39–$95; group sessions: $11–$50, medication evaluations: $18–$55. Evening sessions available. Day treatment programs for mentally ill adults and for children ages 6–12. Special evaluation, counseling, and medication monitoring for older adults. Vocational rehabilitation and placement for mentally disabled clients. Residential treatment programs for chronically mentally ill clients, including homeless clients; support services for residents include case management and mental health services.

Religious-Sponsored Centers:
Emphasis on Concerns of Normal Population

PRESBYTERIAN COUNSELING SERVICE.......(206) 527-2266
564 NE Ravenna Blvd, Seattle 98115
    NCES (Multiple sites throughout King County and Seattle)
Individual, couples, and family counseling focusing on stress and conflicts related to relationships, life changes and loss; issues of growth and individual development; also vocational evaluation and counseling. Sliding scale $30–$100. Marriage and Family Training Clinic (MFT) serves low-income families and trains therapists. Couples and families have the option of reflective team therapy (being observed by therapists in training) or one therapist who consults with experienced clinicians. Sliding scale $10–$30 per session. Seminars, workshops and ongoing groups for marriage preparation and parenting.

JEWISH FAMILY SERVICE ....(206) 461-3240
1601 16th Ave., Seattle 98122
    E 606 110th Ave NE, Bellevue 98004 ....(425)-451-8512
Multiservice agency focusing on (but not restricted to) Jewish clients. Individual, group, couple, family, and child counseling; sliding scale fees: $25–$80 per session. Referral to legal, medical, dental, and other community resources. Kosher meals, visits, health care, and case management for older adults. Social programs, tenant support, residential treatment facilities, advocacy and case management for mentally and developmentally disabled Jewish adults. Jewish Big Pals for children in single-parent families. Resettlement of Jewish refugees. Family life education programs are available. Interfaith marriage support is also offered. Employment guidance is available. Food bank 10am–noon, Wednesdays and Fridays; 2pm–4pm Thursdays. Some services are also available in Russian, Hebrew and Yiddish.

FIGURE 1.1

Comparison of representative religious-sponsored counseling centers and publicly funded mental health clinics in Seattle, Washington.

Note: From *Where to Turn Plus: The Directory of Human Resources,* by Crisis Clinic, 1998, Seattle, WA: Author. Adapted with permission.

Special Training for Pastoral Counselors. Certified pastoral counselors have widely diverse backgrounds and levels of training and experience. Certification has four tracks with varying training requirements, but all four require at least a 3-year professional degree from a seminary. All the tracks also require a certain amount of supervised counseling experience, but only the upper two tracks require that the counselor be state licensed or certified as a professional counselor or marriage and family therapist (AAPC, 2003c).

Many pastoral counseling institutes offer graduate training programs that are affiliated with certain accredited universities or seminaries, such as Vanderbilt University in Nashville, Tennesse, and Garrett Theological Seminary in Evanston, Illinois. The Danielsen Institute in Boston is affiliated with Boston University (Danielsen, 2003). Some universities, such as Loyola College in Columbia, MD, offer an ecumenical pastoral counseling graduate program (Loyola, 2003).

Comprehensive Community Health Centers and Neighborhood Clinics

Comprehensive community health centers and neighborhood clinics of various kinds are developing throughout the country and combining under one jurisdiction counseling, medical, and social services. In these combined programs, counseling services differ from those of the comprehensive community mental health clinics, discussed earlier, which are financed by state and county funds and serve primarily patients with chronic mental illness. These newer centers, designed primarily for persons who are uninsured, service the full range of situational, transitional problems of clients and families. Emerging in communities from the grass roots, these centers vary widely, depending on the needs of particular communities and neighborhoods. Examples are described in chapter 19.

WHAT NEW CHALLENGES FACE THE PROFESSION?

Counseling services emerging in the community have brought about the rise of managed health care programs and Internet counseling services, both of which have raised issues that warrant special attention.

Managed Health Care Programs

Most mental health providers working in the community contract with a managed care organization (MCO) to conduct the administration, financing, and delivery of services (Lawless, Ginter, & Kelly, 1999; Pingitore, Sheffler, Haley, Sentell, & Schwalm, 2001). Originally designed to make health care services affordable to most people and to protect the consumer, MCOs have become bureaucratic systems that tend to stifle rather than enhance health care practices. On the other hand, the many benefits that come with managed care systems can't be overlooked—health care professionals practicing in teams rather than in isolation, lower fees in many cases, and practitioners being held accountable for the nature, duration, and outcome of services.

Of the various managed care organizations, the health maintenance organizations (HMOs) are the most numerous and influential (Cooper & Gottlieb, 2000; Pingitore et al., 2001). An HMO is "an organization that delivers health care to its members for a fixed monthly membership fee. Mental health and medical care are delivered by providers and hospitals associated with the HMO" (Lawless et al., 1999, p. 52). Mental health specialists may be employed directly by the HMO and provide their services at the HMO facility, or more typically, they may contract with HMOs to offer their services in private offices. Most commonly, HMOs contract only with groups of mental health professionals, believing that such groupings cut costs and increase efficiency of services (Bisline, Sheridan, & Winegar, 1991; Giles, 1993).

Managed care services such as HMOs have tried to curtail costs in mental health practice in several ways. They limit counseling and therapeutic services to clients with problems or diagnoses specified by the HMO staff, and they limit the number of sessions permitted each client (usually four to six), thus requiring counselors to use brief therapy techniques regardless of the patient. HMOs further cut costs by a process they call capitation, in which mental health professionals agree to provide services at a flat fee per covered HMO member per month (Giles, 1991; Lawless et al., 1999; Lowman & Resick, 1994). In this system the income of the mental health provider depends on the number of different clients seen rather than the number of sessions per client. This type of reimbursement forces mental health providers to see clients for fewer sessions so as to see more clients per month.

Individuals who belong to a managed care system, such as an HMO insurance program, and who want counseling must often follow a series of complicated procedures. They first must obtain prior authorization from their primary physician, called the gatekeeper. If approved, the individual is referred to a mental health professional who is an approved HMO provider, who must then make a diagnosis of the patient's condition according to the *DSM-IV-TR* (see chap. 7). The provider then submits the diagnosis and a treatment plan to an HMO evaluator, who conducts a utilization review (UR). If the individual qualifies for treatment, the HMO evaluator determines the number of sessions and may modify the treatment plan. If the client is still in need of help after the allotted sessions are used up, the mental health provider must submit a written request—along with a progress report and, at times, case notes—for more counseling sessions. If the HMO evaluator turns down the request, the provider may appeal.

Not all MCOs require such complicated procedures. Belar (2000) points out that managed care systems are very diverse, and many don't employ the methods being criticized—for example, Kaiser Permanente of California, where she was employed as a clinical psychologist. "In my 7 years with Kaiser Permanente I never presented a case for utilization review by either an internal or external group. . . . Nor was there a gatekeeper for access to mental health services; patients could contact the department directly to initiate services" (p. 238). Belar warns that "managed care strategies should not be confused with managed care itself" (p. 237). Further, she adds, those who criticize MCO strategies generally ignore MCO benefits. MCOs, she says, have distinct advantages over unmanaged private practitioners: Services are affordable to most people, and they have access to diverse services through collaborative and multidisciplinary teams of providers (see chap. 3 for further discussion).

Nonetheless, many, if not most, MCOs have problems that need to be addressed. Licensed professional counselors (LPCs) have had difficulty in being approved as mental health providers by MCOs; typically MCOs have contracted with licensed psychologists or licensed social workers. "In states where counselors . . . are faced with insurance companies who do not reimburse licensed professional counselors (LPCs), counselors have exceptional difficulty in being taken seriously by managed care companies" (Smith, 1999, pp. 273–274). In a survey of licensed counselors in four states in different regions in the United States, Danzinger & Welfel (2001) confirmed the difficulty that licensed counselors tend to have in gaining MCO approval: "Nearly three quarters of respondents (71%) reported that they have attempted to become managed care providers and many of them (48%) indicated . . . difficulty in getting approved as providers. In spite of the difficulty . . . 60% of the sample identified themselves as providers for at least one MCO" (p. 142).

Lawless et al. (1999) are optimistic about the future of master's degree counselors as providers for MCO, claiming that master's level practitioners represent the new standard for practice in MCOs. These authors ask, "Why pay a Ph.D. counselor, who demands a higher fee, when you can pay a master's level counselor who is likely to be equally competent?" (p. 62).

Managed care organizations have had a profound impact on mental health practice. Many managed care practices contradict good ethical practice as defined by the professional counseling associations regarding the clients' rights to privacy, the freedom of choice of therapist, confidentiality of client-counselor interactions, counselor control of the type of treatment and duration of counseling, and assurance that the client will not be abandoned by the counselor (see chap. 3). Because of these problems, some mental health providers in private practice choose not to contract with MCOs, but for most this isn't financially possible. "Because of its dominance in the marketplace, eschewing managed care is not an option for most mental health counselors in the foreseeable future" (Danzinger & Welfel, 2001, pp. 137–138).

To cope with these difficulties, many counselors maintain both managed care and self-paying clients. In a survey of California psychologists, a sample that the researchers believe is fairly representative of health care providers throughout the country, Pingitore et al. (2001) found that 37% were not participants in a managed care program. Of those who were, the average number of MCO cases was 50%. Further, these authors found that 33% of psychologists' income came from patients' self-payment. "The evidence also suggests that California psychologists and a significant proportion of their patients have jointly decided to initiate or to continue treatment under a direct-payment arrangement, independent of insurance companies" (p. 595).

Proponents of managed care services claim that this approach forces mental health providers to be more precise and specific in what they do with clients, thus reducing the chance of exploitation by unscrupulous providers who would engage all clients in long-term counseling and therapy, a practice that is costly and unnecessary (Giles, 1993). In addition, managed care organizations generally require providers to form into groups. Provider groups have the advantage of engaging in interdisciplinary case conferences, interstaff consultations, and ongoing in-service training. Further, participating providers do not have to build up their own clientele, as do independent practitioners (Bisline et al., 1991).

Opponents of managed care argue that HMOs tend to make determinations about the type and length of treatment that rightfully should be made by mental health practitioners. Managed care corporations, in their zeal to cut costs, may neglect the individual needs of clients, reduce quality of care, and limit eligibility of clients to those diagnosed as needing medical care (Bloom, 1990). HMOs also ignore clients who can profit from longer-term counseling (Mone, 1994; Whitaker, 1994). And ethical considerations are of concern: Confidentiality and rights of privacy of clients are generally violated when managed care programs require providers to report diagnosis and progress of clients to HMO management.

Internet Counseling

Use of the Internet in the counseling field began in the 1990s and has escalated in all aspects of counseling services, including information search and retrieval, assessment and diagnosis, psychological education, supervision, consultation, record keeping, and, more recently, actual counseling itself, or *online counseling*, also known as *Internet counseling* or *Web counseling* (Guterman & Kirk, 1999; Riemer-Reiss, 2000; Sampson, Kolodinski, & Greeno,1997). Online counseling, in particular, has raised considerable interest and controversy in the field (Remley & Herlihy, 2001; Riemer-Reiss, 2000; Sampson et al.,1997).

The Internet has proven very useful in many aspects of counseling services, most notably in information retrieval, allowing individuals to access a wide range of counseling services, particularly specialized services—career, addiction, spiritual, family, multicultural. The Internet can also facilitate the orientation stage of counseling, which involves record keeping, scheduling, and intake interviewing. And it can facilitate assessment procedures, as well as referrals, supervision, consultations, and conferencing (Sampson et al., 1997).

Some professionals claim that actual online counseling is not only possible, but can be more beneficial in certain cases, particularly for those who are disabled and for those living in remote areas where counseling services are unavailable. Online counseling also allows family members who don't live in the same area to participate (Sampson et al., 1997). Some proponents further claim that online counseling may help certain clients reduce their anxiety about the process because counselor and client preserve a degree of anonymity; and it may improve counselor-client communication because written words offer a more considered means of expression than do oral exchanges (Remley & Herlihy, 2001; Sampson et al., 1997).

But along with the benefits come problems. Sampson et al. (1997) warn that although Internet counseling offers "many new opportunities for clients and counselors, the same possibilities may result in detrimental unintended consequences" (p. 209). Critics have voiced concerns about ethical issues such as the loss of confidentiality and privacy for clients, the increased risk of counselors misrepresenting their professional competence, and the exposure of clients to invalid information and to uncredentialed counselors. Moreover, counselors are less likely to monitor client information searches, and distance counseling limits counselor awareness of the client's social-cultural environment. Critics have also voiced concern over the difficulty in developing effective counseling relationships on the Internet and the lack of counselor availability when clients experience a crisis or trauma (Remley & Herlihy, 2001; Sampson et al., 1997). Ethical concerns and the new codes of ethics that professional associations have drawn up to address online counseling are discussed in chapter 3. The limitations of online counseling in developing an effective counseling relationship are discussed in chapter 4.

SUMMARY

The demand for counseling services has increased rapidly because people are experiencing more conflicts in their everyday lives as a result of escalating social, cultural, and economic pressures and upheavals.

Professional counseling is a unique service in the mental health field, one that focuses on the developmental social-cultural concerns and conflicts of normally functioning individuals, especially during transitional periods throughout their life spans. In this process an experiential relationship develops between counselor and client, an evolving relationship that fosters healing and constructive resolution of personal and interpersonal situational conflicts. This approach generally differs from models used by other mental health providers, in which providers tend to view client problems as symptoms of pathology that require treatment.

In addition to direct counseling, counselors offer outreach services in all work settings—consultation, assessment, psychoeducation, and crisis intervention.

Professional counseling is done by licensed or certified counselors in public schools, colleges, community agencies, employment agencies, and businesses. Regardless of where they work, counselors perform direct counseling and offer various outreach services.

After World War II counseling services developed for the most part only in schools, colleges, and rehabilitation centers but gradually expanded during the late the 1970s and the 1980s into the community. Largely because of limited budgets, however, for many years community mental health services generally had to limit services to persons with severe disturbances.

Increasing numbers of state legislatures have granted licensure to professional counselors, a move that has led to a rapid increase in the number of counselors in private practice and community agencies.

Since the 1980s and 1990s, counseling has spread into important segments of the community—business and industry through employer assistance programs; career counseling centers; pastoral counseling centers and institutes; and comprehensive neighborhood health care centers for the uninsured.

Managed health care programs have greatly impacted the delivery of mental health services in the community. These organizations have brought benefits as well as challenges to counselors and therapists. With the increased growth of the Internet, online counseling continues to expand. Online counseling services include assessment, screening, psychological education, supervision, consultation, record keeping, and actual counseling itself.

PROJECTS AND ACTIVITIES

1. Survey several mental health agencies in your community. Find out how many staff members hold degrees in counseling or social work and how many have psychological or psychiatric training.
2. Attend a meeting of the local, regional, or state counseling association. Also attend meeting of the social workers' association or the psychological association. Compare the types of issues of each program, or compare program brochures of their scheduled meetings.
3. Interview the director of the counseling center at your university; ask about the history of the center and the current policies and practices.
4. Set up a panel of counselors from schools, colleges, and community agencies, all of whom have had training in counseling or counseling psychology. Ask the panelists these questions: What are your major responsibilities? How do these responsibilities tie in with your training? What gaps do you see in services to the general public?
5. Visit a religious-sponsored counseling service near you, or write to such a center for a brochure. Compare its services with those of traditional community agencies. What training have staff members had?
6. Check a directory of community mental health services in a large city, or write for brochures. How many offer mental health services for members of the general public?

REFERENCES

Adler, A. (1927). *Practice and theory of individual psychology*. New York: Harcourt, Brace & World.

AAPC. (2003a). *About pastoral counseling*. Retrieved from American Association of Pastoral Counselors Web site: http://www.info@aapc.org/about.htm

AAPC. (2003b). *Code of ethics*. Retrieved from American Association of Pastoral Counselors Web site: http://www.info@aapc.org/ethics.htm

AAPC. (2003c). *Membership categories*. Retrieved from American Association of Pastoral Counselors Web site: http://www.info@aapc.org/membership.htm

AAPC. (2003d). *Pastoral counseling centers of Tennessee*. Retrieved from American Association of Pastoral Counselors Web site: http://www.info@aapc.org/centers.htm#TN

Baker, S. B., & Shaw, M. C. (1987). *Improving counseling through primary intervention*. Upper Saddle River, NJ: Merrill/Prentice Hall.

Baxter, N. J. (1990). *Opportunities in counseling and developmental careers*. Lincolnwood, IL: V. G. M. Career Horizons.

Belar, C. D. (2000). Ethical issues in managed care: Perspectives in evolution. *The Counseling Psychologist, 28*, 237–241.

Bisline, J. L., Sheridan, S. M., & Winegar, N. (1991). Five critical skills for mental health counselors in managed health care. *Journal of Mental Health Counseling, 13*, 147–152.

Bloom, B. L. (1990). Managing mental health services: Some comments for the overdue debate in psychology. *Community Mental Health Journal, 26*, 107–124.

Brammer, L., Abrego, P. J., & Shostrom, E. L. (1993). *Therapeutic counseling and psychotherapy* (6th ed.). Upper Saddle River, NJ: Prentice Hall.

Brown, S. L. (1991). *Counseling victims of violence*. Alexandria, VA: American Counseling Association.

Bureau of Labor Statistics, U.S. Department of Labor. (2003). *Occupational outlook handbook, 2002–2003 Edition*, Bulletin 2540. Washington, DC: Superintendent of Documents, U.S. Government Printing Office.

Collison, B. B., & Garfield, N. J. (1990). *Careers in counseling and human development*. Alexandria, VA: American Counseling Association.

Cooper, C. C., & Gottlieb, M. C. (2000). Ethical issues with managed care: Challenges facing counseling psychology. *The Counseling Psychologist, 28*, 179–236.

Danielsen. (2003). *The Danielsen Institute*. Retrieved from http://www.bu.edu/danielsen

Danzinger, P. R., & Welfel, E. R. (2001). The impact of managed care on mental health counselors: A survey of perceptions, practices, and compliance with ethical standards. *Journal of Mental Health Counseling, 23*, 137–150.

Dickman, J. F., Emener, W. G., & Hutchinson, W. S. (Eds.). (1985). *Counseling the troubled person in industry*. Springfield, IL: Charles C. Thomas.

Gelso, C. J., & Fretz, B. R. (2001). *Counseling psychology* (2nd ed.). Fort Worth, TX: Harcourt Brace.

Gibson, R. L., & Mitchell, M. H. (1999). *Introduction to counseling and guidance* (5th ed.). Upper Saddle River, NJ: Merrill/Prentice Hall.

Giles, T. R. (1991). Managed mental health care and effective psychotherapy: A step in the right direction. *Journal of Behavior Therapy and Experimental Psychiatry, 14,* 189–196.

Giles, T. R. (1993). *Managed mental health care: A guide for practitioners, employers, and hospital administrators.* Boston: Allyn & Bacon.

Ginter, E. (1989). Slayers of monster-watermelons found in the mental health patch. *Journal of Mental Health Counseling, 11,* 77–85.

Guterman, J. T. (1994). A social constructionist position for mental health counseling. *Journal of Mental Health Counseling, 16,* 226–244.

Guterman, J. T., & Kirk, M. A. (1999). Mental health counselors and the Internet. *Journal of Mental Health Counseling 21,* 300–325.

Herr, E. L., & Cramer, S. H. (1996). *Career guidance and counseling through the life span: Systematic approaches* (5th ed.). New York: Scott, Foresman.

Hershenson, D. B., Power, P. W., & Waldo, M. (1996). *Community counseling: Contemporary theory and practice.* Boston: Allyn & Bacon.

Hillman, J., & Ventura, M. (1992). *We've had a hundred years of psychotherapy and the world's getting worse.* San Francisco: Harper.

Hollis, J. W., & Wantz, R. A. (1993). *Counselor preparation 1993–1995: Program and personnel* (8th ed.). Muncie, IN: Accelerated Development.

Horney, K. (1939). *New ways in psychoanalysis.* New York: Norton.

Hosie, T. W., West, J. D., & Mackey, J. A. (1993). Employment and roles of counselors in employee assistance programs. *Journal of Counseling & Development, 71,* 355–359.

Isaacson, L. E., & Brown, D. (1997). *Career information in counseling and career development.* Boston: Allyn & Bacon.

Kendrick, R., Chander, J., & Hatcher, W. (1994). Job demands, stressors, and the school counselor. *School Counselor, 41,* 365–369.

Lawless, L. L., Ginter, E. J., & Kelly, K. C. (1999). *Journal of Mental Health Counseling, 21,* 50–65.

Levy, D. (1971). Beginnings of the child guidance movement. In M. Levitt & B. Rubenstein (Eds.), *The mental health field: A critical appraisal* (pp. 32–39). Detroit: Wayne State University Press.

Lewis, J. A., & Lewis, M. D. (1986). *Counseling programs for employees in the workplace.* Pacific Grove, CA: Brooks/Cole.

Lowman, R. L., & Resnick, R. J. (1994). *The mental health professional's guide to managed care.* Washington, DC: American Psychological Association.

Loyola. (2003). *Graduate programs in pastoral counseling: Loyola college in MD.* Retrieved from http://www.loyola.edu/academics/alldepartments/pastoralcounseling

May, K. M. (1992). Referrals to employee assistance programs: A pilot analogue study of expectations about counseling. *Journal of Mental Health Counseling, 14,* 208–244.

Mone, L. C. (1994). Managed care cost effectiveness: Fantasy or reality? *International Journal of Group Psychotherapy, 44,* 437–446.

Peer, G. G. (1985). The status of secondary school guidance: A national survey. *School Counselor, 32,* 181–189.

Pingitore, D., Sheffler, R., Haley, M., Sentell, T., & Schwalm, D. (2001). Professional psychology in a new era: Practice-based evidence from California. *Professional Psychology: Research and Practice, 32,* 585–596.

Remley, T. P., Jr., & Herlihy, B. (2001). *Ethical, legal, and professional issues in counseling.* Upper Saddle River, NJ: Merrill/Prentice Hall.

Riemer-Reiss, M. L. (2000). Utilizing distance technology for mental health counseling. *Journal of Mental Health Counseling, 22,* 189–203.

Rogers, C. R. (1939). *The clinical treatment of the problem child.* New York: Houghton Mifflin.

Rogers, C. R. (1942). *Counseling and psychotherapy.* Boston: Houghton Mifflin.

Samaritan Institute. (2003). *Annual report 2002.* Retrieved from http://www.samaritan-institute.org

Sampson, J. P., Jr., Kolodinski, R. W., & Greeno, P. P. (1997). Counseling on the information highway: Further possibilities and potential problems. *Journal of Counseling & Development, 75,* 203–212.

Smith, H. B. (1999). Managed care: A survey of counselor educators and counselor practitioners. *Journal of Mental Health Counseling, 21,* 270–281.

Steenbarger, B. N. (1990). Toward a developmental understanding of the counseling specialty: Lessons from our students. *Journal of Counseling & Development, 68,* 434–437.

Super, D. E. (1955). Transition: From vocational guidance to counseling psychology. *Journal of Counseling Psychology, 2,* 3–9.

Thompson, C. L., & Rudolph, L. B. (1992). *Counseling children.* Pacific Grove, CA: Brooks/Cole.

Whitaker, L. C. (1994). Managed care: Who cares about psychotherapy? *Journal of College Student Psychotherapy, 9,* 7–17.

Wiggins, J. D., & Moody, A. H. (1987). Student evaluations of counseling programs: An added dimension. *School Coungselor, 34,* 353–361.

CHAPTER 2

A Historical Perspective

1900–1920: THE BEGINNINGS OF COUNSELING

Vocational Counseling and Guidance

In 1908 Frank Parsons opened a vocational bureau, the first of its kind, to offer counseling help to those looking for work. It was more than just a placement center that listed job openings. Unusual for his time, Parsons believed that persons have the right to choose their own vocations rather than, say, follow their fathers' line of work, assisting on the farm or in the factory. He implemented this idea by creating the role of *vocational counselor*. By listening to what young persons (generally adolescent boys) had to say about themselves, he countered the prevailing authoritarian attitude that told young people what to do (Parsons, 1909). His belief in the value of listening to their desires and feelings regarding what they wanted to do vocationally was a forerunner of what was to become the essential feature of counseling.

In helping the client self-explore, Parsons developed a unique methodology—that of a self-inventory, perhaps the first questionnaire of its kind. Comprehensive in scope, it probed a person's interests, aptitudes, limitations, moral character, appearance, bodily characteristics, motivations, and disposition. It was a take-home survey with which the applicant could solicit help from family, friends, and teachers (Parsons, 1909). By today's standards it was primitive and unwieldy: The many pages of questions would take hours, if not days, to complete. Questions were simplistic; for example, applicants were asked to mark whether they were honest or dishonest, bold or bashful, sensible or foolish. Interpretation of overall responses was time-consuming and difficult.

But Parsons's concept that a self-survey could be useful in matching one's characteristics to a suitable vocation was unique. Moreover, he believed in the importance of client-counselor interaction; together they interpreted results of the self-survey, going over consistencies and inconsistencies of responses and looking for meaningful patterns. Through such interaction they determined the client's appropriate vocation.

Impressed by Parsons's work, the superintendent of schools in Boston designated 117 teachers as vocational counselors in Boston's elementary and secondary schools. By 1910 approximately 30 cities had programs in vocational planning and job placement. Training in vocational counseling began at Harvard University in 1911. In 1913 the National Vocational Guidance Association was founded (Brewer, 1942).

Parsons and others used the terms *counseling* and *guidance* synonymously, and both methods—counselor-client interaction and advice giving—were used. But after Parsons's death in 1909 and after World War I, interest in this method of self-exploration virtually disappeared and was replaced by occupational information centers. This move was supported by funds from the federal government through the 1917 Smith-Hughes Act, funds primarily for developing vocational guidance in schools.

During World War I the first group standardized tests were developed when the U.S. Army asked psychologists to develop assessment devices to screen out emotionally and intellectually unfit draftees, to place draftees in appropriate jobs, and to select qualified persons for officer training. Psychologists' efforts led to the development of verbal and nonverbal group intelligence tests (the Army Alpha and Beta) and to Woodworth's Personal Data Sheet. Group testing and group assessment proliferated and became a significant force in the growth and direction of applied psychological testing and vocational counseling and guidance (Osipow & Fitzgerald, 1996). The practice of testing became known as *psychometrics* and those who administered and interpreted the tests, *psychometrists.*

College Clinics

Vocational guidance centers had not yet developed on college campuses. Some colleges, however, developed psychological clinics to test children who were having difficulties in public schools. The first psychological clinic was developed by Lightner Witmer in 1896 at the University of Pennsylvania, primarily to diagnose and treat children with learning and behavioral problems. School personnel used this service when their students were experiencing academic, behavioral, or social problems. Other universities then opened similar clinics.

Community Clinics

The first psychiatric clinic was established in Chicago in 1908 by Freudian psychiatrist William Healy. It was called the Juvenile Psychopathic Institute, and services were designed to work with juvenile delinquents. The creation of the institute has a remarkable history. Well-to-do philanthropist Ms. Dunner was appalled by the juvenile crime rate in Chicago, and contrary to prevailing opinion, she believed that social conditions were at the root of the problem. She was part of a group of socially concerned women (including Jane Addams, who developed Hull House) who were noted for their philanthropic endeavors throughout Chicago. In search of a director for the institute, Ms. Dunner insisted on finding the foremost physician on the latest theories of modern psychology

(Levy, 1971). Fellow supporter Professor George Mead, head of the Department of Philosophy at the University of Chicago, consulted with none other than philosopher William James and psychiatrist Adolf Meyer. They recommended psychiatrist William Healy, who was familiar with Freudian methods of psychoanalysis. At that time Sigmund Freud was hardly known in the United States, and psychoanalysis was not designed for children, so hiring Healy was a bold, innovative step. Treatment at the institute followed an interdisciplinary approach, involving a psychiatrist, a psychologist who conducted assessments, and a social worker. In 1917 the Chicago clinic was taken over by the state of Illinois. Healy left for Boston, where he established a similar clinic (Levy, 1971).

1920–1940: THE EARLY YEARS

The field of psychometry blossomed and flourished from 1920 to 1940, and along with it emerged psychologists whose primary tasks were developing, administering, and interpreting tests. During the 1920s the field of educational guidance developed and expanded in schools, but during the 1930s, because of the Depression, the field of vocational guidance expanded in social agencies to serve the needs of large numbers of displaced adults. At the college level in the 1930s, E. G. Williamson (1939) developed what he called *clinical counseling*, based primarily on techniques of testing and diagnosis. A separate movement also emerged during the 1930s; a small but significant group of clinical psychologists practiced relationship therapy in child guidance clinics. That practice influenced Carl Rogers, who went on to develop his client-centered therapy.

Growth of the Testing Movement

During this period the study of individual differences preoccupied applied psychologists throughout the country. At universities and other research centers, psychologists devoted themselves to developing all kinds of tests and measurements. Unlike today, psychologists generally did not practice therapy (Gelso & Fretz, 2001).

Tests were developed to cover all aspects of human behavior—intelligence, personality, various aptitudes, and achievement. Arthur Otis, for example, in 1922 developed the Otis Group Intelligence Scale; E. K. Strong, in 1927, published the Strong Vocational Interest Blank; Clark Hull, in 1928, issued his landmark text describing aptitude testing; and Starke Hathaway developed the Minnesota Multiphase Personality Inventory during the 1930s, publishing it in 1941. The use of standardized tests took hold in psychological, sociological, educational, and vocational guidance services. Business and industry, as well, used tests as a means to screen applicants for jobs.

Educational Guidance in Schools

Progressive education, which was introduced into schools in the 1920s by philosopher John Dewey, exerted a strong influence on school curricula (Woodring, 1953). Proponents believed that schools had the responsibility not only to guide children in their personal, social, and moral development but also to modify the school environment for optimal learning. Insisting that all schoolchildren should receive a well-rounded education, they emphasized broadening school curricula to include personal and social development, as well as academic knowledge and vocational skills.

Leading educator John Brewer, in his landmark book *Education as Guidance* (1932), claimed that guidance and education were synonymous. He proposed that the objective of education is to develop skills in living. Schools should guide young people in individual and cooperative activities, and learning should include citizenship, recreation, personal well-being, and moral development. Teachers were considered guidance specialists who should incorporate life skills into their subject matter. Teachers were to help students "relate themselves to the life of the local community and to that of the nation and the world" (Strang, 1953, p. 143).

Vocational Guidance

During the 1920s most vocational guidance centers were incorporated into school districts and faded from the community as separate agencies. They reemerged in the community during the Depression in the 1930s, however, to assist the large numbers of unemployed. According to Super (1942), schools had proved inadequate settings for vocational guidance because they "were unable to see beyond the narrow confines of the school" (p. 260). He continues,

> With the 1930s new trends somewhat reversed the situation, giving the dominant role to nonschool guidance workers. Social agencies, familiar with the problems of the unemployed and frequently closer to the employer than the schools, seemed to be in the key situation for vocational guidance. . . . Social agencies . . . brought a new emphasis into the literature of vocational guidance, an emphasis on community responsibility and organization. (pp. 260–261)

College Counseling

In 1939 E. G. Williamson published *How to Counsel Students: A Manual of Techniques for Clinical Counselors,* which contained the first theory developed specifically for counseling. This book was an outcome of his work at the University of Minnesota's student counseling center, the first of its kind in the country, at which students were given educational and vocational counseling. Williamson's clinical counseling theory, a diagnostic prescriptive approach, was based on the assumption that personality consists of measurable traits that can be related to occupational choice and success. His term *clinical counseling* paralleled the diagnostic approach that prevailed at this time among clinical psychologists, social workers, and guidance specialists. The popularity of Williamson's theory of clinical counseling as applied to vocational counseling can be attributed, in part, to the testing movement that was flourishing in social agencies and schools.

Child Guidance Clinics and the Beginnings of Therapy

In 1921 child guidance demonstration clinics were established in several strategic cities as a result of increased public interest in the mental health of children. As in Healy's earlier clinics, an interdisciplinary team of psychiatrists, psychologists, and social workers worked with children and parents (Goldenberg & Goldenberg, 2000; Levy, 1971). The team's major task was the testing and diagnosis of children with learning problems and adults with symptoms of mental illness (Hershenson, Power, & Waldo, 1996). Treatment was primarily that of modifying or changing the environment (e.g., placing the child in a foster home) or psychoanalysis by psychiatrists.

This diagnostic and prescriptive model had a few exceptions. Some child guidance clinics practiced relationship therapy as developed by psychiatrist Otto Rank (1936) and popularized by others, such as psychiatrist Frederick Allen and social worker Jessie Taft (Rogers, 1939, 1942). Some clinics also used play therapy as practiced by child therapists such as Fredrick Allen, Dorothy Baruch, Melanie Klein, and David Levy (Rogers, 1939, 1942). This trend in the use of relationship therapy was given impetus by the changes in psychoanalytic treatment made by dissenters of Freud—Alfred Adler and Karen Horney.

During the 1930s Carl Rogers (1939), a clinical psychologist at a child guidance clinic in Rochester, New York, was also practicing one of the new therapies called expressive therapy with children. Although his initial period of training and practice was primarily psychometry, as was customary then for clinical psychologists, he developed a strong interest in the new relationship therapies (Rogers, 1939, 1942). They, in turn, influenced his theory of nondirective and client-centered counseling, which he presented in the following decade.

1940–1960: EMERGENCE OF PROFESSIONAL COUNSELING

A new direction developed in counseling and guidance in the 1940s, one that broke away from the diagnostic prescription approach that had dominated both educational and vocational guidance and clinical treatment centers. The major shift came after Carl Rogers published *Counseling and Psychotherapy* (1942), in which he proposed his *nondirective, client-centered therapy*. A clinical psychologist with many years of experience, in child guidance clinics in the 1930s, Rogers, as described earlier, had been influenced by a process theory of therapy in which the client develops primarily through an evolving relationship with the counselor (Rogers, 1939, 1942). Out of this experience Rogers developed an approach he called nondirective to counteract the directive, diagnostic prescriptive approach prevalent among practitioners at educational and vocational guidance clinics. He later changed the term *nondirective* to *client-centered* (1951; see also chap. 6).

Like other clinical psychologists of his time, Rogers had been steeped in testing and diagnosis. But while practicing in this mode, he also indicated his doubts about relying only on testing as a way of diagnosing. Rogers's approach differed significantly from Williamson's traditional model of guidance or clinical counseling, described earlier. Williamson's method was to gather data, evaluate, and diagnose the problem first and then to "treat" or "counsel" the client. In later years Williamson's system came to be known colloquially as the "test 'em and tell 'em" method (Romano & Skovolt, 1998, p. 463). Debates over the relative merits of Williamson's diagnostic prescriptive method versus the Rogerian client-centered approach continued throughout this period.

Other influences also contributed to a shift in counseling and therapeutic practice at this time. As a result of the Nazi dictatorship, the Holocaust, and the war, many prominent European existentialists and neo-Freudian, psychosocial analysts immigrated to the United States—Otto Rank, Alfred Adler, Karen Horney, Erich Fromm, Erik Erikson, and Victor Frankl. Their approaches counteracted the prevailing American scientific assessment of individual differences, trait factor theory of personality, behaviorism, and classical Freudian psychoanalysis. Their presence in America influenced such leading American psychological theorists as Rollo May, Abraham Maslow, and Carl Rogers.

Origins of Counseling Psychology and Counselor Training Programs

World War II and its immediate aftermath greatly influenced the beginning of professional counseling as we know it today. After the war the general public and the U.S. government recognized that the millions of returning servicemen needed assistance in coping with the uncertainties of their transition to civilian life. Congress, under the G.I. Bill of Rights and through the Veterans Administration (VA), offered full tuition and substantial stipends to returning veterans for the time equal to the months they had served in the military. The VA also provided funding for free vocational counseling for all veterans. Counseling centers sprang up on major campuses, and trained counselors were suddenly needed to fill job openings. These developments supported and promoted the need to provide counseling for the normal concerns of people, the aim that is central to counseling theory and practice today.

In response, the VA initiated and funded university training programs for doctoral degrees in both counseling psychology and clinical psychology. Thus, a new profession termed *counseling psychology* was established (Tolbert, 1982; Whiteley, 1984). Whereas clinical psychologists were trained to diagnose and treat individuals with chronic emotional disorders, counseling psychologists focused on conflicts experienced by normal persons. As Gelso and Fretz (2001) point out, "Counseling psychology was a profession waiting to happen" (p. 34).

Until this time, counseling had been virtually synonymous with guidance—educational and vocational guidance in schools and colleges and vocational guidance in social agencies. Guidance had also been closely associated with the use of tests that measured individual differences, assessing various aspects of a person's characteristics. Moreover, psychological theories at that time focused predominantly on assessing individual differences and personality traits with little regard for developmental processes. The upheavals of the war, however, convinced professionals that social traumas and anxieties during transitional periods influenced and shaped the individual.

Vocational guidance professor Donald Super (1955) readily embraced the new concepts of counseling psychology and promoted the transition from vocational guidance to counseling psychology. In 1946, when Frank Nugent enrolled in the masters program in vocational counseling at Columbia University, Super had just become its director. Super saw himself as part of a new direction for the field of counseling, one that combined vocational assessment, human development theory, social-cultural factors, and the early Rogerian client-centered approach. A long-time specialist in assessment, Super (1949) acknowledged the need to shift away from testing as the primary task of the counselor and lectured on how the Rogerian client-centered approach could be applied when selecting and interpreting tests in vocational counseling.

Super defined the distinction between counseling psychology and vocational guidance in his article "Transition: From Vocational Guidance to Counseling Psychology" (1955). Citing the influence of Rogers's 1942 book, he said that "growth of interest in psychotherapeutic procedures . . . became even greater than interest in psychometrics . . . . [O]ne counsels *people* rather than *problems*" (p. 4). Emphasizing the danger of misusing tests, Super made valuable comments regarding how counselors should use and interpret them properly, warning also that counselors shouldn't overrely on them.

As proponent of one of the earliest human development theories, based on the relatively unknown German scholar Charlotte Buehler, Super (1942) expanded the idea of human development into the vocational field. Vocational development is a lifetime process, he said. Different stages have been studied per se, but "with a few important exceptions [Charlotte Buehler and E. K. Strong] no attention has been paid to persons as they pass from one stage to another" (p. 135).

Another leading educator who promoted the field of counseling psychology was Gilbert Wrenn (1962) at the University of Minnesota. Whereas Super was influential in the 1950s in shifting vocational guidance over to counseling psychology, Wrenn, whose expertise was in the schools, was instrumental in distinguishing school counseling from the old educational guidance models. Like Super, Wrenn opposed the diagnostic prescriptive model of guidance and supported the new developmental, psychosocial, and self theories of human behavior promoted by Erik Erikson, Donald Super, and Carl Rogers (Wrenn, 1962).

Spurred by VA funding, both counseling and clinical psychology training programs were set up in the early 1950s at universities throughout the country. Most of the newly emerging counseling psychologists were to become the future faculty in counseling programs, the practicing counselors in college counseling centers, and the supervisors of the future master's-level counselors-in-training. The majority of counseling psychology programs were established in departments of education or educational psychology; most psychology departments tended to resist the new humanistic, phenomenological, and psychosocial theories of psychology.

Development of Professional Associations

Professional associations were very important to the development of counseling at this time, because the newly formed, fledgling profession was in need of a unifying force that could define its role, nurture its development, and set and implement standards of training. In response to the shift away from guidance and toward counseling psychology and as a result of the VA's creating and funding programs for the new field of counseling psychology, in 1953 Division 17 of the American Psychological Association (APA) changed its name from the Division of Counseling and Guidance to the Division of Counseling Psychology (Woody, Hansen, & Rossberg, 1989). Leaders of APA Division 17 were university professors, such as Donald Super and Gilbert Wrenn, "concerned with dealing with the circumstances of normal development in the personal and vocational areas and factors that interfered with that development" (Woody et al., 1989, p. 8).

Because APA Division 17 was only for psychologists with doctorates, many leaders, including Gilbert Wrenn, who had helped form APA Division 17, were also instrumental in forming the American Personnel and Guidance Association (APGA) (George & Cristiani, 1986). The APGA, in turn, became an umbrella organization for several existing independent associations—for example, National Vocational Guidance Association (NVGA) and American College Personnel Association (ACPA). New subassociations soon formed to address the specific concerns of counselors: the American School Counselors Association (ASCA) and the American Rehabilitation Counseling Association (ARCA). Moreover, to break away from their identity with guidance, counselor educators changed the name of their group from the Association of Guidance Supervisors and Counselor Trainers to the Association for Counselor Education and Supervision (ACES).

Counseling Practice: The Struggle to Clarify and Implement the Counselor Role

College Counseling

Because of the success of VA vocational counseling centers on major college campuses, college administrators converted VA centers (which were terminated in the early 1950s) to student counseling centers, and most remaining college campuses soon opened similar counseling centers. College counseling centers were the ideal places for counselors to incorporate into practice the new developmental, process-oriented, self theories, such as those espoused by Rogers, Maslow, Super, existentialist May, and psychosocial and psychodynamic theorists such as Adler and Horney. Nugent was a part of such a process.

> At the University of California–Berkeley counseling center, where I was a counselor from 1947 to 1950, we practiced the new counseling approaches. Most of our staff were clinical psychologists eager to abandon the old pathological model of diagnosis and treatment and classical Freudianism and try the new psychosocial, developmental, process-oriented therapies. We were eager to work with persons with normal situational conflicts, rather than patients with chronic mental illness. In our counseling sessions we combined the humanistic Rogerian client-centered approach and the psychodynamic theories of Alfred Adler and Karen Horney. The staff welcomed my developmentally oriented, vocational-counseling training under Donald Super at Columbia, and I benefited from their psychosocial backgrounds. Although none of us considered ourselves Rogerian, we were influenced by Rogers's views about the counseling process and the counseling relationship and tried to avoid, for instance, making analytic conceptualizations of client behavior. I learned the benefits of weekly case conferences, which served as an ongoing training laboratory and enabled us to learn from one another. Director Barbara Kirk closely supervised all new counselors, and psychiatrist Leslie Farber (1966), who later became known for his work on existentialism, was the center's consultant and provided perceptive observations regarding the underlying dynamics in the counseling relationship.

School Counseling

Recognition of the need for school counseling was fueled by the turmoil of the postwar years: the population explosion, automation in the job market, changing family patterns, and confusion about values (Wrenn, 1962). Equally important, according to Wrenn (1962), was the impact of the new psychological developmental theories of Super and Erikson, which recognized the crucial transitional period that adolescents go through. Spurred by the success of counseling in colleges, many professionals recognized that students in high schools could also benefit from counseling assistance. Nugent for instance, participated in a new high school counseling program in California.

> At Pleasant Hill High School in California, where I was a counselor in the late 1950s, our staff members were well-trained counselors with master's degrees who developed a program similar to the college counseling programs in which I had worked earlier—that is, voluntary, confidential, and process-oriented with a focus on the client's situational, developmental concerns. This was the counseling role that APGA was to adopt in the early 1960s.

After the Soviet Union launched Sputnik in 1957, Congress passed the National Defense Education Act (NDEA), which provided funds for training high school counselors through special short-term counseling and guidance institutes (Woody et al., 1989). As with any crash program, however, the effect on the practice of counseling was mixed. Generally, counselor educators were hampered both by federal regulations that limited the scope of the training programs and by the short-term nature of the training.

Community Services

Even though professional counseling was spreading rapidly in schools and college counseling centers were springing up throughout the country, this newly defined counseling service was as yet generally unavailable for adults after they left school, with the exception of vocational rehabilitation centers. Family work continued in clinics, where social worker-psychiatrist teams treated primarily children with disturbances.

1960–1980: GROWTH IN PROFESSIONAL COUNSELING

Counseling experienced growing pains during the 1960s and 1970s. It spread so rapidly in schools and colleges that supply could not keep up with demand. Because counselors lacked adequate training, they also lacked a clear understanding of their role and function. Concerned leaders from both APGA and APA Division 17 worked at defining the counselor's unique role and function and developing training standards.

Counseling reached a crisis in the 1970s, as had schools and society in general, triggered in part by the counterculture and personal growth movements and the rise of conflicting values in all segments of society. Many leaders within the profession took sides over humanism versus behaviorism; many others claimed that psychological education should replace counseling. Out of this challenge, professional counselors again clarified their unique role and primary function as distinct from that of educators.

Meanwhile, other therapeutic systems—existentialism, family systems, and cognitive theories—gradually broadened the theoretical base for counselors. During the late 1970s the need for counseling spread into the community and, along with it, the need to develop a terminal master's degree in community mental health counseling, as well as national certification and state licensure to back it up.

Professional Associations Set Standards for School Counselors

Counseling had boomed during the late 1950s and the 1960s, with growth primarily in secondary schools. The number of secondary school counselors had escalated from 6,700 in the early 1950s to more than 30,000 in 1965 (Aubrey, 1982). Elementary school counseling emerged later after the passage of the Elementary and Secondary Education Act of 1965, which authorized grants to school districts for developing elementary school counseling. Even so, those numbers increased more slowly throughout the country than the numbers of secondary school counselors; by the early 1970s the number of elementary counselors had increased to nearly 8,000 (Schmidt, 2003).

Although the new counseling model had been accepted into practice in the late 1950s at some high schools, most schools were slow to adapt their services to accommodate the new counselor role. In a survey of 1200 counselors, Gil Wrenn (1962) found that "preparation in some vital areas is sparse in spite of the large proportion having a master's degree" (p. 164). In his book *The Counselor in a Changing World (1962),* published by APGA, Wrenn proposed a blueprint that clearly defined the school counselor's role and function and provided guidelines for training programs. Wrenn's blueprint was a major departure from the old guidance model. He opposed Williamson's clinical counseling model of assessment, diagnosis, and treatment and was in accord with the new Rogerian model of client-centered counseling and Super's and Erikson's theories of development. Wrenn hoped the term *guidance*, in regard to a counselor, would eventually disappear. The counselor, he said, is a specialist whose role is to counsel students and consult with staff and parents. The counselor role should be nondisciplinarian, and counselor tasks should not include programming, advising, keeping student records, doing clerical work, or supervising the lunchroom.

Wrenn was a strong advocate of the psychosocial belief that persons develop psychologically in relation to their environment. He was also an advocate of the new Eriksonian theory of adolescent developmental transitional stages and the accompanying conflicts and anxieties. Wrenn's proposal for counselor training included a 2-year graduate program with the major core in psychology that included the new psychosocial, developmental, behavioral, and humanistic theories. His proposal also emphasized that students must have adequate and well-supervised practicums and internships.

Wrenn's blueprint was revolutionary. As a follow-up, APGA set up three regional task forces representing APGA, ACES, and ASCA, and from the results of these task forces, APGA published a set of guidelines for counselors (Loughary, Stripling, and Fitzgerald, 1965), which basically agreed with Wrenn's blueprint. Although most APGA, ACES, and ASCA members supported the task force policy statements, many expressed strong doubts that the policies were applicable or workable in school settings. They also warned that most practicing counselors were not prepared to meet these standards.

Despite doubts and objections, Fitzgerald (1965) pointed out, "For the first time there is a statement on the Role and Function of the School Counselor that depicts a consensus from the American School Counselor Association" (p. 41). This statement, he said, could help counselor educators develop appropriate, accredited graduate programs, encourage government agencies to improve counselor certification standards, and stimulate counselors to educate school administrators regarding the professional responsibilities of school counselors. In 1961 APGA, also published a code of ethics that outlined guidelines for counselors' professional responsibilities to clients. Included was the stipulation that the counseling relationship be voluntary and confidential.

It took time for the profession to understand the counselor's unique role and to set training standards. Throughout the 1960s some argued that a counselor was not a guidance specialist, a disciplinarian, a teacher, or an administrator, but rather someone who filled a unique role—that of providing voluntary and confidential counseling for students (Nugent, 1962, 1966, 1969). Professional association members throughout the country struggled to get state certification for school counselors, but in the majority of states certification standards fell short of the criteria recommended by APGA and ASCA. Thus, in many school districts insufficiently trained persons were assigned counseling jobs.

Counseling Centers Spread on College Campuses

During the 1960s increasing numbers of universities offered free counseling services to students who were experiencing problems that interfered with their academic work. By this time Nugent was the director of Western Washington University's counseling center.

> At Western Washington University (WWU) I founded a program in 1962 that was modeled after my experience as a counselor at the UC–Berkeley and Stanford University counseling centers—a program in which counseling was voluntary and confidential, separated from the college administrative and diagnostic testing center, and a program that included weekly case conferences. Our consulting psychiatrist, Buell Kingsley, was eager to work with normally functioning clients and to practice the new model of therapy that de-emphasized diagnosis and avoided pathologizing client behavior. Prior to coming to Bellingham, Kingsley had left his psychoanalytic practice on the East Coast to intern at the Child Guidance Clinic in Philadelphia, known for practicing relationship therapy developed by Frederick Allen, who had worked under Otto Rank (Rogers, 1942). Kingsley came to Bellingham's fledgling mental health clinic only on condition that the psychiatric social worker he interned under, Barbara Smith, be hired as well (B. Smith, personal communication, March, 2000). After I arrived at WWU, we hired Kingsley as our counseling center's psychiatric consultant and formed a liaison with the nearby mental health clinic. Kingsley's and Smith's experience with the new family systems and relational therapies made a significant impact during the 1960s and 1970s in the community and at WWU's college counseling center, where Kingsley's relational approach offset the approaches of behaviorist staff members.

Most counseling centers throughout the country, however, were confused about the purpose of the college counseling center and the role of the counselor. In a national survey of college counseling centers in 1965, the responses of more than 450 center directors confirmed that many centers were not complying with either APGA or APA Division 17 statements about the voluntary and confidential nature of counseling and the role and purpose of counselors: 40% of these centers did not maintain complete confidentiality of counseling records, 65% accepted forced referrals, and 40% were allied with university testing services under the office of the dean of students, an alignment that contradicted the policy of confidentiality in counseling (Nugent & Pareis, 1968).

In response to this confusion, APA Division 17 sponsored a task force chaired by UC–Berkeley Counseling Center Director Barbara Kirk to develop guidelines for university and college counseling centers (Kirk et al., 1971). These guidelines reaffirmed that voluntary, confidential counseling is the primary function of counselors.

In the late 1960s and early 1970s, the counterculture movement also had its impact on counseling centers. With confidentiality guaranteed at the college counseling centers, students overwhelmed by conflicting values regarding the draft, free love, or turmoil brought on by encounter groups flocked to the centers for help.

Counseling Theories Multiply in the 1960s and 1970s

The profession of counseling showed a remarkable ability to adapt to the many new theoretical, therapeutic approaches. Humanistic psychology and therapies—Maslow's theory of self-actualizing, the Rogerian client-centered or person-centered approach, Gestalt therapy—spread rapidly, contending with the prevailing psychoanalytic and behavioristic schools of psychology. The phrase *third force in psychology* was used to describe humanism as distinct from behaviorism and psychoanalysis.

Out of this grew what came to be known as the *human potential movement*. The emphasis on personal growth became very popular and accessible with the emergence of group counseling. Encounter groups, promoted by Rogers (1970), and sensitivity training groups sought to raise consciousness and generated an intense experiential atmosphere that released pent-up emotions.

At the same time behaviorism had become very popular in academic circles. John Krumboltz (1966) edited a book on behavioral counseling with the significant title *Revolution in Counseling*. The opposing views of humanists and behaviorists regarding human nature prompted Carl Rogers and B. F. Skinner to hold debates.

Existential psychology (see chap. 6) made a strong impact on the counseling profession during the 1960s and 1970s (Wrenn, 1973). Although many such as Wrenn have claimed that existentialism is the same as humanism, existential psychoanalysts Rollo May and Irvin Yalom (1995) have clarified distinctions. May sharply criticized the Rogerian client-centered approach, pointing out that the so-called permissiveness of the therapist or counselor during the session was controlling. May and Yalom concluded that this style of therapy "is not fully existential in that it does not confront the patient directly and firmly" (p. 269).

Although very influential during the 1960s and 1970s, existential psychology was essentially philosophical and not readily applicable to practice for most counselors and therapists. Rogers's client-centered counseling and Skinner's behaviorism, in contrast, had been developed into therapeutic systems that could be used by practitioners. These two camps agreed only in their rejection of the third camp, psychoanalytic, whose followers were generally lumped under one person—Sigmund Freud. At that time psychoanalytic dissenters of Freud were virtually ignored—psychosocial analysts Alfred Adler, Erich Fromm, Karen Horney, Otto Rank, Rollo May, and Erik Erikson, not to mention Carl Jung. Like many others, Nugent was influenced by the prevailing schools of thought.

> My clinical training and counseling experience—based on a blend's of Adler's and Horney's psychosocial analytic, Rogerian client-centered, and Super's vocational developmental approaches—kept me from being overly swayed either by the behaviorists or by the human potential movement and Rogerian-promoted encounter groups. Even so, their influence made such an impact on counseling practice that for many years I lost sight of the value of psychodynamic and psychosocial theories.

In the meantime the polarized and narrow Rogerian and Skinnerian views were quietly being offset by other forces that soon would soften their extreme views and add substantially to the theoretical and practical base for effective counseling and therapy. Cognitive theories soon became influential in psychology, the first of which was Albert Ellis's rational emotive therapy (1973). Although Ellis called his book *Humanistic Psychotherapy*, he added a new dimension to humanistic practice by acknowledging that reasoning and emotions are related processes and that one's emotional problems result from illogical or distorted thoughts.

Other developments going on during this period that would later influence the counseling and therapy profession were psychosocial analyst Erik Erikson's life-span developmental theory, George Kelly's personal construct therapy, Alfred Adler's work with families, family systems theories, and the analytical psychology of Carl Jung and his followers.

Psychological Education Emerges

Throughout the 1970s the counseling profession remained unprepared to meet the ongoing counseling boom in schools and colleges. Without enough trained counselors to meet the need, uncertainties arose about counselor effectiveness. Many within the profession who were justifiably unhappy with the quality of both counselor training and counselor practice declared that trained counselors—and all therapists, for that matter—were worse than those with no training at all (Carkhuff, 1972; Rogers, 1973; Szasz, 1971). In an address presented at the 1972 APA convention, Carl Rogers (1973) said,

> I have slowly come to the conclusion that if we did away with "the expert," "the certified professional," "the licensed psychologist," we might open our profession to a breeze of fresh air, to a surge of creativity, such as it has not known in years. (p. 383)

Many leaders in the field claimed that anyone could be a counselor—teachers, professors, student personnel officers, peers. Impetus in this direction came largely from the human potential movement, which was in vogue at the time. Schools of education responded positively to Rogers's (1961) new person-centered (formerly called client-centered) theory and methods, which he claimed would be effective for teachers. Ivey's interviewing skills (1971) and Carkhuff's relationship skills (1972), based on Rogerian principles, were originally developed for counselor training programs but were promoted as skills that could be taught to anyone, with the idea that within a short time anybody could become a counselor. Many leading counseling educators published a rash of articles and books supporting the idea of replacing counseling in schools and colleges with psychological education. The old role of the guidance specialist popular in the 1920s and 1930s had emerged once again under a new term—*psychological educators*. Counselors were seen only as teachers of life skills and relationship skills. Concerned about this trend in school and college counseling, Nugent (1981) wrote that counseling is the counselor's primary role, that psychological education (now known as *psychoeducation*) is the counselor's secondary role, and that these two roles and functions had to be kept distinct.

Community Counseling Emerges in the 1970s

Although counseling services had spread into colleges and schools during the 1950s and 1960s, the need for community counseling lay dormant. By the 1970s, however, the popularity of counseling programs in colleges and schools, despite their shortcomings, inevitably led to an increasingly felt need for similar counseling services in the community.

Community mental health had received a boost when Congress passed the Community Mental Health Act of 1963. Federal funds had become available to states for constructing community-based mental health programs. The chief characteristic was the centralization of all mental health services, including hospitalization of persons with chronic mental illness and preventive services for the rest of the population, based on a model of positive mental health developed by Jahoda (Hershenson et al., 1996; Jahoda, 1958).

At the same time, however, a trend to close state mental hospitals began throughout the country. Federal financing for the comprehensive community mental health programs was gradually decreased, with the idea that communities would take over the cost. Unfortunately, even with state help, most communities did not have the financial capability to maintain the comprehensive programs proposed by the act. As a result, clinics had to cut staff and programs and treat only clients with chronic mental illness.

As counseling needs increased in the community and as state and federal government funds remained tight, nonprofit private organizations emerged, as well as services funded by counties and cities. Crisis centers, drop-in clinics, shelters for battered women, rape relief counseling centers, and centers for runaway youths emerged, all run on small budgets and staffed by paraprofessionals and volunteers.

Volunteer help springing up from the grass roots indicated an obvious lack of trained counselors in the community. To set up private practice in the community, one had to be a psychologist with a doctorate licensed by the state legislature. Most counseling psychologists, however, became counselor educators or worked in college counseling centers or both; their research-oriented training was more suitable for academic settings.

Because APA didn't recognize master's degrees as terminal, APGA developed master's-level community and mental health counseling training programs. Nugent was a part of this effort at Western Washington University.

At WWU I coordinated the development of a 2-year terminal-degree master of science (MS) mental health counseling program, designed for counselors to become licensed practitioners in the community. The program was adopted in 1978 by the WWU psychology department.

Concerned about unqualified practitioners calling themselves counselors in the community, APGA developed guidelines in 1976 for the licensing of master's degree counselors by state legislation. The guidelines were expanded and updated in 1979 and again in 1980. In the state of Washington, Nugent and others established the Washington State Mental Health Counseling Association. After lobbying state legislators for several years, they persuaded them to mandate licensure for professional counselors. Doctoral psychologists had established licensing laws in some states by the 1970s. Many psychologists started entering private practice because it was no longer necessary that they be supervised by psychiatrists. Psychoactive drugs, which were used in mental hospitals to shorten the stays of psychotic patients, were being used as well in clinics and in private practices.

THE 1980S: COMING OF AGE

The 1980s witnessed significant changes in professional counseling and therapy. As counseling in the community increased, the primary focus on the development of professional counseling shifted from school to community. It was gradually being acknowledged that adults of all ages had difficulties adjusting to changes throughout their lives. People of all ages were experiencing increased personal and social stress—drug and alcohol addictions, career changes, increases in divorce rates, job layoffs, midlife crises, homelessness, and unemployment. Vietnam veterans broke silence by expressing in consciousness-raising therapy groups their anguish over their war experiences. Their expressed symptoms became known as *posttraumatic stress disorder* (PTSD).

Counseling was given a substantial boost by the contributions of a wide range of therapeutic approaches. The counseling of the 1970s, dependent primarily on Rogerian client-centered therapy or on behavioristic techniques, had left many counselors disillusioned. The 1980s brought a host of new theories and practices readily adaptable to counseling: Cognitive theories became prominent, with added contributions from Beck (1976) and Meichenbaum (1977). Contributions came from psychodynamic theorists as well: Psychoanalyst Erik Erikson's psychosocial theory of development covering the life span made a strong impact on counseling practice. Family systems theories that had been developed and practiced by psychiatrists and social workers in previous decades now became an important part of counselor training and practice. Out of family systems theory emerged new methods of identifying and working with substance abuse. Another impact on the profession at this time came from gender-based theories and practice raised and developed by the feminist and men's movements and by gays and lesbians. Various ethnic groups began to express counseling needs during this period, each with its own culture-based concerns about traditional methods of counseling and therapy.

Life-Span Development Theories

Erik Erikson's psychosocial stages of human development throughout the life span (see chap. 5), a theory he first published in *Childhood and Society* in 1950, made a strong impact on counseling theory and practice during the 1980s. Carl Jung (1931/1962) had been the first to present a theory of developmental stages throughout life. Then Charlotte Buehler in the 1930s (Buehler & Massarik, 1968) expanded on Jung's ideas. As indicated earlier, vocational counselor educator Donald Super (1942) picked up on her theory and, during the 1940s, created a developmental model of career stages throughout the life span (see chap. 5).

During the 1980s counseling theorists and practitioners reaffirmed that human development theory was central to the definition of counseling and to counseling practice. With the just-mentioned exceptions of Jung, Buehler, and Super, most professionals limited their developmental theories to children and adolescents. Developmental theorists gradually increased their attention to the adult developmental stages through midlife, largely through the work of Levinson (1978) and Gould (1978).

Cognitive Therapies

As Albert Ellis's rational emotive therapy grew in popularity, other cognitive therapies emerged, particularly Beck's (1976), which differed from Ellis's authoritarian approach. While noting the value of the Rogerian client-centered approach, Beck, along with other cognitive therapists, challenged Rogers's view that counselor qualities, congruency, positive regard, and empathy were necessary and sufficient conditions for client change. Beck suggested strategies in which therapists could use the Rogerian client-centered approach while at the same time developing cognitive skills that would enable the client to identify and alter dysfunctional emotions and behaviors (Corey, 2001; see also chap. 6).

Cognitive theories combine well not only with Rogerian theory but also with behaviorism. Recognizing that cognitive theories offered a more comprehensive view of human behavior, behaviorists began developing cognitive-behavioral theories for counseling (Beck, 1976). One of the most successful at this time was Meichenbaum's (1977) cognitive-behavior modification (see chap. 6).

Awareness of Pluralism

In the 1980s awareness of the pluralistic nature of American society increased. Many books and articles on multicultural counseling were published during the 1980s (see chap. 14). McGoldrick, Pearce, and Giordano (1982), for instance, published *Ethnicity and Family Therapy*, in which they describe the need for family counselors to be aware of the special characteristics of more than a dozen ethnic groups when working with families. Counselors are cautioned about their potential biases and are encouraged to become aware of differing social and cultural beliefs and special characteristics of each of the varying ethnic groups.

Gender issues related to human development theories also arose. Female counselors challenged developmental principles based on male norms. Women presented their own developmental theories that emphasized the importance of the self-in-relation as distinct from the male model of separation and autonomy (see chaps. 5, 6, and 14). At the same time the men's movement objected to male stereotyping, and increasing numbers of male counselors became aware of the effects of the male socialization process on their sense of well-being (see chap. 14).

Counseling in Colleges and Schools

Both college and school counseling benefited from the new multidimensional counseling theories and practices that emerged during this period and became available to counseling training programs and practice—the new developmental theories; cognitive and cognitive-behavioral approaches; family systems therapies; and gender-based and multiculture-based perspectives.

College counseling centers were training laboratories for the new therapies and cultural perspectives. At Western Washington University's counseling center, for example, Nugent and his colleagues became a fertile mix of cognitive-behaviorists, psychodynamic counselors, humanists, and phenomenologists, many of whom represented different cultural and gender perspectives, including feminist, African American, and Chinese. College counseling centers in the 1980s, however, showed a decrease in career counseling along with increases in counseling students with severe personal problems, time-limited counseling, and outreach and consultation (Stone & Archer, 1990).

Because of a decrease in funds, both college and school counseling centers curtailed services. In some cases college centers began to charge fees for their services. In elementary and secondary public schools, student-to-counselor ratios increased, and fewer hired elementary counselors. Baker (2000) comments:

> Basic education and school counseling were bombarded by a range of challenges. . . . These challenges included demands that the school curriculum be made more rigorous, drug abuse be prevented, drug users be treated and rehabilitated, exceptional students and culturally different populations be integrated and their differences appreciated, dropout rates be reduced, children of working parents be cared for, students be prepared for more complex and challenging jobs, gender equity be promoted, and local and state taxes for supporting schools be reduced or maintained at existing levels. (pp. 9–10)

New Community Counseling Services

Many new counseling services emerged in the community during the 1980s. The strongest services to appear at this time were the family-oriented counseling and substance abuse programs. For several decades prior to this time, psychiatrists and social workers had been working with families and as a result had developed considerable research and therapy about family dynamics. The new family systems approaches enabled social workers to work effectively with a wide range of dysfunctional families. Counselors made use of this groundbreaking work in developing their own insights and practice in family counseling, which they gradually incorporated into counselor training and practice (see chap. 10).

In their work with families, counselors also became more involved with the impact of substance abuse on families. The profession called attention to the dysfunctions of adult children of alcoholics (ACOAs) and developed healing programs. Family counseling was considered an essential component of drug and alcohol treatment, and closer cooperation among professionals, counselors, and Alcoholics Anonymous (AA) developed (see chap. 13).

In addition, increasing numbers of businesses began to offer employee assistance programs (EAPs) that covered personal and interpersonal stress interfering with job performance. Businesses also offered career development counseling to employees wishing to find more suitable jobs within the company and outplacement counseling to help laid-off employees find new jobs (see chaps. 1 and 19).

Changing Professional Associations

The efforts of APGA and ACES in strengthening their professional identities and their legal status were given a tremendous boost when APGA and the American Mental Health Counselors Association (AMHCA) agreed in 1979 to merge. AMHCA, which had formed an independent association in 1976, now became APGA's largest division. This merger combined APGA's large membership, financial support, and political clout with AMHCA's enthusiasm and devotion to developing counseling in the community. That combined strength enabled master's degree programs in mental health counseling to be set up in universities throughout the country.

In 1983 APGA voted to change the organization's name to the American Association for Counseling and Development (AACD), reflecting the changing emphasis in counseling activity and training. It was a move away from guidance and personnel and toward counseling for the developmental needs of clients. The Association for Adult Aging and Development (AAAD) was formed as an affiliate of AACD.

While AACD was clarifying the professional role of the counselor, APA Division 17 was also acknowledging similar role characteristics for the counseling psychologist. A summary of the general consensus of counseling psychologists at a 1987 annual conference follows:

> . . . attention to promotion of mental health at the level of groups and systems as well as individuals, to development across the entire life span, to adjustment and satisfaction in vocational as well as personal spheres, and to prevention and enhancement as well as remediation. (Rudd, Weissberg, & Gazda, 1988, pp. 425–426)

The difference between APA Division 17 counseling psychology standards and AACD counselor standards lies in their emphasis on academic research. The training model that was endorsed by counseling psychologists is the scientist-practitioner model (Gelso & Fretz, 2001, p. 11).

To further upgrade master's degree training programs, the association, then known as APGA, established in 1981 the Council for Accreditation of Counseling and Related Education Programs (CACREP). As an independent arm of APGA, this agency established criteria to evaluate and accredit master's- and doctoral-level counselor training programs.

In 1982, at a time when state legislatures were slow to pass licensing laws for counselors, APGA established the National Board for Certified Counselors (NBCC). This board certified counselors who met standards of training set by the association. And although it did not have the legal status of state licensing, it did help assure consumers that certified counselors met APGA (later known as AACD, now ACA) training standards. Gradually during the 1980s, the number of states passing licensing laws for master's degree counselors increased, largely as a result of AACD's merger with AMHCA and the increased cooperation among mental health counselors, social workers, and family counselors, all of whom agreed to work toward omnibus licensing to cover all counseling specialists.

THE 1990s AND THE NEW MILLENNIUM: RECENT TRENDS IN COUNSELING

Since the 1990s professional counselors have become well established in both schools and community. Well-trained master's degree counselors have become the norm in many school districts, and increasing numbers of states (currently 47) have licensure laws for mental health counselors practicing in the community. Moreover, counseling theories and practices have expanded to cover diverse elements of the population, addressing the special characteristics of women, men, gays, lesbians, and various cultural and ethnic groups. Comprehensive neighborhood health centers that coordinate counseling, medical, and social services have emerged throughout the country, serving primarily the situational needs of those who are poor or uninsured. The overall success of counseling can be attributed to its unique ability to adapt to a wide range of diverse populations in a pluralistic society, including the older population. Pastoral counseling centers and institutes have emerged to meet the spiritual needs of persons, families, and communities. And the Internet is being used in all aspects of counseling services.

The development of mental health counselors, along with the development of managed care and insurance benefits, has renewed the conflict over the counselor's role and function. Clinical mental health counselors claim that part of the counselor's role and function includes working with mental disorders. Leading mental health counselors reaffirm the long-held definition of counselor as one whose unique therapeutic role is shown through the process-oriented, evolving, and collaborative relationship with the client.

Counseling practice has broadened still further its range of theoretical approaches. A resurgence of psychodynamic therapies modified for the contemporary world has been brought on by increasing cases of trauma victims, violence, addictions, and crises. Growing numbers of counselors have taken an interest in post-Jungian studies largely because of the greater numbers of older clients (see chap. 6). As counselors and therapists work with an ever-wider range of clients and client needs, they acknowledge that adhering to a single model of therapy or developmental theory is inadequate. Increasing numbers of counselors and therapists have been moving toward an integrative theory of development and an integrative theoretical approach to therapeutic practice. Many counselors and therapists have been influenced by postmodern constructivism; its predecessor, personal construct therapy; and social constructionism—approaches that provide alternative constructs and models to the traditional cognitive-behavioral diagnostic, prescriptive approaches.

Pluralism and the Environment

During the 1990s professional counselors recognized the depth and complexity of counseling individuals living in a multicultural society (see chap. 14). ACA and APA Division 17 set up task forces and published special editions of journals covering counseling practice with various ethnic groups, women and men, and lesbians and gays. Multicultural counseling competencies developed by Sue, Arredondo, and McDavis (1992) were adopted in the 1990s by leading professional counseling associations: Association of Multicultural Counseling and Development (AMCD) in 1995; Association for Counselor Education and Supervision (ACES) in 1996; and International Association of Marriage and Family Counseling (IAMFC) in 1997.

As they did in the post–World War II years, increasing numbers of professional counselors have once again recognized the deleterious effect of political, environmental, social, and economic conditions on client well-being. Now taken into account are such social factors as job loss, poor nutrition, abuse, homelessness, and pollution (see chap. 9).

Furthermore, posttraumatic stress, first identified among Vietnam veterans in the late 1970s and the 1980s, has been acknowledged as a disorder for anyone suffering from trauma—all war veterans, refugees, torture victims, victims of domestic violence, and victims of terrorist attacks of all kinds. Likewise, the treatment of alcohol and drug addictions has spread to the treatment of all addictions or compulsive behaviors—eating disorders, sexual abuse, codependency, and gambling (see chap. 19).

School Counseling

As school counselors with master's degrees in counseling have become more common in schools, they have been increasingly asked to intervene in student crises resulting from substance abuse, gang violence, family conflicts, and teenage pregnancies. In many places high school counselors are faced with violent outbreaks in which students are victims or witnesses. Outbreaks have also occurred in both middle and elementary schools. In response, school counselors have had to learn how to intervene in the aftermath of violent outbreaks, as well as to assess violence-prone students and be ready to intervene accordingly.

In many school districts crises have become so prevalent that counselors have often been prevented from serving the normal developmental needs of students (see chap. 17). In an attempt to counter this problem, many school districts nationwide have been designing and implementing comprehensive developmental programs. These programs actually began in the 1970s but spread slowly. During the 1990s, as guidelines became available, school districts throughout the country gradually started adopting programs. That trend has continued into the new millennium in both elementary and secondary schools (Baker, 2000). Such comprehensive programs have helped to enable counselors to provide the important services of individual and group counseling, group guidance, coordination, and consultation.

During the 1990s, largely because of federal legislation, school counselors increased their involvement in career counseling and guidance activities, and more school districts hired career counselors to coordinate new programs in career planning. Federal funds have also helped school districts improve students' career competencies in both technical and academic fields. Eligible students are now able, while still in high school, to attend technical colleges or community colleges. In some states such students can obtain an associate of arts (AA) degree and a high school diploma simultaneously (see chap. 17).

College Counseling

The 1996 and 1997 annual surveys of college counseling centers showed patterns similar to those of the 1980s—a decrease in career counseling, an increase in severity of client problems, and an increase in time-limited, brief counseling. Since the 1990s campus counseling centers have had increased cases of alcohol abuse and sexual assault and more demand for crisis intervention. Today, issues such as clinical depression, anxiety, suicide risk, and substance abuse as well as disorders involving psychosis and other severe pathology are now relatively common among student clients in college counseling centers. Thus, psychological testing, diagnosis, and treatment planning are the norm at many centers. The majority of counselor time continues to be spent in individual and group counseling, and about one fourth in consultation and outreach. Outreach programs such as drug and alcohol abuse prevention, multicultural awareness, eating disorder prevention, and stress reduction are still prevalent (Gallagher, 1996, 1997). Although career issues are commonly related to or affected by clinical problems, career counseling has become separated from many college counseling centers.

Community Counseling

The most significant development in professional counseling has occurred in community counseling services and in counselor training programs. Managed care programs, with their focus on brief counseling, have made a strong impact on community counseling; career counseling centers for adults have proliferated; and neighborhood centers offering counseling to the uninsured and the poor have emerged throughout the country (see chap. 19). At the same time increasing numbers of counselor training programs have expanded their curricula to include courses in spiritual counseling and specializations in gerontological counseling.

Managed Care and Brief Counseling and Therapy

As a result of spiraling costs for therapeutic programs, diminishing financial resources, and increased demand for services, managed health care systems such as health maintenance organizations (HMOs) have proliferated. Health providers running these programs have emphasized the use of brief counseling and therapy or solution-focused approaches in counseling. As these programs have mushroomed, increasing numbers of licensed or certified mental health counselors have become eligible to receive insurance payments for services. Criticisms of managed care have helped modify overly restrictive policies, and constructivists and social constructionists have proposed that managed care allow alternative diagnostic models in addition to the *DSM-IV-TR*.

Career Counseling in the Community

Since the 1990s increasing numbers of adults have changed jobs. Many have been abruptly laid off, or their skills have become obsolete. Highly technical jobs requiring new skills have increased the need for career counseling in the community, and career counseling centers have emerged throughout the country. Career counselor training includes master's-level counselors who not only meet basic requirements but also have advanced specialized work in career counseling. At the same time business and industry have increased career counseling services as part of their personnel programs, which include expanded employee assistance programs. Recently, the sudden drop in demand for high tech jobs left many without work and seeking help from career counseling centers. With fewer job offerings, however, career counseling centers reduced their services.

Counseling of Older Adults

Since the 1990s increasing numbers of developmental theorists have emphasized that older adults have the potential to continue to grow and develop. This life-span perspective has refuted stereotypes about aging that focus on decline and deterioration in one's later years. Counselors have been turning their attention to the 80% of older adults who are self-sufficient and relatively healthy but who nevertheless are experiencing anxiety, depression, or grief resulting from transitions, losses, or sudden changes in life stages (see chap. 15).

Gerontological counseling services increased significantly in the 1990s. Over one-third of counselor training programs include course work in counseling older adults; many of them offer a specialization in gerontological counseling (Myers, 1995). In 1990 NBCC approved a national certification in gerontological counseling as demands for counseling services for older adults increased (see chap. 15).

Spiritual Development

Counseling services sponsored by pastoral counseling centers and institutes have increased steadily (see chap. 1). Many professional counselors have recognized the importance of the client's religious and spiritual concerns and are incorporating theories of spiritual development into counseling practice (Ingersoll, 1997; Kelly, 1995; see also chap. 5). The Association for Spiritual, Ethical, and Religious Values in Counseling (ASER-VIC) is one of the fastest growing divisions in ACA, and ACES set up a task force on spirituality and counseling. Professional activities such as these on the national level have led to increased awareness and interest within the profession regarding the spiritual needs of clients in general (Fukuyama & Sevig, 1997; see also chaps. 1 and 19).

Comprehensive Health Care Centers

In response to the health needs of the poor and the uninsured, comprehensive health care centers that cover counseling, medical, and social services have emerged throughout the country. Typically, they are locally centered, often in ethnic neighborhoods (see chap. 19). These centers serve not only the combined needs of persons but also their situational and transitional concerns, such as job adjustment, family conflict, or death of a loved one. In some areas counselors from school, college, and community have joined forces to work with individuals and families at risk, such as those with problems related to suicide, drug addiction, abuse, and violence.

Introduction of the Internet to the Counseling Field

The use of the Internet in the counseling field began in the 1990s and is now present in all aspects of counseling services, including information search and retrieval, assessment and diagnosis, psychoeducation, supervision, consultation, record keeping, and actual counseling itself, or online counseling, also known as Internet counseling or web counseling (Guterman & Kirk, 1999; Riemer-Reiss, 2000; Sampson, Kolodinski, & Greeno,1997). The Internet has proved to be effective in many areas of counseling services, but some controversy still exists over its appropriateness and efficacy for various aspects of the field.

As mentioned in chapter 1, the primary concerns about Internet counseling involve the confidentiality and privacy of client information. In addition, critics question the ability of counselors to develop effective counseling relationships with clients, and counselor availability may be a concern if a client is experiencing a crisis or trauma. Despite these concerns, however, Internet counseling continues to grow. Professional organizations have attempted to address the potential problems of Internet counseling by adapting the ethical codes of conduct for counselors.

Professional Issues

The ACPA voted in 1991 to disengage from the AACD because ACPA's primary responsibility lies in administrating student affairs, rather than in counseling students. College counselors formed a new affiliate in 1992 called the American College Counseling Association (ACCA). And in 1992 AACD voted to change its name to the American Counseling Association (ACA).

In the late 1990s the AMHCA and ASCA executive boards voted to disaffiliate with ACA. Consequently, in 1998 the ACA governing board made a compromise move by changing its structure to allow members options: join only one division, join only ACA, or join both. At about the same time, ACA issued a revised definition of counseling that included working with the pathology of clients.

The practice of counseling and therapy came under critical review in the 1990s by both the general public and professional practitioners. Crises in confidence brought on by moral issues such as the false-memory controversy motivated the counseling profession to scrutinize and evaluate its members and to assume more responsibility for challenging unethical practices (see chap. 3). In the meantime the profession increased its own self- and peer evaluations. States with counseling licensure laws increased the length of supervised experience required for licensure—as much as 3 years in some states. Increasing numbers of licensed counselors involved in managed care programs have formed group practices with other counselors and mental health providers. Group practice provides counselors with opportunities for case conferences and consultations with other professionals, which are more likely to encourage mutual professional monitoring.

SUMMARY

Counseling services originated in the early 1900s when Parsons developed a community-based vocational bureau for adolescent boys, a program soon picked up by several school districts. About the same time the first child guidance clinic opened for juvenile delinquents in response to the effect of adverse social conditions on youths. World War I stimulated the development of group standardized psychological tests for screening U.S. Army recruits and initiated the field of psychometrics.

After World War I the development of standardized group testing of individual differences became popular for use in schools, colleges, vocational centers, and business and industry. Educators introduced educational guidance into schools, and vocational guidance expanded into community agencies in the 1930s to serve displaced and unemployed persons. Williamson introduced into schools and colleges a clinical counseling model based on testing for individual differences (traits), diagnosis, and treatment. Counteracting this model, some therapists in child clinics started practicing process-oriented relational therapy, a forerunner of Rogerian client-centered therapy.

During the 1940s counseling shifted away from the old diagnostic, prescriptive guidance model and toward the new psychodynamic, developmental, and humanistic theories, including Rogerian client-centered counseling. After World War II college counseling centers emerged to serve the veterans who attended college on VA scholarships. The VA also helped spawn the new profession of counseling psychology, based on a person's situational, developmental concerns.

Whereas college counseling centers flourished during the 1950s, school counseling boomed in the 1960s. Concerned about confusion over the counselor role and untrained counselors in schools, leading professionals of APGA, ACES, and ASCA developed policy statements that defined the role of the professional school counselor and proposed training standards that set the model for counseling.

Reacting to the confusion over the role of school counselors and the inadequacy of counselor training programs, many counselor educators in the 1970s urged counselors to become psychological educators. The onslaught of the counterculture movement, the rise of humanistic person-centered counseling and encounter groups, and the opposing rise of behaviorism further contributed to controversies and confusion of values and roles among professional educators.

During the 1980s as the demand for counseling spread into the community, APGA and AMHCA merged and with their combined strength promoted the development of master's programs in mental health counseling. They lobbied effectively for state licensure of counselors. Erik Erikson's theory of life-span development, new cognitive and family systems theories, and ethnic and gender issues influenced counseling practice. New types of counseling services emerged in the community, including family counseling, employee assistance programs, and substance abuse centers.

Counseling expanded its services in the 1990s to meet the wide range of needs of people in a multicultural society, including career counseling, life-skills development, alcohol abuse, sexual assault, and violence. In the community increasing numbers of counselors have joined managed care programs. Counselors have started offering services to older adults and to those with PTSD. Increasing numbers of pastoral counseling centers and institutes have been appearing in communities throughout the country, addressing the spiritual needs of clients as part of counseling services. Schools have been forming liaisons with community family counseling services and with local universities. Community counseling services have also been forming liaisons with social and medical services in comprehensive neighborhood health centers for the uninsured.

New psychodynamic and post-Jungian therapeutic approaches that acknowledge a person's intrapsychic forces emerged to address the general population's increasingly stressful and traumatic lives. Postmodern constructivist and social constructionist therapies have been challenging traditional cognitive-behavioral diagnostic, prescriptive approaches. Counselors and therapists have been moving toward an integrated theoretical approach to better serve the ever-widening range of clients and client needs.

PROJECTS AND ACTIVITIES

1. Trace the influence of federal funding on the development of counseling from its origins to the present. Explore federal programs currently pending in Congress that relate to counseling. How might these programs affect the profession of counseling if they are passed?

2. Describe the differences and similarities in vocational counseling as defined by Parsons (1909) and Super (1955). How did the notion of vocational development influence the direction of counseling?

3. Super (1955) drew a distinction between clinical and counseling psychologies. Look up preparation programs for each profession at well-known universities. Are the distinctions that Super made consistent with contemporary doctoral and master's degree training programs at these universities?

4. Interview some senior citizens about their perceptions of psychologists, psychiatrists, and counselors. Compare their reactions with those of a group of college students and a group of young adults who are not in school.

5. Community mental health clinics originated in the early 1900s. At that time a psychiatrist, a clinical psychologist, and a social worker constituted the staff in most cases. Their main concerns were working with delinquents and disturbed children and their families. Look up your central regional community clinic, and trace its history in terms of staffing and types of problems handled.

6. Interview a counselor at the college you attend who has been employed there for 15 to 20 years. Ask how the counselor perceives the changes that have occurred and what changes are anticipated.

REFERENCES

Aubrey, R. F. (1982). A house divided: Guidance and counseling in 20th-century America. *Personnel and Guidance Journal, 61,* 1–8.

Baker, S. B. (2000). *School counseling for the 21st century* (3rd ed.). Upper Saddle River, NJ: Merrill/Prentice Hall.

Beck, A. T. (1976). *Cognitive behavior and emotional disorders.* New York: New American Library.

Brewer, J. M. (1932). *Education as guidance: An examination of the possibilities of curriculum in terms of life activities, in elementary and secondary schools, and colleges.* New York: Macmillan.

Brewer, J. M. (1942). *History of vocational guidance.* New York: Harper & Row.

Buehler, C., & Massarik, F. (Eds.). (1968). *The course of human life.* New York: Springer.

Carkhuff, R. R. (1972). The development of systematic resource models. *Counseling Psychologist, 3,* 4–11.

Corey, G. (2001). *Theory and practice of counseling and psychotherapy* (6th ed.). Pacific Grove, CA: Brooks/Cole.

Ellis, A. (1973). *Humanistic psychotherapy: The rational-emotive approach.* New York: Julian Press.

Erikson, E. (1950). *Childhood and society.* New York: Norton.

Farber, L. (1966). *The ways of the will.* New York: Basic Books.

Fitzgerald, P. W. (1965). The professional role of school counselors. In J. W. Loughary, R. O.

Stripling, & P. W. Fitzgerald (Eds.), *Counseling: A growing profession* (pp. 31–41). Washington, DC: American Personnel and Guidance Association.

Fukuyama, M. A., & Sevig, T. D. (1997). Spiritual issues in counseling: A new course. *Counselor Education and Supervision, 36,* 233–244.

Gallagher, R. P. (1996). *National survey of counseling center directors.* Alexandria, VA: International Association of Counseling Services.

Gallagher, R. P. (1997). *National survey of counseling center directors.* Alexandria, VA: International Association of Counseling Services.

Gelso, C. J., & Fretz, B. R. (2001). *Counseling psychology* (2nd ed.). Fort Worth, TX: Harcourt, Brace & Jovanoviche.

George, R. L., & Cristiani, T. S. (1986). *Counseling theory and practice* (2nd ed.). Upper Saddle River, NJ: Prentice Hall.

Goldenberg, I., & Goldenberg, H. (2000). *Family therapy: An overview* (5th ed.). Pacific Grove, CA: Brooks/Cole.

Gould, R. I. (1978). *Transformation: Growth and change in adult life*. New York: Simon & Schuster.

Guterman, J. T., & Kirk, M. A. (1999). Mental health counselors and the Internet. *Journal of Mental Health Counseling, 21*, 300–325.

Hershenson, D. B., Power, P. B., & Waldo, M. (1996). *Community counseling: Contemporary theory and practice*. Boston: Allyn & Bacon.

Hull, C. (1928). *Aptitude testing Yonkers on the Hudson*. New York: World Book.

Ingersoll, R. E. (1997). Teaching a course on counseling and spirituality. *Counselor Education and Supervision, 36*, 224–232.

Ivey, A. E. (1971). *Microcounseling: Innovations in interview training*. Springfield, IL: Charles C Thomas.

Jahoda, M. (1958). *Current concepts of positive mental health*. New York: Basic Books.

Jung, C. (1962). *The stages of life*. In *Collected works* (pp. 387–403). Princeton, NJ: Princeton University Press. (Original work published 1931)

Kelly, E. W., Jr. (1995). *Spirituality and religion in counseling and psychotherapy: Diversity in theory and practice*. Alexandria, VA: American Counseling Association.

Kirk, B. A., Johnson, A. P., Redfield, J. E., Michel, J., Roster, R. A., & Warman, R. E. (1971). Guidelines for university and college counseling services. *American Psychologist, 26*, 585–589.

Krumboltz, J. D. (Ed.). (1966). *Revolution in counseling*. Boston: Houghton Mifflin.

Levinson, D. (1978). *The seasons of a man's life*. New York: Ballantine Books.

Levy, D. M. (1971). Beginning of the child guidance movement. In M. Levitt & B. Rubenstein (Eds.), *The mental health field: A critical appraisal* (pp. 32–39). Detroit: Wayne State University Press.

Loughary, J. W., Stripling, R. D., & Fitzgerald, P. W. (Eds.). (1965). *Counseling: A growing profession*. Washington, DC: American Personnel and Guidance Association.

May, R., & Yalom, I. (1995). Existential psychotherapy. In R. J. Corsini & D. Wedding (Eds.), *Current psychotherapies* (pp. 262–292). Itasca, IL: F. E. Peacock.

McGoldrick, M., Pearce, J. K., & Giordano, J. (1982). *Ethnicity and family therapy*. New York: Guilford Press.

Meichenbaum, D. (1977). *Cognitive behavior modification: An integrative approach*. New York: Plenum.

Myers, J. (1995). From "forgotten and ignored" to standards and certification: Gerontological counseling comes of age. *Journal of Counseling & Development, 74*, 143–149.

Nugent, F. A. (1962). Implementing an appropriate counselor image in schools: An educative process. *Counselor Education and Supervision, 2*, 49–51.

Nugent, F. A. (1966). A rationale against teaching experience for school counselors. *School Counselor, 13*, 213–215.

Nugent, F. A. (1969). A framework for appropriate referrals of disciplinary problems to counselors. *School Counselor, 16*, 199–202.

Nugent, F. A. (1981). *Professional counseling: An overview*. Pacific Grove, CA: Brooks/Cole.

Nugent, F. A., & Pareis, E. N. (1968). Survey of present policies and practices in college counseling centers in the United States of America. *Journal of Counseling Psychology, 15*, 94–97.

Osipow, S. H., & Fitzgerald, L. F. (1996). *Theories of career development* (4th ed.). Boston: Allyn & Bacon.

Parsons, F. (1909). *Choosing a vocation*. Boston: Houghton Mifflin.

Rank, O. (1936). *Will therapy*. New York: Knopf.

Riemer-Reiss, M. L. (2000). Utilizing distance technology for mental health counseling. *Journal of Mental Health Counseling, 22*, 189–203.

Rogers, C. R. (1939). *The clinical treatment of the problem child*. Boston: Houghton Mifflin.

Rogers, C. R. (1942). *Counseling and psychotherapy*. Boston: Houghton Mifflin.

Rogers, C. R. (1951). *Client-centered therapy: Its current practice, implications, and theory*. Boston: Houghton Mifflin.

Rogers, C. R. (1961). *On becoming a person*. Boston: Houghton Mifflin.

Rogers, C. R. (1970). *Carl Rogers on encounter groups*. New York: Harper & Row.

Rogers, C. R. (1973). Some new challenges. *American Psychologist, 28*, 379–387.

Romano, J. L., & Skovolt, T. M. (1998). Henry Borow and counseling psychology: A half-century common journey. *Counseling Psychologist, 26*, 448–465.

Rudd, S. S., Weissberg, N., & Gazda, G. M. (1988). Looking to the future: Themes from the Third National Conference for Counseling Psychology. *Counseling Psychologist, 16*, 423–430.

Sampson, J. P., Jr., Kolodinski, R. W., & Greeno, P. P. (1997). Counseling on the information highway: Further possibilities and potential problems. *Journal of Counseling Development, 75*, 203–212.

Schmidt, J. J. (2003). *Counseling in schools: Essential services and comprehensive programs* (4th ed.). Boston: Allyn & Bacon.

Stone, G. I., & Archer, J., Jr. (1990). College and university counseling centers in the 1990s: Challenges and limits. *Counseling Psychologist, 18*, 539–607.

Strang, R. (1953). *The role of the teacher in personnel work* (4th ed.). New York: Columbia University Teachers College.

Sue, D. W., Arredondo, P., & McDavis, R. J. (1992). Multicultural competencies/standards: A pressing need. *Journal of Counseling & Development, 70*, 477–486.

Super, D. (1942). *The dynamics of vocational adjustment*. New York: Harper Brothers.

Super, D. E. (1949). *Appraising vocational fitness by means of psychological tests*. New York: Harper Brothers.

Super, D. E. (1955). Transition: From vocational guidance to counseling psychology. *Journal of Counseling Psychology, 2*, 3–9.

Szasz, T. (1971). *The myth of mental illness*. New York: Hoeber.

Tolbert, E. L. (1982). *An introduction to guidance* (2nd ed.). Boston: Little, Brown.

Whiteley, J. M. (1984). A historical perspective on the development of counseling psychology as a profession. In S. Brown & R. Lent (Eds.), *Handbook of counseling psychology* (pp. 3–55). New York: John Wiley.

Williamson, E. G. (1939). *How to counsel students: A manual of techniques for clinical counselors*. New York: McGraw-Hill.

Woodring, P. (1953). *Let's talk sense about our schools*. New York: Pergamon Press.

Woody, R. H., Hansen, J. C., & Rossberg, R. H. (1989). *Counseling psychology: Strategies and services*. Pacific Grove, CA: Brooks/Cole.

Wrenn, G. (1962). *The counselor in a changing world*. Washington, DC: American Personnel and Guidance Association.

Wrenn, G. (1973). *The world of the contemporary counselor*. Boston: Houghton Mifflin.

CHAPTER 3

Professional, Ethical, and Legal Issues

COMPONENTS OF A PROFESSION

The profession of counseling is upheld and developed by well-established professional associations—notably, the American Counseling Association and the American Psychological Association Division 17. Through these associations counselors are empowered to define, develop, maintain, clarify, evaluate, and monitor all aspects of the profession, including the counselor role, counselor training standards and curriculum, and performance of services according to professional standards. These associations have developed codes of ethics to protect the rights of clients and to monitor the profession; they also abide by client and counselor legal rights and responsibilities and uphold certain rights and responsibilities for minors.

Professional Associations

The two professional associations whose definitions and standards are specifically designed for counselors are the American Counseling Association (ACA) and the American Psychological Association (APA) Division 17. ACA is the major organization for professional counselors. For psychologists who specialize in counseling, the major organization is APA Division 17 (Society of Counseling Psychology). These professional associations are the only ones whose standards are specifically designed to uphold and train counselors of people with normal developmental conflicts.

ACA

ACA and its divisions have been responsible for setting standards for counselors since the 1950s. ACA was originally the American Personnel and Guidance Association (APGA) and more recently the American Association for Counseling (AACD). As stated in chapter 2, the executive councils of the American School Counselors Association (ASCA) and the American Mental Health Counselors Association (AMHCA) voted in 1995 to disaffiliate with ACA to pursue their own separate goals. In a compromise move, the ACA Governing Council voted in July 1998 to revise the ACA bylaws that provide membership options. ACA President Courtland Lee (1997) commented:

> The bylaws were changed to allow a person to have the option of joining ACA only, a division only, or both ACA and a division. Prior to this action, the ACA Bylaws stipulated that all members had to belong to ACA and at least one division. (p. 5)

This seems to be an unfortunate move. Originally, ACA formed to pull disparate forces together (see chap. 2). Creating role definitions and ethical and training standards for counselors, ACA was the unifying force that established and maintained counseling as a unique profession over the years, providing strength, flexibility, direction, and balance. ACA divisions, along with their major publications, are listed in appendix B.

In the early 1960s ACA's forerunner, APGA, in conjunction with ASCA and the Association for Counselor Education and Supervision (ACES), developed definitions and training standards for the school counselor role (Loughary, Stripling, & Fitzgerald, 1965). APGA also drew up a code of ethics in 1961 to cover counselors in all settings (see chap. 2). In the late 1970s and the 1980s, the association worked with its affiliate, AMHCA, to attain licensure and certification for mental health counselors in the community. ACA also adopted a process of accrediting graduate counseling programs developed by ACES. This accreditation is conducted by the Council for Accreditation of Counseling and Related Educational Programs (CACREP). The standards of ACA and its divisions apply to both master's and doctoral degree programs; graduates, however, obtain the various counseling specialties in the master's degree programs.

ACA publishes the *Journal of Counseling & Development* (formerly the *Personnel and Guidance Journal*) and *Counseling Today,* which include articles pertinent to all divisions. The organization also sponsors yearly conventions, at which workshops and papers are presented. In addition, ACA coordinates national task forces to study and make recommendations about counseling policy and practice, and it lobbies the U.S. Congress to pass legislation to upgrade and fund counseling programs.

APA Division 17

Division 17 (Society of Counseling Psychology) of the APA represents psychologists trained specifically to work with the normal concerns of individuals, groups, and families. Members are psychologists with doctorates. The division, which defined the role of the counseling psychologist, continually works on upholding the professional identity of this group (see chap. 2). APA Division 17 developed *Standards for Providers of Counseling Psychological Services* (APA, 1979). It publishes *The Counseling Psychologist,* a journal related to policy and practice; the *Journal of Counseling Psychology,* dedicated to research; and the Society of Counseling Psychology *Newsletter.* APA Division 17 members adhere to the APA (1992) *Ethical Principles of Psychologists.* Like ACA this association offers workshops, papers, and panels at national conventions and organizes national task forces to work on issues in the field.

Related Professional Associations

Family therapists, social workers, and clinical psychologists each have a separate association that sets standards for training and practice: the American Association for Marriage and Family Therapy (AAMFT), the National Association of Social Workers (NASW), and APA Division 12 (Clinical Psychology).

Unique Counselor Role

Professional counselor training prepares counselors to engage in counseling with individuals, groups, or families experiencing stress in everyday living that results from normal developmental situational conflicts. Counselor training also prepares counselors to engage in psychological education, assessment and testing, consultation, social change, and crisis prevention and intervention (see chap. 1).

In 1985 members of AMHCA who were certified as clinical mental health counselors by the Academy of Clinical Mental Health Counselors (ACMHC) decided that the definition of *counseling* described by ACA and AMHCA, though basic to all counseling, was too narrow to cover the work of clinical mental health counselors. ACMHC therefore drew up its own special definition of *clinical* mental health counseling that includes treating psychopathology from a developmental point of view, as well as working with normal concerns of individuals (Seiler, Brooks, & Beck, 1987).

This new definition of mental health counseling caused considerable controversy within the profession during the 1990s. The Washington State Mental Health Counseling Association, for example, expressed concerns that the emphasis on pathology runs counter to the principles of ACA and AMHCA, which focus on normal developmental concerns. Speaking for mental health counseling (MHC), Jeffrey Guterman (1994) says:

> A seeming consensus has been reached insofar as some writers have suggested that MHC is distinguishable from clinical psychology, psychiatry and social work across key issues. In particular, some have suggested that in contrast with the focus of these other disciplines on psychopathology, MHC takes a developmental approach with clients and is aimed at promoting mental health rather than eliminating mental illness. (p. 226)

Despite this Guterman (1994) notes that "many researchers have pointed out that MHC, like clinical psychology, psychiatry, and social work, still tends to emphasize psychopathology in its conceptualizing and treatment of clients" (p. 226). Protesting this trend, Guterman continues, "Some researchers have argued that emulating clinically oriented providers has impeded the field's attempt at distinguishing itself as a unique core provider" (p. 226). He quotes Ginter (1989) in particular as emphasizing the process-oriented nature of counseling, in which the counselor-client relationship is fundamental to client developmental change. This is in keeping with the definition of the counselor's unique role that emerged in the late 1940s (see chap. 2).

Nevertheless, the trend toward incorporating the clinical approach continues. In 1993 the National Board for Certified Counselors and AMHCA, with the approval of ACA, agreed to merge their certification procedures so that AMHCA would represent both community counseling generalists and clinical mental health counselors. Steinhaus (1993), chairman of the academy's board of directors, writes, "AMHCA will be free to move into the position of representing the counseling generalists as well as the certified clinician, although not primarily the certified clinician" (p. 4). In a related move, the ACA Governing Council (1997) revised its definition of *professional counseling* to include strategies that address pathologies, as well as normal developmental concerns. This latest ACA definition of the counselor role is as follows:

> *The Practice of Professional Counseling:* The application of mental health, psychological, or human development principles, through cognitive, affective, behavioral or systemic intervention strategies that address wellness, personal growth, or career development, as well as pathology.

Counselor Training

Knowledge and Skills of Counselors

In the late 1970s the Association for Counselor Education and Supervision (ACES), a division of ACA, developed training standards for master's and doctoral work in counseling (ACES, 1978). APA Division 17 did the same for counseling psychology students (APA, 1979). Over the years training standards have been upgraded and expanded to include a broader, deeper level of counselor knowledge and skills. In both programs core courses include human growth and development; behavioral dynamics; social and cultural foundations; individual, group, and family counseling theories and techniques; multicultural counseling; lifestyle and career development; appraisal; research and evaluation; and professional orientation. A supervised practicum at the university and an internship in institutions and agencies in the community are essential parts of the training program. Both master's and doctoral students receive these core experiences, although doctoral students generally have longer and more intensive internships, more training in research skills, and more exposure to diagnosis and assessment.

When clinical mental health counselors (CMHCs) developed a new and separate mental health counseling track for clinical mental health counselors, they expanded core courses in counselor training to include additional specialized courses in diagnosis and treatment of mental illness. In addition, increasing interest in the spiritual concerns of clients has led ACES to set up a national task force to develop counselor competencies in spiritual counseling to be incorporated into training standards (Fukuyama & Sevig, 1997).

Counselors-in-training are given a broad philosophical and psychological foundation, enabling them to assess independently the value of contemporary counseling practices and to evaluate new counseling theories and techniques. As the ACA Code of Ethics (1995) states, it is expected that "counselors present varied theoretical positions so that students and supervisors may make comparisons and have opportunities to develop their own positions" (Section F.2.f; see also appendix A). The rationale for this type of preparation is that people who learn only one set of skills are technicians, not professionals, and that their narrow backgrounds limit their ability to expand their knowledge and skills as new discoveries are made in counseling theory and practice.

Practicum and Internship Programs

Counselor training should include two types of supervised experiences: (a) practicum at a university clinic under the supervision of university faculty and (b) internships in a community agency or school under the supervision of agency staff. Effective training experiences work best if both school and community counselors-in-training first engage in practicum at a college training clinic closely supervised by college faculty. Internships supervised by agency staff should then follow at the selected work setting, beginning with small caseloads that gradually increase over time.

In reality, supervised experiences of both types are often the weakest part of counselor training. Some colleges and universities do not have either the counselor educators specifically trained to supervise students or the facilities or videotaping equipment necessary for quality supervision. Thus, school counselors-in-training often do not have practicum experience at a university with faculty supervision. Instead, the practicum is skipped, and students are assigned directly as interns in schools. Unfortunately, interns in school settings are often assigned personnel, clerical, or guidance activities, with little actual counseling experience. In community clinics, although counselor interns do see clients, they are often given heavy caseloads with minimal supervision from either the college or the clinic staff.

Accreditation of Counselor Training Programs

In order to maintain high standards that are consistent in counselor training programs throughout the country, various professional associations have established certain criteria for master's level counselor training programs and accreditation procedures. Accreditation programs include the Council for the Accreditation of Counseling and Related Programs (CACREP), the Council on Rehabilitation Education (CORE), the Commission for Accreditation of Marriage and Family Therapy (COAMFTE), and the American Association of Pastoral Counselors (AAPC) (Hollis & Dodson, 2000).

Accreditation of counselor training programs is a voluntary process initiated by counselor education departments. Each accrediting program requires a separate application for each specialty area, and procedures for each generally take at least 2 years. A counseling training program must meet the guidelines set by the agency and must go through a process of self-evaluation before inviting a team of agency evaluators for an on-site visit. Accreditation must be renewed and reevaluated every 2 to 5 years (Hollis & Dodson, 2000).

Graduates from an accredited counselor training program have certain obvious advantages: Employers prefer to hire graduates of accredited programs; graduates tend to be given preference when applying for an advanced degree; in many states licensure has the same requirements as does accreditation; and national professional counselor certification requirements are essentially the same as those of accrediting agencies (Remley & Herlihy, 2001).

CACREP. In 1991 ACA founded the Council for the Accreditation of Counseling and Related Programs (CACREP); it is the largest accrediting body to evaluate graduate counseling training programs. CACREP accredits master's degree programs in community counseling, school counseling, student affairs practice in higher education, mental health counseling, and marriage and family counseling; it accredits doctoral programs in counselor education and supervision.

To become accredited, a master's program must meet the following CACREP standards (Hollis & Dodson, 2000):

- The program must include at least 2 years and 48 to 60 academic semester hours, depending on specialty.

- Eight core areas must include growth and development, social and cultural foundations, helping relationships, career development, groups, appraisal, research, and professional development.
- Students must complete 100 hours of supervised practicum and 600 hours of internship.
- The program must involve at least three full-time faculty.

Doctoral programs require more hours of supervised internship and more intensive coverage of core areas.

CORE.   The Council on Rehabilitation Education (CORE) is composed of representatives from five different national rehabilitation associations (Hollis & Dodson, 2000). It accredits master's degree rehabilitation programs that include courses in counseling and career counseling theories, psychosocial and medical aspects of disability, job placement and job adjustment, testing, case management, knowledge of community resources, and ethics. Additional requirements are 600 hours of supervised practicum and internship.

COAMFTE.   The Commission for Accreditation of Marriage and Family Therapy Education (COAMFTE) certifies training programs in marriage and family counseling at the master's, doctoral, and postdoctoral levels. A minimum of 60 hours of graduate course work is required, including marriage and family systems, family and child development, assessment, family and marriage dysfunctions, family counseling theories, professional issues, and research. Also required are approximately 900 clock hours of practicum and internship. The average doctoral program requires 80 semester hours of academic work and about 1100 clock hours of clinical experience (Hollis & Dodson, 2000).

AAPC.   The American Association of Pastoral Counselors (AAPC) certifies master's degree pastoral programs that include a clinical counseling specialty with 56 semester hours of counseling and related course work and 610 hours of practicum and internship (Hollis & Dodson, 2000).

Counselor Credentialing: Licensing and Certification

Graduates of counselor training programs have several different types of credentialing available to verify that they have attained a certain level of professional preparation: (a) licensing by state legislatures, (b) certification in specialty areas by state agencies, and (c) certification by national certification boards sponsored by national professional counseling associations.

State Licensure

State legislatures in 47 states and the District of Columbia have enacted bills that require counselors to be licensed in order to engage in private practice in that state. Two forms of licensure exist—a *practice act* and a *title act*. In states with a practice act, counselors cannot practice counseling unless they are licensed. In states with a title act, anyone can practice counseling as long as he or she does not use the title granted to those who are licensed, such as professional licensed counselor. Practice acts are the preferred licensing law.

The advantage of being licensed by the state is that only licensed counselors are qualified for third-party health insurance payments and are accepted as mental health providers by managed care organizations. A disadvantage to this arrangement is that state legislators do not issue licenses for certain counseling specialties. Counselors working in educational institutions or in state or community agencies are not required to be licensed by the state to practice in those settings.

State Agency Certification

Counselors who work in state agencies or institutions must be certified by state agency boards. Unlike state licensure boards, state agency certification boards authorize certification for particular counseling specialties rather than for general counseling practice. Two state agencies that are most active in state certification are state boards of education, which certify school counselors, and state agencies, which certify substance abuse counselors (Remley & Herlihy, 2001).

All 50 states credential school counselors; each state department of education determines the educational requirements and professional experience required to be employed in that state as a counselor in the public schools. Most states require a master's degree in school counseling that includes a practicum in a school setting. Overall, throughout the country credentialing requirements for school counselors are less stringent and uniform than are licensure laws for counselors in the community.

For substance abuse counseling, most state agencies have different levels of counselor certification available for those who don't have master's degrees in counseling.

National Professional Association Certification

The National Board of Certified Counselors (NBCC), under the sponsorship of ACA, and the Commission of Rehabilitation Counselor Certification (CRCC) both offer national certification for counselors. These national professional certifications were set up before state licensing of counselors came into being, as a way of establishing standards for counselor training. Historically, rehabilitation counselors were the leaders in the effort to obtain professional certification. In 1974 the CRCC first set up its system of professional certification (Bradley, 1991), and in 1985 ACA sponsored the NBCC as an independent agency to certify qualified counselors.

Currently, NBCC offers four professional certifications: (a) National Certified Counselor (NCC) for work in all settings, (b) National Certified School Counselors, (c) Certified Clinical Mental Health Counselor, and (d) Master Addictions Counselors. The requirements for NCC certification are a master's degree in counseling with post-master's supervised experience and a written exam. The other specialized certifications require additional training and experience within the area of specialty.

There are both disadvantages and advantages for counselors who are nationally certified by NBCC. In those states that license counselors under a practice act, nationally certified counselors must still be licensed by the state to engage in private practice in the community.

Moreover, national certification does not qualify counselors to receive third-party health insurance payments or to be accepted as mental health providers by managed care organizations. On the other hand, nationally certified counselors have the advantage of being recognized as qualified counselors in all states. Further, national certification recognizes those with counselor specialties, whereas state licensing does not. Many counselors decide to become both state licensed and nationally certified, thus acquiring the advantages of both.

ETHICAL CODES TO PROTECT THE CLIENT AND MONITOR THE PROFESSION

Ethical codes are developed by professional associations to protect the public from unethical or incompetent professionals, as well as to protect the profession from unethical practices by any of its members (Herlihy & Corey, 1996). However, as Corey, Corey, and Callanan (1998) warn, these codes are guidelines; they carry no legal weight. At best, the association can reprimand counselors who behave unethically or can drop them from professional membership.

The ACA Code of Ethics (1995; see appendix A) applies to counselors. The APA's *Ethical Principles of Psychologists* (1992) applies to counseling psychologists. Similar codes have been set by AAMFT (1991) and NASW (1979). Because the ACA code is most representative of general counseling practice, this section highlights the major issues addressed in the ACA Code of Ethics.

Ethics Regarding the Counseling Relationship

When establishing a relationship, the counselor's primary obligation is "to respect the dignity and to promote the welfare of clients" (Section A.1). Counselors work jointly with clients to encourage clients' positive growth and development.

Dual Relationships

At times individuals may ask for counseling from a counselor who is their administrator or supervisor, close friend, or relative. Such requests would require the counselor to serve dual roles which interfere with professional judgment and inhibit the development of trust necessary for successful counseling. For this reason dual relations are unethical. The counselor should refer such individuals to another professional (see Section A.6).

Sexual Involvement with Clients

Counselor-client sexual intimacy is forbidden in the ethical codes of all therapeutic professions (Corey et al., 1998). The ACA Code of Ethics states: "Counselors do not have any type of sexual intimacies with clients and do not counsel persons with whom they have had a sexual relationship" (Section A.7.a). Corey et al. (1998) summarize the damage to clients who became sexually involved with therapists and counselors:

> This harm ranged from mistrust of opposite-sex relationships to hospitalization and in some cases, suicide. Other effects of sexual intimacies on clients' emotional, social, and sexual adjustment

included negative feelings about the experience, a negative impact on their personality and a deterioration of their sexual relationship with their primary partner. (p. 249)

Counselors and therapists who sexually exploit clients not only can be sued for malpractice but also can be jailed on felony charges and lose their licenses, their insurance coverage, or their jobs (Corey et al., 1998).

Countertransference Issues

As the counselor-client relationship develops during the counseling process, the counselor's unconscious, unmet emotional needs invariably arise. This process is called *countertransference.* Counselors must be alert to signs of countertransference and distinguish their affects from those of their clients. Otherwise, the counselors' projected needs will have a detrimental effect on their clients.

The ACA Code of Ethics states: "In the counseling relationship, counselors are aware of the intimacy and responsibilities inherent in the counseling relationship, maintain respect for clients, and avoid actions that seek to meet their personal needs at the expense of clients" (Section A.5.a). Corey (2001) points out, "Ethically, it is essential that we become aware of our own needs, areas of unfinished business, potential personal conflicts, and defenses. We need to realize how such factors could interfere with helping our clients" (p. 44).

Counselors' unconscious, unresolved personal needs that interfere with the counseling relationship show up in numerous ways. Counselors who need approval from clients may be overly solicitous toward them; they may also avoid confronting passive clients. Such counselors may encourage clients' dependence or learned helplessness, or they may exploit clients by delaying appropriate termination of the counseling relationship because they are enjoying a pleasant, need-fulfilling, social interaction with their clients or because they want to continue receiving client fees.

Counselor Values

Values are standards or ethical guidelines that influence an individual's or group's behavior, attitudes, and decisions. A person's particular lifestyle is based on a value system derived from his or her particular religious, philosophical, social, cultural, and political background. Values are fostered by families, ethnic groups, religious organizations, and schools, or they may be arrived at through an individual's personal searching. Value issues come up in counseling when clients have mixed motivations about choices they must make or when their choices conflict with the values of family members, peers, or society (see also "Moral Development," chap. 5).

A counselor's job is to help clients search for various alternative behaviors or attitudes and decide which best contribute to their personal satisfaction and development and still permit effective social interaction. The counselor's task is complex because this search may involve several value systems: those of the clients, the counselor, the school, the society, the clients' peer groups, and the clients' families. These value systems may all be different, even the values of the parents. Counseling is further complicated because the counselor cannot always keep personal values out of counseling sessions. A counselor's particular lifestyle and general behavior suggest clues to his or her beliefs about values in general. A counselor should express personal values when appropriate but allow clients to make their own decisions about alternative values (Corey et al., 1998).

One crucial area of potential values conflict lies in counselor reactions to a client's race, ethnicity, gender, or sexual orientation (see chap. 14). The ACA Code of Ethics specifically states that counselors should respect differences in diverse cultural backgrounds: "This includes . . . how the counselor's own cultural/ethnic/racial identity impacts her/his values and beliefs about the counseling process" (Section A.2.b). These principles also apply to a person's religious point of view, as well as to older adults, those with disabilities or handicaps, and any other aspect that differs in some way from the cultural orientation of the counselor.

According to the ethical codes, counselors must be aware that their own biases might unduly influence a client. In such situations counselors should decide whether to continue working with the client or refer the client to another counselor. Counselors who have certain religious beliefs against abortion, for example, find themselves in a moral bind when a pregnant client contemplates abortion. Counselors must determine whether their moral convictions permit an objective discussion of the issue. If not, the counselors should refer the client to another counselor. Similarly, counselors must not try to persuade a client who opposes abortion to consider abortion as a wise alternative.

Clients' Rights in Counseling

Freedom of Choice and Informed Consent

Both freedom of choice and informed consent relate to the voluntary nature of counseling. The concepts are based on an individual's constitutional right to privacy. Privacy involves "the freedom of individuals to choose for themselves the time and circumstances under which and the extent to which their beliefs, behaviors, and opinions are to be shared or withheld from others" (Siegel, 1979, p. 251). Regarding freedom of choice, the ACA Code of Ethics (1995) states: "Counselors offer clients the freedom to choose whether to enter a counseling relationship and to determine which professional(s) will provide counseling. Restrictions that limit choices of clients are fully explained" (Section A.3.b).

Besides ethical considerations regarding voluntary counseling, experience has shown that most persons profit more from counseling when they agree to, or voluntarily seek out, counseling. Many counseling theorists and practitioners consider motivation to change behavior a first essential step toward a successful counseling outcome.

Informed consent requires that counselors inform clients of the goals of counseling, the services that will be provided, the potential benefits and risks, fees, length of counseling, degree of confidentiality, qualifications of the counselor, procedures and techniques to be used, and clients' right of access to their files. With this information clients can make informed judgments about whether to enter counseling with a particular counselor. Some state licensing laws require counselors to display disclosure statements that spell out these considerations.

When mental health providers in private practice or in community clinics send a diagnostic classification of a client's problem to a health insurance company without informing the client, the client's rights are violated. The client's problems must fit into a particular category of psychiatric or neurotic dysfunction or adjustment disorder for an insurance company to cover costs. These diagnoses are based on psychiatric and psychological categories of disorders listed in the American Psychiatric Association's *Diagnostic and Statistical Manual of Mental Disorders (DSM-IV-TR;* 2000). Corey et al. (1998) state, "Some clients are not informed that they will be so labeled, what those labels are, or that the labels or other confidential material will be given to insurance companies" (p. 122). Providers of mental health services should obtain consent from clients when it is necessary to diagnose them for insurance reimbursement, and diagnoses should be shared with clients once agreement is reached. Through sharing, the diagnoses become a part of therapy, and clients' rights are protected.

Confidentiality

Confidentiality means that counselors will not disclose to others what a client has said in counseling sessions without the permission of the client. This protection is guaranteed by the codes of ethics of professional associations, rather than by law. Guaranteed confidentiality enables clients to develop trust in the counseling relationship and to disclose and explore painful or forbidden feelings and experiences during the healing process. In the ACA Code of Ethics the importance of confidentiality is described as follows: "Counselors respect their clients' rights to privacy and avoid illegal and unwarranted disclosures of confidential information" (Section B.1).

Some counselors say that they are better able to understand and help a client when they share information about the client with teachers or parents or with staff members of other agencies. They claim that because they are doing this to benefit their client, they see no need to request client consent, which the client might refuse to give. This behavior is not only unethical but also counterproductive to professional practice. Too often, counselors who have taken someone else into their confidence are shocked to find that the client in question is later informed of the interaction by that very person. When counselors think that sharing client information with others will be helpful to the client, they can indicate that to the client. Requesting a client's cooperation keeps that person involved, enhances trust, and makes sharing a productive part of therapy. If the client refuses, exploring the reasons for client reluctance can also prove productive.

Exceptions to Voluntary and Confidential Counseling

In certain cases individuals may lose their freedom of choice regarding therapy and have to submit to involuntary commitment if the counselor thinks they may hurt themselves or others. When a client is dangerously suicidal, psychotic, homicidal, or otherwise dangerous to others, the counselor calls on other mental health professionals who can determine whether involuntary commitment is necessary. Likewise, the guarantee of confidentiality may have to be broken. The counselor is legally bound, for example, to report cases of child abuse or to testify in court when summoned. If a counselor is in doubt about the necessity of breaking client confidences, consultation with other professionals is recommended, with action taken only after careful deliberation.

In public schools a student's behavior may become so disruptive or debilitating, the learning problems so acute, or the home situation so poor that administrators may decide that psychological intervention is necessary to determine administrative or therapeutic action. In such cases the student and family lose the right to choose. School psychologists, social workers, and counselors work collaboratively as a team in deciding the best psychological intervention strategies for the student in trouble (Gibson & Mitchell, 1999).

A school psychologist is the primary resource when behavior or learning difficulties that arise in the classroom require administrative psychological intervention and consultation. After assessing the situation through conferences with the student, teacher, and parents, the psychologist may make specific recommendations about treatment. A social worker who works closely with families can tell when family interactions are so poor or school or home relationships so unproductive that intervention is necessary for the student to function in school. On the basis of the social worker's interaction with the family, a referral to marital and family counseling may result. Once these steps are taken, counselors can then work with the student and family.

Counselors also have an ethical duty to warn unprotected third parties when clients with a contagious or fatal disease such as AIDS have not informed and refuse to inform partners about their condition (see Section B.1.d).

Counselors' Professional Responsibilities

Awareness of Degree of Competence

Counselors must be aware of their level of competence. They must not attempt to counsel individuals who have problems that require knowledge or skills beyond the counselors' qualifications (see Section C.2.a). If a counselor is uncertain about his or her ability to work with a particular client or becomes uncertain after seeing the client a few times, the counselor should consult with another professional or refer the client to another counselor or therapist.

Responsibility to the Agency or Institution

Counselors must abide by the policies and purposes of the institutions in which they work. If their own standards of professional conduct are in conflict with institutional policy, the counselors should try to make such changes in institutional policies that will benefit clients (see Section D.1). If counselors are not successful in changing institutional policies that violate good ethical practice, they should report these violations to ethical boards and seek employment elsewhere.

Responsibility to Monitor Effectiveness

The ethical standards of all therapeutic professions include the responsibility of the professional associations to assess, monitor, and upgrade therapeutic practice (see Section C.2.d). In some cases, unfortunately, it takes public outcry, severe criticism from national media, and lawsuits levied against some therapists before the profession scrutinizes questionable practice. Some leading professional journals, such as *Family Therapy Networker* and *Professional Counselor,* have been addressing these issues, challenging therapists and counselors to consider tough moral questions.

The issue over false memory in the early 1990s is a recent example. A central concept in psychoanalytic theory has been that repressed memories of painful childhood traumas contribute to adult client dysfunctions. When therapists help clients recall these experiences and work through their feelings, the clients are generally able to live more productive lives. Therapists have used repressed-memory recall in working with adult war veterans and torture victims suffering from posttraumatic stress disorder (PTSD).

Some therapists misused the practice, however, by inappropriately using methods that induced a client to recall memories of abuse that did not actually happen and were later admitted to be false. Therapist and memory specialist Michael Yapko (Yapko, 1994; Yapko & Whitfield, 1994) took the lead in speaking out on the profession's moral concerns on this issue:

> Many therapists are doing a credible and professional job in their assessment of an individual's sexual history. However, there are also therapists who are unjustifiably inferring a history of sexual abuse on the basis of symptoms that could just as easily be explained in other ways. . . . If the client doesn't accept the diagnosis (of having suffered abuse), he or she is accused of being in denial or worse. . . .
>
>   . . . What counselors unwittingly do is foster the belief in clients that they must have been abused, and then create the conditions that are right for recovering specific memories of abuse that are nothing more than confabulations. (Yapko & Whitfield, 1994, p. 37)

Controversial issues such as the false-memory debate contributed to a crisis in confidence about therapy itself (Butler, 1995; Jacobson, 1995). Such a crisis has been a good opportunity for the profession to engage actively and assess critically all aspects of its therapeutic practices. James Hillman and Michael Ventura's book *We've Had a Hundred Years of Psychotherapy and the World Is Getting Worse* (1992) served as a good model for the 1990s. *Family Therapy Networker* soon followed with a series of special issues over a period of several years that critically assessed professional practice: November/December 1992; September/October 1993; March/April 1994; and March/April 1995. The issue "Fallen From Grace" (March/April 1995), for instance, discusses how "psychotherapy can redeem its tarnished reputation." Even though individual mental health workers have taken stands about the need to monitor professional practice, professional associations representing these professionals have been slow to do the monitoring.

Ethical Considerations in Family and Marriage Counseling

Green and Hansen (1986, 1989) conducted a survey of family therapists in which they were to rank the most significant ethical dilemmas they faced in practice and to indicate whether the AAMFT ethical code was helpful regarding these dilemmas. Following are the six most difficult dilemmas in descending order of significance:

1. Treating the entire family
2. Having values different from those of the family
3. Treating the entire family after one member leaves
4. Professional development activities

5. Imposing therapist values (feminist)
6. Manipulating the family for therapeutic benefit (Corey et al., 1998, p. 374)

Ethical problems for family and marriage counseling are more difficult than for individual counseling (Huber & Baruth, 1987; Margolin, 1982). Responsibility to each family member or to each partner is complex, particularly if members start out with different purposes.

Marriage and family counselors differ in their views of confidentiality. Some believe that counselors should use professional judgment about whether to disclose a particular communication (Corey et al., 1998). However, hidden agendas or fears of hidden agendas can block communication within the family or between spouses. For example, if a spouse confesses to the counselor in secret that he or she has had an affair of which the partner is unaware, the counselor who withholds this information as confidential is colluding with the one spouse. To preserve confidentiality and prevent collusion, the counselor, at the outset, can inform family members that he or she will not keep secrets from those participating; family members can then decide whether they want to work with the counselor.

Huber and Baruth (1987) note potential ethical dilemmas in the following cases: (a) when family therapists redefine the presenting problem in terms of their own therapeutic orientation, (b) when therapists refuse to treat willing members of a family because one member refuses treatment, (c) when deceptive paradoxical interventions are used, and (d) when a therapist overidentifies with one marital partner and sets up triangulation in therapy.

Ethical Issues of Managed Care

Most professional counselors now contract with a managed care organization (MCO) to help facilitate mental health services. But in doing so, most face certain ethical issues in delivering quality care. In a survey of 108 mental health counselors from four regions in the United States, Danzinger and Welfel (2001) found that 75% of respondents reported that managed care presented ethical dilemmas regarding confidential counseling, rights to privacy, free choice of counselor, and informed consent. In a similar survey of 16,000 psychologists, Phelps, Eisman, and Kohout (1998) found that 4 out of 5 psychologists reported that managed care had a negative impact on their professional practice, primarily because of ethical dilemmas similar to those described here.

MCO controlling policies cause numerous ethical dilemmas for mental health providers. The client's freedom of choice in receiving counseling and in selecting a counselor or therapist is limited or nonexistent. Informed consent regarding the nature and duration of treatment is often bypassed. Confidentiality, so important to encouraging constructive self-disclosure, is violated. These unethical practices by many MCOs inhibit the establishment of a trusting counselor-client relationship, the heart of effective counseling or therapy. Furthermore, when mental health providers share confidential case notes with MCOs, neither the provider nor the client has control over what is done with the information. Another ethical issue for the provider concerns the MCO policy of limiting the number of counseling sessions, regardless of the nature of the client's problem.

Not all MCOs are restrictive or advocate unethical practices. Belar (2000), a clinical psychologist and a former employee of Kaiser Permanente's managed care program, claims that Kaiser Permanente, for example, doesn't require utilization reviews. Moreover, she points out that private practitioners are prone to equally unacceptable unethical practices. "Although mainstream psychology seems to view practice in a managed care environment as fraught with more ethical problems than an unmanaged, free-market environment, I am not certain that we can draw such conclusions" (p. 241). Criticisms of MCOs, she points out, have tended to obscure their benefits. She emphasizes that MCOs have a distinct advantage over private practice in that more people, particularly the low-income population, have access to mental health care. Moreover, she adds, clients have access to a full range of services because MCOs encourage collaborative and multidisciplinary teams of providers. And by working collaboratively in clinics, providers are more likely to be held accountable for their services and to observe sound ethical practices.

Many mental health providers and their professional associations have taken steps to consolidate the strengths of both MCOs and traditional private practice and eliminate their respective weaknesses so as to arrive at mental health care delivery that is economical, effective, and ethical. Counseling professionals have made suggestions to practicing counselors on how to proceed in an ethical manner within the MCO system (Cooper & Gottlieb, 2000; Danzinger & Welfel, 2001; Glosoff, Garcia, Herlihy, & Remley, 1999). Regarding the abandonment issue, Glosoff et al. emphasize that it is the counselor's responsibility to continue seeing clients until appropriate referrals can be made. The ACA Ethical Code states

> . . . that counselors are not to abandon their clients (regardless of decisions made by third-party payers) and are responsible for remaking appropriate arrangements for continuation of care that is considered clinically necessary. Because of this counselors may find themselves providing services for little or no fee in order to implement clinically sound and ethical treatment plans. . . . (p.10)

Cooper and Gottlieb (2000) also suggest that clients should be continuously alerted to the restrictions on confidentiality, the uncertainty about what MCO staff do with confidential information, and the degree to which MCOs control treatment protocols and the duration of treatment. Although informing clients of such limitations does help to address the ethical issues in question, such steps often limit effective resolution of client problems. Clients may be reluctant to disclose sensitive personal information, for example, whereas counselors may be reluctant to elicit it.

Glosoff et al. (1999) recommend that counselors who contract with restrictive MCOs should "inform managed care organizations about conditions that interfere with clinicians' ethical responsibilities to their clients or restrictions that limit their treatment effectiveness" (p. 13). Further, these authors say that counselors should "be prepared to make formal appeals of . . . decisions that limit treatment choices and to request the treatment they believe is clinically sound" (p. 13). These authors also believe that counselors should become members of MCO boards of directors in which they can be involved in decision making that will contribute to needed changes.

LEGAL ISSUES

Privileged Communication

Both counselors and clients have certain legal rights, responsibilities, and limitations. *Privileged communication* is defined as "the legal right which exists by statute and which protects the client from having his confidences revealed publicly from the witness stand during legal proceedings without his permission" (Shah, 1969, p. 57). Privileged communication is meant to preserve a well-established relationship so that the client can talk freely without fear of disclosure in court. Privileged communication exists in the following relationships: attorney-client, physician-patient, mental health provider-client, husband-wife, and clergy-parishioner.

Counselors should have a clear understanding of the difference between ethical confidentiality and the confidentiality involved in privileged communication. Privileged communication is specific to counselors testifying in a court of law. It is a legal right granted to clients by a state law, rather than a right guaranteed by a professional association's ethical code. Privileged communication is the *client's* right, not the counselor's.

Because privilege is a client right, clients can waive the privilege and order a counselor or psychotherapist to testify in court. Other exceptions exist in which testimony must be given if a court demands it; Corey, Corey, and Callanan (1993) summarize these exceptions in the literature.

- When a counselor or therapist is conducting a psychological examination in a court-appointed capacity
- When a client files a lawsuit against the counselor for malpractice
- When a client claims a mental condition as a defense against a committed crime
- When a client under age 16 or with a developmental disability at any age is a victim of sexual abuse, rape, or child abuse
- When a therapist evaluates the sanity of a client and determines that hospitalization is necessary
- When clients are considered dangerous to themselves or others or indicate that they intend to commit or have committed a crime (p. 104)

Privileged communication laws do not apply to group counseling or to marital or family counseling (Anderson, 1996; Corey et al., 1998), although Knapp, Vandecreek, and Zirkel (1985) argue that family and marital counseling communication should be privileged unless both spouses choose to waive the privilege.

When the statutory privilege does not exist, counselors can be subpoenaed and required to testify in court about communications with clients in counseling sessions. This often happens with school counselors in child custody cases. Herlihy and Sheeley (1987) recommend that counselors attempt to avoid testifying when they believe it would be harmful to their clients or to their image as trusted counselors. They can request that a judge extend privilege because the counseling code of ethics requires confidentiality, or they can request that their testimony be heard in the judge's chambers.

In most states clients of psychologists and psychiatrists are guaranteed privilege, and counselors, through licensing, are gaining ground. School counselors should also demand this privilege for the students they counsel. Students would be more likely to share their concerns about illegal or asocial acts if counselors were able to guarantee that they could refuse to testify in court about information gained in counseling. Similarly, students involved in child custody disputes in their parents' divorce suits are more likely to seek counseling if the counselor is not forced to testify in court about their sessions.

Child Abuse: A Requirement to Report

Counselors are faced with a dilemma when clients, in confidence, reveal that child abuse is occurring either to them or to someone else. The counselor must report the abuse to child protective services. Laws in all 50 states and the District of Columbia require that a person who suspects child abuse must report it, usually to child protective services although states vary in detail (Camblin & Prout, 1988). Failure to report child abuse is a misdemeanor.

Child abuse includes physical injury, mental injury, sexual abuse, and neglect. The person reporting is given immunity from any civil or criminal liability for breaking confidentiality. When teachers suspect child abuse, it is their legal responsibility to report it to the child protective agency; the counselor should not do the reporting for teachers. This arrangement frees the counselor to develop a counseling relationship with the child and the parents after the reporting is done.

Legal Duty to Warn

In the now famous *Tarasoff* case in 1969, a client at the University of California—Berkeley student health services told his psychologist that he intended to kill his fiancée. The psychologist contacted the police, who questioned the client and then released him as not dangerous. Subsequently, the client killed his fiancée. The fiancée's parents sued the board of regents and the employees of the university. The suit was dismissed in a lower court, but the California Supreme Court ruled in favor of the parents, saying that the psychologist should have warned the client's fiancée.

This issue stirred controversy throughout the mental health community. Many believe that the police overrode a psychologist's opinion about a psychological condition that was beyond the expertise of the police. Furthermore, the police, not the psychologist, should be responsible for warning a potential victim. In that way policing stays in the hands of the police, and therapy remains with mental health providers. In any case when a client is dangerous to others, intervention by the authorities is necessary if the client is unresponsive to treatment. Because states vary considerably regarding the legal duty to warn (Anderson, 1996), counselors should know their state laws. Consultation with other professionals is suggested when counselors are in doubt about their legal responsibility.

Counseling Liability (Malpractice)

If professional counselors do not follow ethical guidelines or legal statutes related to their profession, clients can sue them for failing to act in good faith or failing to care for client welfare. The counselors are then considered professionally negligent, careless, or ignorant in their duties.

In a summary of the literature about malpractice suits, Corey et al. (1998) state that "violations of confidentiality and sexual misconduct have received the greatest attention in the literature as grounds for malpractice suits" (p. 141). Citing Swenson (1997), Corey et al. (1998) note that three ethical issues "pose the highest risks of malpractice lawsuits" (p. 141):

- Violation of clients' personal rights (typically related to sex, privacy, or wrongful commitment)
- Failure to protect others from clients (alleged in failure to warn, failure to commit, and wrongful release cases)
- Incompetent treatment of clients (often alleged in suicide cases)

Counselors can protect themselves from malpractice suits by becoming aware of and abiding by all the preventive measures possible. The following are some of the numerous suggestions offered by Corey et al. (1998): practicing within one's professional competence; honoring confidentiality; issuing a formal disclosure stating limitations of expertise; consulting with other professionals whenever necessary; staying aware of informed consent laws; declaring the pros and cons of treatment approaches; stating, before treatment, fee and fee collection policies; following necessary termination processes; avoiding dual relationships; and keeping accurate, detailed records.

MINORS' RIGHTS

Increasingly, children and adolescents have been granted rights to informed consent and privileged communication in counseling, but in practice these rights remain confusing and complex. To compound the confusion, minors' rights and responsibilities in school differ from those in the community. Thus, minors' rights to seek treatment, to refuse treatment, and to be accorded confidentiality in schools and in the community are discussed separately here.

School Counseling: Free Choice, Informed Consent, and Confidentiality

Although opinions in the literature differ, the general consensus is that children have a right to voluntary counseling in schools, even over parents' objections. Schmidt (1987) presents the case of a fourth grader in counseling whose mother objected to the counseling sessions on religious grounds. The director of counseling in the district concluded that the school ethically and legally should continue counseling if the child wished to continue, even if the parent objected. Acceptance of children asking for and receiving counseling in schools has increased because of the recognition in child abuse laws that children need protection from parents who harm or neglect them (Schmidt, 1987). Children also need protection from parental ignorance (Alexander, 1980).

Regarding informed consent, described earlier, students should have the same rights that adults in the community have. When young children are allowed the same opportunities for informed consent and free choice that are given to older children and adults, their involvement in counseling and their sense of responsibility for their own behavior can increase. Relationships among teachers, parents, counselors, and children can also improve. When students seek counseling on their own and are treated successfully, parents are encouraged to seek counseling themselves (Ohlsen, Horne, & Lawe, 1988).

In discussing confidentiality in child counseling, Van Hoose (1968) says:

> The fact that the counselee is a child in no way gives the counselor the right to violate or betray confidences. In fact, since the child is almost defenseless, the counselor has an even greater responsibility to make certain that he does not provide the adults with a weapon which can be used against the child. The counselor cannot risk making secret deals with the parents and he cannot align himself with either faction in a conflict. (pp. 135–136).

The counselor's first obligation is to consider the child. If a child does not want confidential information given to his or her parents, the counselor should discuss the matter with the child to discover the reasons for the objections, the information that is disputed, and the possible consequences of giving out that information. Thus, the child can contribute to the decision.

In many cases counselors find it important to involve parents in family consultation or family counseling because children's problems generally are part of family interactions (Anderson, 1996). Most parents are cooperative and pleased that counseling is available, but some parents are concerned about their children seeing counselors on their own and about confidentiality. Counselors who meet with parents to discuss the value of such an approach can usually reduce parental doubts and resistance.

To help implement a policy of this sort, a counseling advisory committee composed of interested parents and teachers can be set up. A letter can be sent to parents at the beginning of the year, emphasizing the voluntary and confidential nature of counseling. If parents object, they can have the opportunity to discuss their objections with a counselor. Counselors can also reach out to parents by making presentations to parent-teacher associations and at parent education programs (Schmidt, 1987). The counselor's domain differs from that of school psychologists or school social workers. Because the counselor's primary client is the child, the child's right to confidentiality is honored. For school psychologists and social workers, in contrast, the school is the primary client, and the child's right to confidentiality is waived. According to the ACA Code of Ethics, the counselor's notes on counseling sessions are also confidential and are not part of the school's general student records. Although a student's school records are open to parental review, counseling records are exempt.

Community Counseling

Throughout the country minors generally must have parental consent or must be court ordered to see a counselor in the community. According to Lawrence and Robinson Kurpius (2000), exceptions to this law may vary from state to state and may include mature minors (usually those over age 16); emancipated minors (those over 18 who are self-sufficient and living away from home); minors whose lives are at risk (parents must be informed as soon as possible); minors who seek drug treatment; minors with sexually transmitted diseases; and minors over 12 who have been sexually assaulted. Special rules pertain in certain states to minors of divorced parents: Consent is required of the custodial parent only, and information is released to noncustodial parents only with the custodial parent's consent.

RESEARCH AND EVALUATION

A professional group offering a public service has a responsibility to assess the quality of the service, the degree to which it is helping the public, and its overall effectiveness. In counseling, these assessments generally take the form of research and program evaluations, which differ in their contributions to assessment of the profession. *Research* studies the effectiveness of counseling theories and techniques with clients. *Evaluation* studies the usefulness and efficiency of a counseling program in the community from a practical and budgetary standpoint. Program evaluators, who usually are practicing counselors or counselor educators, determine the utility and efficiency of programs and attach values to their findings. They assess programs through questionnaires, surveys, evaluative interviews, and observations. The main questions they address are, Is the program serving the intended populations? and Is the program efficient and effective? (Posavac & Carey, 1985). Decisions about initiating or changing programs arise from evaluations. At times, *accountability* becomes part of the evaluation. For example, directors may be asked to justify whether their programs warrant funding with taxpayers' monies from state or local budgeting agencies.

Training on how to conduct research and evaluation is included in an effective counseling curriculum. Evaluation and accountability procedures, policies, and problems fit well in supervised internship experiences. Each of these assessment activities, however, raises professional and ethical issues.

Ethical Concerns

Ethical problems that arise from research in the fields of counseling and psychology involve lack of treatment-control groups; failure to obtain informed consent of clients; and coercion, deception, and manipulation of subjects. APA (1973) published ethical guidelines for conducting research with humans, and these guidelines have been incorporated into the ACA Code of Ethics.

In all forms of counseling studies, ethical concerns arise about the use of control and experimental groups. It is unethical to withhold therapy or counseling from a control group to determine whether a matched experimental group profits from counseling.

Another area of concern, *informed consent,* means that research subjects, clients or otherwise, have the right to be fully informed about a proposed study and the right to decide whether they want to participate. Failure to honor these rights is unethical (Corey et al., 1998; Robinson & Gross, 1986). Similarly, it is unethical to deceive research subjects by withholding pertinent material or by otherwise manipulating them so that they are more apt to participate in a study (Robinson & Gross, 1986). An example of unethical deception occurs when a family therapist, to determine progress in later sessions, tapes families in the first session without their knowledge.

Need for Qualitative Studies

Many counseling professionals believe that researchers have been devoting too much time and energy to quantitative research and too little time to qualitative research. The *quantitative* method, which has been the most common type of psychological research, studies the causal effect of an isolated, specific, and observable aspect of behavior. In these studies the behavior being measured can be counted, or quantified, statistically. The *qualitative* method, in contrast, explores the multidimensional qualities of human beings within the context of their environments through case studies and field observations. Practicing counselors generally ignore the largely quantitative research, which they perceive as irrelevant or useless (Goldman, 1989; Howard, 1986; Krumboltz, 1986; Lichtenberg, 1986).

Goldman (1989) recommends that practitioners rely less on experimental, quantitative designs. Krumboltz (1986) argues that students should be encouraged to undertake thesis projects that are relevant to practice. And Howard (1986) recommends expanding scientific research to include more practical methods, such as idiographic studies (i.e., single cases), historical reviews, and other qualitative research methods. In line with these recommendations, counseling psychologists emphasize research methodology that takes into account the social-cultural context of the subjects under study.

In a special issue of *The Counseling Psychologist* on qualitative research paradigms, Hoshmand (1989) recommends three approaches: the *naturalistic-ethnographic,* the *phenomenological,* and the *cybernetic.* The first involves research in natural settings; the second focuses on meaning in human experience; and the third is based on understanding social systems and the process of change in those systems. All three designs involve coordination of researchers and practitioners. More joint research programs by university academicians and practitioners could provide meaningful research.

INTERNET COUNSELING

The rapidly increasing counselor and client use of online counseling—also called web counseling or Internet counseling—has presented new and complex ethical challenges (Remley & Herlihy, 2001; Sampson, Kolodinski, & Greeno, 1997). These include (a) difficulties in maintaining client confidentiality and rights to privacy; (b) increased opportunities for counselor and client anonymity, resulting in potential misrepresentation of counselor credentials and client symptoms; (c) difficulties in determining appropriateness of online counseling for particular client problems; (d) inability to effectively address serious and complex emotional issues; and (e) lack of interstate counselor licensure to monitor interstate counseling (Riemer-Reiss, 2000; Remley & Herlihy, 2001; Sampson et al., 1997).

Aware that existing codes of ethics were not applicable to Internet counseling, professional counseling associations drafted new codes to address the ethical issues. In 1997 the National Board of Certified Counselors (NBCC, 2001) developed a code of ethics specifically for online counseling, called WebCounseling. In 1999 the ACA (1999) published a special supplementary section to its existing code to cover Internet counseling. And in 2000 the revised code of ethics of the AMHCA (2001) included a new section—Principle 14: Internet counseling. Although all the codes address most of the major issues, there are notable distinctions.

Regarding confidentiality, the NBCC code and the ACA code direct online counselors to use appropriate encryption technology to scramble access codes in order to prevent unauthorized access to client-counselor communication. Further, counselors must inform clients when encryption measures are not possible. However, the AMHCA code does not suggest encryption intervention; instead, it states that clients must be informed about the limitations of Internet confidentiality. Both the ACA and AMHCA codes direct that clients be required to sign client waivers acknowledging the limits of client confidentiality in online counseling.

All three codes (NBCC, ACA, and AMHCA) emphasize the necessity of avoiding counselor and client anonymity. Counselors must provide accurate information about their competency, and individuals must identity themselves before being accepted as clients. Online counselors must also arrange for backup professionals in the client's vicinity to cover times when they are unavailable or when clients need emergency help. The NBCC code is the most specific on this point, stating that counselors must contact either the NBCC board itself "or the WebClient's state or provincial licensing board to obtain the name of at least one Counselor-On-Call within the WebClient's geographical region" (Section 9). NBCC also recommends that Web clients be provided with crisis intervention, or hotline, numbers in their locality.

The ACA and AMHCA codes are very similar in their statements about the need to determine whether online counseling is appropriate for a particular client. Both codes say that counselors should conduct intake procedures to determine whether clients are intellectually, emotionally, and physically able to use online counseling. The NBCC code does not direct counselors to screen clients; rather, it specifies that counselors must inform clients that certain presenting problems—such as sexual abuse, violent relationships, eating disorders, and psychotic disorders—are inappropriate for Web counseling. When Internet counseling is inappropriate for prospective clients, the codes direct counselors to encourage them to seek counseling through a traditional face-to-face counseling relationship.

Both the AMHCA and the ACA codes include sections about establishing the online counseling relationship (see also chap. 4, "The Effective Counselor") and again direct counselors to screen clients carefully to determine suitability for online counseling. The codes also state that clients must be warned about the limitations of online counseling as compared to face-to-face encounters. The AMHCA code even requires that clients be given a waiver to sign in which they "acknowledge the limitations that are inherent in a counseling process that is not provided face-to-face" (AMHCA Code, 2001, Principle 14.D).

More difficult ethical issues arise when online counseling is practiced across state lines. The ACA code for Internet counseling (1999) is somewhat unclear: "Professional counselors . . . do not provide on-line counseling services to clients located in states in which professional counselors are not licensed" (ACA, 1999, Establishing the online counseling relationship, Section d). But the AMHCA code is more precise: "Mental health counselors do not provide services to clients in states where doing so would violate local licensure laws or regulations" (Principle 14 F3). And further, "Mental health counselors confirm that the provision of on-line services is not prohibited by or otherwise violates any applicable state or local statutes, rules, regulations or ordinances, codes of professional membership organizations and certifying boards, and/or codes of state licensing boards" (Principle 14G).

Ethical codes drawn up by the professional associations can only begin to address the possible misuse of online counseling. As Remley and Herlihy (2001) put it, "Since Internet counseling is so new, these questions will not be addressed until lawsuits are filed in which Internet counseling was used" (p. 130).

SUMMARY

Over the years counselors have increased their efforts to obtain recognition as a unique professional group, one that is distinct from other mental health providers. Role definitions, training standards, and ethical codes have gradually been developed to define and monitor the profession. Professional organizations have contributed to lobbying state legislatures for licensing and certification.

Ethical codes to protect the client and to monitor the profession include matters that involve the counselor-client relationship, such as dual relationships, sexual involvement, and counselor biases; client rights, such as informed consent and confidentiality; and counselor responsibilities, such as competency awareness, responsibility to the workplace, and self-monitoring. For marriage and family counselors, AAMFT has developed special codes to cover the ethical complexities of family interactions.

Legal considerations regarding the counselor-client relationship include issues of privileged communication, child abuse, and rights of clients. Privileged communication is granted to clients of psychologists in most states; but for clients of counselors, only a small, though growing, number of states grant such privilege. In cases of child abuse, counselors in all states are legally required to report their suspicions to a child protection agency. The law protects the rights of clients in several ways; for example, clients can file a malpractice suit if they believe that a counselor has violated confidentiality or has harassed them sexually.

Certain ethical and legal codes protect minors' rights of free choice and informed consent and confidentiality, but their rights are more protected in the school than in the community.

Counselors have a professional responsibility to assess the quality of their services. A primary way of doing this is through program evaluations that measure the usefulness and efficiency of a program and through research studies that assess the effectiveness of counseling theories and techniques with clients. Professional counselors have suggested that increasing the use of qualitative research designs and reducing reliance on quantitative research would be more meaningful to practitioners.

The increasing use of Internet counseling has presented new and complex ethical issues. Counselors offering online services need to maintain client confidentiality, represent themselves and their credentials accurately, and refer clients to face-to-face counseling if problems are too complicated for online counseling. Professional organizations strongly suggest that counselors carefully abide by the ethical standards for online counseling.

PROJECTS AND ACTIVITIES

1. Write or telephone your state attorney general's office, and ask about the legal status of college, school, and community counselors regarding privileged communications. Are minors covered? Do special regulations for minors cover treatment and pregnancy? Ask for copies of any existing statutes. Begin compiling a loose-leaf notebook on legal concerns.

2. Write or telephone the president or executive secretary of your regional or state professional association, and ask about procedures for reporting unethical behavior of association members. Find out what sanctions, if any, can be applied. Also explore whether the counseling department of your state department of public instruction has policies on unethical behavior of school counselors.

3. Organize a panel of counselors with master's and doctoral degrees in counseling who are working in private practice, schools, colleges, and community agencies. Ask them to discuss the licensing of counselors with master's degrees.

4. Check with your state affiliates of ACA about the licensing of counselors in your state. If licensing exists, what are the stipulations for doctoral and master's degree counselors? If licensing does not exist, are plans to license counselors being considered?

5. APA Division 17 has recommended that counseling psychologists distinguish themselves from other professional counselors as described by ACA. Look over the standards and role definitions. In your opinion, do significant differences emerge? If so, what are these differences? Do they outweigh similarities?

6. Select several agencies with different emphases, such as a child guidance clinic, a halfway house, a crisis clinic, and a public school. Find out whether they employ any paraprofessionals. If so, compare their training programs and duties. How do these duties compare with those of professional persons?

In the following three incidents, assume that you are a school counselor or a licensed community counselor. In each case write a response indicating what you would say or do.

Note: Activities 7, 8, and 9 were written by Dr. Elvet G. Jones, Professor Emeritus of Psychology at Western Washington University, Bellingham.

7. A principal (or agency head) who was once a professional counselor confers with you and tells you that because drug problems in your area have now reached "epidemic proportions," it would be wise for you to let him know about any client who comes to you with such a problem. What do you say to this principal (or agency head)?

8. A 17-year-old comes to see you for the first time. He appears very depressed. He tells you that on May 16, his 18th birthday, he plans to commit suicide; he also tells you in great detail why and how he intends to do so. He further says that he is telling you this because he wants to be sure that no one is accused of doing him in and that because he does not belong to any church and has no priest or minister, you are the only person he is telling. In the light of your role as a counselor and considering the ACA Code of Ethics, how do you proceed in this case?

9. The personnel director at a large, local business calls you about a former client, now 19 years of age. She apparently is on a trip out of the country with her entire family for at least a month and cannot be reached, but she is being seriously considered for a good job, and the director wants to make a decision within 30 days. What the director wants from you is an evaluation of the woman's

personal and emotional adjustment. How do you respond to this request for information that could lead to this young woman's getting a good job?"

10. Search the Internet for online counseling services from a mental health counselor, psychologist, or other licensed helping professional.

Does the site offer information as suggested by the ACA and the AMHCA ethical codes? Identify which ethical issues it addresses (e.g., confidentiality, informed consent, counselor competence, etc.). How would you assess the site in terms of the ethical guidelines?

REFERENCES

Alexander, K. (1980). *School law.* St. Paul, MN: West.

American Association for Marriage and Family Therapy (AAMFT). (1991). *Code of ethical principles for marriage and family therapists.* Washington, DC: Author.

American Counseling Association (ACA). (1995). *Ethical standards* (rev. ed.). Alexandria, VA: Author.

American Counseling Association (ACA). (1999). *Ethical standards for Internet on-line counseling.* http://www.counseling.org

American Counseling Association (ACA) Governing Council. (1997). *Definition of professional counseling.* Alexandria, VA: American Counseling Association.

American Mental Health Counselors Association. (2001). Code of ethics of the American Mental Health Counselors Association (2000 revision). *Journal of Mental Health Counseling, 23,* 2–21.

American Psychiatric Association. (2000). *Diagnostic and statistical manual of mental disorders* (4th ed., text revision). Washington, DC: Author.

American Psychological Association (APA). (1973). *Ethical principles in the conduct of research with human participants.* Washington, DC: Author.

American Psychological Association (APA). (1992). *Ethical principles of psychologists* (rev. ed.). Washington, DC: Author.

American Psychological Association (APA), Committee on Standards for Providers of Psychological Services. (1979). *Standards for providers of counseling psychological services.* Washington, DC: Author.

Anderson, B. (1996). *The counselor and the law* (4th ed.). Alexandria, VA: American Counseling Association.

Association for Counselor Education and Supervision (ACES). (1978). ACES guidelines for doctoral preparation in counselor education. *Counselor Education and Supervision, 17,* 163–166.

Belar, C. D. (2000). Ethical issues in managed care: Perspectives in evolution. *The Counseling Psychologist, 28,* 237–241.

Bradley, F. O. (Ed.). (1991). *Credentialing in counseling.* Alexandria, VA: American Counseling Association.

Butler, K. (1995). Caught in the cross fire. *Family Therapy Networker, 19,* 24–34.

Camblin, L. D., Jr., & Prout, H. T. (1988). School counseling and the reporting of child abuse: A survey of state laws and practices. In W. C. Huey & T. P. Remley, Jr. (Eds.), *Ethical and legal issues in school counseling* (pp. 160–172). Alexandria, VA: American School Counselor Association.

Cooper, C. C., & Gottlieb, M. C. (2000). Ethical issues with managed care: Challenges facing counseling psychology. *The Counseling Psychologist, 28,* 179–236.

Corey, G. (2001). *Theory and practice of counseling and psychotherapy* (6th ed.). Pacific Grove, CA: Brooks/Cole.

Corey, G., Corey, M. S., & Callanan, P. (1993). *Issues and ethics in the helping profession* (4th ed.). Pacific Grove, CA: Brooks/Cole.

Corey, G., Corey, M. S., & Callanan, P. (1998). *Issues and ethics in the helping profession* (5th ed.). Pacific Grove, CA: Brooks/Cole.

Danzinger, P. R., & Welfel, E. R. (2001). The impact of managed care on mental health counselors: A survey of perceptions, practices, and compliance with ethical standards. *Journal of Mental Health Counseling, 23,* 137–150.

Fukuyama, M. A., & Sevig, T. D. (1997). Spiritual issues in counseling: A new course. *Counselor Education and Supervision, 36,* 233–244.

Gibson, R. L., & Mitchell, M. H. (1999). *Introduction to counseling and guidance* (5th ed.). New York: Macmillan.

Ginter, E. (1989). Slayers of monster-watermelons found in the mental health patch. *Journal of Mental Health Counseling, 11,* 77–85.

Glosoff, H. L., Garcia, J., Herlihy, B., & Remley, T. P., Jr. (1999). Managed care: Ethical considerations for counselors. *Counseling and Values, 44,* 8–16.

Goldman, L. (1989). Moving counseling research into the 21st century. *Counseling Psychologist, 17,* 81–85.

Green, S. L., & Hansen, J. C. (1986). Ethical dilemmas in family therapy. *Journal of Marital and Family Therapy, 12,* 225–230.

Green, S. L., & Hansen, J. C. (1989). Ethical dilemmas faced by family therapists. *Journal of Marital and Family Therapy, 15,* 149–158.

Guterman, J. T. (1994). A social constructionist position for mental health counseling. *Journal of Mental Health Counseling, 16,* 226–243.

Herlihy, B., & Corey, G. (1996). *ACA ethical standards case book* (5th ed.). Alexandria, VA: American Counseling Association.

Herlihy, B., & Sheeley, V. L. (1987). Privileged communication in selected helping professions: A comparison among statutes. *Journal of Counseling & Development, 65,* 479–485.

Hillman, J., & Ventura, M. (1992). *We've had a hundred years of psychotherapy and the world is getting worse.* San Francisco: Harper.

Hollis, J. W., & Dodson, T. A. (2000). *Counselor preparation 1999–2001: Programs, faculty, trends* (10th ed.). Philadelphia: Accelerated Development.

Hoshmand, L. T. (1989). Alternate research paradigms: A review and teaching proposal. *Counseling Psychologist, 17,* 3–79.

Howard, G. S. (1986). The scientist-practitioner in counseling psychology: Toward a deeper integration of theory, research, and practice. *Counseling Psychologist, 14,* 61–103.

Huber, C. H., & Baruth, L. G. (1987). *Ethical, legal, and professional issues in the practice of marriage and family therapy.* Upper Saddle River, NJ: Merrill/Prentice Hall.

Jacobson, N. (1995). The overselling of therapy. *Family Therapy Networker, 19,* 40–47.

Knapp, S. J., Vandecreek, L., & Zirkel, P. A. (1985). Legal research techniques: What the psychologist needs to know. *Professional Psychology: Research and Practice, 14,* 435–443.

Krumboltz, J. D. (1986). Research is a very good thing. *Counseling Psychologist, 14,* 159–163.

Lawrence, G., & Robinson Kurpius, S. E. (2000). Legal and ethical issues involved when counseling minors in non-school settings. *Journal of Counseling & Development, 78,* 130–136.

Lee, C. C. (1997). A new world order. *Counseling Today, 40,* 5.

Lichtenberg, J. W. (1986). Counseling research: Irrelevant or ignored? *Journal of Counseling & Development, 64,* 365–366.

Loughary, J. W., Stripling, R. O., & Fitzgerald, P. W. (Eds.). (1965). *Counseling: A growing profession.* Washington, DC: American Personnel and Guidance Association.

Margolin, G. (1982). Ethical and legal considerations in marital and family therapy. *American Psychologist, 37,* 788–801.

National Association of Social Workers (NASW). (1979). *Code of ethics.* Silver Spring, MD: Author.

National Board of Certified Counselors. (2001). *Standards for the ethical practice of InternetCounseling (Online).* http://www.nbcc.org/ethics/webethics.htm

Ohlsen, M. M., Horne, A. M., & Lawe, C. F. (1988). *Group counseling* (3rd ed.). New York: Holt, Rinehart & Winston.

Phelps, R., Eisman, E. J., & Kohout, J. (1998). Psychological practice and managed care: Results of the CAAP practitioner survey. *Professional Psychology: Research & Product, 29,* 31–36.

Posavac, E. J., & Carey, R. G. (1985). *Program evaluation: Methods and case studies.* Upper Saddle River, NJ: Prentice Hall.

Remley, T. P., Jr., & Herlihy, B. (2001). *Ethical, legal and professional issues in counseling.* Upper Saddle River, NJ: Merrill/Prentice Hall.

Riemer-Reiss, M. L. (2000). Utilizing distance technology for mental health counseling. *Journal of Mental Health Counseling, 22,* 189–203.

Robinson, S. E., & Gross, D. R. (1986). Counseling research: Ethics and issues. *Journal of Counseling & Development, 64,* 331–333.

Sampson, J. P., Jr., Kolodinski, R. W., & Greeno, P. P. (1997). Counseling on the information highway: Further possibilities and potential problems. *Journal of Counseling & Development, 75,* 203–212.

Schmidt, J. J. (1987). Parental objections to counseling services: An analysis. *School Counselor, 34,* 387–391.

Seiler, G., Brooks, D. K., Jr., & Beck, E. S. (1987). Training standards of the American Mental Health Counselors Association: History, rationale, and implications. *Journal of Mental Health Counseling, 9,* 199–209.

Shah, S. A. (1969). Privileged communication, confidentiality, and privacy: Privileged communications. *Professional Psychology, 1,* 56–69.

Siegel, M. (1979). Privacy, ethics, and confidentiality. *Professional Psychology, 10,* 249–258.

Steinhaus, J. (1993). I'm not a mind reader. *The Advocate, 16,* 4.

Swenson, L. C. (1997). *Psychology and law for the helping professions.* Pacific Grove, CA: Brooks/Cole.

Van Hoose, W. H. (1968). *Counseling in elementary schools.* Itasca, IL: F. E. Peacock.

Yapko, M. D. (1994). *Suggestions of abuse: True and false memories of childhood sexual trauma.* New York: Simon & Schuster.

Yapko, M. D., & Whitfield, C. L. (1994). Two experts discuss false memory. *Professional Counselor, 8,* 33–38.

CHAPTER 4

The Effective Counselor

Far more is expected of an effective counselor now than was expected in the 1950s and 1960s, the early days of counseling. Since then, the roles and expectations of the counselor have steadily become more varied and complex as counseling theories have multiplied—now based on humanistic, behavioral, cognitive, cognitive-behavioral, contemporary psychosocial, psychoanalytic, psychodynamic, and new postmodern constructivist, and social constructivist approaches. Furthermore, life-span developmental theories have extended counseling beyond the schools and colleges to include older adults.

So, the question, What makes an effective counselor for the 21st century? has become very complicated. One would expect the effective counselor to measure up to the well-developed individual that psychological theorists have formulated. But each of the different psychological theories tends to present its own ideals and its own set of criteria regarding human nature. Moreover, each describes differing processes that help individuals overcome patterns that block effective ways of being.

Thus, these various theories challenge counselors who aspire to be as effective as possible with their clients: Psychoanalysts, for instance, focus on a person's intrapsychic forces, whereas humanists focus on self-actualizing development; cognitive-behaviorists focus on a person's cognitive structure, perceptions, and behavior; and certain feminists focus on the psychodynamics of mutual connections.

Not only have counselor educators and counselors in the field needed to adapt to the steady stream of new theoretical approaches over the years, but they also have had to acquire new and varied competencies as services expanded beyond schools and colleges to the community. As the number of master's degree programs in counseling spread throughout the country and as states established licensure requirements, increasing numbers of counselors began working in private practice and in community agencies. To be effective in these new settings, they have had to become competent in working with families, substance abuse cases, trauma victims, clients with spiritual concerns, and older adults. Ethnic and feminist counselors have emphasized the importance of becoming more aware of one's cultural and gender differences. Increasing needs for crisis intervention and agency requests for diagnostic psychological evaluations have added to the expectations of an effective counselor.

Because of budget cuts, reduced services, streamlined sessions, and the rise of managed care, a sharp rise in brief-therapy programs has occurred, requiring counselors to adapt counseling theories and techniques to short-term counseling sessions. To further complicate the expectations of well-trained counselors, the use of standardized tests, which had declined sharply in the 1960s and 1970s, escalated dramatically in the 1990s, requiring competent counselors to use assessment tools effectively.

With these many new and varied expectations, the counselors' job of making sound moral and value judgments in counseling relationships has become more complex. This, in turn, has made it increasingly important that counselors attend to and cultivate their own personal and professional growth. Aware of their own developmental processes, they are able to know when to seek professional consultation, when to seek professional counseling or therapy, and when to participate in relevant workshops, seminars, and retreats.

PERSONAL QUALITIES

Effective counselors are well-integrated individuals committed to their own continued growth. They tend to be open to new experiences, aware of their own motivations, values, vulnerabilities, and unmet needs. They know when to seek counseling or therapeutic help themselves to maintain growth and meaning in life. These qualities enable counselors to empathize with and support clients struggling through the often-painful steps of self-examination and self-exploration necessary for change and development.

In the 1950s Carl Rogers (1951, 1957) proposed that counselors establish effective relationships with their clients that would lead to client self-actualization. He presented core characteristics essential to an effective counselor-client relationship: empathy (understanding), congruency (genuineness), and unconditional positive regard (warmth) (see chap. 6). *Empathy* describes counselors' ability to experience a client's inner world without identifying with the client. *Congruency* refers to the basic integrity of counselors that permits them to be authentic and honest with clients. Unconditional *positive regard* involves warm, accepting, nonjudgmental attitudes toward clients.

Carkhuff (1969, 1971) proposed two additional core characteristics: respect and immediacy. *Respect* refers to the counselor's high regard for a client's worth as a person. *Immediacy* refers to the counselor's sensitivity to the immediate experiencing of the client. After a review of the literature, Gelso and Carter (1985) concluded that most researchers generally agree that these core characteristics are necessary to facilitate a counseling relationship but do not see them as sufficient to ensure a successful counseling outcome.

Counseling theorists have presented other qualities that also contribute to an effective counselor, such as self-awareness, interpersonal awareness, objectivity, personal integrity, open-mindedness, flexibility, and trustworthiness (Belkin, 1984; Corey, Corey, & Callanan, 1998; Cormier & Cormier, 1998). *Self-awareness* refers to counselors' understanding and acceptance of their own feelings, attitudes, and values; recognition and acceptance of their own vulnerabilities and personal inadequacies; and awareness of the impact these have on others.

Interpersonal awareness, objectivity, and *personal integrity* refer to the counselor's ability to understand a client's struggles and pain. Counselors do not overidentify with or become oversolicitous of their clients, nor do they underestimate and ignore their clients' feelings. Counselors who are aware of their own inadequacies, vulnerabilities, and defenses do not project their own unresolved emotions on their clients; they are able to accept clients' emotional reactions toward them objectively. They are also aware of their position of power with vulnerable, dependent clients and do not abuse it by attempting to control or manipulate client behavior. In addition, they are comfortable with intimacy but are aware of appropriate boundaries in the counseling relationship.

Open-minded counselors are open to new ideas and experiences that stimulate personal and professional growth. They are alert to preconceived notions they may have about a client's experiences, feelings, and values; and they are accepting of client views different from their own. Counselors who are open-minded and unbiased tend to maintain clearer and more accurate perceptions of clients' feelings and actions.

Counselors who are *flexible* are not bound to one theoretical view, nor do they impose one set of techniques on all clients at all times in all contexts. They are thus able to work with a wide range of clients and client problems.

Trustworthy counselors hold confidences shared by clients. They do not deceive clients by misrepresenting their areas of expertise or their theoretical views about counseling, nor do they experiment with new or untried techniques outside their areas of expertise. If a counselor wants to try a new technique within her or his specialty, the counselor should first get the consent of the client.

Effective counselors are also aware of value differences between themselves and their clients when the clients present value conflicts. Counselors help clients seek resolutions that are consistent with the clients' self-growth and effective interactions in society. Counselors do not impose their own values on clients.

Multicultural Awareness

Multicultural counselors have insisted over the years that all counselors must become aware of their own ethnic- and gender-related biases. Counselors should become aware of their own cultural values and beliefs and the ways they differ from those held by others, especially their clients (Arredondo, 1998; Lee, 1995; Locke, 1995; Sue & Sue, 2003). The efforts of these leaders and others like them have led to the inclusion of multicultural competencies in counselor training standards (see chap. 14). Largely because of their influence, the ACA Code of Ethics (1995) includes in its preamble the following statement: "Association members recognize diversity in our society and embrace a cross-cultural approach in support of the worth, dignity, potential and uniqueness of each individual" (p. 1).

Sue (1996) presents three goals that are essential characteristics of effective counselors:

First, we need to become more culturally aware of our own biases, values, and assumptions about human behavior. Second, we need to become increasingly aware of the cultural values, biases and assumptions of diverse groups in our society. Third, we need to begin to develop culturally appropriate individual and system intervention strategies. (pp. 196–197)

Effective counselors are open and responsive to the different socialization and cultural processes and the different views about human nature that exist among the diverse cultures in our multicultural society. Effective counselors are aware that the traditional developmental stages presented by Erikson, Piaget, Kohlberg, and others tend to exclude the majority of the population because they are based on young, white, secular, middle-class, male norms. Counselors open to self-development are familiar with other developmental models (see chap. 5) that take into account women, persons from various ethnic cultures, older adults, and spiritual development. The publications of Ivey and colleagues describe interviewing skills from multicultural perspectives (Ivey & Ivey, 1999; Ivey, D'Andrea, Ivey, & Simek-Morgan, 2002).

Self-Awareness and Growth

Many people now entering the counseling profession have probably had some sort of counseling or therapy themselves. A successful therapeutic experience enables counselors to understand the process of growth and transformation expected in a counseling relationship. If personal counseling were an expected part of their professional development, counselors-in-training would more likely become aware of their own limitations and strengths; they would experience the process of delving into themselves, which could help them relate to clients in more authentic or nonexploitative ways. By learning how to recognize their own unmet needs, counselors-in-training prepare themselves to deal with countertransference reactions when they are working with clients. All counselors would benefit from intermittent or periodic counseling or therapy as they experience transitions, losses, or conflicts in their own lives. Maintaining self-awareness is necessary to remain effective with clients.

Many opportunities exist for counselors to expand their self-awareness and learn new perspectives about relating to clients. Regular case conferences and case presentations can help counselors become aware of countertransference issues and acquaint them with counseling approaches different from their own. In addition, personal-growth workshops and seminars are expected of counselors and therapists on an ongoing basis as a way for them to continue to develop and maintain effective relationships with their clients. Professional associations offer a multitude of workshops at their annual conferences; and counselors and therapists should also take part in therapeutic workshops, seminars, or retreats offered outside their associations or outside their expertise, to broaden their outlook. Schools of social work, spiritually oriented groups, and the Society of Aging, for example, are apt to address issues of which many counseling and psychological associations are probably unaware.

Avoiding Burnout

Most counselors who experience short periods of heightened stress are aware of their condition, are able to work through difficult periods, and can manage to function effectively. If counselors are unaware of or are unable to cope with the stresses of their lives, if they continue feeling anxious and become worn out, and if they become ineffective with their clients, they are suffering from *burnout.*

When burnout occurs, counselors feel "exhausted and depleted, with little energy left for their clients. They tend to manifest negative attitudes about self and work" (Remley & Herlihy, 2001, p. 144). If counselors do not heed and attend to these symptoms, *impairment* is likely to occur. "Burnout is not so much a state or condition as it is a process that, if not corrected, can lead to impairment" (Remley & Herlihy, 2001, p. 144). Impaired counselors are those who may be unaware of their stress level and who have been unable to cope with or resolve emotional stress, resulting in an inability to relate to clients in an effective manner and a likelihood that their ineffectiveness may harm clients. At this stage, since client welfare is at stake, counselors may have to suspend their professional responsibilities until they regain their equilibrium. The ACA Code of Ethics is very clear on this point:

> Counselors refrain from offering or accepting professional services when their physical, mental, or emotional problems are likely to harm clients or others. They are alert to signs of impairment, seek assistance for problems, and, if necessary, limit, suspend, or terminate their professional responsibilities. (Section C.2.g)

Corey (2001) challenges those practitioners who think that counselor burnout is just part of the job. He contends that many counselors who suffer from burnout or impairment tend to blame outside conditions in their lives rather than focusing on their own personal strengths, resources, and limitations. He comments that such an attitude

> often contributes to general feelings of hopelessness and powerlessness. To the degree that professionals continue to blame external factors, they also surrender their own personal power. It is essential that counselors recognize . . . they can be instrumental in bringing about changes, both in their environment and in themselves. (p. 39)

Various conditions lead to counselor burnout or impairment:

- Ongoing feelings of frustration and unresolved countertransference while working with clients
- A highly demanding, poor working environment
- Difficulty with unresolved personal conflicts or crises

Corey (2001) cautions that counselors need to acknowledge their limitations and know when their professional expertise is inadequate for clients with especially complex problems. Effective counselors must be aware of their own countertransference, which inevitably arises during counseling: "Ethical practice requires that counselors remain alert to their emotional reactions to their clients, that they attempt to understand such reactions, and that they do not meet their own needs at the expense of their clients' needs" (Corey, Corey, & Callanan, 1998, p. 49). Effective counselors are able to work through countertransference issues and avoid assuming too much responsibility for clients' progress.

Effective counselors notice signs of potential burnout and take the following steps to alter the situation:

- Confront and attempt to improve stressful working conditions
- Evaluate whether personal issues are interfering with counseling relationships
- Learn their limits and set limits with others
- Engage in professional consultation
- Attend professional workshops to sharpen competencies

- Participate in professional growth activities
- Seek professional counseling
- Broaden interests beyond work

Counselors can establish regular case conferences with peers and attend counseling workshops where they can share strategies about working with difficult client problems. Regarding stressful working conditions, counselors can also discuss with colleagues ways of reducing overload. At the same time they can educate heads of agencies or supervisors about the consequences of counselor burnout, including its impact on client welfare and agency effectiveness. In professional consultation counselors can discuss countertransference issues, doubts or uncertainties about a counseling approach, and concerns about taking on too much responsibility for clients. In addition, personal counseling can help counselors resolve personal issues, doubts about themselves and their competencies, or personal conflicts that are impeding their work.

PROFESSIONAL COMPETENCIES

Professional competencies considered essential for counselors fall into four major categories: (a) knowledge about counseling theories and strategies, (b) interviewing skills, (c) assessment skills, and (d) sound ethical judgment. Additional competencies necessary for counselors in specialty areas—such as family, career, or substance abuse—or in particular work settings—such as schools, colleges, or community agencies—are described in separate chapters in parts 3 and 4.

Knowledge About Counseling Theories and Strategies

It is important for counselors to be aware of the differences among the various theoretical approaches and the value of using these approaches with different client circumstances. It is necessary for counselors to learn all major theories before they decide to specialize in one theoretical orientation, and they must learn the various strategies these theories propose (see chap. 6). Humanists, for example, use strategies to increase clients' insights about themselves and their environment. Among the humanists, Rogerians use interviewing and relationship skills to help clients self-actualize, and Gestaltists use strategies such as visual imagery, body work, or confrontation to provoke feeling responses in clients. Cognitive-behaviorists use strategies such as reinforcement, social modeling, cognitive restructuring, and reframing to correct clients' distorted perceptions about the nature of their problems. Psychodynamic therapists help clients integrate conscious and unconscious processes by helping them become aware of the dynamic, intrapsychic processes underlying their perceptions and interactions.

Although counselors and therapists may eventually specialize in applying certain strategies based on one particular theoretical view, many counselors tend to be *eclectic* and draw upon techniques from a variety of theoretical orientations, depending on the nature of the problem, varying client characteristics, the social context and environment, and the counselor's work setting (Lazarus & Beutler, 1993; see also chap. 6). Although an eclectic approach allows counselors more flexibility, practitioners without a firm theoretical foundation—often the case with inexperienced or minimally trained counselors or therapists—can be dangerous. Such persons are apt to be injudicious in using techniques that go beyond their expertise and training; and when inappropriately applied, techniques that are otherwise potentially beneficial to clients can become damaging. Counselors can avoid the dangers inherent in an eclectic approach by integrating various techniques into a theoretical model (see chap. 6).

An *integrative* theoretical approach is acquired over time as counselors develop a broad and comprehensive understanding of counseling theories and strategies. Through practice, as well as participation in periodic postgraduate training programs, counselors gradually draw on techniques from the different theoretical approaches that are consistent with their fundamental assumptions about human growth and development. They are cautious about using a technique unless they have acquired sufficient training and expertise, but they are willing to take intensive training to learn new strategies that fit their own theoretical model (see chap. 6).

Effective counselors also know when to refer clients to specialists, when client problems require techniques that go beyond their expertise. For example, a counselor who thinks a particular client needs to explore deeper unconscious processes through prolonged therapy would know enough to refer the client to an appropriate psychoanalyst or psychodynamic therapist. Similarly, a counselor whose client has agoraphobic reactions might refer the client to a cognitive therapist specializing in treating phobias.

Interviewing Skills

A significant part of counselor training is the development of effective interviewing skills—a basic component of the counseling process. Allen Ivey (1971) and his colleagues (Ivey & Ivey, 1999; Ivey & Authier, 1978) have been most active in describing the types and uses of interviewing skills that contribute to an effective counseling process. Ivey took the listening and attending concepts that Rogers had emphasized in the counseling relationship and turned them into specific interviewing skills that can be taught to counselors (see chap. 5). During the ensuing years, Ivey expanded and refined these skills and added some new ones. He pointed out that although listening and attending skills were useful in establishing a relationship early in the counseling process, additional skills, which he called *social influencing skills,* were necessary to help move the counseling process along and to encourage clients to change behavior and take action during the later stages of counseling (Ivey & Authier, 1978).

In later writings Ivey and his colleagues (Ivey & Ivey, 1999; Ivey et al., 2002) have taken the lead in applying these skills to multicultural clients, attending to their social-cultural, contextual world. Specifically, counselors should consider such factors as "family, school, and neighborhood, and the impact of broader social issues such as unemployment, poor housing, racism, and ageism" (Ivey & Ivey, 1999, p. 17).

Listening and Attending Skills: Establishing a Relationship

Listening and attending skills, though important throughout the counseling session, are particularly necessary during the beginning stage because they are central to establishing

TABLE 4.1
The Basic Listening Sequence

Skill	Description	Function in Interview
Open questions	"What": facts "How": process or feelings "Why": reasons "Could": general picture	Used to bring out major data and facilitate conversation.
Closed questions	Usually begin with "do," "is," "are," and can be answered in a few words.	Used to quickly obtain specific data, close off lengthy answers.
Encouraging	Repeating back to client a few of the client's main words.	Encourages detailed elaboration of the specific words and their meanings.
Paraphrasing	Repeating back the essence of a client's words and thoughts using the client's own main words.	Acts as promoter for discussion; shows understanding; checks on clarity of counselor understanding.
Reflection of feeling	Selective attention to emotional content of interview.	Results in clarification of emotion underlying key facts; promotes discussion of feelings.
Summarization	Repeating back of client's facts and feelings (and reasons) to client in an organized form.	Useful in beginning interview; periodically used in session to clarify where the interview has come to date and to close the session.

From Ivey, D'Andrea, Ivey, & Simek-Morgan, *Theories of Counseling and Psychotherapy,* 5/e Published by Allyn and Bacon, Boston, MA. Copyright © 2002 by Pearson Education. Reprinted by permission of the publisher.

a relationship (see Table 4.1). When counselors listen intently, clients get the feeling that what they are saying is important. They then feel encouraged to talk more about themselves—the first step in self-exploration. The counselor who is listening attentively is less likely to make premature judgments about the client or the client's problem or to give premature advice, interferences that would spoil the counseling process.

Listening and attending skills serve two different but related functions: The counselor uses *listening skills* to gain information and encourage clients to talk about themselves as well as to help clients express how they perceive themselves and their problems (open and closed questions and encouraging). The counselor uses *attending skills,* in contrast, to understand and clarify clients' feelings and to convey the counselor's feelings of understanding to the clients (paraphrasing, reflection of feeling, and summarization). Counselors who attend closely to their clients also use appropriate eye contact, body language, and tone of voice (Ivey & Ivey, 1999; Ivey et al., 2002).

When using listening and attending skills with multicultural clients, counselors tend to shift focus from facilitating client self-expression or self-understanding to facilitating client understanding of self in a situational context. Multicultural counselors tend to listen for family and contextual issues that affect client expression of self (Ivey et al., 2002). Attending skills, for example, require an awareness of what is appropriate within a client's culture. "With some clients, direct eye contact will be personally or culturally inappropriate, the use of body language will be different, vocal tone may vary" (Ivey & Ivey, 1999, p. 42).

Facilitative Skills: Social Influencing

Once the relationship has developed, additional skills are necessary to help clients explore ways to change behavior. Ivey and Ivey's (1999) *social influencing skills* allow counselors to help clients more deeply explore their problems and take actions that will lead to change (see Table 4.2). These techniques help inspire and empower clients to change undesirable attitudes and behaviors and alter their interactions in detrimental environments. Although these social influencing skills are meant to encourage the client to take action, counselors should not allow their own needs to interfere. In other words, they should not determine for the client what that action should be.

Confrontation is another facilitative tool used to increase client insight and motivation so as to change self-defeating behavior. The counselor may confront clients when they show persistent discrepancies between what they say and how they behave or when they give mixed or garbled messages about their feelings and actions. The intention of confrontation is to invite clients to face themselves realistically so as to examine behaviors or attitudes that are blocking their growth and development (Egan, 1994; Young, 1992).

Egan (1994) prefers the term *challenge* to *confrontation* in order to avoid the idea of a client-counselor battle. Young (1992) cautions that confrontation, though a powerful tool to elicit change, must always be used judiciously and not out of counselor frustration or impatience. Ivey and Ivey (1999) describe effective confrontation as supporting clients while challenging discrepancies or mixed messages in their comments. All authors agree that if confrontations are done in a way that damages self-esteem or humiliates or shames the client, the client's defenses will become even more impenetrable.

Counselors also use *focusing skills* to direct discussion to areas they believe will improve clients' perspectives about themselves, their problems, and the influence of others in their environment. Counselors usually focus first on their clients and their clients' problems; later, counselors change the focus to others in the clients' lives, to the counselor-client relationship, or to cultural-environmental or contextual (i.e., situational or historical) conditions (Ivey & Ivey, 1999).

In some instances counselors may find it helpful to refer briefly to their own beliefs and experiences, a technique called *self-disclosure*. Sharing something about themselves can deepen client-counselor relationships or facilitate client insight or action. Counselors might say, "I get angry at my husband at times," or "I, too, had troubles concentrating in college, but I settled down once I picked a major." Research shows that a moderate amount of counselor self-disclosure has a positive effect on the relationship. However, counselors must be judicious in the timing, depth, and length of time spent in self-disclosure. The sharing must be directed toward helping the client progress and must not occur because the counselor is anxious about the client's feelings or because the counselor overidentifies with the client.

TABLE 4.2
Influencing Skills

Skill	Description	Function in Interview
Interpretation/ reframing	Provides an alternative frame of reference from which the client may view a situation. May be drawn from a theory or from one's own personal observations. *Interpretation may be viewed as the core influencing skill.*	Attempts to provide the client with a new way to view the situation. The interpretation provides the client with a clear-cut alternative perception of "reality." This perception may enable a change of view that in turn may result in changes in thoughts, constructs, or behaviors.
Directive	Tells the client what action to take. May be a simple suggestion stated in command form or may be a sophisticated technique from a specific theory.	Clearly indicates to clients what action counselors or therapists wish them to take. The prediction with a directive is that the client will do what is suggested.
Advice/information	Provides suggestions, instructional ideas, homework, advice on how to act, think, or behave.	Used sparingly, may provide client with new and useful information. Specific vocational information is an example of necessary use of this skill.
Self-disclosure	The interviewer shares personal experience from the past or may share present reactions to the client.	Emphasizes counselor "I" statements. This skill is closely allied to feedback and may build trust and openness, leading to a more mutual relationship with the client.
Feedback	Provides clients with specific data on how they are seen by the counselor or by others.	Provides concrete data that may help clients realize how others perceive behavior and thinking patterns, thus enabling an alternative self-perception.
Logical consequences	Interviewer explains to the client the logical out-come of thinking and behavior if/then.	Provides an alternative frame of reference for the client. This skill helps clients anticipate the consequences or results of their actions.
Influencing summary	Often used at or near the end of a session to summarize counselor comments; most often used in combination with the attending summarization.	Clarifies what has happened in the interview and summarizes what the therapist has said. This skill is designed to help generalization from the interview to daily life.

Ivey et al. (2002) emphasize that counselors using social influencing skills with multicultural clients tend to pay particular attention to the family and cultural context in which the client is experiencing a problem. Counselors are also more likely to encourage multicultural clients to participate, that is, become involved in their community as a way of empowerment.

Link to Theoretical Orientation

Counselors and therapists vary in how they use interviewing skills during counseling sessions, depending on their theoretical orientations (Ivey et al., 2002). All counselor/therapists use listening and attending skills, but they differ in the use of questions: Existential/humanists tend not to use questions; cognitive/behaviorists, on the other hand, frequently ask questions. Counselors and therapists also differ in their choice of social influencing skills: Existential/humanists avoid using reframing skills; for cognitive/behaviorists, "feedback, interpretation, and reframing skills are central" (p. 76), and confrontation is common; and psychodynamic therapists primarily use interpretation, with little attempt to encourage clients to apply new insights and learning to daily life.

Assessment Skills

In the 1930s, 1940s, and 1950s, when the major focus was on vocational and educational guidance and counseling, most counselors were trained to use standardized tests and inventories. During the 1960s and 1970s, largely because of the influence of Carl Rogers, the use of standardized tests declined dramatically. Most counselors used only those interviewing skills that helped clients assess and clarify their problems. During the 1990s the use of standardized tests again increased steadily. Effective counselors today need to maintain an awareness of the increasing numbers of assessment materials available and must develop or upgrade competency skills in the selection and use of standardized tests (see chap. 7, "Assessment: Tools and Processes").

Competent counselors learn to distinguish how and when to use assessment interviewing and tests in counseling and in diagnostic evaluations. During the counseling process counselors may use assessment tools to help clients conceptualize their problems and to encourage deeper self-exploration. In diagnostic evaluations counselors need to know how to assess individuals in three different circumstances: intake interviewing, crisis intervention, and psychological diagnosis for outside agencies (see chap. 7).

Sound Ethical Judgment

Effective counselors work with clients in an ethical and professional manner. Although counselors-in-training learn the codes of ethics of professional behavior, the codes give only guidelines. Counselors must rely on their own good judgment in knowing how to use those guidelines. As discussed in chapter 3, counselors must exercise professional and ethical behavior in maintaining confidential relationships, not imposing their values on clients, refraining from satisfying their own unmet needs in the counseling relationship, and above all, respecting the integrity and welfare of the client.

Kitchener (1984) developed a critical evaluation model to help counselors learn to improve their ethical judgments. This model is based on four underlying moral principles involved in counselor-client relationships: autonomy, beneficence, nonmaleficence, and justice. *Autonomy* means that clients have the right to self-determination, *beneficence* refers to counselors' intent to foster growth in clients, *nonmaleficence* means that counselors avoid taking actions that can harm clients, and *justice,* or fairness, refers to treating clients equally regardless of race, gender, age, or other social or economic differences. Others have since built on Kitchener's model; see Corey et al. (1998) and Cottone and Tarvydas (2003).

Effective training programs use case studies and case conferences to acquaint students with ethical dilemmas and to give them practice in exercising good judgment. When faced with perplexing ethical dilemmas, effective counselors consult with professional colleagues to help them resolve these dilemmas (Stadler, 1990). Counselors who function best in their professional practice also work at resolving their own unmet needs and learn to cope with their own emotional conflicts (Guy, 1987). In addition, as discussed earlier, effective counselors recognize that they are ethically responsible for recognizing their own symptoms of stress and must take steps to deal with or prevent undue stress that could impair their ability to work with clients (ACA, 1995, C.2.g).

Professional Collaboration

Making referrals and forming liaisons with other health care agencies has always been an essential part of the counseling practice. This interaction has evolved over the years into collaborative programs, in which health care professionals from different agencies share or cluster their facilities, not only to cut down on costs, but also to encourage collaboration among health care professionals. The need for health care professionals to work collaboratively has escalated in recent years because of ever more complex sources of stress—psychological, economic, social, and physical—that impact people's lives. As Walsh and Howard (1999) note, there are "new morbidities—poor nutrition, unsafe sex, drug and alcohol abuse, familial and community violence, teenage pregnancy and parenting, lack of job skills, inadequate access to health care, and homelessness" (p. 349).

Health care professionals in all settings now recognize the need to work collaboratively. In the community, comprehensive neighborhood health care clinics combine in one facility the various services provided by counselors, social workers, rehabilitation counselors, physicians, and psychiatrists (see also chap. 19). In Hartford, Connecticut, Hispanic psychiatrist Ramon Rojano, the director of the Department of Social and Health Services, developed collaborative programs involving all segments of the community infrastructure—mental and physical health services, social services, employment agencies, vocational and leadership training programs—to address the needs of low-income ethnic groups and thereby empower them to become effective citizens (see also chaps. 10 and 19).

In a special issue of *Professional School Counseling* on collaboration between school counselors and community mental health workers, Sink (2000) comments: "Our profession can forge proactive links among schools, homes, and communities by embracing 'comprehensive' multifaceted school-wide and community-wide models" (p. ii). In response to research indicating the value of collaborative programs in preventing violence in the schools, Cunningham and Sandu (2000) proposed a school-community team of school counselors, community mental health workers, law enforcement agencies, churches, and other community-based providers to develop and implement a comprehensive violence prevention program. In a similar vein Luongo (2000) recommended that families in which children or youth are using drugs, are victims of abuse, or are violent can best be served by the integrated efforts of school counselors, child welfare workers, juvenile justice personnel, and behavioral health services workers.

Although college and university counseling centers have typically kept networking efforts on campus, many centers are beginning to extend off campus to connect with community health care providers. Almost three fourths of college counseling centers now consult with psychiatric services on campus or in the community (Gallagher, 2001). To encourage off-campus referral services, Central Michigan University Counseling Center hosted a luncheon with community therapists, and in Riverdale, New York, the Manhattan College Counseling Center hosted a successful breakfast for "25 members of local private practitioners, agencies, clinics and hospitals" (Gallagher, 2001, p. 27).

Most notable has been the emergence of collaborative programs in which schools, colleges, and community agencies have arranged to share the same facility, or to form a cluster of facilities, in order to work together more closely. Collaborative programs are as varied as the needs of local communities and neighborhoods. In a unique collaborative effort, for example, the staff of the George Washington University counselor education program developed a GWU counseling clinic in the community neighborhood of low-income groups (see chap. 19). In another example the Redford University counselor education program in Virginia joined forces with Pulaski County High School to form a school-family counseling center next to the high school (see chap. 16).

THE WHOLE COUNSELOR

Counselors-in-practice become effective when they are able to integrate personality characteristics, personal growth experiences, and professional competencies into a cohesive counseling approach consistent with their values in life. In other words, the effective counselor cannot be wholly described through lists of personal characteristics or professional competencies. Counselors are effective when they integrate personal attributes and professional competencies in an ethical manner that benefits clients. They are not self-satisfied, intransigent, or egocentric about who they are and what they know. Instead, they are open and flexible to new ideas and new techniques based on sound judgment and moral principles that safeguard client welfare, all the while resisting impulsive shifts in pursuit of current fads.

INTERNET COUNSELING

Critics of online counseling—counseling by e-mail—have raised doubts about whether an effective counseling relationship can be developed through online counseling. (Remley & Herlihy, 2001; Riemer-Reiss, 2000; Sampson, Kolodinski, & Greeno, 1997). Especially at issue is "the possibility that counselors may operate from erroneous assumptions due to the absence of visual and auditory cues" (Remley & Herlihy, 2001, p. 130).

On the other hand, some professionals claim that in certain cases, Internet counseling provides advantages over face-to-face counseling in establishing and maintaining a counseling relationship. In a review of professionals who have used e-mail, Freeny (2001) enumerates the advantages; (a) individuals reluctant to seek face-to-face counseling find e-mail less embarrassing or threatening; (b) anonymity encourages more candid client self-disclosure and communication; (c) counselors and clients have more time to give considered thought to their comments to each other; and (d) the process is more flexible, allowing clients to work at their own pace. Freeny argues that counselors can develop a caring, nonjudgmental, and empathic relationship with clients through e-mail. Counselors can demonstrate warmth, compassion, and understanding through a "collection of caring words and emotions" (p. 37).

Responsible counselors concur that careful research is needed to determine whether effective relationships can be established in e-mail counseling and whether client self-disclosure is enhanced or inhibited in such relationships (Sampson et al., 1997; Riemer-Reiss, 2000). Some proponents believe that the use of videoconferencing would eliminate these concerns about Internet counseling. According to Sampson et al. (1997), "The use of videoconferencing would allow counselor interpretation of client non-verbal behavior, which is not possible with current telephone counseling or text-based counseling offered over the Internet" (p. 210). With videoconferencing, Freeny (2001) claims that "all the verbal and nonverbal [cues of the client] were available to me: the tone of her voice, her posture and facial expressions, even the deepening pink of her cheeks as she flushed" (p. 32).

Nonetheless, Sampson et al. (1997) caution, "Research on relationship development via videoconferencing in counseling and supervision is clearly needed to clarify relationship development issues" (p. 75). The effective counselor would proceed cautiously in this new arena, carefully evaluating potential benefits and risks.

SUMMARY

Effective counselors are well-integrated individuals committed to their own continued growth and development. They have personal qualities and professional competencies that enable them to develop trusting counseling relationships that foster mutual counselor-client interactions and encourage therapeutic developmental changes.

The personal qualities of effective counselors include warmth, congruency, and positive regard, supplemented by self-awareness, open-mindedness, flexibility, objectivity, trustworthiness, and personal integrity.

Professional competencies acquired by effective counselors include the knowledge and skills necessary to help them guide or encourage clients during the counseling process. Effective counselors are knowledgeable about the major counseling theoretical orientations: humanistic, cognitive-behavioral, psychodynamic, and postmodern constructivist and social constructionist. They are aware of the different helping strategies inherent in each of these orientations, and they select strategies that fit their theoretical orientation and the needs of their clients.

In addition, counselors use two major types of interviewing skills: listening and attending skills and social influencing skills. Listening and attending skills are used to establish a trusting relationship that encourages clients to clarify problems and begin self-exploration. Social influencing skills are used to enable clients to take action in changing attitudes and behavior.

Competent counselors also use assessment skills in two fundamentally different ways: in counseling and in diagnostic evaluations. During counseling, assessment focuses on helping clients clarify their concerns and explore themselves more deeply. Diagnostic evaluations determine and classify behavioral symptoms.

Effective counselors abide by ethical standards that ensure their clients' integrity and welfare: maintaining client confidentiality, refraining from imposing their own values on clients, and refusing to exploit clients to satisfy counselor needs. To remain effective, mature counselors engage in self-growth activities and personal counseling intermittently, thus maintaining and enhancing their self-awareness.

Although there is controversy over the use of Internet counseling, it may have some advantages over face-to-face counseling in terms of counselor effectiveness. Clients may find online counseling less threatening, may feel more inclined to disclose personal information, may have more time to consider their questions or comments, and may find the pace more flexible.

PROJECTS AND ACTIVITIES

1. Select a counselor who you have reason to believe is effective with a variety of clients. Interview the counselor and ask what she or he believes are important characteristics in effective counselors.
2. Talk with the director of the university counseling center or with community mental health counselors. Find out what evaluative roles counselors are expected to carry out.
3. Interview two or three counselors who call themselves eclectic. Ask them about their views on counseling and about the techniques they use most often.
4. Visit a school counseling program. Ask the staff how counselors treat students' emotional crises.
5. Role-play two beginning interviews: one in which the client is nontalkative and the other in which the client, with the same presenting problem, is talkative. Note the differences in listening skills required.

REFERENCES

American Counseling Association (ACA). (1995). *Ethical standards of the American Counseling Association.* Alexandria, VA: Author.

Arredondo, P. (1998). Integrating multicultural counseling competencies and universal helping condition and culture-specific contexts. *Counseling Psychologist, 26,* 592–601.

Belkin, G. S. (1984). *Introduction to counseling.* Dubuque, IA: William C. Brown.

Carkhuff, R. (1969). *Helping and human relations* (Vols. 1 & 2). New York: Holt, Rinehart & Winston.

Carkhuff, R. (1971). *The development of human resources.* New York: Holt, Rinehart & Winston.

Corey, G. (2001). *Theory and practice of counseling and psychotherapy* (6th ed.). Pacific Grove, CA: Brooks/Cole.

Corey, G., Corey, M. S., & Callanan, P. (1998). *Issues and ethics in the helping professions* (5th ed.). Pacific Grove, CA: Brooks/Cole.

Cormier, W. H., & Cormier, L. S. (1998). *Interviewing strategies for helpers: Fundamental skills and cognitive behavioral intervention* (4th ed.). Pacific Grove, CA: Brooks/Cole.

Cottone, R. R., & Tarvydas, S. (2003). *Ethical and professional issues in counseling* (2nd ed.). Upper Saddle River, NJ: Merrill/Prentice Hall.

Cunningham, N. J., & Sandu, D. S. (2000). A comprehensive approach to school-community violence prevention. *Professional School Counseling, 4,* 126–133.

Egan, G. (1994). *The skilled helper: A systematic approach to effective helping* (5th ed.). Pacific Grove, CA: Brooks/Cole.

Freeny, M. (2001). Better than being there. *Psychotherapy Networker, 25,* 31–39, 70.

Gallagher, R. P. (2001). *National Survey of Counseling Center Directors.* Alexandria, VA: International Association of Counseling Services.

Gelso, C. J., & Carter, J. A. (1985). The relationship in counseling and psychotherapy: Components, consequences, and theoretical consequences. *Counseling Psychologist, 13,* 155–243.

Guy, J. D. (1987). *The personal life of the psychotherapist.* New York: John Wiley.

Ivey, A. E. (1971). *Microcounseling and psychotherapy: Innovations in interviewing training.* Springfield, IL: Charles C Thomas.

Ivey, A. E., & Authier, J. (1978). *Microcounseling innovations in interviewing, counseling, psychotherapy, and psychoeducation* (2nd ed.). Springfield, IL: Charles C Thomas.

Ivey, A. E., D'Andrea, M., Ivey, M. B., & Simek-Morgan, L. (2002). *Counseling and psychotherapy: A multicultural perspective* (5th ed.). Boston: Allyn & Bacon.

Ivey, A. E., & Ivey, M. B. (1999). *Intentional interviewing and counseling: Facilitating client development in a multicultural society* (4th ed.). Pacific Grove, CA: Brooks/Cole.

Kitchener, K. S. (1984). Intuition, critical evaluation, and ethical principles: The foundation for ethical decisions in counseling psychology. *Counseling Psychologist, 12,* 43–55.

Lazarus, A. A., & Beutler, L. E. (1993). On technical eclecticism. *Journal of Counseling & Development, 71,* 381–385.

Lee, C. C. (Ed.). (1995). *Counseling for diversity.* Boston: Allyn & Bacon.

Locke, D. C. (1995). Counseling interventions with African American youth. In C. C. Lee (Ed.), *Counseling for diversity: A guide for school counselors and related professionals* (pp. 21–40). Boston: Allyn & Bacon.

Luongo, P. F. (2000). Partnering child welfare, juvenile justice and behavioral health with schools. *Professional School Counseling, 3,* 308–314.

Remley, T. P., Jr., & Herlihy, B. (2001). *Ethical, legal and professional issues on counseling.* Upper Saddle River, NJ: Merrill/Prentice Hall.

Riemer-Reiss, M. L. (2000). Utilizing distance technology for mental health counseling. *Journal of Mental Health Counseling, 22,* 189–203.

Rogers, C. (1951). *Client-centered therapy: Its current practice, implications, and theory.* Boston: Houghton Mifflin.

Rogers, C. (1957). The necessary and sufficient conditions of therapeutic personality change. *Journal of Counseling Psychology, 21,* 95–103.

Sampson, J. P., Jr., Kolodinski, R. W., & Greeno, P. P. (1997). Counseling on the information highway: Further possibilities and potential problems. *Journal of Counseling Development, 75,* 203–212.

Sink, C. A. (2000). Modeling collaboration through caring communities of learners. *Professional School Counseling, 3,* ii–iii.

Stadler, H. A. (1990). Counselor impairment. In B. Herlihy & L. Golden (Eds.), *AACD ethical standards casebook* (4th ed., pp. 177–187). Alexandria, VA: American Counseling Association.

Sue, D. W. (1996). Ethical issues in multicultural counseling. In B. Herlihy & G. Corey (Eds.), *ACA ethical standards casebook* (5th ed., pp. 193–204). Alexandria, VA: American Counseling Association.

Sue, D. W., & Sue, D. (2003). *Counseling the culturally different.* New York: John Wiley.

Walsh, M. E., & Howard, K. A. (1999). School counselors in school-community partnership: Opportunities and challenges. *Professional School Counseling, 2,* 349–356.

Young, M. E. (1992). *Counseling methods and techniques: An eclectic approach* (4th ed.). New York: Macmillan.

Part Two

Theories and Techniques

CHAPTER 5

Human Development Theories

Since the 1950s human development theories have influenced and shaped counseling philosophy, training, and practice and have contributed to counselors' and counseling psychologists' unique professional identity in the mental health field. These theories emphasize helping people of all ages resolve normal conflicts and maintain healthy personal, social, and career development. The Council for Accrediting Counseling and Related Educational Programs (CACREP) mandates that counselors, regardless of specialty, must study human development as one of their requirements. Division 17 of the APA also describes developmental theory as a strong component of counseling psychology practice. Based on human development theories, counseling is clearly distinguished from the remedial emphasis of psychiatrists, clinical psychologists, and social caseworkers.

Many theorists have contributed to these human developmental theories that underlie today's counseling practice. Jean Piaget's (1926) landmark proposal of the cognitive development of children and adolescents emerged in the 1920s and soon had significant impact in Europe. Also in Europe were Carl Jung and Charlotte Buehler, who, in the 1930s, expanded theories of development to include adult development. In America, because of the prevailing Freudians, trait-factor and maturational theorists, and Skinnerian behaviorists, it took several more decades before Piaget, Jung, and Beuhler had an impact.

In the 1950s Erik Erikson offered a more comprehensive, psychodynamic developmental model, which extended from childhood through several stages of adulthood. However, his life-span developmental theory, as well as the Jungian theory of adult development, were overshadowed for a time in the United States by continued attention to child development, particularly with the emerging attention paid to the cognitive development theories proposed earlier by Piaget. In the late 1970s attention to Jung and to Erikson surfaced with the adult developmental theories proposed by Daniel Levinson and Roger Gould, who focused on midlife transitions and crises. Robert Butler (1975) challenged society's stereotypical view of declining older adults by contending that they have the potential to continue to grow and develop intellectually, socially, and psychologically.

Another significant impact in the 1970s resulted from Kohlberg's (1981, 1984, 1986b) theory of moral development. His theory integrated and extended Piagetian cognitive moral development theory and elements of Eriksonian psychodynamic theory of life-span development. Feminists Chodorow (1978), Gilligan (1982), and Miller (1976) added their influence by countering the prevailing theories (e.g., those of Erikson & Kohlberg) that claimed human development is a process of gaining a sense of autonomy and separateness. Feminists claimed instead that human developmental processes are based on developing connectedness and empathic relationships.

James Fowler (1981) added another significant element to human development theory when he proposed stages of faith that addressed spiritual and religious formations as a dynamic relational process of development. More recently, Daniel Goleman (1995) proposed a theory of emotional development, which shows that one's emotions, much like one's cognitive capacities, structurally modify development. One of the first major attempts at forming an integrative developmental model was the developmental counseling and therapy (DCT) model of Ivey, D'Andrea, Ivey, and Simek-Morgan (2002); and Rigazio-DiGilio (2002) followed suit with a systemic developmental counseling and therapy model (SDCT).

Developmental theory has continued to evolve with ongoing critical reviews and suggestions for modifications and new proposals. As discussed later in this chapter, postmodern constructivists and social constructionists propose their integrated life-span developmental models, which encompass the whole person in context with the social-cultural environment. At the same time, several issues have generated debate and criticism: the question of whether humans are the sole agents of their development or whether development is determined by social-cultural influences; the issue of moral universalism versus moral relativism; and criticism over the inadequacies of the stage theory of development.

PIONEERS IN HUMAN DEVELOPMENT THEORY

Early developmental pioneers in the first decades of the 20th century worked only with children and adolescents, and they focused only on biological drives (Freud) or on genetics and maturational growth processes (Hall and Gesell). G. Stanley Hall (1916) and his student Arnold Gesell (1940, 1948), who based their theory only on heredity and the automatic, maturational growth stages of children, introduced a theory of child development that became an influential system of categorizing development into normative stages; that is, "age-related averages are computed to represent typical development" (Berk, 2003, p. 13). Jean Piaget and Carl Jung were the first major theorists to break from these earlier biological determinists and maturationists. Other pioneers worth noting as precursors to contemporary psychosocial life-span development were Charlotte Buehler and Robert Havighurst.

Piaget's Theory of Cognitive Development

Generally considered the giant of the 20th-century psychology of human development, Piaget (1926) held that humans have the innate capacity to restructure their cognitive processes based on interactions with their experiences. He proposed a four-stage cognitive development theory, with each stage dependent on, and flowing into, the next stage: *sensorimotor* (ages 0–2), *preoperational* (ages 2–7), *concrete operations* (ages 7–11), and *formal operations* (ages 11 and above).

Piaget believed that the ability to reason relates to cognitive structures in the mind that become more sophisticated and complex as the individual develops. Cognitive restructuring enables persons to process new experience and data and evolve into higher levels of reasoning, which in turn enable them to solve progressively more complex problems. As individuals mature, they move from the infant's preoccupation with sensorimotor interactions with the world, to the capacity to explore concrete objects and specific events in the environment, to the ability to think symbolically, abstractly, systematically, and logically.

Piaget described two types of processes that occur in cognitive learning at all developmental stages. One, *assimilation,* occurs when individuals incorporate new information cognitively into already-existing knowledge. The other, *accommodation,* occurs when individuals actively apply this new knowledge to changes in their behavior. Piaget believed that cognitive development involves a move from relative disequilibrium or conflict to equilibrium or resolution of conflict. When problems arise that cause discomfort, individuals try to resolve them, a process that leads to change and growth.

Piaget's theory of cognitive development has been a major influence in counseling theory and practice over the years. His many publications in the 1920s and 1930s include *The Moral Judgement of the Child* (1932), which influenced Lawrence Kohlberg (1969, 1981, 1984), who is discussed later and who extended the stages of moral development through adulthood. Piaget also influenced counseling theorists Albert Ellis, Donald Meichenbaum, and Aaron Beck (see chap. 6), who believe that faulty reasoning or distortions in the thinking processes are the major sources of problems. Other theorists influenced by Piagetian theory include constructivists (Neimeyer & Mahoney, 1995). Piaget's work also influenced psychological education activities involving the teaching of cognitive skills, problem solving, and reasoning (Drum & Lawler, 1988; see also chap. 8). Perry (1968) extended Piaget's theory beyond childhood and adolescence to include college students by adding another developmental stage, postformal, and Ivey et al. (2002) followed suit, as discussed later in the chapter.

Carl Jung's Stages of Life

Carl Jung, at the age of 56, wrote "The Stages of Life" (1933) after experiencing a midlife crisis that included personal and vocational upheavals. In this work he differed from other developmental theorists not only in extending the scope of developmental study to those in later life but also in insisting that the period after midlife includes a person's most important years (Jung, 1933, Staude, 1981). Jung conceived of four stages of development: childhood (birth to puberty); youth (puberty to 35 or 40); middle age (35 to 60); and old age (65 and up). He believed that the process of *individuation,* which involves a person's inner search for meaning in life, occurs after midlife rather than during youth or childhood. This theory, though not sharply defined or detailed, was a forerunner of later ideas about stages of life. Jung's conception of life stages foreshadowed Erikson's work in the 1950s and 1960s and is the prime force behind the later adult development theorists, such as Daniel Levinson (1978) and Roger Gould (1978).

Other Pioneers

Charlotte Buehler was probably the first theorist to explore the life cycle systematically (Buehler & Massarik, 1968). She also was probably the first to emphasize the *psychosocial* aspect of human development. In the late 1920s and early 1930s, Beuhler had collected personal documents, letters, and biographies from about 400 people of varying socioeconomic status, national origin, and occupation and had interviewed them. She then identified five psychosocial stages, from early childhood through older adulthood, during which people develop self-realization based on age-related goals.

Buehler is noted for having strongly influenced Donald Super's (1942) career development theory, in which he proposed and, over the years, elaborated on the relationship of personal development to vocational development (see chaps. 2 and 12). Equally important, however, is Buehler's systematic attention to stages in life and her integration of self-theory and human development, which underlies current counseling theory and practice.

Robert Havighurst (1953) also developed a psychosocial life-stage model of development, after conducting longitudinal studies between 1935 and 1950 of individuals at different stages of life. He coined the term *developmental tasks* to describe necessary actions that individuals must take at each stage of life to move to the higher stage of development. Havighurst emphasized that development is based on the person's relationship to the social world and the person's readiness to undergo certain social tasks expected at each stage of life.

CONTEMPORARY LIFE-SPAN DEVELOPMENT THEORIES

As Piaget and Jung were the major pioneers to break from deterministic and maturational theories of development, so were Erikson, Kohlberg, and Gilligan the major figures in the latter part of the 20th century to break from narrow models of child and adolescent development and from narrow cognitive models and male norms of development. Despite Jung's and Buehler's earlier works on life-span development, it wasn't until the last quarter of the 20th century that the counseling and psychotherapeutic profession in the United States acknowledged that human development continues throughout the life span.

Even though Erik Erikson's 1950 theory of life-span development had influenced certain segments of the profession, most continued to adhere to the general assumption that development ceased at adulthood, followed by a gradual decline. William Perry's (1968) work on the cognitive development of college students, which extended development to young adults, gained attention from the profession. But not until the late 1970s, with Daniel Levinson's (1978) and Roger Gould's (1978) work on the midlife period of human development, did the profession acknowledge that human development is a lifelong process. Robert Butler (1975) and others extended developmental studies to include older adults.

As counseling professionals became more aware that adults continue to develop throughout life, counseling services, which initially were only in schools and colleges, expanded into the community. At the same time the general public became increasingly aware that adults continue to be met with transitional challenges when, for instance, they lose a job, get a divorce, decide to seek new lifestyles, retire, or face a terminal illness. As a consequence, they continue to make developmental changes.

Kohlberg's (1981, 1984, 1986b) theory of moral development brought about another major breakthrough and generated ongoing debate and research studies. Not only did his work, along with that of emerging cognitivists, help to highlight the work of Piaget, but he brought the fields of philosophy and social science into dialogue with psychology, and he brought the issues of motivation and meaning of life back into the field of psychology (Kegan, 1986).

Carol Gilligan (1982), influenced by Nancy Chodorow (1978), added another missing link to human development studies by providing the women's perspective of connectedness and empathy for others as a fundamental component. Gilligan and Chodorow and those who followed—such as Conarton and Silverman (1988) and Jordan, Kaplan, Miller, Stiver, and Surrey (1991)—proposed alternative developmental theories emphasizing relational, empathic aspects of human development.

Other major contributions to contemporary development theory came from Fowler's (1981) theory of faith development and Goleman's (1995) theory of emotional development, which indicated the broad, multidimensional nature of human development. Overall, whereas theorists of the past focused on narrow aspects of human development, each ensuing developmentalist took another step in integrating and broadening the various aspects until by the close of the century, theorists were working toward an integrated, multidimensional theory of human development.

Erik Erikson's Psychosocial Life-Span Development Theory

In 1950 psychoanalyst Erik Erikson published his first book, *Childhood and Society,* in which he proposed eight stages of human development. Erikson's theory influenced counseling theory and practice more than any other developmental theory (Blocher, 1974; Brown & Srebalus, 1988; Keat, 1974; Rodgers, 1984). Although he is best known for his attention to identity crises in adolescence and his attention to building one's ego identity, he also had a profound influence on adult development theories throughout the life span. Erikson has since modified his theory, and others have proposed modifications or have rearranged or expanded certain stages. Because Erikson's work over the years has been based predominantly on the healthy psychological and social-growth processes of normal individuals, his theory has undergirded counselors' efforts to establish a unique profession aimed at working with psychologically normal people.

According to Erikson (1950, 1963), human development occurs in eight stages throughout life (see Table 5.1). At each stage individuals work through transitional conflicts as a necessary means of development by undertaking certain developmental tasks. These stages relate to an individual's struggle to balance inner needs with external cultural forces. Erikson describes the conflicts that arise in this process as opportunities for positive growth and change. He perceived these stages as guidelines, not as rigid steps in development. He believed that many environmental forces affect and complicate an otherwise simple pattern of progressive growth (Coles, 1970). In his definitive biography of Erikson, psychiatrist Robert Coles (1970) substantiates Erikson's flexibility: "We do not acquire trust and forever rid ourselves of mistrust or 'achieve' autonomy and thus spare ourselves continuing doubts

TABLE 5.1
Erikson's Eight Stages of Life Development

Stage	Psychosocial Crisis	Significant Relations	Basic Strengths
1 Infancy	Basic trust versus basic mistrust	Maternal person	Hope
2 Early childhood	Autonomy versus shame and doubt	Parental persons	Will
3 Play age	Initiative versus guilt	Basic family	Purpose
4 School age	Industry versus inferiority	"Neighborhood," school	Competence
5 Adolescence	Identity versus identy confusion	Peer groups and out-groups; models of leader-ship	Fidelity
6 Young adulthood	Intimacy versus isolation	Partners in friendship, sex, competition, cooperation	Love
7 Adulthood	Generativity versus stagnation	Divided labor and shared household	Care
8 Old age	Integrity versus despair	"Mankind," "my kind"	Wisdom

Note: From *The Life Cycle Completed: A Review,* by Erik H. Erikson. Copyright © 1982 by Rikan Enterprises, Ltd. Reprinted by permission of W. W. Norton & Company, Inc.

and hesitations" (p. 76). Coles further says of Erikson's views: "What is won can later be lost—and rewon. The body (and in the case of humans, the mind) is not irrevocably set or determined by any one thing—genes, the mother's 'behavior,' the so-called environment—but by a combination of everything and everyone, both within and outside the flesh" (p. 77).

According to Erikson's theory, the formation and dynamics of each sequential stage are dependent on what occurs in the previous stage. If children develop a basic trust in others and themselves, they can develop the will for self-control and responsibility for their own actions (*autonomy*). This autonomy permits children to develop initiative and purpose in life and encourages attainment of productive skills and competence. If these developmental challenges are met, adolescents can develop a coherent sense of self (*identity*), which will lead to tendencies to be true to oneself and others (*fidelity*). These firm foundations set in childhood and adolescence permit the adult to develop love relationships (*intimacy*) over time, altruistic caring for children and concern for the welfare of the next generation (*generativity*), and wisdom about order and meaning in life (*basic integrity*).

Failure to gain adaptive strength at each sequential stage, however, can lead cumulatively to increased behavioral problems. Children who acquire patterns of withdrawal, for instance, are liable to develop confused identities when they reach adolescence and to have tendencies to repudiate themselves and others. As adults such individuals tend to isolate themselves or to become promiscuous and rejective of others. In later life they are apt to be bitter, disdainful, or despairing of life.

Conflicts between the individual and society are central to Erikson's (1968) psychosocial theory; he perceived them as necessary instigators of growth. When conflicts are attended to and resolved in a positive manner, individuals are able to move to a higher stage of development.

> I shall present human growth from the point of view of the conflicts, inner and outer, which the vital personality weathers, reemerging from each crisis with an increased sense of inner unity, with an increase of good judgment, and an increase in the capacity "to do well" according to his own standards and to the standards of those who are significant to him. (Erikson, 1968, pp. 91–92)

Erikson (1968) believed that conflicts can be either positive or negative. Positive conflicts result from individuals' awareness that they are distressed over an ongoing situation—an awareness that motivates them to change themselves or their circumstances in creative and satisfying ways. Negative conflicts differ: "Neurotic and psychotic conflicts are defined by a certain self-perpetuating propensity, by an increasing waste of defensive energy and by a deepened psychosocial isolation" (p. 163).

Eriksonian belief in working through conflicts as a means of developmental growth influenced many developmental theorists, researchers, and psychotherapists, including Conarton and Silverman (1988), Fowler (1981), Gilligan (1982), Kohlberg (1969, 1981), Lyddon (1995), and Steenbarger (1990). That belief is also shared by others. Polish psychiatrist Kasimierz Dabrowski (1964, 1970), for example, developed a theory called *positive disintegration,* in which tension aroused by conflicts represents a healthy awareness that all is not well in one's interactions with others or with one's feelings about oneself. This awareness motivates the individual to change patterns of behavior or to change environmental circumstances that are inhibiting his or her personal or interpersonal growth. Positive disintegration occurs when individuals are able and willing to face conflicts and break down patterns of behavior that are restricting development so that growth can take place. "For the development of higher needs and higher emotions, it is necessary to have partial frustrations, some inner conflicts, some deficits in basic needs" (1970, p. 35). On the other hand, according to Dabrowski, *negative disintegration* occurs when individuals deny or suppress conflicts and their responses to life's challenges become neurotic or pathological. Passive aggression, chronic depression, destructive behavior, and other debilitating symptoms may arise.

The positive potential of working through conflicts has been a consistent, underlying theme of counseling since the 1940s and 1950s. Carl Rogers (1942), for example, claimed that counseling "can be effective only when there is a conflict of desires or demands which creates tension and calls for some type of solution . . . the tension created by those conflicting desires must be more painful to the individual than the pain and stress of finding a solution to the conflict" (p. 54).

More recently, Steenbarger (1990) reaffirmed and amplified Erikson's earlier developmental views on conflict: "Development proceeds through periods of challenge and crisis, which generate new sources of meaning and identity for individuals. Far from being a sign of maladjustment, distress is perceived as a constructive prod and precursor to healthy growth" (p. 435).

Moral Development: Kohlberg and Beyond

Among 20th-century psychological theorists, Piaget (1932) was the first major figure to consider moral development as a fundamental component of psychological development. Freudian psychoanalysis and Skinnerian behaviorism—the two schools of psychology that dominated much of the 20th century—had rejected moral issues as a part of psychotherapy. Freudian theory held that moral concerns came from one's super-ego, determined by authority figures. Behaviorists held that one's behavior is determined by rewards and punishments. Until the appearance of Lawrence Kohlberg's (1969, 1981, 1984, 1986b) publications, Piaget's (1932) work received scant attention from psychologists.

Kohlberg's perspective stemmed from Piaget's premise that moral development is part of one's ability to develop through cognitive structural changes; that is, humans have a self-organizing capacity to restructure their own inner capacities to think and to respond to experiences they encounter in their social environment (Kegan, 1986). Kohlberg expanded Piaget's model by adding more stages, while limiting his study to justice reasoning, or the cognitive capacity of individuals, primarily for research purposes. His theory posited that children, beginning at a very young age, develop morally in a sequence of stages in which they move from a self-centered (preconventional) stage, to a conforming, socially motivated (conventional) stage, and then on to a stage where they employ universal moral principles (postconventional) that consider justice for the good of society. Each stage is hierarchical and must be completed before one can advance to the next stage. Because each structural level "is more comprehensive, differentiated, and equilibrated than the prior structure, each stage is able to do things that prior stages could not" (Kohlberg, 1981, p. 147).

Kohlberg believed that moral development occurs when one is challenged by a moral dilemma in real-life situations: "Moral principles are human constructions arising through human interaction and communication" (Kohlberg, 1986a, p. 542). He developed a series of 11 complex hypothetical stories centering on moral dilemmas; in each the main character is faced with a conflict between personal interest and the good of society and acts to resolve the dilemma. After reading a story, subjects are asked to judge the behavior as right or wrong, and then they are asked questions to determine what reasoning they used to arrive at the judgment.

Kohlberg's research and publications, modified and revised several times, culminated in three volumes—*Essays in Moral Development: Vol. 1. The Philosophy of Moral Development* (1981), *Vol. 2. The Psychology of Moral Development* (1984), and *Vol. 3. Education and Moral Development* (1986b). By the late 1980s the psychological profession could no longer reject morality as an essential component of psychological development.

Kohlberg's work was extraordinary on several counts. It drew international attention from a wide range of academic disciplines, and it drew those schools—social sciences, theology, philosophy, and the various schools of psychology—into cross-discipline dialogues, despite their notoriety for keeping separate domains (Kegan, 1986; Boyd, 1986; Carter, 1986). Motivation and meaning making, so long ignored by the prevailing schools of psychology, resumed their places as essential parts of psychological development (Kegan, 1986; Boyd, 1986). Kohlberg's controversial work generated critical reviews and streams of research studies expanding, replicating, refuting, or modifying his work; studies broadened and extended his narrow concept of morality into all aspects of human development. Addressing the controversy in the mid-1980s was the text edited by Modgil and Modgil (1986), *Lawrence Kohlberg: Consensus and Controversy,* which included a lengthy response from Kohlberg.

One major weakness of Kohlberg's model was the limiting of morality to justice reasoning. Newer research studies have proposed broader models of moral development that cover affective, empathic, intuitive, and faith-based components (Berk, 2003; Fowler, 1981; Gilligan, 1982; Habermas, 1984; Haste, 1993; Kohlberg, 1986a; Locke, 1986; Modgil & Modgil, 1986). Arguing from a feminist perspective, Gilligan (1982) pointed out that caring for the welfare of others takes moral precedence over justice in certain circumstances, as in Kohlberg's (1969) well-known case of a man known as Heinz, who needed to steal some prescription medicine in order to save his wife's life. From Kohlberg's moral justice point of view, Heinz's moral dilemma raises questions in judging Heinz's behavior: Which is more ethical—saving his wife's life or not stealing the drug? Is Heinz responsible for saving his wife's life? Does the druggist have a right to protect his interests?

Based on studies she had conducted, Gilligan (1982) noted that girls consider the relationship between Heinz and his wife and between Heinz and the druggist; thus, they propose solutions that go beyond either stealing the drug or letting the wife die. They suggest, for example, that Heinz should get a loan, find other ways of obtaining money, or continue to appeal to the druggist to delay payment. Since such responses do not suit the (male) norms set by Kohlberg, girls generally scored lower than boys, Gilligan claimed, and thus their moral decisions were regarded as inferior to, or less mature than, those of males.

Conceding this weakness, Kohlberg (1986a) modified his model. Recent research studies show that the revised Kohlbergian model is not gender-based. "Adolescent and adult females display reasoning at the same or higher stages as do their male counterparts. . . . When girls raise interpersonal concerns, they are not downscored" (Berk, 2003, p. 492).

Many others also argued that Kohlberg's use of justice as the universal moral principle was too limited. James Fowler (1981), modeling his faith-based stages after Kohlberg, claimed that moral development has many more dimensions than cognitive reasoning. Kohlberg (1981) conceded that point, saying that the question "Why be moral?" (p. 344) still remains at the sixth stage, but he proposed a seventh stage, which he said is "roughly equivalent" to Fowler's sixth stage of faith (p. 344). Research psychologists, however, rejected his Stages 5 and 6 because they cannot be measured empirically (Rest, Narvaez, Bebeau, & Thoma, 1999).

Many researchers also criticized Kohlberg's claim that young children lack an inherent moral sense: "A key controversy has to do with Kohlberg's belief that moral maturity is not achieved until the postconventional level" (Berk, 2003, p. 497). Since Kohlberg's time, numerous studies of children's cognitive, social, and emotional levels of development show that moral judgments and actions are prevalent among children. At an early age children begin to distinguish between a sense of moral fairness for themselves, a sense of moral justice for others, and a sense of conventional social morality (Berk, 2003).

Consistent with Kohlberg's concern that considerations of moral issues must apply to action, Berk (2003) identifies moral issues pervasive in one's personal and social life.

Using real-life settings as examples of various moral components, she presents various learning strategies (e.g., strategies for enhancing self-control) that can be applied to individuals, families, and social and cultural settings; discusses how patterns of aggression in early and middle childhood lead to aggression in adolescents and adults; explores negative family, social, cultural, and environmental patterns, especially the family "as training ground for aggressive behavior" (p. 509); and discusses intervention strategies for various age levels and settings.

Although Kohlberg considered moral education essential to moral development, he admitted that it was the weakest component of his proposal. Much of the difficulty, he believed, has been the method of teaching moral education, with many educators being prone to adopt either a doctrinaire or a relativist method, neither of which Kohlberg believed is acceptable. Responding in the 1970s to values clarification, the popular movement among psychological educators, he said, "Value clarification is not a sufficient solution to the relativity problem. Furthermore, the actual teaching of relativism is itself an indoctrination or teaching of a fixed belief" (p. 12). Kohlberg emphasized the importance of professional educators becoming aware of their own moral constructs. Without exception everyone has a moral position, including those who claim to be moral relativists.

Kohlberg (1986a) acknowledged, however, that a relativist perspective is often a phase one goes through on the way to the postconventional Stage 5, especially among college students, who question values held by their own cultural traditions as they listen to values held by students of other cultural backgrounds (see the discussion of Perry later in this chapter and in chap. 18). In the Kohlbergian model, however, universal values ultimately supercede social-cultural norms. Numerous cross-cultural studies conducted around the world confirm that different cultures hold similar universal values (Kohlberg, 1981; Boyd, 1986; Berk, 2003). In a review of the literature, Berk (2003) notes that children and adolescents in diverse cultures throughout the world "use the same criteria to separate moral concerns from social conventions" (p. 499). For example, "when asked about acts that obviously lead to harm or violate rights, such as breaking promises, destroying another's property, or kicking harmless animals, cultural differences diminish" (p. 501).

How then has Kohlberg's work influenced counseling practice? His work directly relates to moral conflicts, a crucial component in counseling. Most theorists, educators, and counselors now believe that moral issues are an essential part of human development. Counselors must be aware of their own values, the values of their clients, and the environmental values surrounding both counselors and clients (see chaps. 3 and 4). Many client concerns are presented as moral dilemmas. How individuals perceive right or wrong behaviors influences their feelings about themselves or others and has an effect on self-esteem, career choice, and the types of relationships they seek. Since the 1990s critical debates and alternative proposals on moral development have continued, as discussed later in this chapter under "Trends."

Adult Development Theories

A relatively new field of developmental psychology, adult development, got its major impetus from the work of William Perry (1968), Daniel Levinson (1978), and Roger Gould (1978). Perry studied the intellectual and cognitive development of college-age students.

Levinson and Gould each studied men's development in the later years of life, basing their work on Erikson's ideas about adult ego states and on Jung's writings about life's meaning for older people. Levinson (1986) said, "The study of adult development is, one might say, in its infancy. It has been taken seriously in the human sciences for only the past 30 years or so largely under the impact of Erikson's . . . general writings" (p. 3). In another source (1978), Levinson called Jung the father of adult development because he was the first to state unequivocally that the years after midlife are the most important in life. The recent interest in adult development results from counseling professionals' increased awareness that adults continue to develop throughout life.

William Perry: College Student Development

Believing that adult cognitive development went beyond Piaget's final stage of formal thinking in adolescence, William Perry (1968) studied the cognitive development patterns of college students during the late 1950s and early 1960s (Cavanaugh & Blanchard-Fields, 2002). Students were studied during their undergraduate years to determine their patterns of thinking and the range of their views about the nature of knowledge and the degree to which they depended on authorities or on their own independent thinking for informed views about knowledge (Loevinger, 1976). Perry published his results in *Forms of Intellectual and Ethical Development in the College Years* (1968).

Perry found that beginning undergraduate students tended to rely on authorities to give them valid information and correct answers; they relied on knowledge that was derived from and substantiated by rules of logic. As students progressed through their college years, however, they tended to move from fixed thinking to more flexible forms of reasoning. In progressive steps they moved from the notion that there is one correct view of knowledge, to skepticism about any point of view, to a recognition that there are many different points of view, to ultimately arriving at their own point of view. In the last stage they "recognize that they are their own source of authority, that they must make a commitment to a position, and that others may hold different positions to which they are equally committed" (Cavanaugh & Blanchard-Fields, 2002, p. 279). As students "move through these stages, they integrate their intellects with their identities, resulting in better understanding of their own value systems and related value commitments" (Upcraft & Moore, 1990, p. 47).

Daniel Levinson's Seasons of a Man's Life

Levinson's (1978) interest in adult development was strongly influenced by Jung and Erikson. As mentioned earlier, Levinson called Jung the father of adult development, and he credited Erikson with taking adult development seriously.

Realizing that very little work had been done on adult development, Levinson conducted a study in which he interviewed a diverse sample of adult males over a period of several years. His findings confirmed Jung's and Erikson's view that adulthood is not a plateau but continues to be dynamic. Adult development is what Levinson calls "the evolution of the life structure during the adult years" (p. 42). That life structure comprises all aspects of the self, unconscious and conscious, its interaction with its sociocultural environment, and its participation in the world. Levinson expanded on Erikson's interest in the sociocultural impact on development by attending to how persons interrelate with their environment. Levinson believed that the self is an active force that builds, maintains, reevaluates, and remodels its life structure throughout life.

According to Levinson, adult development is composed of four major periods—childhood and adolescence, early adult, middle adult, and later adult—each period alternating with transitional phases. Individuals go through seasons, or periods, of stability in which they work at building their life structure, alternating with transitions, during which they reevaluate and reorganize their life structure. Levinson emphasized the transitional periods as crucial times in effecting developmental change: "A transition is a bridge, or a boundary zone, between two states of greater stability. It involves a process of change, a shift from one structure to another" (pp. 49–50). Transitions are conflicting and painful, but they also provide the opportunity for growth into the next stage and are a source of healthy change. For each period certain developmental tasks must be met that "are crucial to the evolution of the periods" (p. 53).

Although Levinson is best known for describing the midlife crisis, his theory emphasized that changes and transitional periods occur throughout life. Major conflicts experienced by 70% of his sample during midlife led Levinson to believe that a midlife crisis is inevitable for almost everyone. The major task at midlife, he believed, is to begin to look inward for meaning and unity in life. During the last season (ages 65 and up), adults become caring, compassionate, and attentive to others. Levinson's discussion of the last season is sketchy, however, because no men over age 47 were interviewed.

After publishing his work on adult male development, Levinson, working collaboratively with his wife Judy, conducted a study of adult women during the 1980s. Their work on women—*The Seasons of a Woman's Life* (Levinson & Levinson, 1996), published 2 years after his death—shows that adult women go through similar stages to those of men, although gender issues within the framework are noticeably different.

Roger Gould: Transformations

As he noticed in his practice and personal life that adults continue to undergo changes, psychiatrist Roger Gould (1978) sensed the limitations of his Freudian training and turned to the Jungian view that adults continue to develop. After conducting several research studies, Gould concluded that "adulthood is not a plateau; rather, it is a dynamic and changing time for all of us" (p. 14). After publishing articles on his results and lecturing to professional and lay audiences, he received such an overwhelming response that he developed his work into a conceptual framework, out of which he published his book *Transformation: Growth and Change in Adult Life* (1978).

Gould described six stages of life: childhood, adolescence, young adult, adult, midlife, and beyond midlife. In each stage, he claimed, certain issues based on false assumptions need to be worked on to help transform the individual into the next developmental stage, with each stage leading to increased maturity. "As we grow and change, we take steps away from childhood and toward adulthood. . . . With each step, the unfinished business of childhood intrudes, disturbing our emotions and requiring psychological work" (p. 14). Like Erikson, Gould accepted emotional crises and conflicts as a normal process of adult life; by confronting them, one goes through a process of transformation. "It is about the evolution of adult consciousness as we release ourselves from the constraints and ties of childhood consciousness" (p. 15).

Of particular significance for adult development theory are his last four stages. From ages 22 to 28, individuals transform into young adults as they become committed to their own careers and to raising children. In doing so, they give up the false assumption that parents have all the answers to life's problems. Between the ages of 29 and 34, individuals learn to face their own shortcomings and false assumptions about themselves, their relationships, and their careers. Between 35 and 45, Gould, like Levinson, says a midlife crisis is apt to occur. Persons at this stage confront the false assumption that there is no evil in the world and in themselves, and they confront moral issues about love and death. They also feel a sense of desperation and urgency in trying to attain something meaningful before time runs out. During the next stage, 45 and beyond, older adults settle down, accept life as it is, and become less judgmental or demanding of themselves and others.

At about the time of Levinson's and Gould's works, Gail Sheehy (1976) published *Passages,* which became a best seller. Sheehy interviewed 115 women and men and described the unsettling transitions adults must pass through to attain authentic identities. Sheehy has been criticized because she did not give information about the selection of her sample, method of interviewing, collection of data, and basis for generalizing her findings to the general population (Santrock, 1992). Nevertheless, her work made *midlife crisis* a household phrase and its problems a cultural expectancy.

Older Adult Development

Carl Jung (1933) was especially interested in older adult development and emphasized that this was a creative period in one's life (see chap. 15). But because of the attention given in the United States to child and adolescent development, his theory on the later stage of life was generally ignored in this country for most of the 20th century. In the 1970s and 1980s, when Levinson and Gould were emphasizing midlife development issues, the prevailing view of older adult development was that of gradual, progressive decline and deterioration.

Robert Butler, a renowned gerontologist, challenged this ageist stereotyping of older adults in his landmark publication *Why Survive?* (1975). He noted that people over age 65, who were the fastest growing segment of the population, were living longer, healthier lives and that they were demonstrating the potential to grow and contribute to society in unique ways. A decade later Butler, along with Herbert Gleason, published *Productive Aging* (1985), in which they described how older adults individually and as a group can contribute to the betterment of society. These leaders urged that society change its negative attitudes about aging and foster new social roles and opportunities for older adults to continue to be productive.

After Butler other developmental theorists—Baltes (1987), Cavanaugh (1992), O'Connor and Vallerand (1994), and Schaie (1990)—conducted research regarding development in older adults. They found that older adults do develop capacities in later life quite different from those in their younger days. Tasks involving reflection, judgment, and knowledge relating to meaningful and cultural experiences replaced tasks necessary to younger people, such as abstract reasoning unrelated to experience, timed responses, or rote memorization.

With increased attention to older adults in recent years, the Jungian approach to the later periods of life has gained considerable attention from the general community. Jungian psychiatrist Allan Chinen (1989), for example, proposed three substages of older adult growth: self-confrontation, self-transcendence, and self-transformation. Chinen's proposal and other views of older adult development are covered in chapter 15.

Feminist Human Development Theories

In the 1970s and 1980s feminist development theorists pointed out that Piaget, Erikson, and Kohlberg all based their research on male norms of behavior. Feminists contended that women's and men's developmental processes differ: Whereas women learn to connect with and care for others, men learn to separate and become autonomous (Chodorow, 1974, 1978; Conarton & Silverman, 1988; Gilligan, 1982; Miller, 1976). Much of the early feminist perspective of human development has since been integrated into mainstream developmental theory.

One of the earliest critics of male-dominated theory was Nancy Chodorow (1974, 1978), who wrote "against the masculine bias of psychoanalytic theory" (Gilligan, 1982, p. 8), a theory that emphasized that persons must separate from others to gain their own identity. Traditional psychology had held that women's tendency to relate to and care for others was a sign of inferiority and dependency. However, from research in which she observed small children and their mothers, Chodorow noticed developmental differences between boys and girls emerging early in childhood. Whereas male children break away from their initial bonding with their mothers to find their male identities, young female children maintain connections with their mothers and learn that it is socially acceptable to model their mothers' caretaking patterns (Gilligan, 1982).

Carol Gilligan's landmark book *In a Different Voice* (1982) brought the issue to public attention; she claimed that women, because of their feelings of empathy toward others, speak in a different voice. "Her work on women's development reframes developmental models and brings women's and girls' voices into the center of a new psychology" (Jordan et al., 1991, p. 3). Having taught with Erik Erikson at Harvard and having been strongly influenced by his psychodynamic theory of developmental conflicts (Gilligan, 1982; Wylie, 2002), Gilligan criticized Erikson's theory that humans go through successive stages of separation, an idea influenced by the 19th- and 20th-century American urge for independence and autonomy. She criticized as well his claim that, after having gained independence and autonomy at midlife, one suddenly acquires a sense of caring and intimacy. Instead, patterns of intimacy and caring develop in a long, extended process; by midlife women have developed complex ways of caring for others.

Gilligan (1982) also criticized Kohlberg's theory of moral development for basing the hierarchy of moral reasoning on male norms. She asserted that such a narrow perspective about the morality of justice reasoning cannot be generalized to all cases, that situations differ. Women tend to view moral decisions from a caring perspective, considering relationships and connections with others; and in certain cases the moral option of caring for others takes precedence over justice reasoning. Gilligan, who also taught with Kohlberg at Harvard, collaborated with him on studies and publications on moral development and influenced him to modify his proposal to include caring for others.

At the Stone Center at Wellesley College, women have been doing research and conducting symposia on women's developmental issues since 1981. Their work centers on trying to reach "a new understanding of psychological development in women" (Jordan et al., 1991, p. 4). *Women's Growth in Connection* (Jordan et al., 1991) is a sampling of the writings from that center. The authors pay tribute to Gilligan's close "analysis of the centrality of connection in women's sense of self" (p. 3). They also note that Jean Baker Miller's work *Toward a New Psychology of Women* (1976) "is the single most significant influence on all our work" (Jordan et al., 1991, p. 4). Miller (1991), the director of the center, says that the idea that a girl cannot develop a sense of self because she cannot separate from her mother "is an incredible notion" (p. 14). Miller claims that the literature has ignored the "complexity of the interaction between caretaking and infant" (p. 14). She also says,

> The literature has generally ignored the extraordinarily important character of the interaction—that of attending to and responding to the other. This is the essential feature of what comes to be called "caretaking." It is also the basis of all continuing psychological growth; that is, all growth occurs within emotional connections, not separate from them. (p. 15)

Surrey (1991) uses the term *self-in-relation* to describe women's developmental growth. "The hyphenated phrase 'self-in-relation' implies an evolutionary process of development through relationship" (p. 59). Supporting the theory that a woman's sense of self is enhanced, rather than diminished, through relationships, Surrey says, "the self gains vitality and enhancement in relationship and is not reduced or threatened by connections" (p. 62).

Developmental growth for women evolves in ever more complex modes of relationship throughout one's life. Kaplan and Klein (1991) present core modes of self-development, which they say are laid out by adolescence:

> The relational self grows in complexity, flexibility, sensitivity, and adaptability: The many planes along which this growth occurs include (1) an increased potential for entering into mutually empathic relationships characterized by being able to share one's own affective states and to respond to the affect of others; (2) relational flexibility, or the capacity to permit relationships to change and evolve; (3) an ability and willingness to work through relational conflict while continuing to value the core of emotional connection; and (4) the capacity to feel more empowered as a result of one's inner sense of relational connection to others, particularly to mothers. . . . Thus, the late adolescent woman does not develop "out of" the relational stage, but rather adds on lines of development that enlarge her inner sense as a relational being. (p. 131)

According to Jordan (1991b), the distorted psychological belief that a woman's desire for relationship is a sign of weakness and dependency can be attributed to the early psychoanalytic theory of needs gratification. Twentieth-century psychology was generally based on this theory:

> The relationship based on need gratification has been the keystone in developmental theory. . . . The needs to receive, to be given to, to depend on, and to be loved are well covered in the psychological literature. Much relational exchange and growth, however, is overlooked in this one-sided model. (p. 87)

Another issue explored at the Stone Center is the meaning of empathy (Jordan, 1991a; Kaplan, 1991). Traditional psychological belief, which emphasizes building and

TABLE 5.2
Conarton and Silverman's Feminine Development Theory

Stage	Characteristic Tasks
Phase 1. Bonding	Interdependence with mothers
Phase 2. Orientation to Others	Caring and connectedness to others
Phase 3. Cultural Adaptation	Imitation of males
Phase 4. Awakening & Separation	Beginning search for self
Phase 5. Development of Feminine	Deeper exploration of needs
Phase 6. Empowerment	Exerting power over their own lives
Phase 7. Spiritual Development	Experiencing own interest in life
Phase 8. Integration	Individuation—expanding caring to the world at large

Note: From "Feminine Development Through the Life Cycle," by S. Conarton and L. K. Silverman, in M. A. Dutton-Douglas & L. E. Walker (Eds.), *Feminist Psychotherapies: Integration of Therapeutic and Feminist Systems* (p. 38), 1988, Norwood, NJ: Ablex. Copyright 1988 by Ablex. Adapted with permission.

maintaining ego boundaries, warns that a person who feels empathy toward another is experiencing an affective state that generally means a loss of identity. Jordan (1991a) explains that a person who experiences empathy is using both cognitive and affective responses that preclude the risk of losing one's identity. "In order to empathize, one must have a well-differentiated sense of self in addition to an appreciation of and sensibility to the differentness of self as well as the sameness of another person" (p. 29).

Conarton and Silverman (1988) present a theory of developmental stages for women, that is based on Gilligan's work, Dabrowski's (1964) theory of positive disintegration, and Jungian processes of individuation involving mythic symbolism (see Table 5.2). They emphasize, "The developmental cycle of women must be viewed with the awareness that women's primary striving is for relatedness and connection" (p. 49). Women first bond with their mothers, then expand relationships to others. Of particular note is the adolescent stage of cultural adaptation. During this time a woman's tendency to develop relatedness is broken because she must imitate male behavior in order to compete, first in high school and higher education and then out in the business world. At midlife, Phase 4, she begins to yearn for a return to her feminine nature and starts the journey of self-exploration.

Conarton and Silverman use symbolism to describe the four stages that follow the midlife period, the stages in which a woman journeys into her deep feminine nature. They compare this journey to the four arduous tasks that Psyche, a figure in Greek mythology, had to carry out. In these last stages a woman seeks and develops empowerment to claim her right to be feminine, her right to be recognized as a caring person, and her right to apply her feminine ways of "cooperation, consensus, and mediation" (Conarton & Silverman, 1988, p. 58). She moves toward wholeness and integrates her drives to care for herself and others. Then, in the final stage she turns her caring toward the world, society, and future generations.

Gilligan (2002) also refers to the Psyche myth in her latest book, *The Birth of Pleasure*, which emphasizes again that a woman's perspective differs from the prevailing male-oriented, social-cultural norms. Gilligan uses the Psyche myth to counteract the Oedipal myth, which dominates Western culture and views the human condition as tragic and destructive. Gilligan uses the story of Psyche and Eros to emphasize the striving for and attainment of empathy, love, and regeneration.

Religious and Spiritual Development

For some years now, many counselors and counseling psychologists have indicated that interest in and attention to clients' spiritual concerns has been increasing steadily (Bergin, 1989; Fowler, 1981, 1991; Kelly, 1995; McWhirter, 1989; Worthington, 1989). "The integration of religious perspectives into the professional psychological frame of reference is simply revolutionary" (Bergin, 1989, p. 621).

In his book *Stages of Faith*, James Fowler (1981) proposed a model of faith development that has received considerable attention from counseling professionals and has contributed significantly to the theory of human development. Like many religious leaders of the 20th century, Fowler was concerned about the disenchantment with traditional religious beliefs, the rise of secularism, and the rise of human desire for material gain, wealth, and power. Concerned religious leaders believed it was time to reimagine and redefine faith (Fowler, 1981). Drawing upon the work of theologians Paul Tillich and Reinhold Niebuhr and religious historian Wilfred Cantwell Smith, Fowler defines the meaning of faith, distinguishing it from a fixed religious belief.

> Faith, it appears, is . . . a universal feature of human living, recognizably similar everywhere despite the remarkable variety of forms and contents of religious practice and belief. . . . Faith . . . is not a separate dimension of life, a compartmentalized specialty. Faith is an orientation of the total person, giving purpose and goal to one's hopes and strivings, thoughts and actions. (Fowler, 1981, p. 14)

Combining elements of Eriksonian psychosocial developmental theory of working through conflicts and Kohlberg's and Piaget's structural theories of cognitive moral development, Fowler (1981) proposed a stage theory of faith development, which he believes is relational, interactive, and part of a dynamic process, rather than a matter of acquiring and adhering to a fixed belief system. He sees faith development as triadic, a relationship between the self, the other (the parent), and one's social-cultural world—the shared central values and power.

Fowler (1981) describes faith as "the search for an overarching, integrating and grounding trust in a center of value and power sufficiently worthy to give our lives unity and meaning" (p. 5). Faith is akin to the imagination, he claims, noting the inherent problem with this theory from a research psychologist's point of view, because it is virtually impossible to fit imagination into an objective, empirical style of research. Rather than being externalized and observable, faith stems from a person's own constructs, a view that is consistent with Piaget's and Kohlberg's cognitive structural theories and constructivist theories. Fowler believes, however, that faith development goes beyond one's cognitive constructs to include affective, intuitive components of human development. One of the early proponents of narrative therapy, Fowler believes in storytelling and telling one's story as a matter of faith development. According to E. W. Kelly (1995), Fowler's discipline of faith "is clearly relevant to the spiritual/religious dimension in counseling because it represents people's inner or psychodynamic orientation to questions of meaning and value, that is, to questions that for many people are associated predominantly with spirituality and religion" (p. 70).

Fowler proposed six stages of faith that broadened and extended Kohlberg's stages of cognitive moral reasoning to include affective and imaginal components. In the first three stages of faith development, individuals rely on some authority outside themselves for their faith perspective. During the first stage of faith (*intuitive-projective*), young children follow the beliefs of their parents. They tend to imagine or fantasize angels or other religious figures in stories as characters in fairy tales. In the second stage of faith (*mythical-literal*), older children tend to respond to religious stories and rituals literally, rather than symbolically.

Adolescents enter into the third stage of faith (*synthetic-conventional*), during which their faith begins to form on social-conventional belief systems outside themselves—peer and gang loyalties, dress codes, and so on. They go through identity crises as they search for a sense of themselves in relation to how others think of them, and they feel a need to belong to a group. During this period individuals tend to acquire a conformist acceptance of a faith with little self-reflection or examination of their beliefs. Some critics claim that churches in general represent this conformist stage. Most people and church congregations may remain at this level (Fowler, 1981), but many late adolescents and young adults move on to the fourth stage, particularly when struck with a conflict or a crisis of faith and the need to work through difficulties.

Those individuals who move to the fourth stage of faith (*individuative-reflective*) begin a radical shift from dependence on others' spiritual beliefs to development of their own. Fowler (1981) says, "For a genuine move to stage 4 to occur there must be an interruption of reliance on external sources of authority. . . . There must be . . . a relocation of authority within the self" (p. 179). At this stage individuals are no longer defined by the groups to which they belong. Instead, they choose beliefs, values, and relationships important to their self-fulfillment.

In the fifth stage of faith (*conjunctive*), persons move from the certainty of their beliefs as expressed in logical, propositional affirmations, to a more intuitive understanding of truth beyond reason. This is the midlife period of development in which, in accord with the Jungian view, life appears paradoxical and divided. Individuals become more tolerant and compassionate toward others' beliefs. But Fowler distinguishes tolerance from relativism:

> The relativity of religious traditions that matters is not their relativity to each other, but their relativity—their *relate*-ivity—to the reality to which they mediate relation. Conjunctive faith, therefore, is ready for significant encounters with other traditions than its own, expecting that truth has disclosed and will disclose itself in those traditions in ways that may complement or correct its own. (p. 186)

Individuals who move to the sixth and last stage of faith (*universalizing*) are rare. In this transcendent state of unconditional love and justice, they sacrifice their own self-interests for the sake of others. It is a subversive form of faith, according to Fowler, because the sense of deep justice and commitment to the welfare of others challenges conventional, cultural beliefs. Mother Theresa and Martin Luther King, Jr., are examples of contemporary people who reached this highest form of spiritual development (Fowler, 1981).

In the field of counseling, Ingersoll (1997), Kelly (1995), Fukuyama and Sevig (1997), and Worthington (1989) have been the most outspoken regarding counselors' need to attend to the spiritual development of clients. Worthington (1989) claims that religious and spiritual development has received insufficient attention in counseling; he argues that counselors must become aware of how religious faith relates to both normal development and pathological behavior. Research has shown that more than 90% of U.S. citizens believe in a divine being and that approximately 30% consider themselves strong believers (Spilka, Hood, & Gorsuch, 1985). On the basis of these figures, the majority of clients are embodied with some degree of spiritual and religious belief, conscious or unconscious, as they face emotional crises and try to resolve them. Clients who believe that counselors do not sense the significance of religious or spiritual matters will either be reluctant to bring up their beliefs or will decide to drop out of counseling.

In his comprehensive article "Religious Faith Across the Life Span: Implications for Counseling and Research" (1989), Worthington discusses how the views of Erikson, Jung, and Piaget relate to the spiritual development of people at every stage of life. He also points out how an individual's problems—sex, substance abuse, marital conflicts, poverty, retirement—often have overtones of religious or spiritual concerns. Worthington presents five reasons that counselors need to understand how religious faith influences human development:

1. A high percentage of the population identifies itself as religious.
2. Many people who are undergoing emotional crises spontaneously consider religion in their deliberations about their dilemmas, even if they have not recently been active.
3. Despite their private consideration of religion, many clients, especially religious clients, are reluctant to bring up their religious considerations as part of secular therapy.
4. In general, therapists are not as religiously oriented as their clients.
5. As a result of being less religiously oriented than their clientele, many therapists might not be as informed about religion as would be maximally helpful to their more religious clients. (pp. 556–557)

Some years ago philosopher Harry R. Moody, cofounder and director of the Brookdale Center on Aging at Hunter College, noted that Erikson's developmental stages omitted spiritual growth (Moody & Carroll, 1997). Moody gradually came to realize, however, the correlation between life stages and the stages of spirituality: "Just as there are age-related stages of maturity in each of our lives, I discovered, so there are sequential stages of spiritual opportunity—spiritual passages, as well as social and psychological ones" (pp. 8-9). In *The Five Stages of the Soul: Charting the Spiritual Passages That Shape Our Lives*, Moody and Carroll (1997) note that all the great religions of the world speak of developmental stages: "The notion of stages of the soul, in short, is a universal one" (p. 9). Moody proposes five stages of the soul that "typically occur during midlife and beyond" (p. 33), after a person has experienced enough setbacks in life to question seriously the meaning of life.

1. *The Call*. This stage is familiar to those who experience a conversion, a change of heart, a deep awakening.
2. *The Search*. During this stage the person seeks a teacher, a guide, a way.
3. *The Struggle*. During this stage "the soul's true passage begins" (p. 36). This is the most difficult and longest stage, a period in which the person undergoes many arduous trials and tests and suffers numerous defeats and feelings of despair.
4. *The Breakthrough*. This stage includes illuminating insights. "There are many levels of breakthrough experiences, some small, some great, some lasting, some temporary" (pp. 37–38).
5. *The Return*. "Life goes on as before. . . . There's still work to do. . . . At the same time we now have special knowledge and experience to give back to the world" (p. 38). Persons now have a compassionate outlook toward others, and many become guides and mentors.

Many counselors find it difficult to work effectively with clients' religious or spiritual concerns because they themselves have not explored their own spiritual needs (Fukuyama & Sevig, 1997). Recognizing the need for counselors to become more aware of the spiritual concerns of their clients, the Association for Counselor Education and Supervision (ACES) has appointed a task force to develop counselor competencies necessary for effective spiritual counseling. In line with this effort, Ingersoll (1997) and Fukuyama and Sevig (1997) have proposed new courses covering spiritual issues in counseling.

Emotional Intelligence: A Developmental Learning Process

The concept of *emotional intelligence* emerged as a result of dissatisfaction with the intelligence quotient (IQ) that has dominated psychology since the early 1900s (Goleman, 1995). Critics claim that IQ measures only "a narrow band of linguistic and math skills" (Goleman, 1995, p. 42), which may predict success in school but are unreliable indicators of performance and productivity in the broader field of one's life work. Addressing this lack, Howard Gardner (1993) proposed that humans have *multiple intelligences,* one of which is emotional intelligence. In contrast to the idea of an inherently fixed IQ at birth, Gardner proposes that humans, given sufficient learning conditions, are capable of learning various modes of intelligences (see chap. 7).

Goleman (1995) took Gardner's emotional intelligence component, which Gardner had described from a cognitive perspective, and developed the concept further, describing it from the perspective of emotions. Goleman's thesis is that human emotions can operate independently, beyond reasoning and thinking capacities. Proponents of emotional intelligence challenge the long-held belief that all information gained through sensory experiences goes first to the neocortex, where rational thinking occurs, and then to the amygdala, the seat of emotional responses in the brain. New research shows that when an individual is caught in a dangerous situation, emotional impulses, instinctive fear reactions, are sent directly to the amygdala, in effect short-circuiting the neocortex.

According to Goleman (1995), emotional intelligence results from a learned developmental process that begins in infancy and continues through five sequential stages:

1. Developing awareness of one's emotions through effective parental responses to an infant's emotional needs.
2. Managing one's emotions as the preschooler recognizes and accepts boundaries and limitations.
3. Becoming self-motivated, which Goleman calls the master aptitude—an inner zeal that drives a person to persist despite disappointments.
4. Recognizing and responding empathically to the feelings of others, an essential factor in developing emotional maturity. Empathic development largely unfolds as parental figures attune to the infant or child and convey to the child that they know how the child is feeling.
5. Relating well to others, or acquiring social intelligence, the rudiments of which one begins to learn in preschool. "These interpersonal abilities build on other emotional intelligences" (p. 119). However, persons undeveloped at this stage have difficulty grasping social signals

> for what amounts to a learning disability in the realm of nonverbal messages. . . . The problem can be a poor sense of personal space, so that a child stands too closely while talking or spreads their belongings into other people's territory; in interpreting or using body language poorly; . . . or in a poor sense of prosody, the emotional quality of speech, so that they talk too shrilly or flatly. (p. 121)

Those who experienced severe trauma in childhood tend to feel danger, even when none exists, in any situation that is even vaguely similar to that of the earlier trauma. Yet researchers show that even with adults who are traumatized as children, effective emotional relearning can take place. Those suffering from posttraumatic stress disorder (PTSD) have been conditioned to experience uncontrollable fear at the slightest stimuli that trigger memories of the original trauma; those memories are seated only in the amygdala. Unlike persons who were conditioned to be fearful of, say, spiders and who eventually outgrew their fear reactions, those with PTSD never get over their fear. "Spontaneous relearning fails to occur" (Goleman, 1995, p. 207).

Yet Goleman (1995) claims, "Traumas as profound as those causing PTSD can heal, and . . . the route to such healing is through relearning" (p. 208). Researchers are finding that traumatized children can replay games that "relive a trauma safely, as play" (p. 208). Severely traumatized children can replay the trauma over and over again. Reducing psychic numbing is easier for children because they are accustomed to reenacting imaginatively. For adults the way to recovery is first to regain a sense of safety and "control over what is happening in their body and to their emotions" (p. 211) when certain stimuli trigger reactions of fear.

Ivey's Developmental Counseling and Therapy

Allen Ivey (Ivey, 1986; Ivey, D'Andrea, Ivey, & Simek-Morgan, 2002) modified and expanded Piaget's cognitive theory to include development that continues to occur past childhood and adolescence into adulthood. "We usually think of Piaget's theories as primarily relating to the child, yet they serve as helpful metaphors for the construction of therapeutic theory and method that enables us to examine adult change and development"

(Ivey, 1986, p. 78). Ivey combined Piaget's first two stages and then added a new fourth stage—dialectic/systemic. As Ivey (1986) explains, this new stage is needed because "formal operational thinking as usually defined by Piaget . . . does not adequately account for the complexity of thinking that starts to occur" (p. 104).

Thus, Ivey added a postformal model, similar to that of his predecessors Kegan (1982), Kohlberg (1969), and Perry (1968). In this fourth stage, individuals develop a propensity for reflection and dialectic within themselves, in their relationships, and in their social-cultural environment. Individuals learn to realize that self-reflection and interactions with family and culture provide for constant change and development. "They can recognize the influence of family and cultural systems and see the complexity and variability of emotions and thoughts, can challenge their own assumptions, can transform their thinking in response to changing circumstances" (Rigazio-DiGilio & Ivey, 1991, p. 6).

During this dialectic/systemic stage, individuals "examine relationships between and among things and objects" (Ivey, 1986, p. 120). Individuals at this stage can be in dialogue with their previously developed structural system of development. Individuals, in effect, conduct an evolving transformational process within their basic self structures.

Ivey's model, which he calls developmental counseling and therapy (DTC), emphasizes the importance of the complex, interactive relationship individuals have with others and with their social-cultural environment, that is, "the importance of context" (p. 121). Moreover, this model is particularly valuable for its capacity to encompass both multicultural and older adult developmental issues. Recognizing the dialectical, postformal component in human development and expanding on it, Ivey has contributed a comprehensive, multidimensional, dynamic approach to cognitive development theory.

Sandra Rigazio-DiGilio (2002) expanded Ivey's theory of human development into a therapeutic family systems model called systemic cognitive-developmental therapy (SCDT).

> Systemic cognitive-developmental therapy (SCDT) emphasizes the importance of families as mediators for the culture and the individual. SCDT works to activate and enhance this role by providing suitable therapeutic and consultative environments for facilitating individual, family, and network interaction and growth. (Rigazio-DiGilio, 2002, p. 414)

For a description of how the SCDT model is applied to family therapy, see chapter 10.

TRENDS: TOWARD AN INTEGRATED THEORY OF DEVELOPMENT

Whereas earlier developmental theorists focused on short time spans or only on certain aspects of human development, more recent theorists have been attempting to form integrated models of development that embrace all components of development throughout the life span. Moral development, for example, which was ignored for decades by most psychologists, is now considered an integral part of human development (Berk, 2003; Haste, 1993; Noam & Wren, 1993; Bruner, 1990; Wren, 1990). At the same time, the different schools of developmental thought, such as the cognitive behaviorists and the postmodern constructivists, are carrying on dialogues and debates about similarities and differences (Watts, 2003). Debates also continue over whether humans are the agents of their own development or whether their development is determined by their social-cultural environment. Bridging this divide are those who argue that human development is based on a synthesis of individual capacities, relationships, and social-cultural influences.

Developmentalists now tend to emphasize a world view, claiming that a contextual approach that recognizes multicultural influences is necessary in understanding human development. Cultural psychologist Jerome Bruner (1990) also emphasizes the cultural, historical context in an attempt to make meaning out of experience. "If the cognitive revolution erupted in 1956, the *contextual* revolution (at least in psychology) is occurring today" (pp. 105–106). Rigazio-DiGilio's (2002) SCDT approach emphasizes a multicultural, systemic, contextual model (see also chap. 10). And Steenbarger (1991) proposes a comprehensive model termed a *contextual worldview*, in which human development is affected by individuals' interactions with others, the community, and the world at large.

Many researchers have been challenging or shifting away from the stage theory of human development (Bruner & Haste, 1987; Noam, 1990; Rest et al., 1999; Steenbarger, 1991), with some proposing instead a narrative approach to understanding human development. In light of the overall attempts to integrate theories of development and the ongoing debates over theoretical differences, no single, clear-cut, separate model of human development exists any longer.

Constructivists claim that one's view of the nature of the self has a direct bearing on one's view of human development (Neimeyer & Mahoney, 1995; Neimeyer & Raskin, 2000). They have been strong proponents of exploring the nature of the self and the self's tendency to make meaning out of life's experiences (Kegan,1982; Kelly,1995; Lyddon,1995; Mahoney,1995; Neimeyer,1995). Like Piaget, constructivists believe the self has the self-organizing capacity to make sense of encounters and to reconstruct experiences. This theory of dynamic self-development is opposed to the acquisition of external knowledge (Lyddon, 1995).

Others argue, however, that the self is determined by social-cultural influences. Social constructionists Berger and Luckman (1966) and Gergen (1985) challenged traditional 20th-century psychologists who believed that humans develop as autonomous individuals. They claim instead that human development is determined by one's social-cultural environment. Gilligan (1982), Rigazio-DiGilio (2002), and other leading feminists also advocate that social-cultural influences are a key factor in human development, a perspective that heightens awareness of ethnic diversity and multicultural perspectives of human development.

Bridging the gap between these two positions is cultural psychologist Jerome Bruner (1990), who not only supports social-cultural influences but also believes that humans can act as agents of their own development. Humans find meaning in their experiences, he claims, through a narrative approach to understanding, as opposed to other forms of discourse—logical propositions, conceptualizations, and the use of tests—"as a mode of organizing experience" (Bruner, 1990. p. 43; see also chap. 6 on narrative therapy).

Another attempt to bridge the gap is a model proposed by Helen Haste (1993) that synthesizes the two extremes. According to her theory, development is based on a triadic relationship among (1) the the autonomous, self-organizing self, (2) the interpersonal self, and (3) the self in relation to the social-cultural milieu. This theory is based on a model proposed decades earlier, in the 1930s, by Russian philosopher Lev Vygotsky (1962, 1978), little known in America until recently. Interest in Vygotsky was fueled in the 1980s by sociologists and anthropologists (Bruner & Haste, 1987); he is now highly regarded in professional circles, particularly among child development specialists (Berk, 2003).

Haste's (1993) developmental model, called lay social theory, describes one's social-cultural milieu as a schema with its own complex dimensions, a conceptual framework that humans' do not acquire passively, but gradually grow into, interacting reciprocally in complex ways that affect both the development of the self and the way one interacts with and is affected by the social-cultural milieu. Haste (1993) is among those who believe that moral development is an integral part of human development (Berk, 2003; Noam & Wren, 1993; Bruner, 1990; Wren, 1990). Jerome Bruner (1990), one of the early promoters of narrative therapy, claims that the intention behind telling one's story is to take a moral stand against conventional social mores. "To tell a story is inescapably to take a moral stance" (p. 51).

Although developmental theorists generally have integrated moral development into developmental theory, many are still split over the issue of moral universalism versus moral relativism. Addressing the issue, Haste (1993) proposes a theory of pluralism, "a third option, which goes beyond the dichotomy of relativism and universalism" (p. 179), while at the same time taking into account the many different ways world cultures conceptualize standards of morality. Likewise Bruner (1990), hoping to move the debate beyond that "dreaded form of relativism where every belief is as good as another" (p. 27), advocates a developmental approach in which one "need not fret about the specter of relativism. It concerns open-mindedness . . . . a willingness to construe knowledge and values from multiple perspectives without loss of commitment to one's own values" (p. 30).

A model similar to Haste's is Noam's (1990) integrated model of human development, which regards the self as the organizing core of development in a dynamic relationship with interpersonal interactions and social-cultural influences. Noam's perspective combines constructivist and contemporary psychoanalytic thought, as well as the social-cultural perspectives of Bruner (1986) and Vygotsky (1962). Noam's complicated model of self-development, briefly stated, constitutes a combined system, or two structures, of the self. First, the self develops a biographical structure, or *themata*, involving one's development as a life story, or living biography, to make meaning out of experience; humans form their life stories based on themes, or patterns (constructs). Second, humans have a self-perspective, which develops a self-complexity, or *schemata*, arising from one's interaction with others and the environment.

Noam (1990) argues that a stage theory is an inadequate model of human development because it breaks the human being into a series of collective categories, in which the self is regarded only as an "'epistemic self,' where a multitude of individual and collective life experiences are condensed into a few ideal developmental types or stages" (p. 362). Noam's model, instead, puts the historical, narrative, thematic self in juxtaposition with stages of life encountered in the social-cultural world, such as the child growing into adulthood and the graded learning systems in school programs.

SUMMARY

Human development theories have strongly influenced counseling theory and practice. Piaget's cognitive theory of development underlies the use of cognitive theories of counseling with children and adolescents. Kohlberg's theory of moral development has prompted ongoing dialogue in psychology, philosophy, and social sciences and has opened up discourse among professionals about the meaning of life and the nature of humankind. It has challenged counselors, therapists, and educators to question their own values, and has made moral issues pertinent to clients and students.

Jung and Erikson expanded developmental theories to include a life-span perspective. Levinson and Gould published theories about human development through midlife. Butler then challenged the view that people over age 65 progressively decline. He and other professionals have demonstrated that older adults have the capacity to continue to develop throughout life.

Feminist developmental theorists Gilligan, Conarton and Silverman, and Miller challenged conventional, male-dominated theories, proposing instead that the developmental processes of women and men differ. A woman's tendency to relate to and care for others is not an inferior or immature state, but rather represents a different developmental process.

Attention to spiritual development continues to expand and deepen in the counseling and therapy field after many years of neglect, with increasing interest in Fowler's, Moody's, and Worthington's models of faith or spiritual development. The theory of emotional development proposed by Goleman has also had considerable impact. Among the first attempts at an integrative developmental proposal have been Ivey's model (DCT) and Sandra Rigazio-DiGilio's systemically oriented model (SCDT).

The trend continues toward forming an integrative theory of development, one that encompasses all aspects of human development throughout life. But debates continue to flourish among postmodern developmental theorists over several issues: (1) the nature of the self (whether the self is the agent of development or whether self-development is determined by social-cultural forces); (2) moral universalism versus moral relativism; and (3) the adequacy of the stage theory, with challengers proposing alternative narrative, contextual models as a means of understanding human development.

PROJECTS AND ACTIVITIES

1. Review the literature on conflict in human behavior, and note how conflict is described. Divide the articles into those that describe conflict as a barrier to growth and those that describe it as a potential to growth.

2. If male, place yourself in the developmental stage of Erikson's theory that most describes your stage of life. If female, do the same for the stages of Conarton and Silverman. Do

you find that the crises or conflicts described by Erikson or by Conarton and Silverman are typical of your age and fit your current circumstances? What is similar, and what is different?

3. Interview some retired men and women over the age of 60, asking about any changes in attitudes or behaviors that have occurred in their lives in the last 40 years. Did they

experience any midlife crises? Do you notice differences in the men's and the women's responses?

4. Organize a class discussion around Heinz's dilemma. Does the group believe that responses given by contemporary children or adolescents will differ from those of children 20 years ago? How much influence do

values presented in the media or in behaviors of politicians and public figures have on moral judgment and reasoning?

5. Carol Gilligan poses provocative challenges to developmental theories based on men and generalized to women. Do you see evidence in novels, short stories, or the cinema that support or contradict her view?

REFERENCES

Baltes, P. B. (1987). Theoretical propositions of life-span developmental psychology: On the dynamics, growth, and decline. *Developmental Psychology, 23*, 611–626.

Berger, P. L., & Luckman, T. (1966). *The social construction of reality*. Garden City, NY: Anchor Press.

Bergin, A. E. (1989). Religious faith and counseling: A commentary on Worthington. *Counseling Psychologist, 17*, 621–624.

Berk, L. E. (2003). *Child development* (6th ed.). Boston: Allyn & Bacon.

Blocher, D. (1974). *Developmental counseling* (2nd ed.). New York: Ronald Press.

Boyd, D. R. (1986). The oughts of is: Kohlberg at the interface between moral philosophy and developmental psychology. In S. Modgil & C. Modgil, *Lawrence Kohlberg: Consensus and controversy* (pp. 43–83). Philadelphia: Falmer Press.

Brown, D., & Srebalus, D. S. (1988). *An introduction to the counseling profession*. Upper Saddle River, NJ: Prentice Hall.

Bruner, J. (1986). *Actual minds, possible worlds*. Cambridge, MA: Harvard University Press.

Bruner, J. (1990). *Acts of meaning*. Cambridge, MA: Harvard University Press.

Bruner, J., & Haste, H. (Eds.). (1987). *Making sense*. London: Methuen.

Buehler, C., & Massarik, F. (Eds.). (1968). *The course of human life*. New York: Springer.

Butler, R. N. (1975). *Why survive?: Being old in America*. New York: Harper & Row.

Butler, R. N., & Gleason, H. P. (Eds.). (1985). *Productive aging: Enhancing vitality in later life*. New York: Springer.

Carter, R. (1986). Does Kohlberg avoid relativism? In S. Modgil & C. Modgil, *Lawrence Kohlberg: Consensus and controversy* (pp. 9–20). Philadelphia: Falmer Press.

Cavanaugh, J. C. (1992). *Adult development and aging*. Belmont, CA: Wadsworth.

Cavanaugh, J. C., & Blanchard-Fields, F. (2002). *Adult development and aging* (4th ed.). Belmont, CA: Wadsworth.

Chinen, A. (1989). *In the ever after: Fairy tales and the second half of life*. Wilmette, IL: Chiron.

Chodorow, N. (1974). Family structure and feminine personality. In M. Z. Rosaldo & L. Lamphere (Eds.), *Woman, culture and society*. Stanford, CA: Stanford University Press.

Chodorow, N. (1978). *The reproduction of mothering*. Berkeley: University of California Press.

Coles, R. (1970). *Erik H. Erikson: The growth of his work*. Boston: Little, Brown.

Conarton, S., & Silverman, L. K. (1988). Feminist developmental theory. In M. A. Dutton-Douglas & L. E. Walker (Eds.), *Feminist psychotherapies: Integration of therapeutic and feminist systems* (pp. 37–67). Norwood, NJ: Ablex.

Dabrowski, K. (1964). *Positive disintegration*. Boston: Little, Brown.

Dabrowski, K. (1970). *Mental growth through positive disintegration*. London: Gryf.

Drum, D. J., & Lawler, A. C. (1988). *Developmental interventions: Theories, principles, and practice*. Upper Saddle River, NJ: Merrill/Prentice Hall.

Erikson, E. H. (1950). *Childhood and society*. New York: Norton.

Erikson, E. H. (1963). *Childhood and society* (2nd ed.). New York: Norton.

Erikson, E. H. (1968). *Identity, youth, and crises*. New York: Norton.

Fowler, J. (1991). Stages in faith consciousness. In F. K. Oser & W. G. Scarlett (Eds.), Religious development in childhood and adolescence [Special issue]. *New Directions in Child Development, 52*, 27–45.

Fowler, J. W. (1981). Stages of faith. *The psychology of human development and the quest for meaning*. San Francisco: Harper & Row.

Fukuyama, M. A., & Sevig, T. D. (1997). Spiritual issues in counseling. A new course. *Counselor Education and Supervision, 36*, 233–244.

Gardner, H. (1993). *Frames of mind: The theory of multiple intelligences*. New York: Basic Books.

Gergen, K. J. (1985). The social constructionist movement in modern psychology. *American Psychologist, 40*, 266–275.

Gesell, A. (1940). *The first five years of life*. New York: Harper.

Gesell, A. (1948). *Studies in child development.* New York: Harper.

Gilligan, C. (1982). *In a different voice.* Cambridge, MA: Harvard University Press.

Gilligan, C. (2002). *The birth of pleasure.* New York: Alfred A. Knopf.

Goleman, D. (1995). *Emotional intelligence: Why it can matter more than IQ.* New York: Bantam Books.

Gould, R. L. (1978). *Transformation: Growth and change in adult life.* New York: Simon & Schuster.

Habermas, J. (1984). *A theory of communicative action.* Boston: Beacon Press.

Hall, G. S. (1916). *Adolescence.* New York: Appleton.

Haste, H. (1993). Morality, self, and sociohistorical context: The role of lay social theory. In G. G. Noam & T. E. Wren, *The moral self* (pp. 175–207). Cambridge, MA: MIT Press.

Havighurst, R. J. (1953). *Human development and education.* New York: Longman, Green.

Ingersoll, R. E. (1997). Teaching a course on counseling and spirituality. *Counselor Education and Supervision, 36,* 224–232.

Ivey, A. E. (1986). *Developmental therapy.* San Francisco: Jossey-Bass.

Ivey, A. E., D'Andrea, M., Ivey, M. B., & Simek-Morgan, L. (2002). *Counseling and psychotherapy: A multicultural perspective* (5th ed.). Boston: Allyn & Bacon.

Jordan, J. V. (1991a). *Empathy and the mother-daughter relationship.* In J. V. Jordan, A. G. Kaplan, J. B. Miller, I. P. Stiver, & J. L. Surrey (Eds.), *Women's growth in connection: Writings from the Stone Center* (pp. 28–34). New York: Guilford Press.

Jordan, J. V. (1991b). The meaning of mutuality. In J. V. Jordan, A. G. Kaplan, J. B. Miller, I. P. Stiver, & J. L. Surrey (Eds.), *Women's growth in connection: Writings from the Stone Center* (pp. 81–96). New York: Guilford Press.

Jordan, J. V., Kaplan, A. G., Miller, J. B., Stiver, I. P., & Surrey, J. L. (Eds.). (1991). *Women's growth in connection: Writings from the Stone Center.* New York: Guilford Press.

Jung, C. G. (1933). The stages of life. In *Modern man in search of a soul.* San Diego: Harcourt Brace.

Kaplan, A. G. (1991). Empathic communication in the psychotherapy relationship. In J. V. Jordan, A. G. Kaplan, J. B. Miller, I. P. Stiver, & J. L. Surrey (Eds.), *Women's growth in connection: Writings from the Stone Center* (pp. 44–50). New York: Guilford Press.

Kaplan, A. G., & Klein, R. (1991). The relational self in late adolescent women. In J. V. Jordan, A. G. Kaplan, J. B. Miller, I. P. Stiver, & J. L. Surrey (Eds.), *Women's growth in connection: Writings from the Stone Center* (pp. 122–131). New York: Guilford Press.

Keat, D. B. (1974). *Fundamentals of child counseling.* Boston: Houghton Mifflin.

Kegan, R. (1982). *The evolving self: Problem and process in human development.* Cambridge, MA: Harvard University Press.

Kegan, R. (1986). Kohlberg and the psychology of ego development: A predominantly positive evaluation. In S. Modgil & C. Modgil, *Lawrence Kohlberg: Consensus and controversy* (pp. 163–181). Philadelphia: Falmer Press.

Kelly, E. W., Jr. (1995). *Spirituality and religion in counseling and psychotherapy: Diversity in theory and practice.* Alexandria, VA: American Counseling Association.

Kohlberg, L. (1969). Stage and sequence: The cognitive-developmental approach to socialization. In D. Goslin (Ed.), *Handbook of socialization theory and research* (pp. 347–480). Chicago: Rand McNally.

Kohlberg, L. (1981). *Essays on moral development: Vol.1. The philosophy of moral development.* San Francisco: Harper & Row.

Kohlberg, L. (1984). *Essays on moral development: Vol.2. The psychology of moral development.* San Francisco: Harper & Row.

Kohlberg, L. (1986a). A current statement on some theoretical issues. In S. Modgil & C. Modgil, *Lawrence Kohlberg: Consensus and controversy* (pp. 485–546). Philadelphia: Falmer Press.

Kohlberg, L. (1986b). *Essays on moral development: Vol.3. Education and moral development.* San Francisco: Harper & Row.

Levinson, D. J. (1978). *The seasons of a man's life.* New York: Ballantine Books.

Levinson, D. J. (1986). A conception of adult development. *American Psychologist, 41,* 3–14.

Levinson, D. J., & Levinson, J. D. (1996). *The seasons of a woman's life.* New York: Knopf.

Locke, D. (1986). A psychologist among the philosophers: Philosophical aspects of Kohlberg's theories. In S. Modgil & C. Modgil, *Lawrence Kohlberg: Consensus and controversy* (pp. 21–38). Philadelphia: Falmer Press.

Loevinger, J. (1976). *Ego development.* San Francisco: Jossey-Bass.

Lyddon, W. (1995). Forms and facets of constructivist psychology. In R. A. Neimeyer & M. J. Mahoney, *Constructivism in psychotherapy* (pp. 69–92). Washington, DC: American Psychological Association.

Mahoney, M. J. (1995). Continuing evolution of the cognitive sciences and psychotherapies. In R. A. Neimeyer & M. J. Mahoney (Eds.), *Constructivism in psychotherapy* (pp. 39–67). Washington, DC: American Psychological Association.

McWhirter, J. J. (1989). Religion and the practice of counseling psychology. *Counseling Psychologist, 17,* 613–617.

Miller, J. B. (1976). *Toward a new psychology of women.* Boston: Beacon Press.

Miller, J. B. (1991). The development of women's sense of self. In J. V. Jordan, A. G. Kaplan, J. B. Miller, I. P. Stiver, & J. L. Surrey (Eds.), *Women's growth in connection: Writings from the Stone Center* (pp. 11–26). New York: Guilford Press.

Modgil, S., & Modgil, C. (1986). *Lawrence Kohlberg: Consensus & controversy.* Philadelphia: Falmer Press.

Moody, H. R., & Carroll, D. (1997). *The five stages of the soul: Charting the spiritual passages that shape our lives.* Garden City, NY: Doubleday.

Neimeyer, G. J. (1995). The challenge of change. In R. A. Neimeyer & M. J. Mahoney (Eds.), *Constructivism in psychotherapy* (pp. 11–38). Washington, DC: American Psychological Association.

Neimeyer, R. A., & Mahoney, M. J. (Eds). (1995). *Constructivism in psychotherapy.* Washington, DC: American Psychological Association.

Neimeyer, R. A., & Raskin, J. D. (2000). *Constructions of disorder.* Washington, DC: American Psychological Association.

Noam, G. G. (1990). Beyond Freud and Piaget: Biographical worlds—interpersonal self. In T. E. Wren, *The moral domain* (pp. 360–399). Cambridge, MA: MIT Press.

Noam, G. G., & Wren, T. E. (Eds.). (1993). *The moral self.* Cambridge, MA: MIT Press.

O'Connor, B. P., & Vallerand, R. J. (1994). Motivation, self-determination, and person-environment fit predictors of psychological adjustment among nursing home residents. *Psychology and Aging, 9,* 189–194.

Perry, W. G., Jr., (1968). *Forms of intellectual and ethical development in the college years.* New York: Holt, Rinehart & Winston.

Piaget, J. (1926). *The language and thought of the child.* London: Routledge & Kegan Paul.

Piaget, J. (1932). *The moral judgement of the child.* London: Routledge & Kegan Paul.

Rest, J., Narvaez, D., Bebeau, M. J., & Thoma, S. J. (1999). *Postconventional moral thinking: A Neo-Kohlbergian approach.* Mahwah, NJ: Lawrence Erlbaum.

Rigazio-DiGilio, S. A. (2002). Family counseling and therapy: Theoretical foundations and issues of practice. In A. E. Ivey, M. D'Andrea, M. B. Ivey., & L. Simek-Morgan, *Theories of counseling and psychotherapy: A multicultural perspective* (5th ed., pp. 390–428). Boston: Allyn & Bacon.

Rigazio-DiGilio, S. A., & Ivey, A. E. (1991). Developmental counseling and therapy: A framework for individual and family treatment. *Counseling and Human Development, 24,* 1–19.

Rodgers, R. F. (1984). Theories of adult development: Research, status, and counseling implications. In A. D. Brown & R. W. Lent (Eds.), *Handbook of counseling psychology* (pp. 479–519). New York: John Wiley.

Rogers, C. (1942). Counseling and psychotherapy. Boston: Houghton Mifflin.

Santrock, J. W. (1992). *Life span development* (4th ed.). Dubuque, IA: Wm. C. Brown.

Schaie, K. W. (1990). Intellectual development in adulthood. In J. E. Birren & K. W. Schaie (Eds.), *Handbook of the psychology of aging* (3rd ed., pp. 291–309). San Diego: Academic Press.

Sheehy, G. (1976). *Passages: Predictable crises of adult life.* New York: Bantam.

Spilka, B., Hood, W. R., & Gorsuch, R. (1985). *The psychology of religion.* Upper Saddle River, NJ: Prentice Hall.

Staude, J. R. (1981). *The adult development of C. G. Jung.* Boston: Routledge & Kegan Paul.

Steenbarger, B. N. (1990). Toward a developmental understanding of the counseling specialty: Lessons from our students. *Journal of Counseling & Development, 68,* 434–437.

Steenbarger, B. N. (1991). All the world is not a stage: Emerging contexualist themes in counseling and development. *Journal of Counseling & Development, 70,* 288–296.

Super, D. (1942). *The dynamics of vocational adjustment.* New York: Harper Brothers.

Surrey, J. L. (1991). The self-in-relation: A theory of women's development. In J. V. Jordan, A. G. Kaplan, J. B. Miller, I. P. Stiver, & J. L. Surrey (Eds.), *Women's growth in connection: Writings from the Stone Center* (pp. 51–66). New York: Guilford Press.

Upcraft, M. L., & Moore, L. V. (1990). Evolving theoretical perspectives of student development. In M. J. Barr, M. L. Upcraft, & Associates, *New futures for student affairs: Building a vision for professional leadership and practice* (pp. 41–68). San Francisco: Jossey-Bass.

Vygotsky, L. S. (1962) *Thought and language.* Cambridge, MA: MIT Press. (Original work published 1934)

Vygotsky, L. S. (1978). *Mind in society.* Cambridge MA: Harvard University Press. (Original works published 1930, 1933, 1935)

Watts, R. (2003). *Adlerian, cognitive, and constructivist therapies.* New York: Springer.

Worthington, E. L., Jr. (1989). Religious faith across the life span: Implications for counseling and research. *Counseling Psychologist, 17,* 555–612.

Wren, T. E. (Ed.). (1990). *The moral domain: Essays in the ongoing discussion between philosophy and the social sciences.* Cambridge, MA: MIT Press.

Wylie, M. S. (2002). The untold story: Carol Gilligan on recapturing the lost voice of pleasure. *Psychotherapy Networker, 26,* 46–56.

CHAPTER 6

Counseling Theories and Techniques

THE PURPOSE OF COUNSELING THEORY

Psychological theories are based on how one perceives human nature and the environment. Assumptions about unconscious and conscious processes, development, learning, and socialization are essential components of psychological theories. The theories of professional counseling and therapy, which are based on these psychological assumptions, present systematic ways of understanding a person's psychological framework, the ways problems arise in the individual's development, and methods to help resolve those problems.

An integrated system of beliefs about the counseling process can help counselors improve their professional practice, increase their professional knowledge, and enhance their personal development. A well-integrated theory can guide a counselor through the therapeutic process. It provides the basis for establishing clear-cut counseling goals, a rationale for selection or rejection of particular counseling techniques, a basis for determining ethical counseling procedures, and a framework for conducting and evaluating research on counseling processes and outcomes. Practicing counselors with a sound theoretical basis are able to make evaluations and judgments about new ideas and techniques. Both counselors-in-training and practicing counselors experience personal growth when they explore how their own beliefs and values relate to various counseling theories (Brammer, Abrego, & Shostrom, 1993).

New theoretical approaches have added many new and challenging possibilities for counselors-in-training and those in practice. Because theories have mushroomed at a bewildering pace in this pluralistic era, and many have borrowed from or merged with others, practitioners can no longer adhere strictly to one simple theory. Increasing numbers of counselors and therapists have integrated a variety of theoretical approaches into their practice (see the section "Toward an Integrative Theoretical Approach" at the end of this chapter).

Of the numerous and complex counseling theories in existence today, those chosen for review here have formed the essential foundations of counseling and have generated activity through the years that has contributed to the development of contemporary counseling. Contemporary theories have been selected on the basis of the amount of literature they are generating, the degree to which the literature crosses disciplines, and the degree to which their ideas are accessible to counselors and the lay public.

Theories are classified in this text in six categories: (a) psychoanalytic and psychodynamic; (b) humanistic; (c) behavioral, cognitive, and cognitive-behavioral; (d) constructivist and social constructionist; (e) creative and expressive arts and narrative therapies; and (f) brief counseling and therapy. The first four categories are based on the differing views theorists have about human nature and human behavior. The fifth and sixth categories demonstrate these perspectives in the context of creative and expressive arts and of brief, time-limited counseling sessions.

PSYCHOANALYTIC AND PSYCHODYNAMIC THEORIES

Psychoanalytic and psychodynamic theorists cover a wide range of beliefs, but all believe that the unconscious is part of the governing process of individuals and that intrapsychic, dynamic forces operate in one's interactions with others. The goal of analysis is to help patients become aware of and come to terms with these underlying unconscious dynamic forces.

About 100 years ago Sigmund Freud was developing his theory of psychoanalysis. He believed that a person's unconscious processes are determined by biological, *libidinal,* or *psychosexual* instincts or drives—drives that are potentially destructive unless controlled and channeled. Through psychoanalysis the analyst helps the patient learn to control these unconscious drives. Carl Jung and Alfred Adler once were followers of Freud but later broke with him over his deterministic concept of human nature and his belief that behavior is determined by psychosexual drives. They developed their own theories, claiming that other unconscious forces also govern behavior, such as soul and spirit (Jungian) or the drive to socialize (Adlerian).

Psychoanalysts Karen Horney, Erich Fromm, and Harry Stack Sullivan also objected to Freud's psychosexual model of human nature. Following Adler's belief in the individual's fundamental drive to socialize, they emphasized the individual's psychosocial, or interpersonal, development. Contemporary psychoanalysis is based primarily on later significant contributions that came in the name of ego-analytic and object relations theories, which have been countered more recently by feminist psychodynamic theories emphasizing the nature of connections in relationships.

Classical Psychoanalytic Theory

According to Sigmund Freud (1940/1949), human behavior is determined by unconscious, biological, potentially destructive instincts—the *id.* Id impulses (sex and aggression) often clash with a person's need to adapt to society. As children grow, they develop the ego and the superego. The *ego* is the conscious part of the mind that acts as a mediator between an individual's instinctive, uninhibited id impulses and external reality. As their egos develop, children learn to make compromises between their inner urges and parental and societal controls. The *superego* (conscience) helps persons develop a moral code and an ideal of behavior consistent with traditional values in society.

The ego and the superego develop as part of the personality as children go through psychosexual growth stages—oral, anal, phallic, latent, and genital (Brill, 1938). In the *oral stage* (from birth to about 18 months), gratification centers on feeding. Conflict and anxiety stem from the dependency of the child and the child's demand for immediate gratification. In the *anal stage* (18 months to 3 years), gratification comes from elimination of feces. Toilet training creates conflict and anxiety in child and parent. In the *phallic stage* (3 to 6 years), pleasure centers in the genital area. In this stage the child experiences sexual impulses toward the parent of the opposite sex and sees the same-sex parent as a rival. In the *latent stage* (6 to 12 years), these impulses are relatively dormant. In the *genital stage* (12 to 18 years), the adolescent begins to develop relationships with members of the opposite sex (Baker, 1985).

As the child experiences psychosexual conflicts, the ego runs the risk of becoming overwhelmed either by id impulses or by the superego. To protect the ego, children develop unconscious *defense mechanisms*, which help them survive (Freud, 1966). These defenses can become maladaptive if they contribute to the distortion or denial of reality. Examples of defenses are *repression*, or complete denial of impulses; *projection*, in which people ascribe their own unacceptable behavior to others; *displacement*, in which impulses toward something threatening are redirected toward a safe object or person; and *sublimation*, in which unacceptable drives are channeled into socially acceptable or creative activities.

If parent-child relationships are constructive, children express their impulses in acceptable and satisfying ways. If parents are overly strict, rejecting, or neglectful, children will repress impulses and develop defense mechanisms to deny reality. These defense mechanisms may become overly stringent and lead to neurosis or other personality disorders. Psychoanalysts devote more attention to neuroses than to more severe personality disorders because they believe that persons with neurotic symptoms are more responsive to change. The goal of psychoanalysis is to help clients express, in a safe, therapeutic environment, repressed impulses, fears, and anxieties they experienced as children and to help them learn to channel those energies into socially acceptable behavior.

The therapist assumes an authoritarian position like that of a parent but is neutral or nonthreatening, unlike parents of neurotic individuals. The analyst maintains neutrality and distance by sitting behind the client, who lies on a couch. The therapist then encourages the patient to let thoughts come out regardless of their content through *free association* (i.e., saying whatever comes to mind) and by reporting dreams. As patients bring out repressed memories and emotions, they begin to attach or transfer early unresolved feelings they had toward parents, such as resentment or admiration, onto their therapists. This *transference* is encouraged by therapists as an essential process in therapy. Analysts respond to these distorted feelings in a nonthreatening or nondemanding way, again unlike parents.

Because of their defenses, clients inevitably begin to resist therapy regardless of how motivated they are. *Resistance* is an unconscious process whereby patients prevent repressed impulses and emotions from coming to awareness. Freud believed that resistance blocked the efforts of client and therapist to gain client insights necessary for progress in therapy.

As clients free-associate, report dreams, and experience transference and resistance, the analyst interprets the behavior in a process called *working through*. These interpretations include helping patients see hidden meanings in free associations and dreams, understand the distortions and misperceptions involved in transference toward the analyst, and accept resistance as a sign of progress in therapy. This brings about a nondistorted, real relationship with the analyst and increases client willingness to deal with and resolve unconscious conflicts.

Throughout therapy, therapists must be aware of the possibility of *countertransference*, which is an irrational reaction they may have toward clients that results from the therapists' unresolved needs or conflicts. Therapists may find themselves overprotecting, overidentifying with, or feeling unwarranted irritation toward clients as a result of the therapists' earlier unresolved relationships that may be similar to those of the clients.

Psychosocial Neo-Analytic Theories

Alfred Adler: Individual Psychology

Alfred Adler, a contemporary of Freud, rejected Freud's deterministic, instinct-driven view of human nature and emphasized instead a psychosocial, purposeful perspective of behavior. Moreover, he objected to "Freud's belief that the personality is divided: conscious behavior against unconscious, ego against id and super-ego" (Woodworth & Sheehan, 1964, p. 298). Rather, Adler perceived individuals as unitary, holistic organisms striving to better themselves.

This belief in the unity of personality led Adler to call his theory *individual psychology*—a term that can be misleading, considering his strong advocacy of social forces in human development. The term is clarified, however, in the light of Adler's belief that individuals develop only in the context of their relation to society.

Adlerian theory is best described as follows: "The nucleus of Adler's personality theory is the concept of a unitary, goal-directed creative self which in the healthy state is in a positive constructive, i.e. ethical relationship to his fellow man" (Ansbacher & Ansbacher, 1973, p. 6). A person's unifying and organizing life goal shapes his or her orientation to life, strategies for living, and striving for meaningful goals (Corey, 2001). Individuals have the power to develop their own unique lifestyles, a creative power of self that is "Adler's crowning achievement as a personality theorist" (Hall, Lindzey, & Campbell, 1998, p. 13).

Most significant is the individual's *social interest*. Citing Ansbacher (1992), Corey (2001) says,

> *Social interest* and *community feeling* (*Gemeinschaftsgefuhl*) are probably Adler's most significant and distinctive concepts. . . . These terms refer to an individual's awareness of being part of the human community and to the individual's attitudes in dealing with the social world. Social interest includes striving for a better future for humanity. (p. 111)

Adler believed that individuals strive to develop themselves in relation to their community throughout their lives. Feelings of inferiority or helplessness that all humans experience are instigators for individuals to seek change: "They can seek to change a weakness into a strength, for example, or strive to excel in one area of concentration to compensate for defects in other areas" (Corey, 2001, p. 111).

Adlerian counseling involves counselors and clients in exploring clients' faulty perceptions about goals. Clients then work toward more constructive goals by developing appropriate social interests, by expanding self-awareness, and by creatively modifying their lifestyles.

Adler's approach strongly influenced the views of Karen Horney, Erich Fromm, and Harry Stack Sullivan. Each, in turn, elaborated on Adler's psychosocial emphasis:

> Among those who provided psychoanalytic theory with the twentieth century look of social psychology are . . . Alfred Adler, Karen Horney, Erich Fromm and Harry Stack Sullivan. Of these four Alfred Adler may be regarded as the ancestral figure of the "new social psychological look." (Hall et al., 1998, p. 24)

Adler's belief that individuals develop within a social context led him to focus on family interactions—an emphasis later amplified by Rudolf Dreikurs (see chap. 10 for a discussion of Adlerian family therapy).

Renewed interest in Adler and the move toward integrating various theoretical approaches prompted several cognitive and constructivist professionals to discuss the degree of compatibility of their theoretical models with Adlerian therapy. Richard Watts, as editor, drew together several professionals to engage in an integrative dialogue, the outcome of which is the book *Adlerian, Cognitive, and Constructivist Therapies* (Watts, 2003). Constructivists claim that their core theoretical concepts are remarkably similar to the Adlerian approach (Neimeyer, 2003). On the other hand, while acknowledging that cognitive behavior therapy (CBT) has some similarities with the Adlerian approach and noting that they have much to offer one another, Dowd (2003) points out that CBT differs significantly from Adlerian therapy.

> Adlerian psychology is a subjective, phenomenological approach, which might be described as long on theory and short on data. By contrast, CBT has long stressed the primacy of observable, objective data and the necessity for phenomena to be observable to external agents, to be of scientific interest and psychologically valid. (p. 97)

Karen Horney

Unlike Freud and influenced by Adler, Karen Horney emphasized that social-cultural forces are the major influences in human development. She explored how social influences affect the nature or dynamics of a person's character. An example of this process of character development is exemplified in her own experience when she became aware of her difference from Freud's views about feminine psychology:

> Freud's postulations in regard to feminine psychology set me thinking about the role of cultural factors. Their influence on our ideas and what constitutes masculinity or femininity was obvious, and it became just as obvious to me that Freud had arrived at certain conclusions because he failed to take them into account. (Horney, 1945, pp. 11–12)

Likewise her views about cultural influences on personality were confirmed after she moved from Germany to the United States and noticed that attitudes and neuroses of individuals in Europe differed from those she observed in the United States and that only cultural differences could account for this. Horney believes that the tendency for persons to develop either creatively or neurotically depends on the quality of their interpersonal relationships. Parents thus play a crucial role in the development of their children. When parents are neglectful, indifferent, abusive, or otherwise fail to offer loving guidance, the child develops basic anxiety or, as Horney (1945) puts it, "the feeling a child has of being isolated and helpless in a potentially hostile world" (p. 41). The child, feeling unsafe or insecure, develops a basic hostility toward others, and these feelings further threaten the child.

To assuage this inner conflict, children must develop strategies to repress their impulses in order to maintain a feeling of security. These strategies take the form of three directional interactions with others: *movement toward* others to gain love, *movement away from* others to gain independence, and *movement against* others to gain power (Horney, 1945).

Horney believes that conflicts are an essential and inevitable part of normal human development. She makes important distinctions between normal or situational conflicts and conflicts that are neurotic. Normal conflicts arise out of well-defined, stressful problems related to transitions or to everyday problems in work or family relationships. Normal persons are able to resolve these conflicts and learn from them; they may use any or all of the three orientations toward people in a flexible way. Neurotics, in contrast, are unable to resolve their conflicts; they use inflexible and artificial solutions that do not resolve basic anxiety.

> The normal conflict is concerned with an actual choice between two possibilities, both of which the person finds really desirable, or between convictions, both of which he really values. . . . The neurotic person engulfed in a conflict is not free to choose. He is driven by equally compelling forces in opposite directions, neither of which he wants to follow. (Horney, 1945, p. 32)

Individuals with either normal or neurotic conflicts can learn to become more adaptive through counseling or therapy. Neurotic persons, because of strong repressed contradictory impulses, find it more difficult to change. The emphasis in therapy is to help neurotic individuals become aware of their inflexible strategies with people and to help prepare them to risk changing these patterns.

Erich Fromm

Erich Fromm believes that social-cultural, political, and economic forces play a dominant role in personality development. Exploitative trends in a culture are major causes of pathology. Personal growth, then, is stifled by economic or political forces that prevent individuals from being productive in society.

In his first book, *Escape From Freedom* (1941), which is based on his experiences in Nazi Germany, Fromm presents his view about the human dilemma: As humans have moved from animal-like dependence on instinctual behavior to beings who can reason, think, and choose, they have developed strong ambivalence about this freedom. The world of choices is less secure.

> He has become free but longs for continued dependency and belonging; he has a biological urge to live but his human reason confronts him with the inescapability of death; unlike animals, he has the capacity to solve problems of his world by thought rather than by instinct, but his brief life span makes fulfillment of his potentialities improbable if not impossible. (Woodworth & Sheehan, 1964, pp. 323–324)

Humans try to escape this freedom of choice and the difficulties of solving problems by preferring the security of submitting to authority and to totalitarian systems. Or they themselves become authoritarian and assume power over others, as occurs in male-dominated societies. Another typical mode of escape is to conform to social norms and to peer groups "in which one renounces selfhood by adopting a 'pseudo self' based on the expectations of others" (Hall et al., 1998, p. 142). According to Fromm, humans can learn to cope with the challenges that free choice imposes on their existence by understanding and coming to terms with five basic needs: "the need for relatedness, the need for transcendence, the need for rootedness, the need for identity, and the need for a frame of orientation" (Hall et al., 1998, p. 143).

Harry Stack Sullivan

Harry Stack Sullivan's psychosocial theory is based on the importance of interpersonal relationships in human development.

> Personality is shaped primarily by social forces, with the child's lengthy period of dependence making it particularly vulnerable to influence by others. He posits a powerful human need for interpersonal relationships . . . and he insists that personality exists, and can be studied, only through its interpersonal manifestations. (Ewen, 1998, p. 213)

Sullivan's lasting contribution is his emphasis on the therapeutic interview as a prime example of an interpersonal interaction. The role of the interviewer in therapy sessions, he claimed, is as important as the behavior of the client. "The interviewer becomes the 'participant observer' systematically noting what the patient does, what he says, and how he says it" (Woodworth & Sheehan, 1964, p. 333). Interviewers must also be aware of their own beliefs or attitudes that are incompatible with their clients' (Woodworth & Sheehan, 1964).

Contemporary Psychoanalytic and Psychodynamic Theories

After a lengthy decline psychoanalysis has been experiencing a revival. Many new psychoanalytic books have been published; a new journal, *Review of Psychoanalytic Books*, has been established; and a new Division of Psychoanalysis has been formed in the APA. This renewed activity has been further stimulated by the development of contemporary shorter term psychoanalytic theories.

From the 1950s through the 1970s, psychoanalytic theories were overshadowed by the emergence and domination of humanistic, behavioral, and cognitive approaches. Contemporary psychoanalysis received its major impetus from ego-analytic and object relations theories, both of which have done much to emphasize that interpersonal relationships are fundamental to human growth and development. As Corey (2001) explains,

"The early experiences of the self shift in relation to an expanding awareness of others. Once self-other patterns are established, it is assumed, they influence later interpersonal relationships" (p. 83).

More recently, feminists have developed a revisionist psychodynamic theory regarding the essential nature of connection in relationships as fundamental to human growth and development.

Ego-Analytic Theories

Ego-analysts disagree with Freud's belief that the id, or instinctive drives, essentially govern human behavior and that the ego is a relatively weak servant of the id. They do not believe that the principal role of the ego is to develop defense mechanisms to protect the individual from being overwhelmed by id impulses. Instead, ego-analysts believe that the ego has energies of its own that are not derived from the id. Remembering, thinking, and perceiving are ego processes that influence behavior (Prochaska & Norcross, 2003). The functions of the ego are to adapt to and master the environment as a way of developing the personality structure (Baker, 1985; Ewen, 1998; Ryckman, 1997).

Maladaptive behavior is described as unresolved conflict that results from ineffective or destructive relationships with parents or guardians at some period in psychosocial development. Such persons have not developed strong enough egos to respond appropriately or have lost the capacity to respond. In either case persons move from conscious to unconscious control (Hansen, Rossberg, & Cramer, 1994).

Ego-analysts are concerned more with normal conflicts in development than with pathology. Classical psychoanalytic techniques are used but are modified for shorter term treatment. Ego-analytic therapists tend to be more direct, more active, and more accessible to clients than traditional psychoanalytic therapists are. Transference and resistance are important parts of the relationship, and current aspects of the relationship, rather than past experiences, are emphasized (Prochaska & Norcross, 2003).

Leading ego-analysts are Erikson (1963), Hartmann (1958), and Rapaport (1958). Erikson (1950, 1963, 1968, 1982), the best known of the ego-analysts, published his first landmark book, *Childhood and Society*, in 1950 and continued developing his theory over many years. Affirming the autonomous nature of the ego, he explains, "The ego keeps tuned to the reality of the historical day, testing perceptions, selecting memories, governing action, and otherwise integrating the individual's capacities of orientation and planning" (1963, p. 193).

Erikson believes that psychosocial or ego developmental forces occur throughout a person's life span. At each stage of life, humans are confronted with mastering a developmental task that is of critical importance to maintaining and building the ego while making transitions to the next stage of development (see chap. 5). To master these tasks at each stage, individuals must rely on their ego energies to strike an equilibrium between inner forces and maturational changes and the increasing or changing demands of significant others in society.

Erikson calls such an attempt to master the developmental task at each stage a crisis because the task raises conflicts within the individual and between the individual and others in her or his life. A crisis is equivalent to a turning point, when the individual has the potential to progress or regress. At these turning points one can either resolve one's conflicts or fail to master the developmental task. To a large extent a person's life is the result of the choice she or he makes at each of these stages. Success in resolving these conflicts depends on the degree of ego strength developed in previous stages of life, the degree to which the individual actively works to use emerging abilities and strengths, and the degree of favorable influences in the individual's life (Erikson, 1963, 1968; Ewen, 1998; Ryckman, 1997).

Object Relations Theory

One of the most significant contemporary psychoanalytic approaches is *object relations theory*, which proposes a major restructuring of the classical Freudian instinct-driven theory of human nature. Instead of being governed by id instinctual drives, humans are motivated by their desire to connect or identify with others (i.e., objects).

An early proponent of object relations theory is W. R. D. Fairbairn, who claimed that "the ego's main functions are to seek and to establish relations with objects in the external world" (Hall et al., 1998, p. 180). Similar to the ego-analytic view of the autonomous nature of the ego, Fairbairn's claim was that

> the ego . . . has its own dynamic structure; and it is the source of its own energy. . . . The ego's main functions are to seek and to establish relations with objects in the external world. . . . The central issue in personality development is not the channeling and rechanneling of instinctual impulses, but the progression from infantile dependence and primary identification with objects to a state of differentiation of self from the object. (Hall et al., 1998, pp. 180–181)

One of the most influential of the object relations theorists is Heinz Kohut (Hall et al., 1998). He stressed emphatically the necessity of the nurturing family in development of self, a family whose primary caretaker can sufficiently serve as the responding object to the infant and child. The primary issue for Kohut is

> the presence or absence of empathic and loving relationships. Healthy mirroring and idealizing afford development of the ideal personality type, the person with an *autonomous* self. . . . Exposure to deficient self-objects produces children who possess a noncohesive, empty, or injured self. (Hall et al., 1998, p. 182)

Object relations theory has spawned numerous studies and publications. Attention once more has shifted to early childhood relations as a source of a malformed sense of self, but with a significant difference in inquiry from earlier psychoanalytic thinking. Attention now is focused on the deficiencies of relatedness and the repair thereof.

Feminist Psychodynamic Theory of Connection

Renewed interest in the developing self from the perspective of its relation to others has had a significant impact on the profession—notably, family therapists (see chap. 10) and feminist perspectives of human development (see chap. 5). A growing number of feminists claim that ego and object relations theories have not gone far enough; therefore, women have been providing new theories of their own on the psychodynamic nature of connection in relationships. Even though their theory is based on women's psychological development, they believe that their insights are relevant for everyone.

This theory has been developed over the years by numerous women researchers led by Chodorow (1974), Gilligan (1982), Conarton and Silverman (1988), and Miller (1976) and, more recently, by women at the Stone Center at Wellesley College, led by Jean Baker Miller, Irene Pierce Stiver, Judith Jordan, and Janet Surrey (Jordan, 1997; Jordan, Kaplan, Miller, Stiver, & Surrey, 1991; Miller & Stiver, 1997). Their feminist perspective is based on mutual connection as the primary mode of human growth and development. It is "a relational model organized around the importance of growth-fostering connections in relationships" (Jordan, 1997, p. 4).

Although influenced by the early relations theorists Sullivan, Horney, and Rogers and the contemporary ego-analytic theories of Erik Erikson and object relations theorists, these women researchers differ significantly. Particularly with the Eriksonian and object relations theorists, they disagree with the belief that a person naturally seeks to become an autonomous self (Jordan et al., 1991). To the contrary, they claim that the essential nature of human development is to grow in connection with others. As quoted in Miller and Stiver (1997), Janet Surrey claims, "*Connection* has replaced *self* as the core element or the locus of the creative energy of development" (p. 53).

Moreover, these women disagree with object relations theory that the infant instinctually attaches to an object (food or love object) as the source for growth. In their first major publication, *Women's Growth in Connection* (Jordan et al., 1991), they expressed their differences with traditional contemporary psychoanalytic beliefs and presented a human development model from a woman's perspective (see chap. 5). In a subsequent book, *Women's Growth in Diversity* (Jordan, 1997), they extended their earlier, White, middle-class, heterosexual model to include women from different multicultural backgrounds. In 1996 they founded the Jean Baker Miller Training Institute.

The Healing Connection (Miller & Stiver, 1997) describes their theory as it has since evolved and provides more detail on its therapeutic applications.

> This book is about connections between people, about how we create them and how disconnections derail them throughout our lives. Just as disconnections restrict us and block psychological growth, connections—the experience of mutual engagement and empathy—provide the original and continuing source of that growth. (p. 3)

They point out that their theory "reflects a major shift in our thinking about what creates pain and psychological problems and what fosters healing and growth" (p. 3).

The theoretical position of Miller and Stiver and their colleagues at the Stone Center is unique in that no one person's name can be associated with it, unlike the traditional psychotherapies that have promoted the individual (male) along with the theory. This group of women developed their perspective together, an endeavor that is consistent with their theory—the dynamic nature of mutual connection in relationships. Moreover, they claim that "the powerful role of connections in human growth alters the entire basis of contemporary psychological theory and psychotherapy" (Miller & Stiver, 1997, p. 3).

With connection as the core element of development, other elements specific to this theory include the following: (a) Connections are developed through continual responses and affirmations; (b) relationships involve mutual participants, rather than one person having power over another; (c) all participants become empowered in the relationship; (d) participation, rather than gratification, is the essence; (e) movement occurs in the relationship, a process that evolves over time and provides continuity; and (f) the relationship is something more than the participants and includes what might be called a field, or as Surrey says, *"arenas of growth and learning"* (Miller & Stiver, 1997, p. 213).

Miller and Stiver (1997), in describing the ideal model of mutual connection, say that on the one hand,

> we would form images of relationships that are mutually empathic and give us the means and motivation to act—connections that lead us to more knowledge, that make us feel worthwhile and eager for more connections, that help problematic situations resolve into solutions. (p. 40)

On the other hand, one who experiences too many disconnections

> might form an image of relationships in which feelings cannot be heard, understood, or engaged with mutually; in which she is unable to act or to change a situation; in which she feels less worthwhile and which demonstrate that trying to connect with an important person in her life leaves her feeling more isolated and more alone. (p. 40)

Psychoanalytic Psychotherapy

In the first half of the 20th century, psychology and psychoanalysis had little in common. Operating in entirely different camps, each focused on different aspects of human behavior: Psychoanalysts focused on the person's unconscious; psychologists focused on measurement of individual differences and on conscious behaviors. Each worked in different research settings: Psychoanalysts practiced in clinics; psychologists worked primarily as researchers in academic institutions, observing controlled groups of behaviors that could be statistically measured (Hall et al., 1998).

After World War II a closer relationship developed between psychologists and psychoanalysts as both groups recognized that sharing ideas and concepts would be mutually beneficial. George Klein was a key person who gave impetus to this development (Hall et al., 1998). Expanding on the ideas of David Rapaport (1960), Klein integrated a typical academic curriculum with psychoanalytic training.

> These individuals brought to psychoanalysis the values of laboratory experimentation and quantification and a respect for theory building as well as a firm grounding in cognitive processes. They received from psychoanalysis the kind of theoretical orientation and insights into the person that were lacking in their educational background. (Hall et al., 1998, p. 184)

This rapprochement was further strengthened when psychoanalytic institutes, such as the Menninger Clinic in Kansas, offered psychoanalytic training to postdoctoral psychologists.

Psychoanalytic psychotherapists make assumptions about behavior that are similar to those of ego-analysts. Psychoanalytic psychotherapists are interested in normal developmental problems; they, too, see maladaptive behavior as resulting from repressed needs and rejecting parents. They differ from ego-analysts, though, in that they focus on even shorter, less intensive and less regressive treatment. They tend to see a wider range of clients who are less seriously disturbed, they see clients less frequently, support useful defenses of clients, use a broader range of intervention strategies, and place more emphasis on resolving clients' specific, present-day problems (Baker, 1985).

Carl Jung: Analytical Psychology

Like Freudian theories, Jungian ideas fell out of favor in the United States for several decades, primarily because the dominating psychological theories were following the empirical approach to behavior. Unconscious forces were not recognized as influencing behavior because they could not be measured or observed. Moreover, Jungian theory was even less acceptable than Freudian because Jungian therapists believed that persons are governed not only by biological forces but by other forces as well—mind, spirit, and soul—forces foreign to the scientific empirical model of behavior.

Carl Jung began his career as a psychiatrist before becoming a Freudian psychoanalyst. Early on, Jung broke with Freud primarily because he disagreed with the Freudian theory that a person's sexual drive is the primary force determining psychic life. To distinguish himself from Freudian psychoanalysts, Jung called his theory *analytical psychology*. Jung held that the unconscious contains forces that are potentially positive if they are integrated into consciousness. He believed also that the major force in human behavior is an innate purposive drive to attain wholeness and completeness of self, a process he called *individuation* (Bennett, 1983; Jacobi, 1962; Jung, 1933/1970; Samuels, 1985). Individuation is "a process of integration of the world consciousness with the inner world of unconsciousness. Such action and reaction is inherent in development and growth" (Bennett, 1983, p. 172).

Individuation, or the search for wholeness of self, goes on throughout life and is never completed (Bennett, 1983; Samuels, 1985). Individuation falls into two main stages: the first and the second halves of life. Jung is primarily concerned with individuation of adults in the second half of life (see chap. 5).

> The task of the first half is "initiation into outward reality". . . . it aims at the adaptation of the individual to the demands of his environment. The task of the second half is a so-called "initiation into the inner reality," a deeper self-knowledge and knowledge of humanity, a "turning back" (*reflectio*) to the traits of one's nature that have hitherto remained unconscious. (Jacobi, 1962, p. 105)

Jung's theory developed out of his observations that the images patients see in their dreams and the symbols drawn from them are similar to those found in ancient folklore, myths, legends, art, and rituals (Kaufmann, 1989). From this discovery Jung hypothesized that these images, which he named archetypes, come from the collective unconscious, "the storehouse of latent memory traces inherited from man's ancestral past" (Hall et al., 1998, p. 85).

Among the many archetypes some significant ones for personality development are the *persona* (mask), or adaptive behaviors that are necessary for social conformity; the *animus* and *anima*, which are, respectively, the woman's masculine side and the man's feminine side; the *shadow*, a person's dark, unconscious; and the *self*, a person's inherent tendency to strive for wholeness in life (Kaufmann, 1989). Therapists help patients bring the unconscious to consciousness and relate them to archetypal themes.

Jung (1921/1971) also introduced the idea of two major personality types: the *introvert* (a person oriented to introspection) and the *extravert* (a person oriented to the outer world). He noted, however, that persons are too complicated simply to be divided into two types, so he hypothesized that these can each be further qualified by four typical styles of functioning: *thinking, sensing, feeling,* and *intuitive.* Considerable work has since been done on what is known as Jungian *typology* (Samuels, 1985). The personality inventory Myers-Briggs Type Indicator is based on these Jungian types (see chaps. 7 and 12). It should be noted, however, that Jung objected to classifying people into rigid personality types (Bennett, 1983); he believed that all these character types are inherently in everyone's unconscious and can be drawn into consciousness, a process that is part of individuation. One purpose of therapy is to help the person in this process.

Jung's major procedures were dream analysis and active imagination. Dreams, he believed, are expressions of the unconscious attempting to speak to some situation in the person's conscious life (Samuels, 1985). In *active imagination* therapist and patient plumb the details of a dream, relate the images to ancient myth, and connect them with universal archetypes, as well as with daily events. This process gives meaning to the dream that goes beyond one's ego. Jung distinguished between fantasy and active imagination:

> A fantasy is more or less your own invention, and remains on the surface of personal things and conscious expectations. But active imagination, as the term denotes, means that the images have a life of their own and that the symbolic events develop according to their own logic— that is, of course, if your conscious reason does not interfere. (Bennett, 1983, p. 107)

Jung was virtually ignored in the United States during most of the 20th century (Kaufmann, 1989). Even so, Hall and Lindzey remarked in 1970,

> The originality and audacity of Jung's thinking have few parallels in recent scientific history, and no other man aside from Freud has opened more conceptual windows into what Jung would choose to call "the soul of man." . . . Certainly his ideas merit the closest attention from any serious student of psychology. (p. 112)

More recently, Kaufmann (1989) claimed that "Jung's influence . . . has been enormous, although mostly unacknowledged, and recently there has been a reawakening to his ideas" (p. 126).

Post-Jungian psychology has gained national and international attention in many therapeutic circles. According to Samuels (1985), post-Jungian theories have been classified into three schools: classical, developmental, and archetypal. Each school can be thought of, respectively, as first-, second-, and third-generation Jungian. Samuels argues that differentiating and classifying the various post-Jungian theories can generate more dialogue among the schools, for he says, "a classification . . . into schools can tell us *as much about what is held in common* as about differences of opinion" (p. 18). Adherents of the classical school are those most loyal to Jung, whereas "both the Developmental and Archetypal Schools share an iconoclastic, revisionary attitude that expresses itself empirically in one case, and poetically in the other" (p. 44).

Samuels's book, *Jung and the Post-Jungians* (1985), gives a good look at all three schools. *Archetypal psychology* is discussed more at length here because it significantly differs from traditional psychoanalysis and psychotherapy, and its complex premises and unfamiliar terminology are often misunderstood. Founder James Hillman (1975, 1983, 1989), a Jungian analyst trained in Zurich, continues to challenge the theories and methods of Jungian, post-Jungian, Freudian, behaviorist, cognitive, and developmental thought as well as the very foundations of counseling and psychotherapy. Proponents of archetypal psychology have also attracted attention by their best-selling books of the 1990s: *Women Who Run with the Wolves* by Clarissa Pinkola Estés (1992); *Care of the Soul* by Thomas Moore (1992); and *Iron John* by Robert Bly (1990). Archetypal psychology has stimulated the mythopoetical men's movement and creative and expressive arts therapy.

Hillman (1983) prefers the term *archetypal* to *analytical* because it reflects "the deepened theory of Jung's later work which attempts to solve psychological problems beyond scientific models" (p. 1). More important, he prefers *archetypal* because it "belongs to all culture, all forms of human activity, and not only to professional practitioners of modern therapeutics" (p. 1).

Comparing the principles of archetypal psychology with other psychological theories poses difficulties. The terms central to its understanding—*soul, spirit, psyche, myth, imagination, polytheism*—are foreign to most psychological schools of thought. Moreover, archetypal psychology differs from traditional approaches to psychology in many and complex ways: It focuses on images and imaginable sensibilities, rather than on empirical behavior; relies on a poetic regard, rather than literal analysis of dreams and images; regards an experience in the context of myth, rather than merely as a literal event; emphasizes soul more than spirit; attends to a deepening awareness of soul, rather than to development of self or ego; and accepts the normality of a person's multiple selves, rather than encouraging a person to strive toward an integrated self or ego. Archetypal psychology insists that patients view themselves as part of a larger myth, the myth of society in which they are living, and as responsible for the world's health, the soul of the world (*anima mundi*), rather than their own ego development.

In archetypal psychology "the aim of therapy . . . is the development of a sense of soul" (Hillman, 1983, p. 4). The term *psychology*, or "logos of psyche," Hillman notes, "etymologically means: reason or speech or intelligible account of soul" (p. 16). Soul, of course, is a difficult concept to define. Hillman (1989) says in part:

> By *soul* I mean, first of all a perspective rather than a substance, a viewpoint towards things rather than a thing itself. This perspective is reflective, it mediates events and makes differences between ourselves and everything that happens. . . . The word refers to that unknown component which makes meaning possible, turns events into experiences, is communicated in love, and has a religious concern. (pp. 20–21)

Hillman does not perceive soul in the strict theological sense. Rather, he says, "Religion approaches Gods with ritual, prayer, sacrifice, worship, creed. . . . In archetypal psychology, Gods are *imagined*" (1983, p. 35). In *Care of the Soul* (1992), Thomas Moore emphasizes how persons can express themselves soulfully in everyday life, whether they are doing dishes, making decisions, cooking, or playing music.

Because imagination is the primary activity of the soul, the major focus in archetypal therapy, similar to that of other Jungians and post-Jungians, is to apply active imagination to images sensed in dreams. Instead of analyzing dreams, however, archetypal psychologists help patients deepen their awareness of their dreams or images by reflecting imaginatively on the details of the image. They are encouraged to expand the images by associating them with particular myths that represent archetypal messages. Image work, however, is not easy. In her cogent and comprehensive article on dream work, "An Approach to the Dream"

(1982), Patricia Berry warns, "Our imaginations are untrained, and we have no adequate epistemology of the imagination with which to meet the dream image on its own level" (p. 78).

As with all Jungians, the use of archetypal images is essential in the process of therapy: "Archetypes are the primary forms that govern the psyche. But they cannot be contained only by the psyche, since they manifest as well in physical, social, linguistic, aesthetic, and spiritual modes" (Hillman, 1983, p. 1). Hillman (1989) says, "The archetypal perspective offers the advantage of organizing into clusters or constellations a host of events from different areas of life" (p. 24). The hero, warrior, lover, and king discussed by Moore and Gillette (1990) are examples of archetypes.

Archetypal psychology emphasizes that "for psychology to be possible at all, it must keep the distinction between soul and spirit" (Hillman, 1983, p. 25). The spirit uses scientific objectivity to conceptualize and interpret experiences and to develop rules about behavior (Hillman & Ventura, 1992; Levine, 1992; Moore, 1992). According to archetypal psychologists, effective therapy can more likely occur when patients work imaginatively with both soul and spirit together so as to get a better sense of themselves and of the world.

Most therapists, archetypal psychologists argue, try too quickly to free clients from symptoms or problems by explaining or interpreting their behavior or by using rational problem solving or by administering psychotropic and tranquilizing drugs. Archetypal psychologists suggest that counselors instead help individuals reflect on the symptoms closely and imaginatively for meaning as part of soul work (Moore, 1992).

HUMANISTIC AND EXISTENTIAL THEORIES

All humanists believe to some extent that people possess dignity and worth and are purposeful, active, and capable of shaping and directing their own behavior as they work toward self-actualization. Existentialism and humanism are similar in their belief that human nature is basically good and that persons have free choice to grow and develop. Existentialists, however, "take the position that we are faced with the anxiety of choosing to create an identity in a world that lacks intrinsic meaning" (Corey, 2001, p. 171). In counseling practice the two also share basic similarities. Both believe that "the client-therapist relationship is at the core of therapy. Both approaches focus on the client's perceptions and call for the therapist to enter the client's subjective world" (Corey, 2001, p. 172).

Rogers's Client-Centered (Person-Centered) Theory

Carl Rogers (1942, 1951) perceives humans as possessing a basic, innate drive toward growth, wholeness, and fulfillment. People have a basic need for high self-regard. If unhampered, individuals will organize their inner and outer experiences into an integrated self through a self-actualizing process. Unhealthy social or psychological influences, in contrast, tend to inhibit individuals from achieving an integrated, productive self so that they experience conflicts in expressing their basic needs. According to Rogerian theory, humans have the ability to resolve conflicts but are limited mainly by a lack of awareness about themselves. Conflicts arise when there is a disparity between individuals' basic needs and their needs to gain approval from others.

Rogers (1939, 1942) was impressed with what was called *relationship therapy*, a method he learned in the 1930s during his work as a clinical psychologist in a child guidance clinic in Rochester, New York. It was based on the psychoanalytic concepts of Otto Rank and was promoted by some of Rank's followers, such as psychiatrist Frederick Allen and social worker Jessie Taft. This mode of therapy differs significantly from traditional psychoanalysis in that the therapist does not make intellectual interpretations or conceptual judgments regarding the patient's behavior or expressions, aside from clarifying feelings. "This is a different sort of interpretation" (Rogers, 1939, p. 346). Rogers's landmark book *Counseling and Psychotherapy* (1942) claimed that the counselor role should be *nondirective*, in reaction against the prevailing authoritarian style of counselors and therapists. "Effective counseling consists of a definitely structured, permissive relationship which allows the client to gain an understanding of himself to a degree which enables him to take positive steps in the light of his new orientation" (p. 18).

Acting on the theory that, in the appropriate environment, individuals self-actualize, the counselor is crucial in providing the right atmosphere to help clients self-correct behaviors that block growth and develop new ways of being that foster growth. Thus, in counseling, the counselor focuses on the individual, not on the problem; acknowledges the feelings of the client; places more importance on the immediate situation than on the client's past; emphasizes the evolving nature of the counseling process; and perceives the emotional relationship that develops between counselor and client as a therapeutic growth experience.

Rogers's insistence that the counselor assume a nonauthoritarian, nonadvisory role was a radical departure from conventional therapeutic practice. Without the counselor acting as adviser, the process itself becomes the essence of counseling, a process that can be delineated in a series of stages that indicate the evolving nature of the process itself. The permissive role of the counselor allows the client to explore feelings and develop insights during the ensuing stages. Gradually during the process, the client develops feelings of confidence, begins changing dissatisfying behaviors, and risks taking action in unfamiliar ways. Although these stages have been modified over the years of counseling practice, they have remained essentially the same (Rogers, 1942).

Rogers's 1942 book on nondirective counseling influenced the immediate postwar years. In his next book, *Client-Centered Therapy* (1951), Rogers virtually eliminated the term *nondirective*, a change that implies he realized the term was misleading, a fear he had noted earlier in his 1939 text. Inexperienced practitioners, he worried, would take nondirective to mean that counselors "do nothing" (1939, p. 348). Nevertheless, the term *nondirective* stuck for many years.

Rogers's 1951 text describes in more detail his theory that the counseling process itself is the essence. "He focused more explicitly on the actualizing tendency as a basic motivational force that leads to client change" (Corey, 2001, p. 170). Thus, he describes how clients' feelings both emerge and evolve during the counseling process as clients undergo changes and pass through more complex levels of turbulent feelings, including increased feelings of conflicts, fears, and anxieties.

By focusing on the evolving experiential nature of the therapeutic process itself and by delineating the many characteristic changes the client goes through, Rogers emphasized the sense of movement as the essence of the counseling process. The first part of the counseling session involves changes in client feelings, beginning with a movement from feelings of symptoms to self. This is followed by changes of perception about one's feelings of self-worth and of independence; changes in awareness of denial of experience; changes regarding values; changes in development of an emotional relationship between client and counselor; and changes in client personality structure and organization. The second part of the counseling session involves characteristic changes in client behavior, including increased discussion of plans and behavioral steps to be taken; change from relatively immature behavior to relatively mature behavior; decrease in psychological tension; decrease in defensive behaviors; increased tolerance for frustration as measured in physiological terms; and improved functioning in life tasks (Rogers, 1951).

In 1957 Rogers wrote the article "The Necessary and Sufficient Conditions of Therapeutic Personality Change," in which he elaborated on his earlier views that certain counselor qualities were important in the counselor-client relationship in order to foster client change. These essential counselor characteristics are congruency, unconditional positive regard, and empathy. *Congruency* means that the counselor is an authentic, integrated person. *Unconditional positive regard*, often called warmth, is the nonevaluative, nonjudgmental attitude the counselor has toward the client's thoughts, feelings, and behavior. *Empathy* is the counselor's ability to understand the client's world in the way the client does. When these conditions are present, Rogers claimed, clients can arrive at self-understanding and resolve conflicts (see chap. 4).

With the publication of his book *Becoming a Person* (1961), Rogers expanded his theory of the experiential nature of the counseling process to a person's growth experience during the process of life itself. In the late 1960s Rogers turned his attention to human relationships in all spheres of society and consequently changed from individual to group work. The publication of his *On Encounter Groups* in 1970 promoted a wave of encounter groups throughout the country.

At that same time Rogers started calling his theory *person-centered* and wrote books and articles on a person-centered approach to teaching and educational administration, on encounter groups, on marriage and other forms of partnership, and on the "quiet revolution" that he believed would emerge with a new type of "self-empowered person" (Raskin & Rogers, 1995, p. 136).

Largely because of Rogers's influence, most counselors today, regardless of their theoretical framework, generally regard the counseling relationship as a crucial part of counseling. Moreover, many counselors also acknowledge the therapeutic value of the experiential nature of the process itself.

Gestalt Theories

Fredrick ("Fritz") S. Perls (1969) and Laura Perls (1976) were the major developers of Gestalt theories and techniques. After Fritz Perls's death, Walter Kempler (1973) and Yontef and Simkin (1989) became major proponents of this theory. The purpose of the Gestalt approach is to integrate the person's inner reality (needs, perceptions, emotions) with his or her outer reality (environment). Human experiences always occur in an interactional field (phenomenal field) in which both inner and outer forces are integrated into a whole (called, in German, *Gestalt*). Thus, any inner behavior is immediately responsive to outer behavior and vice versa (Yontef & Simkin, 1989). Humans have potential for functioning in a responsible, genuine way.

Conflict, indecision, or anxiety arises when an inconsistency exists between inner perceptions or needs and demands from the environment. These contradictions can lead to a continual battle between individuals' inherent drive to function authentically, consistent with their inner experiencing self (*self-actualization*), and the need to behave as they believe they should because of expectations of parents and other significant people (*idealized self-actualization*). The goals of counseling are to teach people to become fully aware of themselves and the world and to become mature and responsible for their own lives.

Unlike Rogerians, Gestalt counselors are active teachers who directly confront clients with their inconsistencies. The counselors provoke and persuade clients or manipulate the interview to get clients to correct misperceptions, to express emotions authentically, and to take responsibility for change. The major emphasis is to get clients to respond immediately to experiences. To make clients do so, the counselors confront them with their inconsistencies and with the need to take constructive action regarding unresolved problems related to past experiences (*unfinished business*). This action permits individuals to devote more energy and more awareness to resolving current problems (Corey, 2001).

Besides confrontation Gestalt counselors use many other techniques, including role playing. In contrast with behaviorists' use of role playing, however, Gestaltists emphasize understanding one's own feelings and the feelings of others, rather than practicing behavior. Another strategy is role reversal, in which clients act out behaviors of individuals with whom they are in conflict. Dialogue games are also used in which clients play out both parts of the conflicting feelings or attitudes they are experiencing. Empty chair dialogues may also be used in which clients act out conflicts with other persons who are imagined to be in the empty chair. In this activity clients assume both roles and change chairs as they carry out a dialogue. Gestalt counselors encourage their clients to take responsibility for their emotions by using "I" statements, like "*I* am angry" rather than "*It* makes me angry." Body awareness, massage, visual imagery, and dream analysis are also characteristics of Gestalt therapy. More complete discussions of this therapy are available in Corey (2001); Ivey, D'Andrea, Ivey, and Simek-Morgan (2002); Levitsky and Perls (1970); and Passons (1975).

Existential Counseling and Therapy

Existential theories are rooted in the European philosophies of Heidegger, Kierkegaard, and Sartre and in the existential practice of European psychiatrists. In the United States psychoanalyst Rollo May (1961) and psychiatrists Irvin Yalom (1980, 2002) and Victor Frankl (1963) have applied the existentialist ideas to their analytic practice.

For existentialists humans have the self-awareness and the freedom to make choices that will bring meaning to their lives. This freedom and the responsibility to live with the consequences of these choices lead to existential anxiety—an essential part of living and being. "Existential therapists define anxiety more broadly than other psychotherapeutic groups. *Anxiety arises from our personal need to survive, to preserve our being, and to assert our being*" (May & Yalom, 2000, p. 275).

The well-functioning person is authentically experiencing and expressing needs in a manner not determined by others. People feel guilt and anxiety when they do not take actions they should take or when they do not act responsibly and authentically. Anxieties also arise from an inability to perceive purpose or meaning in life, especially with the realization of death. Existentialists believe that some anxiety is an essential part of life, a condition that encourages people to try to experience life fully and authentically. May (1961) sees awareness of death, for example, as an incentive to live life with zest because people realize that life is only temporary.

Frankl's (1963) views regarding existential philosophy emerged during his terrible experience in Nazi concentration camps in World War II. Through personal experiences and observations of others in these camps, Frankl came to the conclusion that, in the worst conditions of suffering and torture, humans can maintain spiritual freedom, independent thinking, and opportunities for choice. Meaning and purpose in life are maintained through love and suffering. He says that all things can be taken from individuals except two things—attitude and beliefs.

Frankl's (1963) theory is based on the idea that the unity of an individual has three dimensions—physical, psychological, and spiritual. He emphasizes life's spiritual meaning, including death, love, and suffering. Maladjustment arises when a person has conflicts between various moral or spiritual values. Frankl (1963) developed a technique called paradoxical intention, in which clients are encouraged to exaggerate their fears and anxieties, rather than deny them. Paradoxically, this helps dissolve anxiety.

In the post–World War II years, many college students, returning veterans among them, were troubled by existential questions in their search for the meaning of life. At the UC–Berkeley counseling center Frank Nugent's early approach to counseling was strongly influenced by Leslie Farber (1966), who was the psychiatric consultant there and later became known for his work on existentialism.

In 1961 Rollo May published his landmark *Existential Psychology,* and several existential counseling texts were published during the 1960s in which counselors emphasized subjective inner experiencing and a positive outlook on the active, purposeful nature of humans (Arbuckle, 1967; Dreyfus, 1962; Pine, 1969; Van Kaam, 1967). This approach stressed the unique individual who has not only the capacity but also the responsibility to make choices and also emphasized that human beings develop and experience themselves only in relation to other people in the world (Frankl, 1963; Van Kaam, 1967). With the rising popularity of technique-oriented behavior and cognitive behavioral therapies, however, existential counseling faded into the background for a couple of decades until its revival after Irvin Yalom published *Existential Psychotherapy* (1980).

May and Yalom's (2000) existential model draws on psychoanalytic concepts, such as transference and resistance, but they use them in terms of application to current experiencing. In *Gift of Therapy* Yalom (2002) describes how he has applied existential theory and techniques over 45 years of clinical practice. His approach is a combination of existential and psychodynamic theories; he emphasizes that existential therapy is not theory or content driven but instead focuses on the process of the counselor-client relationship. Therapists maintain a nonauthoritative relationship with clients in which they avoid making decisions for clients but help them work through their anxieties about their responsibilities and help facilitate client decisions. Yalom highlights three significant features in the existential counseling process: (a) Counselors help clients attend to the here-and-now, (b) counselors are open and authentic in their interactions with clients, and (c) counselors judiciously use self-disclosure about the mechanics of therapy, about their feelings toward clients in counseling sessions, and, with particular caution, about experiences in their personal lives.

According to Yalom (2002), "Existential psychotherapy is a dynamic approach that focuses on concerns rooted in existence" (p. xvi). By dynamic, he means that conflicts within the individual, conscious and unconscious, generate and influence the individual's attitudes, thoughts, emotions, and behaviors. Clients must be helped to confront death in order to explore meaning in life. "Keep in mind that therapy is a deep and comprehensive explanation into the course and meaning of one's life; given the centrality of death in our lives . . . how can we possibly ignore it?" (p. 125).

The goal of existential counseling is to help clients explore and develop meaning in life. The counselor can help clients recognize their choice-making potential and understand and accept the consequences of choice for their lives and for the lives of others. Counseling is essentially an encounter between therapist and client with an emphasis on understanding and being in an authentic partnership with each other. The problem to be faced is that the world is not necessarily meaningful, unless one makes meaning out of experience. Existentialists like May, Yalom, and Frankl believe that confusion and suffering in the world provide opportunity for growth. Existentialist counselors expect clients to commit themselves ultimately to authentic action and to assume responsibility for the consequences of their actions.

Holistic and Transpersonal Counseling

Holistic counselors perceive good mental health as resulting from physical, emotional, intellectual, and spiritual development—all of which are interconnected. Thus, they bring body, mind, and spirit into the counseling arena (Pietrofesa, Hoffman, & Splete, 1984). Physicians, counselors, and psychologists recognize that emotional stress can contribute to or exacerbate many types of physical illnesses, including migraine headaches, asthma, ulcers, back pain, high blood pressure, heart attacks, and cancer. However, no systematic theories of holistic counseling have been developed.

Holistic techniques are geared to the development of self-awareness and self-monitoring that will promote self-actualization. The best known of these techniques in traditional counseling practice are *biofeedback* and relaxation exercises. Clients are taught to give attention to body functions—such as breathing, body temperature, and body tension—and to monitor functions, such as intrusive or negative thoughts. They are then given instructions to relax through controlled breathing, relaxation exercise, meditation, body exercise, visualization of nonstressful scenes, and recitation of poetry. Meditation, yoga, and massage are familiar because of their popularity with health groups and with some Gestaltists and existentialists. Nutrition education is also considered crucial because a poorly fed body can interfere with a person's sense of well-being, as well as health.

Transpersonal counseling is the best known holistic approach. Its major goal is to help persons learn to expand personal boundaries and to monitor, facilitate, and unify body, mind, and spirit. Transpersonal psychology has become very popular among people seeking fulfillment beyond ego development. It emerged out of Abraham Maslow's principle of self-actualization:

> Transpersonal psychology was called the "Fourth Force" psychology by Abraham Maslow in 1969. It has emerged from mainstream psychology and religious studies as the branch of psychology that studies states of consciousness, identity, spiritual growth, and levels of human functioning beyond those commonly accepted as healthy and normal. (Strohl, 1998, p. 397)

This fourth force follows earlier psychological forces—psychoanalytic, behavioral, humanistic (see chap. 2)—adopting various Eastern philosophies and disciplined meditation to attain higher states of consciousness (Walsh, 2000). Transpersonal psychology is essentially experiential rather than intellectual. Many accredited transpersonal training institutions throughout the country offer comprehensive programs of psychological studies and supervised internships. Counseling procedures are similar to those of humanistic counseling developed by Carl Rogers.

> Transpersonal counselors are generally more concerned with teaching a problem-solving process than with resolving specific problems and complaints. To a transpersonal counselor, conflicts and symptoms are not viewed as illnesses or flaws but as natural consequences of blocked and distorted expressions of one's true identity. They are reminders that the expression of one's deepest truths and potentials . . . [is] being obstructed by poor choice of thoughts and behaviors. (Strohl, 1998, p. 402)

This humanistically oriented approach tends to overlook or ignore the unconscious and intrapsychic forces underlying human motivation and behavior. It is often associated with New Age healing, wherein counselors, therapists, and healers engage in a wide variety of mind-altering practices. New Age spirituality has prompted many professionals to criticize those seeking spiritual enlightenment as a way of escaping their problems and the ills of the world. Clinical psychologist and Buddhist monk Jack Kornfield (1993) warns that most Westerners seeking enlightenment as practiced by Eastern philosophies generally misunderstand such practices. Reaching enlightenment is always temporary, Kornfield says, and just the beginning of one's spiritual practice, which is a perilous and never-ending discipline.

Depth psychologists working with the unconscious, such as Jungian psychoanalyst James Hillman (1975, 1983, 1989) and Thomas Moore (1992), emphasize that one cannot work with spirit without working with soul—terms they are careful to distinguish—without grappling with one's shadow or dark side and confronting one's moral dilemmas. Jungian analysts lead the patient down instead of up; they delve into the depths as a way of bringing the unconscious into consciousness, integrating soul with spirit, rather than aiming only for higher consciousness.

BEHAVIORAL, COGNITIVE, AND COGNITIVE-BEHAVIORAL THEORIES

Behavioral, cognitive, and cognitive-behavioral theorists believe that human attitudes and behaviors are learned in response to one's environment. Maladaptive behavior is best corrected by reinforcing appropriate behavior and/or by reshaping or restructuring perceptions and cognitive processes.

Behavioral and cognitive theories originally developed separately and at different times. Following B. F. Skinner's theory, which became prominent in the 1950s and 1960s, *behaviorists* believe that humans are born *tabla rasa*, a blank slate, without drives or instincts. All behavior is learned, and behaviors that can be scientifically measured constitute the major concern of behaviorists. In contrast, *cognitive theorists*, who emerged some years later, believe that persons' perceptions are instrumental in processing, selecting, evaluating, and responding to external stimuli. The way a person perceives an event determines her or his response or reaction.

Most behaviorists have since adopted cognitive principles and are now generally known as *cognitive-behaviorists*. Likewise, most cognitive theorists, notably Albert Ellis (2000), have adopted behaviorist principles and techniques; Ellis changed his rational emotive therapy (RET) to rational emotive behavior therapy (REBT). Although all tend now to fall under the term *cognitive-behaviorist*, a few continue to remain primarily cognitive, notably Aaron Beck (1976a, 1976b).

Behavioral Theories

For behaviorists observable behavior is the main concern in the counseling process. Because people react to events in the environment, counselors focus on rewarding positive behavior and on extinguishing ineffective behavior by eliminating the conditions that reinforce it. New behavior is then introduced and appropriately reinforced. The counselor is essentially a teacher who helps clients learn new and more adaptive responses to old situations.

Operant Conditioning

The first behavioral approach that focused exclusively on observable, overt behavior was developed by B. F. Skinner (1953) and was called *operant conditioning* and *reinforcement theory*. According to Skinner's operant conditioning theory, an individual learns by reacting to observable stimuli. If the response is reinforced through rewards, the behavior will likely be repeated. If the response is ignored or punished, the behavior usually decreases.

This operant approach was popular in the 1960s in working with disruptive children in schools, those with bed-wetting problems, or persons with mental retardation or schizophrenia (Bijou & Baer, 1965; Patterson & Guillion, 1968). Since then, key persons who have applied this approach to the normal concerns of people in schools and communities are Hosford and DeVisser (1974) and Krumboltz and Thoresen (1976). Counselors have found this theory useful for clients who want to manage or control some undesirable habit or characteristic—such as smoking, overeating, alcohol addiction, or procrastination—or who wish to learn new habits, such as studying effectively, managing time, or improving parenting skills. An important technique is *token economy*, whereby clients gain tokens (positive reinforcement) or lose tokens (penalties), depending on whether they attain a mutually agreed-on target behavior. *Aversive conditioning* may also be used, which pairs an electric shock or some other unpleasant stimulus with thoughts or pictures of undesirable behavior.

Counterconditioning (Desensitization)

Joseph Wolpe (1958, 1969) introduced a behavioral therapeutic approach that reflects the *classical conditioning* work conducted by Ivan Pavlov in the 1920s (Wilson, 1995). Pavlov conditioned dogs to salivate at the sound of a bell. At first he produced the food, which elicited the salivation, at the sound of the bell. Later, the bell alone caused the salivation. Using this same learning principle, Wolpe paired anxiety responses with relaxation exercises so that the relaxation exercise gradually extinguished the anxiety response.

Wolpe (1969) demonstrated that emotionally debilitating behavior can be changed by a technique called *systematic desensitization*, a form of classical conditioning called *counter-conditioning*. *Desensitization* refers to a process that gradually decreases the client's sensitivity to an anxiety-provoking emotion by pairing the emotion with relaxation responses. Wolpe assumed that a person cannot physiologically be anxious and relaxed at the same time. For instance, a client might tell a counselor about an unreasonable fear of dentists that is preventing the client from keeping his or her dental appointments. The client would be taught how to relax through a series of relaxation exercises and then would be told to imagine gradually increasing anxiety-provoking images about dentists. In this way the client would learn to visualize being worked on in a dentist's chair without anxiety and would, it is assumed, ultimately be able to see a dentist without fear.

For persons experiencing unmanageable phobic fears, a desensitization technique is used to encourage them to expose themselves gradually to the feared object in real life under the guidance of the counselor. After progressive exposure clients learn that the consequences of facing the fear are not disastrous. *Flooding*—a technique that should be used with care—involves having clients fully expose themselves to the feared situation so that they eventually realize that their fear is unfounded. *Biofeedback* has also been used to help clients learn to relax by monitoring their physiological responses: breathing, heartbeat, blood pressure, or muscle tension. Clients are wired to a computerized instrument and are taught to reduce tension by observing feedback about their biological responses. They ultimately learn to relax by becoming aware of feedback from their own physiological responses without the machine.

Behavioral Self-Control and Management

Thoresen and Mahoney (1974) broadened the base of behaviorism by teaching clients to modify or manage their own undesirable behavior by using self-administered reinforcement. For example, an overweight person might be taught to implement changes in her or his environment (e.g., keeping records of caloric intake or using smaller plates) and to self-administer a reward if a certain amount of weight is lost in a specific time (e.g., give oneself a gift) and to penalize oneself (e.g., pay a fine) if the weight is not lost.

Cognitive Theories

Cognitive theorists believe that "how one thinks largely determines how one feels and behaves" (Beck & Weishaar, 1995, p. 229). People's thinking, or cognitions, relate to their perceptions about themselves and the world around them. Maladaptive thinking results from faulty perceptions or constructs about oneself and others. Beck (1963) and Ellis (1973) were early pioneers in the development of cognitive theories. In the 1990s Ellis combined his cognitive rational emotive therapy (RET) with behaviorism and changed its name to rational emotive behavior therapy (REBT), which is discussed in the cognitive-behavioral section of this chapter.

Aaron T. Beck's (1976a, 1976b) cognitive theory, following Ellis's early RET model, is similar to it in that clients are helped to recognize and change self-defeating thoughts and cognitions that occur in inner *self-talk* (Corey, 2001). Beck's approach differs from Ellis's, however, in that Beck's cognitive therapy is less confrontational. Beck works together with clients to help them discover their own misconceptions; he assumes that people live by irrational rules that influence distorted thinking, rather than by irrational beliefs (Beck, 1976a). Beck treats obsessions and phobias but is best known for his work with depression.

In treatment of depression, Beck administers the Beck Depressive Inventory (BDI), which is based on typical symptoms and beliefs of depressed persons, to assess the severity of the problem. He then teaches systematic skills in self-observation whereby clients observe their thought-pattern distortions and the faulty inferences, misperceptions, or exaggerations about external events that are not supported by the evidence (Beck, 1976b).

Next, Beck teaches coping skills. If clients are depressed and are withdrawing from activity, he helps them set up a schedule of activities, beginning with nonthreatening tasks that they can complete successfully. In role playing, Beck may play the role of the client and display the client's distorted thinking; with self-critical clients, he may use humor. Beck helps and directs clients to explore and correct misperceptions, list duties and tasks that need to be done, set priorities, and then carry out a realistic plan of action that will reduce depression.

Cognitive-Behavioral Theories

In the 1970s many behaviorists realized that conditioning procedures were too limited to explain behavior adequately and saw the value of combining them with cognitive theories. Cognitive-behaviorists aim to change clients' inaccurate, subjective perceptions about themselves and their environment by uncovering faulty assumptions and beliefs that underlie their thinking and are causing them personal or interpersonal problems. The counselors then teach logical reasoning skills to restructure these thinking patterns and correct the problems. This process is called *cognitive restructuring*.

Ellis's Rational Emotive Behavior Therapy

In the 1970s Albert Ellis (1973, 2000) introduced his theory that most human problems relate to irrational beliefs that arise from illogical reasoning. Believing that thinking and emotion are not separate processes, Ellis claimed that emotional problems result from illogical thought processes. Thus, he coined the term *rational emotive therapy (RET)*. In 1995 he changed RET to *rational emotive behavior therapy (REBT)* because he believed that it more accurately describes his approach.

Ellis lists about a dozen irrational beliefs that he believes plague most people in our culture. These beliefs relate to unrealistic ideas or expectations about themselves, about others, and about the world in general. For example, it is irrational to become very upset over other people's problems or to believe that the world is a catastrophic place when things are not as one would like them to be. These ideas form and are reinforced when a child is exposed to parents and others who model irrational thinking. The goal of counseling is to help clients attain logical approaches to solving problems.

Ellis's famous *ABC principle* emphasizes the importance of one's perception of a stimulus. *A* represents the stimulus, *B* is the belief related to *A* (perception of the stimulus), and *C* is the consequence. For example, a male student comes to counseling complaining that he feels worthless *(C)* because he did poorly on a math test *(A)*. The counselor will try to show him that the failure *(A)* is not really what caused these feelings, but rather his perception of the failure *(B)*. Ellis believes that people use illogical internalized sentences, which he calls *self-talk*. In this case the student thinks *(A)* I failed my math test; *(B)* I should not have failed, for only worthless people fail; and *(C)* I am worthless for failing. The counselor helps the student see that belief *B* is irrational.

After clients go through the *ABC* steps, Ellis helps them change their illogical thinking in a process he calls *disputing (D)*. During this stage counselors teach more rational belief systems; persuasion, cajolery, provocation, and subtle coercion are used where necessary, and homework assignments are given to help clients practice thinking rationally. REBT counselors use other behavioral techniques when appropriate, including self-management, assertiveness training, relaxation exercises, and systematic desensitization (Ellis, 1973, 2000).

Social Learning Theory

Social learning theorists counteracted the behaviorists' conditioning model in the 1960s and 1970s by claiming that learning can occur when individuals imitate the behavior of others, even though the imitation is not directly reinforced. Albert Bandura (1977) has been a major proponent of social learning theory, in which actors, either live or on video, are used to model socially desirable or socially effective behavior. Clients observe and imitate the models' behavior. The modeling of fearless behavior is often effective in treating phobias. For example, children fearful of dentists may be shown films of a friendly dentist interacting pleasantly with cheerful children. Or a client who fears snakes observes a model petting a snake. Video- or audiotape recordings, autobiographies, and typescripts can be used to demonstrate the desired behavior.

The emphasis on external factors makes possible a wide range of techniques. Counselors can demonstrate culturally appropriate behavior by serving as models or by using other persons to model behavior. Problem-solving or logical-reasoning skills can be taught. Another popular approach is role playing, in which counselor and client assume the roles of other persons in the client's life and practice appropriate responses. Clients are given reinforcement, or are taught to reinforce themselves, for desired behavior. Clients can also be trained in specific social skills, such as assertiveness. Homework assignments are considered an essential part of the counseling (Bandura, 1977).

Meichenbaum's Cognitive-Behavior Modification

Donald Meichenbaum (1985, 1993) uses a self-instructional technique called *cognitive restructuring*. Like Ellis and Beck, Meichenbaum (1985) believes that distorted thought processes are behind stress or emotional problems (Corey, 2001).

Meichenbaum also believes that persons are as afflicted by self-talk as they are by explicit comments of others. The goal of counseling, then, is to teach clients the skills to change their maladaptive ways of talking to themselves. Therapy involves teaching clients first to observe their own behavior and listen to themselves, second to develop a new, more adaptive internal dialogue (self-talk), and finally to learn new coping skills so that they will be able to handle stressful situations in real life (Corey, 2001).

A coping-skills learning program usually starts by exposing clients to an anxiety-provoking situation through role playing or imagery. Clients then evaluate their anxiety level and become aware of their anxious self-statements. Next, they make changes in their self-talk and note the decrease in anxiety after the evaluation (Corey, 2001). This procedure is effective for working with those with social or sexual dysfunctions, test or speech anxieties, phobias, or addictions (Meichenbaum, 1985, 1993).

Meichenbaum (1985) teaches stress management skills by means of what he calls *stress-inoculation therapy (SIT)*. As in desensitization, clients are taught to use a graded system in evaluating stress: They start by imagining low-stress situations and then try progressively to imagine more intensely, stressful situations. At each stage they are taught various problem-solving skills: defining the problem, choosing alternatives, making decisions, and verifying outcomes. Meichenbaum encourages clients to use various kinds of relaxation exercises similar to those used by holistic counselors—meditation, breath control, yoga, jogging, gardening, and walking. He believes that stress management training is useful in assertiveness training, anger control, treatment of depression, improving creativity, and treating health problems.

Coping skills learned in the sessions are practiced in real-life situations through increasingly difficult exercises and homework. These activities prepare clients to apply their new learnings after they terminate counseling.

Lazarus's Multimodal Therapy

Arnold Lazarus (1976, 1995) developed a multimodal therapy in which counseling or therapy is tailored to the individual client's needs by the use of techniques taken from all the theories—cognitive-behavioral, psychoanalytic, psychodynamic, and humanistic. Lazarus classifies himself as a social and cognitive-learning theorist because his beliefs are based on empirical principles of learning. He makes the point, however, that he is not theoretically eclectic, but rather technically eclectic.

Maladaptive behaviors or problems are assumed to result from deficient or faulty social learning. The goals of counseling are to bring about, in an efficient and humane way, client-desired change in behavior that will be enduring (Lazarus, 1995).

Using the acronym *BASIC I.D.*, Lazarus describes seven major areas of personality: (a) **b**ehavior (observable action), (b) **a**ffective (emotional), (c) **s**ensation (feelings), (d) **i**mages (imagination), (e) **c**ognitions (thought process), (f) **i**nterpersonal relationships (social), and (g) **d**rugs/biological (physical). A counselor must consider each of these modalities in assessing a person's problem and prognosis. An important feature of this approach is that every individual is considered unique, with her or his own BASIC I.D., so no one theory or set of techniques can work with everyone.

Clients first fill out a life history questionnaire and rate themselves on each modality of the BASIC I.D. Profile. The counselor, after making an assessment based on the client's responses and the counselor's observations, uses a procedure called *bridging*. Bridging means that the counselor first focuses on the client's preferred personality mode before exploring the other modalities. If the client functions predominantly from a cognitive mode, for instance, the counselor at first responds in a cognitive way before responding in another modality.

From among the wide variety of techniques used by behavioral and cognitive-behavioral counselors, multimodal counselors may use reinforcement procedures, assertiveness training, desensitization, biofeedback, and cognitive restructuring, especially in behavioral, affective, and cognitive modes. In physical and imagery modes, multimodal counselors may add Gestalt and holistic techniques, such as the empty chair or role-reversal dialogues; confrontation; abdominal breathing; positive visual imagery; and focusing. In the interpersonal mode, they may use self-management, instruction in parenting, and social skills. With drug and biological considerations, they make certain that appropriate medication is available and that inappropriate medication is curtailed. Like holistic counselors, multimodal counselors encourage good nutrition, physical fitness, and exercise.

CONSTRUCTIVIST AND SOCIAL CONSTRUCTIONIST THEORIES

Constructivism and *social constructionism* emerged from the postmodern era, which was characterized by the gradual breakdown of modernist social-cultural traditions, including the rational, objective, scientific mode of belief. Constructivist and social constructionist thinking arose from different academic disciplines, but "nowhere has this postmodern perspective had more profound ramifications than in the field of psychology" (Neimeyer, 1993, p. 221).

The terms *constructivism* and *social constructionism* are often confused, and debates continue over the fundamental differences between the two. Issues are complex and multifaceted, and the conflicting arguments are often contradictory and difficult to comprehend. "Any close listening to the postmodern chorus reveals a polyphony of voices—not all of which are singing in the same key" (Neimeyer, 1998, p. 140).

Constructivists and social constructionists share the postmodern "rejection of 'objectivist' psychologies" (Neimeyer & Stewart, 1998, p. 141) and the common assumption that a person's beliefs are constructs that can be shaped and reconstructed. Their differences essentially revolve around the nature of the self. Constructivists basically believe that the self has reconstructive capabilities and the integrity and desire to make meaning out of experience. Social constructionists, on the other hand, believe that social-cultural factors determine and modify human beliefs, behaviors, and development. "Although various visions of the self have long served as orienting constructs in psychotherapy, postmodern constructions of identity have posed challenges to a conceptualization of therapy as a straightforward process of self-correction or self-actualization" (Neimeyer & Raskin, 2000, p. 237).

Constructivism

Constructivists theorize that people form constructs to make meaning and order out of their lives on an ongoing basis throughout life. "Human beings are viewed as active creators of constructions that vary in the extent to which they help a person adjust to life's challenges" (Neimeyer & Stewart, 1998, p. 547). Postmodern constructivism challenges traditional models of psychotherapy, especially "therapies having a broadly cognitive orientation" (Neimeyer, 1993, p. 222). In traditional cognitive models, therapy focuses on the client's behavioral problems or emotional distress with the goal of correcting "faulty, unrealistic cognitions that generate emotional distress. Therapy is therefore highly directive . . . or psychoeducational. . . . As such, these therapies are quintessentially modern" (Neimeyer, 1993, pp. 223–224).

> The goal of constructivist therapies is ultimately more creative than corrective, insofar as they attempt to foster the broader development of the client's constructions rather than eliminate or revise cognitive distortions. . . . Accordingly, therapy is likely to be more exploratory than directive. . . . As such, constructivist approaches are quintessentially postmodern, promoting the elaboration of the client's narrative without the convenience of simple criteria for determining what constitutes an acceptable story. (Neimeyer, 1993, p. 224)

Increasing numbers of cognitivists are claiming to be constructivists and postmodern. The cognitivist belief that reality is fixed, objective, and empirical has diminished, and many cognitivists are accepting the constructivist belief that reality is emergent, fluid, evolving, shaped by human/societal constructs (Corey, 2001). Even so, according to Neimeyer (1998, 2003), most cognitivists, including those who claim to be similar to postmodern constructivists, still hold to the traditional cognitive approach that is fundamentally different from the constructivist perspective.

George Kelly's Theory of Personal Constructs

According to Neimeyer (1993), George Kelly's *The Psychology of Personal Constructs* (1955, reissued in 1963) was "the first systematic attempt to articulate a constructivist theory of clinical practice" (p. 224). Aside from Jerome Bruner's praiseworthy review of Kelly's landmark book in a 1956 issue of *Contemporary Psychology* (Bruner, 1990), Kelly's theory of personal constructs and his comprehensive therapeutic system were not generally acknowledged or accepted in professional circles in the United States until about 30 years later (Jankowicz, 1987). Personal construct theory did receive considerable attention, however, in England and Australia.

Since the 1980s personal construct theory has been acknowledged in the United States by increasing numbers of practitioners, and it has been adapted for many specialties. Fransella and Dalton's (2000) book *Personal Construct Counselling in Action* describes how this theory can be applied by counselors (see chap. 9); Jankowicz (1987) explains why it works especially well in the corporate business world; and Viney (1993) describes how it can be used for older adults (see chap. 15). Longtime psychotherapist Efran (2002), in describing the various theoretical influences on his practice, acknowledges that a key influence was Kelly's theory of personal constructs, followed later by the constructivists. Over the years, he says, he keeps coming back to Kelly's original theory and model of practice. "Kelly's constructivist approach left an indelible imprint on the way I practice. Even today, I find myself buoyed by his indefatigable faith in the human capacity to create new alternatives" (Efran, 2002, p. 32).

According to Kelly's (1955) theory, individuals look at the world through patterns of constructs. *Constructs* "are ways of construing the world. They are what enables [individuals] . . . to chart a course of behavior" (p. 9). One can improve one's constructs by increasing, altering, and subdividing them. Often, however, the attempt to alter one's constructs is too great, and individuals seek psychotherapy to help modify or reorganize their construct systems.

Kelly's (1955) "fundamental postulate" is this: "A person's processes are psychologically channeled by the ways in which he anticipates events" (p. 46). This hypothesis is supported by 11 subsidiary structures, or *corollaries*. A person's construct, for example, must replicate itself. Only when a person senses recurrent themes does life begin to make sense. Corollaries speak to the evolving, changing nature of one's constructs; they are individualistic, dichotomous, limited in range, applicable to certain contexts, open to choice as well as to change, part of a complex interrelated system, susceptible to social influences, and subject to incompatibility within the system.

In describing the nature of a construct or the way that one uses one's constructs, Kelly (1955) explains quite simply, "A construct is a way in which some things are construed as being alike and yet different from others" (p. 105). One construes events by comparison and contrast, or more basically by noting opposites. White is the opposite of black. A construct is termed *emergent* when several elements start forming around the similarity pole (i.e., in replication, or recurring patterns). At this point, the individual assigns the pattern a name. The use of symbols, Kelly notes, is "characteristic in the early stages in the formation and use of any construct" (p. 139). Construct theorists are "concerned with finding better ways to help a person reconstrue his life so that he need not be the victim of his past" (p. 23).

Much of the emphasis in therapy is acknowledging that one's constructs are incompatible or inappropriate, out of alignment. Normally, an individual is constantly reevaluating his or her system as he or she encounters new experiences. On the other hand,

> if he fails to reconstrue events, even though they keep repeating themselves, he minimizes his experience. . . . If he is prepared to perceive events in new ways, he may accumulate experience rapidly. It is this adaptability which provides a more direct measure of the growing validity of a man's construct system. (Kelly, 1955, p. 172)

Constructivist Therapies

Numerous scholars and psychotherapists the world over have expanded and elaborated on Kelly's theory of personal constructs, shaping it into the broader concept known as constructivism (Neimeyer, 1993,1998; Neimeyer & Mahoney, 1995; Neimeyer & Raskin, 2000; Presbury, Echtering, & McKee, 2002; Seligman, 2001). The many publications on constructivist psychotherapy include scholars from Australia, New Zealand, England, Spain, and Italy (Neimeyer & Mahoney, 1995; Neimeyer & Raskin, 2000). Constructivism embraces developmental, narrative, and systemic models; it is readily adapted to various therapeutic specialties and can be "applied to a wide range of concerns and settings" (Seligman, 2001, p. 292). Constructivism is being successfully applied in schools (Seligman, 2001), with older adults (Carlsen, 1995), and with attention deficit disorder, posttraumatic stress disorder, and grief (Seligman, 2001; Neimeyer & Raskin, 2000; Lyddon, 1995). With the rising trend to integrate various theoretical approaches, many practitioners are adopting and integrating partial applications but are overlooking constructivism's fundamental theoretical beliefs (Neimeyer (1998, 2003), as discussed later in the chapter.

Constructivists are phenomenological in their approach to counseling and therapy. Constructivist models, which follow Kelly's (1955) tenants of avoiding conceptualizing, are fluid rather than fixed. Therapists avoid being "persuasive, analytical, and technically instructive" (Neimeyer, 1993, p. 224).

> Constructivists view humans as actively imposing their own order on experience and shaping their behavior to conform to their expectations. Thus, a fundamental concern of constructivist psychotherapists becomes the study of the personal and communal *meanings* by which people order their experience, meanings that must be transformed if clients are to envision new (inter)personal realities in which to live. (Neimeyer & Stewart, 1998, p. 550)

One of the most important aspects of constructivist therapies is the belief in a person's capacity to change, as well as the difficulty for persons to undergo change. Thus, the primary role of the therapist is to help the client through this difficult process, which invariably involves conflict and pain; "a premium is placed on forging an intimate therapeutic bond between client and therapist" (G. J. Neimeyer, 1995, p. 114). Above all, the therapist is patient and respectful of the client during the therapeutic process, reflecting "the almost reverential regard that constructivists have for their clients' personal knowing systems" (G. J. Neimeyer, 1995, p. 124).

Whereas other approaches are distinguished primarily by their assessment and procedural techniques, "in contrast, constructivist psychotherapy is characterized by the distinctive mind-set that guides it more than by any particular set of procedures" (Neimeyer & Stewart, 1998, p. 548). Thus, constructivism can best be understood through a discussion of its basic assumptions: (a) the concepts of self and development, (b) the narrative approach to understanding one's experiences, and (c) the systemic perspective of the self in relation to others and to the social-cultural environment.

Fundamental to constructivist thought is the nature of the self and the way it evolves and develops in relation to others. Although constructivists in the Piagetian tradition view "persons as self-organizing systems" (Neimeyer, 1998, p. 141), capable of forming and reforming their own constructs, constructivists don't advocate an autonomous self, but rather a self affected by family and the social milieu. "Kelly . . . went to great lengths to anchor the self in a social context" (Neimeyer & Raskin, 2000, p. 225). Constructivists differ from the Freudian idea that the self is determined by instinctual drives, they differ from the idea that the self is governed by traits, and they also differ from the idea of an actualizing self advocated by Maslow and Rogers. According to constructivist theory, the self develops dynamically (R. A. Neimeyer, 1995) as the individual forms and shapes her or his personal constructs in relation to the family and the social-cultural environment.

One of the primary methods of constructivists is *narrative therapy*, based on the belief that persons make meaning out of their lives by forming stories. "If . . . each of us is in some sense the 'author' of our experience, then the narrative form in which we organize or structure that experience becomes a central concern of psychotherapy" (R. A. Neimeyer, 1995, p. 231). "By rendering an account of experience in personally significant terms, people construct a meaningful story of not only the events that constitute their lives but also themselves as protagonists" (Neimeyer & Raskin, 2000, p. 211). Viney (1993) and Carlsen (1995) use narrative therapy with older adult clients, who are encouraged to seek meaning in their lives by telling their stories, a process known as *life review* (see chap. 15).

Telling one's story fits particularly well with constructivist therapy. When clients and therapists follow the narrative form of self-reflection and exploration, they avoid the use of analytical conceptualizing common to traditional therapies. "Narrative knowing . . . is qualitatively distinct from propositional thought" (Lyddon, 1995, p. 77). "The core of narrative therapy is the constructivist view that all 'knowing' is an act of interpretation" (Presbury et al., 2002, p. 106). Narrative therapy is further discussed later in this chapter.

Constructivists also believe that social interactions with family and society influence one's life. "To a greater extent than traditional cognitive therapies, constructivist approaches to clinical practice . . . situate the self firmly in social context" (Neimeyer, 1993, p. 223). Constructivists, however, have tended to focus primarily on helping to develop the self as the agent within the system. Constructivist therapists have been particularly influenced by the emphasis of family therapists White and Epston (1990) and cultural psychologist Jerome Bruner (1986, 1990) on the importance of social-cultural dynamics in the context of the client's story.

Social Constructionism

Social constructionists assume that human constructs arise from one's social environment. "The notion that personal constructions of understanding are constrained by the social milieu—that is, the context of shared language and meaning systems that develop, persist, and evolve over time—is the essence of social constructionist thinking" (Lyddon, 1995, p. 77).

Social constructionists have made valuable contributions (e.g., Berger & Luckman, 1966; Gergen, 1985) to constructivist psychotherapies through their critique both of the various knowledge patterns inherent in the social systems governing people's lives and of the systems of discourse governing counselors and therapists in practice. The perspectives of social constructionists have come from feminist, ethnic, and older adult groups, whose identities have tended to be subjected to the dominant social order. Those perspectives have shifted the major counseling and psychotherapeutic focus away from the individual and to the individual in connection with the social-cultural milieu, or in Rigazio-DiGilio's (2000) words, the individual in "relational systems" (p. 310). "The majority of constructivist models do not adequately address relational methodologies. . . . All manifestations of psychological distress have a relational component and that only by understanding how the relational systems construct their interpretations and reactions to their distress can therapists hope to understand how individuals and wider communities construe their situations" (Rigazio-DiGilio, 2000, pp. 309–310).

Constructivist and Social Constructionist Dialogues

Acknowledging the shortcomings of both constructivism and social constructionism, Neimeyer and Raskin (2000) go on to point out the positive attributes of both and suggest ways to bridge the gap between the two. Their book *Constructions of Disorder* (2000) attempts to do just that.

Acknowledging that constructivists fall short in recognizing the degree of social influence on the self, Neimeyer (1998) suggests that "fixed role therapies . . . could be expanded to acknowledge the multiple, often contradictory roles we develop and sustain in response to the different discursive contexts we inhabit" (p. 143). At the same time social constructionist approaches are being influenced by constructivist perspectives. "Systemic therapies . . . have become increasingly open to 'importing' concepts from more individual constructivist approaches . . . that help reveal the 'selves' within the system, and that provide a means of tacking back and forth between individual and family level work across the course of a given therapy" (Neimeyer & Stewart, 1998, p. 557).

Ongoing dialogues among constructivists and social constructionists have inspired counselors and therapists to become more open to and reflective of their own theoretical assumptions, which govern their practice. Examining language patterns from a social, cultural, historical perspective has also stimulated healthy dialogue among differing schools of counseling and psychotherapy (Neimeyer & Raskin, 2000).

CREATIVE THERAPIES

Creative and expressive arts therapies are based on the belief that many persons express themselves nonverbally in ways they are unable to do otherwise. Narrative therapy, in which one learns to view one's life as a story, is also a departure from the usual analytical therapeutic approach. Expressive arts and story making, used therapeutically, can reveal one's nature as it evolves over time; can reveal feelings; can release defenses that block or inhibit growth; and as symbolic expression, can reveal one's inner self or soul.

Creative and Expressive Arts Therapies

Creative and expressive arts therapies have rapidly gained favor among counselors and therapists in a wide range of therapeutic settings. Much has been written about creative arts counseling and therapy in which the client works with imagery, drawing, dancing, music, drama, or poetry during counseling and therapy sessions (Levine, 1992; McNiff, 1988). Fleshman and Fryrear (1981) comment, "The art therapies, to a very great extent, have grown from the early seed planted by Jung" (p. 33). Carl Jung's theory of active imagination and archetypes, as well as his use of creative arts in his own life and therapy, was a strong influence in the development of art therapies. Kaufmann (1989) says, "In Jung's consulting room, people danced, sang, acted, mimed, played musical instruments, painted and modeled with clay, the procedures limited only by Jung's inventiveness and ingenuity" (p. 132). Dalley et al. (1987) tie Jung's early work to current creative arts practice: "His technique of active imagination which deliberately mobilized the patient's creativity is an approach that many art therapists use today" (p. 9). Douglas (1995) comments that Jung encouraged arts therapy "as a conscious way to express elements of the unconscious" (p. 118).

Creative arts therapist Stephen Levine (1992) indicates how archetypal psychology, discussed earlier in this chapter, has given impetus to creative arts therapy:

> Given this conception of psychotherapy and its relation to the imagination, it becomes clear why the arts need to enter into the therapeutic process and why, in recent years, different expressive arts therapies have emerged with such vigor. (p. 3)

Unlike Jung, Freud was ambivalent about the idea of using creative arts in therapy and did little with it in practice (Dalley et al., 1987; Levine, 1992). Even so, some of his followers used creative art techniques, primarily drawing and painting, with children (Robbins, 1980).

Among the humanists those most closely aligned with the concepts and techniques of art therapies are the Gestaltists, followed by the self theorists (Dalley et al., 1987; Fleshman & Fryrear, 1981). Because of their emphasis on wholeness of body and mind and the connections between feelings and actions, Gestaltists encourage body movements, dance, massage, drama, acting out dreams, and the use of imagery. Self theorists also encourage their clients to express themselves in poetry, drawing, or dance.

Because of their focus on observable actions of clients and external factors influencing these actions, behaviorists tend to use creative activities as reinforcements or rewards. Cognitive-behaviorists—such as Lazarus, Meichenbaum, and Wolpe—who are concerned about perceptions and distorted thought processes, use imagery as a way of helping clients change behavior (Corey, 2001; Fleshman & Fryrear, 1981; Robbins, 1980).

Personal construct counselors use numerous creative arts therapies to help nonverbal clients become aware of their self-perceptions—the way they construe themselves. Drawings, including interactive drawings between counselor and client, have been effective for those clients who have difficulty talking. Working with clay, music, and dance is also effective.

Narrative Therapy

Narrative therapy has gained significant attention from counselors and therapists in a wide range of disciplines. To constructivists the narrative approach is a fundamental part of therapy. Narratives are forms of client self-exploration that offer clients insights into characteristics of their selfhood and open up ways in which to integrate them. "Clients use these forms of self-exploration to confront important choices in work and in relationships; place past traumas in a more contemporary frame of reference; and give voice to concerns, insights, and new hopes that they may be reluctant to verbalize to another, even to an accepting therapist" (R. A. Neimeyer, 1995, p. 242).

Constructivist therapists believe that emotional distress or disorder results from a gap or break in an individual's life story (Neimeyer & Stewart, 1998). "Clients come to counselors with stories that are outdated, tragic, and rigidified. As a result, these clients experience their lives as repetitive, negative, and unchangeable" (Presbury et al., 2002, p.102). "Most narrative therapeutic approaches share the goal of weaving painful, negative or other unexpected events into the client's dominant life narrative" (Neimeyer & Stewart, 1998, p. 556).

Counselors work collaboratively with clients to help them tell their stories and identify major themes or constructs that are inhibiting or limiting their lives. Constructivist therapies attend to underlying forces that influence one's story: "What seems critical is developing an attitude of attunement to the 'subtext' of the client's writing . . . rather than literally following only the events or 'surface structure' captured by the writing" (R. A. Neimeyer, 1995, p. 234). Clients are then encouraged to revise their stories so as to develop new themes and constructs that are more productive to client growth (Seligman, 2001). Constructivists emphasize that one's story making is a guide, a map that one can alter and change.

Following George Kelly's (1955) early use of narrative form, constructivists encourage clients to see themselves in their stories metaphorically as protagonist and narrator (Neimeyer & Raskin, 2000). Therapists also encourage clients to tell stories from differing points of view or as if they were different characters in the story. Therapists may also help clients project their stories into the future. This process leads clients "to a greater empowerment and the ability to successfully manage their lives" (Seligman, 2001, p. 283).

During the reconstruction of their stories, constructivists ask clients to consider who the audience is. Eventually clients are encouraged to share their stories with a broader audience. "Ultimately . . . narrative therapists assume that the client's preferred identity claims are best authenticated in relation to broader audiences, including family, friends, and perhaps other people struggling with similar problems" (Neimeyer & Raskin, 2000, pp. 234–235).

Another method favored by Kelly (1955), enacting one's story dramatically, is used effectively by many narrative therapists (Efran, 2002; Fransella & Dalton, 2000; Lyddon, 1995). In enactment the client acts the part of a significant person in his or her life, or client and counselor together act out certain parts and then exchange roles. Therapists can then encourage their clients to relate their roles in dramatic play to real life.

> Similar to drama, narrative psychology treats the narrative as an organizing context for human action. From a narrative psychology perspective, people impose socially constituted narratives (or roles) on the flow of their experience and, as a result, are both the authors of and actors in self-narratives—that is, their own personal dramas. (Lyddon, 1995, p. 77)

Another leading advocate of the narrative approach is cultural psychologist Jerome Bruner (1990), well known for his emphasis on the way humans acquire and use language. Since ancient times, he points out, persons applying language as a means of communication formed and told stories as a way of making meaning out of their lives. This basic folk psychology, he says, has been "a system by which people organize their experience in, knowledge about, and transactions with the social world. Its organizing principle is narrative rather than conceptual" (p. 35). The narrative's "unique sequentiality . . . is indispensable to a story's significance and to the mode of mental organization in terms of which it is grasped" (p. 44). Noting the long-standing fragmented nature of the field of psychology, Bruner (1990) remarks that "naturally a reaction has set in against this fragmentation. . . ." (p. xi). According to Bruner (1990):

> What's missing from the field of psychology is the crucial component of the human desire for making meaning of one's life. The central concept of a human psychology is meaning and the processes and transactions involved in the construction of meanings. (p. 33)

Especially important to narrative therapy has been the work of Australian/New Zealand family therapists White and Epston (1990), as described in their seminal book *Narrative Means to Therapeutic Ends* (Presbury et al., 2002; Seligman, 2001). White and Epston introduced a postmodern way of examining how social constructs govern and dominate familial and social patterns (Sharf, 2000). Their narrative therapy enables clients to realize "that our personal realities and self-images are not absolute but are created and maintained by our societies and ourselves" (Seligman, 2001, p. 284). Thus, people are subjected to a *dominant story* (White & Epston, 1990), and client disorder results from this subjection. White and Epston (1990) present ways to help clients restructure and retell their stories so that they become the agents of their narratives, that is, they regain a sense of self (see also chap. 10).

The therapeutic use of listening to stories and of storytelling has also gained attention among professionals. Especially helpful in describing how stories can be used therapeutically are Clarissa Pinkola Estés's book *Women Who Run with the Wolves* (1992), Michael Meade's book *Men and the Water of Life* (1993), and his Mosaic Foundation (2003), which conducts storytelling workshops with inner-city youth (see chaps. 14 and 19).

THEORIES OF BRIEF COUNSELING AND THERAPY

Brief counseling and therapy has increased rapidly in community mental health practice. As the demand for mental health services in the community increased in the 1980s and funding for these services declined sharply, the idea of planned short-term therapy developed. Health maintenance organizations (HMOs) and employee assistance programs (EAPs) emerged with a deliberate emphasis on "brief, highly-focused therapeutic services" (Wells, 1994, p. 3). Managed care soon followed, and brief therapy became a standard model.

In contrast with traditional counseling practices, therapists using brief counseling set specific goals and specify that the number of sessions will be limited. They focus on helping clients develop coping skills that will enable them to anticipate and manage future problems, as well as resolve immediate concerns.

Intermittent counseling is another form of brief counseling. In this approach clients see counselors or therapists off and on over the years as problems arise, rather than spending long periods of time trying to make general personality changes. This model is consistent with the way patients see physicians or dentists; an individual experiencing a particular difficulty sees a therapist or counselor until that problem is resolved and then returns when the problem recurs or another problem arises.

Short-term counseling and therapy has a long history, going back to the earliest Freudian analysts: "At that time, the prevailing mood among psychoanalytic thinkers was that therapeutic intervention could be brief, concise, and effective. Examples abound of therapies being successfully completed in several visits" (Budman & Gurman, 1988, p. 1). Freud at first limited his analysis with patients to 6 to 12 visits, but analysis became more prolonged as clients brought in more complex concerns and as the goals of analysts became more ambitious (Phillips, 1985). Psychoanalysts Alfred Adler, Otto Rank, and Sandor Ferenczi objected as analysis became longer (Garfield, 1989). In later years

Alexander and French (1946) noted that as analysts focused more on the client's immediate conflicts rather than on childhood traumas, fewer sessions of analysis were needed.

A great impetus for brief counseling came with the emergence of the profession of counseling in the late 1940s and 1950s. The emphasis on working with the developmental concerns of normally functioning individuals was geared to short-term approaches–as Nugent experienced in California.

> In the late 1940s, when I counseled at the UC–Berkeley Counseling Center, we found that the majority of our clients could be helped on a short-term basis. In the high school where I practiced in the 1950s, our counseling was naturally brief, and it was naturally intermittent as well because students kept returning to see their counselor during the 4-year period that they were enrolled. So right from the beginning, college and school counseling typically engaged in short-term work because counseling problems centered on transitional, situational concerns that were limited to a student's effectiveness in school.

The chief difference with brief therapy now is that therapy is deliberately planned, and sessions are determined in advance, to be completed within a set period of time. Many counselors and other mental health providers object to this deliberate limitation. Although it is true that many clients profit from short-term therapy, others need longer term help to resolve their problems. A more effective policy is one in which the number of sessions is determined by the client's particular problem, with an extension of sessions available when the client needs it.

Brief therapy is used in both psychodynamic and cognitive-behavioral therapies. Counselors and therapists who use short-term psychodynamic approaches focus on the therapeutic relationship and, unlike long-term analysts, work only with the client's current circumstances. Short-term cognitive-behavioral therapists set specific goals, teach new learning skills, and emphasize practice of new behavior. Currently, particularly in managed care settings, cognitive and cognitive-behavioral approaches are more commonly used.

Common themes with all approaches are that clients have a prior history of adequate adjustment and an adequate ability to relate, but a situational difficulty has arisen that has provoked a dilemma, anxiety, or crisis, such as loss of a job or sudden weight gain.

Psychodynamic Brief Counseling and Therapy

Lewis Wolberg's (1980) *Handbook of Short-Term Psychotherapy* presents a comprehensive and thorough discussion of how psychodynamic concepts can be adapted to brief therapy. Wolberg indicates that it is important to "focus on what is of immediate concern to the patient, such as incidents in life that have precipitated the symptoms for which he seeks help" (p. 99). Thus, therapists focus on some particular situational problem of the client. Feelings of transference and dream content are related to the client's current concerns and circumstances.

Psychodynamic theories getting the most attention are Strupp and Binder's (1984) time-limited dynamic psychotherapy, Sifneos's (1987) short-term dynamic psychology, Davenloo's (1994) short-term dynamic psychotherapy, and Mann's (1973) time-limited psychotherapy (TLP). Mann's TLP relates particularly well to counselors: "This psychoanalytic approach is compatible with counseling psychology's emphasis on client strengths, is suited to work with intact personalities, and places a premium on brevity" (Gelso & Fretz, 2001, p. 316). Furthermore, this approach is consistent with Erik Erikson's human development theory in that Mann recognizes that conflicts happen during transitions that occur throughout life.

Mann's (1973) approach is limited to 12 sessions. He focuses on a central issue, the crisis of separation and individuation that reoccurs in different forms throughout an individual's life. "There are countless experiences throughout life that revive repeatedly the sense of loss and anxiety related to separation-individuation phase. Loss of money, of power, of a relationship, of self-esteem, and of a job . . . are obvious examples" (Gelso & Fretz, 2001, p. 317).

The resolution of the client's feelings of loss and anxiety generally focuses on issues regarding the self. In the initial sessions the therapist looks for the central issue underlying the client's complaint of, say, anxiety or depression. "Mann refers to the central issue as reflecting the client's present and chronically induced pain" (Gelso & Fretz, 2001, p. 318). The central issue involves deeper "underlying self issues that have plagued the client's experience from very early in his or her life" (p. 318). Although the therapist explores the client's past and relates it to the present, this exploration is limited to those experiences that are relevant to the client's central problem.

Therapists employ an empathic approach throughout the 12 sessions, using the counseling process as a positive experience of union and separation. Therapists are understanding of the client's pain but at the same time are unequivocal in resolving the client's dilemma in 12 sessions.

> The two opening moves by the therapist, setting up an empathic bond for which the patient has yearned and then announcing that it will be terminated, build a structure for the therapy that will continue throughout its course with the oscillation between magical fantasies and harsh reality. (White, Burke, & Havens, 1981, p. 250)

"The time limit in TLP addresses the client's desire and need for independence; the treatment helps such a client mature, separate from childhood in a healthy way, and grow" (Gelso & Fretz, 2001, p. 321).

Strupp and Binder (1984) developed time-limited dynamic psychotherapy (TLDP), which involves 25 to 30 sessions, a system similar to Mann's. Earlier, however, Strupp (1981) had expressed cautions about the limitations of psychodynamic brief therapies:

> We have not gone far enough in this endeavor. . . . I believe there are definite limits to what time-limited dynamic psychotherapy . . . can accomplish, and that outcomes depend importantly on patient selection, the goals to which the therapist (and the patient) aspire, and the nature of the therapeutic changes the therapist is able to engender. (p. 238)

Recent criticism of time-limited brief therapy is discussed later in this section.

Cognitive and Cognitive-Behavioral Brief Counseling and Therapy

Cognitive and cognitive-behavioral theories generally are easily adapted to brief counseling and therapy because they are goal oriented and focus on presenting issues or symptoms of relatively short duration. The major brief cognitive and cognitive-behavioral approaches used in mental health practice today are based on the strategic theories of Jay Haley (1987) and Milton Erickson (1980) (see also chap. 10).

Brief Strategic Therapy

Early strategic counselors and therapists used intervention strategies to direct or manipulate changes in clients' repetitive, nonproductive behavior without regard for their emotions or situational factors. Strategic therapists now attend to both client emotions and social context (Cade & O'Hanlon, 1993). They also refrain from using manipulative interventions or interventions that are unethically deceptive or potentially harmful to clients. Cade and O'Hanlon (1993) say, "We have become more concerned with the resourcefulness of our clients and with avoiding approaches that disempower either overtly or covertly" (p. xii).

Genter's Brief Strategic Therapy.   In Genter's (1991) brief strategic model, the counselor defines the problem, establishes goals, designs an intervention, assigns a strategic task, emphasizes positive new behavior changes, and then helps the client learn to incorporate new behaviors into everyday living.

The counselor first asks specific and systematic questions to learn client perceptions of the problem and of social circumstances related to the problem. The counselor also explores attempts the client has made to try to resolve the problem. Goals are specific—only those that can be observed and measured directly. Intervention strategies focus on constructive reframing of the problem and on strategic tasks assigned to encourage the client to make gradual, progressive, positive changes in behavior. The client is then encouraged to try out new behaviors and experiences in everyday life.

Solution-Focused Brief Therapy.   Solution-focused brief therapy has been particularly adaptable to limited therapy as practiced in managed care. Steve de Shazer (1988), one originator of this approach, acknowledges the influence of Weakland, Fisch, Watzlawick, and Bodin (1974), Haley (1987), and Erickson (1980).

Counselors using a solution-focused brief model do not analyze or investigate the presenting problems of clients; talking only about constructing solutions has shortened the time necessary to bring about client change. Counselors "realized that only solution goal talk was necessary, that solution construction was independent of problem processes" (Walter & Peller, 1992, p. 8).

Counselors focus on client strengths and on solutions that are different from the unsuccessful methods that clients have been attempting. They look for exceptions to clients' problem behaviors and aim for small changes. Therapists work with clients who are able to cooperate and who have the ability to solve their problems. They start with changes the clients want, help them select goals that will work for them, and help them choose different tasks when their attempts are not successful (Walter & Peller, 1992).

Traditional Cognitive-Behavioral Models Adapted to Brief Therapy

Burbach, Borduin, and Peake (1988) affirm that cognitive and cognitive-behavioral theories "have much to offer the practitioners of brief psychotherapy" (p. 57) because cognitive approaches have traditionally been based on goal-oriented, short-term procedures. Two cognitive-behavioral theorists described earlier in the chapter—Ellis (REBT) and

Lazarus (multimodal therapy)—have adapted their approaches to fit into a brief therapy model. Ellis (1992) perceives little change from his original position that clients learn to reframe or reconstruct and dispute beliefs that are causing emotional or behavioral problems. In a similar vein, Lazarus (1989), who uses a technical eclecticism to help clients solve problems in the modalities (BASIC I.D.) that are causing difficulties, advocates an intermittent short-term approach so that clients, once they solve a certain set of problems, may seek further help as new problems arise.

Limitations of Brief Therapy

Increasing numbers of counselors and therapists, including advocates of brief therapy, are acknowledging that some clients with more severe symptoms or symptoms that are susceptible to relapse require longer therapy. Erica Goode (1998) discusses the importance of distinguishing those clients needing longer term treatment from those who profit best from brief therapy. She recommends that more studies be conducted to determine to what degree the length of counseling depends on the type of client and/or the client problem.

In addition to considering an increase in the number of counseling sessions, more therapists are suggesting intermittent counseling. Psychiatrist Simon Budman, an advocate of brief therapy, is a proponent of this sort of arrangement. Clients, he says, "may benefit from a longer term with a therapist even if they come in for a session every few months, or a few weeks or every few years" (Goode, 1998, p. 10). Budman may see some patients over a period of years, "intermittently dealing with different problems as they come upon the patient's life" (Goode, 1998, p. 10).

Goode (1998) predicts that exerted efforts by both frustrated practitioners and dissatisfied patients eventually will change policy so that allowances for longer term treatment will be granted when necessary.

TOWARD AN INTEGRATIVE THEORETICAL APPROACH

The 1980s saw a growing trend toward eclecticism among practitioners. At that time, surveys consistently showed that eclectic approaches were the primary theoretical orientation among all mental health professionals (Sharf, 2000). Many professionals in the field have criticized eclecticism, however, charging that inexperienced counselors are apt to adopt eclecticism because they are inadequately trained: "A frequent charge leveled at eclectic practitioners is that they employ various techniques indiscriminately, to the detriment of their clients. . . . there is a tendency to assume that haphazard eclecticism results from an atheoretical orientation" (Neimeyer, 1988, p. 285). According to Sharf (2000), unsystematic eclecticism causes problems because "the therapist acts one way at one time and differently at another" (p. 633).

In response to the criticism of eclecticism, increasing numbers of counselors and therapists have moved toward an integrative theoretical approach in which mental health professionals judiciously select and integrate concepts and techniques from, usually, two theoretical systems (Prochaska & Norcross, 2003; Sharf, 2000). This trend has developed for a number of reasons: (a) Research and experience has demonstrated to counselors that no one therapeutic system has proved to be effective with all clients (Seligman, 2001); (b) clients live in varied cultural and social environments and have varied views about the world and the relative impact of inner and outer influences on their development; (c) clients present a wide range of problems and have differing degrees of support; and (d) a broader theoretical approach encompassing a wide selection of techniques allows counselors different approaches for the different stages of the counseling process.

Sharf (2000) presents three different types of integrative approaches: transtheoretical, theoretical integration, and technical eclecticism. The transtheoretical approach tries "to transcend or go beyond specific theoretical constructs" (p. 630) and works toward selecting those concepts and techniques that are compatible. The concepts and techniques used are "based on client readiness for change, type of problem that needs changing, and processes or techniques to bring about change" (p. 630). In theoretical integration professionals combine personality and theoretical concepts from two or more counseling theories into a systematic theoretical whole. In technical eclecticism the professional uses one theoretical view of personality and selects various techniques from many theoretical orientations. "In contrast to unsystematic eclecticsm," Sharf explains, "technical eclecticism is based on a theory of personality" (p. 633). Lazarus's multimodal theory best represents this mode of eclecticism.

R. A. Neimeyer (1995) warns, however, that counselors and therapists using an integrative approach run certain risks:

> The contrasting approach of theoretical integration of conceptually antagonistic models . . . runs the risk of theoretical incoherence. Even appeals to 'common factors' presumed to operate in all therapies or to a 'common language' to transcend the jargon of different schools are not without problems, because they threaten to reduce multifaceted approaches to their 'least common denominator' and to simplify theoretically rich discourse that is grounded in different traditions of thought. (1995, p. 28)

Neimeyer (1998, 2003) makes a sharp distinction, for example, between cognitive and constructivist theoretical approaches, claiming that their similarities tend to be superficial and cover over the underlying metatheoretical differences. Neimeyer takes issue with those who attempt to integrate cognitive and constructivst narrative therapies. "Simply put," says Neimeyer, "the affirmative, respectful, and celebratory spirit of constructivist therapies in relation to client narratives . . . clashes at fundamental levels with the more critical, suspicious, and editorial attitude of traditional cognitive therapists and researchers toward the same material" (Neimeyer, 1998, pp. 62–63). Likewise Neimeyer (2003) makes a distinction between constructivists and cognitivists in regard to compatibility with Adlerian therapy. As for constructivist and Adlerian approaches, he argues that "a genuine theoretical integration of models seems possible . . . [but] integration of Adlerian and cognitive perspectives . . . is likely to be more superficial or partial" (p.135).

Neimeyer (1995) sees the value, however, in promoting discourse among the adherents of differing theoretical approaches as a way toward integrating those approaches. He proposes a model, called *theoretically progressive integrationism (TPI)*, which would minimize the risks inherent in integrative approaches:

> In the ideal case, a TPI model would suggest that the most progressive mergers would be between approaches that were congruent in their central assumptions about the nature of

human beings, the processes of knowing, and so forth, but that were distinctive at more concrete technical levels—thereby contributing to the extension of therapeutic technique within a consistent, but enriched, theoretical framework. (p. 29)

SUMMARY

Counseling theories represent rationales about human nature and development that provide counselors with the means to create a framework that guides the way they view the counseling process, their clients and the way they interact with them, and their goals and techniques. Counseling theories are divided in this text into six categories: (a) psychoanalytic and psychodynamic; (b) humanistic and existential; (c) behavioral, cognitive, and cognitive-behavioral; (d) constructivist and social constructionist; (e) creative and expressive arts and narrative therapies; and (f) brief therapies.

Psychoanalytic and psychodynamic theorists believe that unconscious, intrapsychic forces within individuals are central to behavior. Freud proposed that instinctual, psychosexual (id) forces shape behavior; later psychoanalytic theorists Adler, Horney, and Sullivan emphasized instead that behavior developed within a psychosocial context.

Following them, ego-analytic theorists, notably Erikson, proposed that the ego has its own energies that drive individuals to develop the skill necessary to become autonomous and to master their environment. Object relations theorists added that relationships help one grow and become autonomous. Women at the Stone Center, contrary to ego-analytic and object relations theorists, believe that growth develops through mutual connections in relationships.

Jung parted company with the Freudian theory that the unconscious is basically deterministic and destructive, theorizing instead that the unconscious can be positive and productive when it is integrated into one's consciousness, an endeavor that can be accomplished through imaginative activity related to myths and archetypes. Post-Jungian archetypal psychologists focus more on a metaphorical awareness of one's experience, one that connects with archetypal images. They acknowledge as well the process of depth psychology that involves developing a sense of soul and moral commitment.

Humanists and existentialists believe that humans have potentialities for positive growth. Humanists emphasize that a self-actualizing process moves individuals to increased self-awareness and development. Existentialists assume that individuals' freedom to determine meaning in life creates anxiety, which can potentially become a growth force.

Behavioral theorists believe that behavior is shaped through reinforcement or imitation. Cognitive and cognitive-behavioral theorists assume that perceptions influence one's thinking, feeling, and actions. They both emphasize that learning is central to development. Postmodern personal construct theorists, constructivists, and social constructionists differ from objectivist cognitive psychologists. Personal construct theorists and constructivists believe that individuals have an innate core-ordering capacity for making meaning from experience by forming constructs that shape the way they perceive (construe) events. Social constructionists believe that one's constructs are formed by social-cultural influences.

According to creative arts theorists, individuals' nonverbal expressions through art, dancing, music, or drama or their narrative storytelling help them express underlying feelings blocking their growth.

Brief therapy and counseling theories, developed by both psychodynamic and cognitive-behavioral theorists, have become prominent in practice because of the rising costs of mental health, limited budgets, and an increased demand for counseling in schools, colleges, and the community.

PROJECTS AND ACTIVITIES

1. Compare Rogers's later writings with his original client-centered theory published in 1942. What are the similarities and differences?

2. Interview counselors in a college, in a school, or in the community concerning how they arrived at their current views about counseling theories.

3. Review the work of the women at the Stone Center at Wellesley College regarding their views about the importance of connections in women's development. Do you agree with them that this perspective could apply equally to men's development? Why or why not?

4. Both social learning theorists and phenomenologists agree that perception is an important dimension of behavior. How do they differ in their definitions of the process of perception and the way it relates to behavior or attitudes?

5. Compare a cognitive-behaviorist with a humanist in terms of their views about human nature and their definition of counseling. How do their beliefs and definitions influence their counseling goals and the type of relationship they establish with clients?

6. List techniques used by each of the following: personal construct theorists and Gestaltists. Determine differences in the type and use of the techniques, and indicate how these differences tie in with philosophical views on human nature and reality.

7. Interview several mental health specialists who classify themselves as psychoanalytic counselors or therapists. Compare their views of the therapeutic process with Freud's original descriptions of psychoanalysis. Find out why they classify themselves as psychoanalytic practitioners.

8. Select the theory you like most and the one you like least. Review the current research about the effectiveness of each theory. Does this research change your attitudes or confirm them?

REFERENCES

Alexander, F., & French, T. M. (1946). *Psychoanalytic therapy: Principles and applications.* New York: Ronald Press.

Ansbacher, H. L. (1992). Alfred Adler's concepts of community feeling and social interest and the relevance of community feeling for old age. *Individual Psychology, 48* (4), 402–412.

Ansbacher, H. L., & Ansbacher, R. R. (Eds.). (1973). *Superiority and social interest: A collection of later writings.* New York: Viking.

Arbuckle, D. (Ed.). (1967). *Counseling and psychotherapy: An overview.* New York: McGraw-Hill.

Baker, E. L. (1985). Psychoanalysis and psychoanalytic therapy. In S. J. Lynn & J. R. Garske (Eds.), *Contemporary psychotherapies: Models and methods* (pp. 19–67). Upper Saddle River, NJ: Merrill/Prentice Hall.

Bandura, A. (1977). *Social learning theory.* Upper Saddle River, NJ: Prentice Hall.

Beck, A. T. (1963). Thinking and depression: Idiosyncratic content and cognitive distortions. *Archives of General Psychiatry, 9,* 324–333.

Beck, A. T. (1976a). *Cognitive therapy and emotional disorders.* New York: New American Library.

Beck, A. T. (1976b). *Depression: Clinical, experimental, and theoretical aspects.* New York: Harper & Row.

Beck, A. T., & Weishaar, M. E. (1995). Cognitive therapy. In R. J. Corsini & D. Wedding (Eds.), *Current psychotherapies* (5th ed., pp. 229–261). Itasca, IL: F. E. Peacock.

Bennett, E. A. (1983). *What Jung really said.* New York: Schocken Books.

Berger, P., & Luckman, T. (1966). *The social construction of reality.* Garden City, NY: Doubleday.

Berry, P. (1982). An approach to the dream. In P. Berry, *Echo's subtle body: Contributions to an archetypal psychology* (pp. 53–79). Dallas, TX: Spring.

Bijou, S. W., & Baer, D. M. (1965). *Child's development* (Vol. 2). New York: Appleton-Century-Crofts.

Bly, R. (1990). *Iron John: A book about men.* Reading, MA: Addison-Wesley.

Brammer, L., Abrego, P. J., & Shostrom, E. L. (1993). *Therapeutic counseling and psychotherapy* (6th ed.). Upper Saddle River, NJ: Prentice Hall.

Brill, A. A. (1938). *The basic writings of Sigmund Freud.* New York: Modern Library.

Bruner, J. (1956). Book review of George Kelly's *The psychology of personal constructs. Contemporary Psychology, 1*(12), 355–358.

Bruner, J. (1986). *Actual minds, possible worlds.* Cambridge, MA: Harvard University Press.

Bruner, J. (1990). *Acts of meaning.* Cambridge, MA: Harvard University Press.

Budman, S. H., & Gurman, A. S. (1988). *Theory and practice of brief therapy.* New York: Guilford Press.

Burbach, D. J., Borduin, C. M., & Peake, T. H. (1988). Cognitive approaches to brief psychotherapy. In T. H. Peake, C. M. Borduin, & R. P. Archer, *Brief psychotherapies changing frames of mind* (pp. 57–86). Newbury Park, CA: Sage.

Cade, B., & O'Hanlon, W. H. (1993). *A brief guide to brief therapy.* New York: Norton.

Carlsen, M. B. (1995). Meaning-making and creative aging. In R. A. Neimeyer & M. J. Mahoney (Eds.), *Constructivism in psychotherapy* (pp. 127–153). Washington, DC: American Psychological Association.

Chodorow, N. (1974). Family structure and feminine personality. In M. Z. Rosaldo & L. Lamphere (Eds.), *Woman, culture and society.* Stanford, CA: Stanford University Press.

Conarton, S., & Silverman, L. K. (1988). Feminist developmental theory. In M. A. Dutton-Douglas & L. E. Walker (Eds.), *Feminist psychotherapies: Integration of therapeutic and feminist systems* (pp. 37–67). Norwood, NJ: Ablex.

Corey, G. (2001). *Theory and practice of counseling and psychotherapy* (6th ed.). Pacific Grove, CA: Brooks/Cole.

Dalley, T., Case, C., Schaverien, J., Weir, F., Halliday, D., Hall, P. N., & Waller, D. (1987). *Images of art therapy: New developments in theory and practice.* New York: Tavistock.

Davenloo, H. (Ed.). (1994). *Basic principles and techniques in short-term dynamic psychotherapy.* New York: Spectrum.

de Shazer, S. (1988). *Clues: Investigating solutions in brief therapy.* New York: Norton.

Douglas, C. (1995). Analytical psychotherapy. In R. J. Corsini & D. Wedding (Eds.), *Current psychotherapies* (5th ed., pp. 95–127). Itasca, IL: F. E. Peacock.

Dowd, E.T. (2003). Adlerian, cognitive-behavioral, and constructivist psychotherapies: Commonalities, differences, and integration. In R. E. Watts, *Adlerian, cognitive, and constructivist therapies: An integrative dialogue* (pp. 91–106). New York: Springer.

Dreyfus, E. (1962). Counseling and existentialism. *Journal of Counseling Psychology, 9,* 128–132.

Efran, J. (2002, May/June). Therapeutic vision. *Psychotherapy Networker, 26*(3), 28–35,70.

Ellis, A. (1973). *Humanistic psychotherapy: The rational-emotive approach.* New York: Julian Press.

Ellis, A. (1992). Brief therapy: The rational-emotive method. In S. H. Budman, M. F. Hoyt, & S. Friedman (Eds.), *The first session in brief therapy* (pp. 36–58). New York: Guilford Press.

Ellis, A. (2000). Rational-emotive therapy. In R. J. Corsini & D. Wedding (Eds.), *Current psychotherapies* (6th ed., pp. 168–204). Itasca, IL: F. E. Peacock.

Erickson, M. H. (1980). *The collected papers of Milton H. Erickson on hypnosis: Vol. 4. Innovative hypnotherapy* (E. L. Rossi, Ed.). New York: Irvington.

Erikson, E. H. (1950). *Childhood and society.* New York: Norton.

Erikson, E. H. (1963). *Childhood and society* (2nd ed.). New York: Norton.

Erikson, E. H. (1968). *Identity, youth, and crisis.* New York: Norton.

Erikson, E. H. (1982). *The life cycle completed.* New York: Norton.

Estés, C. P. (1992). *Women who run with the wolves.* New York: Ballantine Books.

Ewen, R. B. (1998). *An introduction to theories of personality* (5th ed.). Mahwah, NJ: Lawrence Erlbaum.

Farber, L. (1966). *The ways of the will.* New York: Basic Books.

Fleshman, B., & Fryrear, J. L. (1981). *The arts in therapy.* Chicago: Nelson-Hall.

Frankl, V. (1963). *Man's search for meaning.* New York: Washington Square Press.

Fransella, F., & Dalton, P. (2000). *Personal construct counselling in action* (2nd ed.). Newbury Park, CA: Sage.

Freud, A. (1966). *The ego and mechanisms of defense.* New York: International Universities Press.

Freud, S. (1949). *An outline of psychoanalysis* (J. Strachey, Trans.). New York: Norton. (Original work published 1940)

Fromm, E. (1941). *Escape from freedom*. New York: Rinehart.

Garfield, S. L. (1989). *The practice of brief psychotherapy*. New York: Pergamon.

Gelso, C. J., & Fretz, B. R. (2001). *Counseling psychology* (2nd ed.). Fort Worth, TX: Harcourt, Brace & Jovanovich.

Genter, D. S. (1991). A brief strategic model for mental health counseling. *Journal of Mental Health Counseling, 13,* 59–68.

Gergen, K. J. (1985). The social constructionist movement in modern psychology. *American Psychologist, 40,* 266–275.

Gilligan, C. (1982). *In a different voice*. Cambridge, MA: Harvard University Press.

Goode, E. (1998, November 24). When is brief therapy enough? *New York Times,* p. 10.

Haley, J. (1987). *Problem-solving therapy* (2nd ed.). San Francisco: Jossey-Bass.

Hall, C. S., & Lindzey, G. (1970). *Theories of personality* (2nd ed.). New York: John Wiley.

Hall, C. S., Lindzey, G., & Campbell, J. B. (1998). *Theories of personality* (4th ed.). New York: John Wiley & Sons.

Hansen, J. C., Rossberg, R. H., & Cramer, S. (1994). *Counseling: Theory and process* (5th ed.). Boston: Allyn & Bacon.

Hartmann, H. (1958). *Ego psychology and the problem of adaptation*. New York: International Universities Press.

Hillman, J. (1975). *Re-visioning psychology*. New York: Harper & Row.

Hillman, J. (1983). *Archetypal psychology: A brief account*. Dallas: Spring.

Hillman, J. (1989). *A blue fire: Selected writings*. New York: Harper Perennial.

Hillman, J., & Ventura, M. (1992). *We've had a hundred years of psychotherapy and the world's getting worse*. New York: Harper.

Horney, K. (1945). *Our inner conflicts*. New York: Norton.

Hosford, R. E., & DeVisser, L. (1974*). Behavioral approaches to counseling: An introduction*. Washington, DC: APGA Press.

Ivey, A. E., D'Andrea, M., Ivey, M. B., & Simek-Morgan, L. (2002). *Counseling and psychotherapy: A multicultural perspective* (5th ed.). Boston: Allyn & Bacon.

Jacobi, J. (1962). *The psychology of C. G. Jung* (6th ed.). New Haven, CT: Yale University Press.

Jankowicz, A. D. (1987). Whatever became of George Kelly? Applications and implications. *American Psychologist, 42,* 481–487.

Jordan, J. V. (Ed.). (1997). *Women's growth in diversity: More writings from the Stone Center*. New York: Guilford Press.

Jordan, J. V., Kaplan, A. G., Miller, J. B., Stiver, I. P., & Surrey, J. L. (1991). *Women's growth in connection: Writings from the Stone Center*. New York: Guilford Press.

Jung, C. G. (1970). *Modern man in search of a soul* (W. S. Dell & C. F. Baynes, Trans.). New York: Harcourt Brace Jovanovich. (Original work published 1933)

Jung, C. G. (1971). *Psychological types* (H. G. Baynes, Trans.; rev. R. F. C. Hull). (Bollingen Series XX, vol. 6). Princeton, NJ: Princeton University Press. (Original work published 1921)

Kaufmann, Y. (1989). Analytical psychotherapy. In R. J. Corsini (Ed.), *Current psychotherapies* (4th ed., pp. 119–152). Itasca, IL: F. E. Peacock.

Kelly, G. A. (1955). *The psychology of personal constructs*. New York: Norton.

Kelly, G. A. (1963). *A theory of personality: The psychology of personal constructs*. New York: Norton.

Kempler, W. (1973). Gestalt therapy. In R. J. Corsini & D. Wedding (Eds*.), Current psychotherapies* (pp. 251–286). Itasca, IL: F. E. Peacock.

Kornfield, J. (1993). *A path with heart: A guide through the perils and promises of spiritual life*. New York: Bantam Books.

Krumboltz, J. D., & Thoresen, C. E. (1976). *Counseling methods*. New York: Holt, Rinehart & Winston.

Lazarus, A. (1976). *Multimodal behavior therapy*. New York: Springer.

Lazarus, A. (1989). Brief psychotherapy: The multimodal model. *Psychology: A Journal of Human Behavior, 26,* 7–10.

Lazarus, A. (1995). Multimodal therapy. In R. J. Corsini & D. Wedding (Eds.), *Current psychotherapies* (5th ed., pp. 322–355). Itasca, IL: F. E. Peacock.

Levine, S. K. (1992). *Poiesis: The language of psychology and the speech of the soul*. Toronto: Palmerston Press.

Levitsky, A., & Perls, I. (1970). The rules and games of Gestalt therapy. In F. Gagan & I. Shepherd (Eds.), *Gestalt therapy now* (pp. 140–149). New York: Harper & Row.

Lyddon, W. J. (1995). Forms and facets of constructivist psychology. In R. A. Neimeyer & M. J. Mahoney (Eds.), *Constructivism in psychotherapy* (pp. 69–92). Washington, DC: American Psychological Association.

Mann, J. (1973). *Time-limited psychotherapy*. New York: McGraw-Hill.

May, R. (1961). *Existential psychology*. New York: Van Nostrand Reinhold.

May, R., & Yalom, I. (2000). Existential psychotherapy. In R. Corsini & D. Wedding (Eds.), *Current psychotherapies* (6th ed., pp. 273–302). Itasca, IL: F. E. Peacock.

McNiff, S. (1988). *Fundamentals of art therapy*. Springfield, IL: Charles C Thomas.

Meade, M. (1993). *Men and the water of life: Initiation and the tempering of men*. San Francisco: Harper.

Meade, M. (2003). *Mosaic Multicultural Foundation brochure*. Seattle: Author.

Meichenbaum, D. (1985). *Stress inoculation training*. New York: Pergamon Press.

Meichenbaum, D. (1993). Stress inoculation training: A twenty-year update. In P. M. Lehrer & R. L. Woolfolk (Eds.), *Principles and practices of stress management* (2nd ed.). New York: Guilford.

Miller, J. B. (1976). *Toward a new psychology of women.* Boston: Beacon Press.

Miller, J. B., & Stiver, I. P. (1997). *The healing connection: How women form relationships in therapy and in life.* Boston: Beacon Press.

Moore, R., & Gillette, D. (1990). *King, warrior, magician, lover: Rediscovering the archetypes of the mature masculine.* San Francisco: Harper.

Moore, T. (1992). *Care of the soul: A guide for cultivating depth and sacredness in everyday life.* New York: HarperCollins.

Neimeyer, G. J. (1995). The challenge of change. In R. A. Neimeyer & M. J. Mahoney (Eds.), *Constructivism in psychotherapy.* (pp. 11–38). Washington, DC: American Psychological Association.

Neimeyer, R. A. (1988). Integrative directions in personal construct therapy. *International Journal of Personal Construct Psychology, 1,* 283–297.

Neimeyer, R. A. (1993). An appraisal of constructivist psychotherapies. *Journal of Consulting and Clinical Psychology, 61*(2), 221–234.

Neimeyer, R. A. (1995). Client-generated narratives in psychotherapy. In R. A. Neimeyer & M. J. Mahoney (Eds.), *Constructivism in psychotherapy.* (pp. 231–246). Washington, DC: American Psychological Association.

Neimeyer, R. A. (1998). Social constructionism in the counseling context. *Counselling Psychology Quarterly, 11*(2), 135–149.

Neimeyer, R. A. (2003). Two paths diverge in a wood: Cognitive-constructivist contrasts and the future evolution of Adlerian psychotherapy. In R. E. Watts, *Adlerian, cognitive, and constructivist therapies: An integrative dialogue* (pp. 122–137). New York: Springer.

Neimeyer, R. A., & Mahoney, M. J. (Eds.). (1995). *Constructivism in psychotherapy.* Washington, DC: American Psychological Association.

Neimeyer, R. A., & Raskin, J. D. (2000). *Constructions of disorder.* Washington, DC: American Psychological Association.

Neimeyer, R. A., & Stewart, A. (1998). Constructivist psychotherapies. *Encyclopedia of Mental Health, 1,* 547–559.

Passons, W. R. (1975). *Gestalt approaches in counseling.* New York: Holt, Rinehart & Winston.

Patterson, G. R., & Guillion, M. E. (1968). *Living with children.* Champaign, IL: Research Press.

Perls, F. S. (1969). *Gestalt therapy verbatim.* Lafayette, CA: Real People Press.

Perls, L. (1976). Comments on the new directions. In E. Smith (Ed.), *The growing edge of Gestalt therapy* (pp. 221–226). New York: Brunner/Mazel.

Phillips, E. L. (1985). *A guide for therapists and patients to short-term psychotherapy.* Springfield, IL: Charles C Thomas.

Pietrofesa, J. J., Hoffman, A., & Splete, H. H. (1984). *Counseling: An introduction* (2nd ed.). Boston: Houghton Mifflin.

Pine, G. J. (1969). The existential school counselor. *Clearing House, 43,* 351–354.

Presbury, J. H., Echtering, L. G., & McKee, J. E. (2002). *Ideas and tools for brief counseling.* Upper Saddle River, NJ: Merrill/Prentice Hall.

Prochaska, J. O., & Norcross, J. C. (2003). *Systems of psychotherapy: A transtheoretical analysis* (4th ed.). Pacific Grove, CA: Brooks/Cole.

Rapaport, D. (1958). The theory of ego autonomy: A generalization. *Bulletin of Menninger Clinic, 22,* 13–55.

Rapaport, D. (1960). *The structure of psychoanalytic theory: A systematizing attempt* [Psychological Issues Monograph No. 6]. New York: International Universities Press.

Raskin, N. J., & Rogers, C. R. (1995). Person-centered therapy. In R. Corsini & D. Wedding (Eds.), *Current psychotherapies* (5th ed., pp. 128–161). Itasca, IL: F. E. Peacock.

Rigazio-DiGilio, S. A. (2000). Reconstructing psychological distress and disorder from a relational perspective: A systemic coconstructive-developmental framework. In R. A. Neimeyer, & J. D. Raskin, *Constructions of disorder* (pp. 309–332). Washington, DC: American Psychological Association.

Robbins, A. (1980). *Expressive therapy: A creative arts approach to depth-oriented treatment.* New York: Human Sciences Press.

Rogers, C. R. (1939). *The clinical treatment of the problem child.* Boston: Houghton Mifflin.

Rogers, C. R. (1942). *Counseling and psychotherapy.* Boston: Houghton Mifflin.

Rogers, C. R. (1951). *Client-centered therapy: Its current practice, implications, and theory.* Boston: Houghton Mifflin.

Rogers, C. R. (1957). The necessary and sufficient conditions of therapeutic personality change. *Journal of Consulting Psychology, 21,* 95–103.

Rogers, C. R. (1961). *Becoming a person.* Boston: Houghton Mifflin.

Rogers, C. R. (1970). *Carl Rogers on encounter groups.* New York: Harper & Row.

Ryckman, R. M. (1997). *Theories of personality* (6th ed.). Pacific Grove, CA: Brooks/Cole.

Samuels, A. (1985). *Jung and the post-Jungians.* New York: Routledge.

Seligman, L. (2001). *Systems, strategies, and skills of counseling and psychotherapy.* Upper Saddle River, NJ: Merrill/Prentice Hall.

Sharf, R. S. (2000). *Theories of psychotherapy and counseling: Concepts and cases* (2nd ed.). Belmont, CA: Wadsworth/Brooks/Cole.

Sifneos, P. E. (1987). *Short-term dynamic psychotherapy* (2nd ed.). New York: Plenum Press.

Skinner, B. F. (1953). *Science and human behavior.* New York: Macmillan.

Strohl, J. E. (1998). Transpersonalism: Ego meets soul. *Journal of Counseling & Development, 76,* 397–403.

Strupp, H. H. (1981). Toward the refinement of time—limited dynamic psychotherapy. In S. H. Budman (Ed.), *Forms of brief therapy* (pp. 219–242). New York: Guilford Press.

Strupp, H. H., & Binder, J. (1984). *Psychotherapy in a new key: A guide to time-limited dynamic psychotherapy.* New York: Basic Books.

Thoresen, C. E., & Mahoney, M. J. (1974). *Behavioral self-control.* New York: Holt, Rinehart & Winston.

Van Kaam, A. (1967). Counseling and psychotherapy from the viewpoint of existential psychology. In D. Arbuckle (Ed.), *Counseling and psychotherapy: An overview* (pp. 20–52). New York: McGraw-Hill.

Viney, L. L. (1993). *Life stories: Personal construct theory with elderly.* Chichester, UK: John Wiley.

Walsh, R. (2000). Asian psychotherapies. In R. J. Corsini & D. Wedding (Eds.), *Current psychotherapies* (6th ed., pp. 547–560). Itasca, IL: F. E. Peacock.

Walter, J. L., & Peller, J. E. (1992). *Becoming solution-focused in brief therapy.* New York: Brunner/Mazel.

Watts, R. (2003). *Adlerian, cognitive, and constructivist therapies.* New York: Springer.

Weakland, J. H., Fisch, R., Watzlawick, P., & Bodin, A. (1974). Brief therapy: Focused problem resolution. *Family Process, 13,* 141–168.

Wells, R. A. (1994). *Planned short-term treatment* (2nd ed.). New York: Free Press.

White, H. S., Burke, J. D., & Havens, L. L. (1981). Choosing a method of short-term therapy: A developmental approach. In S. H. Budman (Ed.), *Forms of brief therapy* (pp. 243–267). New York: Guilford Press.

White, M., & Epston, D. (1990). *Narrative means to therapeutic ends.* New York: Norton.

Wilson, G. T. (1995). Behavior therapy. In R. Corsini & D. Wedding (Eds.), *Current psychotherapies* (5th ed., pp. 197–228). Itasca, IL: F. E. Peacock.

Wolberg, L. R. (1980). *Handbook of short-term psychotherapy.* New York: Thieme-Stratton.

Wolpe, J. (1958). *Psychotherapy by reciprocal inhibition.* Stanford, CA: Stanford University Press.

Wolpe, J. (1969). *The practice of behavior therapy.* New York: Pergamon.

Woodworth, R. S., & Sheehan, M. (1964). *Contemporary schools of psychology* (3rd ed.). New York: Ronald Press.

Yalom, I. D. (1980). *Existential psychotherapy.* New York: Basic Books.

Yalom, I. D. (2002). *Gift of therapy: An open letter to a new generation of therapists and their patients.* New York: Harper Collins.

Yontef, G. M., & Simkin, J. S. (1989). Gestalt therapy. In R. J. Corsini & D. Wedding (Eds.), *Current psychotherapies* (4th ed., pp. 323–361). Itasca, IL: F. E. Peacock.

CHAPTER 7

Assessment: Tools and Processes

Counselors use assessment tools such as tests, interviews, and observations to help clients in their exploration of themselves and their problems. Although ambiguity exists in the use of the terms *assessment* and *testing* and some individuals use them interchangeably, most experts make a distinction. Cohen and Swerdlik (2002) distinguish the terms as follows: *Psychological assessment* is "the gathering and integration of psychology-related data for the purpose of making a psychological evaluation, accomplished through the use of tools such as tests, interviews, case studies, behavioral observation, and specially designed apparatuses and measurement procedures" (p. 4). By contrast, "a *test* may be defined simply as a measuring device or procedure" (p. 6); and *psychological testing* is "the process of measuring psychology-related variables by means of devices or procedures designed to obtain a sample of behavior" (p. 4).

Psychological tests, called *standardized tests,* originated during World War I, when psychologists developed screening tests for the U.S. Army. The tests flourished with the popularity of psychology of individual differences in the 1920s and 1930s (see chap. 2).

Tests are just one form of assessment among many devices used by counselors. Assessment of one kind or another occurs throughout the counseling sessions. *Evaluation* is another term used frequently in the assessment procedure; it refers to a process that counselor and client use to integrate test scores, the results of other measurement devices, and counselor-client interview comments and observations in order to help the client gain insight into feelings and assess progress in resolving concerns.

In the pre–World War II days of guidance counseling, the primary task for counselors was that of making vocational assessments of clients through the use of standardized tests. The counselors' approach was based on a diagnostic model in which clients were perceived as having fixed personality traits that could be measured through standardized interest and aptitude tests and personality inventories.

Carl Rogers (1942, 1951) objected to this approach because it counteracts the belief that humans are dynamic individuals capable of change. The popularity of his client-centered counseling during the 1950s through the 1970s resulted in a sharp decline in counselors' use of tests and assessments. This change from diagnosing traits to facilitating self-exploration dramatically influenced the direction of counseling. Most counselors who continued to use standardized tests and inventories did so only after a counseling relationship was established and then only to enhance client self-exploration. Effective counselors still hold to this practice today.

Those counselors who continued to use standardized tests in a predictive way were challenged by testing and assessment specialist Leo Goldman in his classic article "Tests and Counseling: The Marriage That Failed" (1972). In a more recent article (1994) he explains:

> The main problem with tests was that they had been developed in the first place for *selection* purposes, and that the typical level of predictive validity that made tests useful for selecting college students or employees had a very different meaning and value when used in *counseling*. (p. 214)

Noting that standardized tests were also narrow and limited in scope, Goldman (1972) suggested that different types of tests should be designed and published that could be used to help clients explore their potentialities. Subsequently, he recommended that a qualitative assessment approach be emphasized in counseling instead of standardized tests:

> Qualitative assessment methods typically are holistic and integrated. . . . Compared with standardized tests, they offer a more active role for clients, a more intimate connection between assessment and the counseling process, and greater adaptability to ethnic cultural, age, gender, and other individual differences. (Goldman, 1990, p. 205)

Goldman suggests that counselors who use tests need to integrate client scores with client self-reports as a way of increasing client self-understanding, a position upheld by Nugent (1981) as well. Goldman (1972, 1992) also objects to most counselors not being adequately trained to use tests. Either they have had insufficient course work in test selection, administration, and interpretation, or they have had courses that emphasize using tests in a diagnostic, predictive manner.

NEW EXPECTATIONS FOR COUNSELORS

Since the 1980s a dramatic upsurge has occurred in the numbers and types of tests used in counseling. "Nearly ten million counselors each year complete 'tests,' 'inventories' and other 'assessments'—and that estimate does not include school achievement tests or college entrance exams" (Prediger, 1994, p. 228). One need only observe the huge booths displaying testing and assessment tools at counseling and psychological conventions or notice the catalogs from over a dozen testing companies to realize how many thousands of psychological tests are now available and in use. Moreover, these companies offer computerized scoring and standardized interpretations that make tests easy and efficient for anyone to use.

Although tests are easier to administer and score, the vast array of types of tests makes selection and interpretation more confusing than ever—especially to the inexperienced or minimally trained counselor, who is apt to overuse or misuse tests or to misinterpret their results. Goldman (1994) is so dissatisfied with the lack of adequate courses about tests and measurements in counseling programs that he recommends, "Standardized tests would be best used by perhaps 10% of counselors who are well qualified in quantitative methods, whereas the 90% would make better use of qualitative assessment methods" (p. 217).

Testing specialist Dale Prediger (1994) responds to Goldman in the article "Tests and Counseling: The Marriage That Prevailed." A long-time advocate of Goldman's position, Prediger concurs with Goldman's feelings of discouragement about the use of testing in counseling. And he agrees with Goldman that the poor quality of tests and the lack of adequate counselor training in their selection, use, and interpretation persist today: "We are still in the snake-oil era of testing. . . . I invite evidence that professional practice has improved" (p. 229).

Prediger (1994) does not think that all is lost, however, in the alliance between testing and counseling. Although he concurs with Goldman's preference for qualitative testing, he argues that using only qualitative assessment is unrealistic for most counselors because it is too time-consuming. Furthermore, he believes that client self-estimates without confirming data may be inaccurate or incomplete. He suggests instead that test score interpretations be used to help clients make more informed and accurate self-estimates: "Ability test scores should not be used as substitutes for ability self-estimates. Instead, they should be used to inform self-estimates/concepts" (p. 232).

DIFFERENT WAYS COUNSELORS USE ASSESSMENT

Today, the use of assessment has become much more complex as counselors have spread into the community, working in a variety of agencies and in private practice. Counselors need to develop or upgrade their assessment skills for a variety of reasons:

- Counselors have sharply increased their use of standardized and nonstandardized tests and inventories, which have proliferated and are both readily available and easy to use.
- Increasing numbers of counselors are expected to conduct intake interviews for prospective clients to determine the most suitable counseling plans for them.
- In all work settings, counselors are increasingly involved in crisis intervention as the number of individuals experiencing emotional upheavals has escalated.
- Increasing numbers of counselors, particularly clinical mental health counselors, are conducting diagnostic psychological evaluations for community and government agencies.
- Increasing numbers of clinical mental health counselors are employed in managed care programs that require the use of the *Diagnostic and Statistical Manual of Mental Disorders* (American Psychiatric Association, 2000).

The types of assessment used in intake interviewing, in counseling, and in career centers are quite different from those used in crisis intervention and in diagnostic evaluation for outside agencies. The primary distinction is that, in the former instances, assessment remains confidential to the client; in the latter, assessment information is not confidential to the client and is generally not shared with her or him.

It is important that counselors who are involved in multiple roles of assessment not mix or confuse their roles. For example, they should not diagnose an individual for another agency who happens to be one of their own clients. Counselors also should not agree to take a person on as a client during a diagnostic evaluation of that person. This separation of duties helps counselors maintain nonevaluative, trust relationships with their clients. It also helps counselors maintain a nonevaluative image for the sake of all people who seek counseling help. For similar reasons university counseling centers should be kept separate from university testing centers. If centers combine the two services, they assume dual roles, which are apt to confuse students and inhibit them from using the counseling center for fear that reports would be submitted to the administration.

Intake Interviewing

An intake interview is used to help determine the most suitable counseling plan for a prospective client. After conducting the interview, the intake counselor assigns the individual to an appropriate counselor. Intake interviewing involves a structured exploration to gain information about a client's presenting problem. Questions typically include what the nature of the problem is, how long the problem has persisted, whether the individual has had previous counseling, what the individual's current career or educational status is, and what current and past interactions have occurred with her or his family.

An intake interviewer then determines which of the counseling staff has the personal characteristics or professional specialization that best fits the prospective client's particular needs. Intake interviewers may recommend that a client be referred to another counseling service that better suits the needs of the individual; for example, a client with a chronic eating disorder might be referred to a clinic specializing in addictions.

If the center has a waiting list, intake interviewers determine when persons can be seen, consistent with the urgency of their problems. Information gained in intake is confidential to the intake interviewer and the assigned counselor.

Assessment During Counseling

The primary method of assessment that counselors use during the counseling process is interviewing. In many cases this assessment method is sufficient to help clients self-explore and also to help them develop joint strategies to resolve problems.

Counselors may decide that information from standardized tests would help supplement and augment information from interviews. Counselors often differ in the extent and type of assessment they use during counseling or therapy, depending on their theoretical orientation. Humanists, as a rule, depend almost entirely on the interviewing process, with only occasional use of self-exploratory measures. Psychoanalysts or psychodynamic counselors or therapists more readily use projective techniques, drawings, stories, or inventories that tap clients' unconscious. Behaviorists and cognitive-behaviorists tend to use structured interviews and instruments that measure observable behavior; they tend to use behavioral rating scales or checklists to assess client behavior. Cognitive behaviorists may use self-monitoring devices to help clients, for example, manage caloric intake or quit smoking.

If testing is agreed on, counselors select appropriate tests of high quality, arrange for administration and scoring of these measures, and then make appropriate, meaningful interpretations. Counselors may administer tests themselves or have psychometrists do them. In public schools scores from standardized tests, which are administered school-wide, are generally available in student cumulative records.

As indicated earlier, most standardized tests have been computerized; in some cases they give not only scores or patterns of scores but also computerized interpretations. Some self-inventories can be easily scored by counselors or clients; a measure like Holland's Self-Directed-Search (SDS) is designed to be self-administered and self-scored.

Learning how to select standardized tests and other assessment methods is only part of the training program in assessment. Learning how to interpret results of assessments and how to interpret clinical observations is the most crucial part of the assessment process. It is also the most misused and neglected. Interpretation involves integrating results from test scores, interviews, and personal observations into a meaningful, accurate pattern that contributes to a greater understanding of the individual and the individual's problem.

Test results should not be used to label clients in ways that will determine or shape the direction of the counseling process. This caution applies especially to computerized interpretations supplied by testing corporations. Assessments of an individual's responses and personality characteristics may change during the counseling process. The counselor makes nonjudgmental, tentative assessments of an exploratory nature and gives feedback to the client that will help clarify the client's feelings and encourage deeper self-exploration. Then counselor and client together make a working hypothesis about the client's problem, a mutual assessment that will help determine a plan of counseling action.

Interpretation of a client's apparent behavioral characteristics often focuses on unraveling and reshaping the client's distorted opinions about his or her behavior. The timing of that interpretation is crucial. Counselors generally withhold making judgments in the initial sessions of counseling, although they are keenly attentive to observing their clients' behavior. These observations provide tentative assessments that will be useful in later interactions during the counseling process.

The mode of interpreting standardized tests differs from that of nonstandardized tests. Interpreting standardized tests is fairly simple and clear-cut; the counselor compares the client's scores with those of an appropriate norm group on which the test was standardized. Percentile scores indicate how well the individual ranks in comparison with the norm group. This simplicity has its dangers, however; counselors must be careful not to rely only on test scores or on commercial interpretations, but rather to integrate them with other assessments.

Nonstandardized assessment is more complex. Counselors must attend to clients' verbal comments, body language, and degree of nervousness; they must avoid making snap judgments about individuals, but instead must observe clients' comments and behavior within the context of the overall counseling experience.

Career Counseling Centers

Counselors in career centers colleges and communities are the ones who most often use vocational interest inventories, aptitude tests, and personality inventories. Their primary focus is to help clients find job placement in the workforce appropriate to their interests, aptitudes, and personality traits. Counselors arrange for clients to take batteries of tests based on client need; integrate results into occupational profiles; and then match these profiles with occupations that require worker traits similar to those of the clients.

Crisis Intervention

In crisis intervention, counselors are suddenly called on to work with individuals who are unable to cope and who are generally not the counselors' clients. The counselors' job involves assessing the persons, determining the degree or severity of their conditions, and then making referrals based on the assessments.

Crisis counselors must first help disoriented or out-of-control individuals regain their equilibrium as much as possible. To accomplish this, counselors direct the interviews to identify and clarify the severity of the precipitating problems while at the same time helping the individuals release emotions and calm down (see "Crisis Intervention" in chap. 8).

Because there is no time to use standardized tests, counselors rely on structured interviews and observations. They need to recognize signs of suicidal intentions, psychotic breakdown, or drug overdose; assessment checklists are available detailing behaviors related to the severity of such crises.

A crisis intervention may involve one or two meetings to enable an individual to stabilize and regain coping skills. Then the crisis counselor can determine whether ongoing counseling or more intensive therapy is needed. If so, the individual will be referred to another counselor in the agency or to a psychiatric service at another agency. In some cases it may be necessary to recommend mandatory psychiatric services to protect individuals from harming themselves or others (see chap. 8).

Diagnostic Evaluation for Agencies

Some counselors and mental health workers perform various kinds of psychological evaluations for community agencies that need to make psychological decisions about certain individuals. These decisions may require clinical assessment to determine, for example, whether the individuals need to be involuntarily committed to a mental institution; whether they are emotionally or mentally competent to stand trial; or whether they are qualified for vocational rehabilitation or for Social Security disability benefits.

In the past, master's degree counselors generally were not involved in diagnostic evaluations for agencies. But as licensing and private practice have increased and diagnostic evaluations have become a lucrative business, more counselors have become involved in this activity. Diagnostic evaluations require special training in the use and interpretation of individual psychological measures. A counselor's recommendations can have a profound and lasting effect on the lives of the individuals being assessed. Clinical mental health counselors now include diagnostic evaluation of pathology in their training programs and list this form of evaluation as one expected competency. Other counselors who want to use the *DSM-IV-TR* should also take special training.

TYPES OF ASSESSMENT

Counselors and therapists assess clients in basically two ways: nonstandardized, or qualitative measures, and standardized, or quantitative measures. *Nonstandardized measures* are informed observations about client behavior or clients' self-reports about their feelings, interests, attitudes, and experiences. The assessments are specific to a particular client, and there are no formal procedures for administering and scoring these assessments. In qualitative assessment, counselors use their clinical skills to interpret observations and self-reports and share the results with their clients. *Standardized measures* are based on statistically derived norm groups, with formal and consistent procedures for administering and scoring. Interpretations are based on a comparison of client scores with those of individuals on whom the measure was standardized.

Nonstandardized or Qualitative Assessment Skills

Client observation is an important skill counselors use to assess clients' emotional frame of mind and readiness to interact with counselors. Clients' degree of anxiety, depression, uncertainty, or resentment can often be gauged by their body behavior: Do they sit slumped in a chair? Do their hands or voices tremble? Are they alert or distracted? However, counselors should guard against automatically perceiving a client's body behavior as a sign of emotional distress. A squirming client, for example, may be sitting in an uncomfortable chair or may have a back problem.

Cognitive-behavioral counselors prefer behavioral observations rather than tests or inventories, which infer underlying client dynamics. They often record their observations in their case notes. Those interested in systematic recording of client behavior can use checklists to mark off whether a client is demonstrating some particular behavior that is considered significant. Some may even use rating scales, ranging from never to always.

Some counselors use client self-reports of various types to encourage client self-observation and self-exploration. These self-reports are as diverse as questionnaires designed to obtain background information, autobiographical or personal essays, or journal keeping. Self-monitoring schedules, in which clients collect and record data of their own behavior, are used frequently. Examples of questionnaires and scales that involve self-reports are the Social Anxiety Inventory, Agoraphobic Questionnaire Cognitions, and the Fear Survey Schedule (Kleinknecht, 1986). Client self-observations contribute to counselors' understanding of client needs or conflicts.

Standardized Tests and Inventories

Unlike informal intuitive procedures, standardized tests and inventories are systematically and statistically designed to give objective information about certain specific client characteristics or behaviors. The two basic types of measurements are tests and inventories.

Tests entail right or wrong answers and measure a person's cognitive, intellectual, or achievement levels. *Inventories,* in contrast, are not concerned with correctness of response, but with descriptive aspects of the client: personality characteristics, values, needs, or degree of emotional well-being or pathology.

A client's scores on a particular standardized test or inventory are compared with the scores of particular groups of people on whom the test was standardized. These comparative representative scores, called *norms,* add meaning to a client's raw scores. Clients' scores on an intelligence test, for example, can be compared with those of an appropriate norm group to determine whether the clients' scores are higher, at the same level, or lower than other representative individuals like them. Norms are usually nationally based, but they can also be regionally or even locally based.

Effective counselors are aware of the possible abuse of norm grouping, particularly with ethnic groups. Multicultural groups have criticized standardized tests whose item choices and norm groups are based on White, middle-class, male youth populations. Of particular concern are intelligence tests and personality inventories. Sue and Sue (2003) say, "The improper use of such instruments can lead to an exclusion of minorities in jobs and promotion, to discriminatory educational decisions, and to biased determination of what constitutes pathology" (p. 48). Cohen and Swerdlik (2002) further explain:

> Items on tests of intelligence tend to reflect the culture of the society where such tests are employed. To the extent that a score on such a test reflects the degree to which the testtakers have been integrated into the society and the culture, it would be expected that members of subcultures . . . would score lower. (p. 247)

To decrease test bias, psychologists attempted to develop culture-fair and culture-specific tests, but they have not proved successful. *Culture-fair tests* include items common to all cultures; a *culture-specific test* contains items expressly related to a specific subculture. Culture-fair tests have had little success as accurate measures of minority groups, and culture-specific tests have low predictive value for the specific cultural group (Cohen & Swerdlik, 2002). According to Cohen and Swerdlik (2002), "Major tests of intelligence have undergone a great deal of scrutiny for bias in many investigations . . . and it has generally been concluded that these tests are relatively free of any systematic bias" (p. 253). Meanwhile, counselors are being alerted to their own biases in selecting and interpreting tests for minorities.

Counselors must also be aware of the reliability and validity of standardized tests. *Reliability* refers to "the degree to which test scores are consistent, dependable, and repeatable" (Drummond, 2000, p. 43). *Validity* refers to the degree to which a test score measures what it claims to measure. For example, individuals who score high on a measure of mechanical ability should be expected to do well on mechanical jobs or in mechanical training.

Reliability can be assessed in three ways: *retest,* in which one administers the same test twice; *parallel form,* in which one administers an equivalent form; and *split-half,* in which two or more equivalent portions are given to determine the internal consistency of the tests (Thorndike, 1997).

Validity, too, can be assessed in three ways: *Content validity,* often referred to as *face validity,* indicates to what extent a test measures what it is supposed to measure. This form is most often used in achievement and ability testing. *Criterion-related validity* measures how well an individual's scores compare to a particular criterion of success. For example, individuals' scores on a spatial aptitude test may be compared to their success as draftsmen. *Construct validity* indicates whether a test measures the particular construct it is supposed to measure. This form of validity is particularly applicable to unobservable constructs, such as personality and interest variables (Cohen & Swerdlik, 2002; Thorndike, 1997).

Counselors generally use five types of standardized measures: three are tests—intelligence, aptitude, and achievement—and two are inventories—interest and personality.

Intelligence Tests

Intelligence tests are designed to measure general academic ability or the ability to perform successfully in academic settings. Such tests fall into two categories: (a) intelligence tests that are designed to be administered only to an individual by a specially trained mental health worker and (b) intelligence tests that are designed to be administered to groups but can also be given to an individual. Also discussed is the theory of multiple intelligences (MI). Many researchers have criticized traditional intelligence tests; most notably, Howard Gardner (1993) challenges the assumption that intelligence is based only on a person's intellectual capacity to perform academically.

Individually Administered Intelligence Tests. The two major intelligence tests that are individually administered are the Stanford Binet and the Wechsler Intelligence Scales. The Stanford Binet grew out of an intelligence scale developed by Alfred Binet in France in 1905 to screen mental retardation in children. It was designed only for use with children and adolescents because of its content and because it is standardized on children and adolescents. It relies only on verbal responses. The Wechsler scales are a variety of tests designed for all ages, including the Wechsler Adult Intelligence Scale (WAIS-III) for ages 16 and older; the Wechsler Intelligence Scale for Children (WISC-III) for ages 6 to 16 years 11 months; and the Wechsler Preschool and Primary Scale of Intelligence–Revised (WPPSI-R) for ages 4 to 6½. The Wechsler scales also differ from the Binet in that they include performance tasks as well as verbal responses. For these reasons the Wechsler scales are widely used for all age levels in measuring intelligence (Walsh & Betz, 2001).

Group Intelligence Tests. Group intelligence tests are often used when counselors and clients decide it is important to obtain a measure of scholastic aptitude. These tests usually measure a component of intelligence. Verbal and numerical reasoning are most often used in school and college settings. A client may be having academic difficulties in a school setting, or a client may be contemplating college with an academic record that is mediocre. The client or the counselor or both may believe that the academic record underestimates the client's true ability, so an intelligence test is used to make comparisons. The most commonly used are the Otis-Lennon School Ability Test, the Henmon-Nelson Tests of Mental Ability (K–12), the California Short Form of Mental Ability, the School and College Ability Tests (SCAT), and the Scholastic Aptitude Test (SAT). A group intelligence test often used in business or in government agencies to help in selecting individuals for job placement is the Wonderlic Personnel Test (Walsh & Betz, 2001).

Multiple Intelligences (MI).   Gardner (1993) challenges the traditional measurements of intelligence, claiming that they measure only an individual's intellectual capacity to perform academically. Years ago he began questioning the method of assessing intelligence:

> There must be more to intelligence than short answers to short questions—answers that predict academic success. . . . The problem lies . . . in the ways in which we customarily think about the intellect and in our ingrained views of intelligence. Only if we expand and reformulate our view of what counts as human intellect will we be able to devise more appropriate ways of assessing it and more effective ways of educating it. (p. 4)

Thus, Gardner (1993) spends considerable time inquiring into the nature of intelligence, challenging the traditional assumption that a person's intelligence is a single entity that is inherited. He and other researchers propose that there are "a multitude of intelligences, quite independent of each other; that each intelligence has its own strengths and constraints" (p. xix).

In his naming of several human intelligences—linguistic, musical, logical-mathematical, spatial, bodily-kinesthetic, and personal—Gardner (1993) warns that these names are only convenient constructs: "These intelligences are fictions—at most, useful fictions. . . . [T]hey exist not as physically verifiable entities but only as potentially useful scientific constructs" (p. 70).

The theory of MI proposes that humans are limited by their cultural domain and by their *field*. In other words, development of intelligences is constrained by the context in which one lives:

> Human beings are born into cultures that house a large number of *domains*—disciplines, crafts, and other pursuits in which one can become enculturated and then be assessed in terms of the level of competence one has attained. (p. xvi)
>
> . . . Once one achieves a certain competence, the *field* becomes very important. The field—a sociological construct—includes the people, institutions, award mechanisms, and so forth that render judgments about the qualities of individual performances. (p. xvii)

MI assessment measures, Gardner emphasizes, are radically opposed to the standard systems of measuring intelligence. First, MI cannot be assessed by a single test taken in an hour or so and out of the context of one's life. Assessment of MI must be conducted over time by observing individuals in the context of their real-life situations. Furthermore, MI can be measured at different times in one's life.

MI criteria, differing from those of standard intelligence tests, focus primarily on the person's problem-solving ability in various situations. Moreover, the criteria vary across human cultures:

> To my mind, a human intellectual competence must entail a set of skills of problem solving—enabling the individual to *resolve genuine problems or difficulties* that he or she encounters and, when appropriate, to create an effective product—and must entail the potential for *finding or creating problems*—thereby laying the groundwork for the acquisition of new knowledge. (Gardner, 1993, pp. 60–61)

Although the process of developing adequate MI assessment measures is fairly new, Gardner is optimistic. Assessment procedures to measure MI would be very useful, he says, because they would measure a much broader aspect of human abilities; moreover, they would present a much broader, clearer picture of an individual's multiple capacities to learn.

Aptitude Tests

Aptitude tests, like intelligence tests, measure an individual's ability to learn but are more specific to given areas of performance. These tests usually include some form of verbal, abstract reasoning, numerical, spatial, mechanical, and clerical ability. Counselors tend to use aptitude tests in career counseling in a variety of settings—schools and colleges, community career centers, employment agencies, and personnel services in business and industry.

Multiple aptitude batteries provide a comparative profile of scores based on the same norm group. The three batteries most often used by counselors are the Differential Aptitude Tests (DAT), the Armed Service Vocational Aptitude Battery (ASVAB), and the General Aptitude Test Battery (GATB). Aptitude batteries are developed to predict how well one will do in specific jobs or training programs. The content of these batteries is determined from analyses of numerous jobs, based on the assumption that different aptitudes relate to different jobs (Thorndike, 1997).

The DAT is specifically designed for high school students exploring career or curricular choices. The ASVAB, originally developed to classify armed services recruits, is now offered by the U.S. Department of Defense to high school students in 15,000 schools at no cost to the students or the school districts. The GATB, used predominantly in state employment services, has for many years been the most widely used battery in career counseling and placement. The GATB also includes performance tests measuring finger dexterity, manual dexterity, and motor coordination—abilities necessary in jobs requiring skills in working with one's hands and with small objects. The GATB currently is administered only in government employment agencies. Counselors in other settings can obtain the results, however, through a written request and with the consent of the client.

Achievement Tests

Counselors use achievement tests primarily in educational settings to help clients explore curricular or career options when proficiency in a specific subject is important. Achievement batteries are given to students in most school districts at specified grade levels; all states use some form of statewide standardized achievement tests in public schools (Thorndike, 1997). The same tests are used either for the entire student body or at a specified grade level, and results are placed in students' cumulative files. Counselors and clients can then make use of them in counseling sessions when students want information about their competencies in various subject areas. Examples of these batteries include the Iowa Tests of Basic Skills (ITBS), used in elementary schools; and the Metropolitan Achievement Tests (MAT), the Stanford Achievement Tests, and the Iowa Tests of Educational Development (ITED), used in elementary and secondary schools.

An achievement test often used by community counselors is the Wide Range Achievement Test (WRAT). This battery—which measures reading, spelling, and arithmetic competencies—has norms from kindergarten to 75 years of age. It is individually administered and is used along with individual intelligence tests to determine whether an individual has a learning disability.

Interest Inventories

When clients are concerned about career choices or are seriously dissatisfied with their jobs, counselors often use vocational interest measures to help them identify a more satisfying choice of job or career. The three major interest measures are Holland's Self-Directed Search (SDS) for high school and college students and adults; the Strong Interest Inventory (SII) for high school seniors, college students, and adults; and the Kuder Occupational Interest Survey Revised (KOIS-R) for high school students. These inventories, in one form or another, compare client vocational interest scores with those of persons in business, professional, scientific, artistic, technical, and social service occupations.

In recent years the SDS has become "one of the most widely used interest inventories" (Drummond, 2000, p. 176). The SDS was published in 1971 and has been revised several times. This self-administered, self-scored, and self-interpreted inventory measures an individual's self-reported occupational interests and classifies responses into six personality types: realistic, artistic, investigative, social, enterprising, and conventional (RAISEC). These personality types are then correlated to more than 1,000 occupational groups (see chap. 12). Although the SDS is designed for individual self-interpretation, it is best used in counseling sessions with a counselor assisting in the interpretation as (Thorndike, 1997).

The SII is the granddaddy of interest measurement tests. Originally published in 1927, it has gone through innumerable revisions. The inventory compares an individual's profile of scores to more than 200 occupational scales and relates them to Holland's six occupational themes (RAISEC). Originally based primarily on professional occupations, its latest revision (1994) added significantly more nonprofessional or vocational technical occupations. In addition, the two separate women's and men's forms were combined into one form to allow responses free of gender bias (Walsh & Betz, 2001).

Another pioneer interest inventory, KOIS-R, which was introduced in 1934 and revised several times, has 119 occupational scales and 48 college major scales. It has norms for high school, college, and adult populations. Compared with the SII, the Kuder scales cover a wider range of occupations and include more nonprofessional and technical occupations.

Personality Measures

Counselors use personality measures (a) to assess client personality traits or characteristics, (b) to compare client characteristics with those of individuals in various occupations or careers, and (c) to assess a client's degree of emotional trauma or pathology. Personality measures are of two forms: objective inventories and projective techniques. *Objective inventories* are self-reports in which clients respond to a series of statements related to their personality characteristics. *Projective techniques* are used to tap a person's unconscious reactions to ambiguous pictures or images or through storytelling or drawing.

Objective Inventories. Examples of objective personality inventories are the California Psychological Inventory–Revised (CPI-R); the Myers-Briggs Type Indicator (MBTI); the Minnesota Multiphasic Personality Inventory (MMPI); and the Edwards Personal Preference Schedule (EPPS). Effective counselors use scores on these measures as indicators of client predispositions capable of change, rather than as fixed, static traits. For example, clients who have low sociability scores and are concerned about their ineffective relationships can be helped to develop social skills, or clients showing obsessive-compulsive behavior can learn to modify their behavior through counseling and therapy.

The CPI-R is used with clients 13 years of age and older. Personal characteristics in the inventory focus on social interactions and feelings of adequacy. Scales presented of desirable characteristics include such areas as sociability, social presence, self-acceptance, sense of well-being, and self-control.

The MBTI is based on Carl Jung's theory of typology. The MBTI was developed by a mother-daughter team, Isabel Briggs Myers and Katherine C. Briggs. Many counselors in colleges and in the community use the inventory to help their clients gain some understanding of how their typology relates to career choices or to personal and social functioning.

Jung's theory of typology is complicated, but basically persons are perceived as either extraverted or introverted. A person is also governed by four functions that are divided into two oppositional pairs: sensory/intuitive and thinking/feeling. Jung's typology is not intended to categorize individuals into personality types that determine their behavior (Pascal, 1992). It is meant to help explore one's inner world, the world of the unconscious, a task usually reserved for the later part of life. The typology serves as a theoretical base from which the analyst can work to help clients develop their inferior functions. In this way clients make changes that lead to wholeness and individuation.

Why is the MBTI so popular among young, career-minded people? Myers-Briggs expanded on Jung's typology system by adding another set of oppositional scales—judgment/perceiving—thus making the patterns of typology more applicable to how one functions in the external world. Spoto (1989) says:

> By developing the perceiving-judging polarity as a separate criterion and then combining it with Jung's basic typological theory and principles, Briggs-Myers implicitly urges users of Jung's original typological theory to be more careful observers of those patterns of behavior relating specifically to the external world. (p. 131)

The MMPI is one of the most widely used personality measures in clinical mental health practice. The inventory consists of eight clinical scales based on psychiatric-psychological symptoms of neurosis or psychosis: hypochondriasis (Hs), depression (D), conversion hysteria (Hy), psychopathic deviate (Pd), paranoia (Pa), psychasthenia (Pt), schizophrenia (Sc), and hypomania (Ma). Scales also measure masculinity and femininity (MF) and social introversion (SI). Four validity scales are scored to detect faking and distorted responses.

The MMPI (revised edition, MMPI-2) is used in a variety of counseling and therapeutic settings to assess the degree and nature of an individual's emotional distress. Counselors and other mental health practitioners in private practice, as well as those who work in mental health clinics or mental hospitals, most often use the MMPI.

The EPPS, with norms for college students and adults, is used when the counselor wants to help clients explore unfulfilled needs that are interfering with their personal, interpersonal, or career functioning. Based on Henry Murray's need theory of personality, it has 28 scales tapping such areas as need for achievement, need for dominance, and need for autonomy.

Projective Tests.   Projective tests are based on psychoanalytic or psychodynamic views about the importance of assessing a person's unconscious motives. In these tests clients react unconsciously to ambiguous pictures, images, or incomplete sentences, or they may draw human figures or objects that are projections of their self-image. The most commonly used projectives in counseling practice are the Thematic Apperception Test (TAT), the Rorschach, the Rotter Sentence Completion Blank, the House-Tree-Person (HTP), and the Draw a Person (DAP). These projective techniques are most apt to be used by doctorate-level mental health practitioners trained in psychodynamic theory and practice.

The TAT consists of picture cards that show one or more individuals in ambiguous settings. The client tells a story about each picture that assumedly reveals something about the client's conflicts or social constraints. The Rorschach is a set of cards with inkblot images; clients are asked what they see in each image.

Counselors using the Rotter Sentence Completion Blank ask individuals to respond to sentence stems, such as "I like . . ." and "I want to know. . . ." The Rotter gives an overall adjustment rating and is used for assessing both how well an individual is functioning and what psychiatric disturbances might exist.

The HTP and the DAP ask clients to draw pictures to indicate unconscious projections of their self-image. These tests are sometimes used by elementary school counselors and community counselors in their work with children. Counselors using these tests need special training in psychodynamic theory, as well as the use of projective tests.

Another drawing test, the Bender Visual-Motor Gestalt Test, commonly called the Bender-Gestalt, is used to assess whether personality disturbances are a result of brain damage. Individuals copy nine abstract designs consisting of dots, curves, and lines; the protocols of individuals being assessed are compared with those of individuals with brain damage. Clinical mental health counselors in the community or in private practice are most apt to use the Bender-Gestalt for this type of diagnostic evaluation.

Statistical Versus Clinical Interpretation of Tests

Counselors can use two different approaches to interpret standardized tests: One is an actuarial or statistical approach; the other is a clinical approach (Cohen & Swerdlik, 2002; Cronbach, 1990). According to Cohen and Swerdlik (2002), the *actuarial approach* is "the application of empirically demonstrated statistical rules and probabilities as a determining factor in clinical judgment and actions" (p. 639). By contrast, the *clinical approach* is "applying a clinician's own training and clinical experience as a determining factor in clinical judgment and actions" (p. 642).

Following is an example comparing the use of these two approaches in interpreting a profile of the MMPI to a client. In an actuarial approach a counselor would generally use a computerized interpretation of the client's profile, provided by a test-scoring company and based on extensive statistical data about clients with similar profiles. Counselors using a clinical approach, in contrast, would use their knowledge about and experience with MMPI profile patterns. They would integrate this information with their clients' observations and comments about themselves and with counselor-client insights gained during the counseling process.

According to Cohen and Swerdlik (2002), the actuarial or statistical approach emphasizes efficiency in making predictions about client behavior, whereas the clinical approach emphasizes flexibility, attention to the client's overall functioning in life, and acknowledgment of the client's individual needs.

Most Frequently Used Standardized Tests and Inventories

The tests discussed here were selected from hundreds of standardized measures used by counselors. The selection was based on the reviews in leading texts on tests and assessment and on two surveys regarding the most frequently used standardized instruments used by counselors in the community.

In Watkins, Campbell, and McGregor's 1988 survey, 66% of counseling psychologists surveyed used tests. In Bubenzer, Zempfer, and Mahrle's 1990 survey of counselors in the community, 70% of doctorate-level counselors and about 50% of master's-level counselors used tests.

Watkins et al. (1988) found that the six most frequently used tests by counseling psychologists were, in descending order, (a) the SCII, (b) the MMPI-2, (c) the WAIS-R, (d) the Rotter Sentence Completion Blank, (e) the Bender-Gestalt, and (f) the TAT. These were followed by the Sixteen Personality Factor Questionnaire (16PF), the CPI, the WISC-R, and the EPPS. These researchers found that vocational interest and objective personality tests were used predominantly in university counseling centers; the WISC-R, in community agencies. Projectives were used more often in private practice, community clinics, and hospitals.

Bubenzer, Zempfer, and Mahrle (1990) found that the MMPI was by far the most commonly used instrument; the next highest were the SCII, the WAIS-R, the MBTI, and the WISC-R. Rounding out the top 10 were the 16PF and the TAT (tied in ranking), the Bender-Gestalt, the WRAT, and the Rorschach and the Multiaxial Clinical Multiple Inventory (MCMI) (tied for 10th). The researchers also compared the use of the MMPI, SCII, WAIS-R, MBTI, and TAT by counselor educational degree and by counselor use (diagnosis, treatment planning, and evaluation). They found that although both doctorate-level and master's-level counselors used these tests, master's-level counselors used them less. They also reported that both master's- and doctoral-level counselors administer all these tests and use them for assessment and diagnosis, treatment planning, and evaluation.

Diagnostic and Statistical Manual of Mental Disorders

For those clients covered by health insurance, community counselors and therapists must use the *Diagnostic and Statistical Manual of Mental Disorders (DSM-IV-TR),* a classification of the various mental disorders, to determine whether a client is eligible for insurance coverage. "The *DSM-IV-TR* is the world's most thorough and widely used system for classifying and describing mental disorders . . ." (Remley & Herlihy, 2001, p. 213). A manual in book form, it classifies mental disorders into 17 categories including childhood disorders, dementia, substance abuse, schizophrenia, mood disorders, anxiety disorders, physical symptoms rooted in psychological problems, intentional faking of disorders, dissociative disorders, sexual and gender disorders, eating disorders, sleep disorders, impulse-control disorders, adjustment disorders, and personality disorders. Normally functioning individuals experiencing stress are classified as having adjustment disorders.

A unique feature of the *DSM-IV-TR* is the therapeutic use of five axes to classify client problems in a comprehensive and informative way; the axes assume a biophysical-social etiology. The therapist assesses the client's condition according to the axes:

Axis I: The major clinical symptom the client is experiencing
Axis II: Any personality disorder or mental retardation
Axis III: The medical condition that may exacerbate the emotional disorder
Axis IV: The psychosocial or environmental problems the client has experienced during the past year that complicate the emotional disturbance
Axis V: A summary or global assessment and a rating of the client's overall level of functioning at the time of the evaluation. The rating scale runs from 1: severe impairment to 100: superior functioning with absence of symptoms.

Following is an example of a *DSM-IV-TR* diagnostic assessment of a particular depressed client suffering from diabetes, recent loss of job, and divorce.

Axis I: *Clinical disorder*—**depression**
Axis II: *Personality disorders and mental retardation*—**obsessive-compulsive**
Axis III: *General medical condition*—**diabetes**
Axis IV: *Psychosocial and environmental problems*—**divorce, loss of job**
Axis V: *General assessment of functioning*—**50 (current)**

The advantages of using the *DSM-IV-TR* in mental health practice are numerous: (a) it offers a universal system of diagnosis that permits dialogue among mental health specialists; (b) it includes attention to cultural, age, and gender features (Sue, Sue, & Sue, 2000); (c) the multiaxial system requires that practitioners consider various physical, psychosocial, and environmental circumstances influencing the client's dysfunction; (d) research and expert opinions were used to construct the classifications.

Despite these advantages practitioners criticize the required use of the *DSM-IV-TR* for insurance purposes for several reasons: (a) it emphasizes pathological symptoms; (b) managed care organizations tend to use *DSM-IV-TR* categories to deny authorization of client treatment for normal conflicts or for longer term care; (c) it has a strong medical orientation even though over half of the classified disorders are unrelated to physical problems (Sue, Sue, & Sue, 2000).

In addition, some managed care companies decline to authorize treatment for some of the diagnostic categories. According to Remley and Herlihy (2001): "Most companies limit in some way the diagnoses for which they will pay benefits. Some companies will not reimburse for V-code conditions, typical developmental transitions, exclusively Axis II diagnosis, adjustment disorders, or family or couple's counseling" (p.237).

Faced with these limitations, counselors may be tempted to assign clients a more severe diagnosis (i.e., up-coding) or a less severe diagnosis (i.e., down-coding) than is clinically accurate so that clients will qualify for health insurance reimbursement. Unfortunately, an inaccurate diagnosis on a client's record can be harmful to the client. "Rather than yield to these temptations, counselors can improve the chances that their treatment plans will be approved by assessing thoroughly, setting realistic treatment goals, and complying with health care companies' recommended treatment protocols" (Remley & Herlihy, 2001, p. 237).

Whether counselors use the *DSM-IV-TR* in their counseling practice, they should be familiar with its classifications. Counselors can better dialogue with other mental health specialists who use the *DSM-IV-TR;* and knowledge of patterns of emotional distress as described by the *DSM-IV-TR* can be useful in intake interviewing or crisis intervention to determine the type of treatment needed and any need for a referral.

Postmodern constructivists and social constructionists offer persuasive arguments in favor of allowing for more than one diagnostic system. Constructivists Leitner, Faidley, and Celentana (2000) express concerns about the use of the *DSM-IV-TR* classifications and labels: "In addition to the conceptual problem inherent with . . . these labels [they] tell very little about understanding a person in ways that lead to treatment options" (p. 117). These authors propose an experiential model called human meaning making diagnosis. Based on George Kelly's (1955) theory of personal constructs, this diagnostic model focuses on how individuals construct meaning in life through their relationships with others. Leitner et al. (2000) advocate "a way of diagnosing the process of meaning making that simultaneously accounts for client distress, respects the lived experience of the person and makes psychotherapeutic interventions understandable and plausible" (p. 201).

Their diagnosis focuses on how clients relate to significant others, or what Leitner et al. (2000) call their ROLE relationships. Difficulties in the way a person relates to significant others indicate ways the counselor can help the client. In determining treatment options, the counselor focuses the diagnosis first on gaining an understanding of what prevented the development of core constructs in early childhood and later impeded the client's ROLE relationships.

The next step in the diagnostic process is to assess "how the client negotiates ROLE relationships" (Leitner et al., 2000, p. 177). This process is done by observing the various ways a person relates to the other in the ROLE relationship: how the person construes others as distinct from herself; the ability to accept mood and behavioral variations in others; the ability to create new ways of interacting in the ROLE relationship; the ability to assume responsibility for her construing interactions and the willingness to reconstrue; the degree of commitment in the ROLE relationship; the willingness to risk continuing ROLE relationships during difficult times; the ability to overcome normal disappointments and injuries; and the ability to maintain a sense of respect for the other's mystery (Leitner et al., 2000).

From the social constructionists' perspective, Gergen and McNamee (2000) ask some tough questions about the overall purpose of the *DSM-IV-TR*. Although acknowledging that the language of diagnostic tools used in the *DSM-IV-TR* allows the profession to better communicate with one another, they ask whether such diagnostic tools were formulated with limited regard for the welfare of the client.

Gergen and McNamee (2000) describe how *DSM-IV-TR* classifications can be harmful to clients: The system ignores social-cultural variations in interpreting client psychological disorders. Clients are given diagnostic labels based on society's negative views about emotional disorders, and the labels stigmatize clients. Further, client psychological disorders are attributed to dysfunctions or flaws in the client, ignoring or underplaying social-cultural factors. Thus, such a method of diagnosing tends to remove the problem "from its normal context of operation; others are encouraged to 'back off,' 'avoid interfering,' and 'let the professionals do their work.' The mental health professions thus disrupt the processes of relational realignment that might otherwise take place within the community" (Gergen & McNamee, 2000, p. 340).

Gergen and McNamee (2000) don't reject the *DSM-IV-TR* as a diagnostic tool; they argue instead that it should not be the only one and advocate for alternative diagnostic measures and treatment as allowable options. They also propose such an alternative, a diagnostic process called *transformative dialogue,* which opens the dialogue beyond the narrow confines of the mental health profession so as to create new "relational networks within the community" (p. 345). Gergen and McNamee suggest that the client's loved ones and family be included as participants rather than obstacles; "problematic behavior should not be placed in the hands of any single profession" (p. 348). A person's dysfunctions should instead be the concern and interest of the rest of the community, including the religious, civic, and business community. "As voices, opinions, interpretations, values, and the like are added to the conversational mix, opportunities become available for moving beyond the tyranny" (p. 345) of a single diagnostic system.

NEED FOR QUALITY TRAINING IN ASSESSMENT

The increase in the use of tests by counselors and the more varied purposes for the use of tests have raised concerns regarding the quality of counselor training, concerns that Goldman (1972, 1982) has expressed for decades. Prediger (1994) concurs: "Unfortunately, the response to student preferences by some counselor educators has been to water down courses, to confine measurement instruction to units in other courses" (p. 228). After surveying mental health counselors' use of standardized tests in agencies and private practice, Bubenzer et al. (1990) concluded that counselor education programs need to improve and strengthen curricular offerings in tests and measurements:

> If master's degree practitioners are using both objective and projective tests and use personality, career, intelligence, and special problem tests for diagnostic and treatment purposes, then it appears that we need to assure, through our accreditation and licensing practices, that they have adequate training and skill. (p. 65)

Counselor training programs need to include comprehensive exposure to tests and measures in ways more complex than the simple testing methods used in the early days. Increasing numbers of counselors are working in private practice, managed care, and community agencies in which insurance companies require a diagnosis from the *DSM-IV-TR* before they will reimburse clients for treatment. Counselors are also exposed to a wide variety of theoretical orientations in which some form of assessment is part of the counseling process. Counselors in private practice are called on to make diagnostic evaluations for agencies; and all counselors, regardless of their work setting, are expected to intervene and assess in crisis situations. The need for using assessment in intervention, family systems, substance abuse, and child abuse has also increased.

As assessment measures have proliferated and are now easily available and as their use has become more varied and complex, counselors-in-training need to be made aware of resources to help determine the quality of tests and their appropriate ethical use. Such resources include *The 14th Mental Measurement Yearbook* (Conoley & Impara, 2001), Anastasi (1996), Cohen and Swerdlik (2002), Thorndike (1997), and Walsh and Betz (2001).

Guidelines for ethical and appropriate use of tests are included in the codes of ethics of counseling and related professional associations. For example, ACA (see appendix A) and APA codes include sections on evaluation and assessment covering such topics as competence to use and interpret tests, interpretation of tests, and test selection and administration. Both codes include the importance of maintaining test security that will uphold the integrity and validity of the tests. Test items and content cannot be modified or reproduced without the permission of the publishers.

An invaluable resource that promotes the ethical use of tests in education and psychology is the *Standards for Educational and Psychological Testing* (1999) developed jointly by the American Educational Research Association (AERA), the APA, and the National Council on Measurement in Education. Anyone using tests should be knowledgeable about these standards.

SUMMARY

In the early days of counseling, the counselor's primary task was to assess the vocational aptitudes and interests of clients through the use of standardized tests. Rogers (1951) and others challenged counselors' overreliance on testing, claiming it was a diagnostic, prescriptive approach to counseling. Rogers claimed that the counselor's role is to develop a trusting counseling relationship to encourage client self-exploration. His views led to a decline in the use of tests for three decades. Many counselors who continued to use tests to assess clients first developed a relationship and then used tests to help their clients self-explore.

For many decades testing specialist Leo Goldman has criticized the profession for not adequately training counselors in the selection, use, and interpretation of tests and assessment. The need for quality training in assessment methods is all the more essential now because the use of tests by counselors has escalated dramatically in recent years. Not only are counselors using more assessments, but they are also becoming involved in new types of assessment with individuals who are not their clients. These newer duties with nonclients include intake interviewing, crisis intervention, and diagnostic evaluation for outside agencies.

Counselors use tests and assessment in a nonjudgmental manner in counseling sessions to help clients clarify their problems and to enhance their self-exploration. Test results are confidential to clients. Appropriately interpreting test results is a key factor in the assessment process. It requires the skills and wise judgment of a trained counselor, one who can integrate information gathered from client test scores, interviews, and personal observations into meaningful patterns and use those appraisals to enhance client self-exploration.

In intake interviews counselors screen prospective clients to determine the best plan of therapeutic action. In crisis intervention, counselors use structured interviews first to help the traumatized individuals gain some equilibrium and then, if necessary, to make an appropriate referral for treatment. In diagnostic evaluations of individuals, counselors work for outside agencies that request their assistance in determining eligibility for benefits, training, or legal disposition.

Counselors use both nonstandardized and standardized types of assessment. Nonstandardized measures include informal observations of client behavior and self-reports of clients about themselves. Counselors use standardized measures based on statistically derived norm groups. The five types of standardized measures include three that are tests—intelligence, aptitude, and achievement—and two that are inventories—interest and personality.

Gardner proposed a theory of multiple intelligences to challenge the use of IQ as the method of measuring intelligence. Counselors and therapists use the *DSM-IV-TR* for diagnostic classification as part of the expectations of managed care programs. Postmodern constructivists and social constructionists, however, point out the shortcomings of the *DSM-IV-TR* and propose alternative diagnostic models as options.

PROJECTS AND ACTIVITIES

1. Visit your university counseling center, and determine the type of assessment procedures the staff uses most often.
2. Talk with a counselor whose major responsibility is crisis intervention. Discuss with her or him procedures used and referral sources available.
3. Interview the counselor or mental health worker assigned to intake interviewing in a community mental health clinic. What are the major assessment tools used? What are the advantages and disadvantages of being an intake interviewer?
4. Use an anonymous questionnaire to survey your class about the types of tests they have taken and their opinions about the value of these measures.

REFERENCES

American Psychiatric Association. (2000). *Diagnostic and statistical manual of mental disorders* (4th ed., text revision). Washington, DC: Author.

American Educational Research Association (AERA), American Psychological Association (APA), & National Council on Measurement in Education. (1999). *Standards for educational and psychological testing.* Washington, DC: Author.

Anastasi, A. (1996). *Psychological testing* (7th ed.). New York: Macmillan.

Bubenzer, D. L., Zempfer, D. G., & Mahrle, C. L. (1990). Standardized individual appraisal in agency and private practice: A survey. *Journal of Mental Health Counseling, 12,* 51–66.

Cohen, R. J., & Swerdlik, M. E. (2002). *Psychological testing and assessment: An introduction to tests and measurement* (5th ed.). Mountain View, CA: Mayfield.

Conoley, J. C., & Impara, J. C. (Eds.). (2001). *The 14th mental measurement yearbook.* Lincoln: University of Nebraska, Buros Institute of Mental Measurement.

Cronbach, L. J. (1990). *Essentials of psychological testing* (5th ed.). New York: Harper & Row.

Drummond, R. J. (2000). *Appraisal procedures for counselors and helping professions* (4th ed.). Upper Saddle River, NJ: Prentice Hall.

Gardner, H. (1993). *Frames of mind: The theory of multiple intelligences.* New York: Basic Books.

Gergen, K. J., & McNamee, S. (2000). From disordering discourse to transformative dialogue. In R. A. Neimeyer & J. D. Raskin, *Constructions of disorder* (pp. 333–349). Washington, DC: American Psychological Association.

Goldman, L. (1972). Tests and counseling: The marriage that failed. *Measurement and Evaluation in Guidance, 4,* 213–220.

Goldman, L. (1982). Assessment in counseling: A better way. *Measurement and Evaluation in Guidance, 15,* 70–73.

Goldman, L. (1990). Qualitative assessment. *Counseling Psychologist, 15,* 205–213.

Goldman, L. (1992). Qualitative assessment: An approach for counselors. *Journal of Counseling & Development, 70,* 616–621.

Goldman, L. (1994). The marriage is over . . . for most of us. *Measurement and Evaluation in Counseling and Development, 26,* 217–218.

Kelly, G. A. (1955). *A theory of personality: The psychology of personal constructs.* New York: Norton.

Kleinknecht, T. (1986). *The anxious self.* New York: Human Services Press.

Leitner, L. M., Faidley, A. J., & Celentana, M. A. (2000). Diagnosing human meaning making: An experiential constructivist approach. In R. A. Neimeyer & J. D. Raskin, *Constructions of disorder* (pp. 175–203). Washington, DC: American Psychological Association.

Nugent, F. (1981). *Professional counseling: An overview.* Pacific Grove, CA: Brooks/Cole.

Pascal, E. (1992). *Jung to live by.* New York: Warner Books.

Prediger, D. J. (1994). Tests and counseling: The marriage that prevailed. *Measurement and Evaluation in Counseling and Development, 26,* 227–234.

Remley, T. P., Jr., & Herlihy, B. (2001). *Ethical, legal and professional issues in counseling.* Upper Saddle River, NJ: Merrill/Prentice Hall.

Rogers, C. R. (1942). *Counseling and psychotherapy.* Boston: Houghton Mifflin.

Rogers, C. R. (1951). *Client-centered therapy: Its current practice, implications, and theory.* Boston: Houghton-Mifflin.

Spoto, A. (1989). *Jung's typology and perspective.* Boston: SIGO Press.

Sue, D., Sue, D., & Sue, S. (2000). *Understanding abnormal behavior* (6th ed.). Boston: Houghton Mifflin.

Sue, D. W., & Sue, D. (2003). *Counseling the culturally different* (4th ed.). New York: John Wiley.

Thorndike, R. M. (1997). *Measurement and evaluation in psychology and education* (6th ed.). Upper Saddle River, NJ: Merrill/Prentice Hall.

Walsh, W. B., & Betz, N. E. (2001). *Tests and assessments* (4th ed.). Upper Saddle River, NJ: Prentice Hall.

Watkins, C., Campbell, V., & McGregor, P. (1988). Counseling psychologists' uses of and opinions about psychological tests: A contemporary perspective. *Counseling Psychologist, 16,* 476–486.

CHAPTER 8

Counseling Outreach: Prevention and Intervention

Besides time spent in direct counseling with individuals, groups, and families, counselors in all work settings are involved in prevention and intervention activities designed to improve the overall mental health climate for everyone in schools and the community. These activities are called *outreach* because counselors usually leave their offices and literally reach out. The major purposes of such activities are to broaden the knowledge and skills of individuals in personal, social, educational, and career development; to improve the school or community environment so that good mental health practices will be encouraged and enhanced; and to assist crisis victims. Thus, outreach serves both a preventive, educational role to improve the mental health of a community and an intervention role to attend to those experiencing crises.

Since the 1970s the number and variety of outreach programs have been increasing in all settings. This expansion is largely a result of the recent proliferation of counseling theories and techniques, including psychoeducation, holistic approaches, wellness programs, and the improvement in crisis intervention programs.

Effective and appropriate outreach activities will not necessarily decrease the number of requests for counseling. Instead, they may tend to increase them. As a counseling center's staff becomes better known and more trusted, more persons may ask for counseling or be referred by others. As teachers or work supervisors become more effective in communication and in relationship and behavioral skills, they not only improve the classroom or work climate but also become more aware of individuals needing professional counseling. Outreach activities may prevent the development of some problems but may also spark a recognition that some individuals are experiencing conflict and might profit from counseling.

COUNSELORS AS CONSULTANTS

Gelso and Fretz (2001) define *consultation* as "a professional service that uses knowledge of human behavior, interpersonal relationships, and group and organizational processes to help others become more effective in their roles" (p. 609). Consultation activities have certain characteristics regardless of the work setting:

- The consultation involves three parties—client, consultant, and consultee.
- The consultation is voluntary and nonjudgmental.
- The focus is on specific issues regarding the client's problem.
- The consultee is free to accept or reject any or all recommendations (Hershenson, Power, & Waldo, 1996; Kurpius & Fuqua, 1993).

In their consulting work, counselors maintain confidentiality and protect the rights of privacy of consultees, just as they do with their clients in counseling. The ACA Code of Ethics (1995) says: "Information obtained in a consulting relationship is discussed for professional purposes only with persons clearly concerned with the case . . . and every effort is made to protect client identity and avoid undue invasion of privacy" (Section B.6.a).

The Consultation Process

Professional counselors offer consultation in their areas of expertise—personal and interpersonal relationships, behavior dynamics, occupational knowledge, appraisal information, and communication skills. In the consultation process the consultant listens to the concerns that consultees have about their interactions with third parties (i.e., clients). For example, a consultee (a fellow counselor) may wonder whether he has sufficient background to work with a client with a severe eating disorder; he may be perplexed about the lack of client response in the counseling sessions; or he may be experiencing feelings of countertransference he does not recognize. The consultant helps the consultee gain insight into the situation and suggests ways to work through it. In some cases consultant and consultee may agree that the client's problem goes beyond the consultee's particular expertise. In these instances the consultee refers the client to another professional.

As a consultant the counselor interacts collaboratively with the consultee on an equal basis; mutual respect and trust characterize their interactions. The goal of consultation is to identify jointly the consultee's problem and collaborate in helping the consultee make use of existing skills or upgrade skills to improve interaction with a third party. In the process the consultee's concerns about the third party are specified; and the consultant and the consultee explore whether the problem relates to a breakdown in communication, a difference in values, or a feeling of inadequacy on the part of the consultee.

Types of Consultations

Consultation activities include the following types:

- With other counselors, other mental health professionals, or other professionals in related disciplines (e.g., psychologists, psychiatrists, social workers, physicians)

- With faculty, administrators, parents, or families in educational settings
- With staff of community organizations serving mental health needs (e.g., crisis centers, senior citizen centers, rape relief services, women's shelters)

With Other Counselors or Other Professionals

When counselors experience problems or need specialized information in working with clients, they may consult with other counselors on their staff or elsewhere in the community. When counselors are uncertain about their work with clients, they have an ethical responsibility to check with a consultant (ACA, 1995). At other times counselors may want technical assistance from an expert in a particular phase of counseling. For example, they may consult with someone who specializes in bulimia, alcoholism, or vocational rehabilitation. In such cases clients should be informed about the need for consultation, and their permission should be obtained prior to the consultation.

In Educational Settings

Faculty, parents, and administrators seek consultation with school counselors when they have confidence in the counselors' professional expertise.

Consultation with Faculty.   Faculty may have problems with individual students or with overall classroom interaction. A student may not be handing in work and may look depressed or agitated, or a student may be disclosing personal concerns beyond a teacher's expertise. Teachers may have personal or marital concerns that are interfering with their class performance, or they may be depressed or anxious about their lives in general.

For problems with students, the process of clarifying the difficulties and determining alternative action follows the consulting procedure previously discussed. If the issue is too difficult to be worked out within the classroom, the counselor may suggest that the teacher refer the student directly to the counselor. If the need is for disciplinary action or a formal evaluation of a student's abilities, the teacher should be directed to an administrator, school psychologist, or social worker. At the college level, faculty should be referred to the dean of students or to the chairs of their departments.

When a faculty member wants to consult about a student, it is wise ethical policy for the teacher to maintain the student's right to privacy and not identify the student. Thus, if the student under discussion is referred to counseling or comes in independently, the counselor will not have prior knowledge about the student. Also, the teacher will be more likely to generalize suggestions about one student's particular behavior to similar behaviors of others.

This approach is feasible in college counseling and in larger high schools because anonymity is fairly easy to maintain. In small schools, however, anonymity becomes more difficult. Nevertheless, it is good policy that a student's name be of secondary importance unless it is determined that the student's behavior is injurious to her- or himself or to others.

Teachers who have personal problems may find it valuable to consult with a counselor for a few sessions. Together they can evaluate the severity of the problem and decide whether counseling is needed. Most often, consultees are apprehensive about whether they need counseling and where to go for the kind of help they need. If counseling is decided on, the counselor can refer the teacher to a professional person whom the counselor respects. It is not considered wise professional practice for counselors to involve themselves in counseling relationships with colleagues. Counselor and teacher might find it difficult to disengage social and/or business interactions from the counseling relationship or to establish the kind of relationship necessary for effective counseling (Corey, Corey, & Callanan, 1998).

Consultation with Administrators.   Administrators are often faced with conflicting demands and pressures from students, parents, and teachers about student behavior and school policy, student rights and responsibilities, and teacher or parent rights and responsibilities. Administrators may, for example, have difficult interactions with parents or with individual teachers or groups of teachers, or they may face a gap between curricular offerings and student needs. Testing programs, appropriate use of school records, and changes in laws about administrator-student interactions are other areas in which school administrators may want consultation.

The counseling staff can offer information and guidelines about the potential consequences of certain administrative actions. Counselors can also use their expertise to ensure that testing and record-keeping policies are in line with the rights and responsibilities of students and adults. And guidelines for an administrator's interactions with parents and teachers can be discussed.

It is not wise professional practice, however, for counselors and administrators to discuss a specific teacher's interaction with students or the teacher's proficiency in teaching. This sort of evaluative interview can raise ethical dilemmas for counselors who are inviting referrals from teachers. On the other hand, if a teacher and an administrator request a joint consultation with a counselor about their interaction, such a consultation may be useful as long as it has no evaluative overtones. And when an administrator is concerned about a teacher's suffering an emotional breakdown or about the safety of others, a consultation with the counselor is in order.

Consultation with Parents.   Consultations with parents can be very effective (Baker, 2000; Gibson & Mitchell, 1999). Parents may request a consultation with a school counselor when they are concerned about their child's or adolescent's poor academic work, lack of friends, poor motivation in school, or unmanageable behavior at home. In these instances it is most effective for the parents or counselor to let the child know that a consultation has been requested and why. If the child objects, the parents may need to resolve the objections before seeing the counselor. The counselor might also talk with the child about the objections, and that discussion in itself might help communication between parents and child. By establishing at the outset effective communication processes based on the right to privacy and confidentiality, the counselor and the parents reduce the possibility that the child will perceive intrigue between the adults. This approach is particularly important because a counseling relationship with the child or the family often arises out of effective consultation (Baker, 2000).

After the consultation, if more intensive work with the family is needed, a referral to a family counseling service is in order. If a psychological evaluation of the child or an evaluation of home conditions seems warranted, a referral to the school psychologist or social worker can be made.

In the Community

Individual consultations may be requested by counselors or directors at mental health community facilities or by staff at various mental health–related services in the community, such as crisis clinics, rape relief centers, senior centers, teenage counseling centers, or women's shelters. Consultations may be requested about individual clients, a particular type of client, ethical policies, or referral services of the organization. Professionals from various work settings may also seek similar consultations—physicians, lawyers, and people from business, industry, government agencies, and religious groups (Boytim, 1986).

In business, supervisors may ask for consultation about a staff member—usually through an employee assistance program (EAP)—or they may want to learn how to refer an employee to counseling (Lewis & Lewis, 1986; Quayle, 1985).

At times family members may ask for consultation with counselors in community agencies regarding a family member, such as an aging parent with Alzheimer's disease. Or family members may request consultation from employee assistance counselors about a relative's alcohol problems or undue emotional strain on the job that is affecting the family (Gerstein & Sturmer, 1993; Hutchison, 1985; Lewis & Lewis, 1986).

PSYCHOEDUCATION

Psychoeducation is another form of outreach in which the counselor educates people in areas of personal, social, career, and educational development (Baker, 2000; Baker & Shaw, 1987; Brooks & Weikel, 1986). Counselors perform the following psychoeducational activities:

- Teaching courses
- Leading workshops and groups
- Training paraprofessionals
- Providing wellness activities
- Offering career education programs

Teaching Courses

Counselors have the background to teach courses in vocational, personal, and social areas. Professional counselors can offer elective, nongraded courses in public schools, colleges, and the community. They can teach classes in conjunction with regular instructors, or they may be invited into classrooms to cover certain topics within their areas of expertise. Counselors typically offer courses in community colleges and in extension and extended-day programs at colleges and universities. Courses or units dealing with career awareness, personal development, and social interactions are common. Also appropriate are courses on such social issues as race relations, cultural differences, mental health issues, sex and marriage, family relationships, individual rights and responsibilities, the changing roles of men and women, and alcohol and drug abuse.

Activities that increase the affective content of school and college curricula are generally called *humanistic education* to differentiate them from academic or intellectual subject matter. Commercial kits, prepared teaching units, recordings, and videotapes are available to counselors and teachers. Some of the more popular programs are the following:

- Group discussions of hypothetical moral dilemmas based on Kohlberg's theory of moral development (see chap. 5).
- Activities to improve personal growth and social interactions (e.g., Besell and Palmores's Structured Human Development Program for elementary grades and Dinkmeyer's Developing Understanding of Self and Others (DUSO) kits of puppets and games for Grades 4 to 6)
- Games to change a behavior (achievement motivation)
- Various strategies to change the classroom environment (sensitivity modules) (Baker & Shaw, 1987)

Counselors who teach courses in personal and social development must be cautious about pushing their personal beliefs or social attitudes onto their students. Psychoeducational courses such as these should not be considered a substitute for professional counseling. The following considerations are offered as guidelines for determining the appropriateness of various humanistic programs in education.

1. Are participants permitted to choose whether they want to be involved in a particular class exercise?
2. Are families' and group members' rights to privacy protected?
3. Are safeguards included so that participants' attitudes are not shaped according to some predetermined values or moral beliefs?
4. Are discussions or exercises of such a nature that they do not provoke psychological or emotional reactions that the instructors are not professionally prepared to handle?
5. Are games or units involving self-disclosure designed to protect individuals from indulging in intimate revelations that may subsequently lead to psychological distress?
6. Are precautions included to ensure that the program does not foster superficial resolutions of student problems or lead to superficial relationships among class members?

Leading Workshops and Groups

Workshops and educational group experiences differ from the instructional units just discussed in that they are usually short term, do not involve academic credit, and are less structured than classroom activities. Counselors often survey students, staff, or members of the community about the types of workshops or group experiences they would like; the workshops or groups are either offered by the counseling staff or arranged for by the staff with outside consultants.

Workshops are typically offered on vocational development, decision-making processes, women and careers, job-seeking skills, assertiveness training, development of self-esteem, communication skills, and parenting skills (Hershenson et al., 1996). In addition, leaders of local or regional ethnic groups may be invited to the school or community agency to discuss improving communication or understanding differing value systems. Workshops on the use and abuse of alcohol or other drugs might be developed by the local alcohol referral center, or the staff of a Planned Parenthood clinic could be invited to describe the clinic's function in the community.

It is important that skill workshops be based on the needs expressed by the population being served, not on the belief of a counselor or counseling staff that everyone needs training in some skill. Thus, if all groups are offered assertiveness training, values clarification, or skills in listening to others, one could legitimately wonder whether the counselor is pushing one system of skills rather than tailoring these experiences to specific concerns expressed by various groups.

Some counselors lead workshops or groups based on the techniques of major counseling theories. For example, counselors might use Gestalt techniques when running workshops on assertiveness training, increasing body awareness, or learning to confront others constructively. Other counselors might develop stress management, study skills, or weight-control workshops based on cognitive-behavioral approaches. Further examples are Gordon's (1975) Parent Effectiveness Training (PET), which follows Rogerian views, and Dinkmeyer's (1976) Systematic Training for Effective Parenting (STEP), based on Adlerian therapy.

Gordon calls his system the no-lose method of resolving conflicts. Parents learn effective management of conflicts by learning how to listen in a nonevaluative way and how to communicate feelings honestly. His system also spells out techniques to change unacceptable behavior by changing the environment. Parents learn how to identify the conflict, generate and evaluate alternative solutions, and decide on the best solution. Then they work out ways to implement the solution and arrange follow-up. Gordon (1977) has applied similar steps to working with Teacher Effectiveness Training (TET) and Youth Effectiveness Training (YET) (Baker & Shaw, 1987).

Groups that develop social interaction skills are sometimes called *sensitivity training* or *organizational development groups*. These are similar to workshops except that they have less structured leadership; counselors take on the role of group facilitator rather than leading the group. In these groups members learn to develop their own system of democratic processes, their own leadership, and their own methods of developing social cooperation. The groups have been used extensively in schools and colleges; they can help student governments function more equitably and can be developed to help improve student-faculty interactions. They also work well in community agencies and businesses.

Structured groups are designed to help group members focus on specific social skills, such as stress management, healthy eating, reducing test anxiety, assertion, and other developmental life skills (Corey & Corey, 2002; Gazda, 1989). As the name implies, these groups are highly structured, with predetermined, specific goals to be accomplished through the use of training and exercises. The process is based on a skill-deficit model; appropriate skills are taught to eliminate the deficiency, thereby increasing social interaction and social use.

Training Paraprofessionals

Counselors provide in-service training for those who want to become counseling paraprofessionals, also called *paracounselors* or *counselor aides*. Paraprofessionals receive training by a professional to perform specific auxiliary duties related to professional duties. Some act as librarian aides in information resource rooms; others learn basic interviewing skills so that they can serve at referral and information desks. Still others are trained to score simple paper-and-pencil tests used in counseling interviews (Hershenson et al., 1996).

Some paraprofessionals are trained for somewhat higher skill levels. In colleges, for example, students are often hired as aides in the residence halls to act as resource persons for students. Through in-service training with professional counselors, these students can learn to be alert to students' problems in the dormitories and to consult with a counselor about whether to refer students.

Counselor aides can also be helpful to professionals when they are trained to provide information about and make referrals to specific community services such as drug or alcohol referral centers or pregnancy counseling centers. In these more complex positions, aides should be forewarned that they are not counselors; training should include avoiding overinvolvement in a person's problems and knowing when and how to refer an individual to a professional. Ivey and Ivey's (1999) interviewing and human relationship skills (discussed in chap. 4) are commonly used in workshop and affective curricula to train paraprofessionals or interviewers, receptionists, and other nonspecialists serving the public in mental health or mental health-related jobs.

Providing Wellness Activities

Counselors who follow wellness models teach individuals how to maintain good health by attending to their physical, emotional, intellectual, and spiritual development. This holistic approach can be applied to groups in educational settings, the workplace, and the community (Hershenson et al., 1996; Myers, 1992). Wellness outreach programs are commonly found in the workplace as part of employee enhancement programs (see chap. 12) and in universities as part of counseling center or health services. Although less common in schools, school counselors have started offering preventive workshops recommended by wellness advocates.

In industry, employees are encouraged to develop healthy lifestyles through educational workshops that cover subjects such as managing stress, developing a healthy diet, learning about the hazards of smoking or misuse of alcohol, monitoring weight and blood pressure, and doing exercises to keep physically fit (Lewis & Lewis, 1986; Witmer & Sweeney, 1992). Some industries provide fitness rooms where employees can do aerobic exercises.

In universities wellness components of student counseling services and/or student health services offer similar types of group experiences. Information and workshops about avoiding sexually transmitted diseases, using safe-sex practices, and reducing chances of date rape are available. Support groups for individuals grieving over losses from death, divorce, or breakups with lovers are common.

Omizo, Omizo, and D'Andrea (1992) discuss the importance of developing wellness activities for elementary students because effective or ineffective lifestyles develop in the early formative years. Omizo et al. conducted a study in which one class of fifth-grade students (the experimental group) was given 10 weekly guidance sessions that covered exercise, nutrition, stress management, relaxation exercises, and good health habits. When compared with another fifth-grade class that received no wellness instruction (the control group), the experimental class showed better scores that were statistically significant on measures of general self-esteem, anxiety level, and knowledge about wellness. Stress management skills can be easily integrated into existing school curricula by using a variety of techniques such as proper breathing, muscle relaxation, imagery and visualization, and biofeedback training (Romano, 1992).

Other programs that contribute to individual wellness are those that teach people to honor the welfare of the planet by encouraging recycling and suggesting ways to help reduce pollution and protect natural resources.

Offering Career Education Programs

During the 1990s increasing numbers of counselors in educational settings and in the community became active in developing career education and career outreach programs. This increased activity in schools stemmed mainly from federal and state funding. In communities the increase in career counseling centers for adults was a response to the demands of the general public for career information and exploration.

Through federal incentives counselors in schools developed curricular activities, workshops, and projects that help students see how their personal characteristics and the environmental factors in their lives influence their occupational choices. These programs focus on career awareness in elementary schools, career exploration in middle schools, and career preparation in high schools (Isaacson & Brown, 1993). For high school seniors these activities include training in writing job applications, developing résumés, practicing job interviews, and visiting, observing, or interning at job sites.

In colleges and universities career education activities are often offered jointly by counseling center and placement center staffs. Typically, these activities are workshops or all-day seminars that include computerized occupational exploration programs, panels of speakers from a variety of occupations, and hands-on workshops to give students practice in writing job résumés and preparing for job interviews. Placement center staff also provide information about job openings and arrange for job interviews.

Career counseling centers for adults in the community provide numerous career education services to their clients, including developing job résumés, preparing for job interviews, and becoming more marketable. Community career centers also provide workshops for clients wishing to change or upgrade jobs or develop their own businesses. Support groups are also formed to help individuals who are displaced homemakers, who suddenly lose their jobs, or who are trying to work through uncertainties about changing jobs.

SOCIAL CHANGE ACTIVITIES

Most outreach programs are social change activities in that they attempt to educate staff in the schools or officials in the community so as to improve general mental health for everyone. In some cases it is appropriate for counseling staffs to make specific suggestions to change the social environment. For example, in a high school a counselor might suggest changes in the curriculum because of ethnic stereotyping, and in the community a counselor might propose ways that area businesses can offer better child care.

Counseling staffs can also affect the social environment in other ways: by helping individuals or groups become aware of the need for changes in policies, curricular offerings, or services or of their right to work for change and to learn procedures by which they can make changes occur. The need for change might be pointed out through workshops in which policies and procedures are discussed and recommendations for change are made to the appropriate officials. Counselors may try to carry out a particularly important social change when administrative policies violate counselor ethical codes, such as breaking confidentiality or ignoring rights of privacy. Other important issues include gender and racial stereotyping, minors' rights and responsibilities, and child care services in colleges and businesses.

It is important that counselors let clients know that change efforts will not always be successful and that participants may come out of the interactions somewhat bruised. Nevertheless, individuals who try to make changes should be given help; they can be shown how to proceed in a fair and firm manner that will best convince the person(s) in charge that a change is necessary. However, even though counselors should support clients' efforts, they should not try to persuade or pressure them in any way to take action. Such decisions and the consequences of those decisions are the responsibility of the clients.

CRISIS INTERVENTION

A *crisis*, or sudden unexpected trauma, can happen to any normally functioning individual. It can cause that person to experience disequilibrium or immobility accompanied by panic, debilitating anxiety, hopelessness, or helplessness. The person may lose the capacity to use coping skills to master his or her responses to the trauma.

Two major categories of stress—external and internal—are liable to produce crises. In *external stress* something or someone in the environment unexpectedly causes disruption, which brings about severe emotional reactions. Such stressors include the sudden death of a loved one, the sudden onset of terminal or serious illness, unexpected loss of a job, rape, assault, abandonment by a loved one, or natural disasters such as floods or earthquakes. *Internal stress* includes suicidal thoughts, severe depression, severe generalized panic, acute alcohol or drug reactions, or psychotic reactions.

Crises occur in educational, community, and business settings. A student may panic in class or on school or college premises and be brought to the counseling center by a faculty member or another student. Similarly, a person in crisis may be brought to a community agency by family members or a friend. The counselor must be available to intervene immediately (James & Gilliland, 2001). In such cases counselors must assess quickly whether individuals might harm themselves or others. If so, counselors have an obligation to take appropriate action to protect others or to arrange protective care for the clients. If no immediate danger exists, counselors can then take steps to help the individuals cope with the crises.

Crisis intervention is not synonymous with counseling; goals are immediate and specific to the crisis. Belkin (1984) aptly and succinctly remarks that "crisis intervention is to counseling what first aid is to medicine, a temporary but immediate relief for an emerging situation presented by an incapacitated client" (p. 423).

The Process of Intervention

The principal goal of crisis intervention is to restore the person to the way she or he was before the crisis occurred. Counselors must be supportive, empathic, and willing to direct the interview (Brammer, Abrego, & Shostrom, 1993; James & Gilliland, 2001). The following steps are important:

1. Help the person express and release emotions through support and empathy
2. Identify and clarify the precipitating problem and the extent of its severity
3. Gather information about the event that caused the crisis
4. Help the client identify her or his coping skills, emphasizing strengths that can help overcome the problem
5. Assess the degree of support for the client from family, friends, and colleagues
6. Explore strategies to improve or resolve crisis-inducing stress
7. Decide whether further counseling is needed and whether a referral to a psychiatrist or another specialist is required

James and Gilliland (2001) specify counselor strategies and the degree of direct action needed (see Figure 8.1). The more immobilized the client, the more directive the counselor should be. In some cases one, two, or three meetings with a client may suffice. But in others the decision may be made to carry out postcrisis counseling either with the counselor or with another mental health specialist.

When a person experiences the death or dying of a loved one, after the initial trauma is eased, the client may need to work through a grief process. Kübler-Ross (1975) developed a system of working with dying people that has also been found appropriate for other losses, such as that of a loved one, a job, or a treasured possession. The stages generally proceed from denial and isolation (in which persons do not accept reality), to feelings of anger at their fate, to attempts to bargain with life, followed by feelings of depression as reality is faced, and finally acceptance. Most persons going through grief stages move back and forth between the stages many times (see chap. 15 on grief work).

Hershenson et al. (1996) point out that a crisis can be a positive growth experience, rather than a disastrous event, if the counselor helps the client cope successfully during the crisis and use it as a *learning experience*.

Suicide Intervention

Suicide intervention is an area of concern for counselors in all settings. An alarming number of teenagers in the United States attempt or commit suicide every year. Among teenagers 15% have seriously considered suicide (Comer, 1996). The suicide rate among young adults is 15% to 24%, now the third leading cause of death for this group (Sue, Sue, & Sue, 2000). Suicide is the highest, however, among the elderly. Almost 25% of individuals who commit suicide in the United States are over age 65. This group also has the highest percentage of completed suicides (Sue, Sue, & Sue, 2000; see also chap. 15).

In instances when someone threatens suicide, the counselor must assess the situation carefully (see Figure 8.1). The counselor must determine the intensity of the depression, anxiety, or disorientation; the frequency of suicidal thoughts; the amount of withdrawal;

FIGURE 8-1

The six-step model of crisis intervention.

ASSESSING:

Overarching, continuous, and dynamically ongoing throughout the crisis; evaluating the client's present and past situational crises in terms of the client's ability to cope, personal threat, mobility or immobility, and making a judgment regarding type of action needed by the crisis worker. (See crisis worker's action continuum, below.)

Listening

Acting

LISTENING: Attending, observing, understanding, and responding with empathy, genuineness, respect, acceptance, nonjudgment, and caring.

1. *Define the problem.* Explore and define the problem from the client's point of view. Use active listening, including open-ended questions. Attend to both verbal and nonverbal messages of the client.

2. *Ensure client safety.* Assess lethality, criticality, immobility, or seriousness of threat to the client's physical and psychological safety. Assess both the client's internal events and the situation surrounding the client, and, if necessary, ensure that the client is made aware of alternatives to impulsive, self-destructive actions.

3. *Provide support.* Communicate to the client that the crisis worker is a valid support person. Demonstrate (by words, voice, and body language) a caring, positive, nonpossessive, nonjudgmental, acceptant, personal involvement with the client.

ACTING: Becoming involved in the intervention at a nondirective, collaborative, or directive level, according to the assessed needs of the client and the availability of environmental supports.

4. *Examine alternatives.* Assist client in exploring the choices he or she has available to him or her now. Facilitate a search for immediate situational supports, coping mechanisms, and positive thinking.

5. *Make plans.* Assist client in developing a realistic short-term plan that identifies additional resources and provides coping mechanisms—definite action steps that the client can own and comprehend.

6. *Obtain commitment.* Help client commit himself or herself to definite, positive action steps that the client can own and realistically accomplish or accept.

Crisis Worker's Action Continuum

Crisis worker is nondirective   Crisis worker is collaborative   Crisis worker is directive

(Threshold varies from client to client)   (Threshold varies from client to client)

Client is mobile   Client is partially mobile   Client is immobile

The crisis worker's level of action/involvement may be anywhere on the continuum according to a valid and realistic assessment of the client's level of mobility/immobility.

Note: From *Crisis Intervention Strategies*, 4th edition by James/Gilliland, © 2001. Reprinted with permission of Wadsworth, a division of Thomson Learning: www.thomsonrights.com. Fax 800-730-2215.

and the responsiveness to counselor overtures of help. The counselor also needs to check whether the individual has made a specific plan to carry out suicide (James & Gilliland, 2001). Counselors should be particularly concerned when suicidal persons start telling others about their specific plans to kill themselves. When the amount of risk is moderate, conselors can discuss alternative actions with clients and, as a follow-up, offer to refer them to a licensed counselor or therapist. In severe cases in which a person remains immobilized, counselors should consult with a psychiatrist, contact the family, and arrange for the client to be taken to the hospital emergency room.

LIAISON ACTIVITIES

By maintaining good professional relationships with other community agencies and specialists, a counseling center can expand its services to clients. Referrals to these agencies and specialists can be made with a minimum of delay or red tape. It is advisable that counselors have lists of referral sources available for clients or consultees. In addition, joint outreach programs in such areas as drug education, AIDS awareness, and career problems can be arranged for persons at various stages of development through communitywide workshops or seminars. And school counselors can have a variety of consultants available for use in the schools.

SUMMARY

In addition to direct counseling, counselors offer outreach services designed to improve the mental health climate for individuals within the community. These services involve prevention and intervention programs that augment and supplement the direct counseling duties of the counseling staff. The four types of outreach most commonly provided by counselors are consultation, psychoeducation, social change activities, and crisis intervention.

Counselors often act as consultants with each other to help gain insights or different perspectives regarding a particular case. They likewise act as consultants with faculty, administrators, parents, and employers regarding matters related to counseling.

Counselors also offer psychoeducational activities in the areas of personal, social, career, and educational development. Counselors may teach courses, offer workshops, or teach groups in schools and in the community. They may also teach personal and social skill building to improve self-image or the ability to relate in social interactions or to prepare for effective job searches. Other psychoeducational activities include training paraprofessionals to serve as aids to the counseling staff.

Counselors may also take direct social action to improve or change administrative policies or procedures that are impeding or stifling good mental health in the community or institutional setting. This step is particularly important if administrative policies involve actions that violate the ethical codes of the counselor.

Direct intervention becomes necessary when individuals experience a sudden, unexpected crisis or trauma that causes panic, severe depression, helplessness, or suicidal thoughts that render them incapable of overcoming the trauma by themselves. Intervention strategies include assessing the problem, calming the individual down, and determining follow-through measures or referrals.

PROJECTS AND ACTIVITIES

1. A school counselor receives a call from a parent concerned that her son is going with the wrong crowd. The student is not, and has not been, a client of the counselor. The parent asks the counselor to call in her son to set him straight. She requests that the counselor not tell her son that she called. How should the counselor respond?
2. Develop an educational and informational program focusing on the culture and customs of a minority group in your locality or in a locality in which you might like to work. How could you involve leaders and other members of the group in the development of the program?
3. Select two psychoeducational programs that have been proposed in the literature for counselors to use in educational institutions, the community, or both. Evaluate these programs on the basis of theoretical orientation,

consideration of rights to privacy, protection against psychological harm, and appropriateness to age level.
4. Discuss how a birth control agency and a counseling center staff in a school, college, or community center could develop a cooperative educational program that would appeal to both females and males.
5. Select and organize a list of books, pamphlets, and films about drug education, sex education, careers, and self-help. Consider the criteria you will use in selecting the material.
6. Interview a career counselor at your university and another at a community career counseling center regarding their outreach activities. Compare the activities in each agency. What are the similarities and differences? Compare also the training and experience of the professional staff at each of these settings.

REFERENCES

American Counseling Association (ACA). (1995). *Ethical standards of the American Counseling Association.* Alexandria, VA: Author.

Baker, S. B. (2000). *School counseling for the 21st century* (3rd ed.). Upper Saddle River, NJ: Merrill/Prentice Hall.

Baker, S. B., & Shaw, M. C. (1987). *Improving counseling through primary prevention.* Upper Saddle River, NJ: Merrill/ Prentice Hall.

Belkin, G. S. (1984). *Introduction to counseling.* Dubuque, IA: William C. Brown.

Boytim, J. A. (1986). The mental health counselor as a consultant. In A. J. Palmo & W. J. Weikel (Eds.), *Foundations of mental health counseling* (pp. 229–232). Springfield, IL: Charles C Thomas.

Brammer, L. M., Abrego, P. J., & Shostrom, E. L. (1993). *Therapeutic counseling and psychotherapy* (6th ed.). Upper Saddle River, NJ: Prentice Hall.

Brooks, D. K., Jr., & Weikel, W. J. (1986). History and development of the mental health counseling movement. In A. J. Palmo & W. J. Weikel (Eds.), *Foundations of mental health counseling* (pp. 3–28). Springfield, IL: Charles C Thomas.

Comer, R. J. (1996). *Fundamentals of abnormal psychology.* New York: W. H. Freeman.

Corey, G., Corey, M. S., & Callanan, P. (1998). *Issues and ethics in the helping professions* (5th ed.). Pacific Grove, CA: Brooks/Cole.

Corey, M. S., & Corey, G. (2002). *Groups: Process and practice* (6th ed.). Pacific Grove, CA: Brooks/Cole.

Dinkmeyer, D. (1976). *Systematic training for effective parenting.* Circle Pines, MN: American Guidance Service.

Gazda, G. M. (1989). *Group counseling: A developmental approach* (4th ed.). Boston: Allyn & Bacon.

Gelso, C. J., & Fretz, B. R. (2001). *Counseling psychology* (2nd ed.). Fort Worth, TX: Harcourt Brace.

Gerstein, L. H., & Sturmer, P. (1993). A Taoist paradigm of EAP consultation. *Journal of Counseling & Development, 72,* 178–184.

Gibson, R. L., & Mitchell, M. H. (1999). *Introduction to counseling and guidance* (5th ed.). Upper Saddle River, NJ: Merrill/Prentice Hall.

Gordon, T. (1975). *Parent effectiveness training.* New York: New American Library.

Gordon, T. (1977). *Teacher effectiveness training.* New York: McKay.

Hershenson, D. B., Power, P. W., & Waldo, M. (1996). *Community counseling: Contemporary theory and practice.* Boston: Allyn & Bacon.

Hutchison, W. S., Jr. (1985). The importance and criticalness of the family systems component of employee assistance programs. In J. F. Dickman, W. G. Emener, Jr., & W. S. Hutchison, Jr. (Eds.), *Counseling the troubled person in industry* (pp. 30–37). Springfield, IL: Charles C Thomas.

Isaacson, I. E., & Brown, D. (1993). *Career information, career counseling, and career development* (5th ed.). Boston: Allyn & Bacon.

Ivey, A. E., & Ivey, M. B. (1999). *Intentional interviewing and counseling: Facilitating client development in a multicultural society* (4th ed.). Pacific Grove, CA: Brooks/Cole.

James, R. K., & Gilliland, B. E. (2001). *Crisis intervention strategies* (4th ed.). Pacific Grove, CA: Brooks/Cole.

Kübler-Ross, E. (1975). *Death: The final stage of growth.* Upper Saddle River, NJ: Prentice Hall.

Kurpius, D. J., & Fuqua, D. (1993). Fundamental issues in defining consultation. *Journal of Counseling & Development, 71,* 598–600.

Lewis, J. A., & Lewis, M. D. (1986). *Counseling programs for employees in the workplace.* Monterey, CA: Brooks/Cole.

Myers, J. E. (1992). Wellness, prevention, development: The cornerstone of the profession. *Journal of Counseling & Development, 71,* 136–139.

Omizo, M. M., Omizo, S. A., & D'Andrea, M. J. (1992). Promoting wellness among elementary school children. *Journal of Counseling & Development, 71,* 194–198.

Quayle, D. (1985). American productivity: The devastating effect of alcoholism and drug use. In J. F. Dickman, W. G. Emener, Jr., & W. S. Hutchison, Jr. (Eds.), *Counseling the troubled person in industry* (pp. 20–29). Springfield, IL: Charles C Thomas.

Romano, J. L. (1992). Psychoeducational interventions for stress management and well-being. *Journal of Counseling & Development, 71,* 199–202.

Sue, D., Sue, D. W., & Sue, S. (2000). *Understanding abnormal behavior* (6th ed.). Boston Houghton Mifflin.

Witmer, J. M., & Sweeney, T. J. (1992). A holistic model for wellness and prevention over the life span [Special issue: Wellness through the life span]. *Journal of Counseling & Development, 71,* 140–148.

CHAPTER 9

Individual Counseling

I ndividual counseling is a process in which a professional counselor and a client develop an interactive relationship that fosters client self-awareness and empowers that person to resolve her or his particular situational problems effectively. Many complex variables influence the nature, intensity, and duration of the counseling process: the counselor's effectiveness, the counselor's particular theoretical point of view, the setting in which the counseling takes place, the client's characteristics, and the nature of the client's problem.

Personal and professional characteristics essential for effective counseling are discussed in chapter 4. Because effective counselors vary in their theoretical approaches, clients need to be aware of a counselor's particular approach to determine whether it is suitable to their needs. Frank Nugent's theoretical framework governs to a large extent how the nature of the counseling process is described here. His model has developed over the years from his work in various settings and is based on working with normally functioning individuals who volunteer to engage in counseling; moreover, it is based on those clients who experience situational conflicts or dilemmas resulting from transitional changes or losses in their lives. In the next six chapters this model is adapted to fit the special needs of clients and, in the last four chapters, is adapted to practical applications in different counseling settings.

THE COUNSELING SETTING

Either clients are in settings—for example, school, college, or workplace—where they can seek counseling help, or they come to a certain counseling agency in the community because of special needs. As discussed in chapter 1, the counseling setting significantly influences the type of counseling offered. In assessing the counseling treatment for particular clients, counselors need to consider the policies of their particular agency or institution regarding type, length, and intensity of services. Counselors also need to inform their clients of the limitations of their services.

Decisions about the length and type of treatment have been important considerations in all counseling settings. Many college counseling centers, because of tight budgets, have for some time limited the number of sessions offered. School counselors have also had to determine whether to work with individuals themselves or refer them to community agencies for more intensive work. In the community, health maintenance organizations and other managed care services advocate or mandate brief counseling and therapy (see chapters 1 and 6).

CLIENT CHARACTERISTICS

Research about client characteristics that contribute to effective counseling outcomes has proved inconclusive. This finding is not surprising because the criteria that have typically been used to describe effective clients are those that generally apply to optimally functioning individuals: willingness to admit problems, verbal fluency, ability to cope, and flexibility (Brammer, Abrego, & Shostrom, 1993; Heilbrun, 1982; Rogers, 1942). Researchers have overlooked the fact that clients who seek help tend to be anxious, doubtful, uncertain, or defensive, especially in an initial therapeutic encounter.

Clients differ considerably in their attitudes about starting counseling. Many clients these days have had previous counseling: Older clients and those who have attended college may have had a series of counseling experiences and may have been exposed to a variety of counseling approaches; some may have had counseling for specific needs, such as career counseling or weight-loss counseling; some may be therapywise, cynical, and wary; some may have formed certain opinions about therapy and about themselves from reading self-help books or taking self-administered personality surveys; even those who have never had counseling may have heard varying reports from friends. Despite the individual circumstances, clients generally approach an initial counseling session with apprehension.

Client apprehension is compounded by the anxieties that compelled them to seek counseling in the first place, symptoms that typically surface when individuals feel particularly vulnerable. One significant characteristic can generally be assumed for all clients, at least for those who voluntarily seek counseling: They recognize that they have difficulties and have the insight, strength, and motivation to seek help.

While developing relationships with clients and planning effective counseling sessions, counselors should consider basic client characteristics that might influence the counseling process: values, view of human nature, worldview. Are they shy or outgoing, articulate or glib or inarticulate? Do they have positive or negative views about human nature, about themselves, and about the world in general?

Other client characteristics that might influence counseling include whether clients believe they have ultimate control of their lives, whether they tend to blame others for their problems, or whether they tend to blame themselves. Attitudes such as these are apt to influence the degree to which clients can bring about changes within themselves or in their environment. Still other client characteristics—the degree of insight they have about their problems, their stated goals, the strength of their defenses—give clues to the degree to which they are able to confront and explore their problems.

These factors are all apt to influence how clients will respond to counseling—how they will interact with counselors, what they will expect to happen in the counseling sessions, and how motivated or capable they will be to make changes for growth. In turn, these characteristics will help counselors decide what goals are realistic for clients and what types of strategies will best help the clients attain those goals.

THE COUNSELING PROCESS

In the counseling process counselor and client develop a trusting, dynamic, interactive relationship that helps empower the client to resolve his or her problem. Counselors and therapists generally agree that a successful counseling outcome occurs when an effective relationship is established between counselor and client (Gelso & Carter, 1985). Moreover, most counselors recognize that an essential role of the counselor is to enable clients to self-explore and develop self-awareness as a way to resolve their problems.

The counseling process evolves through several stages, from the first interview through termination; the process is generally similar regardless of counselor orientation (Brammer et al., 1993; Egan, 2002; Sexton & Whiston, 1994). The counseling process can generally be divided into three overlapping stages: In the initial stage counselor and client develop a relationship that will foster client self-exploration, they clarify the nature of the problem, and they set goals and treatment plans. In the middle stage the counselor helps the client self-explore more deeply to increase insight and understanding of the problem. In the last stage the counselor and client work together in helping the client take action to change behaviors or attitudes in everyday living; they then proceed toward terminating the counseling sessions.

Tracey (1988) points out that the dynamics of the counselor-client relationship change during each of the three stages: In the initial stage counselors relate to clients on client terms, developing rapport, listening, and attending to client needs; in the middle stage counselors challenge clients to explore deeper emotions; in the last stage counselors relate to clients collaboratively as peers.

Initial Stage: Developing a Relationship and Clarifying the Presenting Problem

In the early sessions counselor and client begin to develop the mutual relationship necessary to carry them along on a journey together to resolve the client's problem. Right from the start counselors must convey through their overall manner that they are accepting and understanding. They must also assure their clients that they will maintain confidentiality throughout the counseling sessions. Further, counselors must create an ambience that assures the clients that their welfare is the primary concern during this time. No telephone calls or interruptions are allowed during sessions, counselors are on time for appointments, and counselors' offices are inviting, comfortable but not fancy, and soundproof.

Setting the Tone and Defining Parameters

In the crucial first interview, counselors lay the foundation and set a climate for an effective working relationship. In doing so, they have a somewhat paradoxical task. They must immediately convey an aura of understanding and warmth that assures the clients of trust. At the same time they must clarify the parameters of counseling, as well as gather information about the clients so as to make an initial assessment of the problem.

Clients arrive at the first interview feeling uncertain and ambivalent about talking intimately to a counselor. They may wonder whether they have sufficient strength to undertake the often painful experience of self-exploration. Along with their fears, they come with certain expectations about counselors and counseling (Moursund, 2002). They hope the counselors will not make negative judgments about them, they wonder whether the counselors will hold what they say in confidence, they sense the potential power of the counselors and the possible abuse of that power, and they hope the counselors will have the personal characteristics and expertise to help them.

The first interview can be awkward, particularly when a client is shy or reserved. Making social chitchat to set a client at ease is not recommended; the delay in getting to the reason for counseling can increase anxiety. Usually, a simple statement will suffice: "Tell me what brings you here for counseling." If the counselor has already talked on the telephone with the client, it would be helpful to review that conversation: "Last week, you called and said you had split up with your wife," or "The other day when you phoned, you said you were feeling depressed." If the person has been referred, it is usually helpful to go over how the referral occurred and what the client's expectations are.

During the first interview the counselor generally relies on *open questions* (to bring out general information) and *closed questions* (to obtain more specific information). In the following interchange, for example, the counselor obtains information from the client while also responding to the client's feelings.

COUNSELOR: Have you ever had counseling before? [closed question]
CLIENT: Yes, I saw a counselor about a year ago.
COUNSELOR: What do you think you gained from that experience? [open question]
CLIENT: Nothing much. I was disappointed. My counselor didn't hear what I was saying.
COUNSELOR: You didn't get what you had hoped for, an understanding counselor. [reflection of feeling]

Besides setting a climate of acceptance and warmth and determining the appropriateness of service, counselors explain to clients what they can expect in counseling. Counselors also describe their qualifications and the policies of the agency they work for. They may ask clients what they are hoping for. Confidentiality, rights of privacy, and other ethical and legal considerations also need to be clarified (see chap. 3).

The counselor must make time at the end of the first session to discuss whether the client's concerns are within the counselor's expertise or whether the client believes that the counselor can best serve her or his needs. For example, if the client's main concern is alcohol addiction and the counselor does not work with this problem, then it is necessary to refer the client to someone who does. Or if the client needs more intensive help than the counselor or agency is prepared to provide or the agency limits intensive therapy, then the counselor can suggest an appropriate referral.

Clients at this time may also decide that the counselor's theoretical orientation or approach is not what they were expecting. If so, the counselor can suggest someone more in line with the clients' preferences. In states where counselors are licensed for private practice, it is mandatory that counselors disclose their educational background, theoretical orientation, and the types of techniques they may use. Even when not mandated, this disclosure is a sound idea because counselor and client then have a better idea about their potential compatibility.

Counselors also need to discuss length of sessions, fees, and payment of fees and to arrange regular meeting times. Those counselors in private practice who are eligible for third-party insurance payments also need to explain the expected diagnosis required by the insurance company.

Developing a Mutual Relationship

An effective counseling relationship occurs when trust develops between a counselor and a client and is maintained throughout the counseling process. Trust develops when clients believe that their counselors accept them as worthy persons with dignity and value regardless of what they disclose about themselves. Bordin (1975), who calls the counselor-client relationship a *working alliance,* divides the process of forming that alliance into three parts: (a) establishment of an emotional bond, (b) mutual agreement about goals, and (c) mutual agreement about tasks.

In the early stage of counseling, while client and counselor are getting to know each other and are beginning to establish mutual trust, the counselor listens to the client's concerns and encourages him or her to express the feelings and thoughts that are bothersome; moreover, the counselor fully accepts what the client has to say. This client-centered approach encourages clients to talk more freely and also gives counselors important information to use later when they explore problems more deeply.

A counselor's accepting, nonjudgmental attitude helps clients reveal more about the hurt, pain, or anxiety they are experiencing. In a warm, accepting atmosphere, counselors demonstrate understanding and genuineness and attention to client feelings even as they focus on cognitive processes about what is happening or how clients perceive what is happening in their lives.

A counselor might respond to a client's concerns with a reflection of feeling intended to encourage the client to express more feelings.

CLIENT [a 30-year-old divorcee]:   My whole life collapsed when my husband left me and the children without warning. I'm not sleeping well. I don't have job skills to take care of myself and my two children.
COUNSELOR: You're feeling overwhelmed by it all.
CLIENT: Yes, I am, and I see no way out unless I get some training.

Counselors may also rephrase a client statement to show they are listening and to help the client focus on the concern.

CLIENT: I know it doesn't help my grades when I procrastinate and start projects the night before they are due, but I keep doing it.

COUNSELOR: You know your grades won't improve if you wait until the last minute to begin your project, but up to now you feel unable to change that behavior.
CLIENT: Yes, that's why I decided I need help. I see the problem but not the solution.

To help a client elaborate on the problem, the counselor might ask for clarification.

CLIENT: Sometimes I get a peculiar feeling about myself and my life.
COUNSELOR: Can you tell me more about what you mean by "peculiar feeling"?
CLIENT: Yes, I sometimes feel as though nothing in my life is real, as though I'm in a dream.

Understanding the Client's Problem

Counselors consider several factors about clients and their situational concerns: the severity and complexity of the problem, length and persistence of symptoms, and past stability of the clients. Counselors also consider the context in which clients are experiencing the problem: social and cultural factors, degree of environmental support, and family relationships. These and the other client characteristics described earlier help determine the way counseling will proceed.

Counselors need to consider the functionality of the clients' families of origin, the nature of clients' current familial relationships, the way clients function in their careers or schoolwork, and the types of environmental support available to them. Counselors must also assess how clients' changes in attitudes and behavior will be received by persons close to them. In other words, what will be the consequences of their change?

Counselors must also consider the cultural backgrounds of their clients, particularly those from ethnic groups or from numerous cultural subgroups. Asians, for instance, are made up of distinctly different ethnic groups—Chinese, Japanese, Thai, Korean, Vietnamese, and so on. Moreover, for recent immigrants ethnic identity also depends on whether one is first, second, or third generation in the United States. Where one lives also influences one's cultural identity: Growing up in California is considerably different from growing up in New York City or Alabama. And for Native Americans, growing up on a reservation as a semisovereign tribal nation is a significantly different experience from that of all the other cultural groups. Furthermore, growing up on the Sioux reservation is culturally different from growing up on the Swinomish reservation (see chap. 14).

Forming a Working Hypothesis and Making a Tentative Diagnosis

An important step begins in the first interview and continues during the initial stage of counseling—forming a hypothesis of the client's problem. Using information gained by observing and interviewing the client, the counselor assesses the nature and complexity of the problem to make a tentative hypothesis, or diagnosis of the problem.

For those clients covered by mental health insurance, counselors and therapists must make diagnoses quickly because diagnoses are required in order for clients to qualify for services. In many college counseling centers and community agencies, determining whether clients qualify for services is accomplished in intake interviews.

Counselors must also determine whether clients require a considerable number of sessions or only a few. If symptoms are mild and of short duration, motivation is high, environmental disruption is at a minimum, and the problem is specific and can be resolved in a reasonable amount of time, the counselor can assume that short-term counseling is sufficient. However, if a client has long-term symptoms, complicated or vague problems, strong defenses, confused values, or complex, immobilizing social-cultural conditions, the counselor can assume that deeper, more intensive work is needed before change will occur. To help in these decisions, many counselors use assessment devices such as tests, inventories, behavioral surveys, or schedules.

Use of Tests, Inventories, or Behavioral Assessments.   During the first stages of exploration, a self-inventory may be helpful for clients who have difficulty expressing their needs or talking about their feelings. Nonthreatening personality inventories can measure normal personality characteristics (see chap. 7).

Cognitive-behaviorists tend to use behavioral observations and self-monitoring scales, rather than standardized or nonstandardized tests or inventories, to help them assess clients' problems. Many counselors prefer to make a tentative assessment of a client's difficulty over several sessions in the early phase of counseling. Client-centered counselors following Carl Rogers's (1951) approach do little, if any, diagnosis, believing that it blocks an effective relationship.

Many counselors do not label clients diagnostically but prefer to view diagnosis as a continuous, ongoing process that focuses on understanding clients and on helping them understand themselves. In this approach counselors develop a working hypothesis to help them set goals and establish a productive, flexible plan (Brammer et al., 1993; Corey, 2001).

Personal construct founder George Kelly (1955, reissued in 1963) and his followers, such as Fransella and Dalton (2000), likewise object to labeling client behavior, claiming that such conceptualizations are indications only of the counselor's own theoretical constructs and say little about the client. Personal construct counselors and therapists aim at understanding how clients perceive themselves so as to plan a way to make the necessary changes the clients think are necessary.

> The counsellor must find avenues in the client's construing of the world along which he and the client may move towards a solution of the client's problem. This all leads to our construing any diagnosis as *the planning stage for client reconstruction.* Kelly calls this "transitive diagnosis." (Fransella & Dalton, 2000, p. 35)

The term *diagnosis,* Kelly warns, is not meant in the usual sense of categorizing with a set prescribed treatment for everyone who is similarly diagnosed. He uses the term *transitive diagnosis* for a special reason.

> The term suggests that we are concerned with transitions in the client's life, that we are looking for bridges between the client's present and his future. Moreover, we expect to take an active part in helping the client select or build the bridges to be used and in helping him cross them safely. (Fransella & Dalton, 2000, p. 32)

In determining transitive diagnoses, counselors help clients search for and determine their own personal constructs—that is, self-assessments of the way they see themselves and others. Accordingly, Kelly and other personal construct practitioners who followed him have created an elaborate system for helping clients explore their world. They use numerous techniques—such as repertory grids, laddering, and pyramiding—in which clients in various ways explore and discover their systems of personal constructs. This process can be very time-consuming. The grids and other techniques are optional, however. Counselor can select among them or not use them at all, depending on the client and the circumstances (Fransella & Dalton, 2000).

Use of the DSM-IV-TR.   The *DSM-IV-TR* has become a prominent instrument used by counselors and therapists for clients covered by health insurance. Community counselors and therapists must use diagnostic categories in the *DSM-IV-TR* to justify that a client is eligible to receive insurance benefits (Corey, Corey, & Callanan, 1998). They may also use this instrument to help in assessing the nature and severity of the emotional disorder to determine appropriate treatment or referral (see chap. 7).

Setting Goals and Designing a Plan of Action

Once a client's presenting problem has been discussed and conceptualized, counselor and client work together to set goals and develop a plan of action. Goals need to be as clear and specific as possible, consistent with the complexity of the problem. They must be realistic, flexible, in line with client resources and capabilities, stated in a way that permits continual evaluation of progress, and possible to accomplish in a realistic amount of time (Egan, 2002). Consideration must be given to whether any external circumstances are hindering a client's goal. For example, a client who desires a particular type of training that is only available 3,000 miles away but who cannot leave his family will have to come to terms with his conflicting goals.

Some counselors, particularly behaviorists and cognitive-behaviorists, find it productive to develop contracts with clients. In such cases a contract that includes a statement of goals, the techniques to be followed, and the length of time to accomplish goals can serve as a useful working model for both counselor and client. Goals and treatment plans, however, must be flexible enough to be modified if circumstances warrant a change.

Middle Stage: Exploring More Deeply

In the middle stage of counseling, a shift occurs in the counseling process. Once counselor and client have discussed preliminaries, reached an initial understanding of each other and the client's problem, and agreed on the purpose for working together, they then move into deeper explorations.

For brief, solution-focused, or time-limited counseling, the middle stage is fairly short. Likewise, for those clients who are seeking counseling to solve a particular problem, who have a fairly well developed sense of themselves, and who don't need to go through the complicated process of self-exploration at this time or for this particular purpose, counseling with a brief middle stage is all that is necessary. Counselors and clients can then proceed to the last stage, where they focus on turning new client attitudes and insights into effective behavioral changes in everyday life.

For counseling needs that take more time, however, the process in the middle stage becomes complicated and unpredictable and thus is difficult to describe. As Moursund (2002) points out, in contrast with the fairly predictable first and last stages, the middle stage can go in any number of directions; and the counselor needs to allow clients to explore the numerous avenues under their own volition and at their own pace. "There will be occasions when you literally will not know what the client is moving into, or when you will think you know, only to discover later that you were mistaken. Ambiguity comes with the territory" (Moursund, 2002, p. 86).

Noting Movement and Gaining Emotional Insights

A major characteristic of the counseling process is the sense of movement, accelerating especially in the middle stage of the counseling process (Miller & Stiver, 1997; Rogers, 1942, 1951). Rogers was one of the first to note this aspect (1942), describing in particular the client's gaining of new insights as well as feelings of increasing emotional intensity and turbulence. Expanding on this sense of movement, in his 1951 text Rogers alerted counselors to watch for the various aspects of movement or change that occur in the client during the counseling process. Counselors should watch for changes in perception and changes of feelings; increasing feelings of self-worth and independence; less denial of experience; and changes in values. Rogers also noted the changing emotional relationship between client and counselor.

Over the years, counselors and therapists have confirmed this movement or evolving process that counselor and client experience, particularly the shift from client concerns about external problems to client exploration of inner feelings and emotions.

> The shift from early- to-middle-phase work, then, is marked by a shift from primarily cognitive concerns to an emphasis on emotional work, from focusing on external to focusing on internal events, from talking about relationships outside of therapy to experiencing relationships within the therapy session itself. (Moursund, 2002, p. 76)

In this move from cognitions to emotions, clients begin to take more risks in disclosing their feelings and actions toward themselves and others, and the process shifts to the client-counselor relationship: "Emotional issues begin to take precedence over cognitive ones, and the therapeutic relationship itself is frequently the arena in which these issues are worked through" (Moursund, 2002, p. 76). Therapists and counselors are recognizing that, in the evolving client-counselor relationship, the counselor experiences feelings and new insights as well. These are discussed later in the chapter.

Miller and Stiver (1997), who emphasize developing and maintaining mutual connections in relationships, also note movement as a primary indicator in the therapeutic process. They believe that commencement of movement begins with the awareness of a mutual empathic relationship between patient[1] or client and therapist or counselor. This bonding elicits motion itself, which commences precisely when the patient notices that

---

[1]Miller and Stiver (1997) prefer to use the term *patient* because *client* implies someone in a business transaction. They do not like using the term *patient,* but they say, "It's the best of bad choices" (p. 217). Its original meaning is "one who suffers," stemming from the Latin "to endure."

the feelings she is sharing have an impact on the therapist. The therapist, feeling moved by the patient's experience, responds. Because the patient's dysfunction is based on the denial of feelings by others, therapist responsiveness is a new experience for the client and is precisely what moves them both. With a focus on developing mutual empathic connections, the counseling process begins.

> Participating together . . . is very different from struggling alone without a sense of impact or response, or, alternatively, feeling that you have to hold back parts of yourself because you don't know 'where the other person is' psychologically. This is what we mean by building increasing mutual empathy and mutual empowerment in therapy. (Miller & Stiver, 1997, p. 133)

Personal construct theorists also recognize motion or movement, similar to taking a journey: After the client ascertains his or her current constructs and those parts that are dissatisfactory, client and counselor embark on the path of reconstruing the client's personal constructs in ways that are compatible with the client's circumstances (Fransella & Dalton, 2000). Personal construct counselors note that an increase of emotional reactions is inevitable during therapeutic transitional phases, which they call the *cycles of change.* These counselors watch for increased feelings of anxiety, threat, guilt, hostility, and aggression, signs that the client is experiencing changes. These feelings occur in increasing and decreasing cycles of intensity during the cycles of change (Fransella & Dalton, 2000).

During the cycles of change, clients alternate between loosening and tightening their constructs. They loosen constructs when they lower cognitive awareness, give into experience, and participate without judgment or without holding back. As they use relaxation techniques or engage in free association or dream work, the counselor uncritically accepts the client's trial behaviors. In tightening their constructs, clients raise cognitive processes to a high level by keeping logs of their new experiences, summarizing what happens, evaluating and comparing them to other experiences, and putting them into historical context. Counselors may challenge what the clients mean but are careful not to impose their own differing point of view or their own constructs on the clients (Fransella & Dalton, 2000).

The counselor's primary role is to help guide the client between the alternating loosening and tightening of constructs because of the hazards inherent in going too far either way. Becoming too loose brings on strong anxieties as the client tries unfamiliar ways and experiences chaotic reactions. With premature tightening of constructs, on the other hand, the client is apt to conclude that the new experience was bad and thus will revert back to the safety of familiar old constructs.

Transference. As clients increase their self-disclosure and self-awareness, counselors and clients begin to develop emotional interactions that need to be acknowledged and worked through for counseling to proceed. These interactions are called *transference* and *countertransference* and are described in chapter 6 as cornerstones of psychoanalysis. Even though these concepts are well known in psychoanalysis, many counseling professionals believe that they are universal in all relationships (Brammer et al., 1993; Gelso & Carter, 1985; Young, 1992). Although most counselors, in their focus on short-term situational problems, have not historically dealt with these issues, recently, both counselors and therapists have been attending to problematic transference and countertransference issues that emerge during this stage.

Transference refers to clients transferring onto the therapist emotions developed from an early age toward significant others in their lives. When clients trust a counselor and are encouraged to become aware of their emotions, they begin to express transference feelings—anger, dependency, admiration, love, or hate—toward their counselor. "To varying degrees, transference occurs in probably all relationships. The therapeutic situation, however, with its emphasis on a kind of controlled help-giving, magnifies and intensifies this natural reaction" (Gelso & Carter, 1985, p. 169).

Rogers (1951) discouraged counselors from fostering transference reactions because he feared it would encourage client dependence on the counselor. He thus urged counselors to depersonalize themselves and to avoid making interpretations and giving advice. But his theory has been criticized as not only unnatural but also controlling (May & Yalom, 1995).

Regarding transference, Corsini (1995), a student of Rogers, says that counseling has come a long way since Rogers's time. Watkins (1983) has given attention to the value of transference for counselors; clients with transference issues, he explains, are predisposed to react to others in a set way. "Consequently, the counselee enters a relationship—be it of an impersonal, friendly, or therapeutic nature—with a fixed bent in perceptions and feelings" (Watkins, cited in Dryden, 1998, p. 75). Clients with transference issues thus tend to distort reality. Their set reactions act as a defensive mechanism and prevent self-development. For these reasons, Watkins explains, it is important that counselors address transference issues.

Counselors now generally recognize the value of transference as a natural process. In a therapeutic situation clients who have been projecting feelings and attitudes onto parents and other authority figures start transferring their feelings onto the counselor; with therapeutic help, they become aware of those and similar transference feelings toward other significant persons in their lives. Counselors and therapists help clients express strong feelings by not reacting negatively or making judgments—in contrast with how parents might respond. This accepting attitude reduces client defensiveness and the anxiety related to expressing forbidden feelings.

Brammer et al. (1993) offer suggestions on working through feelings of transference. The counselor might ask a clarifying question, such as, "You seem to be angry with me today. Why is that?" A counselor could also reflect a client's feelings if the client denies them: "You think these feelings might upset me?" Or the counselor may interpret the transference, demonstrating that the client's earlier interpersonal interactions relate to current behavior, while reassuring the client that these feelings are normal: "Perhaps you become anxious when you show anger toward people. Perhaps you are afraid that you are showing too much anger toward me."

Two recent alternative approaches to the concept of transference are the *psychodynamic therapies* of Miller and Stiver (1997) and others who represent the women at the Stone Center and the *personal construct therapies* (Fransella & Dalton, 2000). Because their therapeutic philosophy is based on developing a relationship in which therapist and client engage in a mutual connection (see chap. 5), Miller and Stiver believe that transference experiences are natural and should not be avoided.

> We believe that if the therapist is able to create a new relational context that is empathic and empowering, she will provide a more fertile ground for the essentials of transference to emerge. . . . We see transference as an avenue to learning some of the essentials of past relationships and to seeing how they impact the current therapy relationship. (p. 139)

Moreover, Stiver (1997) emphasizes that "focused attention to transference phenomena provides the central work of the therapy" (p. 38).

Miller and Stiver (1997) point out two objections to traditional approaches to transference. First, they object to the therapist or counselor adopting a neutral role, which runs counter to their theory of mutual connections in relationships. They also object to the therapist or counselor making interpretations of client responses.

> We are not at all persuaded that the therapist offering interpretations about the transference to the patient is necessarily as effective as we were taught it would be. These formulations can often be experienced as highly intellectualized, or as criticisms, and often they are not very meaningful to the patient. (p. 140)

Personal construct counselors also view transference as a useful part of the process if transference is seen as the client casting the counselor in various roles during the changing cyclical process. If, however, the client literally sees the counselor as an object on which the client has become dependent, the counselor needs to reevaluate the relationship and then be alert to such a future possibility before it happens. The counselor needs to guide the client into projecting feelings onto imaginary figures who symbolize persons in his or her life or into enacting roles.

Countertransference.   It is equally important for counselors to recognize their own irrational feelings that they have projected onto clients. When counselors feel uncomfortable with clients or experience irritation or resentment toward them or when they foster client dependence or become too emotionally involved, they must ask themselves why these feelings exist. And if these feelings persist, counselors should consult with another professional. If feelings of countertransference persist with more than one client, the counselor may need counseling or therapy.

Attention has been given to how counselors can use their irrational feelings toward clients to enrich the counseling relationship. In his article "In Praise of Countertransference: Harvesting Our Errors," Taffel (1993) notes that when counselors become aware of and accept their seemingly irrational or inappropriate feelings about clients, they can perceive their projected feelings as "enlightening mistakes and fruitful errors and can make them part of a richer and more realistic vision of the therapeutic experience" (p. 57).

Countertransference issues are a primary consideration for Miller and Stiver (1997) and the women at the Stone Center. They view the therapists' emotional reactions as positive signs, signals for them to come to terms with their own unresolved emotional issues. "Especially when a particular therapy relationship is difficult or confusing, the therapist needs to make certain she has a growthful relational context of herself" (Surrey, 1997, p. 45). They also urge the therapist who experiences countertransference reactions to share them with other professionals, "not as signs of failure but often as necessary arenas for growth and relationship movement" (Surrey, 1997, p. 45).

Personal construct counselors believe that countertransference is a greater concern than transference is. "It is even more vital to be aware of any counter dependency transference, with the counsellor projecting his or her own needs onto the client" (Fransella & Dalton, 2000, p. 107).

Coping with Impasse

During the middle stage, clients begin to make significant changes in their attitudes and outlooks and gain new insights into their problems. They have bonded well with their counselors and have developed trust. Counselors or therapists feel good about the progress. Then, suddenly, right after positive improvements have occurred, clients react, and there's a breakdown. They revert back to old ways, and an impasse develops in the client-counselor relationship that is very frustrating to the counselor (Miller & Stiver, 1997). Some therapists and counselors have recently been dwelling on this period at length because they acknowledge it as the most difficult stage. They have been reconsidering the traditional assessment of impasse and resistance.

Resistance. Impasses as a sign of client defenses have long been known in psychoanalysis and have been considered typical of the therapeutic process. Over the years, therapists have developed strategies to work with client defenses and resistances, which they have perceived historically as a negative factor impeding progress in counseling. More recently, resistance has been recognized as an expected part of therapy that can be used to produce more effective counseling (Brammer et al., 1993; Cormier & Cormier, 1998).

Assuming that the client comes to counseling voluntarily, counselors can recognize that a client's resistance may be signaling that important sensitive feelings are being tapped; defenses arise to prevent feelings of anxiety or pain. Similarly, when a physician pokes a sensitive spot in the anatomy, the patient winces, withdraws, or cries out in pain. Clients naturally will be ambivalent about change, uncomfortable about the need to disclose painful or shameful things about themselves, and afraid to face what the therapist is trying to help them explore.

Client resistance can range from open hostility or antagonism to more subtle, passively resistant behavior, such as being late for appointments or skipping them, misinterpreting what the counselor says, or agreeing with everything the counselor suggests. These manifestations may be perplexing to new counselors, particularly because the client has initiated counseling and is paying a fee for the sessions. But such behaviors make sense when counselors recognize that these behaviors are a means of preventing disturbing feelings from coming into awareness.

Strategies. Many counselors use *social influencing skills* suitable for this stage—such as *interpretation, self-disclosure,* and *confrontation*—to help clients in their self-exploration (Ivey & Ivey, 1999; see also chap. 4). With this approach they attempt to increase the depth of client understanding or encourage clients to comment on the causes of their behavior, the amount of control they have over their circumstances, or the meaning behind their remarks.

Counselors may offer *interpretations* of the clients' defensive attitudes and behaviors that are keeping the clients from becoming aware of painful experiences (Brammer et al., 1993). Interpretations should be offered, however, only after clients are at least aware of the particular emotions they are experiencing and the context in which the feelings arose.

Brammer et al. (1993) suggest that it is wise to focus on attitudes or behaviors that are subject to clients' control, rather than to point out difficulties they are experiencing that they cannot change. Brammer et al. also recommend tentative positive interpretations, rather than a dogmatic negative approach.

Counselors may also use *self-disclosure* to encourage clients to explore feelings. But self-disclosure must be appropriate to client goals, must not burden clients, must not be done too frequently, and must be adapted to a particular client's feelings or circumstances (Egan, 2002).

CLIENT: I'm in a new job, have a new exciting relationship, am moving to a bigger and better apartment. Things are going great, but I feel sick to my stomach.

COUNSELOR: So many major transitions going on in your life all at once can be unsettling and stressful even when they're positive. I recall having butterflies in my stomach when I started my first job in counseling in a new city right after I married.

Other examples of social influencing skills include *encouragement,* in which counselors praise clients' efforts in disclosing more about themselves, and giving *directives* or *information* or *advice* when clients' apparent lack of movement seems related to a lack of appropriate information or experience.

Both psychodynamic feminist therapists Miller and Stiver (1997) and personal construct therapists and counselors such as Fransella and Dalton (2000) object to traditional therapeutic approaches to resistance, in which therapists or counselors blame the clients for not cooperating. They also object to the various strategies that are then employed to break down client resistances, from outright confrontation to subtle and not-so-subtle manipulative strategies.

Miller and Stiver (1997) are emphatic about the necessity for therapists to be aware of patients' needs to hold on to their defenses. The aim of therapists is to be aware of patients' strategies of disconnection. Miller and Stiver emphasize the importance of "respecting these strategies of disconnection rather than viewing them as what therapists typically call defenses—something the therapist hopes to get rid of as quickly as possible" (p. 149). It is so crucial that therapists remain empathic with patients when they shift away and disconnect that Miller and Stiver call their approach the *therapy of honoring the client's disconnecting strategies.*

> Indeed, one way to describe therapy is to say that it is a special place designed for working on disconnections (that's why it can be so hard)—and for learning to move on through the pain of disconnection to new connections, that's why it can be so fulfilling and enlarging for both people involved. (p. 149)

Personal construct practitioners believe that when a client gets defensive or shows signs of resistance, counselors should back off and reevaluate their strategies.

> A client may sometimes appear to 'resist' attempts to persuade her to loosen her construing. . . . It means that the counsellor has not got a clear enough view of what the client is being asked to do. There is a failure of communication between the client and counsellor. There may be too much threat. The client may be having too great a struggle to keep anchors firmly embedded in reality readily to countenance loosening their hold. (Fransella & Dalton, 2000, p. 97)

Although increasingly intense feelings of fear, threat, anxiety, and guilt are signs of movement in transitions, if the feelings are too intense, clients will revert back, resist, and raise defenses. Such signs of resistance alert counselors to pause and try to better understand where clients are coming from.

Counselors have a particularly difficult time working with clients' hostile feelings. Although these feelings can be recognized as part of the transitional process, they may also be signs of patient feelings of threat and chaos. After venturing out aggressively when they have been passive most of their lives, clients may react adversely, feel guilty, and retreat back into old patterns. In such cases counselors can ask clients to describe areas in their lives where they feel secure, where they most feel a sense of themselves. Fransella and Dalton (2000) cite the case of a client who enjoys stamp collecting and who reacts defensively in most situations. However, because the client feels very secure collecting stamps, he can risk trying new possibilities in this domain.

Last Stage: Integrating Client Changes Into Daily Life

As a result of deeper self-exploration and development of a positive relationship with counselors, clients become more self-confident, more assertive, and more authentic in counseling sessions. A "real" counseling relationship emerges in which clients perceive counselors without distortion. This new relationship permits clients to express feelings more authentically, assert their needs, continue to be insightful, and gain understanding of themselves and others (Gelso & Carter, 1985).

In the last stage the counseling relationship becomes collaborative; counselors and clients are peers working together to help the clients reach agreed-on goals (Tracey, 1988). In addition, counselors become more real; they feel free now to offer their own opinions, give advice, and instruct clients in coping or adopting social and self-management skills.

As counselors and clients focus on reaching the goals laid out in the initial stage, the social contexts in which clients will apply their new attitudes and behaviors become a primary counselor-client consideration. With the counselors' help, the clients' major task now is to apply to relationships and circumstances in everyday life the changes in perception, feelings, and behavior generated during counseling sessions.

Clients should be alerted that spouses, other family members, and colleagues, rather than welcoming the client changes, may be puzzled, resistant, resentful, or hostile to them. The counselor has provided an accepting atmosphere to foster and nurture client changes, but these same accepting conditions generally do not exist in the typical client's world. Clients may also be asserting their new feelings in ways that offend others.

Counselors can help their clients consider more effective and less aggressive ways to relate to significant others who are resisting client changes. Counselors can, for example, rehearse with clients effective ways of asserting themselves. And after clients make trial attempts, counselors can give them feedback about the effectiveness of their actions. At the same time counselors can keep their clients from reverting back to their former ways.

Hansen, Rossberg, and Cramer (1994) point out that this is an important stage, a "working through" stage in which the client's new insights and self-understanding are put into constructive action. "The client gains little in the long run from an intellectual understanding of the problem unless she or he is able to try out new methods of behaving" (p. 239).

Counselors differ in the degree of action-oriented strategies and techniques they use in this last stage, depending on their theoretical orientation (see chap. 6). Client-centered counselors, for instance, tend not to use techniques. Psychodynamic counselors tend to focus only on changes taking place within counseling or therapy sessions. Gestaltists use dramatic enactments—role playing, visual imagery, empty chair techniques—as ways for clients to practice changing behavior, but these practices also are confined to counseling sessions.

Cognitive-behavioral and personal construct counselors, in contrast, use many instructional and directive techniques to help clients apply new learning to their everyday actions and relationships. Some even begin earlier, in the middle stage. Personal construct counselors, for example, integrate restructuring strategies into behavioral action in the middle stage because they emphasize the importance of clients applying new insights and attitudes to behavior as they go along in the therapeutic process. "It is in action, in the person's experiments with ways of *behaving* differently that new constructions of events are tried and tested" (Fransella & Dalton, 2000, p. 114).

Cognitive-behaviorists have taken the lead in developing strategies to help clients take action in their everyday lives; Egan (2002) discusses at length how strategies can be worked out effectively. Briefly, they must be specific and realistic, powerful enough to lead to client changes and move clients toward stated goals with a clear, workable plan of action. They must also be actions that clients decide are best for them and are consistent with their values. It is also important to consider the context in which changes in behavior and attitude are practiced. For example, those who have just stopped drinking alcohol should avoid social interactions that center on drinking alcohol. And clients should try out new behaviors in gradual steps.

Counselors can motivate clients to take action by using the social influencing skills described in the previous stage. They would first use strategies that encourage clients to be willing to take appropriate actions; once the clients are willing, the counselors can teach them certain skills to carry out the actions effectively. The numerous social influencing strategies include confronting, probing, offering information, providing feedback about specific behaviors and attitudes, and considering the logical consequences of one's actions. In the following case the counselor raises the question of *logical consequences* when a client impulsively decides to make a major change in life.

CLIENT: I'm fed up. I'm going in tomorrow to let them know I quit.
COUNSELOR: This is the first time you've mentioned this, and you've not explored alternative jobs. How will you support yourself and your wife?

If a client takes no initiative to change after expressing a strong desire to change, the counselor might *confront* the client.

COUNSELOR: You've expressed dissatisfaction with your work, and you've mentioned some alternative jobs. Yet you've said nothing about changing. What's going on?
CLIENT: I've just been too busy to think about it.
COUNSELOR: Are you feeling ambivalent about leaving your job?

Once the client is ready and willing to take appropriate action, the counselor can instruct the client in various skills or strategies to help him or her make changes in daily life. These strategies include conducting behavioral rehearsals in which clients rehearse new behaviors with the counselor; using coping or adaptive skills, such as self-management or self-monitoring skills; modeling behaviors of others; keeping journals; engaging in relaxation exercises; completing homework assignments; and getting feedback from counselors.

Self-management and self-monitoring strategies help clients direct and control their own behavioral change. "Self-management methods involve a combination of behavioral and cognitive-behavioral strategies to increase a client's self-control and ability to change his or her behavior" (Brammer et al., 1993, p. 194). These methods are particularly useful for clients with concerns such as weight loss, anxiety, insomnia, poor interpersonal and communication skills, and nicotine addiction (Miltenberger, 2001). Self-management strategies for addictive persons, for example, involve overcoming barriers that arise when clients try to replace negative behaviors that are immediately gratifying with behaviors that lead to better health but have delayed rewards (Miltenberger, 2001). Obese clients who wish to follow a weight-loss diet might make a self-contract that includes reinforcing themselves with desirable and positive nonfood rewards for sticking to the contract. They also might eliminate easy access to immediately gratifying junk food and increase easy access to nutritious and tasty low-calorie foods and to pleasurable, nonfood activities. Meichenbaum's (1985) stress-inoculation therapy, described in chapter 6, is a well-known self-management strategy in which clients learn and practice coping skills to replace nonadaptive self-statements that accompany stress with more adaptive ones (Miltenberger, 2001).

Counselors can also help clients explore community facilities that offer training in skills they may need—assertiveness training, self-management, weight control. And counselors can help clients search for and evaluate social support systems in the community, such as single-parenting or eating disorder groups.

Close collaboration between counselors and clients is crucial to the success of these programs. Not only are clients expected to initiate changes, but they are expected to monitor their progress as well.

> Self-management programs rely on therapist and client negotiated tasks and homework assignments to both enhance client motivation and structure the change program. . . . Self-monitoring is used to measure progress over time and as an activity that can produce change itself. Clients are taught to administer both verbal and material reinforcers for personal progress. (Brammer et al., 1993, pp. 194–195)

Termination of Counseling Sessions

Effective termination of counseling sessions is a key factor in how successful counseling outcome will be. An otherwise productive client-counselor interaction can be marred if the process is terminated before clients are ready or if sessions continue beyond client need. Successful counseling outcomes are more likely to occur when counselors and clients jointly decide when termination is appropriate, prepare to end the sessions, and attend to the emotional responses that go along with termination.

During the termination stage, counselors help clients review major themes that have emerged during counseling and help them assess their progress in attaining their goals. Counselors also consider how clients can apply and generalize their new learnings and insights to problems that may arise in the future. And counselors can encourage clients to express their feelings regarding the ending of the counseling relationship (Moursund, 2002).

Determining the Appropriate Time

Counselors and clients can determine whether the clients are ready to end the sessions by assessing whether the original symptoms or presenting problems have been resolved. In what specific ways has client stress been reduced? What skills have been developed to help clients cope with concerns? In what ways are clients relating more effectively with others or functioning more constructively in their jobs, academics, or home life? Do clients feel more positive about and more comfortable with themselves?

Fransella and Dalton (2000) list several aspects of client changes or "sufficient psychological movement" to look for: changes in the nature of construing; ability to loosen and tighten construing appropriately; ability to cope with transitional periods of increased anxiety, threat, guilt, and hostility; and the tendency to "move away from the client's 'problems' and his immediate personal concerns into a more dilated field of interest" (pp. 144–145).

If the counselor believes that the client's problem has been resolved, the counselor may raise the issue directly: "I have observed some positive changes in your attitudes, behavior, and relationships. You've made a decision about school, your relationship with your wife has improved, and your work is going well. I wonder if you need any further counseling at this time." If the client agrees, then a termination process can be worked out.

The client may also bring up the idea of termination: "I seem to be doing well on my job and in my relationships. I am sleeping better, and I don't have as many headaches. Maybe I no longer need to see you." If the counselor thinks the client is not quite ready for termination, together they can discuss whether it is advisable to terminate at this time.

Terminating Too Soon

At times counselors or clients initiate termination before the clients have attained counseling goals. Counselors may end a relationship prematurely because they feel resentful toward the client or anxious about whether they can help the client—difficulties relating to countertransference issues discussed earlier. The clients' desire to terminate prematurely may arise from feelings of a lack of progress in the counseling sessions. It may also signal that clients' resistances have not been completely worked through and that clients are not ready for the last stage.

Resisting Appropriate Termination

When they have been in a close and satisfactory relationship, counselor or client or both may resist ending counseling even though all indications show that the client is ready to go. Clients may resist leaving the safety of the relationship because they are anxious about being on their own. Clients with unstable relationships may especially want to hold on to the counselor. In such cases clients' symptoms may flare up, or they may bring in other problems. Counselors need to attend to clients' feelings and reassure clients if termination still seems advisable (Moursund, 2002).

Counselors may also resist termination because they are reluctant to end a satisfactory relationship, are particularly attached to the client, or are overly anxious about the client's ability to function adequately on her or his own. In these cases, counselors must assess their own countertransference feelings.

Leading Up to the Last Session

Sudden termination can be disruptive to client progress even when it is appropriate. A few sessions should be devoted to termination issues before counselor and client say their good-byes in the final session. Personal construct counselors emphasize the importance of the preparation for termination.

> The ending of a period of counseling needs as much, if not more, careful preparation. As at all stages, we need to make predictions about this important part of the process, to ensure that clients are aware of the implications of moving on and able to take into the future the changes in construing which have helped them to overcome current difficulties. (Fransella & Dalton, 2000, p. 142)

Fransella and Dalton (2000) also recommend that sessions not end abruptly but be gradually phased out, with meeting times stretching to every 3 weeks, and then more infrequently, depending on the case.

Moursund (2002) emphasizes that the material brought up during the review of progress and feelings about therapy must be considered in the context of separation. Communication must focus on what it means to the client "who is ending a supportive/ confrontive growth-producing relationship" (p. 107). Moreover, counselors should acknowledge and honor client expressions of positive feelings about the counseling relationship, the counseling experience, and the progress made in gaining new insights and resolving problems.

The end of counseling will mean a transition to a new phase, and transition means some loss, which is usually accompanied by feelings of anger, fear, guilt, or sadness. Moursand (2002) discusses the various client emotions that might emerge as counseling comes to an end. If anger occurs, it may be a defense against feelings of anxiety or a substitute for the more difficult expression of sadness. At this point, Moursand notes, counselors need to help clients see the positive and energizing aspects of their anger. Fear may also emerge prior to termination; counselor acceptance can help reassure clients of their ability to manage their lives.

Sadness often occurs at this time. Not only is there sadness about parting from the counselor, but the experience may also evoke the sadness of earlier partings (Moursund, 2002). As Moursund (2002) points out, however, there is a difference between therapeutic grief and grief over other losses. Here is an opportunity for clients to talk about and work through their feelings of loss with the person they are losing.

Feelings of poignancy may more aptly describe what may be felt during this period, for poignancy does not imply the sense of finality that grief does. And although counseling sessions do end, the possibility of the client's returning is left open, as in intermittent counseling. In personal construct counseling, clients are encouraged to report back 2 years hence and give a progress report. They are also encouraged to renew contact if necessary at any time. So the loss is not a final one, but rather a part of the ongoing life cycle of loss and renewal (Fransella & Dalton, 2000).

Many therapists today, including Dr. Simon Budman, assistant professor of psychiatry at Harvard Medical School, view therapy as intermittent and ongoing, as discussed in chapter 6. With brief counseling, clients work with different problems as they arise in their lives, much as one sees the family doctor (Goode, 1998).

RESEARCH STUDIES ON COUNSELING OUTCOME: META-ANALYSIS

The quantity of research on counseling and psychotherapy outcomes is overwhelming. As an aid, results of outcome studies have been reviewed and summarized through a process called *meta-analysis* (Ivey, D'Andrea, Ivey, & Simek-Morgan, 2002; Parloff, London, & Wolfe, 1986). In this process investigators conduct a systematic search of the literature, using predefined criteria for including studies. Important characteristics of each study— such as client population, type of theory or technique, or type and severity of client problem—are then systematically recorded. Varied statistical devices are used to obtain summary statements about the significance of the results, based on a common key question being studied (Lambert, Shapiro, & Bergin, 1986).

In recent years numerous valid and reliable research studies that sufficiently measure the complex variables of the counseling process have strongly affirmed the effectiveness of counseling and therapy (Ivey et al., 2002). Ivey calls attention to Beutler's (2000) thorough and extensive multilayer study, which indicates that positive therapeutic outcome is highest when (1) counselors develop the trust and acceptance of the client; (2) counselors apply intervention strategies appropriate to client needs; (3) counselors adapt their approach to the client's level of resistance; and (4) counselors maintain a safe atmosphere throughout the counseling process until emotional afflictions are resolved.

SUMMARY

In the process of individual counseling, counselors and clients develop a mutual relationship to help clients gain self-awareness that will enable them to resolve problems effectively.

Factors that influence the counseling process are the counselor's professional and personal characteristics; the type of services provided in the counseling setting; the client's personal attributes, including age, social-cultural background, ethnic identity, and views about gender role; and the overall context in which clients are experiencing problems.

The individual counseling process generally goes through three stages. In the initial stage a counselor-client relationship is established that focuses on understanding client problems; problems are assessed, tentative working hypotheses are developed, and goals are set. In the middle stage a shift occurs in which the client turns inward, exploring feelings and developing insights. Client and counselor experience a sense of movement as they work through the client's emotional turbulence, client and counselor transference and countertransference, and client resistance.

In the last stage counselors help clients apply their new insights and attitudes to their behavior in everyday life. As clients and counselors focus on attaining client goals, the relationship becomes more authentic, collaborative, and instructive. Counselors and clients then work toward effective termination by reviewing what they have accomplished and sharing their feelings about ending the relationship.

Meta-analysis of counseling outcome research indicates that counseling, overall, is beneficial to most clients.

PROJECTS AND ACTIVITIES

1. Compare the resistance of a client who has been persuaded to seek counseling against her will with the resistance of a client who volunteers for and comes regularly to counseling. How would you handle them differently?

2. Interview counselors in a public school, a college, and a community setting. How do they think the policies of their agencies or institutions affect their work with clients?

3. What client characteristics do you think would make it difficult for you to develop a working relationship—for example, a macho male, a militant feminist, a person with fundamentalist religious views, an atheist, a spouse abuser, a spouse having an extramarital affair, an obnoxious client, a very passive client? Play the role of a client who has one of these characteristics.

4. Interview a male counselor and a female counselor with similar background and experience. Ask each of them to describe the major gender issues. Ask them in what way, if any, male and female clients differ. Compare responses. Do you see any evidence of cultural biases?

5. Interview students from two or three different ethnic groups and from a group of multiracial students about the major problems they experience. How willing are they to use counseling services to help them resolve problems?

6. Select a study of counseling outcome from the reviews of research in the chapter. Go to the original source, and evaluate the study. Does it include type of client problem, client characteristics, counselor theoretical views, and techniques used? Was a control group used? How would you improve the study?

REFERENCES

Beutler, L. E. (2000). David and Goliath: When empirical and clinical standards of practice meet. *American Psychologist, 55,* 997–1007.

Bordin, E. S. (1975). The generalizability of the psychoanalytic concept of the working alliance. *Psychotherapy: Theory, Research and Practice, 16,* 252–260.

Brammer, L. M., Abrego, P. G., & Shostrom, E. L. (1993). *Therapeutic psychology: Fundamentals of counseling and psychotherapy* (6th ed.). Upper Saddle River, NJ: Prentice Hall.

Corey, G. (2001). *Theory and practice of counseling and psychotherapy* (6th ed.). Pacific Grove, CA: Brooks/Cole.

Corey, G., Corey, M. S., & Callanan, P. (1998). *Issues and ethics in the helping professions* (5th ed.). Pacific Grove, CA: Brooks/Cole.

Cormier, W. H., & Cormier, L. S. (1998). *Interviewing strategies for helpers: Fundamental skills and cognitive behavioral interventions* (4th ed.). Pacific Grove, CA: Brooks/Cole.

Corsini, R. J. (1995). Introduction. In R. J. Corsini & D. Wedding (Eds.), *Current psychotherapies* (5th ed., pp. 1–14). Itasca, IL: F. E. Peacock.

Dryden, W. (Ed.). (1998). *Key issues for counselling in action*. London: Sage.

Egan, G. (2002). *The skilled helper: A systematic approach to effective helping* (7th ed.). Pacific Grove, CA: Brooks/Cole.

Fransella, F., & Dalton, P. (2000). *Personal construct counseling in action* (2nd ed.). London: Sage.

Gelso, C. J., & Carter, J. A. (1985). The relationship in counseling and psychotherapy: Components, consequences, and theoretical antecedents. *Counseling Psychologist, 13,* 155–243.

Goode, E. (1998, November 24). How much therapy is enough? It depends. *New York Times,* pp. D1, D10.

Hansen, J. C., Rossberg, R. H., & Cramer, S. H. (1994). *Counseling: Theory and process* (5th ed.). Boston: Allyn & Bacon.

Heilbrun, A. B., Jr. (1982). Cognitive factors in early termination: Social insight and level of defensiveness. *Journal of Counseling Psychology, 29,* 29–38.

Ivey, A. E., D'Andrea, M., Ivey, M. B., & Simek-Morgan, L. (2002). *Counseling and psychotherapy: A multicultural perspective* (5th ed.). Boston: Allyn & Bacon.

Ivey, A. E., & Ivey, M. B. (1999). *Intentional interviewing and counseling: Facilitating client development in a multicultural society* (4th ed.). Pacific Grove, CA: Brooks/Cole.

Kelly, G. A. (1955). *The psychology of personal constructs* (Vols. 1 & 2). New York: Norton.

Kelly, G. A. (1963). *A theory of personality: The psychology of personal constructs*. New York: Norton.

Lambert, M. J., Shapiro, D. A., & Bergin, A. S. (1986). The effectiveness of psychotherapy. In S. L. Garfield & A. E. Bergin (Eds.), *Handbook of psychotherapy and behavior change* (pp. 157–211). New York: John Wiley.

May, R., & Yalom, I. (1995). Existential psychotherapy. In R. J. Corsini & D. Wedding (Eds.), *Current psychotherapies* (pp. 262–292). Itasca, IL: F. E. Peacock.

Meichenbaum, D. (1985). *Stress inoculation training*. New York: Pergamon Press.

Miller, J. B., & Stiver, I. P. (1997). *The healing connection: How women form relationships in therapy and in life*. Boston: Beacon Press.

Miltenberger, R. G. (2001). *Behavior modification: Principles and procedures* (2nd ed.). Belmont, CA: Wadsworth/Thomson Learning.

Moursund, J. (2002). *The process of counseling and therapy* (4th ed.). Upper Saddle River, NJ: Prentice Hall.

Parloff, M. B., London, P., & Wolfe, B. (1986). Individual psychotherapy and behavior change. *Annual Review of Psychology, 37,* 321–349.

Rogers, C. R. (1942). *Counseling and psychotherapy: Newer concepts in practice*. Boston: Houghton Mifflin.

Rogers, C. R. (1951). *Client-centered therapy: Its current practice, implications, and theory*. Boston: Houghton Mifflin.

Sexton, T. L., & Whiston, S. C. (1994). The status of the counseling relationship: An empirical review, theoretical implications, and research directions. *Counseling Psychologist, 22,* 6–78.

Stiver, I. P. (1997). What is the role of transference and the unconscious in the relational model? In J. V. Jordan (Ed.), *Women's growth in diversity* (pp. 37–41). New York: Guilford Press.

Surrey, J. L. (1997). What do you mean by mutuality in therapy? In J. V. Jordan (Ed.), *Women's growth in diversity* (pp. 42–49). New York: Guilford Press.

Taffel, R. (1993). In praise of countertransference: Harvesting our errors. *Family Therapy Networker, 17,* 52–57.

Tracey, T. J. (1988). The stages of influence in counseling. In W. Dryden (Ed.), *Key issues for counselling in action* (pp. 63–72). London: Sage.

Watkins, C. E. (1983). Transference phenomena in the counseling situation. *Personnel and Guidance Journal, 62,* 206–210.

Young, M. E. (1992). *Counseling methods and techniques: An eclectic approach*. New York: Macmillan.

CHAPTER 10

Family and Marriage Counseling and Therapy

F amily counseling and family therapy involve an interaction between a professional counselor or therapist and a family during which family members are helped to improve their relationships with one another and, in turn, foster the growth and development of each member. During the counseling process, family members learn to confront and resolve conflicts more productively so that both individual and family development is enhanced.

The terms *family counseling* and *family therapy* are used interchangeably by many professionals writing and practicing in the field (Passmore & Horne, 1991). Generally, *family therapy* designates work with more severe family dysfunctions; *family counseling* is for those suffering from normal situational concerns and conflicts.

In the early decades psychoanalysts (most of whom were Freudian) did not work with families; they worked only with individual patients. The therapeutic intention was to help patients break away from their families, psychologically and literally.

One of the first to break with Freud, Alfred Adler, perceived individuals in the 1920s as being influenced by social interactions. Emphasizing the influence of parental behavior on the child, Adler worked with parenting skills.

Not until the 1950s, however, was the term *family systems* used to describe family social interactions. Building on Adler's early work, psychiatrists and social workers explored the idea that if family influences were contributing to an individual's problems, then working with the family would contribute to the resolution of the individual's problems. While conducting research on schizophrenic behavior at Stanford University in the 1950s, Don Jackson, Jay Haley, Virginia Satir, and others found that schizophrenia arose from schizophrenic patterns of behavior in the family (Foley, 1989; Satir, 1982).

From these explorations family systems therapy, based on the family as a social unit, took hold and has spread since the 1970s throughout the therapeutic and counseling community. The term *family systems* was coined to represent the idea that when one member of a family shows signs of trouble, the symptoms represent problems in and among all members of that family. Although one person is designated as the *identified patient* (IP), the family is perceived as the source of the problem, and the whole family is treated. The family systems model now underlies all schools of family therapy.

FAMILY SYSTEMS THEORIES

The family systems model is based on the general systems theory developed by biologist Ludvig von Bertalanffy (1974), who believed that humans are living systems composed of subsystems that are connected together and dependent on one another; any change in one subsystem produces change in the others. In this model the whole system is greater than the sum of its parts. Family subsystems include smaller units of individual family members who interact and affect the total system. Examples of these subsystems are the interactions between parents, various interactions among siblings, and interactions between a parent and each child.

In equating family systems with general systems theory, Foley (1989) describes three important characteristics: wholeness, relationship, and equifinality. He says, "*Wholeness* means the system is not just the sum of its parts taken separately, but it also includes their interaction" (p. 456). Thus, a family does not consist simply of separate individuals, but rather includes the complex interactions occurring among them. *Relationship* describes the types and quality of interactions going on among family members who are in different subsystems in the family. *Equifinality* is based on the idea that any problem a family member or family is experiencing results from numerous causes, rather than from one particular cause. If an adolescent girl is experiencing an eating disorder, for example, one cannot simply say that it is caused by a rejecting mother. Complex interactions between parents, between parents and daughter, and among the girl and her siblings all contribute. For this reason family systems therapists believe that they can intervene at any time to resolve the family problem. "Regardless of the origin of a problem, any difficulty can be removed if a change is made at any point in time in the system" (Foley, 1989, p. 456). Because of this belief family therapists do not search for underlying causes of family dysfunction, but instead focus on the current interactions in the family that are perpetuating the problem.

Murray Bowen (Papero, 1991), who began his work in the 1950s, was the first family therapist to apply systems theory to family therapy. He originally called his theory "family systems" but in the 1970s changed the name to the Bowen theory because the term *family systems* had become widely used to describe numerous family theories.

Family therapists, regardless of theoretical orientation, follow the general principles of systems theory. They attend to current problems in family dynamics. They explore relationships, alliances, and conflicts within the family and their effects on each member of the family and on the family as a whole. In applying these principles, family therapists tend to be active in the sessions, often acting as instructors, directors, or guides in reorganizing family patterns of interaction. Family therapists differ, however, in the way they work with a family because of differing theoretical positions they have about human behavior.

Because family classification systems are numerous and complex, this text discusses eight family systems theories that represent the basic theoretical approaches presented in chapter 6: (a) object relations, (b) Bowen's family systems, (c) Adlerian family therapy, (d) Satir's process model, (e) Minuchin's structural family therapy, (f) strategic therapy, (g) social learning family therapy, and (h) cognitive-behavioral family therapy. Also discussed under Trends in Family Therapy are several family counseling models from a social-cultural contextual approach.

Object Relations Theory

Object relations has its psychoanalytic roots in ego psychology. Unlike Freud, who specified that instinctual gratification of sexual drives residing in the id is a person's primary drive, object relations theorists believe that humans relate primarily to others. Children develop strong attachments to significant people (called *objects*) to fulfill this need (Atwood, 1992b). Citing Fairbairn (1954) and Klein (1948), Gladding (2002) explains: "According to this theory, human beings have a fundamental motivation to seek objects, that is, people in relationships, starting at birth" (p. 119). Gladding goes on to say, "An **object** is a significant other (e.g., a mother during infancy) with whom children form an interactional, emotional bond. As they grow, children will often internalize (interject) good and bad characteristics of these objects within themselves" (p. 119). Thus, early psychosocial rather than psychosexual relationships influence the development of the child and, later, the adult (Thomas, 1992).

James Framo (1982) is a well-known advocate of this theory. He believes that the emotional responses of each family member and the effects these various emotional expressions have on family interactions are the crux of family dynamics and family functioning. Any unresolved conflicts that exist in either parent's family of origin result in conflicts in relationships in the current nuclear family.

Another important proponent of object relations, Robin Skynner (1981), believes that the family as a unit fosters individual development to the degree that both parents have worked through their own development in their families of origin. When parents request counseling for a problem child, the child's unresolved behavioral problems represent the parents' failure to develop emotional maturity. Skynner believes that when two people marry, each partner brings to the marriage fears and distorted expectations related to blocked developmental processes. Moreover, each partner tries to re-create circumstances in which the undeveloped experience can be reencountered and worked through. He sees these attempts as a great potential for growth in the marriage relationship. But also, he warns, these undeveloped experiences can lead partners to resist individual changes, resulting in unresolved family tensions and dysfunctions.

Object relations practitioners tend to combine treatment of the whole family with treatment of subgroups and individual members of the family. A man and a woman often work together as cotherapists. First, the therapist assesses the whole family to determine the nature and severity of the problem. One family member, usually a child, is designated as the identified patient (IP). After the initial assessment the therapist decides whether to work with the whole family, a subgroup, or the parents alone. If assessment shows that serious marital conflict exists that would impede progress in family counseling, the therapist may first do marital counseling with the parents and bring in the rest of the family later.

The family and the therapist agree on goals, which are usually quite specific. Therapy consists of attending both to the personal problems of each family member and to family dysfunctional patterns. Both parents' unresolved conflicts with their families of origin are included as well.

Therapists recognize that transference and resistance will occur among family members because they are expressing unresolved feelings of anxiety or anger blocked by either the nuclear family or the parents' families of origin. At the same time therapists are observing and interpreting family rules and transactions that are causing family breakdown. Skynner (1981) attempts to let family members express their concerns as spontaneously as possible with a minimum of direct guidance or prompting. "The goal is to facilitate differentiation of the marital partners to the point that they are separate, independent persons enjoying, but no longer simply needing, each other" (Goldenberg & Goldenberg, 2000, p. 226).

Bowen's Family Systems

Murray Bowen (1978) originated the term *family systems* in the 1950s, when he developed his theory of family therapy. He believes that an emotional system exists within a family and that this system influences the degree of separateness (*differentiation of self*) and togetherness (*fusion*) of family members. Bowen's major goal is to develop differentiation, or independence, among family members (Atwood, 1992b).

Differentiation of self, according to Bowen, is crucial for the effective functioning of each family member and the family as a whole. Members of a dysfunctional family fuse identities, become emotionally dependent on one another, and lose their individual selves. Thus, growth, maturity, and emotions are stifled. In an emotionally mature family, he believes, an effective balance of differentiation and togetherness is maintained. Members attain sufficient individuality to make their own decisions without becoming fused, while at the same time showing consideration for others. Bowen claims that it is a mistake for a person to try to resolve fusion problems by isolating from the family through emotional withdrawal, denial of problems, or running away. People who use these escape mechanisms behave immaturely and impulsively and fuse with others (Papero, 1991; Singleton, 1982).

Bowen believes that fusion between members of a family leads to the development of triangles. When two members of a family who are fused enter into conflict with each other, one or the other tries to move out of this locked-in relationship by involving a vulnerable third party, who inevitably takes sides with one of the fused partners (Becvar & Becvar, 1986). In a triangle two members of the family align while the third becomes an outsider and a scapegoat (Singleton, 1982). When tension becomes really unbearable, a fourth person may be drawn in, forcing realignment of the triangle.

When a family first comes in for therapy, members usually blame the family discord on one of the following: (a) one spouse has a problem (e.g., drinking, gambling, or adultery); (b) serious marital discord exists; or (c) a child's behavior is disrupting the marriage and family harmony (Bowen, 1978). Bowen believes that marital conflict in itself does not cause problem children but that problems arise when parents project their anxieties onto their children. This is called *family projection process.*

Bowen believes that patterns of differentiation, fusing, triangulation, and projection are passed from generation to generation in a *multigenerational transmission* process. Problems in a nuclear family can be understood and resolved only if therapy includes exploration of relationships in the families of origin for three generations. Consequently, in therapy Bowen traces dysfunctional patterns through the use of a *genogram,* which demonstrates three generations of family structure, triangulations, and alignments. A genogram is a structural chart showing the relationships of family members, including dates of birth and death, marriages and divorces, and number and gender of siblings.

Once family members understand this pervasive fusing and triangulation, Bowen's main goal is to help all involved differentiate themselves from one another and break the tendency to triangulate. Because the triangles are interlocking, a change in one triangle will cause a change in all triangles.

On the basis of his assessment of the family, Bowen may work with the whole family, with individual family members, or with various combinations of family members representing a family subsystem. If he thinks the conflict between husband and wife is the major factor contributing to a child's symptoms, he may work with the marital discord first before seeing the whole family. If the conflict between spouses is very severe, he may see each one separately until they are able to work together.

Bowen does not give the IP special attention; he believes that the so-called stronger members of the family play a part in fostering and maintaining the sickness in a weaker member. He helps all members become aware of their roles in the family dynamics.

Adlerian Family Therapy

Alfred Adler, originally a follower of Freud, broke with him because Adler believed that a social drive to belong and to relate to others, rather than biological instincts, directed human behavior. He contended that all behavior is purposeful and that the goal is to attain social status in the family and the community (see chap. 6). In the 1920s Adler applied his principles of psychotherapy to work with families in schools and in the community. He emphasized the importance of family dynamics, sibling rivalry, and the birth order of children. He also used consultations with nonpathological families struggling with practical problems in rearing and relating to children. Parents were taught appropriate ways of disciplining their children (Dinkmeyer & Dinkmeyer, 1991).

Because Adler started working with families in the early 1920s, he can rightfully be considered the originator of family counseling and therapy. Nonetheless, he was ignored for many years, overshadowed by Freudian psychoanalysts, humanists, and behaviorists among counselors and therapists. However, a resurgence of Adlerian thought has profoundly influenced psychology in the United States (Mosak, 2000), with credit due largely to Rudolf Dreikurs and then Don Dinkmeyer for carrying on Adlerian thought. The worth and viability of Adlerian psychology can be measured by the amount of research and development it continues to generate and the many Adlerian institutes, professional societies, journals, family-education centers, and study groups that exist. Counselors and therapists have come to recognize the value of Adler because they have become more socially conscious, have moved beyond treating the family in isolation, and are now treating families in the context of their social-cultural environment.

In the 1940s Dreikurs updated Adler's pragmatic theory and style and his focus on non-pathological families struggling to bring up children effectively. A manual for Adlerian family counseling centers—published in 1959 by Dreikurs, Lowe, Sonstegard, and Corsini—became "the bible of Adlerian family counseling" (Dinkmeyer & Dinkmeyer, 1991, p. 385). According to Dreikurs (1968), children are motivated for growth most effectively in groups. They try to attain a place in the group, and if they don't, they develop feelings of inferiority. In severe cases they become discouraged and withdraw from efforts to cooperate.

Even discouraged children, however, try to use creative powers to attain social status. Dreikurs (1968) claims that discouraged children take one of four goal-directed behaviors. They may try to (a) get attention, (b) prove their power, (c) get revenge, or (d) display deficiencies to get special service or exemptions. He does not advocate punishment for misbehavior; instead he proposes that children experience either the natural or the logical consequences of their actions. *Natural consequences* apply when the activity involves only the child—when the child spends all her or his weekly allowance the first day, for example, and has no money the rest of the week. *Logical consequences* occur when two or more people are involved; for instance, children who are frequently late for dinner may not be served dinner whenever they are late.

Dreikurs (1968) points out that when parents, after World War II, began following a permissive style of raising their children, they were at a loss about how to guide or discipline them. Elaborating on Dreikurs's views, Lowe (1982) explains that children in such cases believe that they can make any demand they please, thus becoming irresponsible tyrants, and adults adopt the children's roles. Because they lack methods of disciplining children in a democratic way, parents need help in establishing order. Counseling is meant to give them these methods.

For many years professionals used the term *Dreikurs/Adlerian family counseling and therapy.* Recently, they have been calling this approach simply *Adlerian family counseling and therapy.* Adlerian theory has been used as the basis for a system of parenting skills called Systematic Training for Effective Parenting (STEP), developed by Don Dinkmeyer (Dinkmeyer & McKay, 1976). In addition, Dinkmeyer and Dinkmeyer (1991) applied Adlerian principles to school settings and to parenting groups. Dinkmeyer and Dinkmeyer (1991), Sherman and Dinkmeyer (1987), and Sweeney (1989) published articles and texts describing Adlerian family therapy as a systems approach in both educational institutions and community practice.

Dinkmeyer and Dinkmeyer (1991) emphasize the social aspect of Adlerian therapy. Individuals, they say, strive to gain significance by belonging to a social system, beginning with the family. Family members develop feelings of inferiority when they believe that other family members reject them or deem them unworthy. "All behavior attempts to overcome feelings of inferiority. We seek superiority in part because our earliest experiences surrounded us with superiors" (p. 388). Power struggles then emerge in the family as each member tries to gain social status.

Adlerian counselors and therapists act as teachers, advisers, and facilitators. They help families understand the dynamics of family transactions and the ways each member contributes to the family problems. They help family members recognize their mutual interdependence by directing them to attend to one another's needs and cooperate in constructive give-and-take relationships.

With renewed interest in Adler and with efforts to integrate therapeutic approaches in more comprehensive therapeutic models, both cognitive-behaviorists and constructivists have been in dialogue about the degree of their compatibility with Adlerian family therapy (Watts, 2003; see also chap. 6).

Satir's Process Model

Virginia Satir's model holds that family dysfunction results from faulty communication, a condition directly related to each individual's feelings of low self-esteem. She originally called her theory *conjoint therapy* (1967) to describe the idea that the therapist works with the total nuclear family in counseling sessions.

After completing her work on conjoint therapy, Satir spent time at the Esalen Institute, a humanistic growth center in California. Her exposure to Gestalt therapy, altered states of consciousness, body therapies, and sensory awareness had a profound influence on her, both personally and professionally. From this rich combination of experiences, she developed the *process model* of family therapy (Satir & Bitter, 1991). Satir moved away from her earlier emphasis on pathology, to an emphasis on maintaining the healthiness of normally functioning individuals and wholeness in the family. She used the process model to describe her methods of interacting with individual and family members to help them improve communication styles and feelings of worth. Satir (1982) wrote, "I feel the name 'Process Model' fits how I see what I do. The model is one in which the therapist and family join forces to promote wellness" (p. 12).

Communication and self-esteem are the cornerstones of process therapy (Satir, 1982). Any symptoms displayed by family members result from problems that have blocked their emotional growth, and all members of the family and the family itself have within them the resources necessary to overcome these emotional blocks. Satir's theory emphasizes that the absence of ill health is not the same as the presence of good health. Thus, removing a symptom-producing sickness is not sufficient to ensure positive growth; well-being is directly related to a sense of vitality and to the development of self-esteem.

Because improving communication among family members is the key factor in Satir's approach, congruency between an event and a person's perception of the event is crucial. Dysfunctional family members continually misperceive the behaviors of other family members, resulting in considerable distortions in family communication. Poor communication can also result from family members finding it difficult to accept differences in another member of the family.

When symptoms are observed in families, Satir's model looks for family rules governing the communication in the family system. These rules form the patterns by which children develop their own self-esteem; the system is maintained to preserve all members' sense of self-esteem. Thus, these symptoms have a survival function.

During therapy sessions therapists become models of communication and growth and act as facilitators for each family member and for the family as a whole. They observe interactions, transactions, communication, and responses. They intervene to ask whether messages are clear and correct and how family members feel about a particular comment made by another family member. The therapists interrupt dialogue to check whether each person thinks the communication is correct (Brown & Christensen, 1986). They see themselves as guides, companions, and nourishing educators, rather than as authoritative changers or manipulators. They help families see their nonproductive or destructive patterns and help them engage in health-producing processes.

The goals of Satir's process model are to help each of the family members develop self-esteem and to enable them to grow. Therapists work to change or correct four elements in a family: (a) feelings of self-worth, (b) communication skills, (c) the system of alliances and coalitions, and (d) rules governing the family (Satir, 1982). No one is blamed for the family disturbance; the focus is on the multiple interactions in families. When parents are in conflict, a child often becomes the third angle in a family triangle, and the child must take sides with one parent or another to avoid unbearable conflict.

A major contribution to family therapy is Satir's (1972) classification of styles of communication (see Figure 10.1) and their use in her therapy or counseling. She believes that each individual in a dysfunctional family communicates with the others in one of four ways:

- *The Placater:* Tries to smooth things over, takes blame, apologizes, and tries to please so that other persons do not get angry
- *The Blamer:* Accuses others and finds fault in order to appear strong
- *The Computer:* Gives intellectual reasons, is superreasonable so as to be immune to threats
- *The Leveler:* Tries to be genuine and straightforward in communicating with others, helps resolve conflict

Satir also developed a technique called *sculpting,* in which family members take physical postures that indicate how they are relating and communicating in the family

FIGURE 10.1

Satir's communication stances.

Note: From *Peoplemaking* (p. 83) by V. Satir, 1972, Palo Alto, CA: Science & Behavior Books. Copyright 1972 by Science & Behavior Books. Adapted with permission.

system. As family members exaggerate the postures to represent the four communication styles, the sensory responses help them become visibly and tactilely aware of their communication styles. Family members can also switch roles to experience other persons' styles, and the communication styles of close friends, employers, household help, lovers, and former spouses may be role-played, too.

Another strategy has the family enact a current conflict occurring at home and then use communication games to help members see how family rules or patterns are contributing to the conflict. In this activity Satir uses props such as blindfolds and ropes; for example, family members might use ropes to tie themselves to each other to represent the prevailing pattern and thus become aware of the complexity and dissonance of their relationships.

> Satir sometimes literally tied ends of the rope around all members' waists and selectively asked them to move. In this way, the entire family could experience being tied to one other. They also got a feel for how the movement of one family member influenced the rest of the family. (Gladding, 2002, p. 154)

The family might also role-play a system in which all members are either blamers or distracters and then change to a more productive way of communicating.

Minuchin's Structural Family Therapy

Structural family therapy, one of the most influential theories in the 1970s, originated in the work of Salvador Minuchin at the Philadelphia Child Guidance Clinic. Minuchin was trained as a psychoanalytic psychiatrist and became interested in families in the 1950s, when he was working with juvenile delinquents and lower-socioeconomic minority groups (Atwood, 1992b).

When analyzing faulty family patterns, Minuchin (1974) explores how members of families interact and how faulty communication—repetitive and highly rigid patterns and habits—contributes to family dysfunction. He is also interested in how families under stress use these ineffective behaviors as a means of survival.

According to Minuchin, the family is a social system that develops *transactional patterns,* or family rules, which determine how each member relates to other family members and under what conditions or at what times certain transactional patterns occur (Minuchin, 1974; Minuchin, Lee, & Simon, 1996). In transactions occurring in family subsystems, three factors are involved: boundaries, alignments, and power. *Boundaries* are the rules determining who will participate in a family interaction or transaction and what role each member will play. *Alignments* refer to how various family members form coalitions or alliances to join or oppose another member of a subsystem. *Power* relates to the degree of influence each person has on the family system. A healthy, functioning family has clearly defined generational boundaries; parents are the executives in the family, ensuring that children will not take over parental functions and that grandparents will not interfere (Goldenberg & Goldenberg, 2000). In a healthy family, boundaries and alliances are flexible, and the family can adapt to inevitable changes, such as births, deaths, marriages, or job changes. Alignments are also clear between parents on crucial issues such as discipline; and rules about power are defined so that children know that parents' orders will be enforced.

Minuchin, like Bowen, believes that family dysfunctions occur when family members are either enmeshed or disengaged. In the *enmeshed* family, whose boundaries are diffused, members are tightly interlocked, and any change brought about by one member causes quick resistance from another; in such cases family members become fused and lose personal identity. In the *disengaged* family, boundaries are rigid, and family ties are weak. Members are isolated or disconnected from each other, seldom communicating or making contact with one another. In these cases children run the risk of developing antisocial behavior. In both enmeshed and disengaged families, the power of family members is unclear or inappropriate. Consequently, children may either have insufficient opportunity to express themselves or may tyrannize the family.

Dysfunctional families are resistant to change; when stress arises because of changes in the family, conflict avoidance occurs. In enmeshed families disagreements are rare because conflicts are seen as a sign of disloyalty and as a refutation of love and closeness. In disengaged families the distance that prevents confrontations between members gives a false impression of independence and harmony (Colapinto, 1991). Minuchin believes that whenever conflicts arise, such families use repetitive, stereotyped reactions without modification to preserve family equilibrium at all costs. Thus, instead of resolving conflicts, these rigid responses solidify the dysfunctional family patterns.

A family usually asks for help because of concern about a particular family member (the IP). Minuchin's therapeutic goal is to restructure the transactional rules of the family so that members can communicate and relate in a way that is growth producing for the family and for each of its members. He either tightens or loosens boundaries and helps families make changes in their stereotyped, rigid positions or roles so that they become more flexible in their ways of relating, resolving conflicts, and managing stress related to change. He works on current symptoms and does not involve himself in patterns from the families of origin or in multigenerational transmission of family patterns.

Minuchin is very active in therapy. He uses two basic strategies and a variety of techniques. In the first strategy he joins with the family patterns existing at the beginning of therapy. For example, he may ask the family to enact a conflict that is occurring at home. Using a tactic called *mimesis,* he imitates or models how family members interact with each other. Then in the second strategy, he begins to restructure the family. He may use the technique of *reframing* by putting a positive interpretation on a person's negative behavior. For example, the attempts of a child to run away may be reframed as an attempt to pull the family together in a crisis. Minuchin may also use manipulative intervention if he believes it will alter rigid, unworkable family structures. He may encourage conflicts and actively join alliances or coalitions against other family members to try to induce the family to interact in healthier ways (Minuchin et al., 1996; Roberts, 1992). Therapy is completed when both the therapist and the family think that a new and more effective structure exists, which the family can use in coping with future transactions and stress.

Strategic Therapy

Strategic therapy is defined as "a family therapy in which the therapist devises and initiates strategies for solving the family's presenting problem" (Schilson, 1991, p. 142). The therapist gives family members directives or orders to carry out certain strategic tasks that the therapist believes will eliminate the presenting problem. Strategic therapy is best represented in the work of Jay Haley (1987), a pioneer in family therapy. Haley describes his approach as problem-solving therapy, the goal is to solve the family's presenting problem by using specific techniques and skills within the family structure.

Haley believes that changes in families come not through family members gaining their own insights but from directives given by the therapist. Symptoms are the problem to be treated; current interactions of the family are paramount. No attention is given to historical antecedents in nuclear families or families of origin or to multigenerational patterns. Haley accepts that family symptoms are attempts at survival by family members (Atwood, 1992a). He also agrees with most other family systems theorists that symptoms arise and are maintained because a family cannot deal with changes, such as death, marriage, divorce, illness, or loss of a job. Families cannot solve problems because they are locked into repetitive and nonproductive communication patterns.

The problems, or symptoms, of one family member, the IP, may lead the family to seek help. In confronting the problem behavior, however, Haley focuses on power struggles in the family, assuming that maneuvering for power is inherent in families. He defines *power* as a struggle to determine who is in charge of the relationship. All forms of symptoms—depression, drinking, agoraphobia, work addiction—influence a person's behavior. Thus, the problem of the IP controls family social activities, as well as inter-family interactions.

Rules governing family functioning come under close scrutiny. In a healthy family, rules are clear. If parents become angry with each other, family survival is not threatened, and children do not become involved in their parents' arguments. In a dysfunctional family with ambiguous or unclear relationships, clear-cut rules about who is in power do not exist. Alliances cross generational lines, so triangulations may occur between a parent and a child that prevent resolution of parental conflict. Parents' fights may become violent; children may feel threatened and develop symptoms of anxiety and rebelliousness or depression.

Haley (1987) contends that the family and the therapist are in a power struggle, just as family members are. Gladding (2002) notes that strategic family therapists like Haley perceive themselves as experts who have no need for "collaborative input from client families" (p. 227). The key factor, then, is therapist control. The therapist works to restructure the family system by reestablishing boundaries, changing hierarchies of power and family triangulations, and improving family communication. The therapist does this by using two forms of directives—straightforward and paradoxical. *Straightforward directives* are called *positive cooperative tasks* because they are based on what the therapist has learned about the family, with the expectation that the family members will carry out the tasks and profit from completing them. For example, the therapist tells a husband and wife that they each need more privacy and directs them to spend specific time by themselves. *Paradoxical directives* are called *negative cooperative tasks* and are used on families highly resistant to following the therapist's directives. "The directives are paradoxical because the therapist has told the family that he wants to help them change but at the same time he is asking them not to change" (Madanes, 1981, p. 26).

Three paradoxical interventions have been recommended for use in family therapy by Weeks and L'Abate (1982): (a) reframing the symptom, (b) escalating or inducing a crisis, and (c) redirecting the occurrence of the symptom. *Reframing* refers to relabeling the problem behavior in a positive way. For example, the therapist may describe a child who refuses to do his assigned household chores as someone who may be expressing an urge for independence, a desire that has not been sufficiently recognized. If the child's needs are recognized, then he will probably be willing to do the chores. *Escalating* refers to a strategy called *prescribing the symptom,* in which the client is told to increase the behavior that is presented as a problem. If a child is lying, the child is told to continue lying at every opportunity, to make up better and bigger lies, and to keep a chart indicating success. In *redirection* the client is encouraged to continue the symptom but in altered circumstances. If spouses are continually bickering, for example, they are directed to bicker only at a certain time of day, every day, and to continue bickering without stopping for, say, 2 hours. Clients find it impossible to carry out these directives and end up reducing or giving up the problem behavior.

Weeks and L'Abate (1982) believe that these approaches are best with very resistant families who have severe or chronic problems. They caution, however, against using these techniques in acute crisis situations or with dangerous persons—those who are suicidal, homicidal, sociopathic, or paranoid. For moderately resistive families with less severe or chronic problems, they suggest modifying the procedures and using them with care. For example, the therapist might tell the family what is intended to be accomplished with such a paradoxical intervention.

Behavioral and Cognitive-Behavioral Family Counseling

Behavioral and cognitive-behavioral family theories were considered outside the circle of family systems until fairly recently because they had emphasized working with the individual who was designated as the problem in the family. Contemporary theorists with behavioral and cognitive-behavioral leanings have since moved into a systems approach (Atwood, 1992a; Horne, 1991).

Although acknowledging that these theorists tend to emphasize the identified patient, Goldenberg and Goldenberg (2000) nevertheless say, "There are efforts by some . . . to accommodate a systems/behavioral/cognitive perspective" (p. 269). According to Horne (1991), social learning behavioral counselors are "incorporating systems theory and looking at more interactional circular explanations for behavior change" (p. 472). Atwood (1992c), in her systemic cognitive-behavioral approach to family therapy, also describes cognitive-behavioral models as definitely being within a family systems model. Most contemporary cognitive-behavioral family therapists now perceive the family within a social system and are attentive to family members' interactions. The theories presented here are classified as forms of family systems.

Behavioral and cognitive-behavioral family theories are based on some form of learning theory and are focused on overt, observable behavior. Learning occurs when the individual's response to external stimuli is reinforced or when the individual models the behavior of others. Behavioral family therapists teach and reinforce more adaptive and constructive ways for families to interact. Cognitive-behavioral theorists believe that dysfunctional family members have inaccurate perceptions about themselves and other family members. Those misperceptions lead them to develop illogical or faulty thoughts about their interactions. Counselors following this approach help families correct their perceptions and teach them new reasoning skills.

Social Learning Family Therapy

One of the most prominent groups working with a family behavioral approach is the staff at the Oregon Social Learning Center, directed by Gerald Patterson and John Reid (Horne, 1991), who base their belief on the concept that behavior is affected primarily by *social learning.* This group began its work in an experimental laboratory studying parents and children. Using social learning concepts, the therapists trained parents and teachers to become agents of change. At the Oregon Social Learning Center, they applied modeling, time-out, and reinforcement techniques (Thomas, 1992). They then began working with children and families in their natural environments and with children and teachers in schools, focusing on those children with socially aggressive and antisocial behaviors that were of particular concern to parents and teachers.

Patterson has had a lasting influence on behavioral family counseling.

> Overall, Patterson is credited as playing a critical role in the extension of learning principles and techniques to family and marital problems. His practical application of social learning theory has had a major impact on family therapy. He has influenced other behaviorists to work from a systemic perspective in dealing with families. (Gladding, 2002, p. 173)

Patterson (1971) describes two types of parent-child interactions that he observed most frequently—reciprocity and coercion. He uses *reciprocity* to describe one person's behavior that is followed by a similar behavior from another person. A positive move elicits a positive response; a negative action is followed by a negative response. The other type of parent-child interaction, *coercion,* describes situations that involve either punishment or negative reinforcers. For example, a parent spanks a child who later hits a younger or weaker sibling (Lynn & Garske, 1985). The aggressive behavior of the parent serves as a model for the child, and the child imitates it.

With the social learning approach, counselors meet with the family and make a behavioral assessment in which they identify the problem as precisely as they can, determining with the family the specific behavior needing change. They consider it essential to establish a therapeutic environment and a relationship in which the family will feel safe and comfortable while discussing family problems.

After counselors determine the problem and establish baseline data, they begin a program of intervention, or change, in which all positive or desirable behavior is reinforced. Goals are specific and are limited to changing precise behavior or eliminating presenting symptoms. The counselors use behavioral techniques—such as time-out, modeling, and reward systems—to extinguish undesirable behavior. Contracts between family members and the problem child may be made that detail expected decreases and increases in certain behaviors. After the initial interview counselors help parents learn parenting skills without having the child present.

Behaviorist counselors are basically teachers, they teach skills to parents and train them in reinforcement techniques. Parents are taught to be trainers of child behavior (Goldenberg & Goldenberg, 2000); the counselor helps them make decisions about changing the behaviors of a problem child. Parents and child negotiate a contract specifying behaviors to be changed and rewards or punishments to be given when the child complies or fails to comply (Thomas, 1992). Behaviors to be targeted are specific—lying, stealing, or bullying siblings, for example. Parents monitor the child and give out rewards and punishments. The counselor does a follow-up after therapy is completed.

Cognitive-Behavioral Family Therapy

As discussed in chapter 6, cognitive-behavioral theorists like Beck (1976), Ellis (1982), and Meichenbaum (1985) expanded behavioral counseling approaches to include the influences that cognitive processes—thoughts, beliefs, and attitudes—have on client behavior. These ideas have since been applied to family counseling.

In his rational emotive family therapy, Ellis (1991) uses principles and techniques similar to those of his individual RET approach, now called rational emotive behavior therapy (REBT; Ellis, 2000). Ellis is active, persuasive, and directive; he emphasizes correcting illogical or irrational thoughts. Thus, he assesses family members' illogical ways of relating to one another and explores destructive or irrational inner talk that family members direct toward themselves or others. Without becoming over- or underinvolved, he teaches them how to relate reasonably, logically, and constructively. He assigns homework when necessary.

Alexander and Parsons (1982) developed a cognitive-behavioral family system called *functional family therapy* (FFT). In this approach therapists help family members understand and change thought processes and emotional states that are causing problems in the family system (Fenell & Weinhold, 1989).

Cognitive-behavioral therapists follow three stages in the family counseling process: (a) assessing, (b) facilitating change in the family, and (c) maintaining changes. During the assessment period therapists observe how each family member perceives the problem and how everyone relates to one another. To facilitate change, therapists interpret and clarify family dynamics, reduce blaming, and encourage listening to one another. To maintain changes, families are taught communication skills, ways of monitoring their behaviors, and methods of positive interactions (Alexander & Parsons, 1982; Fenell & Weinhold, 1989).

THE FAMILY LIFE CYCLE

Human development theorists (see chap. 5) assume that individuals go through stages of development throughout their life spans. At each stage individuals usually experience disequilibrium or conflict. In family counseling, these stages are called the *family life cycle* (Carter & McGoldrick, 1999; L'Abate, Ganahl, & Hansen, 1986; Thomas, 1992). Families go through stages or transitions, as do individuals; and individual, family, or environmental changes occur periodically that require adjustment or realignment among family members. This realignment often involves changes in attitudes and behaviors, which, in turn, increase family stress and upset family equilibrium.

Carter and McGoldrick (1999) believe that, at each developmental stage in the family life cycle, each family member and the family as a whole experience changes in status that involve emotional and behavioral consequences. For example, the first stage occurs when the newly married couple must learn to commit to a new relationship together, as well as to the extended families of both partners. In the next stage, when children come along, the married couple must learn to make space for their children and assume joint responsibility for child rearing and for housekeeping tasks. When children become adolescents, the couple must adjust to the next stage, one that requires increased flexibility in family boundaries to give adolescents more independence. When adult children leave home, the family must adjust yet again. In later years grandchildren enter the family, involving new relationships between the older adults and their children and grandchildren. Everyone must learn to adjust to each other's new lifestyles, losses, illnesses, and social roles.

This model readily fits the family systems concept of the family as a social unit; it fits as well the multigenerational concepts of psychoanalytic family therapists. It is also suitable for cognitive-behaviorist family counselors, who can use the model to assess target tasks for their clients.

FAMILY COUNSELING AND THERAPY IN PRACTICE

Family counseling relationships follow predictable stages. Although family specialists may not agree on what specifically should occur in each stage, they describe the following similar processes:

Stage I: Initial stage—developing a relationship and assessing the family problem
Stage II: Middle stage—developing emotional awareness and acceptance of dysfunctional family patterns
Stage III: Last stage—learning how to change the family system
Stage IV: Termination—separating from therapy

Initial Stage: Developing a Relationship and Assessing the Family Problem

Family counseling or therapy usually begins with one family member making the initial contact by telephone. The person may be calling about a family member, the IP, whose ongoing misbehavior is disrupting the family—an unruly or despondent adolescent, a hyperactive child, an alcoholic spouse. Or a person may call on her or his own behalf because of problems with her or his family. These are common examples of the problems presented: "My husband is depressed, and I am worried about him"; "I feel depressed, and my family is upset about my condition"; "My husband is threatening to divorce me"; "The children are completely out of hand, and my wife and I disagree on how to discipline them."

Family counselors generally try to have all family members who live in the home come together at the initial interview. Later, decisions can be made about whether to see only certain family members, whether to involve children, or whether to have separate sessions at times for some family members. At this stage counselors explain the purpose and process of therapy, the counselor's role, and the family members' responsibilities in the session. A counselor might say:

> You are all here because you believe your family is not working together well, and you want to change that. My role is to help you. First, I must learn more about you as a family, hear some history, and find out how you work together. I also want to learn what each of you sees as the major problems in your family. Then we can discuss what changes you'd like to make and work together to make those changes.

In the beginning sessions family counselors or therapists establish rapport, confidence, and trust. They also assess family dynamics or interactions and clarify the central problem. The development of rapport is complex because counselors must build trust relationships between themselves and each member of the family while at the same time helping family members trust one another. As in individual counseling, a warm, empathic, and genuine relationship is essential in family counseling. Counselors must treat each family member as important, insisting that members speak for themselves and listen to one another respectfully. For this reason counselors ask family members to tell, individually, what they think is the major problem and what they expect of the family.

Counselors also observe family dynamics, conflicts, and the quality of relationships. They determine who is allied with whom, what the power structure is, what triangles are present, and what boundaries and rules implicitly function in the family. How enmeshed or disengaged are family members? Faulty communication patterns arising from and contributing to relationship problems are of particular interest. In their assessment counselors must also look for positive resources and strengths in the family (Satir, 1982).

In addition to assessing family dynamics, counselors may explore family history and the reactions of family members to significant earlier family events. During this time it is also important to assess the family's interaction with the extended family, including grandparents and other relatives.

As the family explores itself, counselors begin to reframe the problem as a total family problem and not just the problem of the IP. Resistance to this reevaluation must be met with firmness, patience, and tact. Counselors should point out faulty interactions in current relationships and help the family shift to more constructive patterns.

Once the problem has been refocused successfully, counselors help the family set goals for change, clarify the commitment of each family member, and determine whether family members will be seen together or whether separate sessions for individual members are necessary.

Middle Stage: Developing Emotional Awareness and Acceptance of Dysfunctional Family Patterns

In the middle stage the counselor or therapist helps family members explore and analyze their dynamics to get an understanding of what is causing the problem. The counselor is usually more confrontational, and family members may experience and acknowledge hurt, pain, shame, frustration, and loss. Anxiety increases with emotionally charged self-disclosures, and resistance arises in this middle stage.

In family counseling, as in individual counseling (see chap. 9), resistance is generally seen as a positive sign, one that either indicates the family is closer to confronting its problems or alerts counselors that they are moving too quickly. Fear of change contributes to this resistance. Family members may resist counseling or therapy by remaining silent or by discussing only superficial matters. They may also question the counselor's ability to understand the problem, may come late to sessions, or may complain about the counseling fees. Other types of resistance common at this stage occur when one family member refuses to speak to another or when one family member interrupts another who is beginning to reveal something meaningful. At times the whole family might resist by withholding a family secret pertinent to the problem or by denying that the IP is improving (Solomon, 1969). Transference may also arise as family members project unresolved emotions onto the counselor. The counselor can help family members work through resistance and transference by being patient with them and by being sensitive to and empathic with the anxiety or fear generated by disclosures.

Therapists with a psychodynamic orientation, like Framo (1982) and Bowen (1978), help parents see that some of their problems stem from unresolved conflicts in their families of origin. Role playing or psychodrama may be used; in psychodrama a parent may reenact an experience when, as a child, she was ridiculed by her parents.

Expression of grief is encouraged in this stage of therapy when families have unresolved feelings about losses, such as the death of a loved one, divorce, failure in school, loss of a job, or realization of a childhood loss (Brock & Barnard, 1988; Middleton-Moz & Dwinell, 1986). Shame is another pervasive, unresolved emotion common to dysfunctional families. It needs to be acknowledged and worked through as family members disclose secrets about themselves that they have hidden from others because of deep feelings of unworthiness. For example, a man who has professed only love for his mother may reveal long-standing resentment about her manipulation of him that he has felt ashamed to admit. Once he admits the shame, he can begin to explore his feelings and move from self-hate to self-respect (Fossum & Mason, 1986). In his book *Taming Your Gremlin: A Guide to Enjoying Yourself,* Richard Carson (1983) presents a humorous and keenly perceptive view of how people can become aware of the self-defeating consequences of shame and learn to live more productively.

In this middle stage the family begins to accept that relationships can change and that destructive alliances can be broken without undue loss of security. These acknowledgments lead to changes in family structure: Roles are less rigid, communication becomes more direct and constructive, and feedback to one another about new behaviors within the family is more authentic.

Last Stage: Learning How to Change the Family System

As family members understand and accept how they each have contributed to the origin and perpetuation of problems, they begin to see alternative ways of behaving and communicating. Needing less prompting from the therapist, they begin to intervene, to confront one another constructively, and to give one another feedback on more effective ways of interacting.

Counselors encourage family members to generalize these changes to interactions at home and may assign homework to practice the new behaviors. For example, a mother who has learned to declare in a session her need for boundaries and her own space may be directed to take time off, go on a weekend retreat. Satir (1982) developed communication exercises to help families compare ineffective and effective ways of communicating. For example, two members may sit back-to-back and try, without success, to communicate authentically and then in gradual stages move to looking into each other's eyes and touching hands while communicating fully.

At this point counselors can help the family become aware of resources in the community that can support their efforts to continue new patterns of behavior. For example, a single parent can be encouraged to join a group working on parenting skills. Counselors can also help the family look ahead to upcoming transitions and changes that are likely to occur. They can then help family members consider how to make use of their new attitudes and skills to cope with the anticipated changes.

Termination: Separating from Therapy

Termination in family counseling is considered less difficult than in individual counseling. In successful family counseling, the family has learned to work as a unit to solve its own problems and to give members support. In addition, family members have practiced working on communication skills and relationship issues during the sessions. Thus, feeling less dependent on the counselor, they have fewer problems with termination than do individual clients.

In successful treatment family members show signs that they are ready to terminate when they begin to solve family conflicts at home and when presenting complaints or symptoms are no longer present. Counselor and family members will notice more independent activities, more constructive conflict, and better ways of resolving problems among family members.

Even so, the counselor needs to prepare the family for separation by allowing the last two sessions for the process of termination. A review of what has happened during counseling is helpful. The counselor can also arrange for a follow-up session with the family and convey that the members can return at any time if they feel the need for additional help. The advantage of a well-thought-out termination is significant:

> If conducted over time and with sensitivity, it can help families and family members recognize their growth and development during treatment. It can also help families and their members recognize and accept their feelings, thoughts, behaviors, failures, and accomplishments. (Gladding, 2002, p. 103)

MARRIAGE AND COUPLE COUNSELING THEORIES

Family counseling and marriage or couple counseling overlap considerably, particularly when couples start having children or when young couples are having difficulty disengaging appropriately from their extended families. Most practitioners who identify themselves primarily as family counselors thus include marriage and couple counseling with family therapy. Some of them indicate that they will work with the marriage problem first if they think the marital discord is so severe that it would be impossible to work with the whole family. Some counselors also work with spouses first if they think the IP's problems are primarily a result of marital discord.

Those who specialize only in marriage and couple counseling, however, make certain distinctions between their type of counseling and family counseling. Many couples seeking help do not have children, are undecided about whether to have them, or have decided to remain childless. Other couples have older children who are not living at home and are not available for family counseling even if it seems advisable. These couples seek help because they are not happy with their relationship, not because they are having trouble with problem children. These couples may be having conflicts over gender roles, finances, infidelity, religious values, sexual disharmony, in-laws, retirement, alcoholism, careers, or other problems not related to children. Some marriage and couple counselors also work with premarital couples, cohabiting unmarried couples, and/or lesbian and gay couples. Some specialize in sex therapy.

Theories designed especially for marital and couple counseling had, for many years, come from the social learning school, which emphasized learning skills and educational information. More recently, other theoretical marital counseling models have been developed and now include family therapy approaches such as structural therapy (Minuchin), strategic therapy (Haley), and transgenerational therapy (Bowen), discussed earlier in this chapter. For a discussion of these models, see Brown and Brown's (2002) book *Marital Therapy: Concepts and Skills for Effective Practice.*

Terence Real (2002) became involved in marital counseling after his book on male depression *I Don't Want to Talk About It* (1997) was published. His book triggered numerous phone calls from women who were at the end of their rope, "having already dragged their partners to therapy, veterans of at least one, most often several, failed courses of couples work" (Real, 2002, p. 36). Also impressed by his book was Carol Gilligan (1982; Wylie, 2002), who joined forces with him. Together they developed a marital therapy model called relational recovery therapy (RRT), in which couples attend a 3-day intensive workshop (Real, 2002; Wylie, 2002). Couples attending the workshop understand that they will decide after the workshop to either stay with the marriage or divorce.

According to Real (2002), empowered women have been demanding emotional intimacy in marriage, but men are not prepared to change. "We don't raise . . . boys and men to be intimate partners, but to be strong, competitive performers" (p. 38). Because conventional marriage therapy doesn't work in such cases, Real breaks a major rule during the workshop: He takes sides. He sides with the woman's concerns and focuses first on the man's inadequacies and fears. He confronts him with the truth: that he is avoiding intimacy and connectedness by becoming grandiose, withdrawn, or abusive. Through these confrontations Real helps men take responsibility for their actions, explore and work through shame, express remorse and guilt, and learn steps to maintain intimacy. He then helps women avoid behaviors that reinforce men's tendencies to withdraw while cultivating those that will encourage men to embrace intimacy.

Real (2002) claims that couple counseling as practiced in traditional psychotherapy is ineffective with most couples. Women are aware of difficulties in the marriage and seek help, whereas most men claim to be happy with their marriages and thus go to therapy only because wives demand it. Yet therapists are traditionally trained to assume that both partners are motivated for counseling and desire change. "Pretending that both partners approach therapy equally disturbed is simply a fairy tale. Why do we therapists participate in it? Because, like women, we've been taught to protect men from the truth about themselves" (p. 39). He goes on to say that "the field of psychotherapy has allowed itself to be intimidated. . . . Men's entitlement to withdrawal or attack when confronted" (p. 39) is commonly expected and accepted. Therapists reinforce the male's typical reactions to conflict at home—to avoid, deny, or flee.

In therapy, under the rubric of 'winning the man over,' 'gaining his trust,' 'forming an alliance,' we therapists are taught to cajole, reason, nurture and seduce. We're taught, in other words, to replicate the traditional wifely role. . . . we usually get as far with most men as their wives do.

The subtext is that men, if pushed too hard, will explode, fall apart, or bolt, so it's best to soothe them, win them over, and *then* tell them the difficult truth. (p. 39)

CHANGING FAMILY AND MARRIAGE PATTERNS

Counselors and therapists need to be aware that family counseling theories and practices are generally based on the traditional American (i.e., White, middle-class) nuclear family. Such a model is no longer typical for most American families. In the traditional, idealized model, a married couple rears its own biologically related children, the father acts as head of the household and provider, and the mother is the family's homemaker and nurturer. Today, a majority of children grow up in quite different family patterns. In the majority of families, both parents work outside the home; one third of American children are reared by single parents, usually women; and many families are blended together from remarriages.

Dual-Career Families

In 1988 nearly 75% of women with school-age children were employed—2½ times the rate in 1950 (Basow, 1992). The causes for this sharp increase are many: feminists' objections about traditional gender roles (see chap. 14), rising divorce rates, rising costs of living, and a lower ratio of income to expenses for most wage earners (Hershenson, Power, & Waldo, 1996).

As a result, women are spending less time with their children, and men are expected to spend more (Atwood, 1992c). In addition to job stress for both parents, stress occurs at home. Although both men and women experience stress in dual-career families, women's stress is greater because of expectations that women should continue to handle more domestic responsibilities than men (Basow, 1992). Conflicts in managing the dual role of homemaker and out-of-home worker have made it especially difficult for women to meet their own needs (Zunker, 1994).

With the increase in dual-career families, more than 2 million schoolchildren ages 6 to 13 are self-care (*latchkey*) children, left to themselves after school with little or no supervision (Cole & Rodman, 1987). The professional literature indicates that those children whose mothers work outside the home do not, as a rule, become emotionally disturbed as long as they have had adequate day care and parents who are caring and responsive when they and their children are together (Shaffer, 1993). Shaffer (1993) warns, however, that the research focuses primarily on the ideal norm of the two-parent, middle-class family.

Family counselors must be alert to parents' changing gender roles and to the stresses resulting from a lack of adequate and affordable child care. They must also be aware that family conflicts are exacerbated because the marketplace and communities have not made allowances for dual-career families. Hoffman (1990) and Zucal (1992) urge that family therapists pay attention to Carol Gilligan's views about the differences in women's and men's development (see chap. 5) and become more gender sensitive in their counseling approaches to family conflicts.

Single-Parent Families

Single parents head about one-third of all families—more than triple the number in 1970 (Gladding, 2002). Divorce is by far the leading reason for one-parent families (70%), followed by death of a spouse (14%) and never-married women (10%) (Atwood, 1992c). Of all single-parent families 90% are headed by women. Major sources of stress for single mothers include low income, societal disapproval, and lack of a coparent to help with domestic chores, discipline, and child welfare in general (Basow, 1992). Single parents try to assume the roles of both parents, financial worries are usually worse, children may be expected to assume more responsibilities, and child care services are more necessary (Baruth & Burggraf, 1991).

Walters (1988) says that therapists must help single parents see their problems more as a family issue than as a personal one. The counselor or therapist can help single parents learn to reconstruct their families so that all members, to the extent of their abilities, are involved in overall family functioning.

Atwood (1992c) proposes using a cognitive-behavioral family systems approach to help single parents resolve problems with their children. In this approach the counselor teaches behavior management skills to single parents whereby children are rewarded for completing tasks and taking care of some of their own needs. Single parents are also helped to schedule time in ways that provide nurturing to their children while still maintaining appropriate roles and boundaries. "Part of the family counselor role is to teach the family good child-rearing practices and to help them learn age-appropriate behaviors" (Atwood, 1992c, p. 204).

Attention is given as well to helping single parents work through feelings of abandonment, develop social support groups, and when possible, work toward and maintain civil and respectful contact with former spouses for the benefit of the child or children.

Remarried (Blended) Families

Remarried or blended families are formed when two previously married individuals with children marry each other. Between 40% and 50% of recent marriages will end in divorce, with 80% of men and 75% of women remarrying within a few years. These figures show that increasing numbers of families will be reconstituted into ones in which multiple parents, stepparents, grandparents, and stepsiblings interact (Nystul, 1993; Shaffer, 1993). Because mothers usually gain custody of their children, the stepfamily in which the children live with their mother and her second husband is most common.

Betty Carter (1988), a well-known family therapist, notes the new family patterns that have arisen from complex relationships and roles in remarried families. Role conflicts often occur between the realigned members: Confusion arises over a stepparent's role as disciplinarian, for instance, or remarried families may exclude a biological parent or children not living in the new household. In her counseling model for remarried families, Carter (1988) recommends helping the family develop a flexible system in which it forms permeable boundaries between all family members, including those who do not live together.

CHILD ABUSE AND NEGLECT

The four major types of child abuse are (a) physical or bodily injury, (b) emotional or psychological damage, (c) sexual abuse, and (d) neglect of physical and emotional needs (Brown, 1991; Thompson & Rudolph, 1992). Children are often victims of multiple abuse: Sexual abuse—which involves molestation, fondling, or penetration—generally carries with it emotional abuse and physical abuse. And physical abuse, besides inflicting physical injuries, causes emotional damage. Another form of abuse—verbal assaults, threats, and terrorizing—also causes emotional damage to children, as well as indirect, internalized, physical harm.

With physical neglect parents do not provide adequate supervision of children or safe conditions in the home, or they fail to provide nourishing food or adequate clothing or medical care. Emotional neglect includes parents' withdrawing loving contact from the child, ignoring or dismissing the child's feelings, and preventing the child from developing emotional boundaries. Neglected children suffer from feelings of abandonment; persistent neglect leads to emotional disorders.

Almost 3 million cases of child abuse and neglect were reported in 1992, and 1,261 children died as a result, according to the National Committee for the Prevention of Child Abuse. The number of cases increased by 8% from the previous year, although most instances of child abuse go unreported. In all 50 states family counselors, mental health workers, teachers, principals, and any other professional person working with children must report evidence of child abuse to child protection agencies. If clients reveal that child abuse is happening to them or to others, the counselor has a legal responsibility to inform child protection services, which can take steps to prevent further abuse (see chap. 3).

The Characteristics and Effects of Abuse

The majority of abused children are under 3 years of age (Sroufe, Cooper, & DeHart, 1992). Both male and female parents abuse children physically, emotionally, and through neglect. Sexual abuse occurs more frequently in father-daughter or stepfather-stepdaughter relationships than in any other family relationship. Most female abuse happens in the family; male abuse is more likely outside the family.

Abusers in a family tend to dominate the family and often are substance abusers, have poor relationships outside the family, and have been abused themselves (Brown, 1991; Sroufe et al., 1992). However, there are numerous exceptions. Many who are abusive to spouse and children are not substance abusers, and many abusers seemingly have good relationships outside the home.

Families in which abuse occurs usually have a multitude of stressors: financial problems, lack of jobs, family breakups. In addition, boundaries are unclear or unspecified, and communication is woefully inadequate, with secrecy predominant (Brown, 1991).

If counseling interventions for abused children and their families are not provided, the children can develop serious emotional disorders that carry into adulthood. These disorders include depression and anxiety, codependency, eating disorders, learning disorders, multiple personalities, and sexual or drug addictions (Brown, 1991; Shaffer, 1993).

Abused children tend to be either aggressive or overly withdrawn with other children, resulting in their being rejected by their peers. Posttraumatic stress disorder, including nightmares and flashbacks, often develops and continues into adulthood. The likelihood is also strong that abused children, when they grow up, will abuse their children. Emotionally abused children also maintain a low self-image and gravitate to those who confirm their feelings of worthlessness (Cooney, 1991).

Counseling Families in Which Abuse Has Occurred

With families in which parents have been shown to be abusive, S. L. Brown (1991) emphasizes that treatment must first focus on individual family members. Brown is adamant about the necessity of removing the abused child from the family home. Then, during that time, the counselor works individually with each member of the family until the counselor is fairly certain that abuse will not recur when the child returns to the family or that abuse will not be directed toward other children in the family. Brown further recommends that, after placement in foster homes, abused children should receive counseling to help process the traumatic experiences and work through the shame, guilt, anger, or grief.

On a more optimistic note, Shaffer (1993) points out that many abused or neglected children develop a great deal of resiliency, especially if a supportive, secure relationship is established with a nonabusive parent, grandparent, or other adult in the family. When working with abused children, counselors should look for and cultivate the children's positive strengths.

Rencken's (2000) comments regarding family dynamics and intervention strategies for sexually abused children, abusers, and their families can be generalized to victims of all kinds of abuse. He describes three patterns of boundary breakdowns in families in which sexual abuse occurs. The first is the possessive father who considers his spouse and children to be possessions and does not differentiate among them. He views his daughter in the same way that he views a wife. Second is the immature, irresponsible father who becomes like one of the children. Third is the child who is pushed into becoming a pseudoadult; the child is described as "parentified" (Rencken, 2000, p. 25) when she assumes a substitute mother role, for example, which the mother has abdicated. In treating families in which abuse occurs, Rencken works with three dyads in the following order: mother-child, husband-wife, and father-child. He then works to shift the dyad into a triad of child-mother-father. Finally, he helps clients view their family unit as a whole.

TRENDS IN FAMILY THERAPY

For many years family systems theory neglected to consider the social-cultural impact on the family. Alfred Adler was a significant exception, and in recent years there has been a revival in Adlerian family therapy. Minuchin was another family therapist who recognized the social-cultural impact on the family; his early work with juvenile delinquents in inner-city ghettos was groundbreaking. In retrospect, however, family therapists, including Minuchin, admitted that his method of taking youths out of the slums and treating them away from the community was not successful. After the boys returned to their families and communities, recidivism rates were high. "The overall recidivism rate . . . was high . . . because the moment those kids came back to Harlem, they were sucked into the allure of the streets and the chaotic drama of their families" (Markowitz, 1997, p. 8). More recently, family therapists have been working with disadvantaged youths within their communities. And family therapies have expanded their outlook in a variety of ways to include the social-cultural environment as a significant factor of family dynamics.

Community Family Therapy

Psychiatrist and family therapist Ramon Rojano expanded Minuchin's ideas into what he calls *community family therapy* (Markowitz, 1997). Working with predominantly ethnic families, Rojano emphasizes the value of families working things out within their cultural neighborhoods and communities. He believes that family therapists should focus on helping clients and their families become empowered within their communities. With this approach family therapists help clients use resources in the community, such as schools, public assistance agencies, and employment offices. Some clients are encouraged to take leadership training to enable them to confront inadequacies and injustices in their communities, for example, inadequate school programs or abuse of police power. Other clients are encouraged to enroll in job-training programs (Markowitz, 1997).

Feminist Family Therapy

Feminist therapists are concerned that problems arising from gender stereotyping (see chaps. 6, 14, and 19) are not being given sufficient attention in family systems therapy. They believe that family therapists tend to use an outdated model of the overinvolved, overnurturant mother and the distant, uninvolved father as the accepted cultural pattern. Thus, family therapists, they say, do not pay sufficient attention to the inferior power status of women, thereby perpetuating the inequality of women in our culture (Zucal, 1992). Zucal (1992) believes that family therapists who are aware of these socialized gender differences will be less likely to blame either parent for perpetuating the family problem.

Marianne Walters, Betty Carter, Peggy Papp, and Olga Silverstein, members of the Women's Project in Family Therapy, are family therapists who also have taken into account socialized gender differences. The primary role of the Women's Project over the past 20 years has been to "persuade the field to move beyond the interior of the family to incorporate social and cultural issues into main stream clinical thinking" (Simon, 1997, p. 60).

Known as the "Fearless Foursome" (Simon, 1997, p. 60), the women got together at a time when family therapies were run primarily by men. These women criticized the dominant male perspectives promoted by Bateson, Haley, Bowen, and Minuchin, claiming that the men's views were "more of the same old sexism done up in fancy terminology. . . . Family therapists were too often guilty of perpetuating the same cultural myths about men and women that got families in trouble in the first place" (Simon, 1997, p. 60). In their landmark book *The Invisible Web* (1988), Walters, Carter, Papp, and Silverstein claim their feminist perspectives have yet to make significant changes in mainstream family therapy.

> With regard to these changes in the family, and in women's roles in the family, family therapy theory lags behind the culture as a whole. It is now imperative that there be new approaches in family therapy built on new assumptions about what constitutes a viable family. (p. 15)

In their work with families, Walters, Carter, Papp, and Silverstein focus on issues other than blaming parents, especially the mothers, for the family dysfunction. They concentrate instead on helping family members improve relations with each other and with their extended family, such as the grandparents, and work on forming and maintaining positive connections, rather than encouraging them to become separate and autonomous (see also chap. 19).

Systemic Cognitive-Developmental Therapy

Systemic cognitive-developmental therapy (SCDT) is a model of family systems therapy developed by Rigazio-DiGilio (2000, 2002) as an expansion of Ivey et. al.'s (2002) theory of developmental counseling and therapy (DCT) (see chap. 5). The central theme of SCDT is that all forms of psychological distress are rooted in a relational component among individuals, families, and wider social networks in the community. "Only by understanding how the relational systems construct their interpretations and reactions to this distress can therapists hope to understand how individuals and wider communities construe their situations" (Rigazio-DiGilio, 2000, p. 310). SCDT proposes that the individual, the family, and the wider social network form three key domains in an *interactive triad.* The degree and the quality of communication within this triad influence the effectiveness of family functioning. "SCDT considers family distress to be a natural and logical consequence of developmental and contextual history, and it reframes disorder as the consequence of limiting dialogues that occur among current participating members of the triad" (Rigazio-DiGilio, 2000, p. 312).

According to Rigazio-DiGilio (2000), families function as the primary *socialization matrix* whereby individuals develop and integrate themselves into the culture. The larger social and cultural contexts in which families live and interact play a significant role in enhancing as well as inhibiting family resources.

> This recursive interplay influences how families change to meet the developmental and contextual demands of members and of their multiple ethnic, racial, religious, class, political, institutional, and cultural affiliations. Families must use resources and challenge constraints to maintain a balance of continuity and change. (p. 311).

Encountering the distresses of life, families form what Rigazio-DiGilio calls "illness narratives" to deal with their difficulties. Illness narratives vary widely depending on the level of family disorder, which SCDT has classified on a continuum, with disordered family narratives at one end and ordered family narratives at the other.

Counselors using SCDT focus on strengthening the family's central role in the integration of the individual and the family into the culture. Family therapists help families access and enhance their strengths and assets, expand the use of resources they have previously neglected, and help them reconstruct their illness narratives (Rigazio-DiGilio, 2000).

SCDT practitioners follow the same assessment/diagnostic classification and treatment procedures that are used in Ivey's DCT therapeutic model, described in chapter 5, but adapt them to family concerns. SCDT family counselors assess the family's *collective worldview,* that is, the way the family as a whole construes events (Rigazio-DiGilio, 2002). They also assess each family member's primary and secondary cognitive orientation (i.e., sensorimotor, concrete/situational, formal/reflective, dialectic/systemic) through a structured series of questions. In this way counselors can determine the degree to which families have the flexibility to access other cognitive orientations to improve their opportunities to change. Well-developed families are able to switch back and forth among all four orientations, thereby breaking constraining patterns that would otherwise lock the family into one orientation. The counselor or therapist adopts a certain therapeutic role (i.e., directive, teacher/coach, consultant, or collaborative) appropriate to the family's level of cognitive development. Following is a description of the four cognitive orientations and the appropriate counselor role for each. Therapists start by enhancing the strengths in the family's primary cognitive orientation before helping the family access other orientations that have been neglected.

Sensorimotor-oriented families respond to immediate sensory and emotional experience. If constrained, they may become overwhelmed by emotions, become unstable, and lose sight of environmental considerations. SCDT counselors use a *direct/structured* approach that provides a safe environment so as to increase the family's willingness to access other orientations.

Concrete/situational families can describe their functioning in detail, including explanations about the cause of their distress. When constrained, they adopt a narrow cause-and-effect perspective and persist in actions that perpetuate the problem. Capitalizing on the family tendency to give detailed accounts, SCDT counselors use a *coaching/teaching* role and encourage families to tell their stories from multiple perspectives. In this way, families expand their abilities to access other orientations that will allow them to reflect on their difficulties.

Formal/reflective families are able to explore, reflect on, and analyze family interactions. When constrained, they may bog down in intellectual analyzing and thereby constrict the family's opportunities to change. At this level SCDT counselors act as *consultants* to assist the family in broadening its reflections with practical activities such as constructing and analyzing genograms, to help them reframe their stories.

Families with a *dialectic/systemic* orientation are able to evaluate and integrate the impact of intergenerational, familial, and social-cultural forces on their distress. When constrained, they may become too abstract, lose family identity, and neglect cognitive capacities from sensorimotor or concrete/situational orientations. SCDT counselors adopt the role of *collaborator,* for these families respond to counselor challenges about their worldviews and encouragement to broaden their social-cultural relational perspectives (Rigazio-DiGilio, 2000, 2002).

Postmodern Family Narrative Therapy

Family narrative therapy originated in the collaborative work of family therapists Michael White and David Epston from Australia and New Zealand, respectively. Their approach was strongly influenced by postmodern, social constructionists, notably French philosopher Michel Foucault (1980), who claims that in Western society a person's sense of individuality and independence is an illusion. In reality individuals are subjected to societal or global norms (White & Epston, 1990). White and Epston's family narrative therapy may be the first to apply postmodern, social constructionist thought to therapeutic family practice.

According to White and Epston (1990), people generally are governed by a *dominant story*, a story determined by one's social-cultural milieu. Families come for help because they are at odds with the dominant narratives that control their lives. "In these circumstances, there will be significant and vital aspects of their lived experience that contradict these dominant narratives" (White & Epston, 1990, p. 40). White and Epston's (1990) perspective has helped family therapists view certain family dysfunctions as symptomatic of a social-cultural disorder, rather than simply a problem within the family system (Sharf, 2000).

During therapy sessions the counselor uses a series of questions to elicit new insights, understandings, and perceptions from the family that ultimately lead to more productive alternative narratives. These questions are not designed to diagnose or assess families or gain information. White and Epston (1990) believe that evaluative and diagnostic questioning impedes or hinders the family's progress. Rather than adhering to traditional family therapy models, which believe that the "dysfunction in the family determines the behavior," White and Epston believe that "it is the meaning that members attribute to events that determines their behavior" (p. 3). In this approach counselors and therapists relate to clients as collaborators or partners throughout the counseling process, with the emphasis on the family's important role in how therapy progresses (Seligman, 2001).

The therapeutic process involves several stages: Counselors first help families to mutually agree on the nature and definition of the problem and its influence on the family. The counselor uses a method called *mapping* the problem to help the family learn the extent of the problem's influence, that is, how the problem affects all aspects of their lives—emotionally, physically, behaviorally, and attitudinally. Thus, right from the start, each family member becomes actively engaged in the family story, a problem-saturated narrative. And by arriving at a mutually acceptable perception of the problem, family cooperation is enhanced. In the next set of questions, the counselor asks each family member to undertake the more difficult task of mapping the extent to which he or she influences the problem.

The therapist avoids generalizing or conceptualizing about anything observed but encourages family members to stay with specifics as they map their narratives. The more broadly the map stretches into all areas of their lives, the less narrow the field becomes, thereby allowing the family more options when they later start reconstructing their story.

Next, the family is encouraged to put the problem outside itself in a process called *externalizing* the problem. Families who externalize their problems are liberated from the social-cultural restraints that have made them feel like objects. "When persons learn to separate from problems, they may come to challenge other practices, cultural in origin, that are 'objectifying' or 'thingifying' of persons and their bodies" (White & Epston, 1990, p. 65). Clients may personify their problem, such as naming their depression Gloomy Gus, who is controlling an individual or a family's mood. This strategy helps clients activate their resources to tackle and resolve their problem (White & Epston, 1990).

Therapists also encourage members to look for *unique outcomes,* that is, times when they witness or perform acts that do not contribute to the problem, but instead alleviate it.

> The identification of unique outcomes and the performance of new meanings around these help persons to identify their resistance to the effects of the problem or its requirements. . . . If persons refuse to cooperate with the requirements of the problem, then they are undermining it; refusing to submit to the effects of the problem renders the problem less effective. (White & Epston, 1990, p. 63)

White and Epston (1990) use a wide variety of writing activities to generate the narrative flow with their clients. These activities might include written invitations to therapy sessions when, for example, a family member refuses to attend, written stories that depict a successful endeavor, brief letters between the therapist and family members, letters as narratives in which individuals write a story about a lived experience, and letters about special occasions such as a death in the family.

By exploring the influence of their problem on the family, externalizing the problem, and searching for and acting on unique outcomes, families learn to be responsible for their problems as they become agents of their story. In this way they can resist behaviors that contribute to the problem. And the family learns to develop new alternative narratives that would lead to changes in their lives that might resolve difficulties and improve relationships (Sharf, 2000; White & Epston, 1990).

RESEARCH IN FAMILY AND MARRIAGE COUNSELING AND THERAPY

Gurman, Kniskern, and Pinsof (1986) and Bednar, Burlingame, and Masters (1988) critiqued research reviews on family systems and on behavioral marital and family therapy (BMFT). More recent research has reaffirmed their findings (Gladding, 2002), which are summarized here:

- Regardless of approach, family therapy is more effective than none at all.
- Success rates in marital therapy and family therapy are comparable to those of individual therapy.
- When both parents are involved, outcomes tend to be more positive.
- The therapist's degree of relationship skills shows a relatively high correlation with effective outcomes.
- Behavioral and nonbehavioral approaches are shown to be equally effective for families needing short-term therapy.
- Brief family counseling and therapy has proved to be as effective as long-term family therapy for less severe forms of family problems.

In a review of the literature, White and Allers (1994) note a renewed interest in play therapy (PT) for abused children. Although strongly advocating the value of PT, they found inconsistencies in the research regarding the definition of abuse, the definition of PT, the play therapist's training, and the effectiveness of PTs. They suggest that more consistent research studies and outcomes are necessary before any definite therapeutic system can be recommended.

SUMMARY

Family therapy has flourished in the mental health field since the 1960s, when psychiatrists and social workers first perceived the family as a social unit, or family system. Family systems therapists focus on the family as a whole, rather than on an individual identified patient (IP). As a natural social system, the family is composed of alliances, sets of rules, assigned roles, and prescribed modes of communication.

Because the family is a social unit, when one family member develops problems, the symptoms represent dysfunctions among all family members. Dysfunctional families are enmeshed with or disengaged from one another, cannot communicate directly and authentically, and form alliances among themselves when conflicts arise. Therapists help family members learn to communicate directly and respect one another's boundaries and privacy.

Counselors who specialize in marriage and couple counseling work with married or unmarried couples with or without children, lesbian or gay couples, and those wanting premarital counseling.

Changing family patterns have brought about new considerations for family counselors and therapists. The traditional family pattern, with father as breadwinner and mother as caregiver of their biologically related children, is no longer predominant. In the majority of homes now, both parents work, and about one-third of American families are led by a single parent (mostly women). Many are remarried families with multiple parents, stepparents, and stepsiblings.

Child abuse includes neglect and physical, emotional, and sexual abuse. Family counselors tend to treat the abused child first and then the member of the family who committed the abuse separately before they treat the family together as a unit. Family sessions include issues about boundaries, assuming responsibility for changing behavior, developing support systems, and working to reunify the family.

The recent trend in family therapy has been toward increased consideration of the social-cultural influences on the family. Included in this trend are a community family therapy model, which helps empower inner-city ethnic families; a family model from a feminist perspective; a systemic cognitive development model; and a postmodern family narrative model.

PROJECTS AND ACTIVITIES

1. Interview some counselors who specialize in family counseling. Compare their theoretical backgrounds and the techniques each prefers to use.
2. Practice the technique called sculpting, as used by Virginia Satir. Using other classmates to enact the roles of a family, pose the family to demonstrate its pattern of relating (see Figure 10.1).
3. Interview counselors and social workers in nearby school districts. Find out what family services are offered to parents and students. If none exist, ask how families with problems receive help.
4. Role-play a telephone conversation in which a parent calls to get counseling for an adolescent daughter with "problems." During the conversation it becomes obvious to you that the whole family needs counseling. How would you make this clear to the parent?
5. Consider the pros and cons of using a family systems approach with a single-parent family or a blended family.

REFERENCES

Alexander, J. F., & Parsons, B. V. (1982). *Functional family therapy.* Pacific Grove, CA: Brooks/Cole.

Atwood, J. D. (Ed.). (1992a). *Family therapy: A systemic-behavioral approach.* Chicago: Nelson-Hall.

Atwood, J. D. (1992b). The field today. In J. D. Atwood (Ed.), *Family therapy: A systemic-behavioral approach* (pp. 29–58). Chicago: Nelson-Hall.

Atwood, J. D. (1992c). A system-behavioral approach to counseling the single-parent family. In J. D. Atwood (Ed.), *Family therapy: A systemic-behavioral approach* (pp. 191–205). Chicago: Nelson-Hall.

Baruth, L. G., & Burggraf, M. Z. (1991). Counseling single-parent families. In J. Carlson & J. Lewis (Eds.), *Family counseling: Strategies and issues* (pp. 175–188). Denver: Love.

Basow, S. (1992). *Gender stereotypes and roles* (3rd ed.). Pacific Grove, CA: Brooks/Cole.

Beck, A. (1976). *Cognitive therapy and the emotional disorders.* New York: International Universities Press.

Becvar, D. S., & Becvar, R. J. (1986). *Family therapy: A systemic integration.* Boston: Allyn & Bacon.

Bednar, R. L., Burlingame, G. M., & Masters, K. S. (1988). Systems of family treatment: Substance or semantics? *Annual Review of Psychology, 39,* 401–434.

Bowen, M. (1978). *Family therapy in clinical practice.* New York: Jason Aronson.

Brock, G. W., & Barnard, C. P. (1988). *Procedures in family therapy.* Boston: Allyn & Bacon.

Brown, J. H., & Brown, C. S. (2002). *Marital therapy: Concepts and skills for effective practice.* Pacific Grove, CA: Brooks/Cole.

Brown, J. H., & Christensen, D. N. (1986). *Family therapy: Theory and practice.* Monterey, CA: Brooks/Cole.

Brown, S. L. (1991). *Counseling victims of violence.* Alexandria, VA: American Association for Counseling Development.

Carson, R. D. (1983). *Taming your gremlin: A guide to enjoying yourself.* New York: Harper & Row.

Carter, B. (1988). Remarried families: Creating a new paradigm. In M. Walters, B. Carter, P. Papp, & O. Silverstein (Eds.), *The invisible web: Gender patterns in family relationships* (pp. 333–368). New York: Guilford Press.

Carter, B., & McGoldrick, M. (1999). Overview: The expanded family life cycle. In B. Carter & M. McGoldrick (Eds.), *The expanded family life cycle* (3rd ed., pp. 1–26). New York: Gardner Press.

Colapinto, J. (1991). Structural family therapy. In A. M. Horne & J. L. Passmore (Eds.), *Family counseling and therapy* (2nd ed., pp. 77–103). Itasca, IL: F. E. Peacock.

Cole, C., & Rodman, H. (1987). When school-age children care for themselves: Issues for family life educators and parents. *Family Relations, 26,* 92–96.

Cooney, J. (1991). Counseling and child abuse: A developmental perspective. In J. Carlson & J. Lewis (Eds.), *Family counseling: Strategies and issues* (pp. 225–242). Denver: Love.

Dinkmeyer, D., Jr., & Dinkmeyer, D., Sr. (1991). Adlerian family therapy. In A. M. Horne & J. L. Passmore (Eds.), *Family counseling and therapy* (2nd ed., pp. 383–402). Itasca, IL: F. E. Peacock.

Dinkmeyer, D., & McKay, G. D. (1976). *Systematic training for effective parenting.* Circle Pines, MN: American Guidance Services.

Dreikurs, R. (1968). *Psychology in the classroom.* New York: Harper & Row.

Dreikurs, R., Lowe, R., Sonstegard, M., & Corsini, R. J. (Eds.). (1959). *Adlerian family counseling: A manual for counseling centers.* Eugene: University of Oregon.

Ellis, A. (1982). Rational-emotive family therapy. In A. M. Horne & M. M. Ohlsen (Eds.), *Family counseling and therapy* (pp. 302–328). Itasca, IL: F. E. Peacock.

Ellis, A. (1991). Rational-emotive family therapy. In A. M. Horne & J. L. Passmore (Eds.), *Family counseling and therapy* (2nd ed., pp. 403–434). Itasca, IL: F. E. Peacock.

Ellis, A. (2000). Rational emotive behavior therapy. In R. J. Corsini & D. Wedding, *Current psychotherapies* (6th ed., pp. 168–204). Itasca, IL: F. E. Peacock.

Fairbairn, W. R. (1954). *An object-relations theory of personality.* New York: Basic Books.

Fenell, D. L., & Weinhold, B. K. (1989). *Counseling families: An introduction to marriage and family therapy.* Denver: Love.

Foley, V. D. (1989). Family therapy. In R. J. Corsini & D. Wedding (Eds.), *Current psychotherapies* (4th ed., pp. 455–500). Itasca, IL: F. E. Peacock.

Fossum, M. A., & Mason, J. J. (1986). *Facing shame: Families in recovery.* New York: Norton.

Foucault, M. (1980). *Power/knowledge: Selected interviews and other writings.* New York: Pantheon Books.

Framo, J. L. (1982). *Explorations in marital and family therapy.* New York: Springer.

Gilligan, C. (1982). *In a different voice.* Cambridge, MA: Harvard University Press.

Gilligan, C. (2002). *The birth of pleasure.* New York: Alfred A. Knopf.

Gladding, S. T. (2002). *Family therapy: History, theory, and practice* (3rd ed.). Upper Saddle River, NJ: Merrill/Prentice Hall.

Goldenberg, I., & Goldenberg, H. (2000). *Family therapy: An overview* (5th ed.). Pacific Grove, CA: Brooks/Cole.

Gurman, A. S., Kniskern, D. P., & Pinsof, W. M. (1986). Research on marital and family therapies. In S. L. Garfield & A. E. Bergin (Eds.), *Handbook of psychotherapy and behavior change: An empirical analysis* (3rd ed., pp. 565–624). New York: John Wiley.

Haley, J. (1987). *Problem-solving therapy* (2nd ed.). San Francisco: Jossey-Bass.

Hershenson, D. B., Power, P. W., & Waldo, M. (1996). *Community counseling: Contemporary theory and practice.* Boston: Allyn & Bacon.

Hoffman, L. (1990). Constructing realities: An art of tenses. *Family Process, 29,* 1–12.

Horne, A. M. (1991). Social learning family therapy. In A. M. Horne & J. L. Passmore (Eds.), *Family counseling and therapy* (2nd ed., pp. 463–496). Itasca, IL: F. E. Peacock.

Ivey, A. E., D'Andrea, M., Ivey, M. B., & Simek-Morgan, L. C. (2002). *Counseling and psychotherapy: A multicultural perspective* (5th ed.). Boston: Allyn & Bacon.

Klein, M. (1948). *The analysis of self.* New York: International Universities Press.

L'Abate, L., Ganahl, G., & Hansen, J. C. (1986). *Methods of family therapy.* Upper Saddle River, NJ: Prentice Hall.

Lowe, R. N. (1982). Adlerian/Dreikursian family counseling. In A. M. Horne & M. M. Ohlsen (Eds.), *Family counseling and therapy* (pp. 329–359). Itasca, IL: F. E. Peacock.

Lynn, S., & Garske, J. (1985). *Contemporary psychotherapies.* New York: Macmillan.

Madanes, C. (1981). *Strategic family therapy.* San Francisco: Jossey-Bass.

Markowitz, L. (1997). Ramon Rojano won't take no for an answer. *Family Therapy Networker, 21,* 24–35.

Meichenbaum, D. (1985). *Stress inoculation training.* New York: Pergamon Press.

Middleton-Moz, J., & Dwinell, L. (1986). *After the tears.* Pompano Beach, FL: Health Communications.

Minuchin, S., Lee, W., & Simon, G. M. (1996). *Mastering family therapy: Journeys of growth and transformation.* New York: John Wiley.

Minuchin, S. T. (1974). *Families and family therapy.* Cambridge, MA: Harvard University Press.

Mosak, H. H. (2000). Adlerian psychotherapy. In R. J. Corsini & D. Wedding (Eds.), *Current psychotherapies* (6th ed., pp. 54–98). Itasca, IL: F. E. Peacock.

Nystul, M. S. (1993). *The art and science of counseling and psychotherapy.* Upper Saddle River, NJ: Merrill/Prentice Hall.

Papero, D. V. (1991). The Bowen theory. In A. H. Horne & J. L. Passmore (Eds.), *Family counseling and therapy* (2nd ed., pp. 47–76). Itasca, IL: F. E. Peacock.

Passmore, J. L., & Horne, A. M. (1991). Introduction. In A. M. Horne & J. L. Passmore (Eds.), *Family counseling and therapy* (2nd ed., pp. 1–12). Itasca, IL: F. E. Peacock.

Patterson, G. R. (1971). *Families: Application of social learning to family life.* Champaign, IL: Research Press.

Real, T. (1997). *I don't want to talk about it.* New York: Fireside.

Real, T. (2002). The awful truth. *Psychotherapy Networker, 26,* 34–43, 58.

Rencken, R. H. (2000). *Intervention strategies for sexual abuse* (2nd ed.). Alexandria, VA: American Association for Counseling Development.

Rigazio-DiGilio, S. A. (2000). Reconstructing psychological distress and disorder from a relational perspective: A systemic coconstructive-developmental framework. In R. A. Neimeyer & J. D. Raskin, *Constructions of disorder* (pp. 309–332). Washington, DC: American Psychological Association.

Rigazio-DiGilio, S. A. (2002). Family counseling and therapy: Theoretical foundations and issues of practice. In A. E. Ivey, M. D'Andrea, M. B. Ivey, & L. Simek-Morgan, *Theories of counseling and psychotherapy: A multicultural perspective* (5th ed.). Boston: Allyn & Bacon.

Roberts, E. (1992). The role of fun in family therapy. In J. D. Atwood (Ed.), *Family therapy: A systemic behavioral approach* (pp. 70–87). Chicago: Nelson-Hall.

Satir, V. M. (1967). *Conjoint family therapy.* Palo Alto, CA: Science & Behavior Books.

Satir, V. M. (1972). *Peoplemaking.* Palo Alto, CA: Science & Behavior Books.

Satir, V. M. (1982). The therapist and family therapy: Process model. In A. M. Horne & M. M. Ohlsen (Eds.), *Family counseling and therapy* (pp. 12–42). Itasca, IL: F. E. Peacock.

Satir, V. M., & Bitter, J. M. (1991). The therapist and family therapy: Satir's human validation process model. In A. M. Horne & J. L. Passmore (Eds.), *Family counseling and therapy* (2nd ed., pp. 13–46). Itasca, IL: F. E. Peacock.

Schilson, E. A. (1991). Strategic therapy. In A. M. Horne & J. L. Passmore (Eds.), *Family counseling and therapy* (2nd ed., pp. 141–178). Itasca, IL: F. E. Peacock.

Seligman, L. (2001). *Systems, strategies, and skills of counseling and psychotherapy.* Upper Saddle River, NJ: Merrill/Prentice Hall.

Shaffer, D. R. (1993). *Developmental psychology: Childhood and adolescence* (3rd ed.). Pacific Grove, CA: Brooks/Cole.

Sharf, R. S. (2000). *Theories of psychotherapy & counseling: Concepts and cases* (2nd ed.). Belmont, CA: Brooks/Cole.

Sherman, R., & Dinkmeyer, D. (1987). *Systems of family therapy: An Adlerian integration.* New York: Brunner/Mazel.

Simon, R. (1997). Fearless foursome. *Family Therapy Networker, 21,* 58–68.

Singleton, G. (1982). Bowen family systems theory. In A. M. Horne & M. M. Ohlsen (Eds.), *Family counseling and therapy* (pp. 75–111). Itasca, IL: F. E. Peacock.

Skynner, A. C. R. (1981). An open-systems group analytic approach to family therapy. In A. S. Gurman & D. P. Kniskern (Eds.), *Handbook of family therapy* (pp. 39–84). New York: Brunner/Mazel.

Solomon, M. (1969). Family therapy dropouts: Resistance to change. *Canadian Psychiatric Association Journal, 14,* 22–23.

Sroufe, L. A., Cooper, R. G., & DeHart, G. B. (1992). *Child development: Its nature and course* (2nd ed.). New York: McGraw-Hill.

Sweeney, T. (1989). *Adlerian counseling: A practical approach for a new decade* (3rd ed.). Muncie, IN: Accelerated Development.

Thomas, M. B. (1992). *An introduction to marital and family therapy: Counseling toward healthier family systems across the life span.* New York: Macmillan.

Thompson, C. L., & Rudolph, L. B. (1992). *Counseling children* (3rd ed.). Pacific Grove, CA: Brooks/Cole.

von Bertalanffy, L. (1974). General systems theory and psychiatry. In S. Aristi (Ed.), *American handbook of psychiatry* (Vol. 1, pp. 1095–1117). New York: Brace Books.

Walters, M. (1988). Single-parent, female-headed households. In M. Walters, B. Carter, P. Papp, & O. Silverstein (Eds.), *The invisible web: Gender patterns in family relationships* (pp. 289–332). New York: Guilford Press.

Walters, M., Carter, B., Papp, P., & Silverstein, O. (Eds.). (1988). *The invisible web: Gender patterns in family relationships.* New York: Guilford Press.

Watts, R. E. (2003). *Adlerian, cognitive, and constructivist therapies: An integrative dialogue.* New York: Springer.

Weeks, G. R., & L'Abate, L. (1982). *Paradoxical psychotherapy: Theory and practice with individuals, couples, and families.* New York: Brunner/Mazel.

White, J., & Allers, C. T. (1994). Play therapy with abused children: A review of the literature. *Journal of Counseling & Development, 72,* 390–394.

White, M., & Epston, D. (1990). *Narrative means to therapeutic ends.* New York: Norton.

Wylie, M. S. (2002). The untold story: Carol Gilligan on recapturing the lost voice of pleasure. *Psychotherapy Networker 26* (6), 46–56.

Zucal, B. (1992). Gender issues in couples therapy. In J. D. Atwood (Ed.), *Family therapy: A systemic behavioral approach* (pp. 59–69). Chicago: Nelson-Hall.

Zunker, V. G. (1994). *Career counseling: Applied concepts of life planning* (4th ed.). Pacific Grove, CA: Brooks/Cole.

CHAPTER 11

Group Counseling

Group counseling became popular in the 1960s, when counselors began to realize that individuals who were having problems in their relationships could benefit from sharing their concerns and resolving their problems with others having similar problems. The definition of group counseling by George Gazda (1978), a pioneer in group counseling, remains one of the clearest explanations of the process:

> Group work refers to the dynamic interaction between collections of individuals for prevention or remediation of difficulties or for the enhancement of personal growth/enrichment through the interaction of those who meet together for a commonly agreed-on purpose and at pre-arranged times. (p. 260)

Corey and Corey (2002) point out:

> The broad purposes of a therapeutic group are to increase members' knowledge of themselves and others, help members clarify the changes they most want to make in their life, and to provide members with the tools they need to make these changes. (p. 12)

Group counseling can be useful to persons who are either shy or aggressive in their interpersonal interactions, anxious or uncomfortable in groups, or resistant or conforming to social expectations. Individuals may be having difficulty making or keeping friends, or they may be experiencing friction with peers, parents, faculty, or bosses. Groups can be geared to age-related issues—for children, adolescents, young adults, older adults, and for intergenerational groups, such as mothers/teenage daughters or older adults/young children. Group counseling can be effective for a wide variety of special needs—children of divorced parents, teenage substance abusers, young parents, parents with teenagers, those suffering from grief, abused women, adult children of alcoholics, men needing to learn to control their anger (Corey & Corey, 2002).

Group counseling is inappropriate and inadvisable for individuals experiencing personal or interpersonal conflicts too private to share in a group; it is also unsuitable for those with strong fears about social interactions, for those who might find a group experience traumatic, or for those with low impulse control who might constantly disrupt group interactions (Burlingame & Fuhriman, 1990; Gladding, 2003; Nystul, 1993). In these cases individual counseling may be more suitable until the individuals feel more confident or more in control of themselves.

When clients' problems relate to interpersonal awkwardness, insecurities, or conflicts, group counseling has the advantage of giving members an opportunity to work out their problems in a structured social setting. In this setting they can experiment with and practice new behaviors and receive support for their efforts and feedback from other group members and the counselor. Each member becomes aware of the feelings and experiences of other persons (Nystul, 1993), and each has a chance to help others in the group improve social interactions. Counselors can observe clients interacting with other group members and can interact themselves with each group member (Corey, 2000).

Another value unique to group therapy and counseling is that individuals often experience feelings of isolation as they suffer pain, despair, and/or guilt, even if they share with an understanding counselor or therapist. Expressing painful emotions in a supportive group among those who have experienced similar pain and traumas removes those feelings of isolation and, moreover, validates one's trauma as a communal experience, thus relieving the overwhelming emotional burden carried by lone individuals.

Working psychotherapeutically with depressed males, Terence Real (1997) emphasizes that groups provide significant support for participants. When ready, a volunteer goes to the center of the group circle, where he sits alongside the therapist. Here, in the presence of others, he delves into his deepest fears, conflicts, rage, pain. In one example Real asks a man who enters the circle for the first time how he feels being surrounded by so many others. The man responds,

> "Well, I'm nervous, believe me. But I also feel buoyed up. Like, I feel their energy, man," he clowns. Some men laugh. "No really, though," he continues, "like floating in the ocean."
>
> "It's called support," I say.
>
> "Well, I like it," he says. (p. 215)

Groups do have some disadvantages, though. Clients receive less direct attention from counselors, who must focus on group concerns and group interactions. And some clients may find it difficult to develop the trust in other group members that is necessary for constructive self-disclosure. They may also experience direct or subtle pressure to conform to group norms. In addition, the leadership is weak, group members may experience psychological distress when they reveal more than they are ready to or when they are confronted inappropriately by other group members.

Groups differ in their purposes, goals, and intensity, depending on the severity of the clients' problems or the degree of the clients' dysfunctions. In group counseling literature, these various types of group work are described as falling along a continuum (Gazda, 1989). Growth groups, designed for persons who feel fairly functional but want more meaning in life, are at one end of the continuum. Group counseling, in the middle of the continuum, serves persons who are not living as effectively as they could, who have learned maladaptive ways of interacting with others, or who have negative views of themselves but are able to manage their lives adequately. Group psychotherapy, at the other end of the continuum, includes persons who are more emotionally disturbed and who require intensive remedial work. The goals of growth groups are to educate and train persons in skills and attitudes; the goals of group counseling are to help persons solve problems, develop self-awareness, and improve interpersonal relations; the goal of group psychotherapy is remedial work. In a similar way Corey (2000) differentiates between group counseling and group therapy: "Whereas counseling groups focus on growth, development, enhancement, prevention, self-awareness and releasing blocks to growth, therapy groups typically focus on remediation, treatment, and personality reconstruction" (p. 10).

As with individual counseling and psychotherapy, some overlap exists between group counseling and psychotherapy. Thus, at times the terms *group counseling* and *group psychotherapy* are used interchangeably by theorists and practitioners (Vander Kolk, 1985).

This chapter focuses on group counseling and group psychotherapy. Growth groups, which emphasize specific social skill training (structured groups), interpersonal interactions (sensitivity training or T-groups), and personal awareness (personal growth and encounter groups), are discussed in chapter 8 and in the counseling practice chapters in part 4.

ETHICAL GUIDELINES WITH GROUPS

Ethical guidelines specific to group counseling have been developed by the Association for Specialists in Group Work (ASGW, 1989) and the APA (1973). These guidelines are consistent with the ACA code of ethics for individual and group counseling (1995).

Counselors face different ethical considerations with groups than with individuals. Some of the more important ethical considerations are discussed here: (a) screening for appropriateness for group counseling, (b) allowing freedom to leave the group, (c) monitoring confidentiality among group members, and (d) guarding against group members manipulating or abusing each other (Corey, Corey, & Callanan, 1998).

First of all, group counselors have an ethical responsibility to screen clients for their suitability for the group. If an individual is not psychologically ready for the group or has purposes different from those of the group, the counselor should let the individual know and refer her or him to individual counseling or to a more appropriate group.

Furthermore, group counseling is most effective and ethical when members voluntarily enter a group and have the freedom to leave it. According to the ASGW Code of Ethics (1989), members of a voluntary group "have the right to exit a group; but it is important they be made aware of the importance of informing the counselor and the group members prior to deciding to leave" (Section 5.d). The code recommends that counselors and groups discuss with exiting members the advantages of remaining with the group and encourage them to give their reasons for leaving.

Clearly, a leader has no way of forcing a member to explain why he or she wants to leave the group. And for a member who has never asserted him- or herself before, leaving without explanation may be a sign of newly found strength. Furthermore, such a disruption allows the group to tussle with an actual problem that has occurred within the group.

One example of just such an experience occurred in a university group. The members contemplated sending angry letters to the young man who had abandoned the group. But after working through their feelings and discussing group and individual rights, group members decided to send him cards thanking him for his contributions, telling him they missed him, and letting him know he was welcome to return if he so chose. Although he did not return, he did send the group a letter thanking them for understanding him and explaining that he had learned to assert his needs for the first time in this group, which gave him the courage to break away.

Concerns about whether group members will hold in confidence self-disclosures and group interactions have been expressed frequently in the literature (Corey, 2000; Forester-Miller & Rubenstein, 1992; Gladding, 2003). In accordance with the ACA Code of Ethics (1995, B.2.a), Corey and Corey (2002) state, "Group counselors have an ethical and legal responsibility to inform group members of the potential consequences of breaching confidentiality" (p. 75). Because members tend to unwittingly share their group experiences with close friends or loved ones outside the group, counselors should emphasize that members not share who is in the group or what other members have said. "Group leaders should express the importance of maintaining confidentiality, have members sign contracts agreeing to it, and even impose some form of sanction on those who break it" (Corey & Corey, 2002, p. 75). If counselors clarify the group's responsibilities regarding confidentiality and give reasons for its importance, problems do not often arise. Confidentiality poses more problems in those educational institutions or agencies in which members know one another and share mutual associates and friends. If group sessions are to be recorded or if research based on the group experience is being conducted, confidentiality and rights of privacy require that counselors get written consent from each member (Gazda, 1989).

Attempts by a group counselor or group members to persuade an individual member to behave in a manner the group thinks is desirable is a greater potential problem in groups than is confidentiality. Consistent with professional ethical guidelines (ASGW, 1989), each member in group counseling has the right and obligation to decide how and when she or he wants to participate. Similarly, counselors have an ethical responsibility not to indoctrinate groups with the counselors' values.

In addition, group counselors must always be alert to the psychological risks inherent in group counseling and must conduct groups in a way that minimizes client trauma. Counselors must monitor groups, intervening whenever someone puts pressure on another to self-disclose more than that person is ready to share. Counselor intervention is also necessary when one member makes hostile attacks on another in the guise of confrontation or makes fun of or scapegoats another person.

GROUP COUNSELING THEORIES

Group counseling theories are classified in a manner similar to that of individual and family theories: psychodynamic (transactional analysis and psychodrama), humanistic (group-centered and Gestalt), cognitive-behavioral, and developmental.

Psychodynamic Group Counseling

In psychodynamic group counseling, exploration and analysis of members' unconscious intrapsychic dynamics are emphasized (Hershenson, Power, & Waldo, 1996). Feelings generated by unresolved childhood conflicts are reexperienced, reenacted, and related appropriately to present-day relationships. A counselor must resolve feelings of transference, countertransference, and resistance that arise with each member of the group, as well as with the total group (i.e., group transference). These feelings need to be acknowledged and worked through (Brammer, Abrego, & Shostrom, 1993).

In psychodynamic groups counselors share their interpretations of individual and group emotional reactions with the members of the group. As counseling progresses, members—with guidance from the counselors—share insights about their own behavior and emotional expressions. Insights and understandings lead to more realistic perceptions of early relationships, as well as of themselves, of other group members, and of the counselors. These new and more accurate perceptions help each group member learn more appropriate ways to express and satisfy authentic, legitimate needs in group sessions. In the final stage of counseling, members are encouraged to apply these new insights and learnings to everyday living (Gazda, 1989).

Transactional Analysis

Eric Berne (1961), a psychoanalyst, developed transactional analysis (TA) specifically for groups; TA is based on analysis and understanding of social communication. A transaction refers to the way two people communicate or exchange ideas or feelings, and analysis refers to the interpretation of how adaptive or maladaptive these social exchanges are and how to make them more constructive.

In TA personality structure is seen as consisting of three ego states: parent, adult, and child. The parent is the conscience, or a group of dos and don'ts learned as a child; the adult is the commonsense, reality-oriented portion of the personality; and the child is composed of spontaneous, impulsive feelings—the creative part of the personality. Individuals tend to move from one state to another in their transactions with others.

In 1964 Berne published a best-selling book called *Games People Play,* in which he describes how people behave to get attention, recognition, and physical contact (strokes) in order to flourish and survive. Positive strokes from parents (e.g., warmth and acceptance) lead to healthy functioning; negative strokes (e.g., rejection or severe criticism) lead to dysfunctions; and indifference often results in pathology or severe dysfunctions. Healthy persons give and receive positive strokes in authentic, open, social transactions; maladjusted persons use repetitive sets of social manipulations called games to elicit the strokes they received as children. Through reinforcement with strokes similar to those learned from, and further reinforced by, games they play, persons develop life scripts that control or shape their lives (Berne, 1972).

Counselors use four progressive stages of analysis to help clients: structural, transactional, game, and life script. Most people complete the first three; few go on to life script analysis, in which they desire to change their personality (Berne, 1966). In structural analysis individuals are taught to understand their own personality structures and to be aware when one ego state is excluding another or when one state is intruding on or contaminating another. The adult who always denies the child may become computerlike or develop into a workaholic; the child who always intrudes on the adult may lead the adult to expect immediate gratifications all the time.

In TA what people say to each other (i.e., transactions) is analyzed in the group—thus, transactional analysis. Transactions may be either complementary or crossed. In complementary transactions comments, questions, or requests from one person elicit appropriate and healthy responses from another. Crossed transactions inhibit communication; for example, a request from an adult is responded to as if the initiator were a parent and the responder a child. In TA crossed transactions are converted to complementary ones (Patterson, 1986).

In game analysis people are made aware of the games they play to get strokes (Berne, 1964); game playing is exposed and more authentic relationships taught (Dusay & Dusay, 1989). The final stage, life script analysis, helps group members first recall and reenact childhood experiences and then discover how they acquired and maintained the dysfunctional life script (Steiner, 1974).

Psychodrama

Jacob Moreno (1946) was one of the most influential figures in the development of group work. He coined the terms *group therapy* and *group psychotherapy*. In 1946 he introduced psychodrama, which has had considerable impact on group counseling and therapy in hospitals, community settings, and schools (Blatner, 1995). Psychodrama was the forerunner of several current group theories, including Gestalt, encounter, and some behavioral groups that emphasize action-insight and immediate experiencing.

The purpose of psychodrama is to build a therapeutic setting using life itself as a model. Clients act out conflicts instead of talking about them. Ideally, it is carried out on a psychodrama stage, but more often it takes place in an informal room where staging can occur. The actor-client is aided by a director (the counselor or therapist) and by one or more auxiliary egos (other group members) who act out either persons in the client's life who are not present or the client's imaginations, fantasies, or dreams (Gazda, 1989).

Psychodrama consists of three parts, or stages: the warm-up, the action, and the postaction, or sharing and discussion stage (Moreno, 1983). In the warm-up stage the director describes the procedure, interviews each member briefly, and asks whether the members have present, past, or future situations or relationships they would like to explore. The group may break into smaller groups and practice sharing a conflict. In the action stage a member volunteers to present and act out her problem, with the help of the counselor and one or more persons chosen from the group.

Blatner (1995) describes certain principles of psychodrama. The client must act out conflict rather than talk about it. The actor acts in the immediate present, regardless of when the incident happened in the past or might happen in the future. The client acts out how she feels, regardless of how distorted her perceptions may seem to anybody else.

Clients are encouraged to play the roles of other persons in their lives, as well as their own. In addition, a double, played by an auxiliary ego, may act out the client's feelings, or multiple doubles may portray ambivalent feelings that are hindering free expression by the client-actor. Sometimes an auxiliary ego mirrors the actor's behavior, with the actor observing offstage. The client-actor may also use soliloquy with side comments to group members. Dream work, as in Gestalt groups, involves persons enacting, rather than analyzing, their dreams. The director interprets or suggests changes in scripts or the use of auxiliary egos when necessary. After the performance group members share observations and reactions to the psychodrama in a supportive manner. The actor is encouraged to practice new behavior.

Jacob Moreno introduced psychodrama and sociodrama into schools in 1949. Using these ideas, Heathcote (1971) introduced a model for child drama in 1971. Increasing numbers of elementary school counselors are now using psychodrama with groups of elementary school students (Thompson & Rudolph, 1992). In addition, John Allan (1988), a Jungian counselor, has integrated the principles and processes of psychodrama with Jungian concepts of imagination and individuation to use with elementary schoolchildren who act out.

Humanistic Group Counseling

Person-Centered or Group-Centered Counseling

As they do in individual counseling, Rogerian counselors develop warm, accepting, and authentic relationships with each group member to facilitate positive personal growth. Rogerian counselors accomplish this personal growth by modeling warm, empathic, and congruent attitudes and behaviors toward not only the group but also each member. Thus, an atmosphere is created that fosters these same facilitative characteristics in the interactions of group members with both the counselor and one another. The group works toward building trust and nonjudgmental support for one another, which permits members to drop protective masks and defenses and to face the anxiety of bringing up painful thoughts or shameful acts.

As trust deepens, the counselor helps group members let others know when they are not being genuine, authentic, understanding, or supportive. Misperceptions about self and others are thus corrected, enabling each person to express appropriate needs and relate authentically with others (Corey, 2000; Gazda, 1989). Rogerian counselors believe that substantial personal growth occurs if unconditional positive regard is established.

The counselor expects group members to decide on their individual and mutual group goals; the only direction is that group members ask each other to decide what they want to accomplish. Techniques and games are used sparingly. Trust exercises may be tried but only if the group decides to do so.

Gestalt Group Counseling

Gestalt is an unusual form of group work in that it is a combination of both individual and group counseling with the counselor emphasizing one-to-one interactions with group members as well as facilitating group dynamics (Corey, 2000; Perls, 1969).

In the sessions the typical procedure has been the use of the hot seat, whereby a volunteer agrees to take a seat alongside the counselor in the center of the group circle. The group then observes the counselor/client interactions as the counselor confronts the client's contradictions or inconsistencies or asks the client to describe and act out a recent dream or to role-play with the counselor. The counselor may also initiate group interactions by asking the volunteer to interact with other group members. The counselor allows spontaneous interactions among group members (Vander Kolk, 1985).

As in individual Gestalt counseling, counselors expect group members to attend to immediate experiencing in these sessions, and they expect members to be responsible for themselves. Confrontation and games and gimmicks designed to encourage or goad members to give up dependency and to assume self-responsibility have typically been used (Corey, 2000). By developing awareness in themselves and in others, group members correct distortions in self-perception and perceptions of others.

Critics of Gestalt's method of abrasive confrontation have led practitioners to tone down sessions and be more respectful and supportive of clients' resistance, as well as helping clients learn to manage their emotions. With this in mind Corey (2000) describes a post-Perls Gestalt therapy, in which the hot seat technique is no longer the primary means of raising awareness.

Cognitive-Behavioral Group Counseling

Cognitive-behavioral group counseling is task-oriented. To start off a group session, the counselor first clarifies group procedure, establishes a working relationship, and then assesses each client's problem with input from the other group members. The counselor sets up specific goals with each member for behavioral changes. At the same time group goals consistent with individual goals are determined. As counseling progresses, the counselor teaches and models effective behavior, helps members clarify cognitive misperceptions about themselves and others, and helps change faulty habit patterns. Group members experiment with new behaviors in the sessions and help one another by modeling effective behavior and giving appropriate feedback and reinforcement to one another. Through these interactions, members learn new attitudes, ideas, behaviors, and skills to help them cope and adapt. In the final stages group members learn to generalize the new attitudes and skills developed in group sessions to real life through role playing, behavior rehearsal, and assignments to apply specific new skills at home.

Albert Ellis, a cognitive-behavioral theorist, has been active in group work for many years (Ellis, 1995; Ellis & Grieger, 1977). Ellis attempts to have group members work together under his direction to pick out one another's irrational beliefs, encourage one another to stop self-defeating self-talk, and teach one another to think rationally. He encourages them to practice newly learned behaviors outside the sessions (see chap. 6).

Arnold Lazarus (1976, 1995), another cognitive-behaviorist, believes that his multimodal BASIC I.D. pattern (see chap. 6) works particularly well with groups. He argues that a nonpunitive, nonthreatening group atmosphere enhances the opportunity for group members to correct maladaptive responses across the seven modalities (behavior, affect, sensation, imagery, cognition, interpersonal, and drugs/biological). Under his direction group members can practice new attitudes and behaviors and receive support, feedback, and reinforcement from one another. As in individual work, the counselor is active, uses and teaches numerous techniques that reinforce positive behavior and increase realization, and models appropriate emotional expression and logical thinking.

Developmental Group Counseling

The developmental group counseling approach is based on concepts similar to those discussed in chapter 5. Theorists assume that persons must complete developmental tasks by learning coping skills and playing social roles at different stages in their lives. These tasks arise from individual biological and psychological needs and from society's expectations of certain behaviors at certain ages. If persons fail to perform expected tasks adequately, maladjustment occurs.

Gazda (1989), the major proponent of this approach, attempts to provide a group counseling system applicable to clients at all age levels. Gazda describes the application of developmental group counseling for four groups of different ages: children, preadolescents, high-school-age persons, and adults. Groups are formed around problems related to particular developmental tasks expected for the age group.

Since developmental theorists have subdivided the adult level into several stages, effective groups have also been forming around the needs of young adults, adults at midlife, and older adults. The demand for group counseling with older adults has been increasing, but services have not kept up with demand.

Because of their age, older adults are good candidates for group work. They have a lot of experience on which to draw, and many have developed extraordinary capacities for introspection, deep thinking, and compassion. Group counseling with older adults can be an effective way to help them confront the myths of ageism.

> Counseling groups can do a lot to help older people challenge these myths and deal with developmental tasks that they, like any other age group, must face in such a way that they can retain their integrity and self-respect . . . and offer the elderly the encouragement necessary to find meaning in their lives. (Corey, 2000, pp. 9–10)

Corey and Corey (2000) pay particular attention to groups for grief and bereavement:

> Bereavement is a particularly critical developmental task for older people, not only because of the loss of others who are close to them but also because of the loss of some of their capacities. Although death strikes at children as well as the elderly, facing one's own death and the death of significant others takes on special significance with aging. (p. 402)

THE GROUP EXPERIENCE

Forming a Group

In university counseling centers, public schools, and community agencies where group counseling has already been established, counselors form groups by announcing that a group will be starting at a particular time with a particular purpose. Potential clients then sign up for the group, and other counselors working with individual clients who could profit from group counseling refer them to the group.

If the center, school, or agency has not yet developed a group counseling program, an interested counselor can make a proposal indicating a need for the group, the anticipated goal, the leader's background, and the procedures that will be used. In public schools particularly, the proposal should indicate which topics will or will not be explored and the risks to the clients.

The recommended number of group members varies with the type of group and the group's age range. For college students or adults, the size is about eight persons. A smaller number (three or four) is recommended for groups with elementary children because of their shorter attention span (Corey & Corey, 2002). Some experienced counselors and therapists working with special groups are able to work effectively with large numbers of people. Real (1997), for example, describes working with 40 depressed male clients in a group that meets weekly.

Screening of Group Members

As discussed earlier, careful screening of candidates is necessary for ethical and professional reasons. Screening avoids including group members who would be jeopardized by the experience; who might, because of their personality or behavior, inhibit progress in the group; or who have different purposes from the group's purpose (Brammer et al., 1993; Corey, 2000).

Prescreening prospective group members in individual sessions is the optimal procedure. When the setting does not permit individual screening, however, potential group members can complete questionnaires and be interviewed in small groups. If neither of these options is feasible, a pregroup session can be used as both a screening and an informational procedure (Corey, 2000).

Composition of Groups

Grouping clients with similar concerns and purposes facilitates a working bond and a more cohesive group relationship (Hershenson et al., 1996). Special groups are effective for those with specific problems, such as alcoholism. Grouping in a similar age range permits a group to focus on developmental concerns appropriate for all members (Gazda, 1989). Groups exclusive to men or women are effective ways of exploring gender issues. Special groupings are also effective for abused spouses or spousal abusers.

Frequency and Duration of Sessions

The setting in which group counseling occurs determines the frequency and duration of sessions. In a community agency or college or in private practice, 2-hour weekly sessions are optimal. In school settings shorter times twice a week may be more suitable because students have a shorter attention span and they miss less class time (Ohlsen, Horne, & Lawe, 1988).

In colleges and universities groups usually run about 10 or 14 weeks—the length of a quarter or a semester—because this is a reasonable amount of time for a group to attain goals and it is a convenient time frame for students and counselors. In communities 10 to 20 sessions seems reasonable.

Coleaders

Some group counselors prefer to work with coleaders for several reasons. First, there is apt to be less leader burnout as well as closer attention to group interaction. Second, coleaders can benefit from each other's perceptions of group dynamics and from each other's observations and comments on group members' emotional responses. Third, coleaders can use the way they relate to each other as a model for the group. And fourth, male and female coleaders can, in some cases, better deal with gender concerns (Corey, 2000).

However, one disadvantage of coleaders is the possibility that the group may suffer if coleaders act as rivals, do not trust each other, or try to work out their own relationship struggles in the sessions (Corey, 2000). As in families (see chap. 10), triangulation can occur if a leader sides with a group member against the coleader or if group members work one leader against the other in a power struggle (Vander Kolk, 1985).

Group Stages

Corey (2000) divides the group counseling process into four stages: initial stage (orientation and exploration), transition stage (dealing with resistance), working stage (cohesion and productivity), and final stage (consolidation and termination). Gazda (1989) outlines exploratory, transition, action, and termination stages; and Vander Kolk (1985) describes a beginning and building stage, a conflict and dominance stage, and a cohesive and productive stage. The stages used here are a composite of those models: (a) initial exploratory stage, (b) transition stage marked by resistance and conflicts, (c) working stage marked by cohesiveness and productivity, and (d) consolidation and termination.

Initial Exploratory Stage

In the beginning sessions group members are often strangers to one another. They may be ambivalent about groups; they want help but may be fearful of sounding stupid or disclosing too much about themselves. Thus, the leader often finds many in the group reluctant to talk or able to bring up only superficial topics in an intellectual manner. In addition, members may expect leaders to have authoritative answers to their problems, and some may focus on only themselves and not on other members of the group.

In the early sessions counselors generally respond to the group as a whole to foster group feeling; they also allow time for group members to get to know one another (Vander Kolk, 1985). Group members might be paired off to learn something about one another and then introduce each other to the group. Group members can also be asked to share their feelings about being in a group.

It is important to discuss and set goals in the first session. Group members can help one another clarify goals. For example, a member who says, "I'd like to be less aggressive," can be asked to explain what he or she means by being aggressive.

In the beginning stage counselors facilitate the development of trust, just as they do in individual and family counseling. As in family counseling, group counselors must engender trust between themselves and group members and among all the members as well. Counselors accomplish this by modeling genuineness, warmth, and nonjudgmental attitudes toward all group members and by listening carefully.

Counselors also work on developing those communicative attitudes and skills among group members that will contribute to group cohesiveness, such as self-disclosure and constructive feedback. The leader who discloses immediate feelings and reactions occurring in the group helps the group focus on the immediate experience. When leaders react with positive and negative feedback to concrete, specific, and observable behaviors in a nonjudgmental way, group members more readily accept the feedback (Morran, Robison, & Stockton, 1985).

Transition Stage

As the group moves into the second stage, members begin to realize or are confronted with the need to explore more deeply, to self-disclose more intensively, and to interact more with other group members. Although some trust has been established, the feeling is still tentative, and group members are ambivalent, anxious, and defensive as they realize that they are expected to explore painful emotions and feelings even more deeply. Some wonder whether the group will reject them if they reveal too much, some are afraid that they may lose control and reveal more than they intend, and some are afraid they'll be ridiculed and shamed.

Group counseling professionals describe this stage as being characterized by conflict or rebellion resulting from a struggle for power, control, or dominance among the members and with the counselor (Brammer et al., 1993; Corey, 2000; Gladding, 2003; Schultz, 1973). Schultz (1973) sees it as a time of competition and rivalry, with members testing whether they can trust the leader and other group members.

At this time verbal attacks on the leader may occur, with some members expressing doubts about her or his leadership ability, and others reacting negatively to the counselor's attempts to help them explore their problems. Counselors must recognize that these behaviors represent the resistance to exploring painful feelings that is expected in any form of therapy. Resistance is a sign that members are getting closer to the core of their problems (Ohlsen et al., 1988). On the other hand, conflicts should be resolved.

> If conflicts arise, it is essential that members recognize these conflicts and develop the skills to resolve them. . . . What leaders model when addressing conflict in a firm and respectful manner is every bit as important as what they tell members about conflict resolution. If conflict is not addressed, it then becomes a hidden agenda, which blocks open group interaction. How group leaders intervene is crucial to building trust. (Corey, 2000, p. 484).

Client resistance is a symptom of fears and anxieties and needs to be acknowledged and respected. But the counselor must not ignore the opportunity to help resistive clients become aware of and accept their fears, as well as learn to manage anger and to be respectful of others. Clients should be encouraged to explore their own fears and hostilities rather than projecting them onto others.

> It is also essential that members learn how to respectfully confront others in a caring and constructive fashion. We teach members the importance of talking more about themselves and how they are affected by the behaviors of a member they are confronting rather than telling a member how he or she is, or judging that person. (Corey, 2000, p. 484).

Gladding (2003) views the transition stage as divided into two phases: storming and norming. The time when members become resistant and vent their hostilities and resentments is aptly called the *storming* phase. During this phase the counselor helps members learn conflict management skills and identify different kinds of power plays and different forms of resistance, such as intellectualization, advice giving, dependency behaviors, monopolizing, band-aiding (i.e., being too quick to step in to ease another's pain), and attacks on the group leader, which is "probably the most direct form of resistance that causes groups difficulty" (p. 139).

Norming describes the second phase, when members begin to emerge from struggles for personal identity and move into feelings of group identity. According to Gladding (2003), some of the goals for counselors during this phase are to promote member feelings of cooperation with the group and a sense of collaborative spirit with one another. Skills that can be introduced at this time include supporting, in which members are encouraged to support one another; empathizing, in which members learn to understand another's difficulties in a nonjudgmental way; facilitating, in which the counselor helps members communicate clearly with one another; and self-disclosing, in which members feel safe enough to share their painful feelings (Gladding, 2003).

Working Stage

In the third stage group members develop intimacy and cohesiveness. Group identity is high, and members feel close to one another, more aware of one another's problems. Trust has increased, so members are more willing to take risks in sharing the feelings and thoughts that occur within the group and to give constructive feedback to one another.

However, group intimacy may lead to a false cohesiveness in which members protect one another (Vander Kolk, 1985). An overly supportive group may not encourage members to confront one another authentically, express negative emotions in the group, or challenge one another to make changes in their everyday living. Many groups become stuck in this loving, nonproductive lethargy and never move on.

When a group attains cohesiveness and stability but does not allow itself to remain in a comfortable, secure state, the lengthy working process of the third stage can begin to help group members change. When the group becomes productive, group members are more committed to delving into significant problems and giving attention to interchanges in the group. At this stage group members should challenge one another to convert insights they have gained into action. For example, a group member can confront another who says she recognizes the need to assert herself but remains passive in the group and in her interactions outside the group.

Group members now depend less on the leader, and the group begins to focus on working toward specified individual and group goals. Group members feel free to confront one another and are more willing to accept confrontations as a constructive challenge to change. They are more willing to risk experimenting with new behaviors and giving honest, spontaneous feedback without passing judgment. Conflict among members is effectively dealt with in sessions. As group interactions bring about attitudinal and behavioral changes in the group, members accept challenges to make changes in everyday life.

Group leaders use a variety of techniques to help group members explore their problems, confront one another, and make behavioral changes. Eclectic counselors might use Gestalt techniques such as confrontation, the empty chair, the hot seat, psychodrama role playing, or role reversal to get clients more in touch with their feelings. They might use cognitive-behavioral techniques, as Ellis does, to help persons concentrate on changing self-defeating self-talk or focus on clarifying thoughts through cognitive restructuring. Transactional analysis might be used to improve group members' communication skills. To help members apply new insights to real-life situations, behavioral rehearsal or assertiveness exercises might be tried in anticipation of an encounter outside the sessions or a homework assignment given to carry out a specific new learning.

Consolidation and Termination

In the early years of group counseling, little attention was given to termination of group sessions (Gladding, 2003), but now termination is considered an essential part of group counseling. For effective closure this period of time cannot be minimized. According to Corey (2000), "The initial and final stages . . . [are] the most decisive times [for the group]. . . . It is during the termination phase that consolidation of learning occurs; this is a time for summarizing, pulling together loose ends, and integrating and interpreting the group experience" (p. 128).

Most groups have a termination date fixed in advance of the actual session, particularly in educational settings and clinics. It is wise to start discussions about separation approximately three sessions before the final one to allow time for members to handle psychological or emotional feelings, to work toward transferring new group experiences to the outside world, to work through any unfinished problems in group relationships, and to review what has happened in the group to each member and how each can build on these changes after the group ends (Ohlsen et al., 1988).

Feelings of anxiety, loss, sadness, or anger at losing those with whom group members feel close, safe, and supported must be discussed; it is, after all, the death of the group. The psychological or emotional reactions of significant persons outside the group need to be discussed also, with suggestions about how to deal with those feelings. Family or close friends may resist or be disturbed by changes. In addition, suggestions for further therapy can be made when necessary. Sometimes specific activities—such as joining a support group or a more advanced counseling group, reading, or attending workshops—can increase the chance that learning will continue.

Not all groups will run smoothly through all stages and reach a clear-cut, successful termination. Some groups never pass the comfortable stage. Other groups, because of the personality mix of group members or the leader or both, may not succeed in becoming cohesive. Like individuals, groups have different capacities for growth.

FUTURE TRENDS

Group work is often used now in business and industry to reduce conflict, increase cooperation among coworkers, and improve satisfaction and productivity among employees. One type of group that is effective with coworkers is the quality circle. Its members are employees in the same work area who meet weekly to try to solve problems related to their joint work efforts (Hershenson et al., 1996). Quality circles are described as follows: "Leaders function in a caring capacity offering members support as they examine conflicts and detriments to effective co-worker relations and explore solutions" (Hershenson et al., 1996, p. 220).

Other trends are the increasing numbers of groups that focus on special needs, such as groups for victims of domestic violence, those with PTSD, those with spiritual needs, male depression, grief work, and debriefing witnesses of public violence (see chap. 19).

Research on groups has lagged behind research on individual counseling, a lag attributable to the complexity of studying groups, the lack of effective instruments to measure group process, and the lack of ongoing research into group processes (Gladding, 2003). Although research has indicated that group work is effective, studies haven't yet revealed why this is so (Corey, 2000). However, this situation may be changing: "Increased concern and attention are being devoted to group research. For instance, professional group associations are giving awards and grants for group research" (Gladding, 2003, p. 16).

SUMMARY

Group counseling is helpful to persons having difficulties with interpersonal relationships and social skills. The group counseling environment, which is generally safe and accepting, gives members the opportunity to self-disclose, interact with others, and receive constructive feedback. Group counseling theories are adaptations of theories described in chapter 6—psychodynamic, humanistic, cognitive-behavioral, and developmental, or age-related, approaches.

Ethically, group participation should be voluntary, and group disclosures must be kept in confidence by the group leader. The group leader must also alert group members about the need to maintain confidentiality about group interchanges. Group leaders screen group candidates and generally exclude persons who are highly vulnerable emotionally, overly aggressive, or antisocial. It is unethical for a group leader or group members to persuade or coerce individuals to participate when they are reluctant to do so.

Groups go through stages. The initial stage is exploratory, in which group trust is developed so that clients feel safe enough to participate. This is followed by a transition stage, in which resistance develops among members that must be worked through. A cohesive working stage follows, in which trust is high, self-disclosure is authentic, and feedback is productive. This is followed by the final stage of consolidation and termination of the group sessions.

Trends show increased activity in group work in business to improve worker morale and productivity. Increasing numbers of groups are focusing on persons with special problems—for example, victims of domestic violence, those with PTSD, male depression, grief, and those with spiritual needs.

PROJECTS AND ACTIVITIES

1. Check with a university counseling center and a community clinic about the types of groups offered. Do they distinguish among group counseling, group therapy, and personal growth groups?

2. Assume that you are a leader of a group of college students. One member tells you he thinks another member has been talking about group revelations outside the group. He thinks he knows who the person is but

isn't sure. How would you handle this complaint?

3. A husband and wife, both psychologists, are coleading a group. Some group members ask very personal questions about the husband-wife relationship. The coleaders think they have some right to privacy. How do you think the coleaders should respond to the request for intimate self-disclosures in the group? Role-play a group with coleaders with this type of problem.

4. Trace the history of group counseling. What social, cultural, and psychological factors have contributed to the movement?

5. Select a group population with which you would like to conduct a group experience, such as the elderly, children, adolescents, or battered spouses. Search the literature for

group counseling research findings for this population. Find two studies that you think are statistically sound and two that you think are poorly designed.

6. Debate the merits of having one group leader versus using coleaders. Would the type of group problem, age group, or work setting make a difference?

7. Contact an elementary and a secondary school counselor, and ask whether they handle groups and, if so, what types of groups. What do they see as advantages or disadvantages of group counseling at these age levels?

8. Role-play a group in which a member says she has decided to leave the group because it is a waste of time, the group leader isn't directive enough, and group members are not leveling with one another.

REFERENCES

Allan, J. (1988). *Inscapes of the child's world: Jungian counseling in schools and clinics.* Dallas: Spring.

American Counseling Association (ACA). (1995). *Ethical standards.* Alexandria, VA: Author.

American Psychological Association (APA). (1973). Guidelines for psychologists conducting growth groups. *American Psychologist, 28,* 933.

Association for Specialists in Group Work (ASGW). (1989). *Ethical guidelines for group leaders.* Falls Church, IA: Author.

Berne, E. (1961). *Transactional analysis in psychotherapy.* New York: Grove Press.

Berne, E. (1964). *Games people play.* New York: Grove Press.

Berne, E. (1966). *Principles of group treatment.* New York: Oxford University Press.

Berne, E. (1972). *What do you say after you say hello?* New York: Grove Press.

Blatner, A. (1995). Psychodrama. In R. J. Corsini & D. Wedding (Eds.), *Current psychotherapies* (5th ed., pp. 399–408). Itasca, IL: F. E. Peacock.

Brammer, L. M., Abrego, P. J., & Shostrom, E. L. (1993). *Therapeutic counseling and psychotherapy* (6th ed.). Upper Saddle River, NJ: Prentice Hall.

Burlingame, G. M., & Fuhriman, A. (1990). Time-limited group therapy. *Counseling Psychologist, 18,* 93–118.

Corey, G. (2000). *Theory and practice of group counseling* (5th ed.). Pacific Grove, CA: Brooks/Cole.

Corey, G., & Corey, M. S. (2002). *Groups: Process and practice* (6th ed.). Pacific Grove, CA: Brooks/Cole.

Corey, G., Corey, M. S., & Callanan, P. (1998). *Issues and ethics in the helping professions* (4th ed.). Pacific Grove, CA: Brooks/Cole.

Dusay, J. M., & Dusay, K. M. (1989). Transactional analysis. In R. J. Corsini & D. Wedding (Eds.), *Current psychotherapies* (4th ed., pp. 405–453). Itasca, IL: F. E. Peacock.

Ellis, A. (1995). Rational-emotive behavior therapy. In R. J. Corsini & D. J. Wedding (Eds.), *Current psychotherapies* (5th ed.). Itasca, IL: F. E. Peacock.

Ellis, A., & Grieger, R. (1977). *Handbook of rational-emotive therapy.* New York: Springer.

Forester-Miller, H., & Rubenstein, R. L. (1992). Group counseling: Ethics and professional issues. In D. Capuzzi & D. R. Gross (Eds.), *Introduction to group counseling* (pp. 307–323). Denver: Love.

Gazda, G. M. (1978). *Group counseling: A developmental approach.* Boston: Allyn & Bacon.

Gazda, G. M. (1989). *Group counseling: A developmental approach* (4th ed.). Boston: Allyn & Bacon.

Gladding, S. T. (2003). *Group work: A counseling specialty* (4th ed.). Upper Saddle River, NJ: Merrill/Prentice Hall.

Heathcote, D. (1971). *Drama in education of teachers.* Newcastle, UK: University Printing.

Hershenson, D. B., & Power, P. W., & Waldo, M. (1996). *Community counseling: Contemporary theory and practice.* Boston: Allyn & Bacon.

Lazarus, A. (1976). *Multimodal behavioral therapy.* New York: Springer.

Lazarus, A. (1995). Multimodal therapy. In R. J. Corsini & D. Wedding (Eds.), *Current psychotherapies* (5th ed., pp. 322–353). Itasca, IL: F. E. Peacock.

Moreno, J. L. (1946). *Psychodrama*. Beacon, NY: Beacon Press.

Moreno, Z. T. (1983). Psychodrama. In H. I. Kaplan & B. J. Sadock (Eds.), *Comprehensive group psychotherapy* (2nd ed., pp. 158–166). Baltimore: Williams & Wilkins.

Morran, D. K., Robison, F. F., & Stockton, R. (1985). Feedback exchange in counseling groups: An analysis of message content and receiver acceptance as a function of leader versus member delivery, session, and value. *Journal of Counseling Psychology, 32,* 57–67.

Nystul, M. S. (1993). *The art and science of counseling and therapy*. Upper Saddle River, NJ: Merrill/Prentice Hall.

Ohlsen, M. M., Horne, A. M., & Lawe, C. F. (1988). *Group counseling* (3rd ed.). New York: Holt, Rinehart & Winston.

Patterson, C. H. (1986). *Theories of counseling and psychotherapy* (4th ed.). New York: Harper & Row.

Perls, F. (1969). *Gestalt therapy verbatim*. New York: Bantam Books.

Real, T. (1997). *I don't want to talk about it*. New York: Fireside.

Schultz, W. (1973). *Elements of encounter*. Big Sur, CA: Joy Press.

Steiner, C. (1974). *Scripts people live: Transactional analysis of life scripts*. New York: Grove Press.

Thompson, C. L., & Rudolph, L. B. (1992). *Counseling children* (3rd ed.). Pacific Grove, CA: Brooks/Cole.

Vander Kolk, C. J. (1985). *Introduction to group counseling and psychotherapy*. Upper Saddle River, NJ: Merrill/Prentice Hall.

CHAPTER 12

Career Counseling

C areer counseling involves helping individuals or groups explore career options, make career plans, prepare for appropriate training, and resolve career-related problems. Client concerns include career indecision and uncertainty, dissatisfaction on the job, unsatisfactory integration of life roles, and conflicts with others about career choice or development.

The number of community career centers has been increasing rapidly to meet the growing demand of those reentering the job market, reappraising their work skills, or searching for employment in fields unrelated to their former work experience and training. Isaacson and Brown (1997) comment that this practice

> will grow because adults in our society seem to be relying increasingly on career counselors for assistance. . . . Because of the number of people changing jobs voluntarily and involuntarily, it seems likely that increasing numbers of people will seek assistance from private practitioners in the future. (p. 475)

Supporting this view is a 2000 Gallup poll sponsored by the National Career Development Association. Of the 1003 people surveyed, 70% would get more information about job and career options if they were starting over (Jaffe, 2003).

Commenting on the rapid increase in these services in the community, Isaacson and Brown (1997) describe the multiple services offered by career counselors.

> Career counselors offer a wide variety of services including career counseling with individuals and groups, consultations, job placement, testing, outplacement, resume development, and the development of other employability skills, retirement planning, career/life role integration counseling, spousal relocation training, program evaluation, work adjustment counseling, and vocational appraisal services. (p. 478)

HISTORICAL PERSPECTIVE

Historically, career counseling has been called by a number of different names, including *vocational guidance, occupational counseling,* and *vocational counseling.* By whatever name, career counseling was influential in the development of the counseling profession. Counseling was originally initiated in colleges and schools to help students with vocational and career concerns (see chap. 2). Early vocational counseling in the 1930s and 1940s was primarily influenced by the prevailing emphasis on measuring individual differences. The basic assumption underlying this was that individuals have unique inherent abilities, interests, and personality traits that can be assessed through standardized tests and matched with certain types of occupations. However, as chapter 2 explains, in 1942 Donald Super introduced the idea that persons develop vocationally throughout life, an amplification of Charlotte Buehler's theory of human development. Then Carl Rogers introduced a client-centered approach with an emphasis on personal growth.

Leading vocational counseling professionals at the time—Super (1951, 1955), Ginzberg, Ginzburg, Axelrad, and Herma (1951), Holland (1959), and Roe (1957)—believed that vocational counseling should be integrated with personal and interpersonal counseling. Vocational choice and development, they emphasized, are influenced by and related to personality development. Super (1955), in particular, proposed a theory that integrated vocational development with self-development and related personality factors to vocational concerns. Nugent's experiences supported this approach.

> As a counselor in college and high school counseling centers, a supervisor of counseling interns, and a private practitioner, I, and those with whom I worked, found this integrated approach worked well. We were able to distinguish when a client's concerns were specific to career exploration and when the client's personal conflicts or emotional disequilibrium might be interfering with career exploration. This practice was compatible with the counseling services in the 1950s and 1960s, which existed almost exclusively in school and college settings and encompassed the normal population with its typical conflicts and concerns related to school and thus to vocational issues.

Even so, during the 1970s many college counselors began to focus only on a client's personal growth issues and tended to ignore the client's vocational or career concerns. Humanistic and behavioral theories of psychology prevailed, which did not address problems related to career development. Moreover, counseling expanded to address such issues as family and substance abuse, in which career concerns were generally not the issue. Consequently, at many colleges and universities, placement centers developed into career centers to assist students who needed help in making career choices. And those college counseling centers that no longer attended to clients' career issues referred students with career concerns to the college career centers (Gallagher, 1996).

This primary emphasis on a client's personal and interpersonal concerns was solidified in the late 1970s when the American Mental Health Counselors Association was formed and the master's degree in counseling emerged as a terminal degree. Most agencies that hire mental health counselors in private practice now tend to limit their services to a client's personal and interpersonal concerns. In addition, managed care generally does not allow insurance coverage for career counseling.

THE CURRENT SCENE

Both the ACA and Division 17 of the APA have consistently specified that the counseling profession take a holistic approach and consider career concerns as part of the counseling process. Leading professionals continue to claim that general counseling and career counseling are inseparable, rather than independent, processes (Betz & Corning, 1993; Brown & Lent, 1984; Krumboltz, 1993). Niles and Anderson (1995) found that many adults in career counseling are coping with concerns related to uncertainty, ambiguity, self-efficacy, and personal, as well as occupational, issues. Thus, many researchers now conclude that there are few things more personal than career choice and that the overlap between career and general concerns is substantial (Niles & Harris-Bowlsbey, 2002).

Career development practitioners in the 21st century seek to empower people as they make meaning of their life experiences and translate that meaning into appropriate occupational and other life role choices (Niles & Harris-Bowlsbey, 2002). Because translating experiences into career choices requires people to have a high level of self-awareness, career counseling involves an extensive set of skills to help clients resolve their career dilemmas. Career counseling involves much more than showing clients occupational information books or administering and interpreting tests to advise clients on what occupations they should choose. Indeed, the skills and techniques required for providing career assistance encompass and extend beyond those required in more general counseling.

Need for Professional Training

Presently, career counseling in the United States is provided by many persons in many settings (Herr, 2003). School counselors, college counselors, academic advisers, employment counselors, rehabilitation counselors, mental health counselors, psychologists, and other helping professionals all provide career counseling, although with different purposes and intensity. Because these persons differ in training and knowledge about career counseling, it is difficult to know who can actually provide quality career counseling. Many career counselors have graduate degrees in counseling or counseling psychology with specialization in career development, career assessment, and career planning. These professionals are trained to be alert to signs that a client's vocational concerns might relate to personal or interpersonal conflicts; they are prepared to help the client explore personal concerns as she or he works toward career decisions or, in more serious cases, to refer the client for personal counseling.

Leading career counseling professionals emphasize the need for professional counseling training (Brown, 1995; Brown & Brooks, 1991; Gysbers & Moore, 1987; Isaacson & Brown, 1997; Krumboltz, 1993). Such recommendations, however, are not enforced by licensing or certification laws. Thus, unlike mental health counselors and school counselors, career counselors and placement counselors are allowed to practice without being either licensed or certified. Consequently, many individuals provide career services with little or no formal training in career development theory and practice, and many have no training even in the helping professions (Niles & Harris-Bowlsbey, 2002). Isaacson and Brown (1997) emphasize the "interrelationship of mental health and career concerns" and assert that "counselors and psychologists need to be prepared to deal with both" (p. 496).

Consumers should ask individuals providing career counseling about their credentials (Lee & Shahnasarian, 1998). Specific credentials in career counseling are offered through the National Career Development Association (NCDA), a division of the ACA. These include the Master Career Counselor and the Master Career Development Professional. The *Master Career Counselor* (MCC) is an NCDA member who holds a master's degree in counseling or a related field and has been active as an NCDA member for a minimum of 2 years. In addition, an MCC has at least 3 years of post-master's experience in career counseling and is a national certified counselor (NCC) who either has a state license in professional counseling or is a licensed psychologist. MCCs must also have successfully completed course work in specific educational areas and a supervised career counseling practicum or 2 years of supervised career counseling experience under a certified supervisor or licensed counseling professional. The *Master Career Development Professional* (MCDP) is an NCDA member who holds a master's degree or higher in counseling or a related field and also has been active as an NCDA member for a minimum of 2 years. The MCDP has at least 3 years of post-master's career development experience in training, teaching, program development, or materials development.

Trends in Career Counseling

Herr (2003) reported the following trends in career counseling that will influence the future of the specialty:

- Career counseling will expand as unemployment rates rise, more workers are part-time, and individuals assume responsibility for their own career management.
- Public policy and legislation will continue to provide vital support for career counseling.
- The career counseling profession will address the challenges of using career development activities online and using computer systems and the Internet.
- Researchers will need to develop cost-benefit analyses to document the outcomes of career counseling.

THEORETICAL APPROACHES TO CAREER COUNSELING

Career counseling theories are based on the idea that personal development influences one's choice of and satisfaction in a career.

Developmental Theories

The two most widely known developmental theories are those associated with Donald Super and Eli Ginzburg. As stated earlier, Super (1942) was one of the first to relate personality factors and developmental stages to career development. In 1951, using Buehler's concept of developmental life stages, he described vocational adjustment as the implementation of a person's self-concept. He then outlined (1953) a series of developmental stages throughout life that relate to occupational development (see chap. 2). Super (1961) continued to develop his vocational theory, extending it to include *vocational maturity*. Ultimately, through choices considered mature at each life stage, adults find and establish themselves in appropriate vocations. In 1980 Super expanded his theory further, in what he called a life-span, life-space approach. He proposed that people play numerous roles throughout their life spans that help shape their careers in a broad sense. And he described how various roles interrelate to contribute to career development over the life span (Osipow & Fitzgerald, 1996).

Ginzberg et al. (1951) published one of the earliest theories of vocational choice based on developmental stages. They described the process of career choice as following three stages: (a) *fantasy period* in early childhood, composed of unrealistic ideas; (b) *tentative period,* when children begin to sort out activities they like and can do well; and (c) *realistic period,* when individuals explore realistically and make a specific choice. In 1972 Ginzberg revised his ideas and concluded that vocational choice is lifelong and always open to change.

Trait-and-Factor Approach

The origin of trait-and-factor theory can be traced back to Frank Parsons (1909). It stresses that the traits of clients should first be identified and then matched with factors inherent in various occupations. A more modern form of the trait-and-factor approach is the typology approach developed by John Holland (1997). Holland's typology is considered the most widely used and most influential theory in career counseling practice today (Isaacson & Brown, 1997; Osipow, 1987; Weinrach & Srebalus, 1990). His approach assumes that we can classify individuals into the following six personality types: realistic, investigative, artistic, social, enterprising, and conventional (Holland, 1997). Further, he believes that individuals in each personality type will select jobs or careers that fit their interests, thus forming six matching work environments composed of members who enjoy similar activities and respond to tasks and people in similar ways. Vocational success, satisfaction, and stability, he assumes, depend on how well the individual's personality, as described by interest inventories, matches the work environments selected by the individual.

Table 12.1 presents the descriptions of each personality type along with the matching work environment. From the initial letters of the six personality types, Holland coined the acronym RIASEC to portray the total interest pattern. Because few people are only one type, Holland says, he combines the three most dominant types a person shows on an interest inventory and classifies accordingly. For example, IAE would show investigative interests most strongly, followed by artistic and enterprising. He also classifies working environments by using the same three-letter combinations. These he has listed in a pamphlet called the "Occupations Finder." Holland has conducted extensive longitudinal studies, and results show that personal types and occupational environments do differentiate people. He has used this research to revise his theory over the years (Zunker, 1994).

TABLE 12.1

Holland's Personality Types and Occupational Environments

Personal Type	Personality-Job Theme	Working Environment
Interested in machinery and working with things; not interested in people	Realistic	Skilled trades (machinist, carpenter, mechanic, cook)
Interested in science and abstract analytical tasks; not sociable; independent	Investigative	Scientific/technical job (engineers, chemists, mathematicians, medical technicians)
Interested in creative and imaginative activities; enjoys self-expression	Artistic	Artistic jobs, (artists, musicians, designers, writers)
Interested in helping people and solving social problems	Social	Social service jobs (educators, counselors, nurses, ministers)
Interested in persuading others, leading others; extroverted, dominant	Enterprising	Marketing and promotional jobs (salespersons, public relations specialists, real estate)
Enjoys systematic repetitious tasks and manipulating data	Conventional	Office work (secretary, file clerk, bookkeeper)

Source: Adapted and reproduced by special permission of the Publisher, Psychological Assessment Resources, Inc., 16204 North Florida Ave., Lutz, FL 33549, from *The Self-Directed Search* by John L. Holland, Ph.D. Copyright 1985 by Psychological Assessment Resources, Inc. All rights reserved.

Postmodern Approaches

Recently, attention has been given to career development theories and interventions that depart from the traditional approaches to career development (Niles & Harris-Bowlsbey, 2002). Referred to as postmodern, these approaches emphasize the importance of understanding the plurality of perspectives, contextual impacts, social constructions of reality, and the meaning individuals give to their experiences (see also chap. 6). Proponents of postmodern career interventions focus on exploring the meaning clients place on their careers, rather than simply identifying specific traits of individuals and then placing those individuals in corresponding career categories. Peavy (1997) calls for revisions in the practice of career counseling to reflect the more relevant and postmodern philosophy; specifically, career counseling should acknowledge the multiplicity of realities and contextual influences involved in career development.

As stated in chapter 6, constructivists theorize that people form constructs to make meaning and order out of their lives on an ongoing basis throughout life. Applying this theory to career counseling, counselors help clients identify and evaluate the constructions and meanings in their career decisions; then they can assist clients in reconstructing those meanings (Peavy, 1993). From the constructivist perspective, career counseling outcomes are considered in terms of their "fruitfulness" (Niles & Harris-Bowlsbey, 2002, p. 92), which refers to the assumption that counseling should result in a changed outlook or new perspective on some aspect of life. Career development interventions are framed as experiments conducted both in-session and out-of-session that help clients think, feel, and act more productively in relation to their career concerns. Interventions/experiments can be conducted by using the client's imagination (e.g., guided imagery), or by engaging the client in self-evaluation, simulation (e.g., role playing), and real-world experiences (e.g., job shadowing, job interviewing).

The narrative approach to career counseling emphasizes clients' understanding of their lives by having them form stories and articulate the main character to be lived out in a specific career plot (Cochran, 1997). Stories can help individuals make meaning out of their life experiences by integrating the beginning, middle, and end of the story into a whole. However, stories are never complete, so it is in exploring what is missing in or not told by the story that alternative ways of thinking and acting often appear (Peavy, 1993). In career counseling, stories of self and career can be used by the counselor and client to bring together the client's present knowledge and to help guide forward movement into anticipated futures.

Contextual approaches to career counseling identify ways in which contextual factors (e.g., family, culture, environment) can be incorporated into counseling. A fundamental assumption of the contextual model is that change in one context has the potential to stimulate changes in all other contexts of one's life. Thus, individuals' lives and their career development are intertwined. Using a contextual approach, career counselors would help clients explore how other factors in their lives impact their career development.

CAREER COUNSELING PROCESS

Although many college counseling centers no longer offer career counseling, many still do. Leading proponents reaffirm the value of offering career counseling along with personal counseling for reasons described earlier. Although both career centers and general counseling centers can offer quality career counseling, there are distinctions in the counseling that goes on in the two types of centers.

Super (1993) reaffirms that career counseling and personal counseling are related but proposes that the two entail distinct approaches, which can be treated as a continuum ranging from career counseling with its focus on situational concerns to personal counseling with its focus on inner self-exploration.

> There are in fact two fields: situational counseling, which has subspecialties that focus on differing types of situations (career, family, etc.), and personal counseling, in which the focus is on individuals whose problems are based primarily in their own approach to and coping with situations, not on factors in the situations they encounter. In accepting this dichotomy one should not actually treat it as a dichotomy, but as a continuum of which these are the extremes. (p. 135)

With these differences in mind, well-trained counselors generally function similarly in both settings. As with counseling in general, career counseling requires that the counselor establish a "positive, productive relationship" with clients (Gysbers & Moore, 1987, p. 173) and be able to respond meaningfully to a client's expressed feelings, behaviors, and attitudes (Isaacson, 1986). Counselors must also help the client make use of new insights and understandings to develop more constructive attitudes and behaviors that he or she can use to make decisions and implement them.

Yost and Corbishley (1987) have developed a career counseling process in which they emphasize a procedure similar to the individual counseling process described in chapter 9. First, counselor and client develop rapport, assess client needs, and establish goals. Next, the counselor works to promote client self-understanding through interviews and aptitude and interest inventories. The counselor then helps the client develop appropriate career alternatives, making use of occupational information such as the *Occupational Outlook Handbook (OOH),* which is described later. From these possibilities the counselor helps the client choose a career. Throughout the sessions the counselor helps the client work through obstacles that hinder making choices—such as too few alternatives, not enough information, inappropriate options, or interference from family. Once a choice is made, the counselor helps the client develop job search skills, write résumés, and prepare for job interviews.

Types of Problems

Exploration of Careers

When clients seek counseling help in exploring careers in schools, colleges, universities, and communities, their primary goals are to make appropriate occupational choices and to look into related training programs. In high schools clients are in their formative stages of career exploration; they are exploring types of careers and trying to determine whether to find a job or seek further training. In universities clients seek assistance in choosing majors or in making plans for life after graduation. In community settings clients seek help in exploring the possibility of switching to new jobs, finding job opportunities that fit their interests and training, or seeking further schooling or training.

When a client requests help in exploring career choices, the counselor uses a goal-oriented approach. Together they review occupational history and experience, consider the use of occupational testing, and explore data about occupations or training possibilities as part of client and environmental exploration. As stated earlier, few counselors rely solely on tests and inventories to predict appropriate choices in occupations. Most professional career counselors take into consideration social, cultural, and developmental factors when helping persons make career choices.

Conflicts About Careers

Others' expectations about one's career often contribute to vocational concerns. In high schools, colleges, and communities, parents, spouses, or peers may pressure clients to make choices that are incompatible with their own interests or abilities. In the community, job demands in two-career families or a husband's objection to his wife's desire to start a career may cause marital strife. In addition, conflicts with bosses, supervisors, colleagues, or family members may be interfering with progress or satisfaction on the job.

When clients express strong feelings of anxiety or uncertainty related to work, counselors tend to switch to a client-centered approach in which interviewing skills are used to help clients explore feelings and develop insights. An unemployed woman without work experience might ask for counseling because of marital conflict; her concerns about leaving the marriage may relate to her fears about her ability to support herself and her children. A young man comes asking for career counseling; he would like to major in music but is confused because his parents will not give him financial or emotional support unless he enters a computer training program. In family or marriage counseling, a wife's decision to start a career is causing dissension, or a husband's dissatisfaction with his job is contributing to conflicts with his wife and children. In all these cases both career and personal concerns must be met. However, for clients in acute emotional distress, career exploration is delayed.

To integrate personal and career considerations, counselors must think holistically and skillfully merge a client's career-related concerns with the client's personal concerns. For example, rather than interpreting to the client a whole battery of occupational test results all at once, the counselor might discuss each test result whenever it fits into what the client is working through in the counseling session. Ultimately, a decision about, say, staying with a marriage may include career plans whether or not a divorce occurs. Or a decision about following one's career interest may include changing one's attitudes toward parents.

Clients may also come to career counselors when they are experiencing their own conflict or confusion about their choice of career. A client with strong interests and abilities in two or more areas may become conflicted about which way to go, especially if one choice appears to exclude the other(s). Clients may also experience discrepancies between their interests and aptitudes and their career choices; they may have interest in an occupation but insufficient aptitude, or they may have strong interest in one field and strong aptitude in a different field. In addition, clients' personal values may be at odds with their career choices. For example, an individual may have a strong leaning toward business but also believe strongly that the corporate world discriminates against women and minorities.

Life Transitions

Changes in lifestyles, family moves, or family changes may lead to requests for counseling. A husband who has been the sole provider may suddenly divorce or desert his wife or die. His wife, who has not worked outside the home for years, may need help finding employment to support herself and her family. Moreover, occupations become obsolete, and individuals must find new careers. Or those considering retirement want to explore new possibilities. A stay-at-home mom, after her children are in school, might decide to begin a new career outside the home. Perhaps an employed worker dissatisfied with his job wants to explore a more satisfying career. Or a client laid off from her job experiences uncertainty, apprehension, and bewilderment about how to find a new job.

When clients' personal concerns interfere too much with career issues, the counselor refers these clients to an outside agency for personal counseling or therapy before proceeding with career counseling. Brown (1995) points out that although it is possible for counselors to address career and personal problems at the same time, this becomes impossible when clients' emotional or psychological distress prevents them from engaging in career exploration.

Outreach

Counselors in career counseling centers offer clients a wide range of psychological education and outreach activities. They refer clients with personal concerns regarding careers to workshops or group activities related to stress reduction, assertiveness training, or feelings of loss. They also offer seminars and workshops on preparing job résumés, preparing for job interviews, or learning skills and strategies to improve relationships with supervisors or fellow workers on the job (see chaps. 8 and 19).

The Career Action Center (1997) in Cupertino, California, examplifies the numerous outreach activities that can be offered in addition to counseling. This center is a nonprofit organization staffed by approximately 70 full- and part-time staff, about a third of whom are master's-level counselors and most are specialists in career counseling. A few are nationally certified counselors; the rest are specialists in business and are experienced in career-related concerns such as organizational development, human resources, human relations, and business management. The organization has membership fees that cover free workshops or discounted workshops for members.

Besides offering counseling for self-awareness related to careers, this center offers workshops on how to market oneself when looking for jobs or changing careers, career management and work strategies for those wanting to improve their status in current jobs, and strategy workshops for those wanting to be self-employed. Examples of workshops focused on marketing oneself include conducting a work search, canvassing the area for prospective employers, practicing job interviews, and writing effective job résumés. Career management workshops cover skills in conflict management, active listening, writing skills, assertiveness training, and overcoming anxiety on the job.

SPECIAL TOOLS IN CAREER COUNSELING

Innumerable vocational interest and personality inventories and aptitude tests can help counselors and clients explore client characteristics related to careers. Occupational information resources are also valuable aids to help counselors and clients gather data about occupations, jobs, educational opportunities, or vocational training.

Inventories and Tests

Vocational Interest Inventories

Vocational interest inventories, in which clients compare themselves with groups of people in various occupations, are the most popular measures used in counseling. The Strong Interest Inventory (SII), the Kuder Occupational Interest Survey (KOIS), and Holland's (1994) Self-Directed Search (SDS) are examples of widely used interest inventories (see chap. 7). Other commonly used interest inventories with descriptive data can be found in Isaacson and Brown (1997).

The SII is designed for use with adults, college students, and high school seniors. The client's profile of interests is compared with those of people employed successfully in a wide variety of occupations. These occupations are grouped according to Holland's personality types and environmental structures (RIASEC).

The KOIS also compares an individual's scores with those of people in various occupations, but it includes more occupations in skilled trades and semiprofessions than does the SII. It also includes scores for college majors. The Kuder General Interest Survey—with broad interest classifications, such as mechanical, clerical, scientific, and social service—is appropriate for students in middle schools and the first 2 years of high school.

Holland's SDS is a self-administered, self-scored, and self-interpreted instrument that can be completed in less than an hour. Clients then compare their personal responses with occupations on the basis of Holland's RIASEC categories using the "Occupations Finder."

Personality Inventories

Some counselors administer *personality inventories* if they sense that personal conflicts are interfering with clients' career resolution. The California Psychological Inventory (CPI), the Edwards Personal Preference Schedule (EPPS), the Omnibus Personality Inventory, and the Minnesota Counseling Inventory are representative of personality inventories used in vocational counseling (see chap. 7).

The Myers-Briggs Type Indicator (MBTI), based on Jungian personality types (introvert-extravert, sensing-intuition, thinking-feeling, and judgment-perception), is of interest to counselors who relate lifestyles to career development. However, many Jungians have expressed concerns about an oversimplified use of typology based on the idea that individuals have inherent, unalterable tendencies that determine their lives (see also chap. 6).

Ability Tests

Two aptitude batteries are predominant in vocational counseling: the Differential Aptitude Test (DAT), given widely in high schools, and the General Aptitude Test Battery (GATB), administered most often by state employment offices to the general population. Other aptitude tests commonly used are described in Isaacson and Brown (1997).

The Armed Services Vocational Aptitude Battery (ASVAB) was developed for use in career counseling in the military. It is now used in high schools for exploration of both civilian and military careers (Zunker, 1994). When used in high schools, the battery should be administered and interpreted by school counselors and not by armed services recruiters, because recruiters tend to be biased toward selection of military careers.

Occupational Information

Occupational information is available in resource libraries at centers offering career counseling. Innumerable pamphlets, monographs, audiovisual materials, programmed instruction, computer-based systems, and simulated career games cover occupations, jobs, job families, and occupational fields.

Government agencies—particularly the U.S. Departments of Labor and Commerce—and private companies are the major sources of this information. Educational institutions, professional associations, and commercial outlets also publish information about technical schools, colleges, and continuing education. In addition, state employment agencies can provide information on trends in the labor market, including projections of future job openings.

Two sources that counselors and clients use most frequently for career information are the *Dictionary of Occupational Titles (DOT)* and the *Occupational Outlook Handbook (OOH;* Isaacson & Brown, 1997). The *DOT,* published by the U.S. Department of Labor, provides important client information about almost any occupation in the United States. Included are definitions of occupations, descriptions of jobs in typical industries, and lists of specific skills and worker traits essential to perform these jobs. The *OOH* describes the occupations in more detail, including educational and experience prerequisites, places of employment, employment outlook, earnings, working conditions, chances for advancement, and lists of government resources that provide additional information.

Technology in Career Counseling

Computers have had a powerful impact on the field of career counseling because of their capability to provide career planning and information systems (Niles & Harris-Bowlsbey, 2002). Computer technology related to the career planning process includes tests and inventory administration and interpretation; database searches; cross walking (relating one database to another); standard delivery (delivering the same service to users at any time from any location); monitoring progress of the user through the career planning process; delivering instruction; and linking resources. The combination of these activities is called a *computer-assisted career guidance system* (CACGS).

CACGSs began in the late 1960s. Katz (1963) developed the System for Interactive Guidance Information (SIGI), designed to teach 10 specific work values (e.g., prestige, high income, early entry, leisure, leadership, helping others, variety, and security) and then assist the user in assigning a level of importance to each value. SIGI is used for persons considering enrolling or already enrolled in 2- and 4-year colleges; it is based on the assumption that values relate to choice of occupation. Included are lists of values and related occupations, predictions about grades in required courses, programs for entering training, and help in selecting occupations that fit certain values.

Other systems include DISCOVER and CHOICES. DISCOVER, developed for Grades 7 to 12, includes information about self, a systematic exploration of occupations, decision-making skills, the relationship of information about self to various occupations, and assistance in choosing an occupation. CHOICES, available in colleges and placement offices, follows a practical, step-by-step counseling sequence. The counselor first interviews a client; then the client fills out a self-assessment inventory of interests, aptitudes, and temperament. Then, with the counselor's help and the computer's assistance, the client decides whether to locate specific occupations, compare them and find related ones, or explore occupations generally if the client has limited knowledge about them.

Many career-related tests and inventories are also now available through computer-assisted systems—for example, the SDS, the SII, and the MBTI. Databases containing comprehensive information about occupations, college majors, all types of schools, scholarships, apprenticeships, and jobs are also available through the Internet. Thus, information is available to clients who are ready to compare what they know about their abilities, interests, and personality with occupational lists provided by the computer to match these characteristics.

Computer-assisted career guidance systems are very useful for counselors and clients who are ready to search for career information. It is almost impossible for counselors to gain access on their own to the tremendous amount of information available on occupations, occupational characteristics, and occupational requirements. And computer databases on the Internet can help counselors keep up with the ever-changing trends, projections about jobs, and job descriptions.

However, computers can give only limited help to clients in their explorations about themselves and their interactions with others. Clients generally need a counselor's help in expressing their interests or clarifying perceptions about their own abilities before using a computer. Moreover, material gained from computer-assisted programs is best synthesized and integrated in counseling sessions.

Thus, computers do not replace counselors. Taber and Luzzo's (1999) research found that the most effective means of providing career planning assistance to students or clients is by a combination of computer and counselor. Because technology is used significantly in career counseling, needed counselor competencies include knowledge of computer-assisted software and Web sites; capability to determine whether a computer-assisted intervention is appropriate for a client; capability to motivate the client to use computer-assisted systems or Web sites; ability to help the client process data; and capability to help the client develop an action plan.

COUNSELING PROGRAMS IN BUSINESS AND INDUSTRY

Counseling employees in business and industry has become one of the most rapidly growing specialties in counseling and in counseling psychology (Lewis & Lewis, 1986). As discussed in chapter 1, four programs have been developed for employees: (a) employee assistance programs, (b) employee enhancement programs, (c) job adjustment counseling, and (d) outplacement counseling.

Employee Assistance Programs

As early as the 1940s, a few companies—Dupont, Consolidated Edison, and Eastman Kodak—started offering counseling services for employees who were alcoholics. They realized that it was more profitable and effective to rehabilitate alcoholic workers with good records than to fire them and retrain new workers. These programs were called occupational alcoholism programs (OAPs) (Dickman, 1985). In the 1960s this service spread to other companies. The Kemper Insurance Group expanded its alcoholism program to include marriage and family problems and emotional, financial, or legal concerns. This expansion led to the formation of *employee assistance programs* (EAPs). In the 1970s and 1980s, EAPs continued to expand their services to include employees whose job performance was affected by other personal problems (Smith, Salts, & Smith, 1989). By 1995 the number of EAPs offered in businesses was between 12,000 and 14,000 (Gladding, 2003). As Figure 12.1 shows, the original alcoholism programs expanded their services first to EAPs, known as the broad-brush approach, and then to EEPs (Dickman, 1985).

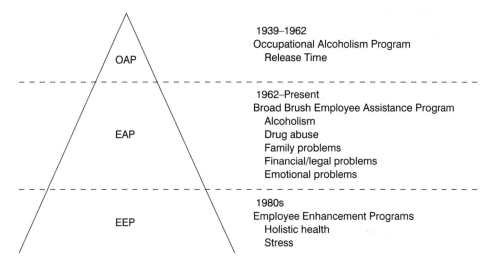

1939–1962
Occupational Alcoholism Program
Release Time

1962–Present
Broad Brush Employee Assistance Program
Alcoholism
Drug abuse
Family problems
Financial/legal problems
Emotional problems

1980s
Employee Enhancement Programs
Holistic health
Stress

FIGURE 12.1
Types of employment counseling programs in business.

Note: From "Employee Assistance Programs: History and Philosophy" (p. 7), by J. F. Dickman, in J. F. Dickman, W. G. Emener, Jr., & W. S. Hutchison, Jr. (Eds.), *Counseling the Troubled Person in Industry,* 1985, Springfield, IL: Charles C. Thomas. Copyright 1985 by Charles C. Thomas. Reprinted with permission.

Characteristics of EAPs

The major purpose of an EAP is to provide professional counseling for employees and their families when the employees are experiencing conflicts or problems that are leading to poor work performance, absenteeism, accidents, or conflicts with supervisors that could ultimately result in job termination if not corrected. In the 1980s representatives of labor and management, national associations concerned with alcoholism, and occupational consultants jointly developed standards for EAPs throughout the United States. Although these standards are voluntary, most practitioners adhere to them (Lewis & Lewis, 1986).

EAPs must have written policies about their philosophy and intent; procedures to orient employees, employers, and supervisors; guarantees of confidentiality to clients; and employee freedom of choice in using the service. In addition, procedures for individuals referred by supervisors or union representatives must be clear-cut, and counselors need to be located in offices that are fairly accessible to all employees.

Hosie, West, and Mackey (1993) surveyed staffing patterns of EAPs throughout the country and found that professionals with master's degrees in counseling and in social work were employed more frequently than individuals with doctoral degrees in the mental health field. Besides the training required of all counselors, EAP counselors need additional experience and training in business organizations and personnel management. Because alcoholism is still a major source of employee problems, training and experience in this area are important, too. Family counseling methods are also needed to meet the increased demand to work with families when individuals are having problems.

Internal and External Programs

Some EAPs are based within the organization (*internal model*); some are run by outside consultants under contract with the company (*external model*) (Lewis & Lewis, 1986). Each model has advantages and disadvantages. Smaller companies usually use outside consultants because they are less expensive.

Almost all early programs were internal, with services provided by counselors who were employees of the company. The advantages of internal models are that the EAP counselor is familiar with the organization, its potential strengths, and its potential problems. The counselor may be more trusted by employees, more joint consultation with supervisors and employees is possible, and more realistic solutions may emerge. Preventive educational programs might also be more easily developed. However, confidentiality might be a problem if counseling facilities are close to administration offices, or supervisors might demand to know about a client's progress.

When companies use outside mental health services, counselors find it easier to maintain confidentiality and to be more professionally objective about company policies and procedures. But they also find it more difficult to integrate these services into the total organizational work environment.

Services Offered

Whether a company runs an EAP or contracts it out, EAP counselors offer services paralleling those offered in other counseling settings. In addition to individual, group, and family counseling, which is usually relatively short term, counselors offer consultation and skills workshops to supervisors and provide psychological education programs promoting good mental health in the work setting. EAP counselors are also trained to make appropriate referrals to mental health agencies or private practitioners when the client's problems require more intensive or extensive work than is allowed by the EAP counselor. In addition, counselors may act as agents of social change in suggesting changes in policies and procedures in supervisor and employee relationships and expectations. EAP counselors anticipate that they will be offering even more comprehensive services in the future, including child care, care for older adult relatives, and planning for retirement (Zunker, 1994).

Employee Enhancement Programs

Employee Enhancement Programs (EEPs) are preventive, or wellness, programs intended to improve the overall mental and physical health of employees and their families. They may be an arm of an EAP or offered as a separate package of services. These programs, when combined with counseling services offered by EAPs under one jurisdiction, can supplement each other as they do in other counseling services.

The purpose of EEP preventive programs is to educate workers about drug and alcohol use, teach stress management and relaxation skills, and provide workshops in other life skills, such as parenting, marriage enrichment, and communication and relationship skills (Lewis & Lewis, 1986; see also chap. 8).

In addition to providing education programs and wellness activities, EEP counselors can explore and help alleviate stressful work conditions:

> Environmental characteristics to examine include physical stressors such as noise level or crowding, as well as such job situations as lack of control, ambiguity and insecurity, family reward systems, overly repetitive work, poor communication patterns, and too little opportunity for growth and development. (Lewis & Lewis, 1986, p. 13)

Job Adjustment Counseling

Career counselors hired by an industry work primarily on helping clients find appropriate placement or job adjustment within the company, exploring the possibilities of changing to a more satisfying job or advancing within the company (see chap. 19).

A career counseling unit can help employees identify career paths in an organization that lead to advancement or to more satisfying jobs. At times career plans do not involve new positions; sometimes employees need to broaden skills or learn new competencies to be successful and satisfied in a particular job. Large companies often have in-service or on-the-job training to enhance and improve employees' skills. Some provide tuition for employees to take college-level courses or technical school training. These programs are expanding in business and industry: "Increasingly, evidence suggests that both employers and employees benefit from these programs" (Isaacson & Brown, 1997, p. 473).

Retirement is one of the most potentially distressing transitions unless planning is started a few years before employment officially ends. Organizations need to provide pre-retirement counseling services to employees, covering both emotional concerns and practical considerations about benefits (Zunker, 1994).

Other painful transitions occur when a worker is suddenly transferred to a new job, promoted, demoted, or moved to a new branch within the company, perhaps requiring a move to another part of the country. In addition, those who have just graduated from technical school and are starting their first real job often experience transition anxiety. Counselors in the workforce who are aware of the vocational pressures and the personal stresses involved can be of help to both employees and company management in easing the strain of those workers in transition.

Outplacement Counseling

Outplacement counseling programs help employees who have been laid off assess their employment experience and skills and search for new jobs (Herr & Cramer, 1996; Zunker, 1994). An increasing number of companies have become interested in helping employees whose jobs were terminated because of bankruptcy, company cutbacks, obsolescence, or other reasons for which the workers are not responsible (Isaacson & Brown, 1997; Zunker, 1994). Companies most often use outside career consultants to help the displaced employees find new jobs and adjust psychologically (Herr & Cramer, 1996); it is important to help these employees, individually or in groups, express their anger. In such situations counselors give personal counseling assistance and help employees learn job-seeking skills, develop effective résumés, and conduct themselves with confidence in job interviews (Zunker, 1994).

EMPLOYMENT COUNSELORS

Employment counselors specialize in helping people find jobs. They work in state employment offices and in college and private placement agencies. These workers are often called *occupational information specialists* or *career information specialists*. As stated earlier, although the national professional association strongly recommends that employment and placement counselors be certified, this is not required by law.

Most placement agencies accumulate job listings from employers through telephone calls or visits. Effective placement counselors spend considerable time cultivating relationships with personnel directors and other hiring officials so that their placement offices will be contacted when firms have job openings.

Employment counselors, particularly those in colleges and private placement offices, also teach clients job search techniques and job interview skills and give them tips on developing résumés (Herr & Cramer, 1996). By role-playing with clients before they go on interviews, the counselor helps them reduce their anxiety and teaches them how to respond and assert themselves constructively with the person in charge of hiring.

Employment counselors in state employment agencies work with challenging and difficult groups of clients, particularly those who have been laid off from their jobs. Clients may need urgent help, especially if they have families to support. Those who have suddenly lost jobs may experience shock, denial, grief, and anger. Those who cannot find work over a long period of time may feel defeated, resigned, desperate, or resentful. Another group, the chronically unemployed, are often difficult to place because of alcoholism, marginal intelligence, or borderline personality functioning. Their motivation is low, and their employment histories are erratic, at best.

To meet the special needs of unemployed clients, it is essential that agencies hire certified or licensed career counselors, who can consider clients' emotional conflicts as they try to help the clients find work. When employment counselors find that clients are so distraught that they are not ready for placement, referrals to a mental health counselor or to a counseling psychologist are in order.

VOCATIONAL REHABILITATION COUNSELING

Rehabilitation counselors help clients with disabilities find appropriate employment and aid them in developing and maintaining as much independence as possible (Herr & Cramer, 1996; Leahy & Szymanski, 1995). State rehabilitation agencies differentiate the terms *disabled* and *handicapped*. Zunker (1994) defines a *disability* as a physical or mental impairment that limits functioning in one or more bodily systems. A *handicap* is described as an inability, related to a disability, to function on a job because of some barrier in the work environment; for example, elevators may be unavailable for a paraplegic worker.

Besides the typical course work expected of all counselors, rehabilitation counselors have course work in the medical and psychological aspects of disability, worker compensation policies, environmental and attitudinal barriers related to disabilities, special considerations in job placement of those with disabilities, and knowledge about the psychological, medical, social, or behavioral services and interventions needed by clients with disabilities (Jenkins, Patterson, & Szymanski, 1992; Leahy & Szymanski, 1995).

The majority of rehabilitation counselors work in public rehabilitation agencies for federal and state governments. These include rehabilitation centers, state employment services, Veterans Administration facilities, prisons and correctional agencies, mental health clinics, hospitals, and Social Security and worker compensation agencies. Recently, privately run rehabilitation services have developed that contract their services with public agencies or the government. In addition, private schools for students with disabilities and some colleges employ rehabilitation counselors. Rehabilitation counselors are also now being hired in EAPs, university-based services for students with disabilities, school-to-work transition programs, and disability management programs in business and industry (Leahy & Szymanski, 1995).

Parker and Hansen (1981) were among the first to describe rehabilitation counseling as a multistep process. Others have followed with similar proposals (Jenkins et al., 1992; Leahy & Szymanski, 1995). This process-oriented counseling generally proceeds as follows: (a) case finding, (b) eligibility determination for services, (c) career counseling, (d) career placement, (e) case management, and (f) termination.

Case Finding and Eligibility Determination for Services

Rehabilitation counselors find potential clients by contacting and setting up referral procedures with other agencies and health professionals who come in contact with persons with disabilities. After a client and a counselor have an initial interview, they review the client's medical, psychological, educational, and vocational background. The counselor is still in the case-finding stage at this point.

Before counseling proceeds, the counselor must evaluate how extensive the disability is, how much the disability is handicapping the person at work, and whether handicapping problems can be corrected through rehabilitation. The counselor coordinates and evaluates the medical, psychological, and vocational assessment and decides on eligibility. If eligibility is denied, the counselor must inform the client of the reason and the right to appeal. A claim may be denied because a client is employable without need of rehabilitation, the disability is not sufficient to warrant benefits, or the client is so severely disabled that vocational rehabilitation would not help. If eligibility is established, the counselor develops written plans that include intermediate and long-term goals and services to be provided.

The client may be eligible for one or more of the following services: counseling, medical treatment, physical restoration (e.g., prosthesis, hearing aid), psychiatric help, prevocational or vocational training, maintenance expenses, transportation, and provisions such as reader services and guide dogs for the blind.

Career Counseling

Throughout the rehabilitation process, counselors must work with the emotional impact of the individual's incapacitating disability. Strategies to accomplish this task must be included in counselor training (Livneh & Sherwood, 1991). Livneh and Sherwood (1991) discuss how counselors can use any number of theoretical approaches with clients with disabilities: psychoanalytic, Adlerian, person-centered, Gestalt, behavioral, and cognitive-behavioral. They recommend that counselors select interventions congruent with their own theoretical orientations and with the nature and setting of the client's disability. Using these interventions, counselors help clients with disabilities gain insight into the psychosocial impact of the disability.

Livneh and Sherwood (1991) point out that persons with disabilities go through phases of adjustment: "Adaptation to disability is not a static concept. It is a dynamic and often protracted process that is composed of several fluctuating and overlapping phases" (p. 525). Synthesizing models presented by other researchers, Livneh and Sherwood describe eight phases of adjustment: "*shock, anxiety, denial, depression, internalized anger, externalized hostility, acknowledgment,* and *adjustment*" (p. 525). These feelings must be acknowledged and worked through if appropriate vocational rehabilitation is to occur.

Career Placement

Placement is a major focus of rehabilitation counseling (Jenkins et al., 1992). Complications may arise because of the negative attitudes of employers, fellow employees, and the clients themselves regarding the disability (Isaacson & Brown, 1997). Some placement agencies have a rehabilitation counselor who specializes in placing persons with disabilities. Such a specialist places clients in jobs after the counselor has helped the clients become ready for the jobs (Parker & Hansen, 1981).

Case Management and Termination

After placing a client on a job, the rehabilitation counselor monitors the client for a few months to see how well he or she is adapting and adjusting to the new work setting. The counselor also consults with the employer and the client's supervisor about how the new employee is functioning on the job; the counselor may suggest changes that are needed in the work setting.

When the counselor, client, and employer are satisfied with the client's progress on the job, the case is terminated. At that time the counselor lets the client know that the case can be reopened if further assistance is needed.

RESEARCH IN CAREER COUNSELING AND DEVELOPMENT

Considerable research has been conducted by counseling psychologists in the area of career development theory, career measurement, and career interventions (Osipow, 1987). Interest measurement and vocational development represent some of the best-developed research areas in counseling psychology (Borgen, 1984). Comprehensive reviews of career research have been presented by Borgen (1984), Brown and Lent (1984), Osipow and Fitzgerald (1996), Spokane and Oliver (1983), and Walsh and Osipow (1983). Presented here are overall trends; readers interested in specific research areas can refer to the resources cited.

Much of career theory began in the 1950s with Super's research on career development and career maturity. These concepts have received much support from researchers (Osipow, 1987).

Holland's person-environment theory has generated more research than any other career theory (Osipow, 1987). Weinrach (1984) also comments, "Probably no theory of career development or vocational choice has been researched or commented on as extensively as Holland's" (p. 71). Osipow (1987) sums up the research on Holland's theory: "Most of the findings point to the theory's vitality and validity for the purposes for which it was designed" (p. 263).

Research on outcomes of career counseling or vocational interventions has been summarized by Spokane and Oliver (1983). They present an integrative analysis of 52 studies about the outcome of vocational intervention and conclude that career counseling leads to positive outcomes. Herr and Cramer (1988) concur that "research studies have repeatedly demonstrated that career interventions do yield positive results and that their general utility is clear" (p. 478).

Likewise, EAPs have consistently shown remarkably high degrees of success in increased worker productivity and the improved physical and emotional health of alcoholic workers (Quayle, 1985). The rapid increase in the number of companies developing these programs attests to their outcome—more productive, satisfied, and healthier workers (Dickman, 1985).

SUMMARY

Career counseling relates to personal and social counseling because the development, choice, and establishment of a career are closely tied to personal needs, social and environmental influences, and personality development. The number of career counseling centers has greatly expanded in the past decade or so in the community and in business and industry.

The major theories influencing the career counseling process are those that relate career development to personal development; those that relate personal developmental characteristics to occupational environments compatible with the individual; and those that emphasize the plurality of perspectives, contextual impacts, social constructions of reality, and the importance of the meaning individuals give to their career experiences. Typical client problems related to careers are the need for career exploration, conflict with others regarding career choices, doubts about choosing or remaining in a career, and disruptive conflicts arising from transitions in work and family.

Community career counseling centers offer numerous and varied outreach workshops and seminars to help clients develop strategies in job searches, upgrade themselves in current jobs, and deal with anxieties or uncertainties during job transitions.

Increasing numbers of counselors are hired by businesses to work with employees whose concerns interfere with their work productivity. Some businesses also hire counselors to help employees find the most suitable career path in the company or find jobs in other companies when their jobs are terminated. Individuals with disabilities benefit from rehabilitation services in career and educational planning. Such services have spread from government agencies to private agencies in the community and to schools and universities.

PROJECTS AND ACTIVITIES

1. Ask one or more people in their 50s who are well-established in jobs why they chose their fields, how they entered them, and what steps they took to get to their current jobs.

2. Sigmund Freud once said that work and love are two of the most important experiences in life. Alfred Adler, another psychoanalyst, agreed. How does this view relate to the theories of career development currently popular?

3. Explore your university's computer-assisted programs for information about careers. Ask to use the programs to gain information about professional counseling. Evaluate the quality and quantity of information obtained.

4. Interview counselors at your local state unemployment and vocational rehabilitation offices. From their comments indicate how you might make use of these agencies as referral sources if you were a counselor in the community.

5. Interview a college placement counselor and a placement counselor in the state employment service. Compare their functions, attitudes, and resources.

6. Explore what employee assistance programs are available in your community. Try to interview both a counselor who works in an internal program and one who is employed in an external agency.

7. Select one career theory or one vocational interest measure (e.g., Strong, Kuder, or SDS), and read a review of the research. Select a study considered sound and one the reviewer considers faulty. Analyze the strengths and weaknesses.

REFERENCES

Betz, N. E., & Corning, A. F. (1993). The inseparability of "career" and "personal" counseling. *Career Development Quarterly, 42,* 137–142.

Borgen, F. H. (1984). Counseling psychology. *Annual Review of Psychology, 35,* 579–604.

Brown, D. (1995). A value-based approach to facilitating career transitions. *Career Development Quarterly, 44,* 4–11.

Brown, D., & Brooks, L. (1991). *Career counseling techniques.* Boston: Allyn & Bacon.

Brown, S. D., & Lent, R. W. (Eds.). (1984). *Handbook of counseling psychology.* New York: John Wiley.

Career Action Center. (1997). *Career action connections: A resource guide to career self-reliance bimonthly.* Cupertino, CA: Author.

Cochran, L. (1997). *Career counseling: A narrative approach.* Thousand Oaks, CA: Sage.

Dickman, J. F. (1985). Employee assistance programs: History and philosophy. In J. F. Dickman, W. G. Emener, & W. S. Hutchison (Eds.), *Counseling the troubled person in industry* (pp. 7–12). Springfield, IL: Charles C Thomas.

Gallagher, R. P. (1996). *National survey of counseling center directors.* Alexandria, PA: International Association of Counseling Services.

Ginzberg, E. (1972). Toward a theory of occupational choice: A restatement. *Vocational Guidance Quarterly, 20,* 169–176.

Ginzberg, E., Ginzburg, S. W., Axelrad, S., & Herma, J. I. (1951). *Occupational choice: An approach to theory.* New York: Columbia University Press.

Gladding, S. T. (2003). *Community and agency counseling.* Upper Saddle River, NJ: Merrill/Prentice Hall.

Gysbers, N. C., & Moore, E. J. (1987). *Career counseling: Skills and techniques for practitioners.* Upper Saddle River, NJ: Prentice Hall.

Herr, E. L. (2003, September). The future of career counseling as an instrument of public policy. *Career Development Quarterly, 52,* 8–17.

Herr, E. L., & Cramer, S. H. (1988). *Career guidance and counseling through the life span: Systematic approaches* (3rd ed.). Boston: Scott, Foresman.

Herr, E. L., & Cramer, S. H. (1996). *Career guidance and counseling through the life span: Systematic approaches* (5th ed.). Boston: Scott, Foresman.

Holland, J. L. (1959). A theory of vocational choice. *Journal of Counseling Psychology, 6,* 35–45.

Holland, J. L. (1994). *The Self-Directed Search: Professional manual* (3rd ed.). Odessa, FL: Psychological Assessment Resources.

Holland, J. L. (1997). *Making vocational choices: A theory of vocational personalities and work environments* (3rd ed.). Upper Saddle River, NJ: Prentice Hall.

Hosie, T. W., West, J. D., & Mackey, J. A. (1993). Employment and roles of counselors in employee assistance programs. *Journal of Counseling & Development, 71,* 355–359.

Isaacson, L. E. (1986). *Career information in counseling and career development* (4th ed.). Boston: Allyn & Bacon.

Isaacson, L. E., & Brown, D. (1997). *Career information, career counseling, and career development* (6th ed.). Boston: Allyn & Bacon.

Jaffe, M. E. (2003). A career center model: Twenty-seven years at InfoPlace. *American Libraries, 34*(6), 65–66.

Jenkins, W., Patterson, J. B., & Szymanski, E. M. (1992). Philosophical, historic, and legislative aspects of the rehabilitation counseling profession. In R. M. Parker & E. M. Szymanski (Eds.), *Rehabilitation counseling: Basics and beyond* (2nd ed., pp. 1–41). Austin, TX: PRO-ED.

Katz, M. (1963). *Decisions and values.* New York: College Entrance Examination Board.

Krumboltz, J. D. (1993). Integrating career and personal counseling. *Career Development Quarterly, 42,* 143–148.

Leahy, M. J., & Szymanski, E. M. (1995). Rehabilitation counseling: Evolution and current status. *Journal of Counseling & Development, 74,* 163–166.

Lee, C. C., & Shahnasarian, M. (1998). Setting the record straight. *Counseling Today, 40,* 18.

Lewis, J. A., & Lewis, M. D. (1986). *Counseling programs for employees in the workplace.* Pacific Grove, CA: Brooks/Cole.

Livneh, H., & Sherwood, A. (1991). Application of personality theories and counseling strategies to clients with physical disabilities. *Journal of Counseling & Development, 69,* 525–538.

Niles, S. G., & Anderson, W. P. (1995). A content analysis of career and personal concerns expressed by career counseling clients. *Educational and Vocational Guidance Bulletin, 57,* 59–62.

Niles, S. G., & Harris-Bowlsbey, J. H. (2002). *Career development interventions in the 21st century.* Upper Saddle River, NJ: Merrill/Prentice Hall.

Osipow, S. H. (1987). Counseling psychology: Theory, research, and practice in career counseling. *Annual Review of Psychology, 38,* 257–278.

Osipow, S. H., & Fitzgerald, L. F. (1996). *Theories of career development* (4th ed.). Boston: Allyn & Bacon.

Parker, R. M., & Hansen, C. E. (Eds.). (1981). *Rehabilitation counseling: Foundations—consumers—service delivery.* Boston: Allyn & Bacon.

Parsons, F. (1909). *Choosing a vocation.* Boston: Houghton Mifflin.

Peavy, R. V. (1993). Constructivist counseling: A prospectus. *Guidance & Counseling, 9*(2), 3–10.

Peavy, R. V. (1997). A constructive framework for career counseling. In T. L. Sexton & B. L. Griffin (Eds.), *Constructivist thinking in counseling practice, research and training.* New York: Teachers College Press.

Quayle, D. (1985). American productivity: The devastating effect of alcoholism and drug abuse. In J. F. Dickman, W. G. Emener, & W. S. Hutchison (Eds.), *Counseling the troubled person in industry* (pp. 20–29). Springfield, IL: Charles C Thomas.

Roe, A. (1957). Early determinants of vocational choice. *Journal of Counseling Psychology, 4,* 212–217.

Smith, T. A., Jr., Salts, C. J., & Smith, C. W. (1989). Preparing marriage and family therapy students to become employee assistance professionals. *Journal of Marital and Family Therapy, 15,* 419–424.

Spokane, A. R., & Oliver, L. W. (1983). The outcomes of vocational intervention. In B. W. Walsh & S. H. Osipow (Eds.), *Handbook of vocational psychology: Vol. 2. Applications* (pp. 99–136). Mahwah, NJ: Lawrence Erlbaum.

Super, D. (1942). *The dynamics of vocational adjustment.* New York: Harper Brothers.

Super, D. E. (1951). Vocational adjustment: Implementing a self-concept. *Occupations, 30,* 88–92.

Super, D. E. (1953). A theory of vocational development. *American Psychologist, 8,* 185–190.

Super, D. E. (1955). Personality integration through vocational counseling. *Journal of Counseling Psychology, 2,* 217–226.

Super, D. E. (1961). Consistency and wisdom of vocational preference as indices of vocational maturity in the ninth grade. *Journal of Educational Psychology, 52,* 35–43.

Super, D. E. (1980). A life-span, life-space approach to career development. *Journal of Vocational Behavior, 22,* 191–226.

Super, D. E. (1993). The two faces of counseling: Or is it three? *Career Development Quarterly, 42,* 132–136.

Taber, B. J., & Luzzo, D. A. (1999). *ACT research report 99-3: A comprehensive review of research evaluating the effectiveness of DISCOVER in promoting career development.* Iowa City, IA: ACT.

Walsh, W. B., & Osipow, S. H. (Eds.). (1983). *Handbook of vocational psychology* (Vols. 1 & 2). Mahwah, NJ: Lawrence Erlbaum.

Weinrach, S. G. (1984). Determinants of vocational choice: Holland's theory. In D. Brown & L. Brooks (Eds.), *Career choice and development.* San Francisco: Jossey-Bass.

Weinrach, S. G., & Srebalus, D. J. (1990). Holland's theory of careers. In D. Brown & L. Brooks (Eds.), *Career choice and development* (2nd ed., pp. 37–67). San Francisco: Jossey-Bass.

Yost, E. B., & Corbishley, M. A. (1987). *Career counseling: A psychological approach.* San Francisco: Jossey-Bass.

Zunker, V. G. (1994). *Career counseling: Applied concepts of life planning* (4th ed.). Pacific Grove, CA: Brooks/Cole.

CHAPTER 13

Substance Abuse Counseling

*S*ubstance abuse occurs when a person overuses alcohol, illegal street drugs, or pre-scribed painkillers, tranquilizers, or stimulants over a sustained period of time, resulting in an impairment in personal and social functioning (Chamberlain & Jew, 2001). These substances are *psychoactive,* in that they alter mood, behavior, and percep-tions and affect the nervous system through chemical changes in the brain. All these sub-stances can lead to physical or psychological dependence (i.e., *addiction*) with repeated use; and withdrawal from them can be devastating to the physical, psychological, and social functioning of the individual (American Psychiatric Association, 2000; Comer, 1998). Because the addicted person develops a *tolerance* to the effects of the substance, main-taining a certain level of euphoria requires increasing dosages, which can lead to more physical and mental damage and more financial burden (Porter, 1998).

Although alcohol, like the other substances mentioned, is technically a drug, society has viewed its consumption differently from that of other drugs. Alcohol is not illegal for adults, and it does not require a prescription, as do most other drugs. Thus, alcohol prob-lems and addictions warrant a separate discussion.

Even though this chapter addresses substance abuse addictions, other addictions are becoming increasingly prevalent in society—such as eating disorders, compulsive gambling, and sexual addictions—and these various addictive behaviors have much in common. Terence Real (1997), speaking on male depression, argues that all addictive behaviors—substance abuse, workaholism, excessive workouts, womanizing, overeat-ing, gambling—act as defenses against male depression (see also chapter 14). Moreover, according to Fossum and Mason (1986) and Kasl (1989), all addictive behaviors share the common underlying feeling of shame that stems from shame-based families. Mem-bers of such families all participate in and maintain the system of shame and addiction.

"One of the most clearly identifiable aspects of shame in families is addictive behavior. The addiction becomes a central organizing principle for the system, maintaining the system as well as the shame" (Fossum & Mason, 1986, p. 123).

COUNSELING PERSONS WITH ALCOHOL PROBLEMS

An estimated 20 million people, including 3 million children and adolescents, suffer from alcohol abuse or addiction. Furthermore, 40% to 50% of highway deaths are alcohol related (James & Gilliland, 2001). Over $100 billion a year is lost in business and to society because of absenteeism or the poor work performance of alcoholics as well as the high cost to law enforcement, the justice system, and social services (Stevens, 2001c). Other sources indicate even higher losses of more than $270 billion (James & Gilliland, 2001). Moreover, many diseases are frequently related to alcohol addiction: cirrhosis of the liver, pancreatic disorders, malnutrition, heart disease, problems of the nervous and muscular-skeletal systems, brain damage, and psychiatric reactions such as depression and paranoia (Goodwin, 1992; Porter, 1998). And the serious interpersonal problems that result from alcohol abuse include domestic violence, child abuse, marital conflict, sexual dysfunction, and dysfunctional social relationships (Bennett, 1992; Stevens, 2001d).

Differences Among Alcoholics, Problem Drinkers, and Social Drinkers

The differences among alcoholics, problem drinkers, and social drinkers are indicated by the degree of dependence on the substance. *Alcoholics* are both physically and psychologically dependent, *problem drinkers* are psychologically dependent, and *social drinkers* are not dependent on alcohol at all (Metzger, 1988; Smith, 2001).

Alcoholics physically and psychologically depend on alcohol to such an extent that they spend most of their waking hours drinking to reduce psychological tension and to prevent *withdrawal symptoms,* the severe physiological reactions when alcohol is withheld. They have trouble holding jobs because of poor attendance and poor performance, and because they are chronically intoxicated, their drinking is obvious to friends and the public. In addition, they deteriorate physically because of malnutrition and the toxic effects that alcohol has on their bodies.

Problem drinkers have a psychological dependence on alcohol. They are apt to drink every day and often excessively. Like alcoholics, they feel compelled to drink as part of their daily routine to reduce tension or anxiety. They differ from alcoholics, however, in that they do not need alcohol to prevent withdrawal symptoms. They do not need a drink, for instance, when they first wake up in the morning to prevent the "shakes." But they sometimes cannot remember what they said or did for brief periods the night before. They may not start drinking until after 5:00 p.m., so they may seem normal most of the time. But their need for a drink every evening is still based on a compulsive urge that is persistent and repetitious. Problem drinkers often deny that they drink excessively and that the drinking causes any problems. Yet their drinking leads to negative physical, economic, and social consequences. According to Belkin (1984), alcoholism is a progressive disease, and problem drinkers are just "one step from alcoholism" (p. 416). Regarding the problem drinker's compulsion to drink at social events, he says, "If you need a drink to be social then you're not a social drinker" (p. 416).

Social drinkers drink a moderate amount of alcohol—perhaps one or two drinks a few times a week—and intoxication rarely occurs (Peer, Lindsey, & Newman, 1982). Social drinkers feel no compulsion to drink; even at parties they are often able to accept or refuse drinks as they please.

In the literature, problems of alcoholics are typically considered more serious than those of problem drinkers. For instance, in comparing the two groups, Belkin (1984) says, "The alcoholic is by far the worse" (p. 416). However, because the difficulties of problem drinkers are less obvious, they are more easily ignored, and thus the problem becomes more insidious.

Families of alcoholics are often forced to seek help because of the severity of the problem: Alcoholics may pass out in public or on kitchen floors, they may lose their jobs, or they may be hospitalized for cirrhosis of the liver. Friends, easily recognizing the problem, are more ready to lend support. Families of problem drinkers are in a more ambiguous position. They are uncertain about the severity of the problem because problem drinkers are often sober a good part of the day. Without clear-cut evidence families are less able to counter the problem drinkers' denials that they have a problem. Friends and relatives, often unaware of the problem, are less ready to understand the family's concerns. Thus, problem drinkers continue their compulsive drinking, and dysfunctional family patterns develop and persist.

The Causes of Alcoholism

Disease Theory

Many believe that alcoholism is a disease caused by genetic or biological multigenerational factors that render persons susceptible to alcohol addiction or compulsive uncontrolled drinking (Erickson, 2001; James & Gilliland, 2001). Many, however, doubt this position. "Today, the full endorsement of the disease model is questioned and is being challenged" (Smith, 2001, p. 336).

Alcoholism, when defined as a disease, is described as "a chronic, primary, hereditary, eventually fatal disease that progresses from an early physiological susceptibility into an addiction characterized by tolerance changes, physiological dependence, and loss of control over drinking" (Mueller & Ketcham, 1987, p. 9). As in other diseases, a process of deterioration and destruction is based on specific causes, and specific characteristic symptoms are evident. Under this description abstinence is essential for recovery.

Psychological Theories

Psychoanalytic and cognitive-behavioral theorists have given more attention to the psychological causes of alcoholism than have humanists (Price & Lynn, 1986). Freudian theorists assume that alcoholism is related to certain pathological personality traits established in early childhood (James & Gilliland, 2001). Object relations proponents emphasize the alcoholic's need to alleviate and deny underlying personal and interpersonal conflicts (Price & Lynn, 1986). Cognitive-behavioral and social learning counselors believe that alcohol addiction occurs because drinking habits are learned and maintained by sociological, psychological, and physiological factors (James & Gilliland, 2001). They hypothesize that drinking serves the seemingly useful purpose of reducing discomfort, anxiety, and tension; this tension reduction reinforces drug usage and increases the possibility of continued usage.

Social-Cultural Theories

Increased attention has been given to social-cultural influences on addictive behaviors—family patterns, neighborhood settings, peer groups, social-cultural milieu. "Attitudes toward alcohol consumption and abuse vary from culture to culture and greatly affect the amount and content of alcohol consumption" (Erickson, 2001, p. 99). Studies show that Jews and Italians have low alcoholism rates, whereas the Irish and French are high on the scale of alcoholism (Calahan, Cisin, & Crossley, 1969; Comer, 1998; Valliant & Milofsky, 1982). Alcoholism is the leading cause of health problems, fatal accidents, and homicide among Native Americans (Robinson & Howard-Hamilton, 2000). The high rates of alcoholism among certain minority groups, such as Native Americans, are attributed to the oppression and poverty imposed by the dominant culture (Sue & Sue, 2003).

Biopsychosocial Theories

Increasing numbers of professionals now acknowledge that a biopsychosocial approach is the most appropriate way to understand the causes of addictive behaviors. Biopsychosocial theories incorporate biological, psychological, and social factors in assessing individuals who are predisposed to substance abuse (Erickson, 2001). These factors include "individual differences in pleasurable reactions to alcohol, psychophysiologic differences, neuro-chemical differences, cognitive functioning differences, temperament or personality differences, and environmental differences within the family, school, community, and peer groups" (Erickson, 2001, p. 104). Attending to these combined biological, psychological, and social factors has gained increasing support from health care professionals. This view is in accord with a multifaceted, comprehensive approach that includes attention to an individual's environment and family dynamics, as well as genetic and biochemical predisposition (Erickson, 2001).

Pretreatment of Persons With Alcohol Problems

Confronting a Person With an Alcohol Problem

Both alcoholics and problem drinkers deny that they have a drinking problem, so they most often respond negatively to suggestions or pleas that they seek treatment. They continue to deny the problem even though family members worry about their secret drinking, gulping of drinks, poor school or work attendance, bad nutrition, or family violence. When family members decide that the excessive drinker must get treatment, they can—in a caring way and with the consultation of alcoholism counselors—confront the alcoholic or problem drinker with the necessity for treatment (James & Gilliland, 2001). This confrontation may convince the drinker to abstain from drinking, join Alcoholics Anonymous (AA), seek counseling, or take a combination of actions.

If the alcoholic or problem drinker continues to deny the problem, then a more forceful intervention technique may be necessary. An alcoholism counselor and, at times, very close friends may join with the family in confronting the person with the alcohol problem about the effects drinking is having on the individual's health and well-being and the well-being of family members and friends (Mueller & Ketcham, 1987). If treatment is still refused, alcoholism counselors may recommend that the family break away from the excessive drinker for the sake of the family's mental health (O'Keefe, 1988).

Confrontation may also occur on the job when work performance is poor or when absenteeism is high because of the worker's alcoholism. Supervisors may confront the worker or may intervene jointly with a counselor in an employee assistance program (EAP) to convince the worker to seek treatment. Such interventions are usually effective because job security is involved (Dickman & Phillips, 1985).

Researchers caution against heavy-handed coercion in confronting the abuser. Making accusations or exhorting confessions from the abuser can lead to increased defensiveness and denial (James & Gilliland, 2001). Miller and Rollnick (1991) have developed a client-centered approach called *motivational interviewing*. Instead of forcing the issue, they discuss the problem with the abuser at an appropriate time and place and give advice rather than make demands. Such an approach gives the person in question a chance to make the decision to remedy the problem. This approach is most successful as an initial step, when persons are being approached for the first time and if they are willing to listen.

Some alcoholics and problem drinkers may be able to abstain from alcohol for a while when they recognize the problem or are confronted. For alcoholics spontaneous abstinence is rare because of withdrawal symptoms; for problem drinkers it is difficult to do for any length of time because environmental pressures from the family or the job often induce persons to revert to drinking. In most cases alcoholics and problem drinkers need counseling help to recover; and their families need counseling to give up behavioral patterns that are reinforcing the addiction.

Assessment and Detoxification

When the person with an alcohol problem agrees to go into treatment, an alcoholism counselor interviews the family and makes an assessment. If the alcoholism is chronic and severe, the person may need to be hospitalized to go through withdrawal under medical supervision. Withdrawal reactions can be severe and even fatal. This precursor to treatment is called *detoxification*. At times the drug disulfiram (Antabuse) is used; it causes nausea and vomiting when taken with alcohol and helps the person attain abstinence (Perez, 2001). Detoxification may take from 3 or 4 days to a week, at which time the person is ready for treatment. During assessment the alcoholism counselor discusses with a spouse and other appropriate family members their own counseling and support needs, indicating when and where these services are available.

Treatment Settings and Goals

Recovering alcoholics and problem drinkers can be rehabilitated through inpatient, outpatient, or partial hospitalization (i.e., day care) services at general or psychiatric hospitals with alcoholic units or at private, nonprofit alcoholism treatment centers. They may also choose to see private practitioners who have expertise in alcohol treatment, or they may receive treatment in community mental health clinics. Frequently, these programs are offered through EAPs, as described in chapter 12. Manfrin (1998) notes the diverse settings in which substance abuse treatment is offered:

> As opposed to mental health settings, which have a moderate range of facility differences, chemical dependency services can be delivered in hospitals, converted houses, basements of nonhospital detoxification centers, jails and prisons, youth centers, community centers, locked and unlocked psychiatric units, rural dwellings, and almost any setting that will house an alcohol or drug counselor with clients. (p. 135)

Inpatient treatment usually lasts about 4 weeks but can last as long as 6 months. Partial hospitalization often runs 5 or more hours a day, 5 days a week, for 4 to 6 weeks. Most researchers and clinicians still believe that for alcoholics abstinence is the primary and essential goal in alcohol treatment (Fletcher, 2001; Smith, 2001). Whether problem drinkers can learn to control their drinking still remains a controversial issue. Most professionals believe that until underlying issues of addiction are dealt with, problem drinkers will continue to be in danger of relapse (Smith, 2001). Fletcher (2001), who offers new solutions to alcohol treatment in her book *Sober for Good,* cautions that for those problem drinkers who have mastered their alcohol problem, only a very few can start drinking again and maintain control. Those individuals who may be able to drink once in a while or moderately are psychologically stable, maintain a stable lifestyle, and have learned to cope well with stress.

After alcoholics and problem drinkers stop drinking, they and their families need counseling help. The term *recovering alcoholic* is often used, as it is here, for both alcoholics and problem drinkers who have stopped drinking. Some professionals have claimed that these people will always remain in the recovery stage because they will always be addicted to alcohol. But more recently, others have found that by treating underlying addictive patterns, patients can overcome their addictive behaviors.

What is agreed is that abstinence alone is insufficient to resolve the alcoholic's or the family's problems. Abstinence does not resolve underlying problems, nor does it immediately improve family relationships. Instead, family problems often become exacerbated when the denial patterns surrounding the alcoholism and the sedative effects of the alcohol no longer exist. And because alcohol is no longer used as a cover-up for family dysfunction, the personal problems of family members and family discord may erupt. Moreover, family members often unconsciously or subconsciously resist changes in the recovering alcoholic, who begins to assert needs and display strengths. Continued counseling is needed to help both the alcoholic and the family form new patterns of behavior.

Counseling services and support groups for both alcoholics and family members can help change dysfunctional family patterns. These services not only help recovering persons abstain but also help them and their family members learn to interact with one another in more productive ways. Counseling helps them understand old behaviors and attitudes, develop coping skills for new experiences in the present, and build a framework for continual future growth, individually and as a family.

Spouse and Family Need for Treatment

Once the alcoholic agrees to treatment, the spouse and other family members also need counseling help. "The attitudes, structure, and function of the family system have been shown to be perhaps the most important variables in the outcome of treatment" (James & Gilliland, 2001, p. 395). As discussed in chapter 10, one member of a family with a problem, represents a problem in the total family system. In the typical family of an alcoholic or problem drinker, the spouse and children have been caught up in a family dynamic of intrigue, in which the alcohol problem has been denied and rarely discussed so that feelings of shame permeate the family. Family boundaries are unclear, family members are enmeshed, and authentic communication is infrequent.

Families that hide their secret unwittingly assume the roles of *enablers,* allowing the alcoholic to continue drinking and not suffer the consequences. The spouse covers up for the alcoholic, takes over duties the spouse should handle, makes excuses for the drinking, pretends the spouse is ill (not drunk), and ends up acting like a martyr (Hogg & Frank, 1992; Schaef, 1986). Meanwhile, children assume different roles to help themselves and the family survive the emotional stress while maintaining secrecy and denial. One may play the hero, who hopes to redeem the family by being successful. Another may hide the pain by acting like the family clown, joker, or mascot. Still another may play the role of scapegoat and act out the family problems. Others may withdraw from stress and act like lost children (Gladding, 2002; James & Gilliland, 2001).

The goals of treatment for spouses and families are to work through their own problems and attitudes and gain sufficient independence so that they can drop the caretaking or enabling roles in which they control, manage, or manipulate one another or the alcoholic (Gladding, 2002). They also need help in overcoming any tendency to continue blaming the recovering alcoholic for all the drinking-related problems in the past. As recovering alcoholics regain strength, family members are apt to feel stronger rage and resentment against them; the members may begin to act out or become physically ill (Stevens, 2001a). "Paradoxically, if the alcoholic makes a commitment to stop drinking, the maladaptive family may become threatened enough to try to reinstitute the perceived homeostasis of alcoholism" (James & Gilliland, 2001, p. 395). This can be quite a problem for recovering alcoholics and is one main reason many take refuge in AA groups—to protect themselves and get the necessary support to remain sober because little support is available from their families.

Codependency

According to alcoholism counselors, the enabling behavior just described occurs because family members have developed mutual codependent relationships (James & Gilliland, 2001; Subby, 1987). In a codependent family, family members have not developed their own independence, cannot express their own needs, and cannot communicate genuine feelings. These characteristics originated in the early experiences of each parent in his or her family of origin.

Codependency is defined as an addiction to a relationship that stifles self-growth and self-expression. According to Wegscheider-Cruse (1985), the codependency addiction closely resembles the alcoholic's addiction to alcohol. Wegscheider-Cruse defines codependency as being dependent on others to such an extent that the dependent person becomes dysfunctional. James and Gilliland (2001) see codependency more generally as arising from prolonged exposure to oppressive family rules that prevent open expression of feelings and straightforward discussion of personal problems. Cermak (1986) describes codependence as a pattern of maladaptive mechanisms in alcoholic families in which control of self and others' feelings and needs is the major way to reduce free-floating anxiety. The shame generated in shame-based families, as discussed later, is considered a major contributor to codependent behaviors (Fossum & Mason, 1986; Subby, 1987). Codependency also involves a lack of clearly defined boundaries within a family, resulting in a loss of personhood.

Scores of characteristics have been published to describe the codependent (Beattie, 1987; Subby, 1987; Wegscheider-Cruse, 1985). Some common behaviors are typical of codependency (Cermak, 1986). Hogg and Frank (1992) list some of these common behaviors:

- *Martyrdom:* Giving up one's own needs in order to meet the needs of others
- *Fusion:* Losing one's identity in an intimate relationship
- *Intrusion:* Controlling the behavior of intimates through excessive caretaking, guilt, or manipulation
- *Perfection:* Holding unrealistic expectations of oneself and others
- *Addiction:* Using compulsive behaviors to manage one's emotions (p. 371)

Concerned about the proliferation of characteristics and the potential for overdiagnosis of codependency, Myer, Peterson, and Stoffel-Rosales (1991) urge that research about the etiology and characteristics of codependency be carried out by mental health counselors.

Alcohol Treatment

As mentioned earlier, most professionals believe that the best results occur if counselors insist that clients with an alcohol problem, whether alcoholics or problem drinkers, abstain from drinking as soon as counseling begins. Otherwise, the counselor becomes an enabler by giving tacit permission for continued drinking. And if alcohol abusers continue to drink, the toxic effects of alcohol on their psychological and physical well-being inhibit the development of a counseling relationship and interfere with or distort communication (Forrest, 1984). After assessment of the severity of the individual's alcohol abuse and after detoxification, if necessary, is completed, the majority of treatment programs, regardless of setting, include individual counseling, family counseling, group counseling, auxiliary services, and support groups (Manfrin, 1998).

Individual Counseling

In individual counseling, recovering alcoholics or problem drinkers and their spouses and appropriate family members receive help to develop feelings of self-worth and responsibility for their own behavior. Most important, they learn to express their own needs more directly. And through exploration of childhood experiences, they get in touch with unresolved feelings of anger, grief, or shame that are affecting their current behavior. They also learn new ways of dealing with stress.

Recovering alcoholics and problem drinkers learn not to depend on alcohol during times of stress. Spouses learn not to assume responsibility for the persons recovering from excessive alcohol use, the spouses must not feel compelled to control or manage them. Above all, the spouses must learn not to treat recovering alcoholics as inferior persons.

Individual counseling approaches vary. Psychodynamic approaches may be used to get at the issues and needs underlying the abuse. Cognitive-behavioral strategies, such as stress management and self-monitoring, may be used to help the abuser develop self-control and prevent relapses (Stevens, 2001d).

Family Counseling

In family counseling sessions family counselors—using a family systems approach as described in chapter 10—help family members become aware of their mutual dependence, dysfunctional communication, and family roles that have exacerbated and perpetuated both the alcohol and the codependent addictions. Family members learn to develop appropriate boundaries by expressing their individual needs for independent action and privacy. They practice communicating personal needs, feelings, and emotions in a direct and authentic manner. They work at giving up the enabling or manipulating roles characteristic of their former dysfunctional interactions. "Just as the family learned to organize itself around the substance use, it must now reorganize itself when there is no substance use in the family. This will require the restructuring of family rituals, roles, and rules" (Stevens, 2001a, p. 217).

Through these sessions family members move from shame to respect for themselves and each other (Fossum & Mason, 1986). They respond to new behaviors with healthy expressions of feelings, rather than with old stereotyped protective interactions. They learn how to live more independently of one another and to get on with their own lives. Nace (1987) uses a family systems approach, as well as psychoeducation activities, insight-oriented therapy for individual family members, and group therapy for family members.

Walters, Carter, Papp, and Silverstein (1988) of the Women's Project, as discussed in chapter 10, criticize the traditional approach to treating family dysfunctions, claiming that gender-based, social-cultural roles are imposed on mothers, fathers, daughters, and sons, roles that cause and perpetuate family dysfunctions. Supporting their position, Real (1997) argues persuasively that family dysfunctions are caused by socially determined masculine and feminine roles.

Group Counseling

Group counseling has always been a very popular and preferred type of treatment for recovering substance abusers. Group therapy is especially effective with those recovering from substance abuse because groups provide social support, empowerment, encouragement to counteract ongoing social pressures to take drugs, and resistance to falling back into addictive behaviors (Fletcher, 2001; Stevens, 2001b). Group counseling is equally effective for other members of the recovering alcoholic's family. Typically, persons with a drinking problem meet with other alcoholics or problem drinkers in one group, and spouses and/or other family members meet with other spouses and family members in a different group (Nace, 1987).

In a group setting all clients get feedback from peers, experiment with new behaviors and social skills, experience emotional closeness to others, learn to assert themselves and confront others, and develop spiritual strength helpful to recovery (James & Gilliland, 2001).

Comprehensive Rehabilitation Models

An example of a widely used comprehensive, interdisciplinary treatment format is the Minnesota model of substance abuse treatment (James & Gilliland, 2001; Perez, 2001). Clients participate in a 28-day treatment procedure in which a team of physicians, psychologists, nurses, social workers, mental health counselors, and substance abuse counselors guide clients through three stages of care: detoxification, rehabilitation, and aftercare (Perez, 2001).

After detoxification, clients enter the rehabilitation treatment phase—a stage that can be either an inpatient or an outpatient service. Group therapy, interaction with support groups, family counseling, self-help groups, and interaction with community resources are included in treatment. Aftercare lasts about a year and may include regularly scheduled weekly or biweekly individual, family, and group counseling. "Aftercare helps clients transition into a sober/clean lifestyle that is lasting and integrated into their everyday lives" (Perez, 2001, p. 158).

Auxiliary Services and Support Groups

Alcoholics Anonymous (AA) and related groups (e.g., Al-Anon and Alateen) have been very successful over the years in persuading alcoholics to give up alcohol and in helping them maintain sobriety. Many counselors and therapists, in working with recovering alcoholics, have used AA as an adjunct to their therapy (Fossum & Mason, 1986; James & Gilliland, 2001). AA is a spiritually based 12-step program in which alcoholics acknowledge that they need a power greater than themselves to maintain abstinence (see Table 13.1). They give themselves into the care of a higher power, acknowledge wrongs, make amends, and continue to admit mistakes. They then help other alcoholics find this spiritual help.

Many counselors insist that the alcoholic join AA (Geller, 1992), and family members are encouraged to join affiliates—Al-Anon for spouses and Alateen for teenagers. AA helps build the confidence needed to remain sober and the skills necessary to interact with family members. The affiliates help family members relate and interact with the person recovering from alcohol abuse. Al-Anon and Alateen also help spouses and children learn how to live with nonrecovering alcoholics or when and how to confront them.

Although many professionals believe that AA involvement is an important factor in recovery, some criticize or express caution about its effectiveness. According to Stevens (2001d), some complain that AA success has been based on white, middle-class groups. Others criticize the 12-step approach as reinforcing the powerlessness of women. According to Fletcher (2001), the two major criticisms of AA concerned the "difficulty accepting the 'higher power'/spiritual concept and dislike for AA's focus on the past and the idea that you're in recovery for life" (p. 114). Other shortcomings noted by Fletcher were that AA doesn't use professional counselors; it is "so strongly male-oriented" (p. 114); and it emphasizes powerlessness and passivity, with little or no attempt to help persons restructure themselves and

TABLE 13.1
The Twelve Steps of AA

---

1. We admitted we were powerless over alcohol—that out lives had become unmanageable.
2. We came to belive that a Power greater than ourselves could restore us to sanity.
3. We made a decision to turn our will and our lives over to the care of God as we understood Him.
4. We made a searching and fearless moral inventory of ourselves.
5. We admitted to God, to ourselves, and to another human being, the exact nature of our wrongs.
6. We were entirely ready to have God remove all these defects of character.
7. We humbly asked Him to remove our shortcomings.
8. We made a list of all persons we had harmed, and became willing to make amends to them all.
9. We made direct amends to such people wherever possible, except when to do so would injure others.
10. We continued to take personal inventory and, when we were wrong, promptly admitted it.
11. We sought through prayer and mediation to improve our conscious contact with God as we understood Him, praying only for knowledge of His will for us and the power to carry that out.
12. Having had a spiritual awakening as the result of these steps, we tried to carry this message to alcoholics, and to practice these principles in all our affairs.

Note: Reprinted with permission of Alcoholics Anonymous World Services.

regain a sense of empowerment. In response to this criticism, some groups have modified the AA steps. But despite the criticisms, AA is still regarded as a significant force in the successful treatment of alcoholics, and many are still making testimonials that AA saved their lives (Fletcher, 2001).

For decades, beginning in the 1930s, AA was the *only* treatment program for alcoholics— a program that dignified the patient's addiction, guaranteed a permanent lifeline of support, and kept the patient in sobriety. Similar treatment programs have recently emerged that provide the positive services of AA without its shortcomings. The problem, however, is that alternative treatment programs are difficult to find, and are nonexistent in many communities, whereas AA is very well known. There are more than 50,000 AA groups in the United States but only about 1,000 groups offering alternative programs (Fletcher, 2001).

Even so, more attention is being given to alternative treatment programs as professionals realize that people respond differently to treatment. Many cannot fit the one mold that AA proposes (Fletcher, 2001). And even though all significant treatment programs insist on abstinence and all believe in a commitment, their recovery methods differ widely. SMART Recovery, for example, is a cognitive-behavioral model in which participants practice cognitive restructuring. "They learn how to challenge irrational, self-destructive thoughts—thoughts that often lead to problem drinking—and replace them with more rational ones so they remain sober" (Fletcher, 2001, p. 124).

Therapists Fossum and Mason (1986) at the Family Therapy Institute in St. Paul, Minnesota, believe that all members of a shame-based family are inherently addictive. Thus, family members need to become aware of and endeavor to overcome their own addictive behaviors before other members of the family can successfully stay in recovery. Fossum and Mason use the various 12-step groups as an adjunct to their own therapy. "These mutual help groups meet regularly and focus on a single problem such as alcoholism, bulimia, narcotics, overeating, etc., with one stipulation for membership, the desire to abstain from the compulsive behavior" (p. 124). They point out that many other groups modeling AA have formed—Narcotics Anonymous, Overeaters Anonymous, Gamblers Anonymous, and Sex Addicts Anonymous.

Adult Children of Alcoholics

Approximately 30 million adults have come from alcohol-dependent families and can be classified as *adult children of alcoholics* (ACOAs). ACOAs are 3 or 4 times more likely to become alcoholics than are persons from nonalcoholic families. Some 50% of women ACOAs with alcoholic fathers marry alcoholics. Also, about 55% of people receiving help in EAPs are ACOAs (Ackerman, 1987; James & Gilliland, 2001).

The personality characteristics of ACOAs are similar to those described earlier for codependents; some writers use the terms *codependent* and *ACOA* interchangeably. After reviewing the literature, James and Gilliland (2001) summarized what professionals generally consider to be ACOA characteristics:

> Upon reaching adulthood, the majority of children of alcoholics continue to experience problems related to trust, dependency, control, identification, and expression of feelings. They are people-pleasers who are not able to trust their feelings or instincts about others. They have difficulty saying no and may be manipulated by others and extend themselves beyond any reasonable human capacity. (p. 365)

Ackerman (1987) and Goodman (1987) are concerned that many counselors perceive ACOAs only negatively. Ackerman claims that many positive characteristics of ACOAs are not acknowledged; he sees them as survivors and believes that counselors have much to learn from ACOAs.

The degree and type of maladjustment of the ACOA depend on the severity and type of parental alcoholism, birth order, gender of the ACOA, gender of the alcoholic parent, stress tolerance of the ACOA, childhood perceptions of the problem, current perception of personal adjustment, and influence of important persons in the ACOA's life. The need for and type of treatment should be based on an assessment of all these factors (Ackerman, 1987). Goodman (1987) makes two further points: (a) One cannot assume that all problems of ACOAs can be attributed to the alcohol problem in the family of origin; and (b) other emotionally repressive factors—such as overcontrol, rejection, severe discipline, or overindulgence by parents—may contribute to ACOA dysfunction.

Treatment for ACOAs

Fossum and Mason (1986), Gravitz and Bowden (1986), and Middleton-Moz and Dwinell (1986) have written specifically about counseling and therapy for this group. Middleton-Moz and Dwinell (1986) emphasize helping ACOAs reclaim personal childhood losses by guiding them through depression, experiences of loss, and expression of grief. The first step is the development of an intellectual understanding of what their lives were like in alcoholic families. Clients make genograms to help attain a perspective of the families of origin. They may draw pictures of how they saw themselves during earlier parts of their lives and as they expect themselves to be in the future. These activities help them move to the next step, a deeper emotional experience. Clients are helped to stop denying their feelings, emotions, and pain about past experiences and to develop a trusting relationship with the counselor. This relationship gives the emotional security necessary for clients as they move to the third step, working through the grief processes connected to their losses. These losses, which clients are asked to list, include the love and acceptance they did not receive from parents, loss of the chance to be a child, and loss of friendships, toys, home, and similar deprivations. Particular attention is paid to the effect of anniversaries, holidays, and birthdays on their feelings of loss. Once grieving has been worked through, behavior and attitudes become more productive.

Gravitz and Bowden (1986) divide ACOA recovery into four stages: (a) survival, (b) emergent awareness, (c) core issues, and (d) integration. In the *survival* stage clients feel pain but do not link it to alcoholism in the family of origin. In the *emergent awareness* stage they begin to identify as ACOAs and break out of the taboo against talking about family interactions. In the *core issues* stage clients are ready to explore feelings and behaviors that led them to seek help. Gravitz and Bowden believe that the primary issue to correct is the all-or-none, or black-and-white, way of thinking about behavior and feelings. Once flexibility is attained, clients move to the *integration* stage, wherein they begin to accept themselves, express needs and wants, and have fun without feeling guilty.

As stated earlier, Fossum and Mason (1986) believe that shame based on dysfunctional interactions within a family is at the core of the development and perpetuation of codependent addictive relationships. This idea is considered a major breakthrough in the treatment of alcoholic addiction and the resultant codependent relationship. Subby (1987) writes, "The private shame and mistaken troubled past festers on into adulthood creating an infection of codependent anxiety" (p. 95).

Fossum and Mason (1986) distinguish guilt from shame. *Guilt* involves acknowledging a specific inappropriate or destructive behavior and making amends. This attitude leaves self-esteem intact. *Shame* is a feeling that one is fundamentally unworthy, bad, or inadequate. An inappropriate behavior that hurts or impinges on others is considered so bad by the offender and is accompanied by painful humiliation so deep that the individual feels rejected as a person. This pervasive feeling of shame leaves little room for repairing damage to others or for learning or growing from a mistake. Shame is fostered, reinforced, and perpetuated in alcoholic families, so children carry these feelings into adult relationships. As adults, then, intimate relationships are difficult to establish.

Fossum and Mason (1986) use a family-of-origin approach to help shame-bound families move to respect for themselves. First, they explore early patterns of communications, interactions, rules, and sources of shame that existed in the original family. Next, they move to a deeper stage in which emotions are the focus. They confront denial of family problems, distinguish guilt from shame, and expose old compulsive patterns of controlling. New feelings and behaviors are experienced and practiced in the group and then generalized to life.

A structured group experience for ACOAs described by Gelso and Fretz (1992) includes helping group members learn to trust others, identify and express feelings, and search out patterns in their dysfunctional families that contribute to their own dysfunction. Genograms are used to demonstrate basic family patterns and to facilitate discussion of their own roles in the family. The characteristics of ACOAs are also presented and analyzed.

Recovering ACOAs and Recovering Parents

The relationship between parents who are recovering from alcohol abuse or codependency and their adult children who are ACOAs is an important, complex, and often neglected relationship. Wegscheider-Cruse (1985) insists that recovering parents and ACOAs must treat each other with dignity and respect. Counseling help is especially recommended for those ACOAs who continue to blame the recovering alcoholic and the codependent spouse for all the problems they caused in the past. ACOAs need help in working through their anger and grief to reach understanding and forgiveness.

It is unusual for recovering parents and recovering ACOAs to receive family counseling together. Often they live miles apart, and each ACOA may have her or his own nuclear family. Nevertheless, counselors can develop effective ways to help both parties engage in long-distance healing.

The characteristics of ACOAs described here, such as codependency and shame, were developed by counselors working with adults who grew up in alcoholic families. Mental health professionals have been noticing these same characteristics in adults who were raised in dysfunctional families where alcohol was never consumed. In such families children were similarly deprived emotionally or abused (Fossum & Mason, 1986; James & Gilliland, 2001).

COUNSELING PERSONS WITH DRUG ABUSE PROBLEMS

Types of Drugs

Psychoactive drugs besides alcohol that alter mood and affect the nervous system include marijuana, stimulants, opiates, depressants, and hallucinogens (Comer, 1998; Erickson, 2001; Porter, 1998). These are not only illegal street drugs such as marijuana, cocaine, and heroin, but also prescription drugs used to help people relax, sleep, decrease their pain, or lose weight. As it does with alcohol abuse, tolerance develops with increased use of these drugs, requiring increased dosages for the desired effects. Overuse can lead to physical or emotional impairment and generally leads to addiction and physical dependence, with withdrawal causing physical and emotional disorientation (Comer, 1998).

Illegal drug use "is a problem that affects everyone, and the costs are staggering" (Stevens, 2001c, p. 15). The sharp rise in street crime—robbery, assaults, murder, and gang wars—is attributed to the trafficking in illegal drugs (James & Gilliland, 2001).

Marijuana

After alcohol marijuana is the most widely used drug and is the most socially accepted of the illegal drugs. Over 9 million individuals in the United States use marijuana regularly

(James & Gilliland, 2001). It is well known that chronic marijuana users often suffer from listlessness and lack of motivation (Comer, 1998; Erickson, 2001). Moreover, persons intoxicated from marijuana can suffer from such side effects as delusions and paranoia, hallucinations, and lack of coordination (Erickson, 2001). Regular use of marijuana can damage the body; like heavy alcohol use, extended marijuana use causes bloodshot eyes and increased heart rate and blood pressure, lung damage, and cancer (Comer, 1998; Erikson, 2001). And like cigarette smoking, marijuana causes bronchitis and asthmatic reactions. Furthermore, users are often unaware that marijuana bought on the street can be laced with other, more potent and toxic drugs (Palfai & Jankiewicz, 1991).

Stimulants

Stimulants increase arousal in the nervous system. Amphetamines, such as Dexedrine and Benzedrine, are stimulants obtained by prescription and are commonly known as speed, uppers, or bennies. Because moderate doses increase alertness and reduce fatigue, some students, truck drivers, and athletes use them to help with stress. Stimulants also curb appetite and are used in prescribed and over-the-counter drugs to help people lose weight (Comer, 1998; Erikson, 2001).

Persons taking amphetamines develop tolerance quickly and need dosage increases as much as 200 times or more to attain a desired effect. When drugs are not available or are withdrawn, users become irritated and suspicious, which can lead to violence. Cocaine, which comes from the *coca* (not cocoa) plant, is an illegal stimulant taken to induce euphoria; over 1½ million people in the United States are cocaine users (James & Gilliland, 2001). It can be inhaled, injected intravenously, or smoked in a highly dangerous compound called *crack* (Erickson, 2001). In the 1970s and 1980s, cocaine was a glamorous status drug used by many upwardly mobile people who believed it to be safer than heroin (Burnett, 1979). Early in that period, cocaine was thought to be nonaddictive, and the dangers of the drug were minimized. Research has since shown cocaine to be addictive; both tolerance increase and withdrawal effects occur. As with amphetamines, after an initial euphoric state, restlessness, irritability, and paranoia follow, ending in severe depression (Porter, 1998). Several prominent athletes have died from brain convulsions or cardiovascular failure after ingesting cocaine. Their deaths dramatically changed public opinion about the danger of cocaine addiction.

Opiates (Narcotics)

Opiates (e.g., opium, morphine, and codeine) derive from the opium poppy. Opium has been used for centuries to reduce pain and induce relaxation (Erickson, 2001; Porter, 1998). Codeine is also used in medicine to control coughs and diarrhea (Landy, 1987). Heroin was developed in the late 1800s as a nonaddictive form of opium. However, after two decades, it was found to be addictive and was declared illegal. Today, it is an illegal street drug ingested by smoking, injecting under the skin, or injecting into the bloodstream (*mainlining*).

It is estimated that about 600,000 to 800,000 Americans are heroin addicts (James & Gilliland, 2001). After feeling euphoric for a few hours, heroin users become lethargic and lose interest in food, health, and personal and sexual relationships (Palfai & Jankiewicz, 1991). All opiate users are highly susceptible to physical dependence on the drug and require high dosages to maintain euphoria. Overdose on heroin can be fatal (Comer, 1998; Sue, Sue, & Sue, 2000).

Depressants (Sedatives/Hypnotics)

Depressants are pharmaceutical drugs prescribed either to sedate or to tranquilize people (Sue, Sue, & Sue, 2000). Barbiturates, such as Seconal and Nembutal, help persons with insomnia; and minor tranquilizers—like Valium, Miltown, and Librium—are used to reduce anxiety (Erickson, 2001). Barbiturates are addictive, causing withdrawal symptoms similar to those of alcohol. Accidental overdosage can lead to death. They are particularly lethal because the death-producing dose remains the same even though addicts must take higher and higher dosages to get an effect (Sue, Sue, & Sue, 2000). Minor tranquilizers can also be addictive for persons prone to avoiding problems and painful situations. Physicians have been criticized for prescribing Valium and Miltown too readily without considering their addictive qualities and monitoring patient's use (Erickson, 2001).

Hallucinogens (Psychedelics)

Hallucinogens include the drugs lysergic acid diethylamide (LSD) and phencyclidine (PCP, angel dust); mescaline, derived from peyote cactus; and psilocybin, derived from a type of mushroom. They produce major alterations in sensation, emotion, and perception (Erickson, 2001). Although many users have described their experiences as wonderful mind-altering trips, these drugs have also caused psychotic reactions requiring extended hospitalization (Sue, Sue, & Sue, 2000). In addition, LSD has caused panic attacks lasting from 2 to 4 days and flashbacks in which a previous LSD trip is repeated even though the person has not taken the drug for months or years. "Flashbacks may occur days or even months after the last LSD experience . . . some people report flashbacks five years or more after taking LSD" (Comer, 1998, p. 422).

Treatment of Drug Abuse

Physical addiction to prescribed drugs occurs when physicians overprescribe stimulants, sedatives, or tranquilizers for persons expressing anxiety or experiencing pain or depression. When some patients become dependent on a drug or need higher dosages, they may obtain duplicate prescriptions from several physicians. Others will shop for a physician who will prescribe a drug when their own physician refuses to do so. If taken over a long period without treatment for emotional or physical disorders, drugs mask a person's turmoil and pain and inhibit opportunities for the person to confront and improve or resolve the cause of the problem.

People become addicted to or dependent on illegal street drugs because the drugs fulfill their need to withdraw or escape from painful reactions to life. Temporary feelings of euphoria and power inhibit confrontation of problems the individuals are experiencing.

A further complication arises when addicts, desperate to buy increasing dosages, end up stealing, selling drugs, or becoming prostitutes to maintain their drug habit. Thus, they become involved in dual criminality—illegal drug use and the resultant criminal acts. Treatment and rehabilitation become even more complex when they are combined with prison terms. Today, drug abusers must also contend with the high probability of becoming afflicted with the human immunodeficiency virus (HIV), which causes acquired immune deficiency syndrome (AIDS), from contaminated needles used to inject drugs (see chapter 14).

Types of Treatment

Treatment programs for drug abuse parallel those of alcohol abuse, described earlier. Individual, group, and family counseling are essential components of treatment. Some drug abuse counselors put a heavier emphasis on inpatient residential treatment programs with a highly structured and protected environment. In part, they believe that these settings protect drug addicts from the influences of drug pushers and peer pressure.

Synanon, the best-known residential treatment center for drug addicts, is run by recovering addicts. The center emphasizes aggressive confrontation, shaming techniques, and complete isolation of addicts until they attain abstinence. After completion of the program, counselors believe that recovering addicts must maintain attachment to Synanon for the remainder of their lives. Other residential treatment programs—Phoenix House and Day-Top Village, for example—are less aggressively confrontational. They encourage patients to disengage from the residence after they complete the program (Comer, 1998).

Residential or semiresidential treatment centers for drug addiction commonly practice behavior modification and social learning theory. Aversion techniques, described in chapter 6, are sometimes used to extinguish the need for drugs; electric shocks may be administered while a person takes the drug or views someone taking the drug. Also, modeling and social reinforcement techniques are used to substitute activities or experiences for drugs in order to satisfy needs (Erickson, 2001).

Methadone, an addictive drug, is used to combat heroin addiction. Persons gradually transfer addiction to the less dangerous and less physically damaging methadone. Dosages are administered to addicts at clinics on a prescribed schedule; and although controversial, methadone treatment is still commonly used with heroin addicts. Outcome research indicates that methadone treatment is more effective when combined with counseling or therapy, family involvement, career counseling, and education (Comer, 1998).

YOUTHS AND SUBSTANCE ABUSE

Concern about teenage substance abuse began in the late 1960s. At that time adolescents were following a trend in American society and experimenting with alcohol and drugs. Since that time teenagers' use of drugs has more than tripled. After reviewing the literature, Schliebner-Tait and Peregoy (2001) summarized the extensive data that point to the seriousness of the problem of alcohol and drug consumption among young people:

Youth involved with alcohol and drugs pose a major problem not only to themselves but also to the community as a whole. . . . Among the graduating class of 1997, 54.3% of students had used an illicit drug by the time they reached their senior year of high school. . . . By eighth grade, approximately 55% of children had used alcohol, 46% had used tobacco, 22% had used inhalants, and 20% had used marijuana. Furthermore, about 25% of all school-age youth are children of alcoholics. (p. 239).

In a study of teenage drinking conducted by the National Center on Addiction and Substance Abuse, it was reported that teenage drinking has become an epidemic (*Bellingham Herald,* Feb. 27, 2002). The Centers for Disease Control reported that binge drinking has increased 17 percent among the general population and 56 percent among 18- to 20-year-olds (*Bellingham Herald,* Jan. 1, 2003).

Marijuana use among young people dropped during the 1980s and early 1990s, apparently because of drug education programs. Recently, however, despite continued drug education, marijuana use has been increasing among young people. According to the National Institute on Drug Abuse (NIDA, 1995, as cited in Comer, 1998), more than 5% of high school seniors smoke marijuana every day.

Substance abuse, particularly alcohol, the leading cause of teenage deaths, clearly points to a crisis in schools and communities, a crisis that is exacerbated now that many youngsters have easy access to automatic weapons. Counselors and health professionals are concerned as well about the effects this abuse has on adolescent development and health. Adolescents who learn patterns of avoidance during formative years will find them difficult to change. In addition, nutritional deficiencies arising from substance abuse are more damaging physically to the growing adolescent than to the mature adult. And adolescents, more than adults, are often away from home when they drink, which means they probably drive while drunk more often than adults do. Although federal, state, and local agencies have been funded to set up clinics, the directors of these clinics complain that funds that would be better spent on treatment are being used to test people for drug use. Counseling services in public schools, colleges, and communities have developed educational and therapeutic programs that focus on teenage substance abuse; these are discussed in chapters 16, 17, and 18.

Almost all drug use begins in preadolescent or adolescent years. Oetting and Beauvais (1988) point out that young people in particular tend to form what Oetling and Beauvais call *peer clusters*—gangs, church groups, Boy Scouts, best friends, and relatives, for example. Such groups contribute to socialization and identity in positive ways, but some also contribute to initiating and maintaining drug use. Drug prevention programs must consider the influence of peer clusters on the drug abuser: These programs will be successful only if new peers are chosen or if peer clusters themselves discourage drug use.

After a review of treatment programs for adolescents with substance abuse problems, Polcin (1992) presented a comprehensive model of treatment that integrates the various programs. That model can be seen at Thunder Road Adolescent Treatment Center in Oakland, California, which is an inpatient facility. Its phases of treatment include orientation and education, dealing with emotional core issues in counseling and family groups, and preparation to leave. Clients are able to practice new coping mechanisms before returning to the community.

SUBSTANCE ABUSE IN OLDER ADULTS

Substance abuse among older adults is an increasing problem in our society, especially as greater numbers of people are living longer. The areas of concern are abuse of alcohol, use and misuse of prescription drugs, and indiscriminate use of over-the-counter drugs to self-medicate (Schliebner-Tait & Peregoy, 2001). Lack of structured activity, separation from family, and loss of spouse and friends can lead to depression, anxiety, and insecurity in older adults, which in turn can lead to substance abuse.

According to the Hazelden Corporation (as cited in Schliebner-Tait & Peregoy, 2001), "20 percent of hospitalized older adults are diagnosed with alcoholism, and nearly 70 percent are hospitalized with alcohol-related problems" (p. 244). Physicians, reinforced by managed care's emphasis on treatment efficiency, are quick to prescribe medication; one-third of the 1.5 billion prescriptions each year are for the elderly, with older adults averaging 13 different prescriptions per year. Assuming that most of these prescriptions serve ongoing chronic conditions of older age, the average older person takes many pills every day. And often no one monitors the interaction of various medicines prescribed by different physicians and/or over-the-counter drugs purchased by older adults. This sort of substance abuse can be not only addictive—but also fatal.

Both older adults and their families need to be educated about the risks involved in substance abuse and self-medication. Both the type and the amount of medication require monitoring. And when substance abuse is diagnosed in older adults, it is crucial that they be referred for treatment: "If the problem is acknowledged and treated, older adults have a very high rate of success in treatment. It is getting them into treatment that is difficult" (Schliebner-Tait & Peregoy, 2001, p. 246).

RELAPSE PREVENTION

One of the most difficult problems in substance abuse treatment is preventing those in recovery from relapsing into their former patterns. After clients leave a supportive treatment environment, they may be influenced by social pressures, increased personal stress, or a return to low self-esteem. If their coping skills are not sufficiently developed, if they have a pessimistic attitude about their ability to control themselves, or if family and community are not supportive, they may relapse into substance abuse.

Thus, strategies to prevent relapse are essential components of treatment plans (Annis & Davis, 1991; Nystul, 1993; Peel, 1988; Stevens, 2001d). Noteworthy relapse prevention models are those that take into consideration psychosocial and environmental factors influencing the recovering individual. Persons with few complicating emotional problems tend to avoid a relapse if they have good jobs and adequate living conditions and they take care of their physical well-being. The availability of counseling to the families of former abusers also cuts back on the possibilities of relapse. Recovering abusers in high-risk situations are those faced with "interpersonal conflict, negative emotional state, and social pressure" (Stevens, 2001d, p. 279). The ease with which individuals can return to their former lifestyle—such as frequenting a certain bar or joining old cronies for drinks—also heightens the risk of relapse (Stevens, 2001d).

According to Fletcher (2001), occasions when the recovering person falls back into a drinking binge can serve as an opportunity for a recovering client to explore with a substance abuse counselor the precipitating factors that led to the relapse (Fletcher, 2001). Social learning and cognitive-behavioral techniques have been used to prevent relapses (Stevens, 2001d). Social learning helps clients build up their own capacities to monitor themselves by keeping logs and journals about their feelings and behaviors. In this way they are more able to anticipate problems and check with counselors. Exploring the feelings that precipitate compulsive urges to drink—such as anger, moodiness, and depression—helps clients gain control of their lives (Fletcher, 2001). Cognitive-behavioral models focus on helping clients make comprehensive changes in lifestyle—changes that involve exercise, relaxation, diet, and cognitive restructuring that will bring about new coping skills. In this way positive habits replace negative ones (Stevens, 2001d).

Many researchers now believe that relapse is inevitable for most recovering addicts until issues underlying addictive behaviors are addressed and remedied. As mentioned earlier, according to Fossum and Mason (1986) and Kasl (1989), feelings of shame that stem from shame-based families underlie addictive behaviors, and all members of the family share and maintain the addiction. If one family member is an alcoholic, for example, the addictive behaviors of other members—such as eating disorders, compulsive spending, gambling, sexual compulsions, or overwork—may not be noticeable. Yet all the compulsive behaviors are similar in that they are meant to overcome the feelings of the family-held shame. Real (1997) concurs with these underlying issues of addiction, claiming further that, as previously stated, all addictive behaviors among males are defenses against male depression (see chapter 14).

Stevens (2001c) comments on the similarities of behavior patterns among those who are addicted. Those with addictive behaviors—those who are compulsively dependent upon a substance or who compulsively enact certain behaviors—have a disorder she terms *process addiction.*

> Process addiction refers to eating disorders, gambling, sexuality, shopping, working, and/or any other process (or behavior) in which one's behavior fits the criteria for 'dependence.' Although there may be some differences in each of these behavioral manifestations, the similarity of behaviors leads many in the field to address these issues as abuse and dependency issues. (p. 26)

She notes further that there is considerable evidence that individuals with this form of addiction typically grew up in families that have a history of substance abuse "and/or have a dual diagnosis of substance abuse/dependency with their process addiction" (p. 26). Stevens (2001c) points out commonalties among those with eating disorders, those who are pathological gamblers, and those who are substance abusers:

> The obvious commonalities of eating disorders with other dependent behaviors is the compulsive behavior, the sense of powerlessness, the obsessive thought of food, and the learned ability to avoid feeling through the abuse of food. . . .
>
> Pathological gambling . . . has much in common with substance dependency. Individuals cannot resist the urge to wager money. The process is chronic and progressive, resulting in unmanageable debt and loss of friends, family, and possibly work. Both eating disorder individuals and pathological gamblers have a high degree of denial as a symptom of the problem. (p. 26)

Some persons have multiple addictions; others fall into a new addictive behavior after overcoming another or develop an addictive behavior after the primary addict in the family, the identified patient (IP), has abstained and is in recovery. Recognizing and treating the underlying feelings of family shame, as well as overcoming the various addictions within the family system, are necessary in preventing relapse (Fossum & Mason, 1986; Kasl, 1989).

TRAINING OF SUBSTANCE ABUSE COUNSELORS

Although the qualifications of substance abuse counselors traditionally have been their personal experiences as former substance abusers and even though many have worked effectively in treatment programs, most professionals now realize the necessity of adequate training programs for substance abuse counselors. Substance abuse cases are increasing in alarming numbers, and addiction issues have become more complex. Yet researchers claim that training programs greatly enhance counselor effectiveness in treating substance abusers (Smith, 2001).

Increasing numbers of universities are offering master's degree training programs specializing in substance abuse counseling. At the same time certification standards for substance abuse counselors have been set up by the International Association for Addictions and Offenders (IAAOC) in conjunction with the National Board for Certified Counselors (NBOC). To obtain a master addiction counselor certification (MAC) under these standards, one must complete a master's degree with a specialty in substance abuse counseling that includes a supervised internship (Smith, 2001). Some states have also set up training standards for individuals who want to work as a substance abuse counselor. To qualify as a certified addiction counselor (CAC), the individual must meet certain state standards that often include a master's degree in counseling, social work, or psychology.

OUTCOME RESEARCH: SUBSTANCE ABUSE TREATMENT

Until Alcoholics Anonymous began in the early 1930s, alcoholism was considered incurable. Currently, alcoholism is considered one of the more treatable problems. More outcome research has been done on alcohol treatment than on other drug treatments. Alcohol treatment programs have also demonstrated more effective results, compared with those of other drug treatments (Smith, 2001).

Research studies on the treatment of substance abuse are limited in number and scope (Smith, 2001). Studies are limited because the causes of substance abuse are complex, treatment methods are varied and not standardized, many substance abusers are involved in different treatments at the same time, and centers using multidimensional approaches often cannot specify which modality is contributing to client change (Smith, 2001). Smith (2001) points out that multidimensional programs are the most often recommended treatment of choice:

Today most substance abuse treatment programs favor a multidimensional approach when dealing with addictions.

Multidimensional or multimodality treatment approaches include a variety of interventions such as detoxification, individual counseling, group counseling, family therapy, inpatient treatment, and education. . . .Yet, research studies demonstrating treatment combinations that might work best as a multidimensional model are nonexistent. (pp. 334–335)

Issues needing more research include the validity of the disease model of alcoholism; determination of whether abstinence is the only acceptable goal; treatment options that take into account gender differences in patterns of substance abuse; the level and type of training for substance abuse counselors; ethical issues over confidentiality; counselor burnout; substance abuse issues related to ethnic minorities; and the use of medications as treatment (Smith, 2001).

SUMMARY

Almost 14 million Americans (more than 7% of adults) can be classified as alcoholics or problem drinkers who have an uncontrollable desire to drink (Fletcher, 2001). "Probably everyone has used/abused, has an abuser in the family, has a close friend that has abused, or knows someone who uses alcohol or other drugs inappropriately" (Stevens, 2001c, p. 1). The major characteristic of an alcoholic is a physical dependence on alcohol, which leads to serious physical reactions when alcohol is withdrawn. Problem drinkers drink excessively and are psychologically dependent on alcohol. Both alcoholics and problem drinkers strongly deny having a drinking problem and resist treatment. Their families may need to confront the alcohol abusers about their problem and explain that they must get treatment if they expect family members to remain with them.

Many researchers claim that substance abuse is one of many addictive behaviors used to mask or alleviate deeper emotional feelings of shame generated and maintained by shame-based families and, with males in particular, used to mask or deny feelings of male depression. Individuals must therapeutically work through underlying issues of shame and depression to overcome addictive behaviors.

The spouses and families of alcohol abusers also need treatment because they typically are involved in family dynamics that enmesh them in a dysfunctional, codependent relationship, which enables the alcoholic to continue drinking. Considerable attention has been given to the problems of adult children of alcoholics (ACOAs) and the codependency in their relationships. Most recently, the influence of shame generated in shame-based families has been recognized as a major contributor to codependency.

Traditionally, abstinence has been the primary pretreatment condition for alcoholics and for the majority of problem drinkers, but a growing number of reports indicate that treatment varies among individuals and, for some problem drinkers, monitored controlled drinking may work. Individual, group, and family counseling is offered by counselors in outpatient and inpatient treatment centers, private practice, or EAPs in business. Support groups such as Alcoholics Anonymous (AA), Al-Anon, Alateen, and a cognitive restructuring program called SMART Recovery are valuable adjuncts to psychological treatment. Collaboration between professional counselors and AA has been increasing.

Drug addiction has reached epidemic proportions. Street crime has increased because addicts may rob, assault, or murder others to get money to pay the exorbitant fees demanded by drug dealers. Treatment for drug addiction parallels that of alcohol treatment, except that for drug addicts heavier emphasis is placed on inpatient residential care.

Because of the increasing crisis in substance abuse among young people, counseling and educational services directed at the prevention and treatment of alcohol and drug abuse have been developed in public schools, colleges, and the community.

PROJECTS AND ACTIVITIES

1. Survey the community in which you live to determine what programs are available for treatment of alcohol and drug dependency.
2. Interview a school counselor in a junior high or middle school and one in a senior high school. Ask for their impressions about the seriousness of the problem of substance abuse in their school districts.
3. Visit an alcohol center and ask the director what procedures are used to confront alcoholics when families request help. Do you consider those procedures consistent with effective counseling practices?
4. Develop a plan you might use if you were a counselor in a school, college, or community to help prevent alcohol or drug abuse.
5. Contact a counselor in a community clinic and one in a school to ask how they handle a client who comes in with a drinking problem or whose drinking problem emerges during the counseling sessions.
6. Try to discover what type of relationship exists between Alcoholics Anonymous, Alateen, and Al-Anon and professional counselors and therapists in schools, agencies, and private practice.
7. The latest theorizing about alcoholism focuses on the family relationships in an alcoholic family. Are agencies or private practitioners in your area involving families in alcohol and drug counseling? What kinds of problems do you see, if any, in involving the family? How can these problems be resolved?

REFERENCES

Ackerman, R. J. (1987). Adult children of alcoholics. *EAP Digest, 7,* 25–29.

American Psychiatric Association. (2000). *Diagnostic and statistical manual of mental disorders* (4th ed., text revision). Washington, DC: Author.

Annis, H. M., & Davis, C. S. (1991). Relapse prevention. *Alcohol Health & Research World, 15,* 175–177.

Beattie, M. (1987). *Codependent no more.* New York: Harper & Row.

Belkin, G. S. (1984). *Introduction to counseling* (2nd ed.). Dubuque, IA: William C. Brown.

Bennett, L. W. (1992). Linking domestic assault and addictions. *The Counselor, 10,* 18–22.

Burnett, M. (1979). Understanding and overcoming addictions. In S. Eisenberg & J. E. Patterson (Eds.), *Helping clients with special concerns* (pp. 343–362). Chicago: Rand-McNally.

Calahan, D., Cisin, I. H., & Crossley, H. M. (1969). *American drinking practices: A national study of drinking behaviors and attitudes.* New Brunswick, NJ: Rutgers Center of Alcohol Studies.

Cermak, T. L. (1986). Children of alcoholics and the case for a new diagnostic category of codependency. In R. J. Ackerman (Ed.), *Growing in the shadow: Children of alcoholics* (pp. 23–31). Pompano Beach, FL: Health Communications.

Chamberlain, L. L., & Jew, C. L. Assessment and diagnosis. In P. Stevens & R. L. Smith (Eds.), *Substance abuse counseling: Theory and practice* (2nd ed., pp. 113–141). Upper Saddle River, NJ: Merrill/Prentice Hall.

Comer, R. (1998). *Abnormal psychology* (3rd ed.). New York: Freeman.

Dickman, J. F., & Phillips, E. A. (1985). Alcoholism: A pervasive rehabilitation issue. In J. F. Dickman, W. G. Emener, Jr., & W. S. Hutchison, Jr. (Eds.), *Counseling the troubled person in industry* (pp. 99–115). Springfield, IL: Charles C Thomas.

Erickson, S. (2001). Etiological theories of substance abuse. In P. Stevens & R. L. Smith (Eds.), *Substance abuse counseling: Theory and practice* (2nd ed., pp. 77–112). Upper Saddle River, NJ: Merrill/Prentice Hall.

Fletcher, A. M. (2001). *Sober for good.* Boston: Houghton-Mifflin.

Forrest, G. G. (1984). *Intensive psychotherapy of alcoholism.* Springfield, IL: Charles C Thomas.

Fossum, M. A., & Mason, M. J. (1986). *Facing shame: Families in recovery.* New York: Norton.

Geller, A. (1992). Rehabilitation programs and halfway houses. In J. H. Lowinson, R. Ruiz, R. B. Millman, & J. B. Langrod (Eds.), *Substance abuse: A comprehensive textbook* (pp. 458–466). Baltimore, MD: Williams & Wilkins.

Gelso, C. J., & Fretz, B. R. (1992). *Counseling psychology.* Fort Worth, TX: Harcourt Brace.

Gladding, S. (2002). *Family therapy: History, theory and practice* (3rd ed.). Upper Saddle River, NJ: Merrill/Prentice Hall.

Goodman, R. W. (1987). Adult children of alcoholics. *Journal of Counseling & Development, 66,* 162–163.

Goodwin, D. W. (1992). Alcohol: Clinical aspects. In J. H. Lowinson, R. Ruiz, R. B. Millman, & J. B. Langrod (Eds.), *Substance abuse: A comprehensive textbook* (pp. 144–151). Baltimore, MD: Williams & Wilkins.

Gravitz, H., & Bowden, J. (1986). Therapeutic issues of adult children of alcoholics: A continuum of developmental stages. In R. J. Ackerman (Ed.), *Growing in the shadow: Children of alcoholics* (pp. 187–207). Pompano Beach, FL: Health Communications.

Hogg, J. A., & Frank, M. L. (1992). Toward an interpersonal model of codependence and contradependence. *Journal of Counseling & Development, 70,* 371–375.

James, R. K., & Gilliland, B. E. (2001). *Crisis intervention strategies* (4th ed.). Belmont, CA: Brooks/Cole.

Kasl, C. D. (1989). *Women, sex, and addiction: Search for love and power.* New York: Harper & Row.

Landy, F. J. (1987). *Psychology: The science of people* (2nd ed.). Upper Saddle River, NJ: Prentice Hall.

Manfrin, C. (1998). Treatment settings. In P. Stevens-Smith & R. L. Smith (Eds.), *Substance abuse counseling: Theory and practice* (2nd ed., pp. 135–165). Upper Saddle River, NJ: Merrill/Prentice Hall.

Metzger, L. (1988). *From denial to recovery.* San Francisco: Jossey-Bass.

Middleton-Moz, J., & Dwinell, L. (1986). *After the tears.* Pompano Beach, FL: Health Communications.

Miller, R. H., & Rollnick, S. (1991). *Motivational interviewing: Preparing people to change addictive behavior.* New York: Guilford Press.

Mueller, L. A., & Ketcham, K. (1987). *Recovering: How to get and stay sober.* New York: Bantam.

Myer, R. A., Peterson, S. E., & Stoffel-Rosales, M. (1991). Codependency: An examination of underlying assumptions. *Journal of Mental Health Counseling, 13,* 449–458.

Nace, E. P. (1987). *The treatment of alcoholism.* New York: Brunner/Mazel.

National Institute on Drug Abuse (NIDA). (1995). *Facts about teenagers and drug abuse.* Rockville, MD: Author.

Nystul, M. S. (1993). *The art and science of counseling and psychotherapy.* New York: Macmillan.

Oetting, E. R., & Beauvais, F. (1988). Common elements in youth drug abuse: Peer clusters and other psychosocial factors. In S. Peel (Ed.), *Visions of addiction: Major contemporary perspectives on addiction and alcoholism* (pp. 141–161). Lexington, MA: Lexington Books.

O'Keefe, P. (1988). When the alcoholic refuses treatment. *Alcoholism and Addiction, 9,* 14.

Palfai, T., & Jankiewicz, H. (1991). *Drugs and human abuse.* Dubuque, IA: William C. Brown.

Peel, S. (1988). A moral vision of addiction: How people's values determine whether they become addicts. In S. Peel (Ed.), *Visions of addiction: Major contemporary perspectives on addiction and alcoholism* (pp. 203–233). Lexington, MA: Lexington Books.

Peer, G. G., Lindsey, A. K., & Newman, P. A. (1982). Alcoholism as a stage phenomena: A frame of reference for counselors. *Personnel and Guidance Journal, 60,* 465–469.

Perez, P. (2001). Treatment setting and treatment planning. In P. Stevens & R. L. Smith (Eds.), *Substance abuse counseling: Theory and practice* (2nd ed., pp. 151–176). Upper Saddle River, NJ: Merrill/Prentice Hall.

Polcin, D. L. (1992). A comprehensive model for adolescent chemical dependency treatment. *Journal of Counseling & Development, 70,* 376–382.

Porter, J. (1998). The major drugs of abuse and their addictive properties. In P. Stevens-Smith & R. L. Smith (Eds.), *Substance abuse counseling: Theory and practice* (pp. 65–96). Upper Saddle River, NJ: Merrill/Prentice Hall.

Price, R. H., & Lynn, S. J. (1986). *Abnormal psychology* (2nd ed.). Chicago: Dorsey Press.

Real, T. (1997). *I don't want to talk about it.* New York: Fireside.

Robinson, T. L., & Howard-Hamilton, M. F. (2000). *The convergence of race, ethnicity and gender.* Upper Saddle River, NJ: Merrill/Prentice Hall.

Schaef, A. W. (1986). *Codependence: Misunderstood—mistreated.* San Francisco: Harper & Row.

Schliebner-Tait, C., & Peregoy, J. J. (2001). Working with selected populations: Treatment issues and characteristics. In P. Stevens & R. L. Smith (Eds.), *Substance abuse counseling:*

Theory and practice (2nd ed., pp. 227–250). Upper Saddle River, NJ: Merrill/Prentice Hall.

Smith, R. L. (2001). Research and contemporary issues. In P. Stevens & R. L. Smith (Eds.), *Substance abuse counseling: Theory and practice* (2nd ed., pp. 321–347). Upper Saddle River, NJ: Merrill/Prentice Hall.

Stevens, P. (2001a). Family therapy and substance abuse treatment. In P. Stevens & R. L. Smith (Eds.), *Substance abuse counseling: Theory and practice,* (2nd ed., pp. 201–226). Upper Saddle River, NJ: Merrill/Prentice Hall.

Stevens, P. (2001b). Individual and group treatment. In P. Stevens & R. L. Smith (Eds.), *Substance abuse counseling: Theory and practice* (2nd ed., pp. 179–200). Upper Saddle River, NJ: Merrill/Prentice Hall.

Stevens, P. (2001c). Introduction to substance abuse counseling. In P. Stevens & R. L. Smith (Eds.), *Substance abuse counseling: Theory and practice* (2nd ed., pp. 1–32). Upper Saddle River, NJ: Merrill/Prentice Hall.

Stevens, P. (2001d). Maintaining behavior change: Relapse prevention strategies. In P. Stevens & R. L. Smith (Eds.), *Substance abuse counseling: Theory and practice* (2nd ed., pp. 277–320). Upper Saddle River, NJ: Merrill/Prentice Hall.

Subby, R. (1987). *Lost in the shuffle: The codependent reality.* Pompano Beach, FL: Health Communications.

Sue, D., Sue, D. W., & Sue, S. (2000). *Understanding abnormal behavior* (6th ed.). Boston: Houghton Mifflin.

Sue, D. W., & Sue, D. (2003). *Counseling the culturally diverse: Theory and practice.* New York John Wiley.

Valiant, G. E., & Milofsky, E. S. (1982). The etiology of alcoholism: A prospective viewpoint. *American Psychologist, 37,* 494–503.

Walters, M., Carter, B., Papp, O., & Silverstein, O. (Eds.). (1988). *The invisible web: Gender patterns in family relationships.* New York: Guilford Press.

Wegscheider-Cruse, S. (1985). *Choice making.* Pompano Beach, FL: Health Communications.

CHAPTER 14

Counseling in a Pluralistic World

Acknowledging that the United States is a pluralistic society, the counseling profession has been making efforts to address the multicultural needs of the population by attending to the social-cultural characteristics of the various ethnic groups (e.g., African Americans, Hispanics, Asians, Native Americans), to the particular gender issues of women and men, and to the special concerns of lesbians, gays, and bisexuals. The professional counseling literature has been giving increasing attention to the ways counselor training can be improved so that counselors can work more effectively with clients from these groups. The major emphasis is on helping counselors become aware of their own potential biases, accept those with differing social and cultural beliefs, and adapt techniques and skills to the special characteristics of persons from diverse groups.

ETHNIC GROUPS: MULTICULTURAL COUNSELING

"An ethnic group is a culturally distinct population whose members share a collective identity and a common heritage" (Baruth & Manning, 2003, p. 9). Because of their differences, ethnic groups often experience discrimination when they interact with others outside their group. Although each ethnic group and each individual within each ethnic group experience varying degrees of discrimination, three common reactions result from these negative interactions: (a) a feeling of powerlessness, (b) a feeling of lack of control over one's environment, and (c) a loss of personal identity (Ponterotto & Casas, 1991; Sue & Sue, 2003).

No other nation in the world has the ethnic diversity of the United States (McGoldrick, Giordano, & Pearce, 1996). In their books on counseling minority client populations, Pedersen, Draguns, Lonner, and Trimble (2002) and Sue and Sue (2003) discuss the four major ethnic groups in the United States: Native Americans, Hispanics, Asian Americans, and African Americans. McGoldrick, Giordano, and Pearce (1996) include not only these groups but also immigrants from Europe, Jewish families, and Slavic families.

Multicultural professionals emphasize that minority groups should not be equated with low-income groups, as is commonly done by the White majority. They say that minority groups are represented at all socioeconomic levels and although proportionally more low-income people are in minority populations, in absolute figures more Whites than non-Whites are poor.

For minorities the everyday stresses that all people experience are exacerbated by political, economic, or religious discrimination. To further the difficulty, if counseling is sought, most ethnic clients see counselors who are from the White middle class. Ethnic counselors and psychologists emphasize that their professions must attend to the concerns of ethnic minorities. Ponterotto and Casas (1991) and Sue, Arredondo, and McDavis (1992) indicate that early in the 21st century, the white majority will become a minority because of increasing immigration rates and decreasing White birthrates. Sue et al. comment:

> The 1990 U.S. Census reveals that the United States is fast undergoing some very radical demographic changes. Projections show that by the year 2000, more than one third of the population will be racial and ethnic minorities, with even higher numbers (45%) in our public schools. By the year 2010, fewer than 20 years from now, racial and ethnic minorities will become a numerical majority, with white Americans constituting approximately 48% of the population. (p. 478)

Definition of Multicultural Counseling

Multicultural counseling, also known as *cross-cultural counseling,* is defined by Sue et al. (1982) as "any counseling relationship in which two or more participants differ with respect to cultural background, values and life style" (p. 47). Similarly, Pedersen (1988) defines *multicultural counseling* as "a situation in which two or more persons with different ways of perceiving their social environment are brought together in a helping relationship" (p. viii). All counseling is, to some degree, multicultural because in every counseling relationship counselors and clients bring different cultural values and influences and different social roles into the sessions. Speight, Myers, Cox, and Highlen (1991) point out that a White counselor working with an ethnic client is only one example of multicultural counseling. "Female counselors with male clients, lesbian counselors with straight clients, Jewish counselors with Buddhist clients, elderly counselors with teenage clients all must answer the question of how to effectively work together regardless of differences" (p. 30). Pedersen (1991) and Ponterotto and Casas (1991) claim that because multiculturalism is relevant throughout counseling, it qualifies as a fourth force in psychology, joining psychoanalysis, behaviorism, and humanism.

Lee and Richardson (1991) are concerned about broadening the definitions of multiculturalism: "As the term has been increasingly stretched to include virtually any group of people who consider themselves *different,* the extent of multicultural counseling theory and practice has become unclear" (p. 6). Locke (1990) also cautions that an overgeneralized view of multiculturalism suggests that "racism is no different from problems experienced by white persons who suffer from social devaluation" (p. 20).

Counselors need to be aware of multicultural differences with all their clients—differences in values, socioeconomic status, gender, and age. At the same time the uniqueness of each client—regardless of race, gender, or age—needs to be acknowledged to prevent stereotyping.

Sue & Sue (2003) offer a comprehensive definition of multicultural counseling:

> Multicultural counseling and therapy can be defined as both a helping role and process that uses modalities and defines goals consistent with the life experiences and cultural values of clients, recognizes client identities to include individual, group, and universal dimensions, advocates the use of universal and culture-specific strategies and roles in the healing process, and balances the importance of individualism and collectivism in the assessment, diagnosis, and treatment of client and client systems. (p. 16)

Early Work

Before the 1970s counseling of ethnic individuals received very little attention. Few persons from ethnic groups were using available mental health services, and those who did showed a significant dropout rate. In a 1977 survey Sue found that 50% of ethnic clients dropped out of counseling after the first interview, compared with 30% of Caucasian clients.

At first, ethnic psychologists made three overall recommendations to reduce the resistance of ethnic minorities to counseling. First, they urged that counselor training be improved so that counselors would become more aware of cultural differences between the White middle class and ethnic groups. Second, they suggested that counselors be highly directive with ethnic clients by giving advice and specific suggestions on how to resolve a problem, rather than by talking with clients about their feelings. Third, they advocated that counselors and clients be matched ethnically to improve the chances of successful counseling outcomes.

Although these suggestions made some improvements in mental health services for ethnic groups, research has shown that they also contributed to a different set of problems. According to Margolis and Rungta (1986), counselor educators and counselors, in their early efforts to overcome stereotypes, only perpetuated the problem. Counselors began responding to ethnic clients as members of a group with specific stereotypical characteristics, rather than treating clients as individuals (Smith & Stewart, 1983). In addition, counselors were perceiving minority differences as deficits, which further contributed to clients' feelings of alienation and powerlessness.

Moreover, in their attempts to use special directive counseling techniques with their minority clients, counselors neglected their clients' individual needs. For example, in writing about Black clients, Smith (1977) objected to the frequency with which direct, task-oriented intervention techniques were recommended specifically for Blacks. Her view was that "once the members of the counseling profession start proposing techniques on the basis of race and socioeconomic class alone, they are surely treading in dangerous waters" (p. 393). She continued, "Black clients should be treated as individuals first and secondly as members of a particular racial group" (p. 394).

Professional Issues

Professional counselors and therapists are now giving considerable attention to the following issues in ethnic counseling:

- Counselor characteristics
- Counselor competencies
- Ethnic client characteristics
- Racial/cultural identity of ethnic clients
- Theories and techniques of multicultural counseling
- Training in multicultural counseling

Counselor Characteristics

The common core elements in a counseling relationship apply to ethnic clients, as well as to White, middle-class clients. Trust must be built in a counseling relationship, in which the ethnic client is seen as a unique individual to whom the counselor responds with warmth, sincerity, and empathy (Draguns, 1996; Thomason, 1993). As in any counseling relationship, counselors need to be open to the values and beliefs of ethnic clients and aware of how the clients' values relate to their own values.

Jones (1985) asserts that empathy and countertransference are two key factors in counseling with Blacks. Empathy permits the White counselor to go beyond superficial cultural understanding to deep cultural insights in which the counselor apprehends more fully the ethnic client's feelings about cultural values, dilemmas, and conflicts. Countertransference often occurs when White counselors react to Black clients with fear, guilt, or denial of differences. White therapists or counselors become more empathic and effective with Black clients when they explore their own needs or motivations that lead to negative countertransference.

Counselor Competencies

In 1992 the Association for Multicultural Counseling and Development (AMCD) approved counselor competency standards for work with multicultural clients, standards that were drawn up by Sue et al. (1992). These standards were endorsed by American Counselor Education and Supervision (ACES) in 1996 and the International Association for Marriage and Family Counseling (IAMFC) in 1997; they were amplified by Arredondo et al. (1996) and also by Sue and Sue (2003). The following summary is taken from Robinson and Howard-Hamilton (2000):

- *Culturally competent counselors are aware of their own assumptions, values, and biases.* They explore the beliefs and values of their own cultural heritage and the impact that heritage has made on them. They are aware of how their own biases can affect minority clients. They acknowledge and respect the differences that exist between their attitudes and values and those of clients of differing racial/ethnic cultures. They are aware of their limitations. When in doubt, they consult with other culturally competent professionals.

- *Culturally competent counselors understand the worldviews of culturally diverse clients; the counselors become knowledgeable about their cultural background, way of life, and everyday living experiences.* Counselors possess or acquire specific knowledge about the cultural values, attitudes, and beliefs of a client's cultural group. They are also aware of societal discriminations that can influence the client's personal development, career choices, psychological problems, and attitudes about counseling.
- *Culturally competent counselors use only those intervention strategies and techniques that are appropriate to the client's cultural values and customs.* They acquire a wide repertoire of appropriate interviewing skills and strategies. They consider the cultural characteristics of clients in their selection and interpretation of assessment and treatment measures and develop an awareness of possible biases in these measures. When counselors become aware of such biases in their professional work, they act as agents of social change to eliminate such practices. Counselors make use of community resources culturally relevant to the client, such as the client's church or neighborhood cultural center.

Ethnic Client Characteristics

Counselors who are sensitive to the needs of ethnic clients consider both individual and cultural characteristics important to developing an effective relationship. McGoldrick (1982) discusses in some detail the major characteristics that are specific to ethnic clients and are listed here.

Individual Characteristics.
- Degree of facility with the English language
- Perception of one's ethnicity
- Client's place of residence—with parents, with an extended family, and/or in an ethnic neighborhood
- Degree of cohesion in the family

Cultural Characteristics.
- Socioeconomic status, educational level, acculturation, and upward mobility of the client and family
- Degree to which the client has value conflicts with the majority society, with another minority group, or with the extended family
- Family's facility with the English language
- Client's position as first, second, or third generation
- Attitudes of ethnic group or family about mental health services
- Client's marriage or partnership inside or outside the culture
- Degree of loyalty expected in nuclear and extended families
- Degree of family ties to country of origin or to cultural traditions or religion
- Ethnic group's designation of certain persons as healers

Factors regarding immigration status are also very important to many groups (Lee & Richardson, 1991). For example, many refugees who left their countries because of repressive or life-threatening governments are trauma victims suffering from posttraumatic stress disorder (see chap. 19).

Racial/Cultural Identity of Ethnic Clients

Racial/cultural identity refers to the degree to which members of an ethnic group have assimilated the values and behaviors of the majority culture and the degree to which they hold to the beliefs, customs, and values of their ethnic culture or heritage (Sabnani, Ponterotto, & Borodovsky, 1991; Sue & Sue, 2003). Awareness that each minority client will differ in the degree of assimilation can reduce the chances of treating every member of an ethnic group in a stereotypical way.

Atkinson, Morten, and Sue (1998) propose a minority identity development model (MID), which describes five stages that members of an ethnic group go through. At first they attempt to identify with the majority culture (*conformity*). Then conflicting self-doubts emerge within the group (*dissonance*). In the third stage (*resistance* and *immersion*), they become disillusioned, resentful, and rebellious. The next is the *introspective* stage, in which they reconsider majority and minority values. In the last stage (*synergistic*), they develop a balanced, integrative awareness of strengths and weaknesses of both majority and minority cultures.

Theories and Techniques of Multicultural Counseling

Contemporary ethnic counselors are less concerned about special theories and techniques for minority clients than were earlier ethnic professionals. Most counselors now attend to both the inner reality and the environmental factors in a client's life. Regardless of counseling theory, counselors can develop credibility and trust with ethnic clients if they work with their clients in a way that is compatible with the clients' beliefs about their culture (Sue & Zane, 1987).

After trust has been established, counselors can help clients reframe the way they perceive their problems. Awareness of clients' individual and cultural characteristics also helps determine whether culture-specific techniques are needed and, if so, which kind should be used. Sue and Morishima (1982) used a culture-specific technique when they followed a common practice in Chinese culture and asked an older uncle to act as an intermediary to help resolve a conflict between an immigrant Chinese daughter and her immigrant mother-in-law. If the client and the mother-in-law had been third- or fourth-generation Chinese Americans, this culture-specific technique probably would have been inappropriate.

Ivey's (1986) developmental counseling therapy theory (DCT) is especially appropriate in multicultural counseling. Ivey emphasizes the importance of moving away from a client focus on self-development to developing the self in relationship to others, a process in counseling he calls a *dialectical/system approach*. Clients who perceive their problems within a situational context of family and culture become aware of how these factors increase the complexity of their experiences, emotions, and thoughts. Problems then are best resolved within these systems (Ivey, D'Andrea, Ivey, & Simek-Morgan, 2002; see also chap. 5).

This view is particularly pertinent to ethnic groups in which family and cultural ties are close and influential. It is consistent as well with feminist views regarding self-development through mutual connections with others (see chaps. 5, 6, and 9). Ivey et al. (2002) recommend using *network therapy* with ethnic groups, which includes counselor intervention with the individuals, their family, extended family, and "community groups, such as schools, church congregations, and service organizations" (p. 404). Network therapy addresses not only changes in the individual and family but also attitude changes in the community that are influencing individuals and families.

Training in Multicultural Counseling

Sue and Sue (2003) express concerns that deficiencies in the cross-cultural components of counselor education programs are contributing to ineffective mental health services for ethnic minorities. They argue that counselor training generally does not include the influences of culture on personality development, career and educational concerns, or behavioral disorders. In addition, they say that counselor-training programs are deficient in teaching counseling skills relevant to the culturally different, use inappropriate training packages of helping skills for ethnic clients, and neglect to give trainees a chance to explore their own subconscious racism.

For over 20 years suggestions have been made to upgrade multicultural counselor training. Copeland (1982, 1983) recommended that training programs for cross-cultural counseling include four components: (a) consciousness-raising, (b) cognitive understanding, (c) affective experiencing, and (d) skill building. In *consciousness-raising,* the counselor is helped to become familiar with a cultural group. *Cognitive understanding* involves teaching counselors to assess demographic data. *Affective experiencing* consists of training counselors to become aware of client and counselor emotions. Counselors are also trained in *skill-building* techniques appropriate for ethnic clients, including interviewing and assessment.

In 1986 Margolis and Rungta recommended that an overall course on multicultural counseling be added to the required core courses for all counselors, rather than a course on each of the predominant ethnic groups, because it is economically infeasible to require several core courses on ethnic counseling. Robinson and Howard-Hamilton (2000) report that the single multicultural counseling course is the most common approach in counselor education programs.

Sue et al. (1992) summarize the following new model of cross-cultural training in their proposal to reform multicultural counselor training:

1. Cultural difference does not mean deviancy, pathology, or inferiority.
2. Biculturalism in racial and ethnic minority groups is acknowledged.
3. Biculturalism involves positive and desirable characteristics that enhance and enrich humans.
4. Obstacles or difficulties interfering with the development of the individual are perceived as existing within the environment and with social-political oppressive forces, rather than within the individual or the minority group.

Several models of multicultural training in counseling and counseling psychology have been summarized by Kiselicka (1998):

Collectively, these models were designed to promote the following: (a) self-knowledge, especially an awareness of one's own cultural biases; (b) knowledge about the status and cultures of different cultural groups; (c) skills to make culturally appropriate interventions, including a readiness to use alternative counseling strategies that better match the cultures of clients than do traditional counseling strategies; and (d) actual experiences in counseling culturally different clients. (p. 6)

Robinson and Howard-Hamilton (2000) present examples of exercises and strategies that can be incorporated into counselor training to improve the multicultural competencies of students. They include facilitating student introspection and awareness of biases, increasing students' learning about other cultures, and improving their skills in relating to persons in other cultures. For example, counseling students might construct their own genograms based on their family history, attend ethnic church services or watch ethnic films and documentaries, and discuss issues related to diverse cultures.

The following four sources give suggestions for improving training in multicultural counseling:

- P. B. Pedersen (1988). *A handbook for developing multicultural awareness.* Alexandria, VA: American Counseling Association.
- P. B. Pedersen (Ed.). (1991). Multiculturalism as a fourth force [Special issue]. *Journal of Counseling & Development, 70.*
- H. F. Myers, P. Wohlford, L. P. Guzman, & R. J. Echemendia (Eds.). (1991). *Ethnic minority perspectives on clinical training and services in psychology.* Washington, DC: American Psychological Association.
- Multicultural counselor training [Special issue]. (1998). *Counseling Psychologist, 26.*

Counseling With Representative Ethnic Groups

Because ethnic groups number more than 53 (Baruth & Manning, 2003), it is not possible to cover them all in an introductory text. The four largest ethnic groups in the United States—African Americans, Hispanics, American Indians, and Asian Americans—are discussed here. However, counselors also need to be aware that members within each group often come from different geographic locations or countries of origin, may speak different languages, and may adhere to different customs (Atkinson et al., 1993). Thus, this is only a general overview. In their book *Ethnicity and Family Therapy,* McGoldrick et al. (1996) cover not only subgroups within these four major groups, but also more than a dozen other ethnic groups, including Italians, Greeks, Germans, Poles, Jews, Irish, Portuguese, and Puerto Ricans. Each section of their book is written by professional counselors or therapists who represent specific ethnic groups and work primarily with clients from these groups. They give insights into intercultural family role behaviors and show how these influence the types of problems that individuals and families might experience. Those particularly interested in counseling with ethnic minority children and adolescents should read *Working With Culture: Psychotherapeutic Interventions With Ethnic Minority Children and Adolescents* (Vargas & Koss-Chioino, 1992) and *Multicultural Counseling: A Life-Span Perspective* (Baruth & Manning, 2003).

Various names are used by members of ethnic groups to designate their cultural identity: African Americans, Blacks, Black Americans; Hispanic Americans, Hispanics, Latinos, Chicanos; American Indians, Native Americans; Asian Americans, Asians/Pacific Islanders.

The names used here are used most often in the ethnic literature. Awareness of the many options makes counselors more sensitive to individual preferences; when in doubt, counselors should ask their clients.

Counseling African Americans

In the United States, African Americans, or Blacks, are the second largest ethnic group, totaling approximately 35 million people (Sue & Sue, 2003). Cross and Fhagen-Smith (1996) observe, "The combinations and permutations of Black life are as infinite as the imagination, and healthy Black adjustment should be expected to vary from one context to another" (p. 122).

Ponterotto and Casas (1991) emphasize that African Americans are a heterogeneous group. Some grew up in the rural South; others in northern cities; some are recent immigrants from the Caribbean. Whereas the literature emphasizes poverty, unemployment, and crime among lower socioeconomic African Americans, a great deal of economic diversity exists among them. "More than one-third of African Americans are now middle-class or higher. . . . [They are] becoming increasingly heterogeneous in terms of social class, educational level, and political orientation" (Sue & Sue, 2003, pp. 294–295).

The literature often ignores the strengths of African Americans and their families while emphasizing broken homes and other problems inherent with lower socioeconomic status. As a group, African Americans are unusually resourceful, having survived centuries of discrimination and oppression (Wilson & Stith, 1993). Their strengths lie in kinship bonds and loyalty to family (Gladding, 1997). Family boundaries are elastic and often include an extended family of aunts, uncles, and other relatives. In addition, children are readily accepted into the family, regardless of the marital status of their parents.

Work and education are also highly valued. Parents expect children to take advantage of education and to seek mental health services because the parents are very concerned about their children's progress in school. Garreau (1988), who sees the emerging Black middle class as a historic change, points out that 81% of Blacks finish high school, compared with 30% in 1960. At the present time African American dropout rates are similar to those of Whites (Sue & Sue, 2003).

Baruth and Manning (2003) emphasize that religion plays an important part in the lives of African Americans, with the church playing a vital role in providing or supporting some sort of mental health service (see chap. 19). They strongly recommend that counselors consider the clergy and church networks to be supportive resources for families in crisis.

Regardless of the socioeconomic status of an African American client, counselors must be aware of possible feelings of powerlessness and rage because of environmental barriers related to discrimination. African Americans of higher socioeconomic status bring in problems similar to those of Whites, which often include self-actualization, improvement of self-esteem, career concerns, and family problems (see chap. 19). Lower-income African Americans are often concerned about factors related to physical and economic survival, such as poverty, unemployment, housing, and health care. Their problems center on depression, alcohol and drug abuse, poor academic performance, acting-out behavior, and juvenile delinquency. Behind all of this is often a desire to improve their quality of life.

Minuchin's family systems approach (discussed in chap. 10) initially worked well in attending to the needs of ethnic families in inner-city ghettos. But according to psychiatrist and family therapist Ramon Rojano, Minuchin's theory of moving clients from the ghettos to better environments for treatment essentially failed in most cases because as soon as individuals returned to their home communities, they fell back into old patterns (Markowitz, 1997). Originally from Colombia and now the director of the Department of Social and Health Services in Hartford, Connecticut, Rojano encourages individuals and families to become empowered within their communities. He believes that family systems therapy must change into a *community systems* therapy. Rojano's theory emerges out of his culture-specific, Hispanic background, which emphasizes close family and community ties; and his programs work particularly well in ethnic neighborhoods (Markowitz, 1997). Because his work has to do primarily with families and their relations to their communities, Rojano's theory and programs are discussed more at length in the chapters on family and community counseling (chaps. 10 and 19).

In any case Jones (1985) says that counselors must pay attention to client characteristics and to the individuality of each client. He states, "There is enormous within-group variability. The question is not how to treat *the* black client but how to treat *this* black client" (p. 175). Schools must start with the premise that African American students are capable of succeeding and want to succeed in school. School officials must then develop alternative strategies to educate these students and to encourage parents to exert a positive influence on their children (Locke, 1995).

> If school counselors are to make significant contributions to the education of African-American students, they must develop an awareness of African and African-American cultures. They must also understand how students are influenced by those cultures. From such awareness, counselors can develop specific strategies that address the unique needs of African-American students. (p. 38)

Counseling Hispanics

The Hispanic, or Latino, population of approximately 35 million represents the largest ethnic minority in the United States. Hispanics are a very diverse group, coming from Mexico (60%), Puerto Rico (10%), Cuba (6%), and Central and South America (28%). A large proportion are poor and unemployed and live in substandard housing in metropolitan areas (Ponterotto & Casas, 1991; Sue & Sue, 2003).

Mental health services have been underused by Hispanics because strong family caring reduces the need for outside help (Baruth & Manning, 2003). However, even though families help buffer stress, at the same time family pressures can intensify difficulties (Padilla & DeSnyder, 1985). Family is the most important social unit for Hispanics, superseding personal identity. Casas and Vasquez (1996) say,

> In traditional Hispanic culture, the family unit (including the extended family) is given great importance; consequently, in that cultural context it is "normal" to deal with the reality and necessity of valuing the welfare of the family higher than one's individual welfare. (p. 57)

Children and adult children thus tend to subordinate their needs to parents' needs, behavior that is reinforced by the teachings of Catholicism—the dominant religion among Hispanics—about respect for parents and family (Robinson & Howard-Hamilton, 2000).

Alcohol and drug abuse, as well as unemployment, are serious problems for low-income Hispanics. School dropout rates are high, often because of language barriers, which interfere with school-family interactions. Hispanic families encourage their children to speak Spanish at home and at school as a means of maintaining cultural identification, whereas school officials generally insist that they speak English (Sue & Sue, 2003).

Hispanic Americans tend to tie emotional difficulties to physical illness; they often take psychological problems to physicians rather than to mental health professionals (Comas-Diaz, 1993). They also tend to seek help from relatives, friends, or spiritualists, or faith healers (De La Cancela & Guzman, 1991; Sue & Sue, 2003).

De La Cancela and Guzman (1991) believe that a social action view of therapy must be included in working with the mental health problems of Latinos. This approach emphasizes the impact of societal or world sickness on the mental health of the ethnic client, rather than focusing on internal sources of maladjustment. This theory is similar to Rojano's community systems theory and the network therapy theory of Ivey et al., discussed earlier. Counselors are urged to use such a community-oriented family counseling system (Baruth & Manning, 2003).

Casas and Vasquez (1996) caution counselors not to neglect the history of Hispanic clients: "The past and present interrelate in such a complex manner, that, for most Hispanics, it is impossible to understand the total individual without an understanding and appreciation for his or her sociohistorical reality" (pp. 158–159). Ponterotto (1987) recommends using a multimodal counseling approach as developed by Lazarus (see chap. 6) because it has the flexibility to be adapted to the wide cultural diversity of Hispanics.

Counseling Native American Indians

The terms *Native American Indian, Native American,* and *American Indian* are used interchangeably in the literature:

> As most scholars know, the term *American Indian* is an imposed ethnic category with little relevant meaning. . . . Somehow, and no one is really certain why, the category continued to be used to the extent that almost all indigenous, native people of the Western Hemisphere are referred to as Indians. . . . For better or worse, the term has become institutionalized and even accepted by the native people themselves. (Trimble, Fleming, Beauvais, & Jumper-Thurman, 1996, pp. 178–179)

According to the 2000 census, approximately 2½ million people in the United States declare themselves to be either Native American Indians or Alaska Natives. There are over 500 federally recognized Indian tribes and 365 state recognized tribes. About 54% of Native Americans live on reservations, the only minority group to do so (Baruth & Manning, 2003). Because most Indian tribes are recognized as nations by treaties with the U.S. government, they have certain sovereign rights and are under federal jurisdiction. Conflicts among local, state, and federal governments regarding the rights and jurisdictions of Native Americans occur in many areas. For instance, these jurisdictional conflicts can lead to confusion about who will fund mental health services, with the frequent result being a lack of adequate funding.

According to Baruth and Manning (2003), American Indians, who are lowest on the socioeconomic scale, have very serious problems of survival, poverty, and unemployment, which often relate to discrimination and stereotyping. On reservations unemployment, poverty, and school dropout rates are significantly higher than the national average. American Indians resist Anglo-American education when it ignores Indian culture. And adolescents in the culture have higher rates of suicide and substance abuse than does any other group of adolescents (Robinson & Howard-Hamilton, 2000; Sue & Sue, 2003).

Alcoholism is a major concern faced by Native Americans. "They are six times more likely to die of alcohol-related causes than the general U.S. population" (Sue & Sue, 2003, p. 322). Domestic violence is also a huge problem, with the rate of abuse for American Indian women 3½ times larger than the national average (Sue & Sue, 2003).

Many problems of Native Americans are affected by a change in socioeconomic status and upward mobility. Those who have college degrees not only have problems similar to those of middle-class Whites but also often find themselves in conflict with members of their tribes. They are often seen as having abandoned their people and their heritage.

Counselors should be aware of the strong extended family system on Indian reservations. Aunts, uncles, and grandparents often serve as parents to nieces, nephews, and grandchildren. Most play a significant part in the upbringing of these children; others take over completely. Family counseling is an effective approach to use with American Indians because of their strong family orientation and kinship (Baruth & Manning, 2003; Trimble et al., 1996). The traditional healing approaches of shamans and medicine men are also used frequently among the American Indian tribes on the reservations, and counselors are urged to cooperate with these healers (Thomason, 1993; Trimble, 1991).

Counseling Asian Americans

Asian Americans are not a homogeneous group, although they are often perceived in that way. Asians who live in the United States come from many cultural heritages, each with a distinct language—Chinese, Taiwanese, Japanese, Filipino, Korean, Samoan, Vietnamese, Cambodian, and Laotian, for example (Kitano & Maki, 1996; Sue & Sue, 2003). Further, large differences exist within Asian American groups in terms of socioeconomic status, primary language, and the recentness of immigration. The Asian American population is about 6 million; and like the Hispanics, Asian Americans are one of the fastest growing groups in the United States because of increasing ratios allowed for Asian immigration (Sue & Sue, 2003; Zane & Sue, 1991). Projections are that Asian Americans will number 20 million in 2020 (Org, 1993).

When working with Asian Americans, the counselor must be particularly aware of their social class, geophysical origin, and level of generation. A bimodal socioeconomic grouping exists in some Asian groups: Half of them are competitive high achievers scholastically, and half are recent immigrants who live in poverty and are unemployed. Because Asian high achievers are more visible to the public, many non-Asians tend to develop a stereotype of Asian Americans as successful, well-educated, and relatively free from mental health problems (Gladding, 1997; Sue & Sue, 2003). Another common stereotypical view is that Asian Americans are nonassertive, a characteristic that is thought to be an inherent part of their personalities. Sue and Sue (1999) claim, however, that such behaviors actually depend on certain situations.

Within Asian American communities strong emphasis is placed on the specific role of each family member. The personal needs of the individual are superseded by the needs of both the elders and the family. Shame is used to reinforce family expectations about appropriate behavior (Kitano & Maki, 1996; Sue & Sue, 2003).

Asian Americans generally feel shame about any need to seek outside help, because they believe that the family is supposed to deal with personal problems. In a study of counseling preferences of Asian American college students, Atkinson, Wampold, Lowe, Matthews, and Ahn (1998) found that they underuse personal counseling services, although they tend to use vocational counseling services more than do college students in the general population. In personal counseling, their shame persists in the form of resistance to talking about themselves (Sue & Sue, 2003).

The problems brought to counseling by Asian Americans of higher socioeconomic status relate to career choice, educational opportunities, independence versus loyalty to family, pressure to succeed, and social isolation (Baruth & Manning, 1999). Immigrant groups have problems with language, depression, unemployment, and housing, problems typical of other low-income groups.

When working with first-generation Asian American clients, counselors must be aware of cultural values that influence the clients' views about mental health. Clients' religious beliefs and traditions are closely tied to their attitudes about mental health and mental illness (Sue & Sue, 2003). Because many Asian American clients are familiar with the use of mediation or negotiation to solve problems, they often respond well to counselors who use such processes. These clients also share the Asian value that family unity comes before the individual's welfare. Counselors need to be aware of these influences when helping clients resolve family conflicts (Kitano & Maki, 1996).

Counseling Multiracial Individuals

Counselors need to be aware of and prepared to deal with complex identity issues confronting children of mixed racial marriages. After the laws against mixed marriages were repealed in 1967, individuals of multiracial descent in the United States increased rapidly (Sue & Sue, 2003). It is estimated that mixed marriages in the United States, which now constitute about 3% of total marriages, will double each decade (Root, 1996). And although mixed marriages are steadily gaining public approval, many children of these marriages feel continued societal pressures from both sides to identify with either one cultural heritage or another. This pressure can lead to confused identity and low self-esteem and to feelings of living marginally between two or three cultures (Sue & Sue, 2003).

In 2000 the U.S. Census for the first time allowed mixed-race individuals to check more than one box for racial identity and to be counted as multiracial (Sue & Sue, 2003). But not all minority groups are pleased with this situation. The National Association of Colored People (NAACP), for example, resists any movements that encourage recognition of multiracial origins "because census numbers of race and ethnicity figure into many calculations involving anti-discrimination laws, voting, and dispersal of funds for minority groups" (Sue & Sue, 2003, p. 364).

Societal stereotypes regarding mixed marriages contribute to the identity problems of multiracial children. Many adults tend to believe, for example, that persons who marry interracially are unstable individuals, heading for unhappy marriages (Sue & Sue, 2003). As a result, they believe their children will develop more psychological and social conflicts than monoracial children. With this mindset, counselors, teachers, and other significant persons attribute multiracial children's' problems to their mixed cultural heritage. To make matters worse, "People of mixed race heritage are often ignored, neglected, and considered non-existent in our educational materials, media portrayals, and psychological literature" (Sue & Sue, 2003, p. 363). "The child or adolescent is often unable to identify his other conflicts and feelings about being multiracial and settles for . . . a monoracial answer that may result in internal disharmony, a false sense of self, social marginality and guilt" (Sue & Sue, 2003, p. 367).

Counselors need to be aware that many multiracial clients do not have the degree of social support that monoracial clients typically have. Monoracial parents who share their children's racial/ethnic heritage tend to be aware of and understand their childrens' concerns about identity. In mixed marriages parents who are monoracial have not experienced the identity conflicts their multiracial children are experiencing. Consequently, they generally lack the understanding or skills to help their children work through identity confusion. Further, multiracial individuals struggling with racial identity may not be accepted or supported by either of their cultural heritage groups (Root, 1996; Sue & Sue, 2003).

Even though all these factors point to more stressful lives for multiracial children, research indicates that there are potential advantages for multiracial individuals who work through the difficulties confronting them (Root, 1996; Sue & Sue, 2003). Among the advantages are these:

> [an] increased sense of uniqueness, better ability to relate to more diverse groups, greater tolerance and understanding of people, ability to deal with racism, enjoying what many groups have to offer, greater variety in one's life, and better ability to build alliances with many diverse people and groups. (Sue & Sue, 2003, p. 373)

Research on Multicultural Counseling

In a survey of articles published between 1983 and 1988 in leading counseling journals, Ponterotto and Casas (1991) found 183 articles related to multicultural counseling and categorized them into five topic areas. In this survey the number of articles about Blacks exceeded the total number of articles on the three other major ethnic groups. Only a few articles were on American Indians, and these were narrowly focused on alcoholism, depression, suicide, and substance abuse.

Ponterotto and Casas (1991) also gathered data from five leading counselor journals during the years 1983 to 1988 on 80 empirical studies on North American racial/ethnic groups. They then evaluated these articles on the basis of 10 criticisms that have been consistently presented in the literature as weaknesses in ethnic research. As Table 14.1 shows, six criticisms were supported by the data, two were only partially supported, and two were disputed.

In 1998 Ponterotto reevaluated these criticisms of multicultural counseling research. He comments, "I believe that in the past decade many of these criticisms have been addressed by researchers to some degree" (p. 63). These criticisms continue to be so pervasive, however, that they still warrant attention.

TABLE 14.1
Results of Survey on Criticisms of Racial Ethnic Research

Six Criticisms Supported by the Data

Lack of conceptual/theoretical frameworks to guide research.

Disregard for within-group or intracultural differences.

The use of easily accessible college student populations.

Reliance on culturally encapsulated psychometric instrumentation.

Failure to adequately describe one's sample in terms of socioeconomic status (SES).

Overreliance on paper-and-pencil measures as dependent variables.

Two Criticisms Only Partially Supported by the Data

Overremphasis on simplistic counselor/client process variables and a disregard for important psychosocial variables within and outside the culture that might impact counseling.

Lack of adequate sample sizes.

Two Criticisms Disputed by the Data

Overreliance on experimental analogue research.

Failure to delineate study's limitations.

Note: From *Handbook of Racial/Ethnic Minority Counseling Research* (p. 94), by J. G. Ponterotto and J. M. Casas, 1991, Springfield, IL: Charles C Thomas. Copyright 1991 by Charles C Thomas. Adapted with permission.

Once again, Ponterotto (1998) emphasizes the need for more qualitative research studies. "I am an advocate of qualitative research methods. The qualitative tradition has been, until quite recently, undervalued in counseling psychology and seldom used in multicultural counseling research" (p. 64). Ponterotto (1998) also recommends that research in the next decade focus on five themes: (a) racial identity development (e.g., oral histories, case studies); (b) multicultural competency assessment; (c) mentoring (e.g., assessing characteristics of effective mentors); (d) model programs (e.g., assessing programs that offer "clinical experience with culturally diverse clients," p. 61); and (e) the role of program diversity in training effectiveness (e.g., taking into account the ratio of culturally diverse students in multicultural classes).

There has long been a concern over the way researchers conduct their studies of ethnic groups. Minorities remember having been exploited by unethical White researchers or "portrayed as deviants" (Sue & Sue, 2003, p. 58). Thus, minorities tend not to trust the motives of researchers: "Whereas social scientists in the past have been able to enter ethnic communities and conduct their studies . . . researchers are now being received with suspicion and overt hostility" (Sue & Sue, 2003, p. 58). Moreover, members of ethnic minorities are annoyed and put off by the abstract language and jargon used by researchers. Minorities believe researchers could better spend their time working on relevant social issues and conditions influencing the lives of minorities; the results of their research could be practically applied to improving the living conditions of minority groups.

Citing APA Guidelines for Ethical Principles in the Conduct of Research with Human Participants, Sue and Sue (2003) raise the following questions:

> Under what conditions is it ethically acceptable to study residents of a ghetto, minority group members, the poor? . . . What are the researcher's motives? Is research conducted for some definable good, or is it opportunistic, exploitative, and potentially damaging to the target population? (p. 59)

COUNSELING WOMEN AND MEN: GENDER ROLE STEREOTYPING

Women and men suffer from stereotypical roles in different ways. Although the prevailing culture expects women's primary role to be that of nurturer and caretaker, such a role has long been considered inferior to the male role. Women have been devalued for their emphasis on developing relationships and connections with others (Gilligan, 1982, 2002; Jack, 1991, 1999; Miller & Stiver, 1997). In the workforce women generally are placed in subordinate positions and experience job discrimination, unequal pay for equal work, and sexual harassment (Basow, 1992; Richmond-Abbott, 1992).

Because of the sustained efforts by the women's movement over several decades, increasing numbers of women have become empowered and have gained self-respect and status equal to that of their male counterparts. Even so, many, if not most, women still feel diminished, trivialized, and disempowered. Emotional problems—such as feelings of a lack of power and control over their lives, a lack of self-confidence and assertion, eating disorders, phobias, and depression—arise from their socialized roles. Women with these problems often become victims of domestic violence, rape, and other forms of sexual abuse (Jack, 1991, 1999; Sue & Sue, 2003).

Stereotypical roles imposed on men lead them to become overzealous in achieving success, requiring them to strive at all times to appear competent, assertive, and invulnerable. Men are trained to disregard emotions related to tenderness, fear, and grief (Kelly & Hall, 1992; Real, 1997, 2002; Robinson & Howard-Hamilton, 2000); they minimize and devalue both their inner self and their relationships. Consequently, their zealous striving for achievement and devaluing of relationships lead to aggression, heart attacks, impotency, violence, and addictive behaviors.

Women and men have organized into various groups to reexamine and modify gender roles and regain a sense of well-being and a caring regard for themselves and others. For women one such group, the National Organization for Women (NOW), works through established channels in society, such as legislative action, to obtain civil rights for women. Another, more radical type of group believes it is necessary to revolutionize society in order to bring about equal rights for women (Basow, 1992). Many women have formed academic research centers for women's studies. Among these are centers to reevaluate traditional psychological theories and propose therapeutic approaches from a feminist perspective. Two such groups are the Stone Center at Wellesley College and the Women's Project in Family Therapy, discussed in chapters 5, 6, and 10.

The men's movement has also formed into various groups, including profeminist and promasculine groups. Profeminists believe that working with women to equalize gender roles will profit men as well as women. Promasculine groups believe that men's foremost need is to form groups with other men to improve their roles (Clatterbaugh, 1990). Male therapists have also been presenting new perspectives on male psychology and masculinity. Terence Real (1997, 2002), for example, argues that male dysfunctions result from coercing boys to adopt so-called masculine behaviors. Other examples are Kenneth Clatterbaugh (1996) and Warren Steinberg (1993).

Although women's and men's groups have differed in their aims and methods to improve gender relationships, leading professionals such as Carol Gilligan (1982, 2002) and Terrence Real (1997, 2002) agree that traditional counseling theories and practice have contributed to gender role stereotyping. They offer alternative ways for counselors and therapists to change their approach to counseling. In recent years women's and men's groups have become remarkably similar in acknowledging that the development of relationships is fundamental and primary for both genders for healthy human growth and development:

> Just as for many depressed women recovery is inextricably linked to shedding the traces of oppression and finding empowerment, for many depressed men, recovery is linked to opposing the force of disconnection, and reentering the world of relationship—to the "feminine," to themselves, and to others. (Real, 1997, p. 158)

A discussion of all of the women's and men's movements with their various aims and actions goes beyond the scope of this book. Those who wish to read more about the movements themselves can start with Susan Basow's *Gender Stereotypes and Roles* (1992), Kenneth Clatterbaugh's *Contemporary Perspectives on Masculinity* (1996), and Warren Steinberg's *Identity Conflict and Transformation* (1993).

Women: Problems With Role Stereotyping

Feminist Theories of Counseling

As women's groups crystallized in the 1970s and 1980s, feminist counselors and therapists began to criticize counseling theories developed by men, which they claimed reinforced the prevailing social and economic status of men and women. In 1970 Broverman, Broverman, Clarkson, Rosenkrantz, and Vogel alerted the mental health professions about therapist and counselor bias toward clients. In their study equal numbers of female and male clinicians were asked to indicate the characteristics of healthy men, healthy women, and healthy adults. Regardless of their gender, all clinicians described healthy men and healthy women in stereotypical ways. Healthy men were described as aggressive, ambitious, decisive, independent, rational, unemotional, and worldly. Healthy women were portrayed as submissive, modest, warm, indecisive, dependent, nurturant, weak, flighty, and emotional. A key finding in the study—a finding that dismayed many women—was that a healthy adult was perceived by clinicians as having the typical characteristics of the healthy man.

On the basis of their concerns about societal and therapeutic restraints placed on women, feminists in the 1970s began to reconsider women's psychosocial development. One of the earliest and most significant efforts was Chodorow's (1974) observation that girls are brought up differently from boys: Girls are encouraged to develop relationships, whereas boys are socialized to separate, become independent and competitive (Gilligan, 1982). Influenced by Chodorow, Gilligan (1982) published her landmark book *In a Different Voice* (1982), in which she affirmed that women have "a different voice," that is, they perceive, experience, and express things differently than do men. The problem, however, is that they're not listened to by the male-dominated, patriarchal society. Female characteristics associated with developing relationships were, at that time, seen as weak, dependent, and submissive.

Early feminists of the 1970s and 1980s agitated to break away from these negative "feminine" images. Women had to learn to assert themselves, stand up for their rights, and be listened to; and the only means was for women to gain a sense of power and autonomy just like their male counterparts. In the ensuing decades feminist theorists carried on gender debates over many issues; some insisted that there should be no distinction between males and females; others debated issues of autonomy versus relationships, and power versus no power. Out of these debates, feminist theorists have generally come to acknowledge the differing strengths of males and females and have developed conceptual distinctions between a male and a female sense of autonomy and power.

Regarding autonomy, "Feminism insists that women must have personal autonomy and both the freedom to direct and the responsibility for directing all areas of their lives; they must decide for themselves what it means to be a woman" (Faunce, 1985, p. 309). According to Young-Eisendrath and Wiedemann (1987), the central theme in all feminist work "has been the fear of personal insignificance" (p. 8). Ballou and Gabalac (1985) say that feminist therapists focus more on developing an egalitarian relationship between therapist and client. Typically, that relationship has been unequal—a strong, authoritarian, male therapist and a weak, helpless female client.

Feminist therapy is a process of building a woman's sense of empowerment—not in the typical male sense of exerting power over someone else, but rather in having the authority to be one's feminine self. "The ability of a woman to validate her own convictions of truth, beauty, and goodness in regard to her self-concept and self-interest is what we call *female authority*" (Young-Eisendrath & Wiedemann, 1987, p. 8). Young-Eisendrath and Wiedemann (1987) are opposed to the medical model approach, "the symptom approach," because of "a sense of hopelessness engendered by the illness model of psychopathology" (p. 5), which focuses on "what is absent, deficient or wrong in a person or situation" (p. 4). They propose a different model, one that enhances the strengths of clients, rather than focusing on weaknesses.

Some of the most notable approaches to feminist therapy in recent years have arison from the feminist developmental theories proposed by women psychotherapists and researchers at the Stone Center at Wellesley College (Jordan, 1997; Jordan, Kaplan, Miller, Stiver, & Surrey, 1991; Miller & Stiver, 1997; see also chaps. 5 and 6). Largely influenced by the pioneer work of Chodorow (1974) and Gilligan (1982), theorists at the center differ from traditional developmental theorists in their claim that forming and maintaining connections in relationships are an essential part of a woman's developmental process. According to Jordan (1991), "The Stone Center model suggests in fact that relationship, based on empathic attunement, is the key to the process of therapy, not just the backdrop for it" (p. 284).

The women at the Stone Center present a new psychology of women based on the belief that women—and all humans, for that matter—grow and develop within mutually connected relationships (Miller & Stiver, 1997). This theory counteracts the prevailing belief among traditional psychological theorists that the goal of human growth and development is to achieve separation and autonomy (see chaps. 5 and 6). Instead of the general tendency to pathologize women's proclivities to nurture relationships and develop connections, women at the Stone Center applaud these characteristics as strengths; indeed, they believe that these characteristics of mutual connections in relationships are necessary to sustain and promote human life and development.

> In reclaiming the knowledge about relationships that women in particular hold, we can begin to form a new model of psychological development *within relationships*, in which everyone participates in ways that foster the development of all people involved, something we might call "mutual psychological development." (Miller & Stiver, 1997, p. 17)

Jack (1991) applies feminist development theory to depression in women, including suggestions for therapy. In her book *Silencing the Self* (1991), which is based on a longitudinal study of 12 clinically depressed women aged 19 to 55, Jack claims that depression in women stems largely from their striving to attain intimacy through behaviors that are culturally defined as feminine—pleasing, self-sacrificing, self-silencing. Instead of creating intimacy, these behaviors lead a woman to experience a loss of self in relationship, lowered self-esteem, and ultimately depression. Jack points out that a woman's negative attitude about her neediness is attributable to the prevailing belief that separation and individuation are the primary goals of development. "As it currently exists, the concept of dependence . . . labels women's orientation to their relationship as weakness or pathology" (pp. 19–20). Instead, Jack argues, women's vulnerability to depression "does not lie in their 'dependence' on relationships or in their depressive response to loss, but in what happens to them within their relationships" (p. 21).

Pointing out that the quality of relationship is the key issue in women's vulnerability to depression, Jack (1991) describes forms of connection, distinguishing between compliance in relationship and authentic relatedness. When, on the one hand, close relationships have high levels of mutual affection, communication, support, and availability, they "create feelings of emotional security" and allow authentic forms of relating (p. 40). When, on the other hand, relationships are characterized by power imbalances, economic disparity, and a lack of sharing the real self with the other, a woman becomes compliant in relationship and hides her real feelings.

Jack expands her thesis on the quality of relationships in her book *Behind the Mask* (1999), an exploration of women's aggression, or the ways they must mask their aggression, a topic that Jack became interested in while she was working on women's depression.

> While a great deal is known about how girls and women silence themselves, we know less about how to change this behavior. Cultural prohibitions against women's aggression, paired with inequality in male-female relationships, often keep women from engaging in positive, creative conflict. Instead, they often turn it into self-reproach, depression, or hostile destructiveness to others. (p. 40)

Although men are admired for being aggressive, women are not, so they must mask their aggression and resort to devious, indirect methods that often become acts of frustrated rage and despair. Jack raises the question of how one's particular outlook can be turned from the destructive rage of hopeless despair to constructive forms of aggression. Women's nurturing, caregiving role is generally seen as submissive and compliant, and generating conflict is seen as wrong and is frowned upon, if not forbidden. Jack emphasizes, however, that women's role of developing and maintaining connectedness in relationships is not a matter of avoiding conflict.

> The ideal for relatedness is not the absence of conflict but the ability to engage in conflict without paralyzing fear or destructive harm. In the closest of relationships conflict is inevitable, and the ability to engage in it positively is fundamental to the survival of an equal, mutually satisfying relationship. Without conflict, one person in the relationship is likely to experience a loss of self, a disappearance of self into the outlines of the other. (Jack, 1999, pp. 39–40)

According to Jack, "Women must be able to call on their aggression to right imbalances in relationship, to stand up for themselves, and to protect themselves. They must bear the threat of separateness if they are not to lose themselves in relationship" (pp. 40–41).

In her best-selling book *Women Who Run With the Wolves*, Jungian psychotherapist Clarissa Pinkola Estés (1992) also claims that women's psychic needs have been overlooked by traditional psychology:

> Traditional psychology is often spare or entirely silent about deeper issues important to women: the archetypal, the intuitive, the sexual and cyclical, the ages of women, a woman's way, a woman's knowing, her creative fire. This is what has driven my work on the Wild Woman archetype for the better part of two decades. (p. 6)

Estés's work in helping women seek their Wild Woman is similar to Robert Bly's (1990) efforts to help men recover their Wild Man. Her work is also similar to that of storyteller Michael Meade (1993) of the mythopoetical men's movement. Estés uses stories as a way for women to reach their innermost selves. She has been using stories therapeutically for more than 25 years:

> Although some use stories as entertainment alone, tales are, in their oldest sense, a healing art. Some are called to this healing art, and the best, to my lights, are those who have lain with the story and have found all its matching parts inside themselves and at depth. (p. 463)

Other feminists urge women to become more politically active in changing the structure of society as part of improving their emotional well-being (Basow, 1992). Ballou and Gabalac (1985) point out that whichever feminist approach one chooses, the assumption is that women have less political or economic power than men and that women's emotional problems result predominantly from external causes. Basow (1992) comments:

> Although there are many variations of feminist therapy, they all have in common the recognition that the social context is an important determinant of human behavior and that the gender roles and statuses prescribed by society are disadvantageous to both sexes, but especially to women. (p. 339)

Counseling Women

Women with problems associated with gender role stereotyping come to counseling for many reasons. They may be depressed or may be feeling inadequate; they may be having trouble changing their roles; they may be experiencing pathological symptoms; or they may be victims of abuse. According to the Stone Center theorists, pathological tendencies in women develop from profound feelings of isolation and loneliness:

> We believe that the most terrifying and destructive feeling that a person can experience is psychological isolation. This is not the same as being alone. It is feeling that one is locked out of the possibility of human connection and of being powerless to change the situation. In the extreme, psychological isolation can lead to a sense of hopelessness and desperation. (Miller & Stiver, 1997, p. 72)

The core psychological problem for women in need of therapy, say Miller and Stiver, is that in their desperate seeking for relationships, they at the same time devise strategies to remain disconnected, "keeping large parts of one's experience and responses out of connection in order to find connections" (p. 82). Miller and Stiver (1997), see this as "*the central relational paradox,* and we believe it is basic to understanding many psychological problems. It is also basic to understanding therapy for these problems" (p. 81). Chapter 9 shows how their therapeutic approach can be incorporated into the counseling process.

Women Who Are Depressed or Feel Inadequate.   Many women clients are concerned with a lack of self-esteem, an inability to assert themselves, and an inability to exert power or control over their lives. Because they have been taught to be compliant, they tend to defer to the needs of their husbands and children and to deny their own needs. When difficulties or conflicts arise between themselves and their husbands or children, women tend to blame themselves and to harbor mixed feelings of guilt, shame, resentment, hostility, and depression (Jack, 1991). Further, because these women generally depend on men to make decisions, they tend to be unequipped to cope with such matters as finances or car maintenance. And after their husbands die or leave them, these women generally feel helpless (Franks, 1986).

As the title of Jack's book *Silencing the Self* (1991) implies, the loss of a sense of self is linked to a "loss of voice in relationship" (p. 36). In helping women recover from depression, Jack emphasizes the importance of the counselor's sensitivity to bringing a woman's voice back into dialogue, first through encouraging it within the therapeutic relationship. "The therapeutic encounter must offer a quality of relatedness that hears the silenced 'I' of a depressed woman and brings it into dialogue" (p. 203). Instead of replicating the traditional hierarchical relationship of therapist (authoritative, male) and client (deferential, female), Jack suggests that the "therapy relationship must provide a different kind of dialogue, one that challenges prevailing interpersonal and intrapsychic patterns" (p. 204). In this way "moving into depression can become a venture into self-knowing to understand the roots of inner division and self-alienation" (p. 193).

The counselor can help clients become aware of the anger and frustration underlying their passive behavior, assist them in asserting their needs, and help them become empowered by teaching them problem-solving and competency skills. Because these women often have not developed sufficient bonding or effective relationships with either their mothers or their fathers, helping them explore their relationships with their families of origin is often necessary. This process helps women confront their unresolved feelings about their parents and recognize that they have been modeling ineffective behaviors.

Women Who Have Trouble Changing Roles.   As with all individuals who undergo personal change, women clients experience conflicts with others when they begin to change their roles. Husbands may object if their wives plan to return to school or get a job or begin to question the husbands' authority. Even more difficult for the women, some husbands may seem to support the changes their wives are trying to make but subtly undermine them.

Many women who have families and take a job outside the home become overstressed when they try to balance their domestic and job responsibilities. Similar problems occur when husbands want their wives to work to supplement family income, but the wives prefer to remain home to care for the children. Another role change imposed on women occurs when they suddenly become single parents. Many feel overwhelmed when the breadwinner and dual-parent roles are thrust on them. In the case of role changes, counselors need to help women develop personal strengths, try new activities, and cope with resistance or anger from family members. In many cases career counseling is necessary.

Women With Pathological Symptoms.   The overrepresentation in mental health clinics of women patients with certain types of pathology can generally be traced to stereotypical roles they and their mothers have been taught. As stated earlier, Miller and Stiver (1997) emphasize that strategies of disconnection are the core of women's pathology:

> This path away from mutual connection, and simultaneously away from the truth of one's own experience, is the path to psychological problems. We believe it underlies many of the problems common to women in particular, including depression, various forms of anxiety, phobias, eating problems, and the so-called personality disorders, such as "borderline personality." (p. 81)

In her book *Behind The Mask* (1999), Jack delves into women's need to mask their aggression in indirect ways that often become destructive or at the very least lead to feelings of guilt and shame. The reasons are obvious enough—unequal power relations, the way girls are brought up, and the need for women to abide by cultural expectations of submission and compliance. Less obvious is how to turn destructive forms of aggression into constructive ways of asserting oneself, the major thrust of Jack's book: how to remove the mask in ways that would be constructive and nonthreatening and would be morally beneficial personally, relationally, and socioculturally.

Like Miller & Stiver (1997), Jack emphasizes the disconnectedness in relations as the core of women's pathological symptoms. Masked, destructive aggression is a consequence of feeling disconnected, having feelings of isolation, hopelessness, despair, and self-hatred. In shifting from destructive to constructive forms of aggression, the goal, as Jack proposes, is to move away from feelings of disconnection toward feelings of connectedness in relationships, a move that does not mean being compliant and submissive to keep the peace.

> Movement toward being able to take a stand in relationships and in the world coincides with a decrease in fear and an increase in confidence. The ability to stand one's ground and enter into conflict constructively is fundamentally related to a sense of worth and strength. (p. 239)

Jack proposes various ways for women to strengthen and empower themselves, ranging from standing one's ground and having courage in relationships, to the aggression of hope. In many cases such ways may mean leaving a relationship, having the courage to seek outside help, or seeking shelter in order to break the patterns of a destructive relationship. Approximately 85% of those with agoraphobia and about 85% to 95% of those with eating disorders are women (Sue, Sue, & Sue, 2000). Persons with agoraphobia suffer from fear and panic when in public, which can ultimately lead to their becoming completely homebound (Sue, Sue, & Sue, 2000). Many professionals agree that these symptoms are associated with a highly developed stereotypical female sex role (Basow, 1992; Richmond-Abbott, 1992).

In a summary of research on the treatment of agoraphobics, Kleinknecht (1991) discusses a treatment called *in vivo,* which he considers the most effective. In this method clients are helped to enter, step-by-step, increasingly anxiety-evoking situations in real life and are encouraged to stay with them until the fear drops.

Eating disorders include anorexia nervosa and bulimia. Anorexics eat so little that they are apt to starve to death, whereas bulimics overeat in binges and then induce vomiting to rid themselves of the food. The stereotypical female sex role that women must be slender and attractive contributes to these eating disorders (Sue & Sue, 2003). Others claim that women with these disorders often come from overcontrolling and repressive parents, or they may be victims of sexual abuse (Nolen-Hoeksema, 1998). As mentioned earlier, Miller and Stiver (1997) point out that eating disorders in girls are the result of social conditioning of disconnectedness, "the path away from mutual connections" (p. 81).

Counselors use a variety of approaches to help these women, including cognitive-behavioral, ego-development, and social-cultural techniques. They work at building self-esteem so that these women can develop responsibility for and control over their own lives (Kleinknecht, 1991; Sue & Sue, 2003).

Victimized Women.   Considerable domestic violence exists in the United States and occurs at all levels of the socioeconomic scale. The number of victimized women far exceeds that of men (Basow, 1992). Numerous psychologists and counselors suggest that many women remain in violent relationships because of low self-esteem, which causes psychological and economic dependence on the abuser (Robinson & Howard-Hamilton, 2000). Others contend that abused women either are powerless or feel powerless to change their situation. The problem relates to sex role stereotyping, which casts men as aggressive and women as submissive.

According to Miller and Stiver (1997), health care professionals and society in general only recently began to acknowledge how extensive and pervasive domestic violence is in our society:

> Only with the emergence of the women's movement has the courageous work of many survivors . . . revealed the widespread existence of incest and the sexual and physical abuse of women and children. Often still working against strong opposition from within and beyond the professions, these survivors and their allies have brought to light how large is the number of women who are battered—or killed—by their husbands or male partners and how large a number of girls are sexually or physically abused most often by male family members. (p. 58)

Jack's (1999) work on women's aggression and the socioculturally determined necessity for them to mask their aggression, discussed earlier, applies especially to victimized women. Being in unequal power relationships, such women experience feelings of extreme disconnectedness, helplessness, and powerlessness, feelings that inevitably lead them to the frustrated rage of despair and self-destruction.

Shelters for battered women have proved successful in helping women leave abusers. Although such shelters are valuable, comprehensive counseling should follow, including work in improving self-esteem and developing inner strengths (Ibrahim and Herr, 1987). In addition, these women need career planning and placement. Basow (1992) recommends that, in addition to having access to shelters, women need to become empowered in relationships by learning assertiveness skills and developing independence. Victimized women benefit significantly from educational and therapeutic group work, including groups for those who are victims of rape, incest, or sexual assault; for those struggling with eating disorders; and for those in need of career counseling (Gladding, 1997).

Men: Problems With Male Stereotyping

Although men who adhere to expected male roles are more likely to develop mental health problems, until recently they haven't, as a rule, sought counseling (Real, 2002; Robinson & Howard-Hamilton, 2000; Scher, Stevens, Good, & Eichenfield, 1987; Silverberg, 1986; Skovholt, 1993; Werrbach & Gilbert, 1987). In a study in which they interviewed women and men therapists about their male clients, Werrbach and Gilbert (1987) found a consensus among the therapists that "traditional male socialization can negatively affect men's relationships and general sense of well-being" (p. 562). Moreover, they found that men are reluctant to seek help and that when they do, they tend to resist a close counseling relationship.

According to Heesacker and Prichard (1992), one aim of traditional counseling—that of trying to help men become more like women in the way they express themselves emotionally—contributes to men's reluctance to seek counseling. They recommend that counselors perceive men as emotionally different from women, rather than as emotionally inferior. They comment, "We do not believe that men are inherently less 'therapizable.' Instead, we believe that when men's emotions are understood more accurately, men will be drawn to therapy in greater numbers and will profit from it to a greater degree" (p. 283). Men traditionally have regarded women's tendency to develop relationships as negative, as a sign of dependency and enmeshment. However, feminists such as Chodorow (1974), Gilligan (1982), Miller and Stiver (1997), Jack (1991, 1999), and others, as discussed earlier, explain how maintaining mutual connections with others is distinctly different from dependency and enmeshment.

Recently, professional counseling journals and books have been addressing men's problems as related to gender role stereotyping and have suggested ways of improving counseling for men. Men traditionally have been reluctant to address male issues because men tend to deny problems, seek counseling less often, and express less dissatisfaction with their roles (Real, 1997, 2002, Silverberg, 1986). More recently, however, many men have been dissatisfied with their lives but, instead of seeking traditional counseling services, have literally taken to the woods. Beginning in the late 1980s, many men throughout the country retreated periodically to special men's gatherings in the wilderness. The most prominent of these groups, the mythopoetical men's movement, stimulated innumerable publications of new perspectives on masculinity and therapeutic approaches to men's problems, including books by Clatterbaugh (1990), Steinberg (1993), and Heesacker and Prichard (1992).

Mythopoetical Men's Groups

The mythopoetical men's movement was immensely popular during the late 1980s and early 1990s. It sprang from the vision of poet Robert Bly, whose work became popular with his best-selling book *Iron John* (1990). Through initiation by older men and close interaction with other men, Bly says, men can reach their deep masculine side. This masculine energy that Bly refers to is different from the shallow drives of the aggressive macho male. Men lost touch with this force, which Bly calls the Wild Man, when our country moved from an agrarian to an industrial society. Instead of working at home, where they could maintain close relationships with their families, most fathers began to work away from home and lost touch not only with their families but also with their creative energies. Out of touch and more inhibited, they developed stifling behaviors based on success, independence, competitiveness, and aggression (Bly, 1988). Like many other men, Frank Nugent was drawn to the mythopoetical movement.

> As a participant in various retreats for several years, I felt the profound need, as did many others, for male bonding and a long-denied opportunity to vent inner anguish in a safe place. Those mythopoetical men's group meetings that I found most successful lasted for a week and were directed by a team of leaders: a storyteller and drummer, a poet, and a Jungian analyst. Musicians who accompanied the leaders' presentations set the men in motion with their music and helped unite isolated individuals in the group (mythic) experience. Such a team provided a Jungian pattern that the leaders believed generated personal transformation (Hillman, 1989; Moore & Gillette, 1990).

Storytelling served as a method of engaging participants in enacting dramatic events. One primary storyteller at these retreats, Michael Meade, describes in his book *Men and the Water of Life: Initiation and the Tempering of Men* (1993) the experiences generated by his storytelling. The story, the group experience, and the conflicts that arose blended and evolved into a dramatic experience for everyone involved. Seeing themselves in the context of a larger story allowed men to release repressed isolated feelings and connect with the felt community of the men gathered closely together at the retreat. Men received support from the group that enabled them to share their vulnerabilities, reexperience old buried wounds and feelings of abandonment and isolation, grieve over lost fathers, examine their flaws stemming from the patriarchal system, and anguish over their inability to connect with wives and children.

The men's movement generated numerous lively responses and debates and stimulated men to delve into new perspectives on masculinity. Through these experiences, men learned to drop their defenses and bond emotionally with other men. This bonding contrasted sharply with the typical male bonding that is task oriented, as in team sports or the military, or that is based on superficial camaraderie in the form of joking or verbal jousting in pubs.

The mythopoetical groups and other similar experiences have expanded men's emotional awareness and have demonstrated that men are willing to acknowledge their need for help and respond well to counseling and therapy if they perceive the experience as inviting and meaningful.

A few cautionary remarks are needed, however, about men's retreats. Some men who start expressing feelings of anger, pain, or tenderness for the first time are met with hostility or bewilderment from spouses, families, or colleagues who are unprepared for the men's changes in behavior. Some men behave aggressively, claiming they are expressing their Wild Man. Even worse, for some, new insights and deep feelings of emotion fade away as soon as they return home and to work, leaving them with vague feelings of depression and loss. Moreover, some men attend one retreat after another as a brief tonic without adequately following through and applying insights to their lives.

For whatever reason, for many men a huge gap exists between what they experience at retreats and what happens after they return home. Such a lack of follow-through prevents them from working through newly experienced emotions. In her therapeutic work storyteller and Jungian psychoanalyst Clarissa Pinkola Estés (1992) estimates that therapeutic work with stories, depending on the story and the individual, takes several weeks or months.

The men's mythopoetical movement has generated a backlash from many profeminists. The idea of males beating drums in the woods, practicing how to become warriors, has touched some raw nerves. The warrior image, however, was meant to serve as a way to explore both the use and misuse of power and the need to turn energy into constructive interactions that go beyond self-serving ends. The primary purpose at male retreats is for men to learn to contain aggressive behaviors, change traditional masculine roles and patriarchal power-over behaviors, learn to use energies constructively, and learn to relate genuinely with loved ones.

> The hairy Wild Man, according to Bly, represents forceful energy and resolve, assertive energy that Bly contrasts to machismo and cruelty. Wild-Man energy is not focused primarily on domination and destruction, but is directed at a constructive engagement with the external world. (Steinberg, 1993, p. 126)

The theory behind both the need for men to find their inner Wild Man and the danger of the misuse of one's energies is quite similar to Estés's belief, as she explains in her book *Women Who Run With the Wolves* (1992), that women must seek their inner Wild Woman to avoid destructive behaviors that arise from neglected inner needs. Estés approaches initiation rituals differently, however. Unlike men, who typically conduct only boy-to-manhood initiation rituals, for women, initiation experiences occur throughout life, Estés says. Women are thrust into ongoing life-death-life experiences; birthing is but one example. Thus, female initiations are cyclical and self-regenerative processes.

Many criticize the mythopoetical experiencing of events as too esoteric. Others are uncomfortable with the variety of interpretations possible with stories and legends:

> For those who are interested in a scientifically grounded theory of masculine development, these anachronistic Jungian theories are not the answer—nor do they claim to be. But as long as the spiritual perspective is kept at the level of spiritual or religious quest (the story that tells stories), and so long as it does not ask scientific questions, it can serve both as a therapeutic device and as a motivator for personal change. (Clatterbaugh, 1990, pp. 102–103)

Still others criticize these men's groups for ignoring political and social issues (Basow, 1992). Although leaders at the men's retreats consistently emphasize that inner transformational changes should be carried over into effective social changes that benefit the community and the world as a whole, efforts to do so are left up to the individuals. One exception has been Michael Meade's (2004) ongoing retreats, described later.

Many counselors have been providing bridges between men's experiences at retreats and their return to families and friends in the community. Counselors can help men who are expressing feelings of anger, pain, or tenderness for the first time to understand why their spouses, families, and colleagues, unprepared for these changes in behavior, often respond with hostility or bewilderment. They can also caution men who behave aggressively toward others because of a mistaken perception of the Wild Man. In addition, counselors can be available to some men who become depressed, frustrated, or at a loss when new deep feelings of emotion and new insights begin to fade in the light of the real world.

Heesacker and Prichard (1992), who are professionally trained counselors, suggest that men clients be encouraged to tell stories, emphasizing that the metaphorical meanings of archetypes and myths can be useful in facilitating men's emotional development. They recommend that counselors be aware of the value of silence or brooding in counseling sessions. Instead of urging clients simply to try to verbalize their feelings, counselors should encourage them to enact their emotions during counseling sessions. The authors suggest that counselors and therapists should join men's groups as a means of consciousness-raising.

Meanwhile, counselors are giving more attention to the value of group counseling with men (Gladding, 1997). A special issue of the *Journal for Specialists in Group Work* published in May 1994 addressed the particular concerns of men. In that issue Hetzel, Barton, and Davenport suggest that group techniques, such as the use of rituals and conflict management, can help men profit from group counseling.

Of the original team, storyteller Michael Meade continues to lead men's retreats. As his book *Men and the Water of Life* (1993) attests, Meade is convinced of the transformational experience of storytelling. His group gatherings continue to evolve. Now organized under the Mosaic Multicultural Foundation, he has been collaborating with men from various ethnic backgrounds and with persons from different cultures, such as Malidoma and Sobonfu Sommé, from Africa, a husband-and-wife team, that helps lead Meade's workshops for men and women. Meade also organizes retreats for youths and adults, as well as for mentors and elders. In the mid-1990s Meade formed the Mosaic Multicultural Foundation to provide scholarship and training programs for disadvantaged youths to participate in his gatherings (Meade, 2004; see also chap. 19).

Counseling Men

Although most men have in the past been reluctant to seek counseling, men are now increasingly willing to see counselors and therapists. Counselors should note that gender stereotyping is usually at the root of their clients' problems. Men seek counseling for many reasons: They may be experiencing personal dissatisfaction or feelings of inadequacy and wish to change; they may be exhibiting addictive behaviors that belie defenses against depression; they may be having trouble with intimate relationships; they may be undergoing transitions in life that require role changes that lead to friction with spouses; they may be developing physiological breakdowns or pathological patterns of violence and abuse of others.

Men Who Feel Inadequate.   Some male clients who are highly successful in their jobs seek counseling because they are emotionally numb, burdened with responsibilities, and dissatisfied with themselves. They often say they think they are frauds and unworthy of their success. In addition, they usually lack the ability to develop personal relationships with both men and women.

Counseling with such men can be difficult because of their strong defenses. They have lost touch with their deep emotions because they have developed masks to cover the feelings of vulnerability that underlie their competent behaviors (Real, 1997, 2002; Silverberg, 1986). These men resist others' attempts to break through their defenses. As clients, they tend to intellectualize their problems while resisting a therapist's attempts to make them aware of their emotional vulnerability (Werrbach & Gilbert, 1987).

Male clients of this type are often troubled by the differences in how they deal with problems at work and at home. On the job they may resolve conflicts in a constructive manner through compromise, arbitration, or consensus. But at home, when conflicts arise, they tend to control relationships either by becoming aggressive or by trying to placate and thus prevent conflict. Counselors can help such clients explore how society's expectations have contributed to these differences in their behavior.

Men With Addictive Behaviors.   According to Real (1997), men develop addictive behaviors to defend against depression. Addictions can take innumerable forms—compulsive drinking, gambling, eating, spending; obsessive sexual urges and behaviors; workaholism; an obsessive desire to watch football and other sports, to work the computer, and so on. These addictions are a form of self-medication; they increase men's disconnection with themselves and with their loved ones and can lead to violent and destructive behaviors toward others.

Real (1997) believes that the problem of male depression is compounded because "we often fail to identify this disorder because men tend to manifest depression differently than women" (p. 23). Because women are permitted by the culture to experience and acknowledge their feelings, they are more likely to exhibit symptoms of depression that correspond to the *DSM-IV-TR* classification of depression (e.g., feeling worthless, immobilized, lethargic, with sudden onset of severe and long-lasting sleeping or eating disorders). Real calls this type of depression *overt depression.*

Male depression, in contrast, is masked and hidden from the person himself and from others around him. Symptoms include numbness of feelings to the extent that the man disassociates and disconnects from others, especially loved ones. Real (1997) calls this type of depression *covert depression.*

Both male and female forms of dysfunction, Real (1997) emphasizes, are similarly caused by early socialization that forces boys and girls to acquire gender-based behavioral patterns. Boys are taught to follow stereotypical masculine patterns of self-reliance and autonomy, strength and dominance; girls are taught to be nurturers and caretakers who must become subordinate to the needs of males. As a result, both boys and girls are traumatized but in different ways: Girls who don't behave according to their expected roles are usually shamed, ridiculed, or enticed into submission. Although girls are allowed to feel anguish and shame and are allowed to cry and weep, they are expected to remain in this weak, submissive role. Consequently, they become disempowered and lose their voice and the ability to assert themselves.

Boys are traumatized even more, Real (1997) claims, because not only are they shamed if they fail to follow expected masculine behaviors but they also cannot show hurt feelings. Thus, boys must deny the pain, the shame, and feelings in general. To maintain a strong masculine image, they adopt defenses to ward off so-called feminine feelings. They are also trained to separate emotionally from their mothers as a necessary step in gaining masculine identity, whereas girls are encouraged to maintain connections with their mothers. Boys thus experience rejection and abandonment, feelings that must be denied. To exert masculine strength, they adopt a false sense of empowerment, asserting themselves as strong and invulnerable. But this aura of grandiosity gives a false sense of self—a self that can and must achieve, must be the best, or as Real says, a self that always needs to feel better than others.

"A common defense against the painful experience of deflated value is inflated value; and a common compensation for shame, of feeling less than, is a subtle or flagrant flight into grandiosity, of feeling better than" (Real, 1997, p. 55). Thus, at an early age, boys seek to gain self-esteem through external recognition and approval of others. Real says that when boys grow up, they are like hollow men lacking feelings of intrinsic self-worth and depending on external achievements and approval from others for feelings of self-esteem.

Boys also tend to identify with the abusive or neglectful father as another means of defending and protecting themselves. In these cases they carry both the shame and the destructive feelings of their fathers or mothers and enact them, in turn, on their own children and spouses. These feelings are called *carried feelings* or *carried shame:* "They are the means by which the wound, the legacy of pain, is passed from father to son, mother to son, across generations. Carried feelings or carried shame are the psychological seeds of depression" (Real, 1997, p. 206).

For men to overcome covert depression, Real (1997) says, they need therapy to help them let go of their addictive defenses, work through the painful withdrawal symptoms, and navigate the long road of recovery: "First the addictive defenses must stop. Then, the dysfunctional patterns in the man's relationship to himself must be attended to. Finally buried early trauma must reemerge and, as much as possible, be reenacted" (pp. 269–270).

The first stage, letting go of addictive defenses, is exceedingly difficult for men. Most men have to be forced into taking the first step; the wife, for example, may leave him. In the second stage, after working through painful withdrawal symptoms, the client disidentifies with the abusing or neglectful parent(s), usually the father. In the third stage the client identifies with two parts of his inner child—the injured, wounded child and the aggressive destructive child, both of whom were introjected, or thrust into his subconcious, by parental behavior. The client essentially learns to nurture and parent himself. At this point Real usually assigns the client to group therapy with other men who themselves are in recovery, working through covert depression. In a form of Gestalt therapy, he uses the hot seat method, whereby the client voluntarily sits on the hot seat in the center of the group. With group support the client is encouraged and coaxed to imagine and enact early childhood traumas and to dialogue with the abusive, neglectful parent(s) and with his injured child. The client then reestablishes a connection with his feminine side, regains a healthy connection with himself and with others, and above all, avoids passing on the toxic consequences of covert depression to his children or spouse (Real, 1997).

Men Who Have Problems With Intimacy.   Terence Real (2002) expanded his work on male depression by exploring the issue of men's inability to develop intimate relationships. Because men in this culture have been brought up to separate from their mothers and become autonomous and independent, they later have trouble with relationships. This male characteristic becomes all the more pronounced with those who suffered ongoing neglect and/or abuse during their childhood from their primary caretakers.

A practicing psychotherapist and teacher for over 20 years, Real (2002) formed a team with Carol Gilligan (1982; Wylie, 2002), who had been impressed by his book on male depression; together they observed couple relationships through a series of interviews and found them severely lacking. "A common story began to emerge—of boys and girls attached to their mothers in pleasure and then losing that connection, of men and women attached to each other in love and then losing that connection" (Real, 2002, p. 37). Real and Gilligan formed a couples therapy program radically different from conventional models with the sole purpose of recovering "relationality" (Real, 2002, p. 36), a therapy aptly called relational recovery therapy. Their model is discussed in chapter 10 under marriage counseling theories.

Men Who Have Trouble Changing Roles.   Counselors also work with men clients who are changing their career or undergoing a major transition in life. Men may experience uncertainty or stress in their work if they are promoted to new and highly demanding jobs, if they lose their jobs and become dependent on their wives, or if their jobs become obsolete and they must seek jobs in fields in which they are untrained. Men who have relentlessly sought success may experience a midlife crisis in which they fear they have wasted their lives (O'Neil & Egan, 1992; Schlossberg & Entine, 1977).

Another time of particular stress for most men comes when they face retirement. A life based on achievement and power suddenly changes, and they feel useless. At the same time they are suddenly put into close daily contact with their wives, a situation unfamiliar to them.

Men also run into difficulties when their wives' roles begin to change. Wives may decide to start careers, or they may express dissatisfaction with their husbands' preoccupation with work and lack of interest in developing the marital relationship. Counselors note that these man usually come to therapy depressed, anxious, frustrated, or angry with women but bewildered about what to do. Clients often say that women want too much or that they don't know what women want (Werrbach & Gilbert, 1987).

Furthermore, changes in men's stereotypical gender roles have led to more men seeking and gaining custody of their children (Grief, 1985; Tillitski, 1992). Consequently, Tillitski (1992) believes that counselors must be alert to an identifiable group of men with postdivorce parenting problems, either as single custodial fathers or as men sharing custody of children with their former spouses.

Men With Physiological and Pathological Problems.

Physiological and psychological disorders often result when men follow stereotypical roles excessively (Skovholt, 1978, 1993; Toomer, 1978). According to Skovholt (1978), workaholic behavior makes men more susceptible than women to ulcers, heart attacks, and high blood pressure. He also notes that more men are alcoholics and that males also outnumber females in completed suicides. Toomer (1978) believes that too much stress can be the cause of an overall shorter life span in men. Men with physical diseases caused by stress respond well to holistic counseling that emphasizes stress reduction, relaxation, and nutrition.

Some men who follow stereotypical aggressive roles excessively may run into trouble with the law. Men commit a high percentage of violent crimes, including gang wars, homicides, rapes, domestic violence, assaults, child abuse, and serial murders. Most voyeurs and exhibitionists are also men, as are most obscene telephone callers (Skovholt, 1978).

More recently, Skovholt (1993) points out that in his many years of counseling men, he has noted a significant change in male response to therapy. Originally, he said, there was little interest among males to enter therapy to deal with their aggression and violence, nor were therapists prepared to work with them. But times have changed.

> Domestic violence intervention programs have grown significantly in recent years. The documented success of these programs . . . represents a major advance in helping men live fuller, healthier, more equitable lives. I have been struck by the response of many men who completed domestic abuse group programs. Often forced into treatment by the courts or a spouse, they later may discuss the benefits of the program and how it has helped them. (Skovholt, 1993, p. 13)

Special rehabilitation programs for treating men with such disorders are offered in community clinics and in prisons and parole offices. Special treatment is also available in clinics and mental hospitals. The Giarretto Institute in San Jose, California, discussed in chapter 19, works with men who have sexually abused their children. It also works with family members in an attempt to restore the families.

Because socialization begins in early childhood, it is important to explore one's family of origin. Aggressive, violent males often come from dysfunctional families in which they routinely experienced emotional neglect, fear of abandonment, or physical abuse. In addition, Skovholt (1993) cites numerous references to the severe loss/grief reactions that men experience when their a female partner leaves them.

> The most dangerous time for males comes from unexpected abandonment. . . . Often a man in this situation becomes extremely depressed and acts out his despair by increasing his attempts to control his situation and his partner through power. This is a pre-abuse and pre-violence stage that suggests active therapist/counselor intervention. (Skovholt, 1993, p. 11)

Many of these men have modeled fathers who themselves were following stereotypical patterns or whose fathers had never bonded with them. As discussed earlier, Real (1997) describes how men carry their fathers' shame and how boys have been taught to devalue their mothers, leaving them seriously unable to relate well to others.

Nonsexist Counselor Training

Fitzgerald and Nutt (1986) claim that special skills are needed to counsel women because of the dangers of stereotyping. In addition, difficulties can arise over the inappropriate gender-match of therapist and client. Many women clients don't respond well to male therapists who have traditional stereotypical expectations of the female role; and female therapists may experience unresolved resentment toward the aggressive acting-out behaviors of male clients (Robinson & Howard-Hamilton, 2000).

Faunce (1985) discusses the importance of including in course work and supervision the principles of feminist therapy, including nonsexist views, an understanding of situational and cultural factors in assessing women's problems, and consciousness-raising of potential gender biases. Heesacker and Prichard (1992) and Williams and Myer (1992) make similar recommendations regarding counselor training and male gender stereotyping in the counseling of men. Corey, Corey, and Callanan (1998) also caution family counselors of the dangers of gender role stereotyping during couples or family counseling. Consciousness-raising through workshops and professional continuing education allows instructors and supervisors to model nonsexist attitudes and behaviors for graduate students and interns in counseling. Instructors can also alert graduate students and interns to any indications of bias or countertransference in their interactions with clients.

Regarding the ethical responsibility of counselor educators, Stevens-Smith (1995) includes gender issues in counselor training programs. She notes that power and equity exist on four levels: "personal, clinical, social, and political" (p. 283). Counselors need knowledge and awareness of their own personal views and potential biases about gender roles. In clinical work counselors must be trained to be aware of their clients' worldviews and know that these worldviews influence their perception of gender roles. Furthermore, the negative impact of the socialization process in our culture on the well-being and emotional maturity of both women and men must be attended to in counselor training. And the political implications of gender cannot be ignored: "A continual refusal to address gender as a political statement may only further perpetuate inequality in power, dependence of women both economically and psychologically and growing resentment among men concerning this issue" (p. 290).

Counselor and Client Match

If counselors are aware of the negative influence of gender stereotyping, they should be better able to counsel clients of either sex (Basow, 1992; Tanney & Birk, 1976). Same-sex counseling may often be more productive, however, assuming that a qualified counselor with suitable personal qualities is available. A woman or man searching for personal identity may respond better to a same-sex counselor; a woman who has just experienced assault, incest, or rape by a man may find it difficult to respond to a male counselor; a man may have trouble relating to a female counselor if he has just experienced a traumatic divorce. Yet even in such cases, counselors of the opposite sex who are understanding, open, and unbiased may sometimes benefit clients who have had consistently negative experiences with members of the opposite sex. A warm, trusting, and productive female-male or male-female counseling relationship may ultimately lead clients to better relationships with members of the opposite sex.

COUNSELING GAYS, LESBIANS, AND BISEXUALS

Surveys indicate that about 10% of the population in the United States, about 22 million people, are gay or lesbian. This figure is considered conservative because some people do not publicly admit that they are gay or lesbian (Baruth & Manning, 2003; Fassinger, 1991; Schliebner-Tait & Peregoy, 2001). Reluctance to acknowledge one's gay or lesbian sexual orientation stems from a history of discrimination and abuse. Negative attitudes began to change, however, after the gay liberation movement developed from the civil rights and women's movements. In 1973 the American Psychiatric Association and in 1975 the American Psychological Association both declassified homosexuality as a form of mental illness. Then, in the mid-1980s, after gay communities experienced the spread of the human immunodeficiency virus (HIV), which causes acquired immune deficiency syndrome (AIDS), former prejudices against gays began to reemerge (Hoffman, 1991). Even though in recent years communities have generally become more accepting of gays and lesbians, "discrimination and violence against these populations remain high" (Sue & Sue, 2003, p. 380).

Several professional journals have featured the counseling needs of gays and lesbians, including the September/October 1989 issue of the *Journal of Counseling & Development* and the April 1991 and September 1998 issues of *Counseling Psychologist.* In 1992 the American Counseling Association (then AACD) published the book *Counseling Gay Men and Lesbians: A Journey to the End of the Rainbow*, edited by Dworkin and Gutiérrez (1992a). These are comprehensive resources from which much of the following discussion is drawn.

The Counseling Process

Gays and lesbians have problems common to everyone, problems related to identity, interpersonal, career, and family issues. These problems are exacerbated, however, for gays and lesbians, who, because of their sexual orientation, must cope with feelings of unacceptance and invisibility. In addition, gay men especially face concerns and problems related to AIDS and to victimization through violence by heterosexuals. Adaptation to a positive gay and lesbian identity (coming out) is often a prolonged, difficult process. Dworkin and Gutiérrez (1992b) summarize the work of O'Bear and Reynolds (1985), who found that a 16-year gap generally exists between awareness of gay feelings, which often occurs during adolescence, and the development of a positive gay or lesbian identity.

Browning, Reynolds, and Dworkin (1991) describe specific issues confronting lesbians, who can be helped through affirmative counseling interventions. Following a similar format, Shannon and Woods (1991) do the same for gay men. Integrating several identity models, Troiden (1989) has developed a four-stage model of gay development: (a) sensitization, (b) identity confusion, (c) identity assumption, and (d) commitment. Troiden presents these stages as a developmental process that usually starts before puberty and ends with commitment when individuals are in their 20s. Individuals who develop awareness of their gay and lesbian feelings later in life generally follow a similar sequence.

Sensitization involves feelings of difference from peers and feelings of social isolation. *Identity confusion* develops when individuals become aware of attitudes and behaviors that could be called gay or lesbian (O'Connor, 1992). This stage is particularly difficult for gay and lesbian adolescents, about 20% to 35% of whom attempt suicide (Herdt, 1989). In the *identity assumption* stage, individuals identify themselves as gays or lesbians. At this stage they find new friends and support groups in gay and lesbian communities; concerns about stigma and family rejection are primary sources of difficulty. In the final stage of *commitment,* gays and lesbians come out to the public. Their way of life includes loving relationships and long-term commitments, rather than a focus only on sexual activities (O'Connor, 1992; Troiden, 1989).

Counselors can help gays and lesbians work through the coming-out process in several ways. Counselors can help clients work through fears and anxieties when they first acknowledge, personally or publicly, that they are gay or lesbian; can help them cope with anger or rejection from family and friends; and can support clients who experience discrimination or violence in social and career interactions. Whereas heterosexuals who experience identity or interpersonal problems usually expect support from their families, gays and lesbians often experience parental rejection or withdrawal of support. Nevertheless, Sue and Sue (2003) caution that counselors should not dwell on issues of sexual orientation when clients are not presenting this as a problem; the counselor's responsibility is to attend to the concerns raised by the client.

Throughout the developmental stages many gays and lesbians explore and work through their own internalized negative feelings about their sexual orientation (i.e., internalized homophobia). Those who are socially rejected or who are uninformed or misinformed about their sexual orientation often experience shame, guilt, and low self-esteem. Murphy (1989) points out that female couples who have affirmed their lesbian identities and have worked through their own internalized homophobia are able to handle parental disapproval and maintain positive relationships with each other.

Bisexuals, whose orientation includes partners of both the same and the opposite sex, have also been receiving attention in the literature. Their numbers are difficult to assess, but it is estimated that they exceed the gay and lesbian populations (Wolf, 1992). Bisexuality has been described variously as a nonentity, a transitional stage toward or away from gay or lesbian tendencies, or a denial of one's gay or lesbian orientation (Wolf, 1992). Wolf (1992) says that bisexual persons come to counseling confused or anxious because they do not feel a part of gay, lesbian, or heterosexual communities. Betz (1991) expresses concern about the lack of attention to bisexuals and believes that gays, lesbians, and heterosexuals all need to give them more support and understanding.

Career Concerns

Like heterosexuals, lesbians and gays, differ considerably among themselves in personality characteristics, abilities, and career interests. Unlike heterosexuals, however, lesbians and gays are faced with deciding whether they want to work in careers in which sexual orientation can cause discrimination or exclusion—for example, in the military, federal government, public schools, or child care (Baruth & Manning, 2003; Orzek, 1992). The counselor's role is to help gay or lesbian clients explore occupations that suit their characteristics and then help them assess the potential risks involved in placement. But ultimately the decisions must reside with the clients.

Couple and Family Concerns

Family and couple counseling with gays involves legal concerns that heterosexuals do not have to face (Fassinger, 1991). Because legalized gay marriages are not sanctioned in society, joint health insurance benefits, joint income tax returns, and legal custody of children are not available to gay couples. Some states prohibit gay parents from adopting children, and gay parents are often refused custody of their children from previous heterosexual marriages. Little support is given to lesbians who choose to have children within a lesbian relationship (Baruth & Manning, 2003; Fassinger, 1991).

Substance Abuse

Research shows that gays and lesbians are more susceptible to substance abuse than are heterosexuals (Schliebner-Tait & Peregoy, 2001). "The psychosocial stress of being a homosexual man or woman (hereafter also referred to as gay/lesbian/bisexual or GLB) in a society dominated by a heterosexual orientation places GLB individuals at high risk for alcohol and drug abuse" (Schliebner-Tait & Peregoy, 2001, p. 232). A major contributing factor is their dependence on the gay bar as the only available place to socialize. Counselors need to be alert to the possibility of substance abuse with gays and lesbians who seek treatment for relationship difficulties, depression, or other symptoms of emotional stress (Faltz, 1992).

Acquired Immune Deficiency Syndrome

Gibson and Mitchell (1999) cite statistics showing that 47% of AIDS cases resulted from male/homosexual/bisexual contact and 21% from intravenous drug use. Statistics also indicate, however, that the percentage of AIDS cases in the heterosexual population is increasing at alarming rates. Women who have sexual relationships with bisexual men or heterosexual men who have had multiple partners are at particular risk.

As of 1997 about 270,000 persons in the United States had AIDS (Stevens, 2001). The majority of persons with AIDS are young: 16% in their 20s, 45% in their 30s, and 26% in their 40s (Gibson & Mitchell, 1999). AIDS develops after a person becomes infected with HIV; it usually takes 6 to 10 years for full-blown AIDS to appear after an individual tests positive for HIV.

Counseling with AIDS clients presents more challenges and difficulties than does counseling with clients in general (Geratz, 1995; Hoffman, 1991). Client feelings of isolation and rejection are aggravated by illness and the fear of dying. AIDS victims may also deny their illness. Hoffman (1991) puts it vividly: "It is about the loss of one's health, vitality, sensuality, and career—and most profoundly, the letting go of the future as one had envisioned it" (p. 468).

Hoffman advocates a psychosocial counseling model in working with persons with AIDS (PWAs) because the disease affects all aspects of the individual's life and has traumatic effects on family and friends. In her model she includes the importance of addressing the stigma attached to AIDS, the degree of interpersonal and institutional support, situational factors related to the source and progression of the disease, and client psychosocial characteristics and competence (gender, race, lifestyle).

Allers and Katrin (1988) propose an AIDS psychosocial counseling model (APCM) that involves five phases: (a) overcoming the initial fear of the disease, (b) redefining relationships, (c) modifying lifestyles, (d) reevaluating life's meaning, and (e) adjusting to the physical and social limitations (p. 235). Price, Omizo, and Hammett (1986) recommend a similar psychoeducational model of treatment, in which clients are encouraged to take an active role. They suggest that clients engage in safe sex; but they also recommend that clients develop emotional intimacies with partners, rather than emphasizing sexual encounters. In addition, they encourage clients to refocus on activities that cut down on feelings of isolation. Especially beneficial for AIDS clients is the supportive atmosphere of group counseling, which provides a feeling of family togetherness and gives an opportunity for positive role modeling. Counselors must also be familiar with social agencies to which they can refer clients for legal, medical, or economic aid.

A biopsychosocial model for counseling clients with AIDS is proposed by Geratz (1995). He believes that a comprehensive treatment program should include (a) information and education about the illness, (b) a comprehensive biopsychosocial assessment, (c) crisis intervention services when appropriate, (d) brief or long-term counseling or both, (e) group intervention, and (f) comprehensive and thorough case management with detailed follow-up procedures (p. 16).

Families of AIDS victims may also need counseling to overcome their misapprehension that the disease may be contagious, which can lead to their rejection of the patient. Grief counseling can help them complete their relationship with the dying AIDS patient and rid themselves of the guilt and remorse that often follow the death of a loved one (Dworkin & Pincu, 1993; Williams & Stafford, 1991).

Parents of Gays and Lesbians

Since the late 1980s, articles have been appearing in the professional literature about counselor interaction with parents or families of gays and lesbians. Murphy (1989) has written about helping lesbians deal with parental attitudes, and Teague (1992) discusses the need for services to be available to families of gays and lesbians. Hammersmith (1987) proposes an interactionist sociological approach to working with families of gays. Teague and Hammersmith both discuss the importance of acknowledging family fears about stigmas and the need to provide families with information and resources. Parents especially need emotional support and the availability of counseling to work through their doubts and concerns when their children come out as gays or lesbians. Support groups can help them share experiences and learn new attitudes and skills in relating to their children and their children's partners.

Counselor Training

Some authors have pointed out that training programs inadequately cover the counseling of gays and lesbians (Betz, 1991; Buhrke, 1989; Buhrke & Douce, 1991; Sue & Sue, 2003). These authors suggest that core courses in counselor training need to include discussions about the special concerns of gays and lesbians. They also recommend that some counseling theories and techniques be modified and that courses in career counseling include issues about discrimination of gays and lesbians. Moreover, instructors, supervisors, and graduate students in counselor training programs need to become aware of their own latent or potential biases toward gay and lesbian clients (House & Holloway, 1992; Baruth & Manning, 2003).

All counselors should differentiate those clients who are expressing confusion about sexual orientation from those who have confirmed their gay or lesbian identity. In the first case counselors should allow clients the freedom to explore their own sexual identities. In the second case counselors should support a client's particular orientation.

Few counselor training programs include courses or field experiences in AIDS treatment. In a survey of APA-approved graduate programs in counseling and clinical psychology, Campos, Brasfield, and Kelly (1989) found that 75% of programs responding did not include training for counseling AIDS patients. In their study Crawford, Humfleet, Ribordy, Ho, and Vickers (1991) found that counselors and psychotherapists were reluctant to accept AIDS patients. Crawford et al. conjecture that negative attitudes might be generated by feelings of professional inadequacy, as well as by ignorance. In any case they recommend that training programs and in-service training include information about AIDS and skills to work with PWAs. They also recommend training counselors to be aware of the countertransference that is apt to happen during counseling, when they may tend to overidentify with the client's trauma, either by avoidance or by oversympathizing. Because the sufferings of AIDS patients are so complex, counselors working with these clients need "training in cultural diversity, empowerment strategies, medical information, gay and lesbian issues, counseling clients on death and dying issues and . . . a greater degree of knowledge . . . in psychology and psychiatry disciplines" (Geratz, 1995, p. 16).

Counselor and Client Match

A majority of gay, lesbian, bisexual, and heterosexual clients choose counselors with the same sexual orientation. Even so, many mental health professionals do not believe that only gay counselors must work with gay clients or that only heterosexual counselors must work with heterosexual clients. Sexual orientation is not an essential match characteristic as long as the client is willing and as long as gay, lesbian, bisexual, and heterosexual counselors are aware of their own potential biases and are understanding of gay, lesbian, and bisexual difficulties. In their guidelines for appropriate counselor training, Buhrke and Douce (1991) give the following cautions: "Do not refer all gay and lesbian issues to gay or lesbian faculty or staff. Do not assume their only expertise is gay and lesbian issues. Such practice tokenizes and ghettoizes gay and lesbian people" (p. 230).

SUMMARY

Counseling professionals are increasingly aware that they must prepare themselves to work with the complex, diverse needs of growing numbers of multicultural individuals whose needs, values, and beliefs differ from those on which traditional counseling theories and techniques have been developed. Special attention is now being given in counselor training to increasing counselors' awareness of their potential biases toward clients.

The professional literature has been reflecting more understanding of diverse social-cultural characteristics, including the various ethnic minorities, men and women, gays, lesbians, and bisexuals.

Ethnic counselors and psychologists have been especially active in discussion and research about counselor attitudes, racial identity, and individual and cultural characteristics. Female counselors have developed feminine counseling theories and techniques to counter the negative impact of gender stereotyping and to help female clients develop themselves through relationships and connections with others. Professionals acknowledge that gender-based socialization processes cause dysfunctions in males as well; male counselors are applying new theories of masculinity to counseling practice. Counselors, also help gays, lesbians, and bisexuals develop their own identities and cope with the biases of relatives, colleagues, and society in general. For AIDS victims, counselors help clients work through feelings of isolation, denial, anger, and grief.

PROJECTS AND ACTIVITIES

1. Role-play an opening counseling session with a counselor and a client of the opposite sex. The prospective client says she feels shy and intimidated in her interactions with the opposite sex. Then reverse the roles of counselor and client. Share reactions to the feelings engendered in counselor and client.

2. Invite a panel of speakers who are members of various ethnic groups and are community mental health specialists and school counselors to speak to your class about problems in reaching ethnic clients. Invite suggestions on how to improve communication with these groups.

3. Explore the traditional healing approaches of a particular ethnic group. Invite such a traditional healer (e.g., a Native American shaman or medicine man) to speak to the class about her or his views of mental health and treatment.

4. Invite professionally trained female and male counselors to class to discuss the types of problems their clients present that are specifically related to gender role conflict. Ask them to discuss how they go about helping these clients.

5. Invite lesbian, gay, and bisexual persons from a campus advocacy group and the director of the university counseling center to class, or interview each person separately. How does each think the gay advocacy group and the counseling center uniquely help gays? Do they overlap? Are cross-referrals made?

6. Invite professionally trained counselors from various minority groups to discuss with your class or group the issues related to the counseling of minorities—for example, counseling by whites, differences and similarities in minority group values and their influence on counseling, and the problem of culturally biased tests.

REFERENCES

Allers, C. T., & Katrin, S. E. (1988). AIDS counseling: A psychosocial model. *Journal of Mental Health Counseling, 10,* 235–244.

Arredondo, P., Toporek, R., Brown, S. P., Jones; J., Locke, D. C., Sanchez, J., & Stadler, H. (1996). Operationalization of the multicultural competencies. *Journal of Multicultural Counseling & Development, 24,* 42–78.

Atkinson, D. R., Morten, G., & Sue, D. W. (1993). *Counseling American minorities: A cross-cultural perspective* (4th ed.). Dubuque, IA: William C. Brown.

Atkinson, D. R., Morten, G., & Sue, D. W. (1998). *Counseling American minorities* (5th ed.). Boston, MA: McGraw-Hill.

Atkinson, D. R., Wampold, B. E., Lowe, S. M., Matthews, L., & Ahn, H. (1998). Asian American preferences for counselor characteristics: Application of the Bradley-Terry-Luce model. *Counseling Psychologist, 26,* 101–123.

Ballou, M., & Gabalac, N. (1985). *A feminist position on mental health.* Springfield, IL: Charles C Thomas.

Baruth, L. G., & Manning, L. M. (1999). *Multicultural counseling and psychotherapy: A lifespan perspective* (2nd ed.). Upper Saddle River, NJ: Merrill/Prentice Hall.

Baruth, L. G., & Manning, M. L. (2003). *Multicultural counseling and psychotherapy: A lifespan perspective* (3rd ed.). Upper Saddle River, NJ: Merrill/Prentice Hall.

Basow, S. A. (1992). *Gender stereotypes and roles* (3rd ed.). Pacific Grove, CA: Brooks/Cole.

Betz, N. E. (1991). Implications for counseling psychology training programs. *Counseling Psychologist, 19,* 248–252.

Bly, R. (1988). The mystery of the wild man. *Resurgence, 128,* 8–10.

Bly, R. (1990). *Iron John: A book about men.* Reading, MA: Addison-Wesley.

Broverman, I. K., Broverman, D. M., Clarkson, F. E., Rosenkrantz, P. S., & Vogel, S. R. (1970). Sex-role stereotypes and clinical judgments of mental health. *Journal of Consulting and Clinical Psychology, 34,* 1–7.

Browning, C., Reynolds, A. L., & Dworkin, S. H. (1991). Affirmative psychotherapy for lesbian women. *Counseling Psychologist, 19,* 177–196.

Buhrke, R. A. (1989). Incorporating lesbian and gay issues into counselor training: A resource guide. *Journal of Counseling & Development, 68,* 77–80.

Buhrke, R. A., & Douce, L. A. (1991). Training issues for counseling psychologists in working with lesbian women and gay men. *Counseling Psychologist, 19,* 216–234.

Campos, P. E., Brasfield, T. L., & Kelly, J. A. (1989). Psychology training related to AIDS: Survey of doctoral graduate programs and predoctoral internship programs. *Professional Psychology: Research and Practice, 20,* 214–220.

Casas, J. M., & Vasquez, M. J. (1996). Counseling the Hispanic: A guiding framework for a diverse population. In P. B. Pedersen, J. G. Draguns, W. J. Lonner, & J. E. Trimble (Eds.), *Counseling across cultures* (4th ed.). Thousand Oaks, CA: Sage.

Chodorow, N. (1974). Family structure and feminine personality. In M.Z. Rosaldo & L..Lamphere (Eds.), *Woman, culture and society.* Stanford, CA: Stanford University Press.

Clatterbaugh, K. (1990). *Contemporary perspectives on masculinity: Men, women, and politics in modern society.* Boulder, CO: Westview Press.

Clatterbaugh, K. (1996). *Contemporary perspectives on masculinity: Men, women and politics in modern society.* (2nd ed.). Boulder, CO: Westview Press.

Comas-Diaz, L. (1993). Hispanic Latino communities: Psychological implications. In D. R. Atkinson, G. Morten, &

D. W. Sue (Eds.), *Counseling American minorities: A cross-cultural perspective* (4th ed., pp. 245–263). Dubuque, IA: William C. Brown.

Copeland, E. J. (1982). Minority populations and traditional counseling programs: Some alternatives. *Counselor Education and Supervision, 21,* 187–193.

Copeland, E. J. (1983). Cross-cultural counseling and psychotherapy: A historical perspective, implications for research and training. *Personnel and Guidance Journal, 62,* 10–15.

Corey, G., Corey, M. S., & Callanan, P. (1998). *Issues and ethics in the helping profession* (5th ed.). Pacific Grove, CA: Brooks/Cole.

Crawford, I., Humfleet, G., Ribordy, S. C., Ho, F. C., & Vickers, V. L. (1991). Stigmatization of AIDS patients by mental health professionals. *Professional Psychology: Research and Practice, 22,* 357–361.

Cross, W. E., Jr., & Fhagen-Smith, P. (1996). Nigrescence and ego identity development: Accounting for differential black identity patterns. In P. B. Pedersen, J. G. Draguns, W. L. Lonner, & J. E. Trimble (Eds.), *Counseling across cultures* (4th ed., pp. 108–123). Thousand Oaks, CA: Sage.

De La Cancela, V., & Guzman, L. P. (1991). Latino mental health service needs: Implications for training psychologists. In H. F. Myers, P. Wohlford, L. P. Guzman, & R. J. Echemendia (Eds.), *Ethnic minority perspectives on clinical training and services in psychology* (pp. 59–66). Washington, DC: American Psychological Association.

Draguns, J. G. (1996). Humanly universal and culturally distinctive: Charting the course of cultural counseling. In P. B. Pedersen, J. G. Draguns, W. J. Lonner, & J. E. Trimble (Eds.), *Counseling across cultures* (4th ed., pp. 1–20). Thousand Oaks, CA: Sage.

Dworkin, S. H., & Gutiérrez, F. J. (Eds.). (1992a). *Counseling gay men and lesbians: Journey to the end of the rainbow.* Alexandria, VA: American Counseling Association.

Dworkin, S. H., & Gutiérrez, F. J. (1992b). Introduction: Opening the closet door. In S. H. Dworkin & F. J. Gutiérrez (Eds.), *Counseling gay men and lesbians: Journey to the end of the rainbow* (pp. xvii–xxvii). Alexandria, VA: American Counseling Association.

Dworkin, S. H., & Pincu, L. (1993). Counseling in the era of AIDS. *Journal of Counseling & Development, 71,* 275–281.

Estés, C. P. (1992). *Women who run with the wolves: Myths and stories of the wild woman archetype.* New York: Ballantine Books.

Faltz, B. G. (1992). Counseling chemically dependent lesbians and gay men. In S. H. Dworkin & F. J. Gutiérrez (Eds.), *Counseling gay men and lesbians: Journey to the end of the rainbow* (pp. 245–258). Alexandria, VA: American Counseling Association.

Fassinger, R. E. (1991). The hidden minority: Issues and challenges in working with lesbian women and gay men. *Counseling Psychologist, 19,* 157–176.

Faunce, P. F. (1985). Tracking feminist therapies: Integrating feminist therapy, pedagogy, and scholarship. In L. B. Rosewater & L. E. A. Walker (Eds.), *Handbook of feminist therapy: Women's issues in psychotherapy* (pp. 309–320). New York: Springer.

Fitzgerald, L. F., & Nutt, R. (1986). The Division 17 principles concerning the counseling/psychotherapy of women: Rationale and implementation. *Counseling Psychologist, 14,* 180–216.

Franks, V. (1986). Sex stereotyping and diagnosis of psychopathology. *Women & Therapy, 5,* 219–231.

Garreau, J. (1988). The integration of an American dream. *Washington Post National Weekly Edition, 5,* 6–8.

Geratz, E. (1995). A biopsychosocial paradigm for counseling clients with AIDS. *Counseling Today, 37,* p. 16.

Gibson, R. L., & Mitchell, M. H. (1999*). Introduction to counseling and guidance* (5th ed.). Upper Saddle River, NJ: Merrill/Prentice-Hall.

Gilligan, C. (1982). *In a different voice.* Cambridge, MA: Harvard University Press.

Gilligan, C. (2002). *The birth of pleasure.* New York: Alfred A. Knopf.

Gladding, S. T. (1997). *Community and agency counseling.* Upper Saddle River, NJ: Merrill/Prentice Hall.

Grief, G. L. (1985). *Single fathers.* Toronto: Heath.

Hammersmith, S. K. (1987). A sociological approach to counseling homosexual clients and their families. *Journal of Homosexuality, 13,* 173–190.

Heesacker, M., & Prichard, S. (1992). In a different voice revisited: Men, women, and emotion. *Journal of Mental Health Counseling, 14,* 274–290.

Herdt, G. (1989). Gay and lesbian youth: Emergent identities and cultural scenes at home and abroad. *Journal of Homosexuality, 17,* 1–42.

Hetzel, R. D., Barton, D. A., & Davenport, D. S. (1994, May). Helping men change: A group counseling model for male clients. *Journal for Specialists in Group Work, 19,* 52–64.

Hillman, J. (1989). *A blue fire: Selected writings.* New York: Harper Perennial.

Hoffman, M. A. (1991). Counseling the HIV-infected client: A psychosocial model for assessment and intervention. *Counseling Psychologist, 19,* 467–542.

House, R. M., & Holloway, E. L. (1992). Empowering the counseling professional to work with gay and lesbian issues. In S. H. Dworkin & F. J. Gutiérrez (Eds.), *Counseling gay men and lesbians: Journey to the end of the rainbow* (pp. 307–324). Alexandria, VA: American Counseling Association.

Ibrahim, F. A., & Herr, E. L. (1987). Battered women: A developmental life-career counseling perspective. *Journal of Counseling & Development, 65,* 244–248.

Ivey, A. E. (1986). *Developmental therapy.* San Francisco: Jossey-Bass.

Ivey, A. E., D'Andrea, M., Ivey, M. B., & Simek-Morgan, L. (2002). *Counseling and psychotherapy: A multicultural perspective* (5th ed.). Boston: Allyn & Bacon.

Jack, D. C. (1991). *Silencing the self: Women and depression.* Cambridge, MA: Harvard University Press.

Jack, D. C. (1999). *Behind the mask: Destruction and creativity in women's aggression.* Cambridge, MA: Harvard University Press.

Jones, E. E. (1985). Psychotherapy and counseling with black clients. In P. Pedersen (Ed.), *Handbook of cross-cultural counseling and therapy* (pp. 173–179). Westport, CT: Greenwood Press.

Kelly, K. R., & Hall, A. S. (1992). Toward a development model for counseling men. *Journal of Mental Health Counseling, 14,* 257–273.

Kiselicka, M. S. (1998). Preparing Anglos for the challenges and joys of multiculturalism. *Counseling Psychologist, 26,* 5–21.

Kitano, H. H. L., & Maki, M. T. (1996). Continuity, change, and diversity: Counseling Asian Americans. In P. B. Pedersen, J. G. Draguns, W. L. Lonner, & J. E. Trimble (Eds.), *Counseling across cultures* (4th ed., pp. 124–145). Thousand Oaks, CA: Sage.

Kleinknecht, R. A. (1991). *Mastering anxiety: The nature and treatment of anxious conditions.* New York: Plenion Insight.

Lee, C. C., & Richardson, B. L. (1991). Promise and pitfalls of multicultural counseling. In C. C. Lee & B. L. Richardson (Eds.), *Multicultural issues in counseling: New approaches to diversity* (pp. 3–9). Alexandria, VA: American Counseling Association.

Locke, D. C. (1990). A not so provincial view of multicultural counseling. *Counselor Education and Supervision, 30,* 18–25.

Locke, D. C. (1995). Counseling interventions with African American youth. In C. C. Lee (Ed.), *Counseling for diversity* (pp. 21–40). Boston: Allyn & Bacon.

Margolis, R. L., & Rungta, S. A. (1986). Training counselors for work with special populations: A second look. *Journal of Counseling & Development, 64,* 642–644.

Markowitz, L. (1997). Ramon Rojano won't take no for an answer. *Family Therapy Networker, 21,* 24–35.

McGoldrick, M. (1982). Ethnicity and family therapy: An overview. In M. McGoldrick, J. K. Pearce, & J. Giordano (Eds.), *Ethnicity and family therapy* (pp. 3–30). New York: Guilford Press.

McGoldrick, M., Giordano, J., & Pearce, J. K., (Eds.). (1996). *Ethnicity and family therapy.* New York: Guilford Press.

Meade, M. (1993). *Men and the water of life: Initiation and the tempering of men.* San Francisco: Harper.

Meade, M. (2004). *Mosaic Multicultural Foundation brochure.* Seattle, WA: Author.

Miller, J. B., & Stiver, I. P. (1997). *The healing connection: How women form relationships in therapy and in life.* Boston: Beacon Press.

Moore, R., & Gillette, D. (1990). *King, warrior, magician, lover: Rediscovering the archetypes of the mature masculine*. San Francisco: Harper.

Multicultural counselor training [Special issue]. (1998). *Counseling Psychologist, 26*.

Murphy, B. C. (1989). Lesbian couples and their parents: The effects of perceived parental attitudes on the couple. *Journal of Counseling & Development, 68*, 46–51.

Myers, H. F., Wohlford, P., Guzman, L. P., Echemendia, R. J. (Eds.). (1991). *Ethnic minority perspectives on clinical training and services in psychology*. Washington, DC: American Psychological Association.

Nolen-Hoeksema, S. (1998). *Abnormal psychology*. Boston: McGraw-Hill.

O'Bear, K., & Reynolds, A. (1985, March). *Opening doors to understanding and acceptance: A facilitator's guide for presenting workshops on lesbian and gay issues*. Workshop and manual presented at the American College Personnel Association Convention, Boston.

O'Connor, M. F. (1992). Psychotherapy with gay and lesbian adolescents. In S. H. Dworkin & F. J. Gutierrez (Eds.), *Counseling gay men and lesbians: Journey to the end of the rainbow* (pp. 3–22). Alexandria, VA: American Counseling Association.

O'Neil, J. M., & Egan, J. (1992). Men's gender role transitions over the life span: Transformations and fears of femininity. *Journal of Mental Health Counseling, 34*, 305–324.

Org, P. (1993). Twenty-million in 2020. In *The state of Asian Pacific America* (pp. 11–24). Los Angeles: LEAP Asian Pacific American Public Policy Institute and UCLA Asian American Studies Center.

Orzek, A. M. (1992). Career counseling for the gay and lesbian community. In S. H. Dworkin & F. J. Gutirrez (Eds.), *Counseling gay men and lesbians: Journey to the end of the rainbow* (pp. 23–34). Alexandria, VA: American Counseling Association.

Padilla, A. M., & DeSnyder, N. S. (1985). Counseling Hispanics: Strategies for effective intervention. In P. B. Pedersen (Ed.), *Handbook of cross-cultural counseling and therapy* (pp. 157–164). Westport, CT: Greenwood Press.

Pedersen, P. B. (1988). *A handbook for developing multicultural awareness*. Alexandria, VA: American Counseling Association.

Pedersen, P. B. (Ed.). (1991). Multiculturalism as a fourth force [Special issue]. *Journal of Counseling & Development, 70*.

Pedersen, P. B., Draguns, J. G., Lonner, W. J., & Trimble, J. E. (Eds.). (2002). *Counseling across cultures* (5th ed.). Thousand Oaks, CA: Sage.

Ponterotto, J. G. (1987). Counseling Mexican Americans: A multimodal approach. *Journal of Counseling & Development, 65*, 308–312.

Ponterotto, J. G. (1998). Charting a course for research in multicultural counseling. *Counseling Psychologist, 26*, 43–68.

Ponterotto, J. G., & Casas, J. M. (1991). *Handbook of racial/ethnic minority counseling research*. Springfield, IL: Charles C Thomas.

Price, R. E., Omizo, M. M., & Hammett, V. L. (1986). Counseling clients with AIDS. *Journal of Counseling & Development, 65*, 96–97.

Real, T. (1997). *I don't want to talk about it*. New York: Fireside.

Real, T. (2002). The awful truth. *Psychotherapy Networker, 26*, 34-43, 58.

Richmond-Abbott, M. (1992). *Masculine and feminine: Gender roles over the life cycle*. New York: McGraw-Hill.

Robinson, T. L., & Howard-Hamilton, M. F. (2000). *The convergence of race, ethnicity and gender*. Upper Saddle River, NJ: Merrill/Prentice Hall.

Root, M. P. P. (Ed.). (1996). *The multiracial experience: Racial borders as the new frontier* (2nd ed.). Thousand Oaks, CA: Sage.

Sabnani, H. B., Ponterotto, J. G., & Borodovsky, L. G. (1991). White racial identity development and cross-cultural training. *Counseling Psychologist, 19*, 76–102.

Scher, M., Stevens, M., Good, G., & Eichenfield, G. A. (1987). *Handbook of counseling and psychotherapy with men*. Newbury Park, CA: Sage.

Schliebner-Tait, C., & Peregoy, J. J. (2001). Working with selected populations: Treatment issues and characteristics. In P. Stevens & R. L. Smith (Eds.), *Substance abuse counseling: Theory and practice* (2nd ed., pp. 227–250). Upper Saddle River, NJ: Merrill/Prentice Hall.

Schlossberg, N. K., & Entine, A. D. (1977). *Counseling adults*. Monterey, CA: Brooks/Cole.

Shannon, J. W., & Woods, W. J. (1991). Affirmative psychotherapy for gay men. *Counseling Psychologist, 19*, 197–215.

Silverberg, R. A. (1986). *Psychotherapy for men: Transcending the masculine mystique*. Springfield, IL: Charles C Thomas.

Skovholt, T. (1978). Feminism and men's lives. *Counseling Psychologist, 7*(4), 3–10.

Skovholt, T. M. (1993). Counseling and psychotherapy interventions with men. *Counseling & Human Development, 5*, 263–283.

Smith, A., & Stewart, A. (1983). Approaches to studying racism and sexism in black women's lives. *Journal of Social Issues, 38*, 1–15.

Smith, E. J. (1977). Counseling Black individuals: Some stereotypes. *Personnel and Guidance Journal, 55*, 390–396.

Speight, S. L., Myers, L. J., Cox, C. I., & Highlen, P. S. (1991). A redefinition of multicultural counseling. *Journal of Counseling & Development, 70*, 29–36.

Steinberg, W. (1993). *Identity conflict and transformation*. Boston: Shambhala.

Stevens, P. (2001). Introduction to substance abuse counseling. In P. Stevens & R. L. Smith (Eds.), *Substance abuse counseling: Theory and practice* (pp. 1–32). Upper Saddle River, NJ: Merrill/Prentice Hall.

Stevens-Smith, P. (1995). Gender issues in counselor education: Current status and challenges. *Counselor Education and Supervision, 34,* 283–293.

Sue, D., Sue, D. W., & Sue, S. (2000). *Understanding abnormal behavior* (6th ed.). Boston, MA: Houghton Mifflin.

Sue, D. W., Arredondo, P., & McDavis, R. (1992). Multicultural counseling competencies and standards: A call to the profession. *Journal of Counseling & Development, 70,* 477–486.

Sue, D. W., Bernier, J. E., Durran, A., Feinberg, L., Pedersen, P., Smith, E. J., & Vasquez-Nuttall, E. (1982). Position paper: Cross-cultural counseling competencies. *Counseling Psychologist, 10*(2), 45–52.

Sue, D. W., & Sue, D. (1999). *Counseling the culturally different* (3rd ed.). New York: John Wiley.

Sue, D. W., & Sue, D. (2003). *Counseling the culturally diverse: Theory and practice* (4th ed.). New York: John Wiley.

Sue, S. (1977). Community mental health services to minority groups: Some optimism, some pessimism. *American Psychologist, 32,* 616–624.

Sue, S., & Morishima, J. K. (1982). *The mental health of Asian Americans.* San Francisco: Jossey-Bass.

Sue, S., & Zane, N. (1987). The role of culture and cultural techniques in psychotherapy. *American Psychologist, 42,* 37–45.

Tanney, M. F., & Birk, J. M. (1976). Women counselors for women clients? A review of the research. *Counseling Psychologist, 6,* 28–32.

Teague, J. B. (1992). Issues relating to the treatment of adolescent lesbians and homosexuals. *Journal of Mental Health Counseling, 14,* 422–439.

Thomason, T. C. (1993). Counseling Native Americans: An introduction for non-Native Americans. In D. R. Atkinson, G. Morten, & D. W. Sue (Eds.), *Counseling American minorities: A cross-cultural perspective* (pp. 171–187). Dubuque, IA: William C. Brown.

Tillitski, C. J. (1992). Fathers and child custody: Issues, trends, and implications for counseling. *Journal of Mental Health Counseling, 34,* 351–361.

Toomer, J. E. (1978). Males in psychotherapy. *Counseling Psychologist, 7,* 22–25.

Trimble, J. E. (1991). The mental health service and training needs of American Indians. In H. F. Myers, P. Wohlford, L. P. Guzman, & R. J. Echemendia (Eds.), *Ethnic minorities:*

Perspectives on clinical training and services in psychology (pp. 43–48). Washington, DC: American Psychological Association.

Trimble, J. E., Fleming, C. M., Beavias, F., & Jumper-Thurman, P. (1996). Essential cultural and social strategies for counseling Native American Indians. In P. B. Pedersen, J. G. Draguns, W. J. Lonner, & J. E. Trimble (Eds.), *Counseling across cultures* (4th ed., pp. 177–209). Thousand Oaks, CA: Sage.

Troiden, R. R. (1989). The formation of homosexual identities. *Journal of Homosexuality, 17,* 43–73.

Vargas, L. A., & Koss-Chioino, J. D. (Eds.). (1992). *Working with culture: Psychotherapeutic intervention with ethnic minority children and adolescents.* San Francisco: Jossey-Bass.

Werrbach, J., & Gilbert, L. A. (1987). Men, gender stereotyping, and psychotherapy: Therapists' perceptions of male clients. *Professional Psychology: Research and Practice, 18,* 562–566.

Williams, J., & Stafford, W. B. (1991). Silent casualties: Partners, families, and spouses of persons with AIDS. *Journal of Counseling & Development, 69,* 423–427.

Williams, R. C., & Myer, R. A. (1992). The men's movement: An adjunct to traditional counseling approaches. *Journal of Mental Health Counseling, 14,* 393–404.

Wilson, L. L., & Stith, S. M. (1993). Culturally sensitive therapy with Black clients. In D. R. Atkinson, G. Morten, & D. W. Sue (Eds.), *Counseling American minorities: A cross-cultural perspective* (4th ed., pp. 101–111). Dubuque, IA: William C. Brown.

Wolf, T. J. (1992). Bisexuality: A counseling perspective. In S. H. Dworkin & F. J. Gutierrez (Eds.), *Counseling gay men and lesbians: Journey to the end of the rainbow* (pp. 175–187). Alexandria, VA: American Counseling Association.

Wylie, M. S. (2002). The untold story: Carol Gilligan on recapturing the lost voice of pleasure. *Psychotherapy Networker, 26,* 46–56.

Young-Eisendrath, P., & Wiedemann, F. (1987). *Female authority: Empowering women through psychotherapy.* New York: Guilford Press.

Zane, N., & Sue, S. (1991). Culturally responsive mental health services for Asian Americans: Treatment and training issues. In H. F. Myers, P. Wohlford, L. P. Guzman, & R. J. Echemendia (Eds.), *Ethnic minority perspectives on clinical training and services in psychology* (pp. 49–58). Washington, DC: American Psychological Association.

CHAPTER 15

Counseling Older Adults

For the first time in history, most people can expect to live well into their 70s and 80s with considerable vigor and self-sufficiency. Trends indicate that increasing numbers of people will live into their 90s and beyond. The increase in life expectancy has been truly remarkable. Whereas early in the 20th century only a small percentage of the population lived past 45, life expectancy now is in the mid-70s. By 1990 those over 65 constituted 12.7% of the total U.S. population. By the year 2030 this age-group is expected to increase to over 21% (Cavanaugh & Blanchard-Fields, 2002; James & Gilliland, 2001). In the United States people over 85 years of age are the fastest growing age-group.

As life expectancy has increased, developmental theorists have recognized that older adults have the potential to continue to grow and develop until they die. Stereotypes about aging, however, interfere with the recognition of the growth potential of older adults and contribute to the reluctance both of older adults to seek counseling and of mental health workers to serve them.

STEREOTYPES OF OLDER ADULTS

The overriding stereotype is that as adults age, they automatically start deteriorating and declining physically, psychologically, and socially. They are thus considered an emotional and economic drain on society. Paradoxically, however, another prevalent stereotype is the belief that most older people are well heeled, wasteful spenders who indulge in frivolous activities, using up the resources of their heirs. Yet another misperception is the belief that older people live in a blissful golden age with few hassles and conflicts, contentedly reclining in rocking chairs or peacefully withdrawing from society as they wait for death. Older adults are also mistakenly perceived as being a homogeneous group very much alike in characteristics.

Of all these stereotypes the most devastating to the welfare of older adults is equating aging with decline and deterioration. In her book *The Fountain of Age* (1993), Betty Friedan claims that most of the faulty perception is perpetuated by physicians, nurses, psychologists, and gerontologists. Over 75% of recently published articles and books written by health care professionals about aging deal only with those who are physically incapacitated, chronically emotionally disturbed, or victims of Alzheimer's disease. Publications about older adults generally cover only those living in nursing homes, even though only about 5% of older people live in these facilities (Bee, 1996; Cavanaugh & Blanchard-Fields, 2002; Myers, 1990; Perlmutter & Hall, 1992).

Actually, over three-quarters of this age-group are self-sufficient. Relatively free of heavy responsibilities such as child rearing and career development, most older adults are able to pursue creative, self-fulfilling activities in the community. Rather than languishing through a long period of physical and mental decline, increasing numbers of older people are realizing the potentialities and possibilities of living two or three more decades with healthy growth and development.

Friedan (1993) emphasizes that ageism comes from society's tendency to compare older adults to an ideal-youth model. This attitude, she says, contributes to older adults trying to emulate youths and despairing as a result. She also emphasizes that the increasing numbers of active, healthy people over age 65 constitute a potentially powerful and positive social force in society—a force, however, that has not as yet been defined.

NEW PERSPECTIVES ON OLDER ADULTS

New perspectives on older adults allow for a positive image of aging. Longitudinal designs by researchers and life-span developmental theories indicate that older adults continue to develop. Studies about cognition and memory also indicate that intellectual capacities continue to develop as one gets older.

Older adults are difficult to categorize because they represent the most heterogeneous and diverse developmental group. Whereas young people are noted for looking, dressing, and acting like their peers, and those in the workplace follow certain dress codes and patterns of living, older adults tend to develop pronounced differences. They tend to go their separate ways. Some, for example, become more deeply involved in specialized hobbies, such as raising orchids or collecting miniature train sets; others become engrossed in skydiving or car racing; and some spend all their time traveling in their camper vans while others stay put in the same home and devote themselves entirely to their grandchildren. And some never retire, particularly self-employed persons and professional artists and musicians.

Developmental theorists have recently been countering the prevailing tendency to lump all older people into one age-group—the elderly—which extends over three decades (65 to 90 and beyond), the widest span of all age-groups. Those in their 60s, for instance, generally have very different concerns from those in their 80s. And those in their 70s tend to have very different concerns from those in their 90s. Some have suggested three substages within this span: *young-old* (ages 65–75), *old-old* (ages 75–85), and *oldest old* (age 85 on) (Bee, 1996). Unfortunately, such terms imply little sense of development except for that of decline.

Change in Research Designs

The stereotype of the declining older adult results largely from gerontologists using cross-sectional research that compares older adult performance with that of younger people (Friedan, 1993). Moreover, the subjects of such studies were primarily older adults living in nursing homes or other caretaking institutions—a select group of persons with physical or mental incapacities (Bee, 1996; Myers, 1990; Wellman & McCormack, 1982).

Life-span developmental psychologists have since made significant methodological changes in their theoretical and research designs. Using longitudinal instead of cross-sectional approaches, they test the same subjects over a long period of time, or they may use a sequential design that combines cross-sectional and longitudinal methods. These approaches permit researchers to look at changes or consistency among cohort groups—groups of individuals who were all born about the same time and who share similar contextual or historical experiences (Bee, 1996; Cavanaugh & Blanchard-Fields, 2002; Harrigan & Farmer, 2000; Knight, 1996). Those who were teenagers during the Depression, for instance, grew up with attitudes different from those of teenagers during the upheavals of the 1960s. Longitudinal and sequential research on aging, when carried out with normally functioning older adults, shows that older persons continue to maintain their capacities to learn, instead of going through a steady period of decline and deterioration as they age.

Emergence of Life-Span Developmental Theories

Until the 1950s developmental psychologists theorized only about child and adolescent stages of development. With the exception of Carl Jung (1933), gerontologists and psychologists believed that people started declining after they reached adulthood. Another exception, Donald Super (1942), followed Charlotte Buehler's life-span developmental theory and introduced a vocational development theory in which he outlined vocational tasks appropriate at different life stages (see chap. 12). In this early model, however, he followed the prevailing view that individuals over age 65 simply decline. In later years Super (1990) softened his position. Although he no longer described older adults as being in decline, he did see older adults only in nonoccupational roles. Exploration for older adults, he said, consists merely of looking for a suitable retirement home; he saw little need for society to cultivate a pool of occupational talent among older adults.

Psychoanalyst Erik Erikson (1950), influenced by Carl Jung, published an eight-stage life-span developmental model in which he proposed that people continue to develop throughout the life span (see chap. 5). At that time, however, he included only two adult stages: the *generativity* stage from age 30 through midlife and the *integrity* stage for everyone over age 65. Even so, these two stages became classic models for the older adult. During the generativity stage adults are in their caring, nurturing, reproductive years; during the integrity stage older adults work through despair and disintegration toward reintegration and a renewed sense of meaning in life. In the 1970s Gould (1978), Levinson (1978), and Valliant (1977) elaborated on Erikson's life-span developmental theory, but emphasized only the midlife crises of 40- and 50-year-olds.

Robert Butler (1963, 1975) took the lead in focusing on the developmental tasks and concerns of older adults. To challenge prevailing opinion that older adults sink into steady decline, he issued the landmark book *Why Survive?* (1975), declaring that elderly persons serve a vital purpose in society. His book *Productive Aging* (Butler & Gleason, 1985) explores new roles for older adults and the means by which they can best serve society.

In the days when Erikson (1950) first proposed his stages of development, he believed that the process of searching for and finding new meaning in life—gaining integrity—was sufficient as the last stage of life: One is then ready to die. Some have since criticized Erikson's integrity stage for being the so-called last stage of development; many older adults in their mid-60s still have 20 to 30 more healthy years to live. Friedan (1993) believes there must be more to life for older persons after they reach the integrity stage. She suggests that generativity, which Erikson proposed as occurring during the midlife period, should extend for the rest of life but with a different emphasis. Whereas younger adults in the generativity stage focus on bearing children, parenting, and serving others in the workplace, older adults serve the needs of the community at large in meaningful, generative ways.

Erikson (1978, 1980, 1982) continued to revise and develop his work, but his original theories stuck in the public mind. In his later work he emphasized that older adults, as they become more reflective, draw on their resources developed in earlier stages; generativity, rather than being a stage one leaves behind as one moves into the last stage, is an ongoing process but differently expressed. At the integrity stage one reviews prior stages on an ongoing basis, drawing on one's resources—a dynamic, regenerative practice that also reaffirms one's sense of self, or integrity.

Joan Erikson (1997), Erik's wife, added a ninth and last stage to Eriksonian theory. In her 90s she speaks eloquently about this final stage, which describes those in their 80s and 90s, who realize that their feelings of hope and trust, the foundations of development, are constantly being challenged as they start losing what was gained in previous stages—losses without hope of gains. Paradoxically, as one relinquishes these aspects of oneself, the remaining qualities, hope and faith, enable one to transcend material needs, except for what is immediately present—enjoying a child's laughter, enjoying the scent of roses, searching for one's glasses. The final stage—wisdom, or *gerotranscendence* as she calls it—is similar to transcendent states expressed in Jungian and Eastern spiritual practices. In this seeming withdrawal from life, one becomes more keenly present:

> This type of 'withdrawal,' in which one deliberately retreats from the usual engagements of daily activity, is consciously chosen withdrawal. Such a stance does not necessarily imply a lack of vital involvement; there may be continued involvement despite disengagement—as Erik says, a 'deeply involved, disinvolvement.' This paradoxical state does seem to exhibit a transcendent quality, a 'shift . . . from a materialistic and rational vision.' However, when withdrawal and retreat are motivated by a disdain for life and others, it is unlikely that such peace of mind and transcendence will be experienced. (p. 125)

Jungian psychoanalyst Alan Chinen (1989) has subdivided the latter stages into several developmental stages in which the older adult undergoes tasks and attains renewal and growth. In his book *In the Ever After*, he uses elder fairy tales as an appropriate mode of describing psychological development in the later years. The first group of tales depicts the first stage in which older persons confront their own foibles. The next series of tales shows how older persons replace self-centered, ego-building needs essential for youth with concerns about resolving issues for the long-term benefit of others. Self-transcendence culminates in the third stage; they become elders, a stage of wisdom and compassion.

Another Jungian psychoanalyst, Clarissa Pinkola Estés (1992), proposes a series of developmental stages that continue throughout life past 100. Although she refers to women, similar stages, she says, can be considered for men. The stages occur at 7-year intervals, and each requires a set of tasks, thus counteracting the usual view of aging as passively moving through life, governed only by time. "Each age represents a change in attitude, a change in tasking, and a change in values" (p. 447).

Developmental Characteristics

Physical and Cognitive Capacities

As they age, people generally start losing physical agility and endurance; many cannot hear or see as well as they used to; and many suffer from crippling arthritis and need canes or walkers. Such physical losses, however, have been wrongly perceived as affecting all older adults. As mentioned earlier, part of the problem is society's tendency to lump all seniors together, even though the older population represents more than a 30- to 40-year span. The physical capacities of 65-year-olds are usually very different from those of people in their 80s, and 70-year-olds are usually more agile than 90-year-olds. "As much variation exists in the type, rate, quantity and the impact of biological changes for the elderly as for younger age cohorts" (Harrigan & Farmer, 2000, p. 29).

Further misconceptions about the degree of physical deterioration in older adults may arise from misdiagnosis. The lack of mobility or agility in many older adults may result from high dosages of medications, poor nutrition, or lack of exercise. Physicians, nurses, gerontologists, psychologists, and other health care professionals may incorrectly attribute an older person's physical afflictions to the normal aging process.

On the positive side, although adults tend to acquire more physical limitations as they age, they also have more time and leisure to attend to good nutrition and to engage in physical fitness programs. Moreover, loss of some physical or sensory capacities tends to enhance other sensory capacities. Blind persons, for instance, are noted for their acute sense of hearing. Those persons slowed down by walkers or canes tend to observe more keenly everything around them, as is so poignantly portrayed in Terry Kay's book *To Dance With the White Dog* (1990).

Recent studies show that intelligence does not decline with age. Reports in earlier studies that intelligence scores dropped in adulthood were based on the use of intelligence tests standardized to youth-oriented tasks. These tests emphasized speed-based performance and abstract reasoning unrelated to experience. Researchers then began to compare the subscores of intelligence tests of older adults and youths. They found that older adults outperformed younger adults on meaningful tasks involving knowledge, judgment, and experience (e.g., verbal reasoning, performance tests, information), whereas younger adults did better on speed tests, memory tasks, and abstract reasoning unrelated to meaningful or cultural experiences (Bee, 1996; Cavanaugh & Blanchard-Fields, 2002; Friedan, 1993; Schaie, 1990).

Older people generally become concerned about losing their memory—an essential component of intelligence and reasoning. Studies have tended to show a slowdown, as one ages, in working memory, which involves the capacity to hold information in mind while at the same time using the information to solve problems or to acquire new learning (Bee, 1996; Cavanaugh & Blanchard-Fields, 2002; Craik & Jennings, 1992; Harrigan & Farmer, 2000).

But research also shows that memory differences between younger and older adults are insignificant when the material to be memorized is relevant and meaningful and when older adults are motivated (Cavanaugh & Blanchard-Fields, 2002; Knight, 1996). Younger people are quicker than older adults in memorizing nonsense syllables and digits, but older people may be insufficiently motivated because they do not sense the relevance of rote memorizing tasks. Aside from the idea that older persons may be too wise to bother learning meaningless symbols, the question remains whether they have the cognitive capacity for rote memorization. Researchers have found that normally functioning, motivated older adults can regain skills on speed and memory tests with practice (Cavanaugh & Blanchard-Fields, 2002; Friedan, 1993; Knight, 1996).

In 1993 Friedan challenged the prevailing belief among psychologists and gerontologists that human brain cells automatically deteriorate as the adult grows older. She cites the work of Diamond, Johnson, Protti, Ott, and Kajisa (1985), who studied brain cell deterioration in rats, including very old rats. Placing rats in a large cage in an enriched environment with loving care from attendants and with games and mazes to play with, the researchers compared these rats with other rats who were in an empty cage without loving care or an enriched environment. Those in the enriched environment increased their number of brain cells, whereas the brain cells of isolated rats withered.

The latest research findings run contrary to the traditional view that the brain stops developing after childhood and adolescence. Studies conducted by the brain research team at Princeton, headed by Elizabeth Gould (Gould, Reeves, Graziano, & Cross, 1999), found that in adult macaque primates, the brain continues to generate neurons that migrate to several regions of the neocortex, the area of cognitive functioning, learning, and memory. There in the neocortex the immature neurons differentiate and mature. Wylie and Simon (2002) support these findings in a review of the literature on brain research. "That the brain produces brand-new cells in maturity—has become generally accepted, as has the idea that the brain is changing and growing continuously throughout life, shaped as much by experience as genetic heritage" (p.28).

Rybash, Hoyer, and Roodin (1986), who support the importance of accumulated experiences over the years, believe that older adults set up a type of expert processing much like a computer. Knight (1996) comments on this view:

> With the accumulation of experience, older adults have a considerable store of knowledge about how things are and how things work, especially in their individual area of expertise, informed by work experience and family experience. In these expert domains, the more mature may tend to outperform the young. (p. 6)

Recent literature challenging the criteria for measuring intelligence throws new light on the question of whether a person's intelligence automatically declines with age. The standard measurement system, known as IQ, has been criticized for some time, most recently and significantly by Gardner (1993). In his book *Frames of Mind: The Theory of Multiple Intelligences,* he proposes that persons are not born with a single type of intelligence, but rather develop multiple intelligences over time through learning. His theory, described in chapter 6, explains how intelligence manifests itself in a variety of ways: linguistic, musical, logical-mathematical, spatial, bodily-kinesthetic, and personal. The main criteria for assessing intelligence, he claims, should apply to various cultures around the world and, moreover, should focus primarily on problem-solving abilities, which entail resolving "genuine problems" and "finding and creating problems" (p. 10). Thus, older adults in certain cultures are esteemed for their high level of elder intelligence.

Psychosocial Development

Prevailing views about the aging process have held that as people get older, they become increasingly inflexible in their attitudes and behavior. Older people are stereotyped as adhering to old patterns of behavior, resisting new experiences, and being unwilling or unable to adapt to change.

In reality, however, older adults have gone through many transitions and varied relationships and upheavals throughout their lives, tasks that require considerable adaptation and flexibility. After they retire and their children leave home, older adults experience loss of status, change in housing, loss of friends and spouses, and loss of physical agility. Coping with these many changes requires fundamental adjustments in attitudes and perspective (Chinen, 1989; Friedan, 1993; Neugarten, 1977).

Another general misconception has been that older people are expected to withdraw voluntarily from society as an inevitable step toward a new life filled with contentment and peace. This disengagement theory, developed by Cummings and Henry (1961) and considered a significant psychosocial process of aging, dominated the thinking of professionals and the general public for decades. Cummings and Henry declared that older adults who detached themselves from society were following a natural and optimally healthy process.

Recent research, however, indicates the opposite. Those who are least disengaged have higher morale, are healthier, and display more satisfaction (Adelmann, 1994; Bee, 1996). Healthy, normally functioning older adults tend to be well informed about current social issues and participate in worthwhile community activities (Cavanaugh & Blanchard-Fields, 2002). Older adults who desire to serve the community do face barriers, however. Unlike earlier stages of development in which roles and tasks are laid out (e.g., careers, university degree programs, raising a family), older adults must carve out roles for themselves in untracked, innovative ways and must do so in a manner that keeps them maintaining a sense of freedom, independence, and control over their lives.

Optimal Aging

Although humans have the capacity to continue to live meaningful, creative lives throughout their life span, many older adults do not attain this form of optimal aging. Instead, many are apt to spend their later years in humdrum, meaningless activities that lead to stagnation, depression, or immobilization. Professionals have been raising questions concerning why some older adults maintain a high quality of life while others do not. They've been exploring the characteristics, strategies, habits, and environmental conditions that differentiate optimally aging persons from those who are not.

In 1961 Neugarten, Havighurst, and Tobin made the first major attempt to define successful aging when they developed a measure called the Life Satisfaction Index consisting of five components: "zest (as opposed to apathy), resolution and fortitude, congruence between desired and achieved goals, positive self-concept, and mood tone" (Nussbaum et al., 2000, p. 330). Following this early work, other research studies were conducted, revealing by the mid-1980s "the multidimensional nature of aging" (Nussbaum et al., 2000). According to Ryff (1986), however, the research had generally failed because of little understanding of the aging process and an overall stereotypical view of the declining older adult. To counteract this approach, she proposed six criteria that represent successful aging based on an integration of life-span developmental and personal growth theories. Called an integrated model of personal development, her criteria are self-acceptance, positive relations with others, autonomy, environmental mastery, purpose in life, and personal growth (Nussbaum et al., 2000). In Ryff's view successful creative older adults are independent, willing to question and rebel against stifling societal norms, and proactive in shaping the environment to fit their needs.

Another perspective on successful aging is proposed by Rowe and Kahn (1998), who define it as the ability to maintain three coordinated and integrated personal characteristics: a low risk of disease and disease-related disability, high mental and physical functioning, and active engagement in life. They emphasize that older adults need to follow a good diet, keep fit, and maintain a social network of friends and family while continuing productive activities that are valuable to society.

None of these proposals about optimal aging, however, include the importance of spirituality and transcendence beyond oneself as important factors in creative aging. Noting this gap in the literature on aging, some professionals have attended to these aspects in their descriptions of optimal aging. Citing McFadden (1996), Cavanaugh and Blanchard-Fields (2002) say, "For many adults, their relationship with God is a key aspect of their identity. . . . When faced with the daily problems of living, older adults use their religious faith more than anything else, including family or friends, as a coping mechanism" (p. 357).

In their quest for meaning, older adults do tend to focus on spiritual concerns and issues. Many undertake a healthy disengagement—not only the very old, those in their 80s and 90s, as discussed earlier, but also those in their 60s and 70s seeking an inner spiritual path. The spiritual quest is generally made in solitude; the older person disengages from the outside world, a tendency often misunderstood in an extraverted, ego-centered, secular-minded society. Older persons who retreat into themselves are judged as fading out, losing their minds, or getting senile, not only by caring loved ones but also by most health care professionals. Even many religious organizations are unprepared to acknowledge and enhance the spiritual inner journey the older person takes. In his book *To Dance With the White Dog* (1990), Terry Kay eloquently describes such a man in his 80s who has lost his beloved wife of 60 years. When he adopts an imaginary white dog as his preferred companion for his inner journey, his overconcerned adult children believe he's not in his right mind and consider sending him to an old folks home; he finally convinces them to see things his way.

In their spiritual search older persons face their own sense of mortality, part of the Eriksonian despair/integrity process described earlier (see chap. 5), a difficult yet essential developmental task for older people. Schachter-Shalomi and Miller (1995) put it this way: "Release from myopic self interest brought on by the terror of death, elders can now serve others. Having acquired a broader philosophic perspective and a rootedness in the continuity of time, they can act as custodians of humanity's wisdom" (p. 91).

In many other cultures elders are honored and revered and are given special recognition as persons of wisdom. Baruth and Manning (1999) comment: "Many Japanese Americans equate old age with prestige and honor. Respect for elders is evident in the language used when addressing the elderly and in . . . bowing to them" (p. 180). Similarly, in Native American and Hispanic families, elders are not expected to withdraw, but rather play the role of mentor to younger generations (see chap. 14).

In writing about optimal aging, Friedan (1993) extends and adapts Erikson's concept of generativity to include older adults:

> Older leaders . . . as if driven by some larger generative impulse may move beyond the battles of special interests, the politically correct agenda or ideological imperatives . . . . they seem almost driven to use their wisdom to reconcile implacable differences that are consuming and wasting our human resources. (p. 617)

As an example of becoming more active and innovative participants in the community, seniors are beginning to develop and run their own programs at some senior centers, rather than merely following programs determined and administered by a younger staff. At the Whitney Senior Center in St. Cloud, Minnesota, for example, octogenarian Willis E. Dugan (1993) developed a remarkable senior activity project for the Retired Senior Volunteer Program (RSVP). This project engages seniors in a meaningful social activity that involves and benefits multiple generations: Senior citizens assist frail, elderly nursing home residents in constructing wood blocks and toys for children. (This project is described more fully in chapter 19.)

In 1994 more than 285,000 older adults participated at 1,900 elderhostels worldwide—evidence that elders are eager for learning but in ways that differ from those at conventional youth-oriented college campuses. The success of these hostels is attributable, in part, to older persons' sense of freedom to choose to learn what they want and need. It fits their personal quest, their inner journey to acquire a renewed sense of meaning in life, a zest for learning that surpasses that of the average college student.

The success of elderhostels that began in 1975 surprised even the founders. At a symposium on productive aging, elderhostel founder Marty Knowlton (1996) said in his keynote address that he never expected the unbelievable response and progress in the development of elderhostels worldwide: "We didn't know with whom we were dealing. They are marvelously responsive, extremely mentally alert, open, friendly, challenging." He pointed out that the key to the success of the experience is how challenging older people can be to their professors: "It hones the college professor to be sharper and sharper" every time he or she engages with an older-adult student. Permanent year-round learning institutes are forming as part of the Elderhostel Institute Network. Called the Institute for Learning in Retirement (ILR), hundreds are now located in the United States and Canada (see chap. 19 for a description).

THE COUNSELING NEEDS OF OLDER ADULTS

Many gerontologists and other professionals have been discussing the paradox of aging in our culture: a rapidly growing group of healthy, vigorous, older adults eager to learn and wanting to carve out new roles for themselves in a society that stereotypes them as no longer competent or as standing in the way of younger people (Butler & Gleason, 1985; Cavanaugh & Blanchard-Fields, 2002; Friedan, 1993; Gutman, 1987).

As scholars have become more interested in the developmental aspects of aging, the counseling profession, too, has become more interested in the counseling needs of normally functioning older people (Myers & Schwiebert, 1996). Jane Myers (1989, 1990) has been instrumental in changing the attitudes and practices in mental health counseling with older adults.

> Mental health counseling with older persons is an emerging specialty stimulated by changing demographics and dramatic increases in the number of older persons during this century. Because most mental health counselors can expect to encounter older persons and their families with increasing frequency, an understanding of normative and developmental issues and transitions is imperative. (Myers, 1989, p. 245)

Largely through Myers's efforts, a national gerontological counselor certificate was established in 1990 by the National Board of Certified Counselors. Since then, more than one-third of counselor training programs have added or expanded course offerings in counseling older adults (Myers & Schwiebert, 1996).

In a review of the literature on aging and counseling, Myers (1990) notes that counseling services for normally functioning older people do not meet the current need. She claims that considerable numbers of older adults have mental health concerns that could be responsive to treatment. Whereas older persons constitute 15% of the U.S. population, older adult clients represent only 2% to 6% of mental health clients in outpatient services (Flemming, Rickards, Santos, & West, 1986; Myers, 1990). In contrast, the 10% to 15% of older adults who are chronically or severely mentally ill take up the major proportion of inpatient mental health resources. Myers (1990) comments: "Although older persons are under-represented in outpatient care, they are over-represented in inpatient mental health populations. More than 60 percent of public mental hospital beds are occupied by persons over age 65" (p. 251).

The latest viewpoints and research about older adults denote a much more optimistic view about therapeutic work with the elderly than the traditionally held attitudes among professional gerontologists and other health care professionals. Increasing numbers of counseling professionals are exploring their attitudes about counseling older adults. Myers (1990) and Knight (1996) have given attention to the unique counseling needs of older adult clients; Waters and Goodman (1990) have presented counseling strategies particularly useful in empowering older adults. Knight (1996), Myers (1990), and Waters (1990b) have discussed how counselor attitudes toward older adults influence the counseling relationship.

Other counseling practitioners have presented special techniques, such as life review and reminiscing, appropriate for counseling this age-group (Crose, 1990; Knight, 1996; Sweeney, 1990; Waters, 1990a). As mentioned earlier, Jungian psychiatrist Allan Chinen (1989) presents the special technique of using elder fairy tales to guide older persons through a series of developmental tasks that help lead them through various transformational stages.

Characteristics of Older Adult Clients

Older adult clients—programmed by society as useless, weak, or incapable of learning—generally feel despair. Many are unaware of their potentialities to learn new skills, grow personally, and adapt to the many transitions in their lives. Nevertheless, older adults are potentially good prospects for counseling: They have had more complex and varied experiences in relationships, transitions, and losses than younger clients. They tend to have deeper insights and give more considered thought to issues. They have a longer time span of past experiences to process and reflect on. They are apt to be more judicious and more contemplative in selecting a method to resolve their problems because they see more alternatives than do younger clients. Knight (1996) says:

> The development of expertise through life experience will, in general, be an asset when working with older adults. Older adults often have expertise that is relevant to the problem that was brought to therapy. Their accumulated knowledge of people and relationships can be brought to bear on current relationship problems. (p. 26)

Knight comments further about the rich psychological history older adults bring into counseling: "If the issue has been of concern for some time, there are probably examples of many different ways that the client has approached the problem in the past, with various patterns of success and failure" (p. 40). He perceives that the challenge for counselors and clients is to take as much as possible from these past experiences and help clients see them from a perspective that is relevant to current needs.

Furthermore, postretirement individuals often have more time and energy to explore new behaviors, interests, skills, and relationships than do younger clients. Most are no longer committed to full-time jobs, nor are they involved in raising or supporting families. (That is changing, though, with so many adult children returning home to live with their parents and so many older adults now raising their grandchildren.)

Because older people are far more divergent in their outlook and experience and they span a far broader age range, they are just as diverse as younger persons in their attitudes and reactions to counseling and therapy. Elders in their 60s and 70s are usually more favorable toward counseling than are elders in their 80s and 90s. Those in their 80s and 90s, who grew up at a time when counseling was considered to be only for crazy people, are generally reluctant to seek or accept counseling. On the contrary, many in their 60s probably have had counseling of some sort or another. Some may be quite willing to seek counseling; others may be too therapy-wise and cynical about therapists.

With these considerations in mind, one can make some generalizations about the concerns of older adults that differ from those of younger clients. Adolescents, young adults, and midlifers are concerned by and large with strengthening their egos, developing careers, and raising families. The roles they play are fairly well established and reinforced in society. Older adults must contend with several complex changes that are unique to the later stage of life. Transitions that older people go through require changes in long-standing habits and lifelong patterns of living in a society that offers few prescribed roles to help guide them through the necessary adaptations. Some older people think their skills are obsolete and are unaware of latent talents they may have that could be developed. Others who are eager and optimistic about applying their skills in new ways and developing latent talents in worthwhile endeavors find resistance from employers, training institutions, family, and peers, influenced by prevailing stereotypes about aging.

When they are no longer involved in maintaining careers or responsible for rearing children, many older adults are quite happy to be free from responsibility and enjoy taking trips, vacationing, or following a life of leisure. Many others, however, sensing that they are no longer needed either as parents or as valued employees, feel useless and full of despair. Erikson (1950) believes that these feelings of despair are central to the later stage of life-span development. He proposes that older persons faced with despair and disintegration no longer focus on outward or external connections as a way of finding meaning in life. Typically, their search for meaning turns inward. As discussed earlier, they reassess their past experiences and reintegrate them with the present to achieve new meaning, acquiring a renewed sense of self. Butler (1963) elaborates on this process of integration in which one looks back on life, in what he terms a life review.

Coping With Changes In Spousal Relationships

After children leave home and one or both spouses retire, the relationship between spouses often changes. The husband may hang around the house, getting in his wife's way. The wife is unaccustomed to having her husband underfoot; besides, she may be preoccupied with caring for her 90-year-old mother, who lives 50 miles away. In another scenario described more fully later in the chapter, one spouse may become seriously ill and require constant caretaking by the healthier spouse—a role the caretaker spouse may find emotionally and physically exhausting.

The death of a spouse also forces changes, new responsibilities, and challenges into the life of the surviving spouse at a time when she or he is in shock and grieving. The remaining spouse may have to take on unfamiliar household tasks previously carried out by the other spouse. The spouse may lose contact with previous friends and be uncertain about new roles as a single person.

Changing Intergenerational Relationships

Older adults' relationships with their adult children also go through changes. In many instances adult children may not know how to respond to their parents' new patterns of living. In other numerous instances adult children in their 30s are not yet economically established and are returning to live with their parents. Older adults are unaccustomed to such a phenomenon, and many are unprepared for such interruptions in their lives. In earlier days elder parents passed away soon after adult children set up their own households and started raising families; certain predictable static relationships sufficed in those conventional lifestyles and shorter life spans. Now, however, intergenerational relationships take on complicated twists and are unpredictably fluid. Many older adults and their adult children are in contact with each other every day. At the other extreme many are no longer in contact with each other at all. As with any dynamic interaction, loved ones experience strain and conflict. Working through the conflicts and resolving the misunderstandings are necessary parts of the developmental process.

New Roles in Grandparenting

In numerous cases older adults are having to take on full-time care of their grandchildren. According to the U.S. Bureau of the Census, 3.7 million children (18 years or younger) are living in households headed by grandparents (Morrissey, 1997). Grandparents are often called upon to take over caring for grandchildren in situations where one parent has died or has left the family; is incapacitated by mental or physical illness, alcohol or drug addiction; or is abusive or neglectful of children. In these situations the other parent, usually the father, is unwilling or unable to be responsible for parenting (Peterson, 2001). Many grandparents who become caregivers for their grandchildren find the job emotionally and financially taxing. Many who had put parenting behind them are once again faced with the challenges of child rearing, often with children who are emotionally damaged. Further complications arise because of confusion or ambiguity in the legal status of grandparents who want to enroll children in school or who want access to children's school or medical records (Peterson, 2001).

Another problem facing some grandparents involves their legal right to visit their grandchildren. Grandparent visitation may be refused or restricted when the parents divorce and an ex-spouse has full child custody or when, less often, there are irreconcilable differences between grandparents and their son or daughter.

Over the past 30 years grandparents have gained legal visitation rights to grandchildren in all 50 states. More recently, however, because of concern that parents' rights with their children are being eroded, one-third of the states have tightened their laws to reduce grandparents' visitation rights. As a result, more grandparents who have been suing for visitation rights have been losing out in court (Gearon, 2003).

Changing Perspectives Toward Siblings

Sibling relationships among older adults often undergo marked changes as well. A brother or sister may suddenly take on added significance in one's later years. Sibling bonds differ from parent-child bonds: Siblings are more than peers; not only have they known each other longer than anyone else, but they are also blood relations, kinfolk who share a significant past. Older adults often seek out siblings whom they have not seen for years. Their high expectations of bonding as they used to may turn out to be a disappointment, or they may develop deep, fond relationships they never had when they were young.

Coping With Physical Disabilities

Physical afflictions of various kinds are a major area of concern for older adults. Although many elderly individuals are physically fit and are involved in exercise programs, run marathons, and go on long bicycle treks, 75% of older people are physically limited in one way or another (Cavanaugh & Blanchard-Fields, 2002). Many have had hip operations, mastectomies, or heart bypass surgeries; many suffer from such chronic health problems as arthritis or back pain. Although some older adults with physical problems retreat to a sedentary, inactive lifestyle, many others partake in preventive health care programs by joining physical fitness clubs and eating healthful, nutritious meals. Many older adults learn to adapt to their physical limitations and increase activities that use other physical or sensory capacities. A once physically active older person now confined to a wheelchair may, for example, turn inward, develop a vivid imagination, and become a beloved storyteller.

Coping With Diminishing Financial Resources

In most cases older adults' financial status determines their ability to adapt successfully to the many changes of later life, learn new skills, keep physically fit, and continue to be productive and self-sufficient. Whereas many older people are comfortable financially, many others, trying to survive on Social Security checks, worry about how to make ends meet. Their overriding concerns are about the rising costs of medical and dental care and their diminished income, as well as holding on to adequate housing for themselves.

Counselor Characteristics

Increasing numbers of counselors are working with older clients in mental health clinics, health centers, senior centers, and private practice (Waters, 1990b). Counselors' earlier reluctance to work with older adults has decreased as the counseling profession has begun to dispute ageist stereotypes, while giving more attention to growth and development in older adults.

Counselors who work effectively with older adult clients have additional characteristics and skills that supplement those described in chapter 4. They should be familiar with the economic, social, and political times that older adults have lived through; they should be aware that older adults have experienced many more complex transitions and have endured longer-term relationships than younger adults have. Counselors with such awareness help older clients perceive their strengths and coping skills, which they have developed over the years, and apply or adapt them to resolve current dilemmas. Counselors should also be aware of previous counseling experiences older adult clients have had and the effect of these encounters on the clients' current attitudes about counseling.

The mental health of older adult clients is closely tied to their physical, social, and economic well-being. When working with older clients, counselors find it particularly important to network with other professionals and agencies serving elders in the community. For example, consultations with or referrals to physicians, physical therapists, or nutritionists—with the client's knowledge—often contribute to more successful counseling results.

The Counseling Process

The counseling process for older adult clients follows the stages described in chapter 9. Although this process parallels that used with younger clients, there generally are some differences with older clients, particularly in the types of counseling goals, transference and countertransference relationships, encouragement of client action, and the termination of counseling.

Counseling Goals

A major counseling goal is to help empower older adults to gain control of their lives. When they enter counseling, older clients typically express feelings of helplessness and hopelessness; they generally feel overwhelmed by losses, transitions, and changes in life. Such a goal can help older clients explore previously acquired coping skills and learn to use them in new ways. Older clients feel empowered when counselors help them refute ageist stereotypes, a necessary first step as they strive to carve out new roles and new relationships despite resistance from society or from those close to them.

Spiritual questions and concerns are often raised by older adults when former roles and long-held commitments are no longer existent or satisfying. The older client's goal in these instances is to explore new meanings and purposes in life that transcend immediate personal needs.

Another counseling goal particularly important to older clients, who generally feel isolated or lonely, is that of seeking out community support groups. Persons working through grief over the death of a spouse, spouses heavily burdened with caretaking duties, or individuals cut off from family or career relationships can profit from appropriate support groups.

Transference and Countertransference

In all counseling relationships, counselors and clients develop feelings toward each other based on unconscious attitudes arising from unresolved relationships in the past. Client feelings toward counselors are called transference; counselor feelings toward clients are called countertransference (see chap. 6). Until recently, therapists, following Sigmund Freud's original views, considered these feelings barriers to successful counseling. Therapists now believe that awareness and acceptance of feelings of transference and countertransference offer opportunities for both client and therapist to work through unresolved feelings, thereby strengthening the counseling relationship and rehearsing a process for developing more effective relationships in everyday life (Corey, 2001; Gelso & Carter, 1985; Genevay & Katz, 1990).

Successfully working through transference feelings with an effective counselor can help older adults clear up unresolved power issues between themselves and their adult children; work through unrealistic or negative expectations about relationships with grandchildren; or work through unresolved guilt feelings, jealousies, or power struggles with spouses or siblings either living or dead (Knight, 1996).

Genevay and Katz (1990) have taken the lead in exploring countertransference with older adults. In their book *Countertransference and Older Clients,* they point out that counselors can be more effective with older clients when counselors recognize and make therapeutic use of these feelings.

> We come face to face with thoughts, memories, feelings and unresolved issues from our own lives. . . . We can connect our feelings and experiences with those of the patients and clients we serve; and we can provide better diagnosis and treatment in the process. Out of our own observations of ourselves and our aging families we can become more effective professionals and more sensitive to the people we help. (p. 13)

Counselor countertransference is a particularly important and complex part of the counseling process with older clients because clients are apt to be older than the counselors. Thus, counselors may overreact to client concerns on the basis of experiences they themselves have had or are having with their own aging parents; they may overreact to their own fears about aging or to society's neglect of elders. At times these counselor feelings may arise in reaction to the type of problem the older client is confronting—suicidal thoughts, declining physical or mental capacities, or death.

When an older client reminds a counselor of his or her mother or father, the counselor may become oversolicitous if the client seems frail. Or if the client disagrees or takes issue with what the counselor says, the counselor may feel threatened and think his or her expertise is being challenged. The counselor may become more authoritative, determined to point out the client's faults or need to change, or the counselor may distance him- or herself from the client and become indifferent to the dynamics of the relationship. When the age differential is large, the counselor may regard the client as a grandparent; countertransference reactions may then evoke protective feelings in the form of "a basically positive feeling for a somewhat fuzzily perceived older person who must be protected from the middle generation's interference" (Knight, 1996, p. 71).

Counselors need to be alert to the pressure of negative countertransference when, for example, they become convinced that a client is too old to profit from therapy, they consistently misdiagnose depression as dementia or Alzheimer's disease, they insist without evidence that medication will be more satisfactory than therapy, or they feel bored, anxious, or unable to help (Genevay & Katz, 1990; Knight, 1996).

Encouraging Client Action

In the final stages of counseling, counselors and clients work jointly to search out new resources or new opportunities for growth and change based on insights gained in earlier sessions. This stage is particularly important for counselors and older clients because society tends to be unprepared for, unresponsive, or even resistant to older adults developing new social and career roles.

Older clients can take action to change their lives by making use of talents and skills in new and innovative ways. Retired history or language teachers, for example, may lead tours to foreign countries; retired biologists may lead nature treks. Others might develop talents they had put aside early in life, such as playing a musical instrument, renewing their skills by taking lessons, becoming proficient, and/or joining the community orchestra. Someone who has collected antiques over the years might open an antique shop.

Terminating Counseling

Counselors working with clients considerably older than themselves tend to find terminating sessions the most difficult part of counseling. Knight (1996) says, "It is virtually always the therapist rather than the client who experiences termination as very difficult" (p. 96). Older clients, Knight says, often are reassured by termination, seeing it as an indication of having completed something successfully. They often have had more experience with endings and so are more used to them. Therapists, in contrast, tend to be more reluctant to end sessions because they fear that older persons may be too frail to deal with problems on their own or will experience loneliness or feel abandoned. Nevertheless, counselors do need to be alert to any client feelings of sadness, fear, resentment, or anxiety that might occur during the terminating stage of counseling. Counselors need to address these issues to the satisfaction of their clients before counseling is concluded.

Life Review: A Special Technique With Older Adults

In 1963 Robert Butler proposed that *life review* is a natural process experienced by older adults—a process in which a person reviews and reflects on past experiences, achievements, joys, and sorrows as a way of searching for a renewed sense of meaning in life.

Butler's life review is an amplification of Erikson's original view of the major developmental task of older adults. Erikson proposed that when older adults feel despair, they review and reevaluate their past and gain integrity, or a sense of coherence, in their lives. In later writings Erikson and other developmental theorists expanded the life review concept as a means whereby elders can develop new, productive ways of living (Harrigan & Farmer, 2000; Friedan, 1993; Knight, 1996; Whitbourne, 1985). Knight (1996) says that "life review is not an end in itself, but rather a process that improves the life history as a step toward creating the future" (p. 161).

Life reviews are truly meaningful if older adults use them in life-enhancing, generative ways. They have become a popular technique in counseling and therapy with older adults. Crose (1990), Disch (1988), Knight (1996), Sherman (1991), Viney (1993), Waters (1990a), and Whitbourne (1985) have all written about life reviews and their appropriate use in counseling and therapy.

Life review activities are also led by those who are not counselors or therapists; writers and biographers often lead such workshops for older adults. The purpose and approach of noncounselors is quite different, however, because they use life review nontherapeutically. In this discussion life review is used therapeutically by professionally trained counselors and therapists for those clients who express a need for it.

A counselor cannot expect a client to come forth with a complete life review that encompasses many decades of life. Knight (1996) sees the counselor as a directive in helping the client through the life review process. According to Knight, counselors should note any large gaps in client stories to encourage deeper exploration of areas that clients might be avoiding. Counselors act as editors in helping clients make choices about what areas are important to cover. Knight recommends that positive elements be emphasized if the goal of counseling is to help clients improve their sense of well-being. If the aim is to change long-standing behaviors, counselors may have to work on hidden negative experiences that need to be acknowledged and worked through. Consideration of how lifetime stories tie in with clients' future ways of life is essential (Knight, 1996; Waters, 1990a; Whitbourne, 1985).

In contrast with Knight's directive approach, many counselors prefer to act as guides, rather than as editors, in the life review process. Rather than trying to influence or shape the content of older adult recollection, they encourage clients to talk about memories that are important to them. Further, they encourage clients to do their own interpreting of these remembrances.

Life review should be done by well-trained counselors. Disch (1988) has expressed concern that mental health practitioners who are untrained in adult development might misuse or overuse life review. Waters (1990a) considers it a valuable tool for counselors but cautions that "life reviews may trigger sadness and depression for people who feel extreme dissatisfaction with their lives" (p. 277).

Knight (1996) also believes that life review should not be used indiscriminately. He suggests that it is not typically appropriate or useful for problem-focused concerns related to specific situational changes that do not unduly disrupt the older adult's life. He recommends using life review when older adults are grieving and need to develop new perspectives about their lives or when they are experiencing new emotions that must be integrated into the self. Further, he sees life review as a useful technique when older adults themselves raise doubtful, despairing questions about how well they have lived their lives and wonder how they can continue to live productively.

Life review techniques have been incorporated into some well-established counseling approaches—for example, Gestalt, Adlerian, personal construct, and Jungian. Gestalt techniques can be used during a life review to help delve into unfinished business (Crose, 1990). Clients are encouraged to reexperience their past stories by enacting them. The older person may be asked to dialogue with someone who is dead or otherwise unavailable and so resolve conflict with that person (the empty chair technique). Alfred Adler believed that individuals' earliest recollections are essential clues to understanding their unique styles of life. In line with this view, Sweeney (1990) encourages older adults clients to use purposeful reminiscing as a means toward modifying their lifestyles in a positive way.

Personal construct theory (see chaps. 6 and 9) can also be effectively applied during the life review process (Viney, 1993). This approach is based on the assumption that elders have acquired complex constructs of meanings from the events they have experienced over the years. These constructs are reconstrued and modified during the therapeutic process, enabling clients to experience change or transformation. Commenting on a personal construct approach to elders, Viney (1993) says,

> They are also seen like all adults, as actively handling their own flaws of experience, being able to reflect on that process and to recognize that they are, themselves, agents of it. They are also able to integrate separate aspects of this experience over time in the stories they construct and to reintegrate it when events make such change appropriate by retelling their stories. (p. 9)

Viney (1993) believes that reconstruing and reintegrating experiences is at the core of psychological development. This integration can best be accomplished by listening to elders tell and retell their stories in therapy. Through this process elders can "work through grief and guilt, getting in touch with strengths, both personal and interpersonal, and unleashing creativity and enjoyment as well as that most fulfilling sense of integrity" (p. 50).

Jungian psychiatrist Alan Chinen (1989) uses the telling of elder fairy tales as an imaginative way to help older adults review their lives. In working through the messages of the elder fairy tales, Chinen says, "The elder embraces the past, not to regress but to illuminate all of life. The end is the beginning transfigured" (p. 137). Chinen (1989) makes a sharp distinction between youth fairy tales, in which the young hero is the protagonist in search of achievement and glory, and elder fairy tales, in which the older person is the protagonist in search of maturity and wisdom. Youth tales, common in our culture, focus on ego identity and achievement—essential developmental tasks in the first half of life. Heroes and heroines conquer dragons, witches, and evil older people to achieve perfect love and a kingdom. End of story. Elder tales, on the other hand, which begin where the youth-oriented tales end, are concerned with essential developmental tasks in the second half of life: self-confrontation, self-transcendence, and emancipation—tasks that lead to compassion and wisdom.

Life review can be effective in group counseling, as well as in individual counseling. When working with groups, stimuli such as music or memorabilia such as newspaper clippings or old family photographs can be used to trigger recollections (Waters, 1990a). Sharing stories is another way of evoking memories. As in any group counseling, however, counselors need to be certain that neither they nor any group members pressure or try to persuade another group participant to share memories that she or he is not ready or willing to share.

Special Problems of Older Adults

Depression

Depression has become the major mental health problem of older adults (Comer, 1998). It is estimated that 20% of the elderly have some sort of mild or moderate depression (Myers, 1990). Clinical chronic depression among older adults is relatively uncommon, those suffering from chronic depression tend to have intense and persistent sadness and pessimism not obviously related to anything specific in their lives. These intense feelings interfere with their ability to function adequately socially or physically. Those with mild or moderate depression feel sad or in a down mood because they are suffering from specific losses or transitions that are stressful or unexpected. They are, however, usually able to meet daily responsibilities (Schmall, Lawson, & Stiehl, 1993)

Depression in older adults is often overlooked or misdiagnosed. Health care professionals tend either to misdiagnose depressive symtoms or to overprescribe antidepressant medication and ignore the value of counseling and psychotherapy. Stooped posture, minimal physical activity, sleep disturbances, and reduced appetites, all of which are typical symptoms of depression, are also characteristic of many frail, sickly older people who are not depressed. In addition, misdiagnosis may occur because many older adults who are depressed deny and cover up their feelings because they are afraid they would be diagnosed as crazy. At times symptoms of depression such as weakness and fatigue may be misdiagnosed as a sign of a particular physical illness. Furthermore, some older depressed people exhibit temporary memory problems and confusion that mimic dementia or Alzheimer's disease. If mental health workers are unaware of this similarity, they may make incorrect diagnoses of dementia (Schmall et al., 1993). Ageism may also contribute to misdiagnosis. Professionals who automatically equate older age with cognitive loss fail to consider other factors, such as feelings of depression, lack of exercise, or malnourishment.

The misuse or overuse of medication for depression has particular ramifications for older adults. Physicians and mental health workers who believe that older adults are not responsive to counseling because of their age tend to prescribe only medication. This occurs despite statistics showing that psychotherapy or counseling, along with medication, has a higher success rate than medication alone (Jakubiak & Callahan, 1996).

Suicide

If an older adult's depression goes unrecognized or is misdiagnosed as dementia, the person may become suicidal. Counselors must be particularly attentive to the possibility of suicidal intentions in depressed older adults. The average rate of suicide among those over age 65 is the highest of any age-group (Bee, 1996; Belsky, 1990; James & Gilliland, 2001).

Factors that contribute to the high risk of suicide in older adults include severe losses, such as the death of a loved one; prolonged feelings of hopelessness, helplessness, or isolation; prior attempts at suicide; heavy alcohol or drug use; an expressed desire to kill oneself; and the availability of a lethal weapon (Schmall et al., 1993). Most of these symptoms are similar to those of suicidal younger people. In older adults, however, chronic physical ailments, adverse reactions to multiple prescription drugs, losses, and isolation play a bigger part. Moreover, older people are more determined to follow through with the intent to kill themselves, and they are more likely to complete suicide attempts.

Elder Abuse and Neglect

Elder abuse or neglect by caretakers has only recently come to the attention of mental health counselors and other professionals. Elder abuse occurs in various ways—physical and psychological abuse, financial exploitation, and neglect. Caretakers may physically or verbally assault elders, steal or misuse elders' money or property, leave elders in unsanitary or hazardous living environments, or withhold appropriate care.

Elder abuse is as prevalent as child abuse but is a well-kept secret, scarcely reported in the professional literature or public media (Callahan, 1988). According to Cavanaugh and Blanchard-Fields (2002), "Estimates are that nearly 500,000 elders experience abuse or neglect with another 150,000 suffering self-neglect" (p. 372). Older persons are most likely to be abused by their adult children and by their spouses. But abuse also occurs all too often in nursing homes. Pillemir and Moore (1989) surveyed more than 500 nurses and nurse's aides working with older adults in nursing facilities. Results showed that 10% of respondents said they had physically abused a resident, and 40% reported they had psychologically abused a resident. When they were asked about their observations of how other staff members treated elderly patients, however, the levels of abuse rose dramatically: 36% reported they had observed other staff members physically abusing elderly patients, and 81% reported witnessing acts of psychological abuse.

Abuse or neglect of the elderly is more likely to be detected and prevented in long-term care facilities than in private homes. For those elderly people who live in private homes, abuse rarely gets reported (Sue & Sue, 2003). The elderly often are powerless when spouses or sons or daughters abuse or neglect them. Overcome with shame or fear of abandonment and impaired by physical disability, they are reluctant or unable to report abuse. Shelters are available where abused children or abused spouses can escape for protection, but unfortunately no such emergency facilities are available for older abused persons who need to be separated from their abusers.

Elder protective services have been mandated in all states to serve older adults who are being neglected or abused. Whenever health care professionals notice signs of elderly abuse in clinics or in long-term care facilities, they are required to report it to elder protective services. When abuse is reported to protective services and the circumstances are assessed, several actions are possible. Arranging for alternative care is one option; another is determining whether the abuse was precipitated by a caregiver who was overstressed. Caretakers can be helped to assess the degree of overload and can be taught how and where to seek help when stress levels escalate (Sue & Sue, 2003).

Respite care is available in most communities to give overburdened caretakers assistance, relief, and time-out. Arrangements can also be made for visiting nurses or other health care professionals to come to the home at regular intervals to bathe the patient, check on medication, change bedding, and attend to other similar tasks. These services are particularly helpful when the caretaker is physically unable to lift or move the elder. In addition, caretakers can get help in preparing meals or in doing household chores. These services ease stress and permit caretakers to have some time to themselves, run errands, or engage in their own social activities. Many caretakers could also benefit from counseling, which can help them work through feelings of helplessness, anger, grief, or guilt when strained relationships reach a breaking point (see "Counseling Needs of Caretakers" later in this chapter).

When professionals become aware that an elderly person is being exploited financially, they can assist the elder in getting legal advice and legal protection. Reputable attorneys now specialize in elder law. In these instances counseling can help the older person work through feelings of anger, depression, or grief at the betrayal of a trusted adviser, loved one, or caretaker.

Loss: Death and Dying

Losses can happen any time during a person's life—loss of one's job, loss of a home, loss of a loved one, or, for the terminally ill, the imminent loss of one's own life—but such losses generally occur more often in the later stages of life. Individuals suffering from losses such as these without an opportunity to go through the process of grieving can experience emotional and physical problems (James & Gilliland, 2001; Marino, 1996). Depression, disorientation, and anxiety disorders result from unresolved grief (Marino, 1996). Many therapists claim, however, that those suffering from losses develop new strengths as they work through the grieving process (James & Gilliland, 2001); it enables them to realize new opportunities for growth. Accepting change in life empowers and revitalizes.

Confronting one's own mortality and facing one's own death are the ultimate stage of development (James & Gilliland, 2001; Kübler-Ross, 1974; Rando, 1984). In her classic book *On Death and Dying* (1969), Elizabeth Kübler-Ross points out the general denial of death among most people in our culture. She explores the need for greater understanding of the emotional problems—the fears and denials—of terminally ill patients and their families.

Through interviews with 200 terminally ill persons, Kübler-Ross found that most people go through five emotional stages: denial, anger, bargaining, depression, and final acceptance. She perceives that *denial* is a normal stage of getting ready to die. After accepting the reality of death, patients then experience *anger* and resentment, which are generally projected on family and caregivers. In the next stage, they try *bargaining* to delay or postpone death. When they realize that this is futile, *depression* sets in, followed by *final acceptance* of the inevitability of death and a sense of peace. In a later publication, Kübler-Ross (1974) cautions against considering these steps to be fixed stages that everyone experiences at the same time. The process of emotional response may differ significantly in individuals.

When working with a client who is dying, counselors need to consider the client's degree of physical pain and deterioration, psychological outlook, the number and nature of interpersonal attachments, and the amount of energy and degree of hope (Cavanaugh & Blanchard-Fields, 2002; Corr, 1991–1992). Counselors also need to take into account the setting in which the client is being cared for—at home, in a hospital, or in a long-term care facility. Cavanaugh and Blanchard-Fields (2002) recommend using a form of life review in which counselors encourage clients and family members to write narratives about earlier life experiences, which can help them work through emotional blocks to grieving.

The most valuable contribution that counselors and other mental health workers can make is to help dying individuals maintain some semblance of control and independence in their lives. Whenever possible the dying person should be involved in all end-of-life decisions. (Cavanaugh & Blanchard-Fields, 2002; Schulz & Ewen, 1993). These considerations are especially important to older adults because these people are particularly susceptible to feelings of helplessness.

Hospice Care.   Until the 1940s most terminally ill older adults spent their last days at home, being cared for by family members and friends. From the 1940s through the 1970s, most dying persons died in impersonal, clinically oriented institutions, isolated from loved ones and family and with little or no attention to their emotional and psychological needs (Cavanaugh & Blanchard-Fields, 2002).

In 1967 in reaction to the sterile, isolating institutional approach, St. Christopher Hospice was established. This center emphasized a more humanitarian approach to caring for the terminally ill, a method that combined institutional and home care. This movement spread quickly throughout North America and Europe; today, there are more than 1,500 hospice programs (Bee, 1996).

The major focus in hospice care is involving family members in the care of the dying person in a warm, personal atmosphere. Hospice services generally work out of a patient's home or a family home. Cared for in familiar surroundings and in significant contact with family and friends, the patient can attend to her or his impending death with less fear and apprehension. Not only are family and friends more involved in daily caretaking, but they also are able to visit with the patient more often, listen to the patient's stories, and offer comfort and reassurance in the patient's last days. The patient and loved ones have more opportunities to say good-bye and to let go of past conflicts through reconciliation and forgiveness.

Professional assistance is provided by an interdisciplinary team of professionals, which may include physicians, visiting nurses, social workers, and counselors. Assistance is also given at regularly scheduled times with such caretaking tasks as bathing the patient, preparing meals, and doing household chores. A counselor can be particularly helpful when family members experience undue stress from caretaking, express unresolved conflict with the terminally ill patient, or experience debilitating grief over losing their loved one.

The Grief Process and Grief Counseling. Kübler-Ross (1969) suggests that the family members of the dying person go through similar stages of grieving: denial, anger, guilt, preparatory grief, and the final stage of saying good-bye. Their emotional reactions and behaviors, however, are quite different from those of the dying patient. Family members may shop around from physician to physician, hoping for a different diagnosis, or they may feel guilty that they did not do more for the patient. Counseling family members during the early stages of grief can help them continue to work through the grieving process after their loved one dies. For those patients who are terminally ill, family members have some time to anticipate and begin the grief process. Sudden, unexpected deaths, however, have the additional impact of shock and a lack of opportunity to say good-bye or to resolve unfinished business.

Whether death is expected or unexpected, counselors must consider various factors when assessing the intensity and duration of a client's grief. How central was the deceased in the client's life? How troubled was the client's relationship with the deceased? Has the client recently experienced other deaths or serious losses? Does the client have unresolved grief reactions from earlier stages of life?

More recently, some counselors and other mental health professionals have questioned the value of the stage model of grieving based on Kübler-Ross's work. Grief work specialists Neimeyer and Worden believe that the stage theory implies a passive process that clients go through over a period of time. They propose instead a more active mode in which persons actively resolve grief (Marino, 1996). Worden (1992) has developed a series of grief work stages that he believes allow clients that more active role. Termed *emotional tasks,* the stages are (a) accepting the reality of the loss, (b) experiencing the pain of grief, (c) adjusting to an environment in which the deceased is missing, and (d) withdrawing emotional energy from the lost relationship and investing it elsewhere.

Marino (1996) describes how Robert Neimeyer has adapted Worden's approach and has developed what he calls an *active adaptation model* of grieving. Neimeyer has clients face denial by encouraging them to tell the stories of their loss and share their loss with family and friends. He helps clients acknowledge the pain, not only of the initial loss but also of the suffering afterward from the deprivation. Clients are then helped to adapt to new environments without the loved ones. In the case of the loss of the spouse, this adaptation often includes taking on tasks that had been done by the partner. Suddenly faced with unfamiliar responsibilities, the survivor often has to learn quickly to manage finances, prepare meals, repair the house, or learn to drive. In the last stage of grief counseling, clients are encouraged to connect with other people and to develop new interests and activities in life.

Feelings of guilt are the most complex emotional experiences a survivor must work through, especially if the death was sudden and traumatic or the result of suicide or if the relationship with the lost one had been troublesome. Caretakers are apt to feel guilty when they experience relief after a patient dies. Or a grieving widow may believe that she neglected the dying husband or was unnecessarily difficult with him (Knight, 1996; Worden, 1992). In these cases Gestalt techniques are recommended, such as role playing or the empty chair dialogue, in which the client has imaginary discussions with the deceased over unresolved issues (Knight, 1996; Worden, 1992). Psychodrama also works well in a group setting in which the client enacts scripts with other group members, one of whom portrays the deceased person (Worden, 1992).

Grief specialist Gary Price believes that this active adaptation model works best in group counseling (Marino, 1996). The process of having group members share stories of loss helps normalize the grieving process, offers mutual support to group members, and expedites the resolution of conflicts resulting from the loss.

Abnormal Grief Reactions.   Sorrow, sadness, loneliness, denial, anger, disbelief, guilt, and depression are all natural and expected emotional reactions to loss. What distinguishes normal from abnormal reactions, however, is not the type of emotion being expressed but rather the intensity and duration of the response (Cavanaugh & Blanchard-Fields, 2002). Persons suffering from guilt and self-blame that persist over a long time are experiencing abnormal grief reactions. These feelings disrupt the individual's life and turn into long-term depression, which may manifest itself in chronic fatigue or tension or may include obsessional thoughts about the deceased long after the person has died. The grieving individual may refuse to move the deceased's belongings or may resist developing new relationships long after a reasonable time of mourning has passed (Cavanaugh & Blanchard-Fields, 2002; Knight, 1996).

Counseling in Long-Term Care Settings

Increasing numbers of counselors are working with older adults in long-term care (LTC) settings. Counseling may occur in nursing homes, residential centers, adult day care centers, or clients' homes (Ganote, 1990). These older adults may be experiencing emotional distress related to a disability; grief over a loss or conflicts with caretakers or family members; or depression or difficulty in adjusting to the restraints of LTC settings.

For various reasons the counseling needs of older adults in LTC have not been adequately met. Nursing homes have replaced mental hospitals as the major institution caring for older adults with mental illness; as a result, about two thirds of the elderly in these facilities have some form of psychiatric disorder (Jakubiak & Callahan, 1996). Of the remaining elderly residents, those with developmental concerns tend to be ignored. Thus, neither group receives psychiatric help or counseling, Nursing home surveys in the 1980s show that only 2% of nursing home patients received care from a mental health professional (Jakubiak & Callahan, 1996).

In the 1990s counseling in nursing homes increased following the enactment of the Omnibus Budget Reconciliation Act (OBRA) in 1987 (Jakubiak & Callahan, 1996). Subsection C, entitled Nursing Home Reform, deals with the regulation of activities, services, and certification of nursing homes. This act calls for monitoring the quality of life in nursing homes and screening persons with mental illness and mental retardation before admission. The act also specifies that counseling and therapy services must be offered by trained professionals.

Counseling in LTC settings differs in some ways from counseling in most other settings. In LTC most of the counselor's work is done outside the office, through a lot of brief, intermittent counseling and response to crises. Counselors must also work closely with physicians because older adult clients usually have medical problems accompanying their psychological concerns. It is particularly important that counselors be aware of the various medications clients are taking and their effects on the clients' physical and emotional well-being.

LTC clients generally show anxiety or depression and feel helpless as a consequence of having lost autonomy and independence. Feelings of loss are central in the lives of LTC elders: the loss of spouses, relatives, and friends as well as the loss of independence and control. In these instances counselors help clients work through emotions such as denial and anger—feelings that are a normal part of the grief process. Working through grief, as discussed earlier, permits clients to explore ways of adapting to life as LTC patients.

Older LTC adults may be referred to counseling because they are striking out at caretakers or other residents or are yelling, swearing at others, or otherwise being disruptive (Ganote, 1990). The counselor's role is to provide a safe place for them to vent their feelings of helpless rage and frustration and to suggest ways they can gain some sense of control over their lives (James & Gilliland, 2001). Counselors can consult with caretakers about allowing clients to have more options and be able to make choices in their daily lives. For example, clients may be involved in menu selection, choice of recreational activities, or decisions about the number of visitors allowed or the timing of the visits. At the same time counselors can encourage clients to express their feelings about their disability. Counselors can also discuss ways clients can approach their daily activities in new ways.

Professional counselors working with LTC clients use relaxation techniques, cognitive restructuring, Gestalt techniques focused on naming and expressing emotions, and life review (Ganote, 1990; Knight, 1996; Waters, 1990a). Relaxation exercises can be effective with older adults who are overly anxious. The exercises can focus on relaxing muscles, deep breathing, or light exercise. Clients generally find it easier to explore their feelings or concerns after therapeutic body work.

Cognitive restructuring can be helpful with clients who are depressed or who have exaggerated feelings of helplessness. A realistic appraisal of their physical and emotional concerns helps them confront their problems directly and reduces their tendency to exaggerate or overgeneralize their symptoms (Knight, 1996). For LTC clients who appear stoic, strained, and tense because of losses, Gestalt techniques can help them identify and express emotions. For example, while clients bring up painful feelings, they are encouraged to notice their bodily sensations and emotional reactions.

Life review can be effective with older LTC clients who express concerns about a lack of meaning in life or who express interest in exploring their past. Gestalt techniques can be helpful in the life review process. Clients can reenact past experiences as if they were in the present or can have an imaginary dialogue about an unresolved conflict with someone who has since died, bringing forth painful past experiences into the present. These activities permit new perspectives and new meanings to reshape memories of past experience (Crose, 1990).

Counselors can work closely with caretakers when counseling LTC clients, but as in all other settings, maintaining confidentiality between counselor and client is essential to the integrity of the counselor-client trust relationship. Only if clients are in danger of harming themselves or others may counselors share information without client consent.

Counseling Needs of Caretakers

When older adults require long-term intensive care, family members, especially spouses, are the most common and preferred source of caretaking, followed by friends, volunteer agencies, and lastly nursing home and other caretaking agencies (Kropf, 2000). About 54 million Americans, many of whom are also working, are involved in the caretaking of older adults. By 2020 it is estimated that 40% of the workforce will be caretakers (Bruzzese, 2001; Schneider, Kropf, & Kisor, 2000). Caregivers often are spouses who themselves may have some degree of physical incapacity. Many middle-aged adults also do some form of caretaking of one or more of their parents (Bee, 1996), according to Bee (1996), about 37% of middle-aged women will do some caretaking. Many of these women will be caught in a generational squeeze, having to care for both their children and their ailing parent(s).

Older adults requiring long-term intensive care generally have higher morale and more peace of mind when family members are the major caregivers. Family members who provide such care out of love and concern give generously of their time and energy. But caretaking can also become overtaxing financially, physically, and emotionally (Kropf, 2000). When the demands of caretaking become overwhelming, caregivers often become overstressed and depressed (Bee, 1996; Belsky, 1990; Bruzzese, 2001; Gwyther & George, 1986). Factors other than the actual duties of care often contribute to that pressure. For instance, if caregivers feel a lack of appreciation or support from other family members, if their relationship with the older person has always been troublesome, of if they have not learned problem-solving strategies, the burden of care may become particularly stressful (Belsky, 1990; Gwyther & George, 1986).

Counselors can help caretakers deal with the ongoing stress of caretaking by helping them explore and work through feelings of resentment and entrapment. These feelings often result from countertransference when the patient makes unrealistic demands on the caretaker or becomes overly dependent or manipulative (Delmaestro, 1990; Katz, 1990). Counselors can also suggest ways to reduce stress, such as making arrangements for respite care. In addition, caretakers can be encouraged to talk with health care professionals about ways to manage caretaking more efficiently. Counselors can also refer them to caretaker support groups, if available in their community, where feelings and suggestions about caretaking are shared.

Counselors should become informed about support networks in the community that specialize in working with older people. Local hospitals often have social workers on staff who can arrange regular visiting nurse and housekeeping services for older people in their homes. Counselors can also help caretakers develop and make use of support services that help with shopping, meals, and housekeeping. In addition, churches and synagogues often provide supplementary caretaking services for older adults (Kropf, 2000).

During counseling, caretakers may come to realize that they are unable to continue giving personal care to loved ones. Counselors can then help clients express and work through the feelings of guilt or ambivalence about giving up the caretaking and help them make alternative caretaking arrangements for their loved ones.

Because of frustration, caretakers in LTC facilities at times get overly angry at residents when they are disruptive or unmanageable or when they curse or hit at staff and other residents. In reaction some staff members have resorted to subduing residents by applying physical restraints (e.g., tying patients to beds or wheelchairs) or sedating them heavily with drugs. Counselors can help caretakers in LTC facilities acknowledge and work through their feelings of anger and frustration when elderly patients make unrealistic demands or become overly dependent or manipulative (Delmaestro, 1990; Katz, 1990). When caretakers work through their own countertransference feelings with a counselor or therapist, they can better assess and understand elderly patients' feelings of helpless frustration and anger. Caretakers then are more responsive to counselor suggestions regarding ways to prevent the emotional or physical outbursts of their elderly patients.

CONSULTATION WITH FAMILIES OF OLDER ADULTS

In addition to offering counseling services to older adults or to the caretakers of older adults, counselors offer counseling services to family members who have concerns about their aging parents. One example is helping adult children determine whether their parents are capable of living independently or whether they need care. If they need care, then the type of care needs to be explored. Should the older adults live with their children, get full-time or part-time help from visiting nurses, or move to an assisted-living center or a nursing home? A counselor can also help adult children of the elderly recognize when the children may be overanxious about their parents' welfare and when they realistically need to intervene on their parents' behalf.

OUTCOME RESEARCH

In a review of research on counseling outcomes with older adults, Smyer and Intrieri (1990) concluded that few studies exist and that what little research there is focuses on time-limited therapy with depressed elderly clients. They recommend that counselors conduct research with adults who have less severe emotional disorders, that they study the effectiveness of individual counseling with older people, and that they explore the use of preventive psychological education and support activities.

Part of the reason for the meager amount of research in gerontological counseling is that funds for research in all aspects of gerontology are inadequate. Carol Schutz (1995), executive director of the Gerontological Society of America, says that growth and support for gerontological research are increasing but that "it still remains underfunded and important, 'break-through' ideas may be languishing for lack of funds" (p. 34). As gerontological research in general increases, one can anticipate an increase in gerontological counseling research.

SUMMARY

Healthy older adults have become a significant force in society as life expectancy has increased dramatically since 1900. By the year 2030 older adults will represent more than 21% of the total population. The increased longevity of healthy older adults stimulated human development scholars to explore the unique developmental processes of people over age 65. Contrary to general belief, they found that most individuals continue to develop and grow throughout their life spans.

Stereotypes about older adults interfere with their growth potential. The most detrimental stereotype is that of equating aging with decline and deterioration. This stereotype is based on society's tendency to idealize and emulate a youth model.

As more and more older adults are living longer and healthier lives, the demand for older adult counseling services has increased. Counselors can help older adults adapt to the many changes and transitions they experience in the later part of life. They can guide older adults in their search for new and productive roles and activities.

The counseling process with older adults is similar to that used with clients at other age levels. Some aspects, however, are unique to counseling older adults: (a) Counseling goals focus on helping clients regain control over their lives; (b) countertransference issues related to ageism and to the fear of getting old are common among counselors working with clients who are much older than they; (c) counselors need to help clients overcome barriers in society that interfere with their carving out new roles in their lives; (d) life review, in which a person reflects on and reevaluates past experiences to gain new meaning or purpose in life, is particularly suitable for older adult clients.

Gerontological counselors must be aware of problems that are especially troublesome for older adults. Their rates of depression and suicide are the highest of any age group. Elder abuse or the neglect of frail elders, often unreported, occurs frequently in the elders' own homes, as well as in long-term care facilities. Losses of loved ones, careers, and family responsibilities are commonplace in older adults. The numbers of those suffering from terminal illness increase with older age. Grief work counseling helps older adults and their loved ones work through suffering and loss. In the case of terminally ill patients, counselors work with hospice services specifically developed to care for dying persons and their families.

Gerontological counselors also offer valuable services to individuals who are long-term caretakers. They can help caretakers work through countertransference, recommend ways of reducing stress, and refer them to appropriate support groups.

PROJECTS AND ACTIVITIES

1. Interview one of your grandparents or someone old enough to be your grandparent regarding his or her views about the transitions, changes, or conflicts he or she has experienced in the later years. How consistent are these views with the views discussed by developmental theorists?

2. Select an individual over age 65 who you believe is functioning optimally and another who seems to be having difficulty coping with changes in life. What factors may be contributing to their differences in functioning?

3. Interview two counselors, one male and one female, regarding their views about counseling older adults. Do you notice any differences in their views about the developmental processes of older adults? If so, what are they?

4. Visit a senior center. Notice whether any activities are related to counseling or preventative services.

5. Check television, newspapers, and films and note any stereotypes of older adults.

REFERENCES

Adelmann, P. K. (1994). Multiple roles and physical health among older adults: Gender and ethnic comparisons. *Research on Aging, 16,* 142–166.

Baruth, L. G., & Manning, M. L. (1999). *Multicultural counseling and psychotherapy: A lifespan perspective.* Upper Saddle River, NJ: Merrill/Prentice Hall.

Bee, H. L. (1996). *The journey of adulthood* (3rd ed.). Upper Saddle River, NJ: Prentice Hall.

Belsky, J. K. (1990). *The psychology of aging* (2nd ed.). Pacific Grove, CA: Brooks/Cole.

Bruzzese, A. (2001, July 31). Help workers manage caretaking. *Bellingham Herald.*

Butler, R. N. (1963). The life review: An interpretation of reminiscence in the aged. *Psychology, 256,* 65–76.

Butler, R. N. (1975). *Why survive? Growing old in America.* New York: Harper & Row.

Butler, R. N., & Gleason, H. P. (Eds.). (1985). *Productive aging: Enhancing vitality in later life.* New York: Springer.

Callahan, J. J., Jr. (1988). Elder abuse: Some questions for policymakers. *Gerontologist, 28,* 453–458.

Cavanaugh, J. C., & Blanchard-Fields, F. (2002). *Adult development and aging* (4th ed.). Belmont, CA: Wadsworth.

Chinen, A. B. (1989). *In the ever after: Fairy tales and the second half of life.* Willamette, IL: Cheron.

Comer, R. (1998). *Abnormal psychology* (3rd ed.). New York: Freeman.

Corey, G. (2001). *Theory and practice of counseling and psychotherapy* (6th ed.). Pacific Grove, CA: Brooks/Cole.

Corr, C. A. (1991–1992). A task-based approach to coping with dying. *Omega, 24,* 81–94.

Craik, F. I. M., & Jennings, J. M. (1992). Human memory. In F. I. M. Craik & T. A. Salthouse (Eds.), *The handbook of aging and cognition* (pp. 51–110). Mahwah, NJ: Lawrence Erlbaum.

Crose, R. (1990). Reviewing the past in the here and now: Using Gestalt therapy techniques with life review. *Journal of Mental Health Counseling, 12* (3), 279–287.

Cummings, E., & Henry, W. E. (1961). *Growing old.* New York: Basic Books.

Delmaestro, S. (1990). Sharing despair: Working with distressed caregivers. In B. Genevay & R. S. Katz (Eds.), *Countertransference and older clients* (pp. 123–135). Newbury Park, CA: Sage.

Diamond, M., Johnson, P. E., Protti, A. M., Ott, C., & Kajisa, C. (1985). Plasticity in the 904-day-old male rat cerebral cortex. *Experimental Neurology, 87,* 309–317.

Disch, R. (Ed.). (1988). *Twenty-five years of the life review: Theoretical and practical considerations.* New York: Haworth Press.

Dugan, W. E. (1993). *Wood block and toy project: Designed for diversely-abled senior volunteers.* St. Cloud, MN: Retired Senior Volunteer Program.

Erikson, E. (1950). *Childhood and society.* New York: Norton.

Erikson, E. H. (1978). Reflections on Dr. Borg's life cycle. In E. H. Erikson (Ed.), *Adulthood* (pp. 1–32). New York: Norton.

Erikson, E. H. (1980). *Identity and the life cycle.* New York: Norton.

Erikson, E. H. (1982). *The life cycle completed.* New York: Norton.

Erikson, J. M. (1997). *The life cycle completed: Erik H. Erikson.* New York: Norton.

Estés, C. P. (1992). *Women who run with the wolves: Myths and stories of the wild woman archetype.* New York: Ballantine Books.

Flemming, A. S., Rickards, L. D., Santos, J. F., & West, P. R. (1986). *Report on a survey of community mental health centers* (Vol. 3). Washington, DC: Action Committee to Implement the Mental Health Recommendations of the 1981 White House Conference on Aging.

Friedan, B. (1993). *The fountain of age.* New York: Simon & Schuster.

Ganote, S. (1990). A look at counseling in long-term settings. *Generations, 14,* 31–34.

Gardner, H. (1993). *Frames of mind: The theory of multiple intelligences.* New York: Basic Books.

Gearon, C. J. (2003, February). Visiting the 'kids' gets harder. *AARP Bulletin,* p. 6.

Gelso, C. J., & Carter, J. A. (1985). The relationship in counseling and psychotherapy: Components, consequences, and theoretical antecedents. *Counseling Psychologist, 13,* 155–243.

Genevay, B., & Katz, R. S. (Eds.). (1990). *Countertransference and older clients.* Newbury Park, CA: Sage.

Gould, E., Reeves, A. J., Graziano, M. S. A., & Cross, C. G. (1999). Neurogenesis in the neocortex of adult primates. *Science, 286,* 548–552.

Gould, R. (1978). *Transformations: Growth and change in adult life.* New York: Simon & Schuster.

Gutman, D. (1987). *Reclaimed powers: Toward a new psychology of men and women in later life.* New York: Basic Books.

Gwyther, L. P., & George, L. K. (1986). Caregivers for demented patients: Complex determinants of well-being and burden. *Gerontologist, 26,* 245–247.

Harrigan, M. P., & Farmer, R. L. (2000). The myths and facts of aging. In R. L. Schneider, N. P. Kropf, & A. J. Kisor (Eds.), *Gerontological social work: Knowledge, service settings and special populations* (2nd ed., pp. 26–64). Belmont, CA: Brooks/Cole/Thomson Learning.

Jakubiak, C. H., Jr., & Callahan, J. J., Jr. (1996). Treatment of mental disorders among nursing home residents: Will the market provide? *Generations, 19,* 39–42.

James, R. R., & Gilliland, B. E. (2001). *Crisis intervention strategies* (4th ed.). Belmont, CA: Brooks/Cole.

Jung, C. G. (1933). The stages of life. In *Modern man in search of a soul.* San Diego, CA: Warcourt Brace.

Katz, R. (1990). Using our emotional reactions to older clients: A working theory. In B. Genevay & R. S. Katz (Eds.), *Countertransference and older clients* (pp. 17–26). Newbury Park, CA: Sage.

Kay, T. (1990). *To dance with the white dog.* New York: Washington Square Press.

Knight, B. G. (1996). *Psychotherapy with older adults* (2nd ed.). Thousand Oaks, CA: Sage.

Knowlton, M. (1996, March). *Evolution of a new old age.* Speech delivered at Productive Aging Conference, Vancouver, British Columbia, Canada.

Kropf, N. P. (2000). Home health and community services. In R. L. Schneider, N. P. Kropf, & A. J. Kisor (Eds.), *Gerontological social work: Knowledge, service settings and special populations* (2nd ed., pp. 167–190). Belmont, CA: Brooks/Cole/Thomson Learning.

Kübler-Ross, E. (1969). *On death and dying.* New York: Macmillan.

Kübler-Ross, E. (1974). *Questions and answers on death and dying.* New York: Macmillan.

Levinson, D. J. (1978). *Seasons of a man's life.* New York: Knopf.

Marino, T. W. (1996). Grief counseling broadens its definition. *Counseling Today, 39,* 13.

McFadden, J. (1996). A transcultural perspective and reaction to C. A. Patterson's "Multicultural-Counseling: From diversity to universality," *Journal of Counseling and Development, 74,* 232–235.

Morrissey, M. (1997). More grandparents raising grandchildren. *Counseling Today, 39,* 1, 4.

Myers, J. E. (1989). *Adult children and aging parents.* Alexandria, VA: American Counseling Association.

Myers, J. E. (1990). Aging: An overview for mental health counselors. *Journal of Mental Health Counseling, 12,* 245–259.

Myers, J. E., & Schwiebert, V. L. (1996). *Competencies for gerontological counseling.* Alexandria, VA: American Counseling Association.

Neugarten, B. L. (1977). Personality and aging. In J. E. Birren & K. W. Schaie (Eds.), *Handbook of the psychology of aging* (pp. 311–335). New York: Van Nostrand Reinhold.

Neugarten, B. L., Havighurst, R., & Tobin, S. (1961). The measurement of life satisfaction. *Journal of Gerontology, 16,* 134–143.

Nussbaum, J. F., Pecchioni, L. L., Robinson, J. P., & Thompson, T. L. (2000). *Communication and aging* (2nd ed.), Mahwah, NJ: Lawrence Erlbaum.

Perlmutter, M., & Hall, E. (1992). *Adult development and aging* (2nd ed.). New York: John Wiley.

Peterson, K. S. (2001, August 6). Grandparents' labor of love. *USA Today,* pp. D1–2.

Pillemir, K., & Moore, D. W. (1989). Abuse of patients in nursing homes: Findings from a survey of staff. *Gerontologist, 29,* 314–320.

Rando, T. (1984). *Grief, dying, and death.* Champaign, IL: Research Press.

Rowe, J. W., & Kahn, R. L. (1998). *Successful aging.* New York: Pantheon.

Rybash, J., Hoyer, W. J., & Roodin, P. A. (1986). *Adult cognition and aging.* New York: Pergamon.

Ryff, C. D. (1986). *The failure of successful aging research.* Paper presented at the Annual Meeting of the Gerontological Society of America, Chicago.

Schachter-Shalomi, Z., & Miller, R. (1995). *From age-ing to sage-ing: A profound new vision of growing old.* New York: Warner Books.

Schaie, K. W. (1990). Intellectual development in adulthood. In J. E. Birren & K. W. Schaie (Eds.), *Handbook of psychology and aging* (3rd ed., pp. 291–310). San Diego: Academic Press.

Schmall, V. L., Lawson, L., & Stiehl, R. (1993). *Depression in later life: Recognition and treatment.* Corvallis: Oregon State University.

Schneider, R. L., Kropf, N. P., & Kisor, A. J. (Eds.). (2000). *Gerontological social work: Knowledge, service settings and special populations* (2nd ed.). Belmont, CA: Brooks/Cole/Thomson Learning.

Schulz, R., & Ewen, R. B. (1993). *Adult development and aging: Myths and emerging realities* (2nd ed.). New York: Macmillan.

Schutz, C. A. (1995). Professional organizations in aging: Where have we been and where are we going? *Generations, 19,* 33–34.

Sherman, E. (1991). *Reminiscence and the self in old age.* New York: Springer.

Smyer, M. A., & Intrieri, R. C. (1990). Evaluating counseling outcomes. *Generations, 14,* 11–14.

Sue, D. W., & Sue, P. (2003). *Counseling the culturally diverse: Theory and practice* (4th ed.). New York: John Wiley.

Super, D. E. (1942). *The dynamics of vocational adjustment.* New York: Harper.

Super, D. E. (1990). A life-span, life-space approach to career development. In D. Brown & L. Brooks (Eds.), *Career choice and development: Applying contemporary theories to practice* (pp. 197–261). San Francisco: Jossey-Bass.

Sweeney, T. J. (1990). Early recollections: A promising technique for use with older people. *Journal of Mental Health Counseling, 12,* 260–269.

Valliant, G. E. (1977). *Adaptation to life.* Boston: Little, Brown.

Viney, L. L. (1993). *Life stories: Personal construct therapy with elderly.* Chickesler, UK: John Wiley.

Waters, E. B. (1990a). The life review: Strategies for working with individuals. *Journal of Mental Health Counseling, 12,* 270–278.

Waters, E. B. (1990b). Why counseling? *Generations, 14,* 5–6.

Waters, E. B., & Goodman, J. (1990). *Empowering older adults: Practical strategies for counselors.* San Francisco: Jossey-Bass.

Wellman, F. E., & McCormack, J. (1982). Counseling older persons: A review of outcome research. *Counseling Psychologist, 12,* 81–96.

Whitbourne, S. K. (1985). The psychological construction of the life span. In J. E. Birren & K. W. Schaie (Eds.), *Handbook of the psychology of aging* (2nd ed., pp. 594–618). New York: Van Nostrand.

Worden, J. W. (1992). *Grief counseling and grief therapy: A handbook for the mental health practitioner.* New York: Springer.

Wylie, M. S., & Simon, R. (2002). Discoveries from the black box. *Psychotherapy Networker, 26,* 26–37, 68.

CHAPTER 16

Counseling Programs in Elementary Schools

Children's mental health has declined sharply since the mid-1980s as a result of changing family patterns, an unstable society, rapidly changing values, and deteriorating home life. During the same time the numbers of reported cases of alcoholism, domestic violence, and child abuse have been increasing (Gibson, Mitchell, & Basile, 1993; Myrick, 1997; Thompson & Rudolph, 1992). Approximately one in five children and adolescents experiences the signs and symptoms of a *DSM-IV-TR* disorder during the course of a year, but only about 5 % of all children experience what professionals term "extreme functional impairment" (DHHS, 2000).

Children's psychological problems are most evident in classrooms, where children generally spend most of their waking hours under adult scrutiny and supervision. Emotional stress interferes with children's academic and social progress and causes children to withdraw from or disrupt classroom activities. School counseling programs can help address students' emotional problems that may impact academic and social performance, as well as benefit parents, teachers, administrators, and the overall community as well (ASCA, 2003). Although it is important to improve mental health services for children in the community, schools offer a special opportunity for children to obtain help. First, children or their parents do not have to pay fees for school counseling programs, as they do for services in the community. Second, teachers who are with the same children all day are likely to spot those who are experiencing problems and refer them to counselors.

When children request or are referred to counseling in elementary schools, counselors have options: They can work with children who can respond to short-term or intermittent counseling, or in more severe cases they can contact parents and arrange for further assessment by the school psychologist or counseling with a mental health counselor in the community. Counselors can also be instrumental in helping to improve the mental health climate in the school by offering children psychoeducational activities or acting as consultants with teachers, parents, and administrators. Although the focus in this chapter is on counseling in elementary schools, most of the activities and approaches discussed are also applicable to mental health counselors working with children in the community.

Even though high school counseling spread rapidly during the 1960s, elementary school counseling didn't get under way until the 1970s. The delay can be attributed to various factors. First, counseling initially focused primarily on vocational development. Second, it was widely believed that elementary school teachers could adequately serve as counselors because they knew their students well and because special training for school counselors was not considered necessary at that time. Third, school psychological services were considered sufficiently covered by school psychologists, whose job consisted of testing children and diagnosing learning and/or emotional disabilities, and by school social workers, who were prepared to intervene in difficult family-school relations.

In 1965 the Elementary and Secondary Education Act, an extension of the National Defense Education Act also in 1965, authorized grants to school districts for developing elementary school counseling. Such funding had been previously available only for secondary school counseling. By 1969 elementary counselors were employed in all 50 states, and by the early 1970s the number of elementary counselors had increased to nearly 8,000 (Schmidt, 2003). The number of counselors in elementary schools continued to grow in the 1980s, most likely as a result of the *A Nation at Risk* report of 1983, which included recommendations for counselors to be placed in all elementary schools.

THE ROLE OF THE ELEMENTARY SCHOOL COUNSELOR

As a national association representing the interests of school counselors, the American School Counseling Association (ASCA, 2003) has defined the role of the professional school counselor as a certified/licensed educator who addresses the needs of students comprehensively through the implementation of a developmental school guidance program. School counselors are specialists in human behavior and relationships who provide assistance to students through four primary interventions: counseling (individual and group); large-group guidance and instruction in skill development in academic, career, and personal-social areas; consultation; and coordination (ASCA, 2003). *Counseling* is defined as a confidential relationship in which the counselor meets with students to help them resolve or cope with their problems and developmental concerns. *Guidance* involves instruction and psychoeducation. *Consultation* refers to the collaborative partnership among school counselors and parents, teachers, administrators, school psychologists, social workers, visiting teachers, medical professionals, and community health personnel to plan and implement strategies to help students be successful in school. Lastly, *coordination* is defined as a leadership process in which the counselor helps organize, manage, and evaluate the comprehensive school counseling program.

Counselors are hired as part of the school staff and usually work in the school building. Their presence makes them easily available to students, teachers, and administrators. Appropriate facilities are important for effective counseling; counselors need a soundproof office in which confidential counseling can be carried out and another room set aside for group counseling and parent or family consultation.

ASCA recommends a ratio of 1 counselor to 100 to 300 elementary school students. This ratio is sufficient only if other psychological and educational specialists and community mental health resources are available to students and only if sufficient secretarial help is available to counselors. According to Baker (1996), "Universal ratios are difficult to dictate because of individual differences associated with the severity of student problems, amount of available secretarial and clerical assistance, curriculum options, and referral support" (p. 360).

Comprehensive School Counseling Programs

A comprehensive school counseling program consists of the four primary interventions—counseling, consultation, coordination, and assessment—in response to the identified needs, goals, and objectives of the school and community. Developing such a program involves a series of processes that include planning, organizing, implementing, and evaluating procedures (Schmidt, 2003).

Planning typically occurs at the beginning of the school year when school counselors make an assessment of students', parents', and teachers' needs. From this assessment counselors begin to select goals and objectives for their counseling programs. *Organizing* is a continuation of the planning process and involves selecting major goals and objectives and determining which services can best achieve these goals. *Implementing* is considered the action phase of a comprehensive school counseling program. It is during this phase that various services—for example, counseling, teacher and parent consultation, classroom guidance, testing, crisis intervention, and referrals—are provided by school counselors. *Evaluating* involves procedures that help counselors determine whether their services have been successful and what program changes would be recommended for the future.

One of the most prominent comprehensive school counseling program over the years has been the Gysbers and Henderson (2001) model. According to their model, a larger proportion of time is allotted for guidance and psychoeducational activities (35–45%) than for individual and group counseling (30–40%) in elementary schools, with the proportion of time for counseling decreasing for high school students (25–35%) as the need for advisement, consultation, and collaboration increases (Gysbers & Henderson, 2001). Myrick's (1997) comprehensive developmental school guidance and counseling program allows a more balanced distribution of counselor time—about 50% for individual and group counseling and 50% for the various other counselor tasks (guidance, advisement, psychoeducation, consultation, and coordination). That balance of time in Myrick's model is preferred in this text because students who receive counseling to work through developmental conflicts are more likely to benefit from academic learning and skill development in the classroom, as well as from group guidance and psychoeducational programs.

According to research conducted by Sink and MacDonald (1998), school districts have tended to adopt existing counseling guidelines and programs without reviewing the programs and without questioning the basic assumptions of human development underlying the various components of the counseling model being adopted. Sink and MacDonald

(1998) recommend that professionally trained counselors participate in reviewing the existing models used in or proposed for their school district, clarifying their role as counselors and suggesting changes where necessary. Most importantly, they point out,

> State and district models should principally reflect the best theory and practice in human development. . . . Rather than replicating earlier models, state programs may need to be modified in light of current developmental theory and research as well as the general concerns and needs of constituents. Future investigations on the comprehensive guidance movement should further examine the developmental nature of these programs and their long-term effectiveness. (p. 93)

As a complement to comprehensive school counseling programs, ASCA developed national standards to better define the role of school counseling programs in American educational systems (Dahir, 2001). The standards are based on three interrelated content areas: academic development, career development, and personal-social development. Each content area contains three standards designed to support student success and promote student achievement. These standards help school counselors implement school counseling program strategies designed to maximize and support student development.

Academic Development: Academic development includes students acquiring attitudes, knowledge, and skills that contribute to effective learning in school and across the lifespan; employing strategies to achieve success in school; and understanding the relationship of academics to the world of work and to life at home and in the community.

   Standard A. Students will acquire the attitudes, knowledge, and skills that contribute to effective learning in school and across the life span.

   Standard B. Students will complete school with the academic preparation essential to choose from a wide variety of substantial postsecondary options, including college.

   Standard C. Students will understand the relationship of academics to the world of work and to life at home and in the community.

Career Development: The standards for career development guide professional school counselors as they implement school counseling program strategies and activities to help students acquire attitudes, knowledge, and skills to successfully transition from grade to grade, from school to postsecondary education, and ultimately to the world of work.

   Standard A. Students will acquire the skills to investigate the world of work in relation to knowledge of self and to make informed career decisions.

   Standard B. Students will employ strategies to achieve future career success and satisfaction.

   Standard C. Students will understand the relationship between personal qualities, education and training, and the world of work.

Personal-Social Development: The standards for personal-social development guide professional school counselors in helping students with acquisition of attitudes, knowledge, and skills to help them understand and respect self and others, acquire effective interpersonal skills, understand safety and survival skills, and develop into contributing members of society.

> *Standard A*. Students will acquire the attitudes, knowledge, and interpersonal skills to help them understand and respect self and others.
>
> *Standard B*. Students will make decisions, set goals, and take appropriate action to achieve goals.
>
> *Standard C*. Students will understand safety and survival skills. (Dahir, 2001)

Developmental Needs of Children

An appreciation of normal development is essential to understanding mental health in children. What might be perceived as abnormal by someone who has contact with a child (e.g., teacher, parent, counselor, or school administrator) might fall within the established range of what is considered normal for that child's age or situation (Ginter & Glauser, 2004). In the life of a child, many situations erroneously construed as a serious mental disorder can easily be conceptualized as a developmental crisis. Research focusing on normal and abnormal child development helps school counselors identify behaviors and emotions that deviate from expected cognitive, social, and emotional developmental norms.

Awareness of a child's cognitive development is important for elementary school counselors. According to Piaget's cognitive development theory (Piaget & Inhelder, 1969), children at age 5 are verbal in their thinking but usually can handle only one concept at a time. From 7 to about 11, children tend to think concretely. Then they begin to think abstractly and can consider various ways of solving problems and learning to deal with the future, as well as focusing on the present. As they grow, children undergo more complicated, structural cognitive processes until they reach adulthood (see chap. 5). The value of Piaget's work is well known and accepted among educators:

> Understanding how children think enables counselors to choose developmentally appropriate activities for individual and group counseling and for classroom guidance. . . . Knowledge of cognitive development is also useful for counseling with teachers and parents, for example, in determining possible reasons for frustration in classrooms, lack of completion skills and low motivation. (Gibson et al., 1993, p. 29)

Counselors working with children also need to be aware of the psychosocial stages of children from ages 5 to 12 as proposed by Erik Erikson (1950; see also chap. 5). Whereas Piaget emphasizes structural cognitive development, Erikson focuses on the psychosocial development of individuals in their interactions and relationships with others. According to Erikson's *psychosocial theory*, 5-year-olds who are functioning adequately have passed through the development of trust and are at the stage of sensing their own individuality. They are developing a conscience and have a concept of right and wrong. From 6 to 12, children become more responsive to socially acceptable activities. Less self-centered, they become more interested in and involved with other people. Some children, however, do not pass through these stages successfully. A counselor may see, for example, a child of 11 who has not developed sufficient trust, autonomy, or individuality. The counselor's job, then, is to help the child develop these qualities. Gibson et al. (1993) note that "psychosocial theory provides counselors with a useful framework for understanding the dynamic impact of the school and home settings on personal and social development" (p. 39).

In addition to Erikson's theory, several other theories exist to explain many of the social, emotional, and cognitive elements of a child's development (Ginter & Glauser, 2004). One such theory of human development is attachment. *Attachment* is defined as the type of emotional bond established between a child and a parent or caretaker that creates a secure condition, feeling, or both (Bowlby, 1969, 1973a, 1973b). Normal attachment develops during a child's first 2 years of life. Problems with the parent-child relationship during that time, or breaks in the consistent caregiver-child relationship, prevent attachment from developing normally. If the caretaker is warm and responsive on a consistent basis, then the relationship is characterized as a *secure* attachment. *Insecure* attachment, on the other hand, is characterized by "caretaker inconsistency or rejection of the infant's bids for attention and care" (Schreiber & Lyddon, 1998, p. 358). There are a wide range of problems and varying emotional disturbances in children associated with insecure attachment, including immature behavior; chronic lying, cheating, or stealing; hyperactivity; poor concentration; learning disabilities and delays; destructive behavior to self or others; cruelty to animals; preoccupation with fire, blood, and gore; and poor social skills. These problems may become apparent in the classroom, or parents may turn to school counselors for help in how to deal with their child at home. Because treatment for attachment disorder in children includes family therapy, school counselors usually refer the child and family to a mental health counselor or marriage and family counselor in the community.

Laura Berk's (2003) considerable contributions to child development theory include the importance of moral development in children. According to Berk's summary of research (see chap. 5), a young child with a well-developed sense of self, known as the *personal domain,* will be more likely to develop morally in the domain of social conventions as well as in the domain of moral imperatives. Berk emphasizes the crucial roles that parenting, cultural environment, social learning, and cognitive development have on the moral development of children. Without adequate exposure in all realms, especially the parenting environment, children are in danger of acquiring aggressive, violent behaviors, which will be difficult to overcome. Adequate parenting allows children to develop the moral internalization and self-control necessary to navigate through moral challenges; it also allows cognitive and emotional development and "the ability to think of themselves as separate, autonomous beings who can direct their own actions" (Berk, 2003, p. 503).

Assessment and Evaluation

Assessment encompasses the instruments and procedures used to gather data for student appraisal. Educational tests, psychological evaluations, interest inventories, interviews, and observations are examples of assessment procedures used by school counselors (Schmidt, 2003). Standardized tests measuring intellectual ability, achievement level, and reading ability are available to elementary school counselors for use in improving students' self-understanding (see chap. 7). Some commonly used tests (and the grades for which they are appropriate) are the California Short Form Test of Mental Ability (K–8), the Otis-Lennon Mental Ability Test (K–9), the Primary Mental Abilities Test (K–6), What I Like To Do (4–7), the California Test of Personality (K–8), and the Early School Personality Questionnaire (1–3).

Nonstandardized self-report techniques—such as autobiographical essays, diaries, and questionnaires—are other assessment techniques to help counselor and child jointly participate in exploring the child's attitudes, self-esteem, and personal characteristics.

Some elementary school counselors prefer to use individual personality measures that involve drawings made by the child, such as the House-Tree-Person Test (H-T-P) (Allan, 1988; Keat, 1974). In other instances the counselor simply asks children to draw what they please and then has them tell stories about their pictures. The counselor may also ask children to draw pictures of their families.

An important distinction exists between testing for diagnostic purposes and testing for counseling. In the first case diagnostic testing is done by the school psychologist to determine a child's learning or emotional disabilities and to help in administrative decisions about a child's placement in a school or other institution. In counseling, testing is done in confidence by counselors to help improve a child's self-understanding. Counselors use tests to help set counseling goals, help the client make a decision, help explore new areas of client interest, facilitate counselor-client interactions, or help prepare the client for future counseling sessions (see chap. 7).

Although some believe that the only legitimate assessment functions for school counselors are those to achieve counseling goals (Baker, 1996), school counselors, in this age of accountability, must accept responsibility for identifying the important services of their programs and evaluating the effectiveness of those services (Schmidt, 2000). There are countless ways that counselors can carry out program evaluation. For example, the counselor may (a) ask students to assess their participation in particular services or activities, (b) request that parents and teachers provide feedback about changes they have observed in students who have participated in specific programs, (c) collect pretest and posttest data to measure outcome in an anger management group, or (d) compare absentee rates at the beginning of the year and at the end of the year if a goal of a particular program is to increase student attendance for the school year. Regardless of the methods used, school counselors have the responsibility of evaluating their overall program, reporting the results, and suggesting changes to address the findings of the evaluation process (Schmidt, 2000). The accountability process allows counselors to more accurately address the needs and expectations of students, parents, teachers, and administrators.

COUNSELING CHILDREN IN ELEMENTARY SCHOOLS

Counselors preparing for elementary school positions have a more difficult time defining their potential counseling populations than do counselors in secondary schools. Whether children are in a K–4, K–6, or K–8 school, the difference in sophistication is much greater between the youngest and the oldest students than it is between freshmen and seniors in a high school. Elementary school children vary much more in independence, motivation, judgment, and developmental abilities than do adolescents of high school age.

Nevertheless, elementary counselors have considerably more opportunities than do secondary school counselors or community counselors to engage in a counselor role consistent with that described by ASCA and the Association for Counselor Education and Supervision (ACES)—for example, doing direct counseling and consultation. According to

Hardesty and Dillard (1994), elementary school counselors perform fewer administrative and clerical activities than do secondary and middle school counselors. Elementary counselors also engage in more consultation and coordination activities and work more consistently and systematically with families, teachers, administrators, and professionals in the community (Gibson et al., 1993; Schmidt, 2003). In addition, unlike community counseling services, school counseling services do not charge fees, nor are they hampered by managed care restrictions.

Referral Sources

Elementary school teachers generally refer more children for counseling than do secondary school teachers because elementary teachers have the same children in class for most of the day for the entire school year. Thus, elementary school teachers have a better opportunity to observe children's lack of motivation, perceive children's uncertainties about themselves, or sense when children's home situations are not going well. They are also more aware of children's withdrawal and are more affected by children's nuisance behavior (e.g., constant fidgeting, getting out of their seats at the wrong times, lying, getting into fights). Stealing or other antisocial behavior can be observed more readily, too.

Because elementary schools tend to be smaller than high schools, principals and vice principals have more interactions with the children and the teachers. Consequently, elementary school administrators are more likely to refer children to counselors than are administrators in other schools.

Furthermore, if it becomes clear to children, even very young ones, that a counselor is available to them, they will begin to seek counseling on their own (Gibson et al., 1993). Administrators, teachers, and parents should encourage children to do so by letting them know that they can talk to a counselor if something is bothering them. In addition, students who have had successful experiences with a counselor often suggest that their friends see the counselor. It is also quite common for students to bring their friends with them to their counseling sessions because their friends need help.

Additional referrals come from both children and teachers as counselors make themselves more visible through informal classroom visits and as they help teachers present classroom units related to child development or mental health. Sometimes counselors teach the units themselves.

Counselors should recognize that some children who are nonverbal or resentful or whose ethnic background is different from their own may be reluctant or unwilling to see a counselor. Counselors must be visible to these children and approach them in noncoercive ways. A feeling of trust is more likely to grow with such an approach than it would through either indifference or attempts to cajole, persuade, or force such children into counseling.

Individual Counseling

School counselors often work with students individually to help address particular problems or concerns. The process of individual counseling is consistent with that described in chapter 9. A counselor's first step is to develop trust and rapport with a client. Then the counselor clarifies the problem, explores options to resolve the issue, and chooses a plan or strategy to solve the problem (Schmidt, 2003).

Although children generally express or act out emotions more easily than adults, they have difficulty labeling them. Counselors can help children become aware of and label their emotions. For example, if a child says with strong feeling, "I hate my teacher," the counselor can respond, "You sound like you're very angry with your teacher, so let's talk about your anger."

The counselor should let the child control the distance between them by using a corner of a desk or table, rather than having a desk between them or sitting in opposing chairs with no barrier. The child is then free to come closer when she or he is ready. Nonverbal explicit behavior on the part of the counselor is important in communicating with young children. For example, counselors may leave their own chairs and sit in smaller chairs when talking with children. Counselors should make specific suggestions to help their clients resolve their problems but should emphasize that any course of action must be determined by the children.

Elementary school counselors see students who identify a variety of concerns that may require different approaches in individual counseling. Counselors addressing behavior problems in students typically use behavioral strategies. For example, counselors may use positive reinforcement and extinction, whereby appropriate behaviors are rewarded but inappropriate behaviors are purposely ignored and are not reinforced through adult attention (Baker & Gerler, 2001). Other behavioral strategies include modeling, roleplaying, and desensitization.

One of the most widely used counseling approaches in elementary schools is Adlerian counseling, which emphasizes that all children's behaviors are goal directed. Sweeney (1998) focused on helping teachers and parents understand that the issues underlying children's misbehavior include attention, power, revenge, and inadequacy. The use of encouragement as well as natural and logical consequences is recommended to change inappropriate behavior. For instance, a logical consequence for a child who disrupts others in the classroom might be for the teacher to move the child to an isolated location, thereby preventing further disruption (Baker & Gerler, 2001, p. 295). Adlerian counseling also focuses on birth order, family constellation, feelings of inferiority, and lifestyle assessment (see discussion of Adler in chaps. 6 and 10).

Keat (1990) modified Lazarus's multimodal counseling approach and applied it to counseling children. Lazarus (1989) defined seven potential problem areas, or modes, of personality—**b**ehavior, **a**ffect, **s**ensation, **i**magery, **c**ognition, **i**nterpersonal relationships, and **d**rugs—which he called BASIC I.D. Keat renamed these personality modes to better describe children's problems—**h**ealth, **e**motions, **l**earning, **p**ersonal relationships, **i**magery, **n**eed, and **g**uidance of actions, behaviors, and consequences—and used the acronym HELPING (see Table 16.1). After an initial interview using the modified multimodal approach, Keat outlines and ranks the child's major concerns and then uses counseling approaches or techniques to resolve them in order of the ranking. Table 16.2 shows an example of this procedure.

Often, because young elementary school children may have limited verbal skills, traditional counseling that relies on verbal interactions between counselor and student may

TABLE 16.1
Multimodel Evolution

Letter	Helping Modes	Basic I.D. Modes
H	Health	Drugs-Diet (D)
E	Emotions-Feelings	Affect (A)
L	Learning-School	Sensation-School (S)
P	People-Personal Relationships	Interpersonal Relations (I)
I	Imagery-Interests	Imagery (I)
N	Need to Know-Think	Cognition (C)
G	Guidance of Actions, Behaviors, and Consequences	Behavior (B)

Note: From *Child Multimodal Therapy* (p. 10), by D. B. Keat, 1990, Norwood, NJ: Ablex. Copyright 1990 by Ablex. Reprinted with permission.

TABLE 16.2
HELPING Children Change

Mode	Rank	Concern Number	Concern	Intervention
Health	5	H1	Pain	Avoid/relief
		H2	Sickness	Wellness
Emotions	2	E1	Anxiety	Stress management
		E2	Anger	Madness management
		E3	Feeling down	Fun training
Learning	6	L1	Deficiencies	Life skills
		L2	Failing	Study skills
		L3	Sensory shallowness	Music
Personal Relationships	1	P1	Getting along (adults)	Relationships enhancement (RE)
		P2	Lacks friends	Friendship training
Imagery	4	I1	Low self-worth	IALAC (I Am Lovable and Capable); Storytelling
		I2	Coping lacks	Heroes (cartoons)
Need to Know	7	N1	Despair	Hope
		N2	Mistaken ideas	Cognitive restructuring
		N3	Lack of information	Bibliotherapy
Guidance of Actions, Behaviors, and Consequences	3	G1	Behavior deficits	Modeling
		G2	Motivation	Contracts

Note: From "Change in Child Multimodel Counseling," by D. B. Keat, 1990, *Elementary School Guidance and Counseling, 24*, p. 250. Copyright 1990 by American Counseling Association. Reprinted with permission.

not be effective (Schmidt, 2003). Thus, school counselors may use other counseling approaches, including play therapy and creative and expressive arts therapy.

Play Therapy

Young children under the age of 12 have relatively limited ability to verbalize their feelings and thoughts and to use abstract reasoning; thus, traditional talk therapy may not be effective. Because play is thought to be the natural language of young children (Landreth, 2002), play therapy may be a more effective means of working with elementary age children in helping them play out their experiences and feelings (Landreth, 1987). *Play therapy* is a counseling approach in which the counselor uses toys and play as the primary vehicle for communication (Kottman, 2004). The goals of play therapy include increasing client self-esteem, helping the client learn about self and others, helping the client explore and express feelings, improving decision-making ability, practicing self-control, and learning social skills.

Although there are many different theoretical approaches to play therapy, the two primary approaches are nondirective and directive. *Nondirective* play therapy emphasizes the client-counselor relationship and the innate ability of children to solve their own problems in their own time. Nondirective play therapists depend on the skills of tracking, paraphrasing, reflecting feelings, returning responsibility to the child, and setting limits (Landreth, 2002; Landreth & Sweeney, 1997). They avoid leading the child in any way, through interpretation, design of therapeutic metaphors, bibliotherapy, or any other more directive technique. *Directive* play therapy, on the other hand, involves the counselor facilitating or directing the counseling process in a way that he or she believes would be appropriate for the child and the goal of counseling. A variety of play media is used to create the play situation, "attempting to elicit, stimulate, and intrude upon the child's unconscious, hidden processes or overt behavior by challenging the child's defense mechanisms and encouraging or leading the child in directions that are seen as beneficial" (Gil, 1991, p. 36). Nondirective and directive play therapy are two ends on a continuum; other theoretical approaches to play therapy often fall between these two extremes.

Play therapy occurs within a counseling room called the playroom. Unlike traditional counseling rooms, the playroom contains a variety of toys and play materials within easy reach of children. The counselor needs to select toys and play materials to help children express a broad range of emotions, encourage mastery experiences, establish positive relationships with the counselor, test limits, increase self-control, enhance understanding of self and others, and improve self-image (Landreth, 2002). Kottman (2001, 2003) suggests that the playroom should contain toys that represent each of five distinct categories: family/nurturing toys, scary toys, aggressive toys, expressive toys, and pretend/fantasy toys.

Most play therapists, regardless of theoretical orientation, use several generic, basic skills (Kottman, 2004). These include tracking, paraphrasing, reflecting feelings, returning responsibility to the child, using the child's metaphor, and limit-setting. *Tracking* involves the counselor narrating the child's behavior during the counseling session; the purpose of which is to build rapport and a relationship with the child (Kottman, 2001).

Paraphrasing involves restating what the child has just said but in the counselor's words. *Reflecting feelings* is similar to paraphrasing but with an added feeling word within a statement. Often children project their feelings onto toys or objects in the playroom; thus, counselors reflect the underlying, deeper feelings expressed through the child's play. In *returning responsibility to the child,* the counselor, when appropriate, encourages the child to make a decision for herself or himself or accomplish a task during the counseling session. *Using the child's metaphor* means that the counselor uses the child's symbolic expression of her or his experiences without imposing the counselor's interpretation of the meaning of the story. *Limit-setting* is used to keep the child and the counselor safe in the playroom, stop the child from deliberately breaking toys or damaging the playroom, keep the child from taking home play materials, keep the child from leaving the session before the scheduled time, and stop the child from staying in the session after the time limit has expired.

Creative and Expressive Arts Therapy

Other nonverbal means of counseling that school counselors can use with children are the creative or expressive arts. These include music, dancing or movement, imagery, visual arts, literature and writing, and drama and psychodrama. The use of expressive arts in counseling adds a sense of playfulness to the process, promotes the client-counselor relationship, improves client-counselor communication, promotes client self-understanding, and helps nonverbal clients participate meaningfully in the counseling process (Arnheim, 1990; Gladding, 1998).

Because they take naturally to creative activities, children tend to respond spontaneously and creatively as long as they have not been unduly inhibited. Music therapy can be very helpful with children, particularly those in elementary school, because they seem to love music and spontaneously sing, listen, or play musiclike instruments (Gladding, 1998). Dance helps children get in touch with their bodies and with the relationship of their physical beings to the environment, as well as allowing a creative release of energy. Imagery increases divergent thinking and activates the imagination. Painting and drawing are safe ways for children to express suppressed feelings on paper or to "tell" what has been forbidden to talk about (Riley, 1997). Children's literature—for example, storybooks, fairy tales, and nursery rhymes—provides a mythic plane that reveals meaning usually unavailable in ordinary observable events. Puppets help children act out dreams that manifest inner conflicts with families and others.

Therapists encourage children to act out stories based on Moreno's (1946) psychodrama. With younger children, acting out dramas with toys or talking to puppets is usually safe and fun for them and revealing for counselors (Gladding, 1998). Children can make up stories about their family by using puppets, they can use role plays to act out a variety of real-life situations, or they may enjoy writing and producing their own plays or skits.

For culturally diverse students Cochran (1996) recommends using both play and art therapy. Elementary school children from different ethnic groups may have difficulty expressing themselves verbally because of language and/or cultural differences but can express themselves more freely through play activities, art, music, dance, and drama.

Brief Counseling

Brief counseling, as discussed in chapters 6 and 9, is a method whereby a counselor meets with a client for a limited number of sessions to discuss specific problems. Intermittent brief counseling is particularly appropriate in elementary schools because counselors can see the same students off and on throughout the many years the students are there. In addition, counselors can easily follow up on their work with children, observe changes as they occur, and build on previous counseling contacts when new problems arise.

Solution-focused counseling is another approach to brief therapy that has been used in school counseling. The goal of solution-focused counseling is to help students recognize the strengths in themselves and their lives by focusing on "what is right" rather than "what is wrong" with them (Harrison, 2000, p. 92). The counselor's task is to ask students to identify exceptional times—past, current, or future—and to encourage the use of non-problem behaviors (Osborn, 1999). A variety of questions can help students focus on positives: "What will happen if you wake up tomorrow morning and you no longer have this problem?" or "What will be different and how will you know the problem is solved?" (Schmidt, 2003, p. 145). Solution-focused counseling is effective with reluctant/resistant students because its positive focus helps minimize students' resistance to the counselor and to the overall counseling process.

Group Counseling

The school counseling literature has encouraged the use of group guidance and counseling since the late 1950s. Today, the ASCA identifies group counseling and guidance as primary services of elementary and secondary school counselors (Schmidt, 2003).

Group counseling and group guidance are two processes used by school counselors to address a wide range of student concerns and interests. The primary difference is that *group counseling* creates a confidential and personal relationship among group members, and *group guidance* (also referred to as classroom guidance) is instructional and informational in nature (Schmidt, 2003). Group guidance is described later in this chapter.

Group counseling provides a setting in which students can share their concerns, learn and practice new behaviors, identify with common issues held by other group members, and develop effective listening skills. It can be useful for children who have conflicts with family or peers or whose shyness or aggressiveness interferes with social development (Ohlsen, Horne, & Lawe, 1988). Group counseling can also be effective for groups of children who are experiencing similar problems, such as anger control, grief, the effects of divorce or single parenting, or alcohol and drug abuse. Students having academic difficulties can also benefit from group counseling.

Group counseling methods and processes that are used for adults and adolescents apply to children as well; however, counselors must adapt techniques to fit the developmental stages of children. The size of groups in elementary schools is usually no more than five students. In addition, because elementary school children have short attention spans and lack social maturity, group counseling sessions typically last from 20 to 30 minutes.

Addressing Cultural Diversity

Special considerations in counseling ethnic groups are discussed in chapter 14. Ethnic children, especially, face many difficulties when attending a school at which the student body and the teachers are predominantly White middle class or most of the other children are from ethnic groups other than theirs. Language barriers and barriers attributed to differing family and cultural values and expectations especially affect young children.

Although it would be ideal if representative ethnic counselors served each of the various ethnic groups in every school, that is not fully possible. Thus, counselors must develop resources to bridge the cultural gap between the staff and the schoolchildren and their families. Counselors should have available bilingual interpreters from the community and consult regularly with respected members of various ethnic neighborhood communities.

Several authors have written or edited books on multicultural counseling that include discussions about counseling ethnic children, along with case examples (e.g., Baruth & Manning, 1999; Lee, 1995). In one such example Jesse Zapata (1995) describes the case of an 8-year-old immigrant Mexican boy, usually a good student, who stopped doing his schoolwork and whose attendance declined. After unsuccessfully attempting to discipline the boy and trying to contact his home, the teacher referred the boy to the counselor. After talking with the boy and asking about his parents, the counselor learned that the boy's mother had left him with his aunt, who spoke no English and had returned to Mexico for 2 weeks to attend her mother's funeral. She also had taken along her older son, who usually acted as the interpreter for the family. A consultant from the Hispanic neighborhood was able to help the counselor and the teacher understand that it was quite normal, in this cultural context, for the mother to handle things in this way. The counselor and the teacher arranged for an interpreter to work with the family during this time and a tutor to help the boy catch up.

PRESENTING PROBLEMS OF ELEMENTARY SCHOOL CHILDREN

Vocational/Educational Problems

Elementary school children are not likely to enter counseling with vocational concerns as a presenting problem unless the school goes to the eighth grade. During counseling sessions, however, while discussing relationships or parental expectations, children may reveal attitudes about work, occupational values, or occupational stereotypes. These discussions can then contribute to children's awareness of the multiple factors in career choice and thus help move the children toward more effective vocational planning in the future.

The pressure on young children regarding occupational choice is greater and more common than most people realize. Some adults push elementary school children to specify what they are going to be when they grow up. In these cases counselors need to reduce that pressure by encouraging children to explore vocational options. Indeed, in these situations dealing with parents' inappropriate pressure is usually more important than career exploration. Children may also be confused when parents express distaste for their own jobs or talk about occupations only in terms of social status.

Early educational interests and abilities may contribute to the vocational direction that children take later. However, their expressed interests and performance may also lead to premature parental expectations about their choice of an occupation. At this stage of development, occupational stereotypes based on gender or on ethnic group usually develop. These stereotypes can cause conflict for a young child—male or female—who is showing interest in an area traditionally considered appropriate only for the other gender. Stereotyping also inhibits a young person from following natural inclinations in exploring vocational possibilities.

The idea that vocational development is part of total personality development and self-concept development has implications for elementary school counseling. Exploring and understanding one's interests, aptitudes, and values are processes that start early in life and should receive attention in elementary school.

Referrals for learning difficulties are usually more numerous in elementary schools than are referrals for vocational concerns. Like vocational concerns, however, these problems are often tied in with personal values, attitudes, and interpersonal problems. Teachers tend to refer children who lack the motivation to begin or complete work assignments or who are not working up to their estimated ability. Children may seek out a counselor and complain that they are bored with school or that they find the work too difficult.

The counselor can help children explore the reasons for their difficulty with schoolwork. Children may be feeling undue pressure from teachers or parents over the quality of their academic performance, or conversely, teachers or parents may not be paying sufficient attention to the child's work. The counselor can help determine whether a child is being expected to do work above his or her ability; if so, the teacher can be alerted to modify expectations. The counselor can also recommend referral to a school psychologist if the educational difficulty looks severe or puzzling enough to warrant psychological assessment for possible placement in a special education or learning disability class. If the home situation is contributing to the lack of educational progress, family counseling might prove helpful. Or if the home situation is chaotic and the children are suffering from neglect, referral to a social worker is in order. In any case the counselor might still continue counseling with the child or the family or both. The school psychologist or the social worker and the counselor might also work jointly with the child and the family.

Following are examples of problems students typically present to counselors and some possible approaches counselors can take.

Client 1: Allison is a fourth grader referred to the counselor by her teacher because she is not working at the level her teacher believes she should. Allison has above-average ability and superior scores on reading and standardized achievement tests. She does not hand in assignments on time, is careless in her work, and generally acts bored. Allison is apparently willing to see the counselor but seems uninterested during the first counseling session.

Response C–1: Allison has been referred by her teacher, so her motivation for counseling may be minimal. The counselor may find it helpful to clarify with the student why the referral was made, whether the student agrees with the teacher's appraisal, and whether the student believes that a problem exists. The counselor could explain to Allison that she does not have to continue with counseling if she prefers not to but could come back whenever she felt she needed to. If she decides to continue, then counselor and client could discuss her classroom attitude, feelings, and behavior.

If Allison has difficulty expressing herself, the counselor might use play media, such as free drawing or puppets, as a means of helping her relax and start talking. Her drawings or puppet play might give some clues to her feelings about herself and her interactions with others. If she talks freely, instead of using play media the counselor could rely on client-centered listening to help her explore the reasons for her lack of interest in school.

Because her teacher made the referral, the counselor might suggest to Allison that the teacher would find it useful to receive some feedback about thier discussions. The counselor and Allison could decide together what to share with the teacher and who would share it.

Client 2: Brett, a fifth grader, has asked the secretary for an appointment for counseling. When he comes in, he tells the counselor he is having trouble with mathematics and science. He expresses little interest in them. His mother is a physicist and his father a biologist. Brett thinks they are disappointed in him. He prefers English, social sciences, and art.

Response C–2: In talking with Brett, it is important to help him first explore whether his belief concerning his parents' expectations is accurate. This exploration could include encouraging Brett to talk with his parents about their aspirations for him. Role-playing a dialogue with his parents as a form of behavior rehearsal might be helpful. If his discussion with his parents indicated they would not be concerned if he did not follow scientific paths, the focus of the counseling sessions could be on cognitive restructuring to clarify his expectations about himself. If, however, his parents proved to be set on his making top grades in mathematics and science, the counselor could ask Brett whether it would be helpful for the counselor to talk with them.

Client 3: Billy is a second grader who is referred by his teacher because he does not seem to be able to comprehend the reading assignments in class. The teacher is dubious about his ability to learn second-grade material and wonders whether he belongs in a special education class. He is new in the school district, and no records of intellectual capacity or achievement are available.

Response C–3: Billy has been referred by his teacher for a psychological evaluation for the possibility of placing him in a special education class. The referral is inappropriate. It should have been made to the school psychologist after the teacher consulted with the principal and obtained permission from Billy's parents. The school psychologist is the learning specialist who is trained to make psychological evaluations and diagnoses.

However, even though the referral is inappropriate, the counselor might ask Billy whether he knows why the teacher referred him to the counselor and how he feels about it. The counselor could explain that the teacher wondered whether he was assigned to the right class because he is new at the school and no previous records are available. The counselor could invite Billy to come back if he ever wanted to talk over what was going on. In this way the counselor can serve as a resource to Billy and his parents, whether he is relocated or remains in the same class.

Personal Problems

Children experience feelings of loneliness, inadequacy, rejection, and self-hate similar to the feelings experienced by adolescents and adults. They have doubts about their intellectual ability and worry about their classroom or playground behavior. Some children express beliefs that they are dumb, unattractive, or worthless. In other cases anger, disappointment, or bewilderment may be felt but not recognized or articulated. Counselors need to help children express, understand, and label these feelings and work toward more productive perceptions of themselves.

Client 4: Marcus, a second grader, is referred by his teacher because he has difficulty in his interactions with other children. He is very sensitive to criticism and breaks into tears when students tease him or the teacher corrects his work. The teacher has talked with his parents. The mother is overprotective and blames the teacher and other children for picking on Marcus; the father acts uninterested.

Response C–4: Marcus may readily agree to talk with a counselor because he wants to do what he is asked and not risk disapproval. Because he may have strong feelings of inadequacy, however, he may find it difficult to open up about his negative feelings or impulses. At any rate Marcus needs a nonevaluative, trusting relationship in which he can express his doubts about himself and his apprehensions about others' opinions. Play media may be useful during the sessions. The counselor should help him explore whether his expectations and/or the expectations of his parents are unrealistic.

The counselor should try to help Marcus become aware of and label his feelings when he cries. It is likely that his tears reflect unexpressed feelings of anger and frustration, as well as hurt and shame. If Marcus responds well, the counselor might suggest a conference with his parents.

Client 5: Dave, a third grader, sees the school counselor in an assembly and asks for an appointment later in the day. When he comes in, he says that he has been having bad dreams and that he gets stomachaches. His schoolwork is not going as well as he would like, and he is not making friends easily. His two older siblings have good academic records and seem socially secure. Dave has superior academic ability, but he calls himself dumb.

Response C–5: Dave apparently is experiencing depression and stress related to concerns about his capabilities and may be having some physical reactions to the pressure. As with any client expressing physical symptoms, the counselor should recommend a medical examination to determine any physical basis for the stomachaches.

Dave has initiated counseling and is open about his concerns, so the chances of helping him are favorable. Some of Beck's techniques might prove helpful for breaking tasks into manageable units in which success is assured. Dave's teacher can cooperate in applying Beck's methods in the classroom (see chap. 6). Family consultation or counseling might also be helpful.

Social Problems

A significant portion of referrals in elementary school result from children's problems in interacting with teachers, parents, and peers. Teachers may refer a child they constantly have to discipline. Friction may build up because of a child's distracting behavior or a teacher's impatience or both. Teachers may be concerned by excessive shyness or may believe that a child's home situation is contributing to overdependence, nuisance behavior, or underachievement. Picking fights and calling others names are common ways for children to express their frustration and anger. Children may ask for counseling because they are unhappy, lonesome, or frustrated at school or home; parental, sibling, or peer interactions may not be going well.

Client 6: Carrie, an eighth grader, comes to the counselor's office in tears. She has had a fight with her best friend. Now her friend is giving a party and has not invited her.

Response C–6: Peer friction occurs frequently with children at this age and most often quickly disappears if adults do not complicate matters. If Carrie has good interpersonal relationships and this incident is simply a spat, the counselor should listen sympathetically but not overreact. Carrie will probably figure out a way of resolving the conflict. However, the counselor can help her deal with her feelings of disappointment at not being invited to the party. On the other hand, if Carrie has had persistent problems with her peers, the counselor should explore what is contributing to the ongoing friction. Carrie might benefit from group counseling with students who are having similar problems.

Client 7: Christie, a third grader, runs up to the counselor in the hallway during recess and asks to see the counselor sometime during the day. When she comes in, she exclaims that she is both angry with and afraid of her teacher. She says that her teacher picks on her and blames her for things she hasn't done. The teacher also yells at the class, which upsets her.

Response C–7: Christie presents a type of problem that requires the counselor to be diplomatic. If teachers perceive that a counselor takes the students' side in teacher-student conflicts, the staff becomes resentful. If students perceive that a counselor takes the teachers' side, they will probably avoid the counselor. A counselor's goal is to help improve relationships between teachers and students.

In Christie's situation the counselor should try to help decrease the friction. If the teacher is approachable and Christie has the ego strength, the counselor should encourage her to discuss her concerns with the teacher. Role-playing might prove useful. If Christie's behavior is contributing to the friction, the counselor should ask her how she might change her behavior to improve the interaction. If the teacher is not willing to consult with the counselor, the counselor may have to help Christié learn strategies to minimize stress in that classroom.

Persons at Risk

Antisocial Behavior

Children's antisocial behavior includes stealing, defacing school property, being truant, breaking windows, cheating on tests, chronic lying, and hurting themselves or others. In the lower grades throwing rocks at other children or at buildings or cars is a common problem. Drug or alcohol use may occur in the higher grades. When children seek out counselors to confess that they have been involved in antisocial behavior, the counselors should not necessarily turn the children over to authorities unless the children are dangerous to themselves or others. Instead, counselors can help the children control antisocial impulses and direct them into constructive avenues before these impulses overwhelm them. In addition, if disciplinary action is not automatically meted out, other children with similar impulses will be more likely to see the counselor.

However, if children endanger themselves or others because of their behavior, the counselor is ethically bound to tell them that their families and other mental health professionals must be contacted so that they can get more intensive help.

> **Client 8:** John, a fourth grader, tells the counselor he set a fire in the wastebasket in a lavatory. He was angry at a teacher and an administrator because he thought he was being treated unfairly. This was the first time he had set a fire, and he immediately put it out. His own behavior scared him.

> *Response C–8:* Because John's behavior is not chronic and he is concerned about his own impulsive act, the counselor is not required to report his behavior. The counselor should work with him about his reasons for believing that he was being treated unfairly and help him express his anger more constructively. If he has some justification for his feelings, the counselor might arrange for a three-way conference with the teacher or administrator or both. The counselor should also explore with him his family dynamics, to see whether his behavior was aggravated by poor family interactions.

> If John had expressed irresistible urges to set fires and had set other fires, the counselor should have discussed the need for him to receive more intensive help because that kind of behavior is potentially dangerous to others. The counselor should have contacted his parents and arranged psychological or psychiatric consultation. The counselor would still have tried to be a source of help to John both during and after his treatment.

Attention-Deficit/Hyperactivity Disorder

Counselors in elementary schools are often called on to work with children diagnosed with attention-deficit/hyperactivity disorder (ADHD), one of the most frequently diagnosed psychiatric disorders of childhood. The *DSM-IV-TR* cites the prevalence rate of ADHD at 3% to 7% for school-age children; it is more prevalent in boys than in girls. ADHD is characterized by persistent and developmentally inappropriate problems with attention, impulsivity, and hyperactivity. Students with ADHD consistently drift off task; are distractible; act with no forethought to consequences; overreact; refuse to obey instructions, commands, or requests; are disorganized; experience learning problems, academic underachievement, and school failure; have social skills problems; and have low self-esteem (Erk, 2004).

The hyperactivity component may not always be readily observable in a counseling session, because children with ADHD are able to maintain attention in one-to-one situations that are unique or novel, such as individual counseling sessions (Erk, 2004). Thus, counselors are often apprised of ADHD-related problems in children by their parents. To diagnose ADHD, referral to the school psychologist for a thorough assessment is recommended.

School counselors can implement multidisciplinary-multidimensional treatment for children or adolescents with ADHD, coordinating the efforts of parents, school staff, and physicians. Counselors can also provide ADHD workshops for parents and school staff and can become advocates of ADHD children in the community. Erk (2004) recommends parent training and counseling, teacher education, individual counseling, group counseling, behavioral interventions, self-esteem education, social skills education, and family counseling for children with ADHD. He also recommends referral to a family physician, pediatrician, or psychiatrist to inform the family about medication as a possible addition to treatment.

Wicks-Nelson and Israel (2000) report that the effectiveness of traditional individual counseling and play therapy with children with ADHD is not documented. They also report that pharmacotherapy and behavioral interventions are the treatments of choice. The most commonly used medications for ADHD are stimulants (Greenhill et al., 2002)—for example, Ritalin, Concerta, Dexedrine, and Adderall. Although much controversy surrounds the use of stimulants, an estimated 75% of medicated children show increased attention and reduced impulsivity in activity level, both in the laboratory and in natural environments that illicit ADHD behaviors (Whalen & Henker, 1998).

Some health care professionals, such as psychiatrist Peter Breggin (1998), are alarmed at the unquestioned use of Ritalin without regard for the serious side effects of the drug and its long-term effects. Some are worried that teachers and counselors are encouraging its use to maintain order in classrooms. "Some parents, educators and doctors wonder if schools are encouraging students to take Ritalin because they need it or because it is easier to teach rambunctious kids if they are medicated" (Gannett News Service, 1998b, p. C1). Since 1990 there has been a steep increase in the use of Ritalin in the United States. As an alternative to using the drug to calm hyperactive children, Breggin suggests "de-stressing the environment by looking at ways the home, school and entertainment media may be promoting difficult behavior" (Gannett News Service, 1998a, p. C1).

Client 9: Kenny, age 9, was not considered a bad child by his parents, but he had always been overly active. Starting at age 3, he was in constant motion, rushing from one activity to the next, leaving a trail of toys behind him. He was reckless and impulsive: He would run into the road without looking for cars, no matter how many times his mother explained the danger or scolded him. He chattered nonstop at mealtimes and frequently did not follow through on his parents' requests, although this seemed not to be deliberate. At recess his tendency to overreact—like hitting playmates for simply bumping into him—had already gotten him into trouble several times. He couldn't concentrate on his schoolwork and was in danger of failing his grade. His parents didn't know what to do.

Response C–9: In working with Kenny, the counselor should begin by interviewing his parents and getting information about him and his family's history, the degree of stress the family is experiencing in caring for him, and his behavior problems and strengths. The counselor should also interview teachers to obtain information on learning and academic problems and on peer interaction. The counselor should then refer the parents to their family physician, pediatrician, or psychiatrist for a medical evaluation for potential pharmacotherapy. The counselor should also refer the family to a community mental health counselor to help the parents learn behavioral interventions to use with Kenny at home. The counselor should suggest that teachers implement behavioral interventions in the classroom, too, such as token reinforcement, time-outs, and contingency contracting. A daily report card could be sent to the parents to promote communication between the teacher and the parents and to inform them of the Kenny's performance so he could be rewarded for progress.

Child Maltreatment

In 2001 approximately 903,000 children were found to be victims of child maltreatment—57% suffered neglect, 19% were physically abused, 10% were sexually abused, and 7% were psychologically maltreated. Child abuse is reported more frequently in elementary schools than in other settings because of teachers' close interactions with the children. Physical signs of child abuse include bruises, fractures, and burns; however, many signs of abuse do not have physical indicators. Some behavioral signs of abuse include withdrawal, aggression, hypervigilance, difficulty concentrating, and poor school performance.

As indicated in chapter 3, counselors must report incidents of physical abuse, neglect, or sexual abuse. In addition, school counselors are increasingly called upon to coordinate counseling services for abused students and to develop child abuse prevention programs for their schools. School personnel have learned to rely on counselors when confronted with procedural and legal concerns regarding the subject of abuse (White & Flynt, 2000). Although school counselors are mandated to report suspected child abuse, counselors need to work diligently to maintain the relationship with the child so that ongoing counseling services can continue after the crisis is over and/or referral to appropriate community agencies is made. In addition, school counselors can work with nonoffending family members in collaboration with community agencies to help them deal with the trauma.

Client 10: Sarah's fourth-grade teacher, Mrs. Johnson, consulted with the school counselor to discuss Sarah's behavior in class. Mrs. Johnson had noticed that Sarah's schoolwork, which usually had been good, had declined significantly in the last few months. Sarah seemed preoccupied in class and unable to concentrate on assignments. One day Mrs. Johnson noticed Sarah eating alone during lunch and asked her how she was feeling. Sarah was quiet, but she stated she wasn't feeling well because she hadn't slept the night before. When asked why, Sarah became more withdrawn but stated something about being afraid of her father when he drank beer.

Response C–10: In this case the student has not disclosed a specific incidence of child abuse. However, approximately half of all cases of abuse happen at the hands of substance-abusing perpetrators, so the counselor should keep in mind that abuse is a possibility. The counselor should initiate individual counseling with Sarah to build a relationship and assess the reasons for her recent poor school performance. The counselor should provide informed consent information to Sarah, describing the limits of confidentiality. The purpose of counseling would be to provide Sarah with an opportunity to express and be validated for her feelings and to teach her coping strategies. If Sarah was relatively nonverbal in the sessions, the counselor could engage her in nondirective play therapy. If she disclosed child abuse, the counselor would remind her of the legal and ethical requirement to report what she had disclosed and would then make a report to the appropriate authorities. The counselor should continue to see Sarah individually to provide support for her in the possibility of an upcoming investigation.

Substance Abuse and Violence

Children born of drug-abusing parents enter elementary schools every day, and children are becoming involved with drugs and alcohol themselves at alarmingly younger ages (Schmidt, 2003). "Substance abuse is not a problem of just the adult world or even the adult and adolescent world . . . it has already dramatically invaded the elementary school years as well" (Gibson et al., 1993, p. 103). A significant amount of pressure to drink alcohol comes from peers. Use of marijuana and other drugs also occurs at this level.

Along with substance abuse, violence in the schools has also escalated. Although more common in secondary schools, violence in the lower grades is increasingly being reported. The third leading cause of death of elementary and middle school children is homicide. Greater numbers of children have been carrying weapons to school, and shootings both by outsiders and by schoolchildren are increasing. Elementary counselors must therefore be prepared to offer interventions to individuals, students, groups of students, the student body as a whole, and families.

Juhnke (1997) uses a critical incident stress debriefing (CISD) approach with elementary and middle school students suffering from postviolence emotional trauma after experiencing or witnessing a violent scene at school. Counselors first meet with parents to share feelings about the traumatic event and to introduce them to the debriefing process. Then they form joint sessions of parents and students with no more than five or six children and their parents at a time. Parents sit behind their child, sometimes putting their hands on their child's shoulders. A counselor then encourages each of the children to talk about what they remember and to express their feelings as they experienced the trauma. The counselor then asks all the children to come together and share their memories and feelings about the event. Afterward, counselors arrange follow-up individual and group counseling for those who need it.

OUTREACH ACTIVITIES

Psychoeducation: Group Guidance

Group, or classroom, guidance is educational and differs from group counseling in terms of the depth of interaction. It isn't intended to explore or encourage confidential, personal sharing among group members. Instead, group guidance typically involves the school counselor presenting instructional material to small groups (10 to 15) or large groups (25 to 30) of students, usually situated in a classroom. School counselors create instructional units around general topics, including school success, social skills, dealing with peer pressure, conflict resolution, career planning, safety from strangers, drug education awareness, and assertiveness skills (Wittmer, 2000). As with group counseling, group guidance sessions are typically 20 to 30 minutes in length and are conducted once or twice per week for a total of four to six sessions, depending on the information being delivered.

Comprehensive career development programs, proposed and funded by the National Occupational Information Coordinating Committee (NOICC), include career awareness at the elementary level. In such a program the counselor helps children become aware of their uniqueness, gives them a perspective about the role of work in society, and introduces a survey of different occupations. School counselors and teachers often work together to plan joint activities in the classroom that will provide career information and career self-awareness. Speakers from various occupational fields within the community may be invited to share their experiences. Field trips to local businesses may also be used to supplement curriculum activities.

Crisis Intervention

Most children are faced with crises at one time or another, and some children are chronically in crisis through no fault of their own. For young children crises generally revolve around family disruptions—severe illness or death of a parent, divorce or threat of divorce, remarriage of a single parent, a parent's loss of a job, drug or alcohol abuse, or homelessness. Loss of a pet or loss of a close friend who suddenly moves away can also unduly disturb a child. When a child comes to a counselor in crisis, the counselor first calms the child down and attends to her or his immediate concerns. The counselor then decides whether further counseling is appropriate or, if the child still needs emergency help, whether to notify staff and family to make further arrangements.

Consultation

Consulting is a major function of school counselors. It involves providing information, presenting instruction, giving suggestions for handling situations, and facilitating planning processes (Schmidt, 2003). Simply stated, consultation is "a process whereby the first party (consultant) assists a second party (consultee) in finding a solution to a problem that concerns the third party (client)" (Harrison, 2000, p. 183). In other words, the school counselor in the consultant role helps teachers, parents, or administrators find a solution to a problem that involves a student. Consultation is considered an indirect service to students through direct involvement with teachers, administrators, and parents. In the consulting role school counselors assess problems, determine goals, explore alternatives, and choose appropriate courses of action. The communication skills used in consulting are similar to those in counseling and include open questions, paraphrases, and summaries.

Elementary school teachers who trust their counselors often request consultations with them about classroom interactions. At times the focus centers on children; at times, on the teachers themselves. Following are two examples of concerns that teachers might bring to their school counselor, along with suggested responses.

Teacher 1: Mr. Colby, a sixth-grade teacher, complains about two disruptive children in his class. They talk out loud, answer insolently at times, and in general demonstrate rudeness and disrespect. The class laughs and becomes restless when these children act up. When one or the other or both are absent, the class works smoothly. Mr. Colby has had similar difficulties before. He prefers trying to change his behavior, rather than sending the children to the administrator for disciplinary action.

Response T–1: The school counselor can show Mr. Colby how to set limits with disruptive students and can give him guidelines on how to stick with those limits. The counselor can also encourage him to confront the students about their behavior and set up an agreement or contract outlining what is acceptable classroom behavior.

Teacher 2: Mr. Fletcher drops into the counselor's office and sits down heavily. He appears to be highly perceptive but a little unsure of himself. He is being evaluated for tenure. His administrator visited his class and told him afterward that he is well organized but too distant with his students. The administrator recommended that he be more outgoing and friendly—characteristics of the administrator. Mr. Fletcher senses some need to be more approachable with students but cannot see himself emulating the effervescent administrator.

Response T–2: The counselor should support Mr. Fletcher's reluctance to emulate another personality. The counselor can also discuss with him the reasons for his uncertainty about his professional ability and possible ways he can capitalize on his sensitivity to students' needs to make him more approachable for students.

Collaboration and Coordination

Although school counselors have the primary responsibility for developing comprehensive school counseling programs, they cannot accomplish this task fully without collaborating with professionals in the community (Schmidt, 2003). School counselors initiate collegial relationships with a variety of educational, medical, and counseling agencies that provide outside services to school populations. When problems come to their attention that are beyond the scope of services the school can offer, elementary school counselors need to be aware of the resources available for family and marriage counseling. When a child demonstrates serious emotional difficulties or when a severe crisis leaves a child with lingering emotional problems, a referral for outside counseling is usually in order. By knowing the community's facilities and authorities, counselors will be ready when they need to report child abuse and can make arrangements for cooperative treatment efforts. They will also be better able to arrange joint outreach programs in drug education, suicide prevention, and parenting skills.

One such example is the unique partnership between two elementary schools in Maryland and the Department of Counseling and Human Services at Johns Hopkins University in Manford (Keep & Bemak, 1997). The program was developed in economically disadvantaged communities with high crime rates "as a way of addressing issues of violence and aggression within the school and community" (p. 259). A mental health team was formed, including persons from school, family, and community. Johns Hopkins faculty provided training and consultation to elementary counselors and to community participants who jointly identified student and family problems and developed cohesive prevention programs.

WORKING WITH FAMILIES

Parent Consultation

Parents want their children to succeed in school. They usually want their children to behave well in school at all times, too (Harrison, 2000). Counselors in a consultant role can assist parents by teaching them effective ways of promoting positive behaviors in their children.

A difficult situation faced by almost all school counselors is the dreaded phone conversation with a parent whose child has been disciplined by the teacher and/or school administrator. As a consultant the school counselor should not choose sides between the parent and the teacher/administrator. Although it is a precarious balance, allying with both parties is important in getting all parties working together to help the child. The counselor needs to (a) use basic counseling skills—especially paraphrasing and reflecting feelings—to build rapport with the parent and ease the tension, (b) assure the parent that everyone in the school wants the best for the child, (c) express appreciation for him or her as a concerned parent, and (d) suggest a strategy, such as a meeting with the teacher. If a parent-teacher conference is suggested, the counselor may need to facilitate such a conference to help the teacher and parent develop appropriate problem-solving strategies. A follow-up consultation with the parent can be carried out by telephone. If it is apparent that family counseling is needed, a referral can be made.

Parent Education

Elementary and middle school counselors offer training in parenting skills to groups of parents from basically functional families. Parent Effectiveness Training (PET; Gordon, 1975) and Systematic Training for Effective Parenting (STEP; Dinkmeyer, 1976), an Adlerian approach, are most common. In these programs parents meet weekly for a school semester to discuss mutual problems of discipline or communication and to learn techniques in child rearing. Some schools offer similar classes for single parents, divorced parents, or parents who are recovering alcoholics.

Conroy and Mayer (1994) developed a 2-year parent education program in a primary school in Durham, North Carolina. During the first year, groups of parents met with a counselor for six sessions to discuss how the parents could help their children become more responsible and cooperative in school and at home. In the second year, through a series of evening meetings, parents discussed ways to discipline children appropriately and, at the same time, build their self-esteem. During this time a parent resource library was available for their use. A majority of parents believed that the program had improved their parenting skills, with consequent positive changes in their children's behavior at home and at school.

SUMMARY

Duties of elementary school counselors are similar to those of counselors in other settings, except that counselors in elementary schools do more consultation with parents, families, and teachers and are more involved with crisis cases.

Along with traditional counseling approaches, elementary school counselors often use play therapy and creative and expressive arts therapy with nonverbal children to increase child openness and spontaneity. Group guidance activities are conducted more frequently in classrooms in elementary schools than in other educational settings. These activities focus on building self-esteem, improving personal growth, and learning communication skills. Confidentiality and rights of privacy should be honored with children in elementary schools to maintain their trust and to increase their feelings of self-involvement in counseling. Brief counseling is well suited for elementary school counselors. Elementary school counselors have been increasing their attention to multicultural counseling and to family counseling and consultation.

PROJECTS AND ACTIVITIES

1. Interview elementary school counselors, school psychologists, and school social workers who are working in the same school district. How does each group perceive its unique responsibilities? How well do the various specialists work together?

2. A teacher tells a counselor that she wants to talk to him about a child in her class who is in counseling. The counselor explains that he wants to obtain permission from the child in order to preserve confidentiality. Later, the principal tells the counselor that the teacher is upset because he acted as though she could not be trusted. Consider how this situation could be handled to preserve confidentiality and yet not antagonize the teacher.

3. Assume that a new counselor is meeting with a group of teachers to discuss her role and to suggest guidelines for referral. A teacher tells the counselor that he is confused about to whom he should refer children who are creating discipline problems. He asks the counselor when he should refer a child to the principal and when he should refer to the counselor. How should the counselor respond?

4. Suppose that Marcus (Client 4) has a teacher who you believe is hypercritical, but the teacher is unaware of her behavior. How might you involve the teacher to improve the classroom environment for Marcus and the other students in the class?

5. Invite an elementary school counselor and a counselor working with children in a community agency to talk with your group about the types of children's concerns with which they work. Ask them to discuss their use of play media.

6. You are asked to talk at a PTA meeting about your role as an elementary counselor. Outline what you believe would be important considerations to include. Compare your ideas with the role definitions presented in this book.

7. Compose a memo that could be sent to parents at the beginning of the academic year that defines your role and duties as a counselor. In the memo include confidentiality and freedom of choice as important components in counseling.

8. With another student role-play your initial interchange with Allison (Client 1) as she walks into your office, a willing but uninterested referral.

REFERENCES

Allan, J. (1988). *Inscapes of the child's world: Jungian counseling in schools and clinics.* Dallas: Spring.

American School Counseling Association (ASCA). (2003). The ASCA national model: A framework for school counseling programs. *Professional School Counselor, 6*(3), 165–168.

Armheim, R. (1990). The artist as heater. *Arts in Psychotherapy, 17,* 1–4.

Baker, S. (1996). *School counseling for the 21st century.* Upper Saddle River, NJ: Merrill/Prentice Hall.

Baker, S. B., & Gerler, E. R. (2001). Counseling in schools. In D. C. Locke, J. E. Myers, & E. L. Herr (Eds.), *The Handbook of Counseling* (pp. 289–318). Thousand Oaks, CA: Sage.

Baruth, L. G., & Manning, M. L. (1999). *Multicultural counseling and psychotherapy: A lifespan perspective* (2nd ed.). Upper Saddle River, NJ: Merrill/Prentice Hall.

Berk, L. E. (2003). *Child development* (6th ed.). Boston: Allyn & Bacon.

Bowlby, J. (1969). *Attachment and loss: Vol. 1. Attachment.* New York: Basic Books.

Bowlby, J. (1973a). *Attachment and loss: Vol. 2. Separation: Anxiety and anger.* New York: Basic Books.

Bowlby, J. (1973b). *Attachment and loss: Vol. 3. Loss.* New York: Basic Books.

Breggin, P. (1998). *Talking Back to Ritalin: What doctors aren't telling you about stimulants for children.* Monroe, MA: Common Courage Press.

Cochran, J. L. (1996). Using play and art therapy to help culturally diverse students overcome barriers to school success. *School Counselor, 43,* 287–298.

Conroy, E., & Mayer, S. (1994). Strategies for consulting with parents. *Elementary School Guidance and Counseling, 29,* 60–66.

Dahir, C. A. (2001). The national standards for school counseling programs: Development and implementation. *Professional School Counselor, 4*(5), 320–327.

Department of Health and Human Services (DHHS). (2000). *Mental health: A report of the surgeon general.* Rockville, MD: Author.

Dinkmeyer, D. (1976). *Systematic training for effective parenting.* Circle Pines, MN: American Guidance Service.

Erikson, E. H. (1950). *Childhood and society.* New York: Norton.

Erk, R. R. (2004). Counseling treatment for children and adolescents with DSM-IV-TR disorders. Upper Saddle River, NJ: Pearson/Merrill/Prentice Hall.

Gannett News Service. (1998a, March 12). Psychiatrist criticizes rising use of Ritalin on children. *Bellingham Herald,* p. C1.

Gannett News Service. (1998b, March 19). Ritalin worries parents, educators. *Bellingham Herald,* p. C1.

Gibson, R. L., Mitchell, M. A., & Basile, S. K. (1993). *Counseling in the elementary school: A comprehensive approach.* Boston: Allyn & Bacon.

Gil, E. (1991). *The healing power of play: Working with abused children.* New York: Guilford.

Ginter, E. J., & Glauser, A. S. (2004). Assessment and diagnosis: The developmental perspective and its implications. In R. R. Erk (Ed.), *Counseling treatment for children and adolescents with DSM-IV-TR disorders.* Upper Saddle River, NJ: Merrill/Prentice Hall.

Gladding, S. T. (1998). *Counseling as an art: The creative arts in counseling.* Alexandria, VA: American Counseling Association.

Gordon, T. (1975). *Parent effectiveness training.* New York: New American Library.

Greenhill, L., Pliszka, S., Dulcan, M. K., & Work Group on Quality Issues. (2002). Practice parameter for the use of stimulant medications in the treatment of children, adolescents, and adults. *Journal of the American Academy of Child and Adolescent Psychiatry, 41, Supplement,* 26S–49S.

Gysbers, N. C., & Henderson, P. (2001). Comprehensive guidance and counseling programs: A rich history and a bright future. *Professional School Counseling, 4,* 246–256.

Hardesty, P. H., & Dillard, J. M. (1994). The role of elementary school counselors compared with their middle and secondary school counterparts. *Elementary School Guidance and Counseling, 29,* 83–91.

Harrison, T. (2000). Brief counseling in the K–12 developmental counseling program. In J. Wittmer (Ed.), *Managing your school counseling program: K–12 developmental strategies* (pp. 85–94). Minneapolis, MN: Educational Media.

Juhnke, G. A. (1997). After school violence: An adapted critical incident stress debriefing model for student survivors and their parents. *Elementary School Guidance and Counseling, 31,* 163–170.

Keat, D. B. (1974). *Fundamentals of child counseling.* Boston: Houghton Mifflin.

Keat, D. B. (1990). *Child multimodal therapy.* Norwood, NJ: Ablex.

Keep, S. G., & Bemak, F. (1997). School-family-community linked services: A school counseling role for changing times. *School Counselor, 44,* 255–263.

Kottman, T. (2001). *Play therapy: Basics and beyond.* New York: Guilford.

Kottman, T. (2003). *Partners in play: An Adlerian approach to play therapy* (2nd ed.). Alexandria, VA: American Counseling Association.

Kottman, T. (2004). Play therapy. In A. Vernon, *Counseling children and adolescents* (3rd ed., pp. 111–136). Denver: Love.

Landreth, G. L. (1987). Play therapy: Facilitative use of child's play in elementary school counseling. *Elementary School Guidance and Counseling, 21,* 253–261.

Landreth, G. L., (2002). *Play therapy: The art of the relationship* (2nd ed.). New York: Brunner-Routledge.

Landreth, G. L., & Sweeney, D. S. (1997). Child-centered play therapy. In K. J. O'Connor & L. M. Braverman (Eds.), *Play therapy theory and practice: A comparative presentation* (pp. 17–45). New York: John Wiley.

Larans, A. (1989). Brief psychotherapy: The multimodal model. *Psychology: A Journal of Human Behavior, 26,* 7–10.

Lee, C. C. (Ed.). (1995). *Counseling for diversity: A guide for school counselors and related professionals.* Boston: Allyn & Bacon.

Moreno, J. L. (1946). *Psychodrama.* Beacon, NY: Beacon Press.

Myrick, R. D. (1997). *Developmental guidance and counseling: A practical approach* (3rd ed.). Minneapolis: Educational Media.

Ohlsen, M. M., Horne, A. M., & Lawe, C. F. (1988). *Group counseling* (3rd ed.). New York: Holt, Rinehart & Winston.

Osborn, C. J. (1999). Solution-focused strategies with "involuntary" clients: Practical applications for the school and clinical setting. *Journal of Humanistic Education and Development, 37*(3), 169–181.

Piaget, J., & Inhelder, B. (1969). *The psychology of the child.* New York: Basic Books.

Riley, S. (1997, Winter). Children's R. and narratives: An opportunity to enhance therapy and a supervisory challenge. *The Supervision Bulletin,* 2–3.

Schmidt, J. J. (2000). Counselor accountability: Justifying your time and measuring your worth. In J. Whittmer, *Managing your school counseling program: K–12 developmental strategies* (2nd ed., pp. 275–291). Minneapolis, MN: Educational Media.

Schmidt, J. J. (2003). *Counseling in schools: Essential services and comprehensive programs* (4th ed.). Boston: Allyn & Bacon.

Schreiber, R., & Lyddon, W. J. (1998). Parental bonding and current psychological functioning among childhood sexual abuse survivors. *Journal of Counseling Psychology, 45*(3), 358–362.

Sink, C.A., & MacDonald, G. (1998). The status of comprehensive guidance and counseling in the United States. *Professional School Counseling 2*(2), 88–94.

Sweeney, T. J. (1998). *The Adlerian counselor.* Muncie, IN: Accelerated Development/Taylor & Francis.

Thompson, C. L., & Rudolph, L. B. (1992). *Counseling children* (2nd ed.). Pacific Grove, CA: Brooks/Cole.

Whalen, C. K., & Henker, B. (1998). Social impact of stimulant treatment for hyperactive children. *Journal of Learning Disabilities, 24,* 231–241.

White, J., & Flynt, M. (2000). The school counselor's role in prevention and remediation of child abuse. In J. Wittmer (Ed.), *Managing your school counseling program: K–12 developmental strategies* (pp. 149–160). Minneapolis, MN: Educational Media.

Wicks-Nelson, R., & Israel, A. C. (2000). *Behavior disorders of childhood.* Upper Saddle River, NJ: Merrill/Prentice/Hall.

Wittmer, J. (2000). *Managing your school counseling program: K–12 developmental strategies.* Minneapolis: Educational Media.

Zapata, J. T. (1995). Counseling Hispanic children. In C. C. Lee (Ed.), *Counseling for diversity: A guide for school counselors and related professionals* (pp. 85–108). Boston: Allyn & Bacon.

CHAPTER 17

Counseling Programs in Middle and Secondary Schools

A dolescents face developmental transitional challenges in which they struggle with their identities, make important educational and career decisions, develop intimate peer relationships, and try to become more independent and self-sufficient. Because adolescents spend most of their waking hours in school, school personnel have considerable impact on their lives. Having a well-trained staff of counselors in secondary schools is essential. Although school counselors have a variety of roles and activities in the schools, we believe that their primary function is that of professional counselor.

The first counselor role definitions and training standards for secondary school counselors as we know them today were developed in the early 1960s by the American Personnel and Guidance Association (APGA, now ACA) and the American School Counselors Association (ASCA; see chap. 2). In contrast with the earlier advice-giving guidance role that prevailed in the years before World War II, these standards defined the counselor role as helping the client work through developmental, situational concerns in a nonjudgmental and client-centered way. Since that time, these standards have served as guidelines for counselors in all specialty areas. For this chapter the term *secondary counselor* will refer to counselors working in both middle and high schools, although distinctions will be made between the two when appropriate.

In the early postwar decades, secondary school counselors had difficulty implementing effective counseling programs largely because significant numbers of counselors were not adequately trained and because administrators, parents, and teachers were resistant and confused about counselor roles. Counselors were burdened with course scheduling, college placement, and academic record keeping. Although the present-day secondary school counselor's role is changing, the typical secondary counselor continues to assist students by providing information about course selections, career opportunities, test results, colleges, and scholarships (Schmidt, 2003).

STUDENT DEVELOPMENTAL NEEDS

According to Erikson's psychosocial developmental theory, individuals go through eight developmental stages throughout their life span (see Table 5.1 in chap. 5). In adolescence young people go through the fifth stage, during which they develop a sense of identity. Adolescents are searching for an *identity* that will enhance their feelings of self-esteem, as well as provide reassurance from others that they are valued. This stage serves as a bridge between the childhood and adult stages. To be ready to develop a sense of identity, individuals must have adequately worked through and integrated the challenges confronting them in earlier stages—building trust relationships, strengthening feelings of autonomy, striving for achievement, and taking initiative. A strong identity then prepares them for the next stage, which requires that individuals develop love, intimacy, and caring. "The emerging ego identity, then, bridges the early childhood stages, when the body and the parent images were given their specific meanings, and the later stages, when a variety of social roles becomes available and increasingly coercive" (Erikson, 1980, p. 96).

Feminist developmental theorists—including Gilligan (1982), Conarton and Silverman (1988), and Jordan, Kaplan, Miller, Stiver, and Surrey (1991)—have taken issue with Erikson's model as a description of women's stages of development (see chaps. 5 and 6). Particularly at the adolescent stage, they claim, a girl's natural pattern of development goes unrecognized. If they have to follow the male model of separation and autonomy that Erikson describes in order to compete, adolescent girls begin to feel thwarted, confused, and defeated.

THE MIDDLE SCHOOL COUNSELOR

Middle schools are fairly recent educational organizations that have replaced junior high schools in many communities across the country (Schmidt, 2003). The age range of middle school students is usually between 10 and 13 and includes Grades 6 through 8. This particular age-group is caught in the difficult developmental stage between childhood and adolescence. In addition to experiencing the normal problems that occur in family, school, and community, middle school children also have to adjust to changes in their bodies, pressure from peers, pressure in school, and other problems in establishing self-identity (Gladding, 2004).

The primary function of the middle school comprehensive counseling program is counseling. In fact, middle school counselors are increasingly viewed as the school-based mental health professionals and are often called upon to work collaboratively with community-based mental health care providers to develop treatment plans and provide therapeutic interventions for students with mental disorders (Baker, 2000, p. 50). Thus, middle school counselors need to be familiar with common childhood behavioral disorders and *DSM-IV-TR* diagnostic classifications.

Middle school counselors perform the same functions as other school counselors in a comprehensive school counseling program. They work with students individually and in groups, consult with teachers and administrators, collaborate with community agencies, and consult with parents to address the specific needs of their children. Middle school counselors must also intervene in crisis situations, including parental divorce, death of a student, death of a student's family member(s), family violence, child abuse, homelessness, peer conflicts, substance abuse, academic failure, teen pregnancy, incarceration, and medical problems.

THE HIGH SCHOOL COUNSELOR

Since the 1980s, as increasing numbers of professionally qualified school counselors have entered the field, they have been in a better position to clarify their role in their school districts. More than either elementary or middle school counselors, however, high school counselors "have performed [and often still do so] clerical and quasi-administrative duties such as entering scheduling data in computers, checking the number of credits students have accumulated, posting test scores into cumulative folders, organizing the senior prom, and so on" (Coy & Sears, 2000, p. 56). Often, the role of the high school counselor is still defined by school administrators, rather than in a comprehensive school counseling program or by the ASCA (refer to the ASCA national standards in chap. 16).

Helping other school personnel understand the role of and the services provided by the school counselor is an important aspect of the job. Many high school counselors find themselves supervised by individuals who have more responsibilities than they can handle, little knowledge of the role of the school counselor, and little time to manage a school counseling program (Coy & Sears, 2000). Effective counselors take charge of their own programs to ensure program progress. If there is more than one counselor in a school, counselors can rotate the lead role in the management process.

Also important for counselors is to become involved in drawing up or amending their districts' comprehensive school counseling program, for which the first step would be to define the counselor role (Sink & MacDonald, 1998). The comprehensive program includes not only individual and group counseling but also other important counselor functions, including such outreach activities as group guidance and psychoeducation, career information, development and planning, consultation, and coordination. In the face of multiple responsibilities, counselors need to ensure that an adequate proportion of time is allotted to individual and group counseling (see also chap. 16).

COUNSELING STUDENTS IN MIDDLE AND SECONDARY SCHOOLS

The trend toward creating comprehensive school counseling programs (see chap. 16) began in the 1970s and has continued into the new millennium (Baker, 2000). Although some secondary school counselors may spend a significant amount of time doing quasi-administrative duties, they are still expected to provide the important services of any comprehensive school counseling program: individual counseling, group guidance and counseling, coordination, and consultation.

A minimum of 1 counselor to 300 high school students is recommended by the ASCA. This ratio is optimal when the following other resources exist: (a) psychological specialists and community resources; (b) a registrar who deals with registration, scheduling, and student activities; and (c) career guidance specialists and substance abuse counselors who supplement the counseling staff. A few school districts in Washington State, for example, have hired registrars to oversee and manage student personnel work to free counselors for counseling.

Effective counselors encourage students to ask for counseling on their own. They also make their services well known. They visit classrooms, publicize their services in a brochure or school newspaper, and otherwise make themselves visible to faculty, students, and parents. In this way teachers, administrators, parents, and students become valuable referral sources because they understand the nature and availability of counseling services.

Individual Counseling

Secondary school counselors generally follow the individual counseling process described in chapter 9. A trusting relationship is established between client and counselor, in which the student client explores the nature of his or her problem, gains new insights, and takes steps to help resolve the problem. In their struggle for identity and independence, adolescents may respond to adults with ambivalence, fear, suspicion, and rebellion. With this age-group, counselors should expect transference, resistance, and countertransference. When problems are seen in the context of normal developmental growth that adolescents experience during this major transitional stage, counselors can understand where the adolescent client is coming from. Seen in this context, the counselor can then help bridge the gap that usually exists between adolescents and adults.

With many students of this age-group experiencing major social and emotional concerns, secondary school counselors often find themselves dealing with more complex problems. Substance abuse, teen pregnancy, threats of suicide, and physical and sexual abuse are common concerns of too many of today's youth (Coy & Sears, 2000). Because these problems are more complex, more intensive and long-term counseling is often needed, for which referrals to community mental health services are usually made. However, less intensive individual counseling is provided by school counselors as a more remedial and short-term approach to helping students with less severe issues. Three common approaches often practiced by school counselors are Adlerian therapy, brief counseling, and choice theory, or reality therapy (Dollarhide, 2003). Chapters 6, 10, and 16 contain further information on Adlerian therapy and brief counseling.

Choice theory was begun by William Glasser in the 1960s as "reality therapy," which is now considered the "process" of choice theory. It focuses on two general concepts: the environment necessary for conducting counseling and the procedures that lead to change. Described as an internal control psychology, choice theory is the complete opposite of behavioral theory, an external control psychology (Glasser, 1998). The basic tenets of choice theory are that almost all behavior is chosen and that we are driven to satisfy five basic needs: survival, love and belonging, power, freedom, and fun. The most important need is love and belonging; closeness to and connectedness with the people we care about is required to satisfy all other needs. Glasser believes disconnectedness, that is, the lack of love and belonging, is the source of almost all human problems, including mental illness, drug addiction, violence, crime, school failure, and spouse and child abuse.

The role of the counselor using choice theory is primarily one of teacher and model, accepting the client in a warm, involved way and creating an environment in which counseling can take place (Gladding, 2004). The counselor immediately seeks to build a relationship with the client and focuses on behaviors the client would like to change, as well as ways to go about making these changes occur, without the use of any behavioral techniques such as reinforcement. The process of choice theory encourages the client to self-evaluate her or his own behavior by asking questions such as "What are you doing now?" "Is it working?" and "What are the consequences?" The counselor does not focus on early childhood experiences, insight, blame, or excuses for behavior, but rather emphasizes aspects of the client's life that she or he can control. Because of its emphasis on what the client can choose and can control, choice theory is well-suited for working with students in the secondary school environment.

Group Counseling

Although secondary school counselors generally do less group counseling than elementary school counselors do, group counseling should be encouraged in secondary schools. Adolescents' strong urges to affiliate with and be accepted by peers and to develop intimate relations strongly suggest they would respond well to group counseling. Although adolescent group counseling can be similar to adult group counseling, there are some significant differences. Counselors generally are more active with adolescents, particularly in the group's initial stages. Adolescents want to understand the structure of the group and its process, as well as the value of the experience. They prefer an informal setting where they can sit on the floor. Adolescents in a group tend to watch and question the counselor's behavior or techniques and also tend to model the counselor (Ohlsen, Horne, & Lawe, 1988).

Role playing is a particularly effective technique in adolescent groups. Group members can role-play with the counselor to help work through feelings of transference or to rehearse an interaction with an adult. They can also role-play with one another or use the empty chair technique and play two people. In these cases students select the characters and the scenario. Ohlsen et al. (1988) encourage soliloquies and side remarks, techniques used in psychodrama, when students play characters who speak and behave one way but feel (and make asides) another way (see chap. 11).

Providing educational and career information in a group guidance format is another important function of secondary school counselors (Coy & Sears, 2000). The most common group guidance topics for middle and high school students are life skills, interpersonal skills, conflict resolution skills, and career development.

Addressing Cultural Diversity

It is essential that counselors in schools attend to the developmental, transitional concerns of a rapidly increasing number of ethnic students. In 1998 the U.S. Bureau of the Census predicted that by the year 2050 the U.S. population will be 24.5% Hispanic, an increase of 13.1%; 52.8% non-Hispanic White, a decrease of 19.0%; 13.6% non-Hispanic Black, an increase of 1.4%; 0.9% non-Hispanic American Indian, Eskimo, or Aleut, an increase of

0.2%; and 8.2% non-Hispanic Asian or Pacific Islander, an increase of 4.3%. In addition, new immigrants continue to find homes in the United States. Leading African American counselor and educator Courtland Lee (1995) comments: "Among the contemporary issues facing school counselors and related helping professionals, addressing the developmental needs of the growing number of students from culturally diverse backgrounds, is perhaps the most challenging" (p. 3).

Increasing numbers of counselors consider it imperative that school counselors incorporate a multicultural perspective into the developmental approach underlying the current counseling process (Baruth & Manning, 1999; Faubert, Locke, & McLeod, 2000). Even as they validate differing groups' uniqueness and appreciation of self, counselors need curricula that will enhance appreciation of diversity. Counselors have a unique opportunity and responsibility to prepare students to value difference, which will be an important component of a well-functioning society in the 21st century.

> Adolescents often develop individual and cultural identities under difficult circumstances involving racism, discrimination, and injustice. The "culture of poverty" image may influence Native Americans' identities; similarly, African Americans, hearing repeatedly that their culture is "inferior," may develop negative identities. (Baruth & Manning, 1999, p. 90)

Lee (1995) describes how school counselors can integrate psychosocial development and multicultural diversity to benefit adolescents and children. "Children and adolescents must master psychosocial developmental tasks through their socialization within a cultural context" (p. 8). When working with the adolescent development of ethnic students, counselors must learn to understand these students' particular cultural backgrounds—family and community characteristics, gender role definitions, and religious or spiritual beliefs.

The program Getting on the Right Track was developed in a North Carolina school system for African American ninth-grade students who were having difficulty reaching their academic potential (Locke, 1995). Counselors, teachers, and parents worked together to improve the students' motivation to learn through activities that strengthened their African American identity, as well as their academic skills. During a 3-year period students met biweekly. During the first year "they were instructed in African American history and culture; basic communication techniques (e.g., the importance of eye contact and assertiveness); study techniques; and strategies for successful interracial interactions" (Locke, 1995, p. 34). In their sophomore year students served as peer mentors to freshmen beginning the program. Junior year activities consisted of writing their family histories, volunteering in the community, and exploring the programs of at least five colleges or universities.

Another example occurred in a high school in New Orleans, where the counseling staff presented a unique psychoeducational program that developed cultural awareness of the three major ethnic groups represented in their high school (Carter & Vuong, 1997). Entitled Unity Through Diversity, the program was designed after a student survey showed that most students felt a need to understand the various cultures represented in the student population. Students from the three major ethnic groups planned and presented three different assemblies at intervals throughout a semester. In addition, social studies teachers were given cultural material to use in classroom units, relating both to the cultural group being highlighted and to an appreciation of multicultural diversity. Evaluation by the students afterward was highly favorable (Carter & Vuong, 1997).

PRESENTING PROBLEMS OF MIDDLE AND SECONDARY STUDENTS

Adolescents who come in for counseling have value conflicts and confusion regarding who they are, what they want to be, and how they want to relate to others in an increasingly complex and rapidly changing society. Changes in family patterns and values contribute to their uncertainties. Peer pressure to drink or take drugs is increasing. In a world where job security is lacking, adolescents see adults constantly anxious about losing their jobs, making ends meet, meeting the rising costs of education, and obtaining adequate and affordable health care for their families. Many adolescents come from single-parent families or suffer from domestic violence. Many are homeless; some have no parents. Ethnic adolescents have further complications because of stereotyping, prejudicial treatment, and a lack of understanding from other cultural groups.

Much of the counseling literature and the media emphasize the most extreme problems facing adolescents—alcohol and drug abuse, teenage pregnancy, depression, suicide, and violence. These important issues are discussed later in the chapter. But first, our emphasis is on the normal, troublesome areas of adolescent development that characterize this major transitional stage, areas that relate to career/educational, personal, and interpersonal issues.

Career/Educational Issues

Secondary students put top priority on vocational or career exploration and choice. They are approaching the time when they must become financially independent and, in so doing, must find a suitable and satisfying job or decide on and prepare for a challenging career or life work. After high school approximately two-thirds of graduating students will enter the labor market. The other one-third will go either to college or to vocational school. While in high school, these students must decide on the institutions to which they will apply and the kind of training they wish to begin.

Decisions about occupational choice or education beyond high school are more complicated than they were a few decades ago. Male students then were expected to be preoccupied with their careers because they were perceived as the primary breadwinners. Relatively few women pursued careers. The women's movement has helped change this pattern. Many women now prepare themselves for suitable jobs, whether they plan to marry or not. More complex choices about occupational and family roles must now be made by both men and women.

More career avenues have also opened for ethnic groups. These increased options can lead to more productive and satisfying lives, but they can also lead to conflicts as new patterns replace old stereotypes. Opportunity may involve upheaval in personal relationships if individuals select options that displease people close to them. Life can become more fulfilling but also filled with more anxiety.

Career counseling is a complex process that is interwoven with total personality development and is a part of total lifestyle. Students generally present their questions about vocational/career or educational plans in one of three ways: (a) They may ask for vocational/career information, (b) they may present a conflict they have with others over a vocational choice, or (c) they may want to resolve some self-conflict or confusion regarding two or more occupational plans.

Career Exploration

Client 1: Gail, a sophomore, pops her head in the counselor's office and asks for an appointment. She is trying to work out her junior year program. Her grades are very good, and she likes all subjects. She says she wants to go to college but is not sure what career to consider. She would like to explore interests and aptitudes to get some ideas about vocational direction.

Response C–1: Gail appears likely to be highly responsive to tests; she may even ask for them. Her question relates to a general career exploration, so a Kuder Occupational Interest Survey and a Differential Aptitude Test would be appropriate. If the personal and test data bring up exploratory career patterns, Gail could be given something to read about these occupations. If not, she could be encouraged to look into a variety of courses and return for more career consideration at a later date.

Client 2: Aaron is perplexed. He is a freshman trying to decide whether to take a college preparatory curriculum or look for apprenticeships and attend a technical school. He enjoys drafting and machine shop. He has discussed the question with his industrial arts teacher, who has given him some occupational information and recommended that Aaron talk with a counselor.

Response C–2: The counselor should probably not bring up tests and occupational material with Aaron right away. It would be preferable to have him express some of his ambivalence about life planning and lifestyle. Discussion about tests and the use of occupational information resources can be introduced later.

Attempts would be made in these interviews to help the students consider and explore their perceptions about themselves and the world of work, their values about work, and the lifestyles they imagine for themselves. The counselor might also explore with the students their parents' views about their future. The degree to which parents support student's plans and the degree of their financial support often determine the direction students will take. The counselor can then suggest that the students take standardized interest inventories and aptitude tests if further exploration is necessary. However, the counselor should refrain from introducing tests too quickly, to allow students to explore their own feelings, attitudes, and values regarding career aspirations and not to depend on tests to provide all the answers.

Conflict With Others About Career Plans

Client 3: Bob is interested in acting and has demonstrated talent in several plays. He is thinking of directing and writing, as well as acting. He is verbal, expressive, and articulate. His father is a successful pipeline contractor who wants Bob, his only child, to come into the business. He scoffs at drama as an effeminate occupation. Bob's mother is quiet and unassuming but subtly supports Bob. His father refuses to support him in college if he persists in drama. Bob thinks he is letting his father down. At the same time he wonders whether drama is a realistic choice economically.

Client 4: Sholanda, a senior, is referred by her social studies teacher. She is an excellent student who has a scholarship to an out-of-state college. She is thinking of law.

Her boyfriend is registering at the local community college. He is distressed because she has decided to leave the state. He says she apparently does not care enough for him to change her plans. Sholanda feels guilty and wonders whether her educational plans are selfish.

Response C–3/4: These students' questions about career concerns are complicated by their interactions with or the expectations of significant people in their lives. They see the counselor because they are uncertain about how to cope with the differences between their own expectations and the expectations of others. These conflicts have contributed to their confusion or doubts about vocational planning. The counselor should probably not begin vocational testing or appraisal with either Bob or Sholanda until any dependency/independency conflicts and ambivalences in their relationships with significant others have been explored.

Through increased knowledge of self, occupations, and relationships with others, Bob and Sholanda may become convinced that their career planning is correct and may successfully change the minds of the dissenting persons. It is also possible in either of these cases that both the student and the other party involved may modify their positions and reach a reasonable compromise. If Bob and his father are willing to meet with the counselor to discuss their differences, the chances of a compromise are enhanced. For example, Bob might continue with drama but work during the summers for his father to learn a practical trade and explore further his interest in some phase of the business. Sholanda's opportunities for compromise are fewer. The compromise might consist of an agreement that she and her boyfriend will visit on holidays to determine whether they will continue their relationship. Or perhaps her boyfriend could decide to attend a school closer to hers because he would not lose a scholarship by changing schools.

Another possible outcome is that the clients may become convinced that their choices are correct, but the others involved may be so adamantly opposed that a breach in their relationships occurs. For Bob this could mean disruption in the family relationship and withdrawal of economic support. For Sholanda the decision to persist in her plans despite objections could mean the end of a love relationship. If an impasse developed between Bob and his father, the counselor could discuss with Bob the possibility of arranging counseling sessions with him and his parents, using a family systems approach. Or they could be referred to a family counselor at a community agency.

Personal Conflict About Career

Students often come to a counselor about vocational planning when they have strong interests and abilities in two or three areas and are in conflict about which path to follow. Strong interests and abilities in two or three areas can become confusing, especially if it appears that one choice excludes the others. In other situations personal values and goals may seem at odds.

Client 5: Stefan is referred by a local minister who knows the counselor. Stefan, a senior, is expressing value conflicts related to occupations. He is a warm, outgoing person who enjoys working in social services. He is considering the ministry or YMCA work. He believes, however, that he wants to make good money in a job. His lifestyle includes material rewards that he thinks social service will not give him. Yet business does not appeal to him. His mother is in banking, and his father is a social worker. They encourage him to make his own decisions.

Response C–5: This conflict stems from the student's ambivalence or contradictory motivations or values. The counselor should first explore with Stefan the alternatives he presents, the various values and motivations each choice represents, and the reasons that he is having difficulty in deciding. Counselor and client should explore the extent to which external pressures are influencing the situation and consider whether these alternatives are truly mutually exclusive. Directly expressing conflict in values is an important step for Stefan and should be followed up. His perception of his mother's and father's values may be contributing to his confusion. As counseling progresses, the counselor might give him a vocational interest inventory and a personality inventory to help him determine the direction he wants to go.

Personal Problems

At times students present problems related to their attitudes and behavior, which are causing inner conflicts, tension, indecision, or confusion. The central feature of this type of presenting problem is that students are expressing ambivalence, uncertainty, or guilt about their attitudes, feelings, or behavior.

Conflict

Client 6: Jane is an intense person who talks rapidly. She has an impressive 3.9 grade point average. She transferred here as a junior at the beginning of this year and got straight *A*s her first semester. She wants to see a counselor about applying for scholarships. In the course of the dialogue, she says that she has continual headaches and has seen her physician, who calls them tension headaches. She feels upset with herself; she says she spends all her time on her schoolwork.

Response C–6: The counselor can readily help Jane with scholarship applications. But Jane revealed other problems. How is she fitting in as a new student? The counselor might simply conclude that she needs to get more involved in social activities and take relaxation exercises to reduce tension. But the counselor should also explore what else might be underlying her tension headaches. How does she feel about her high achievement record? Do gender issues have any bearing on this case? According to feminist researchers, high-achieving female students tend to have lower self-esteem than high-achieving male students. What are her career aspirations? To which universities is she applying? How do her parents feel about her plans? Has she made friends at school who have similar aspirations? Perhaps it would be helpful to arrange for her to have group counseling with other females with similar interests and abilities.

Doubts or Confusion

Client 7: Ernie speaks his mind freely. He is the first one to volunteer answers in class and to offer opinions at meetings. He wonders whether he sounds off too much. He thinks his enthusiasm sometimes ruffles others. He asks whether he should assert himself less.

Response C–7: Ernie needs to explore both the nature of his uncomfortable feelings when he is expressing himself in groups and the reasons that these feelings arise. If discussion indicates that he is misperceiving the reactions of others because of his own uncomfortable feelings about assertion, cognitive restructuring may be helpful to correct his misperceptions, or client-centered techniques might help him get in touch with his lack of self-assurance. However, if discussion indicates that he is dominating other group members, the counselor should help him explore reasons that he needs to call attention to himself. Assertiveness training could help him distinguish between aggressiveness and appropriate assertion of ideas, and role-playing communication skills might improve his group interactions. Group counseling might also help him practice social skills.

Client 8: Frank is restless. He wonders what life is all about. Who am I? What's the purpose of it all? he asks himself. School and life seem meaningless; courses do not make sense. He sees himself as alienated. He says he has no religious convictions, but he is curious about religion.

Response C–8: Frank's presenting problem is generally termed *existential* because he is concerned with broad questions about life or existence. If he is articulate, the interviews may involve a good deal of careful listening and reflecting by the counselor in client-centered fashion. If Frank has difficulty expressing himself, however, the counselor should not hesitate to ask questions or make observations to help him confront the source of his concerns. Religious or spiritual questions about the meaning of life begin to surface as adolescents question their parents' beliefs or lack of beliefs and ponder how the world is being governed. The counselor's task is to help clients with spiritual or religious concerns explore their doubts, questions, or aspirations without influencing or inhibiting these explorations with the counselor's own religious or spiritual convictions.

Social Problems

In cases of interpersonal conflicts and feelings of social inadequacy, clients are troubled by the differences between their needs or expectations and the needs or expectations of other persons in their lives. They may also indicate that they feel socially inept and ask for help in developing skills to interact with others.

Interpersonal Conflicts

While searching for identity and working through dependency/independency relationships, adolescents can be expected to run into conflict with the usual authority figures—teachers, parents, and administrators. They also feel social pressure from the groups, cliques, or gangs that form in high schools. Peer groups have varying expectations of conformity, and engaging in certain behaviors gains approval from these groups. The adolescent who decides to behave in a manner different from that of the peer group or gang often feels conflicted or anxious. Gaining independence helps adolescents develop inner strength, but it also increases the likelihood of friction, disapproval, and rejection.

When clients say they are having conflicts with others, counselors should avoid becoming their advocates in the disagreements. Counselors are not arbiters or referees. Nor are they defenders of teachers, parents, or the establishment. Rather, they help students express and clarify the conflict and explore both their own expectations, values, and feelings and the attitudes or values of those with whom they are in conflict. Alternative actions and the consequences of these actions can then be evaluated. Counselors can quickly lose effectiveness or become involved in conflict if they assume the stance of advocate.

Client 9: Juan stomps into the counselor's office between classes and asks for an appointment after school; he is angry at his social studies teacher. He complains that the teacher picks on him, criticizes him, and is sarcastic. He claims that the teacher belittled him in front of the class by calling him a clown.

Response C–9: It would be easy to agree with Juan if the teacher was known to be sarcastic, but if the teacher was a friend and was well liked by other students, the counselor might be tempted to defend the teacher. Rather than take sides, however, the counselor should permit students like Juan to express their anger and frustration and then assess the situation with them.

One way to start is by carefully discussing the specific behavior that Juan is complaining about, as well as assessing how he behaves in class. He might then feel able to cope in class, or he might decide that a talk with the teacher might help. If the teacher and Juan prefer a joint consultation with the counselor, the counselor should emphasize that her or his role is to keep Joel and the teacher's dialogue open and not to act as a referee. Teachers and students are often surprised at the success of a direct discussion. However, if the relationship between the teacher and Juan is beyond a reasonable discussion or if the teacher has had difficulty with other students and has not been amenable to change over the years, Juan may be able to drop the course. If that is not possible, then he can be helped to cope with the teacher so as not to provoke or reinforce the attacks. Rational emotive techniques to assist him in handling an unpleasant reality might prove constructive.

Client 10: Jason is a school leader and a good student who is popular with both sexes. He is concerned because he and his girlfriend constantly clash. She is highly independent; she refuses to let him pay her way on dates and becomes annoyed if he opens doors for her. He admires her independence yet feels irritated when she asserts herself. Jason's friends are highly sociable, enjoy traditional male-female relationships, and see his girlfriend as an odd feminist.

Response C–10: Jason is confronted with changing expectations in male and female gender roles. Here's a chance for him to examine his ambivalence about his girlfriend's independence when he puts such a high premium on his own. He appears attracted to, and yet bewildered by, her attitudes. Another factor contributing to his confusion is the difference between her behavior and the behavior of other girls in his social group. Exploring his attitudes about his girlfriend is important to his future attitudes toward and relationships with women and with social groups in general.

Feelings of Social Inadequacy

At times students express feelings of inadequacy about social awareness, social ease, or social skills. Teachers also may find that a student's behavior is immature or uncertain.

Client 11: Rosa expresses concern about her inability to make friends, attract dates, or feel part of her own peer group. People do not dislike her, she says. It is worse: They are indifferent. She describes herself as shy and wants to learn to be more outgoing.

Response C–11: Many students express a desire to change specific behaviors or attitudes. Because of this specificity, some counselors immediately suggest that clients take assertiveness training classes or some other kind of training in communication skills. It might be preferable to determine first whether the problem lies in a lack of social skills or a low self-image. If a lack of skills is paramount, the counselor can proceed with assertiveness training, role playing, or some other appropriate technique. Students can practice relatively safe interactions with others between counseling sessions. At this stage it is important for clients to realize that when they begin to assert themselves or to act differently, they may get negative reactions from others.

If Rosa's concerns are more complicated than she originally presented, the counselor should first explore personal and social issues. If her problem stems mostly from inexperience, the counselor should help her develop social skills early in the sessions. Group counseling might also be useful for Rosa to practice interacting with others in the group who are experiencing similar concerns.

Students at Risk

Antisocial Acts

Client 12: Elena is a quiet, somewhat withdrawn student who keeps to herself much of the time. She has difficulty talking about why she made the counseling appointment. Finally, she blurts out that she has shoplifted articles in downtown stores on two occasions and has given them to friends as gifts.

Client 13: Greg has been in a few times to discuss poor study habits. He shares that he received an *A* in a history course, but the counselor notices that he is uncomfortable. When the counselor mentions this, Greg stammers that he got the *A* by cheating on the final. He admits that this was not the only time he has cheated.

Response C–12/13: The counselor need not involve parents, other authorities, or professionals in either of these situations. The behavior is not chronic, and the students are serious about seeking help. they should be commended for recognizing the need for help and given full opportunity to express their anxieties. The counselor should make it clear that he or she cannot protect them from legal or disciplinary action if their behavior continues and is discovered while they are in counseling. The counselor might also explain that if parents or the authorities do discover the behavior, they will most likely be pleased that the students have already voluntarily sought help.

The counselor should try to help the students explore the factors contributing to the antisocial behavior but should make no attempt to condone or excuse stealing or cheating on the basis of emotional factors. Rather, counselor and client should explore the reasons for Elena's efforts to buy friendship and Greg's feelings about grades. Often in these situations counseling brings out evidence of poor family interactions that are contributing to the problem behavior. Students who admit to cheating sometimes want to let the specific teacher(s) know about the cheating. The counselor should help students take such a step. However, it should be perceived as part of the counseling process, rather than as a confession intended to relieve guilt and eliminate the need for further counseling.

Alcohol and Drugs

The Bellingham School District in Washington State developed a program of drug and alcohol awareness, prevention, and intervention. The district hired three substance abuse counselors to serve several schools in the district. The program was introduced into the schools by counselors, who held 2- or 3-day awareness workshops for administrators, counselors, teachers, and office staff. They discussed the severity of the overall problem, outlined ways of identifying specific problems, and worked on intervention strategies and ways of making constructive referrals to the substance abuse counselors. In this program a teacher who suspects an alcohol problem refers the student to the drug/alcohol counselor. If an assessment by the substance abuse counselor indicates that the student needs treatment, then the student may work with the substance abuse counselor. If inpatient treatment is required, the student is referred to an alcohol or drug treatment center. While students are in treatment, tutoring is available to them. After they return to school, they are offered a support class taught by the substance abuse counselor to help them resist peer or environmental pressures that might lead to further drinking or drug abuse.

Suicide

Every year 5,000 to 6,000 adolescents take their lives, and another 500,000 make abortive suicide attempts (Popenhagen & Qualley, 1998). In other terms one out of three adolescents has considered suicide, and one out of six has attempted it (Steinberg, 1993). Counselors can provide school-based programs that train parents, school staff, and students on how to detect early signs of suicidal behavior—for example, talk about committing suicide, talk about specific plans for suicide, or depression that prevents normal functioning. In these cases a counselor should be consulted. As described earlier, counselors can intervene, make further determinations about the severity of the problem, and/or refer students for more intensive help (see also chap. 8).

Another example from the Bellingham School District demonstrates how school and community counselors and other mental health specialists can work together effectively in a suicide prevention and intervention program. That program has three modes. The first mode, led by mental health counselors from the community, involves half-day work-shops for all school staff to discuss recognition of suicidal symptoms and effective ways of intervening. The second mode, led by school counselors and included in the classroom curriculum, teaches students how to be aware of signs of suicidal behavior and how to bring disturbed students to the attention of adults. The third mode, led by community mental health specialists, trains suicide response teams composed of school counselors. Each team is prepared to help a school population handle the trauma of a suicide in the school. This group is also available for other types of crises that affect total school popu-lations, such as an accident in which several students are killed, the murder of a student, or the sudden death of a teacher.

Violence

Youth gangs are increasing in number and size throughout the United States (Omizo, Omizo, & Honda, 1997). Gang members often abuse their powers—assaults, use of guns and other weapons, destruction of property, use of drugs, and drug trafficking. The long-range effects of gang membership have shown a decrease in the ability to develop skills necessary to reach adulthood or gain marketable job skills.

> The increase in the size and violence of youth gangs makes it imperative that teachers, coun-selors, administrators, and social service professionals recognize the variables which contribute to an adolescent's decision to join a gang. Effective preventative interventions that address these factors must be developed to deter youth from turning to gangs. These interventions should look at ways of channeling and redirecting the positive aspects of gangs into more con-structive, socially acceptable outlets. (Omizo et al., 1997, p. 39)

To explore the phenomenon of youth gang membership, Omizo et al. (1997) con-ducted a study of eight male high school gang members in Oahu, Hawaii, a region where police have identified 45 gangs with more than 1,000 members. In a series of interviews, they found that the boys joined gangs because they felt a sense of belonging, an increase in self-esteem, protection from other gangs, and an outlet for social and recreational activ-ities.

When counselors are aware of adolescent needs to affiliate with others, they can help channel teenagers into more constructive group activities. In addition to providing indi-vidual and group counseling to gang members, counselors can offer parenting skills activ-ities to parents. Joint school and community services can also be offered to educate the general public about the characteristics of youth gangs and ways they can help gang members rechannel their energy.

Several mass killings have occurred in secondary schools, in which a student has shot teachers and fellow students without warning. In these tragic cases counselors can serve in two ways. First, with the aid of community specialists, they can work with traumatized students, families, and school staff to deal with their shock, anguish, and fears. This is called *debriefing.* Second, counselors can become trained by specialists in violence pre-vention to detect the symptoms of individuals with the potential for violence so that they can intervene before disaster occurs. In turn, counselors can work with other school staff and with families to alert them to the danger signals in adolescents prone to violence.

Social Change

Students in secondary schools are for more able to change inappropriate or unfair school policies and procedures than are children in elementary schools. Counselors can help secondary students consider options and consequences and inform them of procedures for making complaints in accordance with school policy.

One example of an affective change process occurred in a high school in Whatcom County, Washington. A client told her counselor she was unhappy that her high school had no women's swim team. The student complained that this deprived her and others of engaging in swim competition, and she wanted to do something about it. She and her counselor decided that her first step should be to talk with the principal, who responded positively and suggested she talk with the superintendent. The superintendent recommended that the issue be brought before the board of education. After the student presented her rationale to the board, the board decided to hire a women's swim coach in midseason.

The same student had more difficulty when she tried to persuade the athletic director to include women's sports on a wallet-sized schedule of men's sports. The director gave evasive responses and numerous rationalizations as to why the change could not be made. However, with the counselor's encouragement, the student persisted, continuing to make appointments and telephone calls. After a year of continuous pressure, the change was made, in line with affirmative action regulations.

OUTREACH ACTIVITIES

Psychoeducation

As with elementary school counselors, secondary school counselors also provide group guidance to students (see chap. 16). As one form of group guidance, *psychoeducational groups* have a predetermined goal, include a significant educational component, and focus on developing knowledge and coping skills. Group leaders typically plan the topics and structured exercises for each session in advance, as they would develop a curriculum. Many sources of group exercises on a wide range of topics are available to counselors; the primary job for counselors is identifying and appropriately sequencing those topics. Because psychoeducational groups are typically short-term, can be used with a variety of populations in a variety of settings, and have a significant educational component, they are ideal for working with adolescents in schools.

Jones and Robinson (2001) developed a model to help counselors plan and design psychoeducational groups. The first step is to brainstorm as many group session topics as possible and find appropriate related group exercises. Next, the counselor needs to assess each topic/exercise in terms of intensity—for example, does the topic or activity evoke anxiety among group participants, challenge group participants to self-disclose, increase awareness, focus on feelings, concentrate on the here and now, and/or focus on threatening issues? Then the leader must plan the sequence or order of the sessions: Psychoeducational groups are planned with less intense topics/exercises in the beginning stage of the group, more intense sessions in the middle or working stage of the group, and less intense again during the ending stage of the group. This model can help counselors develop psychoeducational groups on any topic.

Crisis Intervention

As teenage drug addictions, suicides, gang wars, possession of guns, and sexual assaults have become common occurrences, high school counselors have become increasingly involved in crisis cases. Figure 17.1, on page 441, shows a log of a high school counselor's typical workday; crisis cases dominate the counselor's time. Crises can occur whenever sudden, radical changes disrupt an individual's life or environment. The individual can become seriously disoriented, depressed, or agitated. Crises require prompt and direct intervention to avoid the possibility of serious consequences or further deterioration (see chap. 8). Groups of students, as well as individuals, can have crises that require intervention from school officials. Hundreds of gangs exist in the United States, and "more than 135,000 students in this country carry handguns to school every day" (Murray, 1993, p. E1).

In schools the counseling center is usually the first call when emergencies arise. Counselors are generally expected to take steps to calm a person down and to take immediate action when necessary. Counselors then determine whether to work with the student or make a referral to a community agency (see chap. 8). With cases involving several students, such as gang-related crises, counselors might arrange conferences with all those involved and perhaps their families and establish follow-up psychological education programs.

In crisis situations counselors should remain calm while they talk with students to determine whether any disorientation has been caused by psychotic or drug reactions or whether sudden, acute depression or confusion has been caused by upsetting circumstances, such as a sudden death in the family or the breakup of a relationship. If a student is so disoriented, depressed, or agitated as to be suicidal or dangerous to others, administrators and parents need to be informed. If a student is in a state of shock, the counselor first needs to help the student recover from the initial shock. The counselor usually sets up counseling sessions to help the student express grief, anger, or frustration and confront the reality of the event. Psychiatric and psychological consultation should be readily available, from either a consultant hired by the school district or a consultant from a community mental health clinic. If necessary, the counselor should refer the case to a community agency.

Consultation

Counselors serve effectively as consultants with teachers and administrators. They are particularly needed in this capacity in secondary schools because teachers who teach five or six classes to different sets of students have little opportunity to work through conflicts with students or to observe those needing help. Likewise, administrators' interactions with students, especially in large high schools, are usually limited to those who are always in trouble or are outstanding scholars, athletes, or leaders.

Teacher 1: Ms. Adams approaches a counselor in the teachers' lounge and asks whether he has time to talk with her. The counselor suggests taking their coffee to his

1. Sexually abused student living away from home wants to quit school. I have talked with two of his teachers repeatedly.

2. Girl who was in a fight yesterday arrived throwing up, with bruises, scratches on face, hurt nose, swollen foot—arrangements were made for the sick room and a ride to the doctor. We called her mother. The girl's father and many relatives are Vietnam Vets. Many people close to her have died this year.

3. Student with an unusually severe sexual assault case came to make arrangements for a leave to appear in court, and also to contact her Rape Relief advocate. This girl's mother is a drug addict with AIDS. She does not live at home.

4. Student who had recently had an abortion came in with very unusual symptoms. I had her call her doctor immediately.

5. A multiple abused person who had been hospitalized for mental illness came in (after her Mom called me about her low grades and defiance). We addressed the past abuse enough to figure out how her behavior was changing and have her agree to return to her psychiatrist and later we discussed her high ability and how her grades and career plans might all fit together.

6. Got a call from special ed. about a family in emergency housing with two special ed. kids here. I have talked repeatedly for 2 years with teachers, administrators, CPS workers, police, counselors, housing admin. and drug and alcohol counselors. This move was cleared with the superintendent.

7. Talked with (a colleague) about legal issues of the assault. Gave a note to a teacher of the assaulted student about missing a test. Talked with Mom again about our plan here to resolve the dispute.

8. Discussed with (a colleague) the 9 kids who are still seriously depressed over their friend's death.

9. Laid out pamphlets for display on STD's [Sexually Transmitted Diseases] in outer office.

10. Proofread a scholarship recommendation.

11. Talked to a student about a class transfer. Sent the student to talk with his teacher.

12. The assaulted student reappeared from the doctor with a fractured bone in her foot, and perhaps in her nose. On her (and her mother's) request, we sent for her adversary and attempted to make a temporary truce. However, both girls were clearly not ready to do much more, so I sent the 1st girl home to rest (doctor's orders) and talked with the second about the incident. It appears alcohol is possibly an issue here, too. Will approach that tomorrow. We decided to resume sometime next week after some time away from each other. We established ground rules for this week to quell rumors and avoid conflict.

13. A mother came in about (her son). This student is in the middle of a bitter custody battle.

14. A new student arrived and needed to be enrolled in classes and oriented.

15. I resumed trying to find the teacher for the previous case and succeeded. Then I couldn't find the principal.

16. I checked with a student who is trying to switch her classes because of her baby, which she just put up for adoption today. This girl has been repeatedly abused and has been in the foster care system for years.

17. I talked to one of my pregnant girls—just checking in.

18. A father called after talking to his daughter's teacher at my request. We decided to drop one of her classes. I need only talk to the (missing) principal. This girl has had multiple sex abuse experiences and much loss. She does not live with her parents.

19. I talked to a student just returning from (X) for multiple suicide attempts about how he's doing, and we formed plans as to how to work with his teachers. A teacher came in later to report he missed class today.

20. I talked to a student who took 23 pills (antidepressant) and some other drugs who is in our recovery class, and recently went through treatment and extensive CPS work. This girl is protected from her mother by a court order. Her Dad is a Vietnam Vet with symptoms of PTSD [posttraumatic stress disorder].

21. I brought in and changed the student's schedule whose father called me earlier. Talked with teacher about student's attendance problem.

22. We ordered 5 personal allotment books on Learning Styles, Grief Counseling in Schools, and counseling Victims of Violence.

23. Talked to a teacher about the girl who had the abortion—5 student request slips left on spindle, 20 students to see for second semester scheduling.

FIGURE 17.1

A log of a high school counselor's typical workday.

Note: To protect the people involved, the names of persons and the name and location of the school district have been withheld or altered. This high school is located in a relatively stable, self-contained, small, established town. The community is surrounded by farmland with some heavy industry nearby and is made up of middle-class Whites and two ethnic minorities.

office, where they can talk without being overheard. There she tells the counselor that she is concerned about a student who is not handing in his assigned papers but who scores high on standardized intelligence and achievement tests. He is polite, presents no discipline problems, and promises to hand in his papers. Ms. Adams, a young, energetic, first-year teacher, feels frustrated and annoyed.

Response T–1: Ms. Adams is trying to encourage an underachiever, who is probably resisting because of fear of failure. Thus, encouragement to try to measure up to the teacher's expectations, which he is uncertain he can meet, is leading to further withdrawal. In this case the teacher might try setting smaller, achievable, sequential steps in the mode of Beck's stress theory.

Teacher 2: Mr. Baker is a high school teacher just out of college. He looks and dresses like the average student. He perceives himself as their friend and goes out of his way to show personal interest. A sophomore has a crush on him and finds all kinds of excuses to see him. Some harmless, prank telephone calls have been made to his home. He is convinced that she made the calls.

Response T–2: Mr. Baker should be encouraged to explore whether he is subtly contributing to the uncomfortable relationship by his overly friendly manner. A discussion of his interactions with all students might reveal his anxiety about assuming an authoritative role, his awkwardness because of his youthful age, and his need to be liked and approved of by the students. He should be encouraged to drop the buddy role with students and increase social interactions with people his own age.

Administrator 1: Ms. Karpinski, the principal of a high school, asks for consultation because she is considering revamping the curriculum to meet the students' needs more effectively. The town has changed from a suburban residential area to a semi-industrial one during the 10 years since the last curriculum overhaul. She wonders whether the students' vocational aims are being served.

Response A–1: A counseling staff can help the principal improve the curriculum by giving some general feedback about student requests for courses and some ideas about student prospects after graduation. The counseling staff can offer to conduct a survey of students about their curriculum needs and a follow-up study of graduates.

Counselors also serve as consultants and resource persons for schoolwide testing programs mandated by the state or by school districts. In effective school counseling programs, counselors do not administer or record test scores. Rather, they are consultants helping administrators evaluate the type and quality of tests being used and set appropriate and ethical policies on appropriate administration and use of tests. Counselors also are consultants to teachers in interpreting test results and relating scores to data in student cumulative folders.

Collaboration and Coordination

In light of the large number of crisis cases and the serious personal and educational problems of students, coordinating or collaborating with individuals or agencies in the community to provide mental health counseling in the school is an important function of secondary school counselors. High school counselors report that "more and more community-based programs are operating in the schools" (Coy & Sears, 2000, p. 61)—for example, community substance abuse agencies working within the school. The services are much more effective when the school counselor actively collaborates with the outside agency.

Working With Families

Secondary school counselors, like elementary school counselors, are in a favorable position to provide family consultation and brief family counseling services. In high schools this approach can be valuable in assessing and treating adolescent developmental concerns, as well as alcohol and drug abuse, eating disorders, and adolescent depression.

One remarkable example of a family counseling center for high school students and their families is the School/Family Counseling Center (SFCC) in Pulaski County, Virginia. This unique collaborative program was developed by high school counselors at Pulaski County High School and university counselor educators at Radford University (Miano, Forrest, & Gumaer, 1997). After meeting together and designing a proposal, they received a grant to develop a program to reduce the dropout rates of students at risk. At-risk students included academic failures, substance abusers, those suffering from family conflicts and/or sexual abuse, pregnant girls, and those with persistent disruptive behavior.

In their collaboration the high school and university counselors engaged the services of high school students in vocational classes to construct a school/family counseling center next to the high school. The SFCC is supported by the school, families, community, and university; comprehensive counseling services are offered to both students and their families. The center is staffed by two full-time high school counselors, as well as counseling interns from the university who are supervised by university faculty. Counseling is also provided in the evenings once or twice a week by the supervised counseling interns. Initially set up for individual and family counseling, SFCC has now expanded to include group and couple counseling.

Training School Staff

Training school staff to facilitate their personal and professional development is another primary function of today's secondary school counselor. School counselors possess many skills that teachers need—for example, communication skills, conflict resolution skills, and stress management. By conducting regular in-service sessions, counselors can train staff, especially teachers, so that they can master the skills needed to work with students more effectively (Coy & Sears, 2000, p. 61). For instance, counselors can provide training in interpersonal communication skills, such as active listening, genuineness, acceptance, open-ended questions, paraphrases, reflecting feelings, and summarizing.

In-service programs can be tailored to provide teachers with information that will enhance their understanding of their students (Dollarhide, 2003). Topics on resiliency, child abuse, at-risk students, working with ADHD children and families, and ethics are just a few of the many topics that would be valuable for teachers. In-service training for school administrators would also be beneficial, particularly as a way of educating them about comprehensive school counseling programs.

Peer Facilitators

Students are often actively involved in a school counseling program, not as clients, but rather as peer facilitators. Peer facilitators can be trained to provide a variety of services, including peer mediation, peer helping, peer tutoring, peer orientation, and peer facilitation of groups (Dollarhide, 2003). Peer facilitators need to be carefully screened for appropriateness, and special training needs to be provided in the helping process, communication skills, the basics of confidentiality, and facilitation of interaction. In addition, peer facilitators have to be well trained about the limits of their involvement so that they know to contact the school counselor immediately if any problems are beyond their helping ability.

The benefits of peer facilitators are numerous. They can provide feedback about the progress of the student being helped, serve as a role model for other students, and assist with some of the logistics of running the school counseling program. Benefits to the peer facilitator include the development of helping and leadership skills, as well the opportunity to experience what it's like to work in the school or the helping profession.

Career Development

Outreach programs in career exploration and development expanded extensively in secondary schools when the National Occupational Information Coordinating Committee (NOICC, 1989a, 1989b) provided ongoing federal and state funding as well as guidelines to develop programs. Freshmen and sophomores now explore vocational interests and aptitudes and learn to find and use occupational information; juniors decide on certain job or career options and begin to develop specific skills necessary for these jobs; seniors learn to conduct job searches, write job résumés, practice job interviewing skills, and serve as interns in the workplace.

Further support to career education was provided through the School-to-Work Opportunities Act passed by Congress in 1994 (NOICC, 1994). Under that program, which is administered by the National School-to-Work Office under the joint direction of the U.S. Departments of Labor and Education, states are given grants to provide career education to help high school students make the transition from academic training to the world of work. The program features a work-based learning component that involves job training and on-site work experiences. Participating students have two mentors—one from the school staff, the other an employee in the work setting. The school mentor works jointly with counselors, teachers, and employers to direct students' progress; the workplace mentor instructs and guides students on the job. Students also learn how to conduct job searches, develop résumés, practice for job interviews, and the like. Further, counselors and career specialists can arrange for students to observe workers firsthand; students can spend a day shadowing an employee in a particular profession to learn about the characteristics of the job.

Another national career development program, Tech Prep, is designed to help students finish high school with improved skills for job placement. Through the joint efforts of high schools and community/technology colleges, students take course work in high school that earns community college credit.

Paralleling these federal programs, the State of Washington has developed a unique career development program called Running Start, whereby qualified juniors and seniors in high school take tuition-free courses at a community college and earn both high school and college credit. Qualified students are thus able to earn an associate's degree at a community college by the time they graduate from high school.

ASSESSMENT AND EVALUATION

Innumerable tests are available to help students explore their career interests and aptitudes. Because career exploration is such an important developmental task, interest inventories, aptitude tests, and personality measures are important counselor tools. These tests and inventories are described in chapter 7, along with cautions about their limitations.

Briefly, the Kuder Occupational Interest Survey (KOIS) is used in early high school; the Strong Interest Inventory (SII) is used in upper high school grades. Holland's Self-Directed Search (SDS) is applicable throughout high school. The Differential Aptitude Test (DAT), the Armed Services Vocational Aptitude Battery (ASVAB), and the General Aptitude Test Battery (GATB) are most often part of career exploration. Personality measures include the California Psychological Inventory (CPI), the Personality Orientation Inventory (POI), the Tennessee Self-Concept Scale, the Junior and Senior High School Personality Questionnaire, and the Mooney Problem Checklist. Computer programs such as DISCOVER and SIGI are also designed to help students understand their interests, lifestyle choices, and possible career options.

A DAY IN THE LIFE OF A SCHOOL COUNSELOR

A log describing a day in the life of a school counselor in Washington State (see Figure 17.1) was submitted in 1993 by a high school counselor who was concerned by the preponderance of crisis cases in her daily schedule. This high school has a team of well-qualified counselors whose administrators have, over the years, responded to their requests to develop and maintain a professional counseling center in the school. The center tends to draw many students who need help.

In a recent follow-up interview, the counselor said that some significant changes have occurred: The school brought in two new counselors to ease the overload; moreover, federal and state funds have created new career development programs that allow, among other services, accelerated academic tracks for some students, including Tech Prep and Running Start (both described earlier).

Although the counselors spend more time now with student developmental concerns, the typical day still has a preponderance of similar crisis cases. Nevertheless, an increased percentage of counselor time is now spent in execution of programs that foster academic, career, and social success and safety. In addition, more community resources outside the school are now accessible for the medical, psychological, and social support of students. Leaders from various ethnic communities are also becoming more actively involved with their youths and with school programs. Counselors, therefore, have more opportunity to focus on K–12 program planning, including methods to address developmental needs more adequately, create violence prevention programs, and introduce 4-year career planning and development procedures for students starting in the ninth grade.

SUMMARY

Although secondary schools were one of the earliest places to offer counseling services, for many years school counselors had difficulty gaining a professional identity because they lacked sufficient training, were unclear about their role, and were bogged down in administrative work. Recently, with increasing numbers of well-trained counselors and changed attitudes about counselor roles, counselors have been spending more time in professional counseling and counseling-related activities.

Adolescents go through major developmental, transitional changes, which naturally cause anxiety, confusion, fear, and aggression. Adolescent developmental needs center around a search for identity. Their confusion and value conflicts relate to changing family patterns and cultural upheavals in a rapidly changing, uncertain world. In working with adolescent clients, counselors expect to encounter ambivalence, conflict, fear, and rebellion.

During the 1990s secondary school counselors spent an increasing amount of time dealing with student crises that involved suicide threats, gang wars, sexual abuse, and substance abuse. Special programs funded by federal and state governments during the 1990s have allowed counselors to spend more time helping students explore careers, engage in on-the-job internships, and enroll in accelerated programs.

The need for school counselors to address the developmental needs of ethnic students has become urgent, particularly because ethnic groups will soon make up the majority of students in the United States. Counselors need to be aware of the tendency for most ethnic persons to identify closely with their particular cultures and families.

High school counselor efforts to forge liaisons with community agencies have proved effective; such liaisons are becoming more common and are especially helpful in addressing the increase in crisis cases in schools. School and community networking services for youths and their families help build community participation in working with adolescents, as well as reducing gang violence, alcohol abuse, and suicides in the adolescent population.

PROJECTS AND ACTIVITIES

1. Interview some high school counselors near you about their interest in and use of inventories, personality measures, and intelligence and aptitude tests.
2. Evaluate two computerized career information systems developed for use with high

school students. If possible, use a computerized program yourself to explore areas of interest to you.
3. Develop a list of agencies in the community that appear to be essential as resources for the school system. Then determine how

many of these agencies actually exist in nearby communities.

4. Conduct a survey of the literature or of adolescent students about adolescents' contemporary concerns. Are counselor preparation programs with which you are familiar geared to meet these needs?

5. This activity will require a tape recorder and another interested student who will team up with you for a series of role-playing counseling interviews. Use the activity to experiment with the different types of possible counselor responses to a client's remarks. You and the other student should each take a few minutes to work out a possible counseling situation. Then one of you acts as a client who presents your concern (with the recorder on) to the other person, who acts as the counselor. Then you will reverse roles. Role-play for at least 10 minutes so that the person playing the counselor makes several responses. Then replay the tapes and summarize what was said by the client and by the counselor. Classify the counselor's responses. Here are some suggested categories:

a. Probing for more facts and details by questioning

b. Giving advice or telling the client what to do

c. Judging or interpreting responses

d. Making responses that facilitate the expression of the client's feelings

(NOTE: This activity was written by Dr. Elvat G. Jones, Professor Emeritus of Psychology at Western Washington University, Bellingham.)

6. Role-play an interview with Sholanda, Client 4, using first a female as the counselor and then a male. What differences were felt when the counselor was a male and when the counselor was a female?

7. Explain how a client-centered counselor would work with the concerns of Gail, Client 1, about career exploration.

8. With two other students, role-play a three-way interaction with Juan (Client 9), his counselor, and his teacher.

REFERENCES

Baker, B. B. (2000). Middle school counseling in the new millennium: A practitioner's perspective. In J. Wittmer (Ed.), *Managing your school counseling program: K–12 developmental strategies* (pp. 49–55). Minneapolis: Educational Media.

Baruth, L., & Manning, M. L. (1999). *Multicultural counseling and psychotherapy: A lifespan perspective.* Upper Saddle River, NJ: Merrill/Prentice Hall.

Carter, R. B., & Vuong, T. K. (1997). Unity through diversity: Fostering cultural awareness. *Professional School Counseling, 1,* 47–49.

Conarton, S., & Silverman, L. K. (1988). Feminine development through the life cycle. In M. Dutton-Douglas & H. E. Walker (Eds.), *Feminist psychotherapies and feminist systems* (pp. 37–67). Norwood, NJ: Ablex.

Coy, D., & Sears, S. (2000). The scope of practice of the high school counselor. In J. Wittmer (Ed.), *Managing your school counseling program: K–12 developmental strategies* (pp. 56–67). Minneapolis: Educational Media.

Dollarhide, C. T. (2003). Partnering with students: Counseling in the three domains. In C. T. Dollarhide & K. A. Saginak

(Eds.), *School counseling in the secondary school: A comprehensive process and program* (pp. 133–158). Boston: Allyn & Bacon.

Erikson, E. H. (1980). *Identity and the life cycle.* New York: Norton.

Faubert, M., Locke, D. C., & McLeod, P. W. (2000). The counselor's role in teaching students to value cultural diversity. In J. Wittmer (Ed.), *Managing your school counseling program: K–12 developmental strategies* (pp. 49–55). Minneapolis: Educational Media.

Gilligan, C. (1982). *In a different voice: Psychological theory and women's development.* Cambridge, MA: Harvard University Press.

Gladding, S. T. (2004). *Counseling: A comprehensive profession* (4th ed.). Upper Saddle River, NJ: Merrill/Prentice Hall.

Glasser, W. (1998). *Choice theory: A new psychology of personal freedom.* New York: Harper Perennial.

Jones, K. D., & Robinson, E. H. (2001). Psychoeducational groups: A model for conceptualization. *Journal for Specialists in Group Work, 22*(2), 356–365.

Jordan, J. V., Kaplan, A. G., Miller, J. B., Stiver, I. P., & Surrey, J. L. (Eds.). (1991). *Women's growth in connection: Writings from the Stone Center.* New York: Guilford Press.

Lee, C. C. (1995). School counseling and cultural diversity: A framework for effective practice. In C. C. Lee (Ed.), *Counseling for diversity* (pp. 3–17). Boston: Allyn & Bacon.

Locke, D. C. (1995). Counseling interventions with African American youth. In C. C. Lee (Ed.), *Counseling for diversity* (pp. 21–40). Boston: Allyn & Bacon.

Miano, G., Forrest, A., & Gumaer, J. (1997). A collaborative program to assist at-risk youth: *Professional School Counseling, 1,* 16–20.

Murray, P. (1993, May 23). Guns, kids, and pain. *Seattle Post-Intelligencer,* p. E1.

National Occupational Information Coordinating Committee (NOICC). (1989a). *The national career development guidelines: Local handbook for high schools.* Washington, DC: Government Printing Office.

National Occupational Information Coordinating Committee (NOICC). (1989b). *The national career guidelines project.* Washington, DC: Government Printing Office.

National Occupational Information Coordinating Committee (NOICC). (1994). *Program guides: Planning to meet career development needs in schools-to-work-transition programs.* Washington, DC: Government Printing office.

Ohlsen, M. M., Horne, A. M., & Lawe, C. F. (1988). *Group counseling* (3rd ed.). New York: Holt, Rinehart & Winston.

Omizo, M. M., Omizo, S. A., & Honda, M. R. (1997). A phenomenological study with youth gang members: Results and implications for school counselors. *Professional School Counseling, 1,* 39–42.

Popenhagen, M. P., & Qualley, R. M. (1998). Adolescent suicide: Detection, intervention, and prevention. *Professional School Counseling, 1,* 30–36.

Schmidt, J. J. (2003). *Counseling in schools: Essential services and comprehensive programs* (4th ed.). Boston: Allyn & Bacon.

Sink, C. A., & MacDonald, G. (1998). The status of comprehensive guidance and counseling in the United States. *Professional School Counseling, 2*(2), 88–94.

Steinberg, L. (1993). *Adolescence.* New York: McGraw-Hill.

CHAPTER 18

Counseling Programs in Colleges and Universities

Young adults of college age are faced with developmental transitional challenges related to adjusting to academic life, developing academic skills, and planning a career, as well as struggling with the personal identity, developing social relationships, learning to live with roommates, and forming intimate, romantic partnerships. Counseling centers are available to students at most universities and colleges to help with these challenges.

As more fully explained in chapter 2, counseling centers as we know them today developed after World War II, originally to meet the needs of returning veterans. These new postwar counseling centers focused on integrating the client's vocational concerns with personal and psychosocial developmental needs. This approach was influenced by Super's (1953) view that vocational development is an intrinsic part of total personality development and by Rogers's (1942, 1951) emphasis on client-centered approaches and on personal growth. Prior to the formation of these new college counseling centers, colleges had generally relied on the faculty to conduct academic and vocational advisement, functions that were not considered counseling according to those professionals who were part of this new movement. Although confusion existed over the nature of college counseling and about those best equipped to deliver it, these early college counseling centers became models for the creation of role definitions and training standards for professional counselors in all settings.

College counseling centers flourished in the 1960s, expanding and spreading to colleges and universities throughout the country. To clarify the counselor role, Kirk et al. (1971) published the article "Guidelines for University and College Counseling Services," based on input from counseling centers throughout the United States. These guidelines affirmed that counseling focused on students' developmental needs is the primary function of counselors.

449

The 1960s and 1970s witnessed the Civil Rights movement, the women's movement, and the breakdown of social barriers to higher education for minorities and women. In addition, large numbers of older students with families entered colleges and universities, resulting in more diverse and complex campus environments. Concurrently, the student services field expanded to keep pace with the evolving needs of students. Administrative functions traditionally performed by faculty were reassigned to student affairs (Hodges, 2001). During this time counseling for college students emerged on campuses throughout the country as a separate professional service offered only by counseling professionals with specialized training.

During the 1980s many new, comprehensive therapeutic approaches and techniques were incorporated into counseling practice—psychodynamic family systems approaches, psychosocial life-span developmental models, various cognitive theories and techniques, and new theoretical approaches to gender, ethnic, and multicultural issues (see chaps. 2, 5, 6, and 10). To address the transitioning from late adolescence into early adulthood among college students, counselors adopted developmental approaches to counseling, emphasizing interpersonal, emotional, physical, and spiritual dimensions. These approaches will be discussed later in the chapter. In addition, career (i.e., vocational) counseling that had emerged after World War II as part of college counseling services was largely taken over by campus career advisement and placement centers.

In 1991 college counselors formed their own professional organization called the American College Counseling Association (ACCA). They had formerly been affiliated with the American College Personnel Association (ACPA), which focused on overall student personnel work. But when ACPA disaffiliated from the ACA, college counselors who wanted to continue to identify with ACA formed the ACCA as a new division of ACA. In 1998 ACCA published the first issue of its new journal, *Journal of College Counseling*, with its goal, according to Benshoff (1998), "to create a professional publication that recognizes the importance and potential contributions of both research and practice to our profession" (p. 4).

Today, an increase in the number of clients with more severe problems has necessitated that many college counseling centers move away from the traditional developmental approaches to a more clinical approach. Recently, even small college counseling centers have seen an increase in psychological pathology (i.e., diagnosable mental disorders) among the student population (Hodges, 2001). Issues such as clinical depression, anxiety, suicide risk, and substance abuse, as well as disorders involving psychosis and other severe pathology, are now relatively common among student clients in college counseling centers. Thus, confidential psychological testing, diagnosis, and treatment planning are the norm at many centers. Although career issues are commonly related to or affected by clinical problems, career counseling remains separated from many college counseling centers.

ORGANIZATION AND ADMINISTRATION OF COUNSELING CENTERS

College counseling centers are typically under the jurisdiction of a vice president of student affairs or a dean of students. As a part of student services, counseling centers work together with the student affairs office to facilitate students' general welfare and academic progress.

Besides the counseling centers, student services include resident life management, financial aid, health services, student life activities, academic advisement, registration, admissions, and special programs for foreign students, minorities, and disabled students.

Although closely interrelated with other student services, counseling centers maintain their unique role with clients by remaining autonomous and separate from other student services. They differ significantly from other services in that counselors develop a confidential, voluntary, and nonauthoritarian relationship with clients in order to best help them resolve personal doubts and conflicts that are interfering with academic, personal, or social functioning. Although some student services, such as health services and academic advisement, may have some similarities to counseling, those services are primarily diagnostic, prescriptive, advisory, or instructional. Only those counselors trained in mental health counseling or counseling psychology are qualified to work in counseling centers. Counseling centers can prevent confusion with other student services by clearly defining the counselor's unique role and clarifying its distinction from other student services.

The counselor's role in college counseling centers also differs from that of counselors in campus career centers. Career exploration as an integral part of personal development, as discussed earlier in chapters 2 and 3, has been the hallmark of college counseling since its inception. Unfortunately, since the 1970s the number of college counseling centers offering career counseling has declined. In the authors' opinion career counseling fits well within college counseling centers, since many emotional or behavioral issues clearly impact career decision making and job functioning. On campuses where counseling centers no longer offer career counseling, career placement services respond to student needs by expanding their services, hiring professional counselors specializing in career counseling, and changing their name to career counseling services.

College counseling services are provided by well-trained counselors, social workers, and psychologists who, for the most part, are available at no fee to help students work through their issues. In addition, most counseling centers serve as resources for the placement of counselor interns from the departments of psychology, educational psychology, and counselor education and, less frequently, from schools of social work. These counselor interns are at either the master's or the doctoral level and are supervised by full-time counselors at the center. College counselors may also train resident aides and counselor aides in interviewing skills so that they can interact effectively with students and instruct them in referral policies and procedures.

Individual and group counseling is the most common treatment modality; however, college counseling centers continue to address academic problems by offering outreach activities, such as consultation with faculty, psychoeducational groups and workshops (e.g., stress management, time management, study skills, conflict resolution), and crisis intervention. Each center has a director, typically an experienced counselor with a doctoral degree, who hires, oversees, supervises, and consults with staff. The director is also responsible for carrying out center policies, budgeting, setting up counseling loads, and overseeing the supervision and training of new staff members and student interns. Most directors also take on a small caseload of clients. The student records kept by counselors are confidential and unavailable to college administrators and faculty.

Because of the escalating need for counseling services among students and the lack of resources to hire needed counselors, many centers refer clients to off-campus community counseling centers. In a 2001 survey Gallagher found a ratio of 1 counselor to 1,600 students in college counseling centers. The ratio generally recommended by counseling center directors is 1 counselor to 750 to 1,000 students. This latter ratio is minimally sufficient only if other necessary psychological personnel services are available to students. Adequate on-campus psychiatric services can reduce the number of people with crises or chronic problems who would otherwise need to use counseling centers. Well-staffed minority affairs offices and alcohol or drug information and referral services also reduce pressure on college counseling centers.

College counseling staffs spend about 61% of their time in individual and group counseling, with brief counseling the most commonly used approach. Various outreach programs take up the rest of their time—psychological education, crisis prevention and intervention, consultation with faculty and administration, and supervision of interns and aides. Crisis services have expanded to deal with the increasing numbers of students afflicted with traumatic crises, students addicted to alcohol, and students suffering from violence, abuse, and sexual assault (Gallagher, 2001).

Collaboration With Student Services

As stated earlier, college counseling centers are clearly distinct from other student services. However, students are best served when all student services, while maintaining their separate identities, actively collaborate with one another. Counseling services can effectively collaborate with other student services through cross-referrals. For example, when student clients at the counseling center need to explore career options, they can be referred to the career center. Likewise, when students at career centers express doubts and conflicts that interfere with career choice, they can be referred to the counseling center.

Cross-referrals also work effectively between counseling centers and health services. Counselors can refer clients to health services when they are experiencing symptoms of physical or mental illness. Likewise, health services can refer students to counseling when students are under the type of emotional stress that does not require hospitalization or medication. Counseling centers can also collaborate effectively with other services by offering joint psychological education workshops. They can work jointly with career placement in planning a career fair, or they can work jointly with health services in offering educational programs on alcoholism.

Maintaining Referral Networks

Most college campuses are self-contained minicommunities for students, featuring health services, counseling services, financial aid, housing, dining, and recreational facilities, as well as student centers and associations for various religious, cultural, ethnic, and social-political action groups. Even so, many students feel isolated and out of touch with campus student support groups. A good cross-referral system among all student services and student associations helps reduce student feelings of isolation.

As mentioned earlier, collaboration is an essential function of campus organizations. Counseling center staffs use a variety of ways to inform the campus community about counseling services—for example, distributing brochures, featuring services in the school newspaper, and having open houses. Excellent sources of referral to counseling centers are the directors of residence halls and their aides, student services personnel, and the various student support groups and associations.

Counseling centers can also set up guidelines for faculty and administrators on when and how to refer students. The University of Maryland, for example, has developed the Take a Faculty to Lunch program to orient new faculty to services offered by the center. At these sessions counselors describe to faculty how to determine whether a student needs counseling help and how to make a referral (Westbrook et al., 1993). Faculty are in a key position to refer students whose academic difficulties seem related to signs of emotional blocking or distress.

Regarding administrative referrals, counseling centers must continually keep administration officials informed about the center's role. Administrators responsible for students' scholastic standing and discipline may see the counseling center as a place to which they can refer students who are on academic probation or who have broken campus regulations. However, counseling in such cases should still be voluntary; a student whose grade point average has fallen below the university's minimal standards should not be required to get counseling in order to remain in school.

University Testing Services

University testing services are generally under the jurisdiction of academic services, separate from the counseling center and student services. In some universities, however, counseling and testing services are combined, raising concerns about jeopardizing and compromising the counseling relationship. Again, the roles of the two services are very different. The function of campus testing services is to manage a variety of tests for the university: administering and scoring entrance examinations for applicants to various graduate programs, administering and scoring student evaluations of faculty, and scoring and making statistical analyses of classroom exams for professors. These screening and evaluative types of tests are not counseling or counseling-related functions and should not be confused with the psychological testing provided at many college counseling centers. Test scores from the former are not placed in students' confidential records but belong to the administration and faculty. Testing services such as these should be offered by a separate testing bureau with the sole function of administering tests and evaluations and giving feedback to administrators, department heads, and faculty.

COUNSELING COLLEGE STUDENTS

Developmental Needs of College Students

During their college years students continue to develop cognitively, intellectually, emotionally, and spiritually. It is important that counselors view student issues in light of developmental needs. According to Erik Erikson's (1950, 1968) psychosocial developmental theory (see chap. 5), students of college age continue to develop a sense of ego-identity as they move into the next stage of developing relationships. As they focus on developing their academic, personal, and social competencies, they are also absorbed in developing and maintaining close relationships. As was true with adolescents, college students who have not adequately worked through Erikson's earlier stages—that is, trust, autonomy, achievement, and initiative—need to confront and work through these challenges so that they can develop an authentic sense of identity and effective interpersonal relationships.

William Perry (1970) came up with nine stages of college student development, focusing primarily on intellectual and moral development. Extending Piaget's cognitive development theory to include late-adolescent college students, Perry listed the steps by which students progress from a simplistic, categorical view of the world to more complex forms of thought about the world, their disciplines or areas of study, and the self. The nine positions, grouped into four categories, are described here:

Dualism/Received Knowledge

1. *Basic duality:* All problems are solvable; therefore, the student's task is to learn the right solutions.
2. *Full dualism:* Although some authorities may disagree, there are right solutions to problems; therefore, the student's task is to learn the right solutions and ignore the others.

Multiplicity/Subjective Knowledge

3. *Early multiplicity:* Students learn that there are two kinds of problems: those whose solutions we know and those whose solutions we don't know yet. The student's task is to learn how to find the right solutions.
4. *Late multiplicity:* Most problems have solutions that we don't know yet; therefore, it doesn't matter which (if any) solution the student chooses. At this point students may become frustrated and either enter an educational program like math that has clear answers or drop out of college.

Relativism/Procedural Knowledge

5. *Contextual relativism:* All proposed solutions are supported by reasons; the student's task is to learn to evaluate solutions.
6. *Precommitment:* The student sees the necessity of making choices and committing to a solution

Commitment/Constructed Knowledge

7. *Commitment:* The student makes a commitment.
8. *Challenges to commitment:* The student experiences the implications of commitment and explores issues of responsibility.
9. *Ongoing commitment:* The student realizes that commitment is an ongoing, unfolding, evolving activity.

Perhaps the most widely known and applied theory of student development is Arthur Chickering's (1969; Chickering & Reisser, 1993) psychosocial model. Based on Erik Erikson's identity-versus-identity confusion stage of development, Chickering proposed seven vectors along which traditionally aged college students develop. Chickering and Reisser's revised 1993 model shows some significant changes from Chickering's (1969) earlier model, which had indicated that achieving autonomy is a significant feature of development. The revised model indicates that becoming autonomous is only one step in moving toward forming relationships, a change influenced by the relational theories of the feminist theorists, discussed later.

1. *Developing competence:* Student confidence that they have the ability to cope with any situation and can successfully achieve what they set out to do; includes intellectual competence, physical and manual skill competence, and interpersonal competence.
2. *Managing emotions:* Finding ways of balancing negative or painful feelings with positive, uplifting emotions and integrating feeling with thought and action; bringing self-control and self-expression into balance; managing two major impulses, aggression and sex.
3. *Moving through autonomy toward interdependence:* Some level of separation from parents and increased reliance on peers, authorities, institutional support systems, and self.
4. *Developing mature interpersonal relations:* Tolerance and appreciation of difference and the capacity for intimacy.
5. *Establishing identity:* Growing awareness of competencies, emotions, and values; confidence in standing alone and bonding with others; moving beyond intolerance toward openness and self-esteem; comfort with body and appearance; comfort with gender and sexual orientation; and a stronger sense of self.
6. *Developing purpose:* Increasing ability to be intentional, to assess interests and options, to clarify goals, to make plans, and to persist despite obstacles.
7. *Developing integrity:* Clarifying a personally valid set of core beliefs and values and matching those values with socially responsible behavior.

During the critical period of late adolescence, college students question their ethical and moral values and the meaning of life. According to Kohlberg's (1981) theory of cognitive moral development, as discussed in chapter 5, college students raise doubts and become skeptical of their own conventional beliefs as they dialogue on moral issues with other students who come from different social-cultural backgrounds. Kohlberg (1981) acknowledged Perry's theory that during their college years students acquire relativistic moral attitudes as they learn to accept their fellow students' differing value systems. However, Kohlberg said that this period of moral relativism is a transitional phase as individuals move on to postconventional Stage 5.

Adolescence has long been a particularly difficult time for women (Chodorow, 1978; Conarton & Silverman, 1988; Gilligan, 1982; Jordon, Kaplan, Miller, Stiver, & Surrey, 1991; Miller, 1976). During adolescence girls are expected to break away from their developmental inclinations of relating and caring for others if they are to survive the academic system and the business world that are geared to male standards of competitiveness, autonomy, and dominance. Girls thus go through what Conarton and Silverton (1988) call "cultural adaptation" (see chap. 5).

Following their predecessors Chodorow (1978) and Gilligan (1982) (see chap. 5), feminist theorists at the Stone Center, Jordan et al. (1991), challenge Erikson's developmental model, claiming that, for women, developing relationships is a necessary component of developing a sense of identity and therefore precedes the developmental stage of forming one's identity. Likewise, Gilligan (1982) criticized Kohlberg's (1969) cognitive model of moral development, a model limited to justice reasoning, for excluding the relational, caring considerations of women as crucial components of moral decision making (see chap. 5). Kohlberg (1986) consequently modified his model to take into account women's empathic perspective. Further counteracting the male-oriented, cultural expectations of women's development, Kaplan and Klein (1991) advocate a model of women's relational developmental patterns, which evolves in ever more complex modes of relationship throughout life. Their core modes of self-development are laid out by adolescence, however. "The late adolescent woman does not develop 'out of' the relational stage, but rather adds on lines of development that enlarge her inner sense as a relational being" (p. 131).

College students are also very interested in exploring spiritual issues, questioning, expanding, and deepening their faith perspectives. According to Fowler's (1981) theory of faith development (see chap. 5), students at the college level go through a period of doubt and skepticism, similar to Perry's model of college development, as they exchange ideas with others in the dynamic process of faith development. In their hunger to explore the meaning of life, college students redefine their faith as distinct from doctrinal religious creeds. Fowler considers faith development an ongoing process, "a dynamic existential stance, a way of leaning into and finding or giving meaning to the conditions of our lives" (p. 92).

Brief Counseling

Counseling centers have been limiting the number of counseling sessions available to clients, much as managed care programs have done in the community. In 1996 about half of counseling centers surveyed reported this practice (Gallagher, 1996). According to a study conducted by Gage and Gyorky (1990), college students with specific situational developmental concerns related to academics, careers, and relationships are appropriate for time-limited counseling. Clients who have mild disturbances and are capable of focusing on specific goals are generally able to benefit from brief counseling.

Brief counseling historically has worked well in college counseling centers ever since its inception in the early post–World War II years (see chaps. 1 and 2). What's different now is the limit of 10 sessions imposed in advance in all cases, as well as the focus on a single, specific goal. Nugent experienced this limitation firsthand recently.

> I first tried brief counseling with mandated limited sessions as a visiting counseling psychologist at the Center for Counseling and Psychological Services at Pennsylvania State University. I was dubious about its constraints: Having the agency impose limits on my counseling sessions and having to ask for permission to extend the sessions for certain cases ruffled my feathers. I did find, however, that making specific goals at the initial stage and following them worked well for most students. Essential to the success of the system was that, for those who needed it, we could, with permission, extend the sessions. I had no trouble extending sessions at this particular center, although this may not always be the case at other centers.

Use of Tests and Inventories

College counselors use standardized tests and inventories in the counseling process when they and their clients agree that information gained from these measures can help client self-exploration (see chap. 7). These tests and inventories are confidential and are kept separate from the entrance exams or student evaluations of faculty discussed previously. Tests and inventions are often used to augment interviews when client concerns are related to career choice and exploration (see chap. 12), but they can also be helpful when clients are exploring interpersonal relationships, are identifying a specific clinical syndrome like depression or anxiety, or are seeking deeper self-awareness. The use of tests has increased over the last several years because of the need to evaluate the effectiveness of counseling services and to accurately provide a *DSM-IV-TR* diagnosis for the client.

Common clinical tests used for evaluation and diagnosis include the Outcome Questionnaire–45, the Beck Depression Inventory, and the Substance Abuse Subtle Screening Inventory. For those students requesting career counseling, the following interest and personality inventories are generally used: the Strong Interest Inventory (SII), the Kuder Occupational Interest Survey (KOIS), and the Self-Directed Search (SDS). The Edwards Personal Preference Schedule (EPPS) and the Alport Vernon Study of Values are also popular for both career and interpersonal and personal concerns. In some centers, the Minnesota Multiphasic Personality Inventory (MMPI) and the Wechsler Adult Intelligence Scale (WAIS) are used with persons experiencing personal problems or academic difficulties.

Online Counseling

Internet usage for private counseling and for online instruction (e.g., counselor education courses) is growing. Many colleges and universities have tried to decide how to provide counseling services online for the convenience of all students—both on campus and off; such services meet the needs of students with limited time and access to in-person counseling.

The definition of *counseling services* in the college setting is neither clear nor universal and often encompasses both psychological counseling and student services. Thus, online counseling often simply addresses general questions regarding education or academic goals, questions about transcripts, graduation checks, financial aid information, and so on. Some colleges and universities integrate psychological services into online counseling services by providing online screenings and assessments. Although they are not a complete evaluation, these screenings can help students determine whether counseling services with a professional counselor are needed. A typical online screening includes demographic questions about the student and a symptom checklist, typically assessing depression, eating disorders, anxiety, or substance abuse. Screening results are provided within a few minutes, and students are given recommendations regarding seeking professional consultation. Although demographic information is gathered, screenings usually do not collect any unique identifying information such as names, e-mail addresses, or Internet addresses; thus, the confidentiality of the student is protected.

Addressing Cultural Diversity

College counselors are in a uniquely favorable position to work with the concerns, transitions, and issues of ethnic and multicultural students. College campuses typically draw a wider variety of multicultural groups than do many public schools or communities; ethnic students mingle with nonethnic students in dormitories, classes, and social activities. Moreover, diverse ethnic groups tend to come together to raise issues and discuss multiracial, multicultural problems. Although most college counseling centers include ethnic counselors on their staffs, few have all major ethnic groups represented at any one center. Counseling centers continually need to explore ways of modifying counseling to meet the divergent needs of ethnic students, work out outreach programs, and develop support groups on campus.

Effective counseling with the major ethnic groups discussed in chapter 14 applies as well on college campuses. Not covered earlier but especially evident on college campuses and in concentrated numbers are multiracial and international students, whose presence raises issues that need to be attended to by college counselors.

Multiracial Students

A group of students from seven different multiracial backgrounds formed a support group at the University of Memphis. The special challenge facing these students was studied by Nishimura (1998), who formed groups and asked them to express their concerns. From their responses she developed common themes confronting them. The students' major concern was their difficulty establishing a racial identity that could help them define themselves and communicate that image to others. They were not comfortable in monoracial groups, often feeling "challenged to 'prove' their ethnic membership" (p. 50). They also felt a lack of models or mentors who could guide them in identity development. To them, race was an ever-present issue. College counselors need to be aware of and sensitive to the complex identity issues of multiracial students. They also must examine their own attitudes and values about interracial marriage and the children of interracial marriages (Nishimura, 1998).

International Students

Increasing percentages of the college student population are from foreign countries (Pedersen, 1991). For them the usual stresses encountered in college are compounded. When students come from different political or socioeconomic systems, the cultural or values differences they face become more complex than those of ethnic groups in the United States. These differences may show up in how faculty and students interrelate, how much medical care is expected, how much freedom the individual has to choose a major, and how males and females interact. Feelings of isolation and alienation may overwhelm these students when family support is not available. In addition, the following special areas of concern for international students are specified by Orpeza, Fitzgibbon, and Baron (1991): culture shock, changes in socioeconomic status, expectations about academic performance, and family-related pressures. Many students also face worry and concern about political unrest in their home countries, fear about deportation, grief over a family death, or anxiety about family problems back home.

Overall, the theories, techniques, and attitudes discussed in chapter 14 for working with ethnic groups in the United States apply to students from foreign countries. Counselors must be aware of any stereotyping of clients, and they need to be alert to cultural differences without losing sight of the individual. In a review of the literature on counseling international students, Leong and Chou (1995) conclude: "From our review, it seems particularly important to develop creative alternative modalities for international students, given some of the cultural barriers and inhibitions about seeking professional psychological help" (p. 238). They suggest as well outreach activities such as time management and language skill workshops, pretherapy orientation sessions to acquaint them with Western counseling approaches, and training of residence hall advisors.

Working With Groups

About 85% of university counseling centers offer group counseling (Gallagher, 1997). The special characteristics of young adult groups that counselors should consider are discussed by Budman, Michael, and Wisneski (1980) and Ohlsen, Horne, and Lawe (1988). The groups tend to center on difficulties in developing intimate relationships and with consequent feelings of loneliness and isolation. Many young adults who lack the capacity to be open and trusting with others exacerbate the problem by giving up, withdrawing, or overintellectualizing. The opportunities to socialize that are readily available on college campuses may aggravate a student's feelings of isolation and loneliness. With older students, ages 36 to 50, groups address anxieties that relate to doubts about being in school, a lack of peer support, conflicts with spouses or children, the pressure of changing careers, and stress that results from separations, divorce, or broken relationships.

Personal growth groups, called *structured groups,* focus on behavioral and skills training that reduces stress, develops relationships, and handles transitions related to normal life development (Gazda, 1984). The group leader defines the problem, assesses how participants are functioning, provides a rationale for learning, and uses direct instruction, modeling, role playing, cognitive restructuring, biofeedback, and more to accomplish goals (Ohlsen et al., 1988). Examples of prevention groups for a college population are described by Drum (1984). He presents four comprehensive programs: stress awareness, relationships, future forecast, and transitions. In transitions, for instance, he outlines more than 25 panels and workshops, including academic adjustment, gender roles and relationships, coming out as a gay or lesbian, minority culture transitions, intimacy, changing religious values, and career choices.

Dendato and Diener (1986) have effectively used cognitive/relaxation techniques and training in study skills in structured groups to reduce test anxiety. In six 1-hour sessions deep muscle relaxation and Ellis's rational emotive strategies were taught to reduce tension and to challenge irrational beliefs about the consequences of examination grades. Some counseling centers offer relaxation and stress reduction programs. Rhode Island University is developing a stress management laboratory using computerized EEG biofeedback, and Salisbury State College and the University of Louisville have set up relaxation rooms for clients that do not require a staff member to be present (Gallagher, 1997).

Working With Families

College counselors work with families infrequently. Because college students still have conflicts with parents, however, and because their problems may stem from earlier experiences in dysfunctional families, college counselors need to be familiar with family systems theory and family dynamics (for further discussion see chap. 10).

Lopez (1986) describes the links between the nature of the family structure and depression in college students. He recommends that counselors assess the family structure with the depressed student and discuss troublesome family interactions, such as parental disputes and the student's role in the disputes. Different and more effective patterns of response can then be developed. A family systems approach called *systemic theory,* based on Haley's strategic therapy (see chap. 10), is recommended for college counseling (Searight & Openlander, 1984). In this approach counselors pay attention to family structure and use paradoxical directives to change self-defeating behavior.

A comprehensive model for counseling ACOAs in college counseling centers is described by Crawford and Phyfer (1988). They believe that ACOAs who voluntarily seek counseling have attained sufficient awareness of the problem that counselors can use Gestalt techniques (see chap. 6) to elicit feelings related to unfinished business about family interactions. They also recommend the following: family sculpting, developed by Satir (see chap. 10), so that long-denied emotions can be acted out; cognitive restructuring and behavior rehearsal to develop new ways of thinking and behaving; and counseling techniques specific to adult children who assumed roles of hero, scapegoat, lost child, or mascot in the family of origin.

More older students are requesting marital counseling. Significant numbers of students live together or consider marriage before graduation. Premarital, marital, or postmarital counseling and couple counseling for heterosexual and gay and lesbian couples are services available to students.

PRESENTING PROBLEMS OF COLLEGE STUDENTS

Presenting problems of college students generally parallel those of high school students. Both groups are in educational settings with requirements they must fulfill to graduate and policies they must agree to follow in order to remain in school. College students differ from high school students, however, in that most are of legal age and so are primarily responsible for their behavior. They also are not legally compelled to attend school. In addition, college students usually have more choice of instructors than do high school students.

Although they are legally adults, most undergraduates remain in a suspended state of semi-immaturity and dependence, compared with persons of the same age who do not go to college but begin careers, have a steady income, get married, and start raising families. For college students who work, jobs are usually part time and involve menial tasks. If they decide to go on to graduate school, they generally experience further delays in developing a stable economic life and permanent relationships.

Many college students must obtain student loans that put them into considerable debt. They are under constant stress to perform optimally in their academic work; poor relationships with an instructor may hinder or delay graduation or jeopardize entrance into graduate school. Attending college may also place a strain on intimate relationships, particularly when one partner wants more time and commitment from the other.

Even with the available on-campus special interest support groups, many students feel isolated and lonely. Many come from far away, from places where they are accustomed to close identification with family and community. This description may be particularly apt for ethnic students and international students, whose concerns are addressed later in the chapter.

With the increased numbers of older students on campus and the return to college of women who left to raise children, college counselors are now working with older people and must be aware of the issues and developmental needs of persons in their 30s, 40s, and beyond. Counselors should know theories of family and marital counseling even though they work less directly with families than do counselors in other settings. Problems concerning marriage, career change, aging parents, and child care show up more often in 2-year community colleges than in 4-year colleges because the average age of students in community colleges is higher.

Career/Educational Concerns

During the period of intense student activism and the push for alternative lifestyles in the late 1960s and early 1970s, many students were less interested in exploring traditional career choices or attaining high grade point averages than they were in personal growth and encounter groups. Thus, some counseling centers either neglected career counseling or considered vocational concerns of students to be secondary. As discussed previously, that trend has continued steadily throughout the years, resulting in a continuous decline in the number of counseling centers offering career counseling. In 1996 a national survey of college counseling center directors showed that 30% of campuses offer career counseling primarily through counseling centers, 55% through career counseling and placement offices, and the remainder through both counseling and career centers (Gallagher, 1996).

This trend is disturbing and ironic because career exploration as an integral part of personal development has been the hallmark of college counseling (see chaps. 2 and 12). Leading counseling professionals continue to insist that general counseling and career counseling are inseparable (Isaacson & Brown, 1997; Osipow & Fitzgerald, 1996; Zunker, 1994). When counseling centers abandon this heritage, they not only do an injustice to students but also take on the image of a mental health clinic—quite different from their original identity.

The cases presented here are typical of career concerns that clients bring to counseling centers still involved in career counseling. If career counseling is done in a separate career counseling center, the procedures laid out here apply as well. Career concerns and academic success appear to be foremost in students' minds today. Faced with the high-tech revolution and stiff competition, many students react with dismay and even panic. Jobs in some professions are not readily available at graduation, and entrance requirements of professional schools have become challenging. Many students are concerned about entering graduate school; some have two or more interests that appear to conflict. Other students may have difficulty choosing majors; some parents try to persuade a daughter or son to select a particular major whether or not she or he has any interest or ability in that area.

Increasing numbers of women have decided to return to school after raising families. Many of them express doubts about their ability to do academic work. Some are in conflict with husbands who are ambivalent about their wives going back to school. Other college students who made top grades in high school are flunking out of college. Some students may want to discuss the advisability of dropping out of school.

Counselors often see students who may be in the wrong majors, may be unsuited for college, may be working too many hours, or may lack motivation because they see no purpose in attending college. In addition, many students experience anxiety reactions and block when taking tests, doing mathematics assignments, presenting speeches before a class, or writing English themes or term papers.

Client 1: Janet, age 32, requests counseling because she is concerned about her academic progress and her vocational goals. She has returned to college after 13 years of marriage. Her children are 11 and 9 years old; her husband is a busy executive in a local advertising agency. Janet says he supports her attending college but is too busy to give much help at home. She finds schoolwork stimulating but overwhelming, particularly because she must make arrangements for child care and must still assume the major responsibility for the home. She also is not sure what career she wants; law and environmental science are two possibilities. She looks anxious and fatigued.

Response C–1: The counselor first needs to help Janet reassess how she and her husband are sharing household tasks. Counselor and client need to discuss the degree to which her husband is willing to share responsibility for the home and the children and the degree to which Janet has been able to accept his help. Any residual guilt feelings about leaving the children or any doubts about her academic ability must be worked through. After these factors are clarified, career options can be explored from the standpoint of how her interests, abilities, and values relate to law, environmental science, or other fields. Interest inventories, personality inventories, and other appropriate testing might be used. If Janet appears to need support, the counselor might suggest that she join a group for older women students on campus.

Client 2: Neil, a freshman, is taking a mathematics course required for graduation. He was referred to the counseling center by his mathematics teacher. Neil says that he does well in his homework assignments but he blanks out on tests. He studies hard, but as soon as the test is handed out, he becomes immobilized. The teacher is sympathetic and believes that Neil understands his work, but he has no option but to fail him on tests.

Response C–2: Blocks, or anxiety reactions, are common among students and occur most frequently in mathematics, speech, and English classes. Neil's immobilization on mathematics exams may represent anxiety about the consequences of failing or the need to be perfect, or it may be a fear conditioned by poor teaching in earlier mathematics classes. Ellis's rational emotive techniques, which involve logical reasoning, are often used in these situations (see chap. 6). Some counselors might use Wolpe's (1973) desensitization techniques, which are discussed with Client 5.

Personal Concerns

College students have continuing questions about traditional social mores, sexual patterns, and lifestyles. Many students are exploring religious, spiritual, and philosophical beliefs. As students move away from the immediate jurisdiction of their parents, their behavior changes as they encounter new experiences.

Self-doubt and uncertainties are as frequent in college as in high school. Homesickness, if severe, may lead some students to drop out of school. Students may also worry about why they are floundering while others their age are doing well. Anxieties may increase as students near graduation. In addition, questions and concerns about homosexuality and bisexuality are more frequently raised by college students than by high school students.

Client 3: Vivian is a 20-year-old junior who feels attracted to some women. She has dated men and has had intimate and pleasant heterosexual relationships. However, in a discussion with members of the campus gay advocacy group, it was suggested that she seek counseling because of her ambivalence.

Response C–3: Vivian is expressing a need to clarify her sexual orientation in a nonjudgmental, neutral atmosphere. A client-centered approach seems appropriate in helping her sort out her feelings, attitudes, values, and concerns. The counselor should help her confront her ambivalent feelings and explore more directly the quality and quantity of her relationships with men and women and any pressure she might be receiving from either lesbians or heterosexuals. No attempt would be made to sway her in one direction or the other.

Client 4: Georgia is a 20-year-old junior who describes herself as lacking motivation and self-discipline. Neither college nor social life is stimulating. She has done well academically but is beginning to have trouble in some courses. She attended a women's consciousness-raising psychoeducation group, jointly sponsored by the student affairs office and the counseling center. Her apathy prompted leaders of the group to refer her for counseling.

Response C–4: Georgia appears to be depressed. The counselor should notice that she has already taken two proactive steps: attending a women's group session and coming in for counseling. The counselor should help her explore uncertainties she has about herself academically, personally, and socially. Workshops based on behaviorally oriented theories help clients confront the degree of reality of their concerns. They also help change negative reinforcers to positive ones and use techniques to spur the depressed person into action. Beck's approach to depression (see chap. 6) is also appropriate.

Client 5: Al says he has a phobia about going to a dentist. He has been told that further neglect of his teeth may lead to serious gum problems. He makes dental appointments and then manages to talk himself out of going.

Response C–5: Al's fear of dentists might be reduced effectively by Wolpe's desensitization techniques. The counselor should help him develop a list of situations that elicit varying degrees of anxiety related to keeping a dental appointment. Then they should work together to rank these situations in a hierarchy of severity, with his highest anxiety presumably being that of sitting in the dentist's chair and having his teeth worked on. Al would then be taught to relax various muscles progressively until he is capable of relaxing himself fully in a few minutes. Next, he would be taught to visualize increasingly anxious situations while relaxed, until he is able to visualize himself in a dentist's chair and remain calm. After Al becomes desensitized through imagined actions, the counselor helps him take actual steps toward seeing the dentist.

Client 6: Gina is a freshman who was referred by a resident aide because she is experiencing severe homesickness. She feels nauseous, has periods of crying, and has missed classes. She has been thinking of dropping out of school. She has telephoned her parents, who have tried to convince her to work it out on campus.

Response C–6: A counselor should work closely with Gina to help reassure her and to help her stay in school. Gina might require more than one counseling session a week for a while. The counselor should talk with her about any concerns—ability to do the work, inability to make friends, guilt about leaving her family, and any other sources of unhappiness, such as an uncooperative roommate, an intimidating professor, or an overload of classes. In most cases when a student is given support and reassurance, homesickness wanes. Cooperation between resident hall personnel and counseling center staff, albeit with due regard for confidentiality, can be a plus for a student's ultimate resolution of the problem. A support group can also be helpful.

Interpersonal Conflicts and Concerns

Students in dormitories often seek counseling because of friction with roommates. To get along with roommates, students must learn to accept different values and different lifestyles. They also must learn appropriate ways of asserting themselves if roommates behave in an inconsiderate way or take unfair advantage of them.

Premarriage, marriage, or couple counseling also occurs fairly often. When couples break up, for instance, problems may be difficult to overcome because both may live on campus, and it may be difficult for them to avoid seeing each other. In addition, they must often contend with roommates or acquaintances on campus who want to know about the breakup and/or help them somehow.

Even though the majority of students at many colleges live away from home, much of college counseling relates to parent-student relationships. Parents may subtly or directly threaten to withdraw financial support or disown a student who behaves in a way that displeases them. This displeasure can occur over anything from the choice of friends or career to drinking habits to general ways of living. Many college students also worry about their parents' problems, such as divorce, illness, or loss of a job. Counselors can often help students and parents work through the difficult process of confronting their differences, resolving conflicts, and developing more constructive relationships.

Client 7: Carla, a freshman, is having problems with her roommate. Unlike Carla the roommate is friendly and sociable but is also untidy and brings in friends at all hours without checking with her. Carla expresses fondness for her roommate and wishes she could have the dates and social contacts of her friend. However, she dislikes her roommate's inconsiderate behavior but cannot express it directly to her. Her resident director referred her for counseling.

Response C–7: Roommate problems often result from students' inability or reluctance to assert themselves with their roommates. In Carla's case the counselor can help her confront her roommate constructively. Assertiveness training might be appropriate. Gestaltists might focus on her ambivalence about her roommate. She may need help developing social skills other than assertion. As counseling progresses, if communication between roommates reaches an impasse, Carla may decide to move. The counselor can refer her to another dorm if that plan seems appropriate.

Client 8: Matt has an excellent grade point average but is having trouble with a professor who teaches a required course in his major field. Matt believes that his midterm grade, which was below average, was unfair. He describes the professor as belligerent. Consequently, his motivation to work on assignments is low. The counseling staff has received similar complaints from other students about this professor. However, this professor is the only person teaching the course.

Response C–8: The counselor needs to clarify with Matt what he hopes to gain from counseling. If he wants to develop ways of interacting with the professor, then counseling is in order. The counselor could help him confront the professor in a constructive manner. Role playing might be used to help Matt practice the proposed interaction. The counselor might explore why the professor has had such a bad effect on Matt's motivation. Ways of coping with similar situations could be discussed. If Matt wants to register an administrative complaint, the counselor can suggest that Matt talk with the head of the department. However, the counselor should not intervene; it is not the counseling center's role to report a professor's behavior to the authorities.

Client 9: Bert is a 26-year-old graduate student living with his mother in an apartment off campus. His mother is in her early 60s. She cooks for him, cleans house, and waits up for him when he dates. Bert wants to move out on his own. However, when he mentions this to his mother, she worries about being able to take care of herself; she has felt this way ever since her husband's death 10 years before. Bert feels frustrated and guilty.

Response C–9: The counselor can help Bert confront his mother with the importance of his developing his own life and of her developing her own. Guilt feelings must be explored. If Bert's mother continues to express anxiety about his deserting her and about her inability to take care of herself, counseling for her might be suggested. Bert could also join a men's group. This experience, combined with individual counseling, would help him take constructive action that would be beneficial to both him and his mother.

Gender Issues

Gender issues are generally expressed most intensely on college campuses. Women study gender role concerns in courses and tend to join together to object to discrimination or harassment from faculty, administrators, or male students. Women also question the social-cultural stereotyping that contributes to depression, domestic violence, and career discrimination. Gender issues are discussed at length in chapters 5, 6, and 14.

A trend that continues to raise implications for college campuses and counseling staffs is the large number of women returning to college after they have fulfilled homemaking responsibilities (Padula, 1994). A comprehensive literature review was conducted by

Padula (1994) regarding women who return to college (i.e., reentry women) at a nontraditional age after prolonged absence for as much as 35 years. Studies show that these returning women tend to have significantly higher grade point averages and higher educational aspirations than do traditional students. Studies also indicate, however, that they have less confidence in themselves and in their career planning, suffer from role conflict and emotional distress from family demands, and express significant dissatisfaction with advisement and counseling services. Positive attitudes and support from family, friends, and professors are particularly important (Padula, 1994).

Padula (1994) concluded that career counseling programs need to be improved for these women: Counselors need to become aware of the special needs and concerns of older women and provide counseling, support groups, and psychoeducational programs that address their particular needs. Women reentering educational institutions do have characteristics and needs that are different from those of traditional students. Reentry women are also very concerned about vocational, family, and financial issues, as well as issues of personal development. These concerns underline the necessity for the development of counseling, advisement, and educational programs that will meet the needs of these reentry people.

Antisocial Acts and Alcohol Abuse

College students come to counseling because of antisocial, aberrant, or illegal acts similar to those of secondary students and persons in the community. Shoplifting, drug or alcohol abuse, and sexual aberrations occur in all settings wherever counselors work. Misbehavior and illegal acts occurring primarily on college campuses include cheating on exams, creating havoc in a dormitory or elsewhere on campus, harassing teachers, and stealing exam questions. When students voluntarily seek counseling, confidentiality is upheld. No report goes to the office of the dean of students or the vice president for student affairs unless the students are endangering others or themselves.

Antisocial behaviors generally come to the attention of a dean in the student affairs office who decides whether disciplinary action is necessary. The dean may recommend that the person receive counseling without taking disciplinary action. In these cases it is important that the counselor let the student know that she or he cannot be protected from legal proceedings or disciplinary action if the illegal or inappropriate behavior continues.

Alcohol abuse increased dramatically on college campuses throughout the country during the 1990s, with serious consequences for student drinkers, fellow classmates, and school officials (Prendergast, 1994; Steenbarger, 1998). Recent research suggests that alcohol abuse is widespread among college students, with approximately 20% of all students qualifying as heavy drinkers and over 40% of students reporting at least one binge-drinking episode in a given 2-week period. This kind of drinking is associated with a number of adverse consequences, including sexual misconduct, damage to property, academic difficulty, drunk driving, unsafe sex, and suicidality (Steenbarger, 1998, p. 81). In a Carnegie Foundation survey, college presidents claimed that the biggest problem on campuses is alcohol abuse (Eigen, 1991). The sharp increases in sexual assaults, date rapes, and gang rapes on college campuses are often related to alcohol abuse (Gallagher, 1997).

Steenbarger (1998) believes that the existing college counseling programs are ineffective in treating alcohol abuse because of the prevalence of brief counseling. "Even when alcohol abuse is identified, the forms of treatment offered on many campuses are too abbreviated to be effective and rely on approaches that are associated with poor outcomes" (p. 89). Professionals recommend that counseling centers offer ongoing longer-term group work, the type that has proved effective in alcohol treatment. They also recommend broadening counseling services to include motivational counseling techniques for clients in denial and teaching coping skills to clients who have stopped drinking and want to prevent relapse (Miller & Rollnick, 1991; Steenbarger, 1998).

In 1989 Rutgers University established the first campus-based alcohol and drug rehabilitation center in the United States. Student substance abusers there can now continue their education while receiving treatment. Since then, other campuses have adopted similar alcohol and drug treatment programs (Steenbarger, 1998).

Crises

Because the number of college students who are experiencing serious emotional problems has increased considerably since the mid-1980s, college counselors have been learning effective intervention procedures (Stone & Archer, 1990). Crises arising out of suicides or suicide attempts or threats are fairly frequent; college students have a higher suicide rate than the general population (Comer, 1998). In a review of demographic studies about suicide rates among college students, Comer (1998) indicated that the suicide rate of adolescents and young adults has doubled since 1955. He concluded from his review that many aspects of college life are stressful: competition for grades, lack of support, indifferent or hostile reactions from professors, jockeying for academic and athletic honors, and increased use of drugs and alcohol. Further, he notes that the weakening of nuclear families and rapid, volatile social and economic changes have also contributed to a dramatic upsurge in suicide. In addition, anxiety attacks or acute psychotic reactions requiring immediate counseling, hospitalization, or drug therapy are also common on college campuses. Students may collapse under academic pressures, the need to make too many decisions, traumatic breaks in relationships, feelings of loneliness and isolation, or the death of a relative or friend.

Cooperative emergency policies and procedures should be developed among the staffs of counseling centers, student personnel offices, student health services, residence halls, and mental health clinics. In residence halls, where emergency situations most often occur, immediate intervention is necessary to determine whether a crisis is of short duration or whether the student appears too incapacitated to continue in school. Further decisions may be necessary about hospitalization, drug therapy, and notification of the student's family. If the crisis is temporary, follow-up counseling may be appropriate. If the student needs hospitalization and the family must be informed, the student personnel officer in charge should take the necessary steps.

Psychiatric services and consultation to help counseling center staff working with clients in crisis are available on two-thirds of college campuses. These are offered in the counseling centers, student health services, or both. Counseling centers average about 18 hours of psychiatric consultation per week for staff members (Gallagher, 1997).

For students experiencing crises after hours, emergency on-call services are provided by counseling centers at about three-fourths of campuses. Counselors on call are reached by beepers, regular telephone, or emergency lines (Gallagher, 1997).

OUTREACH ACTIVITIES

The outreach programs designed to improve student mental health environments at colleges and universities usually take the form of group activities or consultation with faculty and administrators. Similar to those in secondary schools, the two types of psychological education groups are developmental education and crisis prevention and intervention.

Developmental Programs

Career Education

Funding provided by the National Occupational Information Coordinating Committee (NOICC) has increased career education programs in colleges and universities. NOICC (1992, 1994) includes guidelines for career development programs in higher education. A variety of programs are now offered:

> To help students/clients choose/change a major and/or identify potential occupations, colleges provide assessment of interests, aptitudes, values, and work styles . . . furnish . . . career libraries providing materials about colleges, graduate and professional schools as well as a full array of occupational data . . . provide career development classes, and individual and group counseling. (NOICC, 1994, p. 10)

NOICC has also enabled career placement offices to help students explore internships or other on-the-job experiences, which provide opportunities for students to clarify their career choices. As a further result of ongoing NOICC funding, career centers have developed programs that teach students how to write résumés, how to embark on a job search, and how to conduct themselves in job interviews (NOICC, 1994). Counseling centers and placement office staff members often work jointly to help students with these activities. For older returning students, counselors develop workshops or group sessions about how to reenter the workforce successfully or how to explore new, more satisfying careers.

Personal Growth

Despite increased demands that college counselors work with more serious psychological problems and with crisis intervention, counseling centers should continue to provide programs directed toward personal growth and development (Stone & Archer, 1990). Westbrook et al. (1993) describe psychoeducational programs offered by the counseling center staff at the University of Maryland, College Park. "Psychoeducational programs in the classroom are small-group procedures that are designed to assist students in reducing stress, relieving test anxiety, relaxing or acquiring other circumscribed goals" (p. 686). Westbrook et al. also emphasize the necessity for counseling centers to develop workshops and classes regarding racism.

Romano (1984) describes a credit course in stress management at the University of Minnesota—Psychology and Management of Stress: Theory and Application. After presenting psychological stress theories, he uses a combination of holistic and cognitive-behavioral approaches. Students use a holistic approach to practice progressive relaxation, breathing, and biofeedback; they learn behavioral approaches such as Meichenbaum's stress-inoculation training, assertiveness training, and some of Ellis's cognitive restructuring to reduce stress-producing attitudes and behavior (see chap. 6). In evaluation 56% of students reported lower stress levels.

Prevention and Intervention Programs

At colleges and universities the major risk groups are students with alcohol and drug problems, adult children of alcoholics (ACOAs), suicidal students, and perpetrators and victims of violence.

Alcohol Abuse

The heavy drinking patterns of college students require that college counseling services focus on extensive prevention and intervention programs to supplement the alcohol abuse treatment programs discussed earlier. Steenbarger (1998) presents five steps to improve outreach alcohol prevention programs: (a) increase early screening, (b) enhance campuswide education regarding available services, (c) offer and promote more alcohol-free residence halls, (d) expand counseling services to include more and improved group prevention activities and intervention services, psychoeducational courses, and support programs, and (e) broaden services to include coping skills for those who have stopped drinking and want to prevent relapse. "A combination of targeted educational, environmental, and programmatic structural group interventions holds significant promise in promoting the health of our campus communities" (p. 89).

In response to heavy student drinking on college campuses, Steenbarger (1998) reviewed preventive programs that have been developed on campuses throughout the country. He notes that almost 70% of college campuses have developed on-campus alcohol abuse prevention programs, many of which include policies regulating the use of alcohol in fraternities and residence halls. A comprehensive alcohol education program at the University of Cincinnati includes strategies to alert faculty, staff, and student leaders to the need to regulate alcohol consumption on campus (Coyne, 1984). Interventions are focused on groups that are the worst alcohol abusers—typically, fraternities. Counselors conduct a series of workshops with two volunteer fraternities, in which they discuss alcoholism, appropriate house rules for drinking, and alternatives to alcohol. A psychoeducational group for ACOAs at Colorado State University shared hidden family experiences, confronted denial, and retrieved and restructured suppressed feelings (Downing & Walker, 1987). Self-help strategies were included during the eight group sessions. Afterward, some members joined Al-Anon, and others sought out individual or family counseling.

Suicide

The increasing rate of suicide requires that counseling centers plan comprehensive outreach, prevention, and intervention programs. Counseling staff have a prime responsibility to explore conditions on campus that are contributing to student suicide and to take what steps they can to ameliorate the problems. Educational programs regarding tell-tale signs of suicidal symptoms can be made available to faculty and staff, along with discussions about the need for mentoring students anxious about their academic progress and consultations with administrators about the effects of faculty abuse and harassment of students. In addition, because students away from home and lacking family or community support often experience feelings of loneliness, isolation, and despair, counselors can offer workshops about how to cope with such issues as broken relationships and academic pressure and can encourage and develop support groups to deal with and help alleviate feelings of isolation.

At a graduate dormitory at Indiana University, after several suicides had occurred in the dorms, four friendship-development seminars were held during the year (Fondacaro, Heller, & Reilly, 1984). Problems contributing to social isolation were identified and shared. White and Rubenstein (cited in Gilliland & James, 1997) describe how the Cornell University Psychological Services Center collaborated with local radio stations to broadcast messages about their services aimed at high-risk suicidal students. The program was successful in increasing high-risk student self-referrals to the center.

Violence

Some university counseling centers have set up programs related to violence prevention or intervention in response to increased numbers of sexual and physical assaults on campuses. California State College at San Francisco has developed a plan of action with academic departments to deal with potentially dangerous students on campus. Southwest Texas State University has set up a Victory Over Violence week to educate students about antiviolent activities on campus (Gallagher, 1996). To work with the aftermath of violence or tragedy on campus, the State University of New York at Cortland has developed a post-traumatic stress debriefing procedure in conjunction with the local hospital psychiatric unit (Gallagher, 1997).

Consultation and Collaboration

Faculty may consult with counselors about concerns or conflicts with students, administrators, or others. They may also raise questions regarding personal problems.

Professor 1: Professor Drake has built good trust relationships in her physics class. A student confides that she thinks she is pregnant. Another confesses that he has tried cocaine and is worried about it. Still another student shares deep concerns about his alcoholic parents. Professor Drake wants to maintain openness with her students but feels overwhelmed and ill-equipped to handle the students' problems.

Response P–1: Professor Drake can be helped to differentiate between the roles of caring teacher and professional counselor. She can be given guidelines on how to refer students to a counselor when it appears necessary. She then can be a bridge for students to the counseling center.

Consultation with college administrators includes department chairs, deans of student affairs, and other student personnel workers.

Administrator 1: Professor Ramos, department head, asks for a consultation about a faculty member who is depressed and has mentioned suicide. The faculty member has asked that the information be kept confidential but has also been reluctant to seek professional help. Professor Ramos is worried about the teacher and about her own responsibility for the teacher's welfare.

Response A–1: The counselor can help Professor Ramos realize that the teacher in question is placing an undue burden on her. The counselor can suggest that Professor Ramos tell the teacher that she cannot keep this information in confidence unless the teacher seeks help. The counselor should offer to see the teacher and help arrange appropriate treatment. If the teacher refuses help, the administrator, with the teacher's knowledge, should notify the teacher's family and arrange for sick leave.

Administrator 2: Dean Brown, dean of the School of Education, asks the counseling center director whether the center can help coordinate efforts to screen, select, and retain students who are candidates for the teacher training program.

Response A–2: Dean Brown should be told that the counseling center could jeopardize its voluntary, confidential nature if it became involved in evaluations for departments. However, the counseling center can suggest how the department can interview prospective students and how it can set specific procedures for determining student suitability for the program. Referrals to the counseling center would be appropriate only as long as interactions between students and counselors remained strictly confidential.

College counseling centers should also maintain good communication and effective cross-referral procedures with other services on or off campus, such as community mental health clinics, community hospitals, marriage and family centers, alcohol and drug treatment centers, rape relief centers, women's shelters, and Planned Parenthood.

SUMMARY

College and university counseling centers closely follow professional counseling association recommendations that well-trained professional counselors provide services geared to persons with normal developmental concerns. Students' flexible schedules and close proximity to campus services make it relatively easy for students to get counseling.

Counseling services include individual and group counseling, various outreach prevention and intervention services, supervision of interns and resident aides, referral networking, and collaborating with health and social services on and off campus. Counselors see clients about concerns related to careers, personal doubts about themselves and their academic ability, relationship conflicts, gender issues, antisocial behavior, alcohol abuse, and suicide and violence.

Counselor outreach through psychological education programs includes classes and workshops regarding career education, personal growth, and interpersonal relationships. Because gender issues arise more intensely on college campuses, more clients are likely to raise those issues in college counseling sessions than in other counseling settings. College counselors need to continue to address the special concerns of the wide variety of ethnic, multiracial, and international students on university campuses.

Although most college students do not live with their parents, many still depend on them for financial support, and many are still suffering the residual effects of earlier faulty parent-child interactions. College counselors thus need to be familiar with family theories and techniques. Marital, couple, and family counseling is becoming more common on college campuses as older married persons are returning to school.

PROJECTS AND ACTIVITIES

1. A counselor in a college counseling center receives a visit from a roommate of one of her clients. The roommate tells the counselor that he is concerned that the client is not leveling with the counselor about his real problem. He offers to give background information about his friend that he believes will be helpful. How should the counselor respond?

2. The director of a college counseling center notices that the proportion of minority students seeking counseling is significantly lower than their proportion of the student body as a whole. What steps can the director take to be sure that minority students who need help will receive it?

3. Referrals from faculty and other professionals on campus are encouraged by the directors of counseling centers. Some faculty members who have referred students to the center call and ask whether the students have shown up and what has happened. What should a counselor do in these instances?

4. An official of a government agency telephones the director of a college counseling center and asks whether a certain student has had counseling, because the official wants an evaluation of the student regarding security risks. How should the director respond in a manner consistent with professional standards?

5. A residence hall director refers a student to a counselor. The student, who is underage, has been drinking in the dorm. The student is willing to receive counseling. After a few sessions the residence hall director calls and tells the counselor that the student is still drinking and wonders what to do. How should the counselor respond?

6. A student who is a resident aide calls the counseling center to explain that a student on his floor appears to be in a serious emotional state. The student refuses to leave his room, eat meals, or attend classes; he is incoherent and seems to be hallucinating. The college has no psychiatrist on staff, and the health center offers primarily first-aid treatment. How should the counseling center staff respond?

REFERENCES

Benshoff, J. M. (1998). On creating a new journal for college counseling. *Journal of College Counseling, 1*, 3–4.

Budman, S. H., Michael, J., & Wisneski, M. J. (1980). Short-term group psychotherapy: An adult developmental model. *International Journal of Group Therapy, 30*, 63–76.

Chickering, A. W. (1969). *Education and identity.* San Francisco: Jossey-Bass.

Chickering, A. W., & Reisser, L. (1993). *Education and identity* (2nd ed.). San Francisco: Jossey-Bass.

Chodorow, N. (1978). *The reproduction of mothering.* Berkeley: University of California Press.

Comer, R. J. (1998). *Abnormal psychology* (3rd ed.). New York: Freeman.

Conarton, S., & Silverman, L. D. (1988). Feminist developmental theory. In M. A. Dutton-Douglas & I. E. Walker (Eds.), *Feminist psychotherapies: Integration of therapeutic and feminist systems* (pp. 37–67). Norwood, NJ: Ablex.

Coyne, R. K. (1984). Preliminary prevention through a campus alcohol education project. *Personnel and Guidance Journal, 62*, 524–529.

Crawford, R. L., & Phyfer, A. Q. (1988). Adult children of alcoholics: A counseling model. *Journal of College Student Development, 29*, 105–111.

Dendato, K. M., & Diener, D. (1986). Effectiveness of cognitive/relaxation therapy and study-skills training in reducing self-reported anxiety and improving the academic performance of test-anxious students. *Journal of Counseling Psychology, 33,* 131–135.

Downing, N. E., & Walker, M. E. (1987). A psychoeducational group for adult children of alcoholics. *Journal of Counseling & Development, 65,* 440–443.

Drum, D. J. (1984). Implementing theme-focused prevention: Challenge for the 1980s. *Personnel and Guidance Journal, 62,* 509–513.

Eigen, L. D. (1991). *Alcohol practices, policies, and potentials of American colleges and universities: A white paper.* Rockville, MD: U.S. Department of Health and Human Services, Office for Substance Abuse Prevention.

Erikson, E. H. (1950). *Childhood and society.* New York: Norton.

Erikson, E. H. (1968). *Identity, youth, and crises.* New York: Norton.

Fondacaro, M. R., Heller, K., & Reilly, M. J. (1984). Development of friendship networks as a prevention strategy in a university megadome. *Personnel and Guidance Journal, 62,* 520–523.

Fowler, J. W. (1981). *Stages of faith: The psychology of human development and the quest for meaning.* San Francisco: Harper & Row.

Gage, L. A., & Gyorky, Z. K. (1990). Identifying appropriate clients for time-limited counseling. *Journal of College Student Development, 31,* 476–477.

Gallagher, R. P. (1996). *National survey of counseling center directors.* Alexandria, VA: International Association of Counseling Services.

Gallagher, R. P. (1997). *National survey of counseling center directors.* Alexandria, VA: International Association of Counseling Services.

Gallagher, R. P. (2001). *National survey of counseling center directors.* Alexandria, VA: International Association of Counseling Services.

Gazda, G. M. (1984). *Group counseling: A developmental approach* (3rd ed.). Boston: Allyn & Bacon.

Gilligan, C. (1982). *In a different voice.* Cambridge, MA: Harvard University Press.

Gilliland, B. E., & James, R. K. (1997). *Crisis intervention strategies* (3rd ed.). Pacific Grove, CA: Brooks/Cole.

Hodges, S. (2001). University counseling centers at the twenty-first century: Looking forward, looking back. *Journal of College Counseling, 4*(2), 161–173.

Isaacson, L. E., & Brown, D. (1997). *Career information, career counseling, and career development* (6th ed.). Boston: Allyn & Bacon.

Jordon, J. V., Kaplan, A. G., Miller, J. B., Stiver, I. P., & Surrey, J. I. (Eds.). (1991). *Women's growth in connection: Writings from the Stone Center.* New York: Guilford Press.

Kaplan, A. G., & Klain, R. (1991). The relational self in late adolescent woman. In G. V. Jordan, A. G. Kaplan, J. B. Miller, I. P. Stiver, & J. L. Surray (Eds.), *Women's growth in connection: Writings from the Stone Center* (pp. 122–131). New York: Guilford Press.

Kirk, B. A., Johnson, A. P., Redfield, J. E., Free, J. E., Michel, J., Roston, R. A., & Warman, R. E. (1971). Guidelines for university and college counseling services. *American Psychologist, 26,* 585–589.

Kohlberg, L. (1969). Stage and sequence: The cognitive-developmental approach to socialigation. In D. Goslin (Ed.), *Handbook of socialigation theory and research* (pp. 347–480). Chicago: Rand McNally.

Kohlberg, L. (1981). *Essays in moral development: Vol. 1. The philosophy of moral development.* San Francisco: Harper & Row.

Kohlberg, L. (1986). A current statement on some theoretical issues. In S. Modgil & C. Modgil, *Lawrence Kohlberg: Consensus and controversy.* Philadelphia: Falmer Press.

Leong, F. T. L., & Chou, E. L. (1995). Counseling international students. In P. B. Pedersen, J. G. Draguns, W. J. Lonner, & J. E. Trimble (Eds.), *Counseling across cultures* (4th ed., pp. 210–242). Thousand Oaks, CA: Sage.

Lopez, F. G. (1986). Family structures and depression: Implications for the counseling of depressed college students. *Journal of Counseling & Development, 64,* 508–511.

Miller, J. B. (1976). *Toward a new psychology of women.* Boston: Beacon Press.

Miller, W. R., & Rollnick, S. (1991). *Motivational interviewing: Preparing people to change addictive behavior.* New York: Guilford Press.

National Occupational Information Coordinating Committee (NOICC). (1992). *The national career development guidelines project.* Washington, DC: Author.

National Occupational Information Coordinating Committee (NOICC). (1994). *Program guide: Planning to meet career development needs.* Washington, DC: Author.

Nishimura, N. J. (1998). Addressing the issues of multiracial students on college campuses. *Journal of College Counseling, 1,* 45–53.

Ohlsen, M. M., Horne, A. M., & Lawe, C. F. (1988). *Group counseling* (3rd ed.). New York: Holt, Rinehart & Winston.

Orpeza, B. A. C., Fitzgibbon, M., & Baron, A., Jr. (1991). Managing mental health crises of foreign college students. *Journal of Counseling & Development, 69,* 280–284.

Osipow, S. H., & Fitzgerald, L. F. (1996). *Theories of career development* (4th ed.). Boston: Allyn & Bacon.

Padula, M. A. (1994). Reentry woman: A literature review with recommendations for counseling and research. *Journal of Counseling & Development, 73,* 10–16.

Pedersen, P. B. (1991). Counseling international students. *Counseling Psychologist, 19,* 10–58.

Perry, W. G. (1970). *Forms of intellectual and ethical development in the college years: A scheme.* New York: Holt, Rinehart Winston.

Prendergast, M. L. (1994). Substance use and abuse among college students: A review of recent literature. *Journal of American College Health, 43,* 99–114.

Rogers, C. R. (1942). *Counseling and psychotherapy.* Boston: Houghton Mifflin.

Rogers, C. R. (1951). *Client-centered therapy: Its current practice, implications, and therapy.* Boston: Houghton Mifflin.

Romano, J. L. (1984). Stress management and wellness: Reaching beyond the counselor's office. *Personnel and Guidance Journal, 62,* 533–536.

Searight, H. R., & Openlander, P. (1984). Systemic therapy: A new brief intervention model. *Personnel and Guidance Journal, 20,* 381–391.

Steenbarger, B. N. (1998). Alcohol abuse and college counseling: An overview of research and practice. *Journal of College Counseling, 1,* 81–92.

Stone, G. L., & Archer, J., Jr. (1990). College and university counseling centers in the 1990s: Challenges and limits. *Counseling Psychologist, 18,* 539–607.

Super, D. (1953). A theory of vocational development. *American Psychologist, 8,* 185–190.

Westbrook, F. D., Kandell, J. J., Kirkland, S. E., Phillips, P. E., Regan, A. E., Medvene, A., & Oslin, Y. D. (1993). University campus consultation: Opportunities and limitations. *Journal of Counseling & Development, 71,* 684–688.

Wolpe, J. (1973). *The practice of behavior therapy* (2nd ed.). New York: Pergamon.

Zunker, V. G. (1994). *Career counseling: Applied concepts of life planning* (4th ed.). Pacific Grove, CA: Brooks/Cole.

CHAPTER 19

Counseling in the Community

Before 1960 mental health care for the general population was not considered a responsibility of local communities. Persons with mental illness were placed in state-run asylums located in "rural settings, housing thousands of patients for years, sometimes decades, on end" (Wylie, 1992, p. 14). Affluent people could afford to see a psychotherapist or seek care at a private clinic. However, Wylie (1992) says, "there was very little in the way of health care for the vast majority of Americans" (p. 15). After humanistic, developmental, family systems, and cognitive-behavioral therapies were introduced in the 1950s, 1960s, and 1970s, increasing numbers of counselors and therapists became interested in working with the normal concerns of people. A national survey in the early 1960s indicated that "far more people felt they needed help with marriage and family, and 'non-job adjustment problems in the self' than any other causes, but only one person in seven ever sought such help" (Wylie, 1992, p. 15).

In 1963 Congress passed the Kennedy Comprehensive Community Mental Health Act. Based on the idea that mental health care should be a community responsibility, this bill proposed setting up 2,000 mental health centers throughout the United States. It was designed to cover the full range of services for those with normal emotional problems, as well as those with severe and chronic mental disorders (Randolph, 1978). Each center was to serve about 250,000 persons in a particular region (Wylie, 1992). Under this act persons who had previously been sent to mental institutions outside the community were to be treated in inpatient local facilities. Other proposed facilities were to include outpatient clinics that would attend to the counseling concerns of the general population, halfway houses for transitional care, crisis clinics, hot lines to handle emergencies, and such preventive measures as education and consultation. In 1965 Frank Nugent was serving as the board chairman of a community clinic.

The psychiatric director and the board of the Whatcom Community Mental Health Clinic envisioned a comprehensive center in our community, so we applied for and were granted federal funds to start building a community mental health center. Unfortunately, however, the Kennedy Act mandated that federal funding for these comprehensive programs would be cut annually, with the stipulation that states gradually take over the funding. As we worked out plans to develop the facility, federal funds dwindled, and the Washington State legislature was unable or unwilling to provide what was needed. As a result, completion of the facility was delayed for almost 10 years, and it ultimately consisted only of an outpatient clinic serving those with severe or chronic mental disorders. No provisions were made for any other needed services. In addition, our nearest state mental hospital was closed even though inpatient facilities were unavailable in the community. The local hospital eventually provided a limited number of beds for temporary inpatient care.

Similar failures to develop comprehensive community mental health services were happening throughout the country, even as most state-run mental hospitals were permanently closed nationwide. Local clinics thus had the extra burden of monitoring psychotropic medications and managing the chronically ill. To fill the gap, crisis clinics, hot lines, and halfway houses emerged; facilities operated on shoestring budgets by well-intentioned, overworked, and mostly untrained volunteers. These agencies have continued to grow and improve staff and services, but no central agency coordinates them. The services have had only informal connections with the community mental health clinics and have vied with them for local funding. The degree of cooperation has depended on individual effort to develop communication networks. To supplement the limited funds from local and state governments, directors of community counseling services use alternative sources, such as the United Way, grants from local and regional corporate foundations, individual contributions, and fund-raisers. Although this type of financing draws in support from the local community, staff directors and/or their assistants must spend a great deal of their time seeking funds.

In the 1980s and 1990s even more severe cuts in federal and state funding caused a further move away from the original idea of community mental health clinics providing comprehensive coverage for everyone. State-funded community mental health clinics have continued to focus on serving only those with severe and chronic mental illnesses.

CURRENT STATUS AND TRENDS

Unlike counseling services in schools and colleges, community mental health services are not centralized. Community mental health is a hodgepodge of services scattered throughout the community. Moreover, individuals in the community, unlike students in schools and colleges, are not automatically eligible for free or even partially free counseling. Counseling services in the community serve mostly those who can afford to pay. For those who have health insurance, limited services may be only partially covered through managed care and EAPs (see chap. 1).

A wide variety of counseling services are available in the community, however. Unencumbered by a single institutional policy and any restrictions other than those imposed by managed care, community counseling offers a wider, more complex, and eclectic array of counseling services than is available in schools and colleges. Community counselors generally can work in a more flexible milieu than can counselors in educational settings.

The number of professionally trained community counselors has been steadily increasing. Most states now have some form of licensing for professional counselors. Moreover, increasing numbers of universities throughout the country offer master's degree programs that train counselors to work in the community.

Counseling services are also available in the workplace through EAPs for those employed in large companies. Various religious groups, as described in chapter 1 and later in this chapter, have also taken steps to provide counseling services for those who have no insurance and who cannot afford to pay high fees.

Many counselors and therapists acknowledge the impact of the social-cultural environment on the mental and physical health of individuals, families, and communities. Some family therapists, as discussed later, have extended family relationship issues into the broader social context. Likewise, some of those who have lost a loved one and some who are terminally ill are sharing the grieving process with community support groups, a sharing that continues well beyond the memorial service.

Increasing numbers of ethnic counselors have been making a significant impact on community counselor training and practice. They have been successfully leading the drive to incorporate multicultural counseling competencies into counselor training programs. They have also been raising counselor awareness about the need to consider and appreciate differences in the values, customs, and lifestyles of various ethnic groups in the community. Moreover, their emphasis on the dynamic interaction of individual, family, and community has been influencing the profession as a whole (see also chap. 14).

As part of this growing community awareness, neighborhood counseling services are emerging that range from teenage counseling centers to counseling in senior centers. At the same time in some communities various health agencies, heretofore separate, have been combining services: Some neighborhood medical facilities now include mental health services, and spiritual counseling is being combined with counseling and therapy as well as with medical care. Individual needs are being treated in conjunction with one's extended family, workplace, neighborhood, and community.

As part of the therapeutic healing process, war veterans, POWs, refugees, and torture victims are sharing their stories with others, and their stories are being integrated into the larger social-historical context of the country as a whole. Special therapeutic clinics and support groups have also formed in the community for those with addictions, those with attention-deficit-hyperactivity disorder, and those suffering from violence.

Community counseling has come to acknowledge that people are faced with transitions related not only to age, but also to marriage and family issues; loss of a job or home; a sudden death; spiritual needs; social, cultural, and economic conditions; and political upheavals.

AGE-RELATED COUNSELING

Because community counselors work with clients of all age levels, they must be familiar with the developmental needs, conflicts, and transitional phases of children, teenagers, young adults, adults in midlife, and older adults.

Children and Teenagers

Over the years schools have steadily improved their counseling services to meet the ever-growing needs of students. In recent years, however, professionals have realized that schools should not be the only place, nor have the sole responsibility for, offering counseling services to those at-risk children whose behavior dysfunctions tend to be generated and perpetuated by malfunctioning social conditions in the community.

Joint services have been successfully developed in many communities. A noteworthy example is the family counseling and therapy center built conjointly by Radford University and the Pulaski County High School in Virginia, as described in chapter 17.

Another example of joint services between school and community is an innovative program developed by high school counselor Bob Osterman in Bellingham, Washington, to help abused youths 10 to 18 years of age with anger management problems. The program, called Creative Concepts Ice Project, gained national attention in the ACA newsletter *Counseling Today*. The project teaches ice hockey to at-risk youths to help them express their anger constructively. The youths are referred by the Washington Department of Children and Family Services, private practitioners, and state juvenile probation officers and are first taught ice hockey skills by a retired professional hockey player, skills that build up their self-esteem. Osterman (cited in Guerra, 1998b) says:

> Ice hockey releases pent-up feelings of anger and frustration in a positive way. With the penalty box time and peer review, these kids learn ways of dealing constructively with the anger they feel. . . . These penalties are not only for violating ice hockey rules like high sticking or fighting, but for not doing homework, getting into a fight at school, and so forth. (p. 32)

Osterman carries out individual counseling during the game and group counseling after the game. When a youth is put into the penalty box for a specific time because of an infraction, Osterman goes over with him what was wrong and why it was wrong. Group counseling follows in the locker room after each game. The boys go over a videotape of the game to check on their playing skills and to review with Osterman and each other any infractions or misbehaviors that occurred in the game. The program is funded by state grants and by donations of money and ice hockey equipment from business and industry.

Some community agencies offer troubled youths a full range of services unavailable in the more limited, academically oriented school settings. One such example is Youth Eastside Services (YES) in Bellevue, Washington, a nonprofit neighborhood center that offers teenage counseling services. Fees are determined by use of a sliding scale; people are not refused services if they cannot afford to pay (R. Fitzgerald, personal communication, May 4, 1990).

Although its major focus is on treatment of alcohol and drug abuse, YES offers services to teenagers and their parents in such other areas as individual, group, and family counseling; crisis intervention; psychological education; consultation and support services; physical or sexual abuse; and general family conflicts. Groups and classes include support groups for children of alcoholics and/or drug-dependent parents, classes for families on drug/alcohol abuse, a support group for incest victims, anger management for youths, a group for adolescents with separated or divorced parents, a gay/lesbian adolescent group, and a class in building self-esteem for adolescents. YES staff, under the direction of the youth employment coordinator, also run workshops on job searches. Staff are given in-service training to work with diverse racial and cultural groups. YES staff have formed cooperative relationships with the schools, consulting with the school personnel and teaching courses in nearby school districts, particularly on drug and alcohol education. Casework and advocacy services are free to families who need help finding medical, legal, or financial services.

Another approach is taken by Michael Meade's (2004) Mosaic Multicultural Foundation, which offers troubled youth from inner-city ghettos weekend retreats throughout the year at various wilderness or urban centers in the Pacific Northwest and California. Impressed by what Mosaic has to offer troubled youth, poet Luis Rodriguez has been participating in their workshops and retreats for several years. "I haven't seen anything like it before. It's really about how to bring back the broken pieces of community through story, poetry, singing and other forms of art and practice. Each time Mosaic had a conference or retreat I could see these young people changing their lives. Something fundamental was happening for them" (Scher, 2002).

Young Adults

Only one-third of high school students go on to college. Thus, after age 18 most young adults lack free and easily accessible professional counseling services to explore career possibilities and deal with conflicts regarding personal development and social interactions and commitments. Now that counseling services have increased significantly in the community, they need to become more accessible and affordable to these young adults. Persons in their mid-20s and early 30s who have finished college or graduate school are also confronted with beginning a career, starting a family, developing relationships, rearing children, and developing personally and creatively.

Career Concerns

Client 1: Maggie is 18 years old and divorced. She dropped out of school to get married when she became pregnant, but she lost her baby in childbirth. After that, her marriage deteriorated. She has been working part time as a waitress and has been on and off welfare. She is discouraged about herself and her life so far and is worried about being overweight. She is looking for a full-time job but is uncertain about her job qualifications.

Response C–1: Maggie has taken a positive step by seeking help. Her problem has three related facets: (a) She lacks feelings of self-esteem, (b) she is seeking vocational help, and (c) she wants to lose weight. While exploring vocational opportunities, Maggie needs to explore family relationships that have contributed to her low self-esteem and self-defeating behavior. Another consideration is whether she has worked through feelings of grief about the loss of her baby. Vocational exploration could include using the Kuder Occupational Interest Survey (KOIS), the Self-Directed Search (SDS), and the General Aptitude Test Battery (GATB). The counselor should assess with Maggie her concerns about her weight. How much overweight is she? Has her weight increased during this period of unusual stress? If it appears that her weight gain is significant and interferes with her health and that she wants to take the steps necessary to lose weight, the counselor could refer her to another counselor who specializes in weight loss.

Client 2: Michael, who is 29 and single, is referred by the state employment office. He is a chemist who has held five jobs in the past 3 years. He is bright, energetic, and sardonic. He says that he has yet to find a good boss; he has either been fired or has left jobs because of friction with supervisors. He is not sure that chemistry is the right profession.

Response C–2: Most noticeable in Michael's case is his difficulty with authority figures. Anticipating that he will transfer these feelings to the counselor during counseling sessions, the counselor should confront him constructively about his relationship problems. Helping him assert his needs and express his feelings appropriately and constructively would constitute an important part of counseling. It might be helpful for him to role-play actual conflicts he has had with his bosses. While his relationship problems are being addressed, his career concerns can also be explored. Why did he choose chemistry? Was there any parental pressure? How competent and interested was he in his various jobs? The counselor could use interest and aptitude measures and explore occupations related to chemistry via a computerized occupational program.

Personal Concerns

Client 3: Nina is a 27-year-old lawyer. She is single, lives alone, and is a leader in the community. Her major concern relates to her uncertainty about what she wants for her future. She has made friends and enjoys their company but is reluctant to become involved in a long-term relationship. Yet she says she would like to have children and admits to feeling lonely at times.

Response C–3: Nina appears satisfied with her career; her main focus is on developing constructive relationships. A key factor is her ambivalence about committing herself to a long-term relationship. Exploration of family patterns may be productive in working with clients like Nina. How does she perceive her mother and father's relationship? Did she feel enmeshed in or too separate from the family? How well did the family communicate? These explorations could help reach her fears about commitment and her concerns about loneliness. Discussions are appropriate about the characteristics of the friends she cultivates and the quality of her relationships with them.

Client 4: Mona, 19, makes an appointment for counseling because of her inability to handle her grief over the loss of her mother and father in an automobile accident more than a year ago. She has frequent crying spells and is finding it difficult to handle her job as a clerk in a bank.

Response C–4: Mona needs help working through the feelings of loss at her parents' deaths. Grief counseling, which would permit release of anger and helplessness, is needed. In this process exploring the relationship with her family and family dynamics is important. Because sharing grief with other support persons can help her work through the grieving process, the counselor should refer her to a grief support group.

Interpersonal Conflicts and Concerns

Client 5: Mark, a 19-year-old, reveals that he has recently recognized and accepted that he is gay. He is having difficulty, however, telling his parents and friends about his sexual orientation. He is an only child and is concerned that his parents will oppose him.

Response C–5: Mark needs to consider whether he is ready to confront his parents at this time because he only recently recognized and accepted that he is gay and he is uncertain about how strongly his parents might react. The counselor should first help him explore his relationship with his parents to evaluate how flexible they actually are and whether this is an appropriate time to tell them. The counselor might role-play with him so that he can practice expressing his feelings authentically. He also needs help considering the consequences of rejection. If he decides to confront his parents and they do reject him, further counseling regarding his feelings of loss and abandonment will be necessary. If the family is ambivalent, family counseling may be helpful.

Adults at Midlife

The developmental concerns of middle-aged individuals relate primarily to job changes and loss of loved ones. Individuals may suddenly be faced with losing a job. Or they may experience the loss of parents, a divorce, or the breakup of the family. It is a time when individuals take stock of their accomplishments or lack of them, and for many persons it is a time ripe for a midlife crisis.

In the early 1990s persons faced with the high-tech revolution had to be retrained or retire. Job loss became a real concern for many middle-aged individuals. That trend has continued. Corporate mergers in an effort to downsize have caused further upheavals in the labor market. In the early 2000s the collapse of the high tech industry, the unexpected loss of pensions, and the recent trend of hiring skilled labor overseas while laying off white collar workers here have left abnormally high numbers of unemployed middle-aged workers. That ongoing job instability has seriously disturbed the well-being of many families and communities.

Adults in midlife also start evaluating their abilities as parents. They may feel troubled or guilty if their children have not become successful or happy adults or have not developed values or lifestyles compatible with their own.

Likewise, adults are troubled and anxious when they see their aging parents, who have been their models, become physically disabled or senile. Thus, besides coping with the developing needs and conflicts of their own children, they are having to decide how best to care for their aging parents as they become more incapacitated (see "Working With Aging Families" later in the chapter).

Another issue of primary concern for middle-aged adults is the change in gender roles that may begin to emerge at midlife. Men looking ahead to retirement may reduce their attention to work and begin to focus on home life. Women may show increasing interest in channeling their energies outside the home after the children leave. These reversals can lead to conflicts and friction in a marriage.

Career Concerns

The need to make a midlife career choice or career change may be complicated by related factors that arouse anxiety and apprehension. Counselors must have the professional capacity to help clients make decisions about career planning but must also possess the background to help them confront and work through personal uncertainties about their capacities to handle new demands in life.

Client 6: Jolene, 38, has been referred to the community counseling clinic by a friend. She has two children in school and has expressed interest in trying to develop a career. Jolene has had 1½ years of college and then worked for 2 years as a cashier in a department store before marriage. She is considering college or vocational training. Her husband is supportive but ambivalent. She, too, expresses ambivalence. She is anxious about her ability to do well in school and is uneasy about whether she is being fair to their children.

Response C–6: Jolene may need help recognizing that her anxious feelings about getting training and her ambivalent feelings about her responsibility for her own growth and her family's welfare are not unusual. She is contemplating a significant change in lifestyle that will take cooperative effort from the whole family. The counselor should help her explore her ambivalence about her plans. Does her uneasiness about the children have to do with what her husband and society expect from her as a mother and a wife? Counselor and client should discuss issues of child care, the sharing of household duties, and other necessary adjustments in lifestyle. Assuming that her and her husband's ambivalence is resolved and she decides she wants to go back to school, the counselor should help her explore career possibilities by suggesting that she take vocational interest and aptitude tests.

Client 7: Boris, 52, has been referred by the counselor at the Division of Vocational Rehabilitation. Boris worked as a repairer of heavy equipment until he suffered a heart attack. His physician told him that he could not continue in his current job but that he would be able to handle lighter jobs. Boris is quite shaken by his disability and the news that he can't resume the work he had enjoyed. His despondency has affected his relationship with his wife. He expresses a need to be employed but feels hopeless about the prospects of alternative jobs.

Response C–7: The counselor should help Boris express and work through his grief, anger, and despair at having to give up a job he enjoyed and help him express his feelings of anxiety about his physical incapacity and the need to begin a new, unfamiliar job at midlife. At the same time the counselor should help him start exploring alternative job possibilities by first asking him to describe the characteristics of his previous job that appealed to him and that he could still safely do now. Discovering that he can still perform valued tasks will serve as a significant motivator. The counselor can then help him explore occupational informational sources that match his interests and aptitudes. Boris's job skills and interests may be clear-cut enough to match with specific job alternatives. But if doubts arise, the counselor can suggest that he take interest and aptitude tests. After he has decided on some suitable alternative jobs, the counselor should send that information to the rehabilitation counselor, who will then arrange for appropriate job training or placement.

Personal Concerns

Client 8: Fran, a 49-year-old widow, is referred by her physician. She is a registered nurse who enjoys her work, but she expresses feelings of loneliness. Her husband died suddenly 2 years ago, and her two children have left home. She has doubts about how good a parent she has been; neither child finished college, and her daughter recently went through a difficult divorce. Fran has very few women or men friends. She feels uncomfortable with the few married couples she and her husband knew.

Response C–8: Fran has been left on her own after a long married life. Because she likes and functions well on her job, the counselor should concentrate on her concerns about loneliness and relationships and should refer her to group counseling for recently widowed women. The group offers an opportunity for her to bond with other women, work through her grief, share her uncomfortable feelings in social situations, and practice skills relating to others. In a group like this, her feelings of inadequacy as a parent can also be shared.

Interpersonal Conflicts and Concerns

Client 9: Kirstin and Joe are a couple in their 40s. Kirstin's mother, in her late 70s, has been living by herself since her husband died 6 years ago. She is losing her eyesight and her memory and sometimes becomes disoriented. Kirstin is considering taking her mother into their home; Joe believes that a retirement home or nursing home would be better. He has experienced friction over the years with his mother-in-law, and he says that Kirstin has suffered from headaches when she and her mother have been together. Kirstin works full time as a librarian, sometimes evenings and weekends.

Response C–9: The problem confronting Kirstin and Joe is very common. Although older persons often move into assisted-living quarters, such facilities are expensive and frequently inadequate. Kirstin's and Joe's differing attitudes about her mother need to be addressed. Kirstin's compassionate desire to care for her mother in Kirstin and Joe's home, which counters the trend of institutionalizing older people, should be recognized. Joe's emotional reactions to his mother-in-law need to be explored. Are his feelings distorted, or is he being more realistic in the light of their situation? The counselor should help them address their differences as they consider their options, including the degree of care her mother needs, the suitability of retirement and nursing homes in their area, available space in their home, adjusting Kirstin's work schedule to care for her mother, the availability of day care facilities for older people, and the availability of visiting nurses who assist older people in their homes.

Older Adults

Older adults are the most heterogeneous of all the age-groups. They span an age range of about 30 years and represent a multitude of individual differences in socioeconomic status, experience, knowledge, skills, health, intergenerational family relationships, and motivation. For this reason a separate chapter (see chap. 15) deals with their diverse needs.

Because 80% of older adults are self-sufficient and healthy enough to take care of themselves, the major concern for most older people is finding ways to stay productive and useful in a society that has retired them out of the occupational mainstream. The counseling and therapy profession and other health care professionals have started to address their needs, but retraining has been slow. Gerontologists, for example, who have been considered the specialists of older adults, have been trained by and large to work with long-term care patients in assisted-living facilities. Thus, they tend to view all older people as being in need of assistance in one way or another.

The goals of counseling—helping older adult clients exercise control over their lives, become empowered, and find new opportunities to grow—should be the same for older adults as they are for younger people (Waters, 1984). Counselors can help older adults cope with the many transitions they go through in later life, including changing their relationship with a spouse when one or both retire, developing new relationships with their adult children, working with grief over the loss of a spouse or friends, dealing with uncertainties about new grandparent roles, moving from a long-time home to a smaller apartment, and overcoming fear of abandonment.

Counselors must be prepared to notice signs of despondency among older people. Suicide rates are highest among the elderly over 75, increasing among those in their 80s (Westefeld et al., 2000). Reasons for the high rates of suicide among older adults are complex: feelings of helplessness and hopelessness, chronic disabilities and pain, and adverse reactions to prescription drugs. Suicide can claim even those older adults who have loving support from family and friends (Westefeld et al., 2000; see chap. 15).

Senior centers are excellent places for counseling services for older adults. Sue Grady (1990), a certified counselor at the Mature Minglers Multipurpose Senior Center in Birmingham, Michigan, points out that the senior center is an essential part of the community and therefore can respond to clients' problems in the social context in which the seniors live. Moreover, a well-trained senior center staff can reduce the negative influence of ageism. The staff can assume the roles of change agents or can be advocates for seniors by encouraging community leaders to improve social services such as transportation systems and home care. The staff can, as well, use nontraditional counseling methods that fit the particular needs of the senior centers. For example, the staff can welcome drop-ins, carry on counseling outside the office, and set up spontaneous support groups or visit homes when necessary.

Senior centers are also the obvious place to offer group counseling, a particularly effective way for older adults to express their concerns, because a group can share common losses and gain intimacy and a renewed sense of community spirit. Groups can be organized around specific topics, such as grieving, health, loneliness, creative expression through music or art, or life review (Thomas & Martin, 1992; see also chap. 15).

An excellent example of a worthwhile and productive senior center activity was mentioned briefly earlier. At the Whitney Senior Center in St. Cloud, Minnesota, retired counselor educator and octogenarian Willis E. Dugan created an innovative work project called the Wood Block and Toy Project. This project allows both able-bodied senior citizen volunteers and nursing home and adult care elderly to engage in a productive activity—making toys for children (Dugan, 1993). "This is an example of a type of senior volunteer activity that produces feelings of belonging, a sense of contributing and improved self-esteem on the part of elderly participants" (Willis E. Dugan, personal communication, July 12, 1997).

Twice a month senior volunteers meet at the Whitney Senior Center Workshop with patients from nursing homes and adult care centers. Under the supervision of retired senior volunteers, these elderly patients sand and paint precut wood blocks and toys. The toys are then distributed to children at the holiday season. "The block sets and wooden toys are distributed by United Fund to Head Start programs, libraries, church schools, Woman houses, medical clinics, welfare offices and schools" (Willis E. Dugan, personal communication, July 12, 1997).

Significantly, Dugan, who was 88 at the time of our interview, was one of the oldest living professional counselor educators, a long-time leader in the field who had served as executive director of APGA (now ACA) from 1966 to 1971. Acting as a model elder counselor educator, he demonstrated how retired professional counselors can continue to help others be productive and generative in the community.

Client 10: Fred, who is 67, makes an appointment because he is feeling restless, bored, and mildly depressed. He retired after an active career as a salesman but had not made any plans for retirement. He expresses general malaise and a recent sharp decrease in sexual potency. His wife, 55, is employed at a travel agency. She enjoys her job and has a great deal of contact with people. He says he is happy about her job but also feels some resentment about her constant activity.

Response C–10: Fred made an appointment for counseling on his own, a positive first step. He needs an opportunity to express his feelings of loss of identity and loss of purpose in life, which occur to most people when they retire. He also needs an opportunity to develop attitudes and strategies for building a revised lifestyle that will include sufficient activity to help him regain self-respect. He can explore how to use the talents, attitudes, and experiences that contributed to his success as a salesman to develop activities that will give him personal satisfaction and social recognition, such as involvement in community service. He also needs to confront how he can become involved in the home. Then he might more fully support his wife's activities, and she might better understand his confusion and help him work through his resentment and uncertainties. To attain this mutual understanding, Fred and his wife could profit from marital counseling as a supplement to individual counseling.

FAMILY COUNSELING AND THERAPY

Work with families and couples is paramount in community mental health services, especially because public schools and colleges do only limited amounts of family and marital counseling. Families have a great variety of presenting problems. Persons with alcohol and drug problems, children of alcoholics and adult children of alcoholics, the aging and the adult children of the aging, children with emotional and behavioral problems, pregnant teenagers, and families of gays and lesbians may all involve family counseling or consultation. Counseling services for normally functioning families have become increasingly available, including state and county youth and family agencies, religious-sponsored counseling centers, EAPs, HMOs, and privately sponsored family centers. Some feminist and ethnic family counselors, as described later, approach family counseling differently from the approach of traditional family therapists.

Job-Related Family Issues

Until recently, family counselors and therapists in the community had generally ignored the relationship of work issues to family breakdowns or dysfunctions (Bielski, 1996):

> Until very recently, most therapists considered the practical details of their clients' work lives not much more relevant than the color of their curtains, or only worthy of passing attention if they revealed spillover symptoms of deeper relational problems. (p. 25)

After interviewing several prominent family counselors, Bielski (1996) concluded that during the 1990s increasing numbers of therapists began to recognize the importance of work-related pressures on family dynamics. He writes that nationally known family therapist Betty Carter became aware of these issues in the early 1990s:

> Betty Carter remembers her own dawning recognition some years ago that the lived experience of work, and the enormous social and personal pressures work encompassed in the late 20th-century America, were as important to consider in therapy as family-of-origin issues, marital interaction or substance abuse. (p. 25)

Family therapists shared with Bielski (1996) incidents from their practices in which family dysfunction or marital friction related to work issues: an executive losing a high-powered job through company downsizing with no commensurate job available; a 20-year employee being laid off with no new job in sight; individuals who overidentified with jobs at the expense of their relationships; women overworked in two-career families. That career- and job-related issues have an impact on personal development and well-being has long been acknowledged by professional counselors and counseling associations in their definitions of counseling and the counselor role. That family therapists are incorporating these ideas into family dynamics is a noteworthy occurrence in the counseling and therapy field.

Working With Aging Families

According to Sandmaier (1998), "Working with aging families is a major frontier of family therapy. It is where we ourselves must come of age" (p. 25). Many family therapists are undergoing fundamental changes in their approach to issues of adults and their aging parents; some now advocate that it is possible to facilitate growth and development, particularly as it relates to changing their relationship. "The question at hand, then is how can this juncture in the family life cycle be transformed from an emphasis on adjusting to loss and disappointments to a focus on growth and possibility?" (p. 26).

Family therapist Terry Hargrave (cited in Sandmaier, 1998) explains that the key to counseling aging families is to shift the relationship so that there is more give-and-take, more of a mutual caregiving, with the elder person still considered worthy of providing wisdom and nurturance to his or her adult child. "Hargrave is convinced that the recognition of an older person's continuing capacity to give to their families is absolutely critical to successful work with older families" (Sandmaier, 1998, p. 29).

Family therapist Virginia Abrams (cited in Sandmaier, 1998) concurs. Abrams believes that this late stage in the aging parent and adult child relationship is a crucial time for engendering renewal:

> At no other juncture in life's journey . . . were children asked to so profoundly alter their roles vis-à-vis their parents. So nearly universal is the need to negotiate this shift that it is considered a bona fide adult developmental stage—achieving "filial maturity." (p. 30)

For most, she contends, intergenerational conflicts and misunderstandings between middle-aged adults and aging parents can be attended to with effective therapeutic help. A staff clinician at a community mental health center in Manhattan called Support Program for Older People, Abrams doesn't let distance between parties deter her. In some cases she reaches out by telephone to help reconnect and heal old wounds between an adult child and an elderly parent in her effort to generate last-chance attempts for renewal.

Ethnic Family Counseling

In working with ethnic families, counselors must be aware of differing cultural values; varying cultural expectations regarding gender roles; the degree of involvement of the extended family; the influence of religion; residence in an ethnic neighborhood; the recentness of immigration; and the effects of socioeconomic status.

Most African American families traditionally have had strong bonds of kinship that offer support to family members who are struggling for economic and social survival. "Therapists must . . . be willing to expand the definition of family to a more extended kinship system. Relations often live in close proximity and expect to rely on one another in time of need" (Baruth & Manning, 1999, p. 153). However, family counselors are working with increasing numbers of single-parent African American families headed by women. Conflicts between husbands and wives escalate when families move away from their kinship roots and when there is high unemployment, alcoholism, and poverty.

African American counselors recommend using pragmatic approaches in family counseling:

> Therapies with the most promise for African American families set aside abstract theoretical notions of how to conduct family therapy. Models that adopt active, intervention-oriented strategies emphasizing social functioning over inner feelings are more appropriate. (Baruth & Manning, 1999, p. 153)

The insistence of Asian American families on loyalty to the family tends to make these families unwilling to engage in family counseling. The father is typically the spokesman for the family, so children and wives may be reluctant to bring up significant problems in the family to avoid shaming the father (Baruth & Manning, 1999).

Hispanic families tend to respond more positively to family counseling than to individual counseling because of their strong family ties and the feeling that family members have a responsibility to help each other. Close-knit Hispanic families respond well to counseling (Baruth & Manning, 1999; Garcia-Preto, 1982). Family therapist Ramon Rojano (Markowitz, 1997), as the director of the Department of Social and Health Services in Hartford, Connecticut, capitalized on his Hispanic roots and effectively extended the concept of family counseling to family community counseling (see chaps. 10 and 14).

Native American families, particularly those living on reservations, are also close-knit, with considerable intergenerational bonding. Family members and extended family tend to work together to resolve their problems. They generally refrain from seeking counseling, but when they do seek it, their close kinship tends to bring about positive results beyond those of individual counseling (Baruth & Manning, 1999; Trimble, Fleming, Beauvais, & Jumper-Thurman, 1996). In a review of the literature, Trimble et al. (1996) found that counselors who work with Native Americans and who include the family's social network tend to be more effective. Baruth and Manning (1999) note:

> When the counselor is able to engage the family, he or she should proceed cautiously to allow family members to deal with problems at their own pace. Also, an overbearing or manipulative counselor will almost certainly alienate Native American clients. (p. 366)

Feminist Family Counseling

Back in the late 1970s family therapists Betty Carter, Peggy Papp, Olga Silverstein, and Marianne Walters formed what came to be called the Women's Project in Family Therapy. They got together to counteract family therapy's male-dominated perspective and to develop alternative approaches to family therapy (see chap. 10). In so doing, they have persuaded family therapists over the years to move family issues beyond the narrow confines of a family system to include the family's social-cultural milieu. They also have encouraged family therapists to help their clients move beyond simply airing personal grievances against their parents, beyond playing the victim, and help clients begin to take responsibility for their lives. "Therapists have been accused in recent years of encouraging a culture of grievance in which everybody blames their problems on somebody else and sees him or herself as a victim" (Simon, 1997, p. 66).

As part of this task, they have challenged family therapists who encourage clients to blame the parents, especially the mother. But it has not been easy, they say, to change the long-held attitudes of most family therapists. Just when they think that professional family therapists have changed the way they think about gender issues in general and mothers in particular, Marianne Walters says that "some therapists will show a tape where a mother is blamed or put down or ignored or even humiliated, and much of the audience will not even notice" (Simon, 1997, p. 60).

In working with family and relationship cases, the primary issue for these family therapists is to help clients reassess their attitudes toward their mothers. Olga Silverstein says that during counseling she notices the way a man relates to his wife and from that draws links to the way he relates or related to his mother: "I believe that the basic essential relationship in which a man cuts off emotionally is the one with his mother" (quoted in Simon, 1997, p. 63).

As Betty Carter points out, males have been brought up in the culture to separate and become autonomous from their mothers. So how can they know how to relate well or connect with their wives? Carter adds that men typically learned to block their feelings in their relationship with their parents. The father was usually wrapped up in his work, and the mother kept her distance emotionally because that was what she thought she was supposed to do. Carter generally starts with the man's relationship with his father because the man wants to, and it's easier for him, too. Then, later, she shifts to his relationship with his mother, a more difficult task but more to the crux of the problem.

> Then I shift to the mother, which is a tougher deal, but that's where the real payoff comes. I've had any number of turned off men who, when they finally did go back to the mother that they were maligning or ignoring or whatever, found her eager to respond and to validate them. . . . [I]t often changes the man's whole way of relating to everyone. (quoted in Simon, 1997, p. 63)

Sexual Abuse Family Counseling

One community-oriented treatment program for sexually abused families is the Giarretto Institute, a private, nonprofit clinic and training center in San Jose, California, founded by Henry Giarretto and his wife, Anna. Over the years they have expanded their work to other clinics throughout the country; the Giarretto model has been used in 160 clinics worldwide (Berry, 2003). Therapists, probation officers, county officials, and former patients work together to treat the family and also to create a sense of extended family. The goal is to change destructive family dynamics while reunifying or keeping the family intact (J. Szybalski, personal communication, June 12, 1993).

The core of the Giarretto treatment program is its unusual type of group counseling, in which each family member joins separate groups: fathers with fathers, mothers with mothers, and children with children. Another unique feature about this institute is that former patients serve as an extended family support system. Former client families living in the community are coupled with families in treatment and are involved as consultants, models, and support for each family member and the family as a whole. Former clients give lectures and workshops in the community to publicize the treatment program and to raise funds.

Group treatment for mothers of incest victims is described by Landis and Wyre (1984). The group therapist is a woman, and group members are self-referred or are referred by a state agency or other counselors or therapists. The women range in age from 25 to 45 and may be single, remarried, or still married to the spouses who committed the sexual abuse. Issues include anger and lack of trust toward men, poor communication with abused daughters, and difficulty developing intimate relationships. Inappropriate roles and communication styles learned in families of origin are discussed. These women confront their own passivity and its role in failing to protect their daughters. They are taught how to approach their daughters about their maternal feelings. Male partners join the women in the later stage of the group.

Domestic Violence Therapy

Innovative psychoeducational programs have been developed for women who are domestic violence victims. One such program, conducted by family therapist Rhea Almeida at the Institute for Family Services in Somerset, New Jersey, breaks with traditional practice in that the abusers, as well as the abused, are involved in group psychoeducational activities (Wylie, 1996). About 60% to 70% of abusers enter the program voluntarily. The remainder are court-mandated.

Unlike some therapeutic interventions that legal authorities and women's rights advocates alike distrust for allegedly "coddling" abusers, the Institute combines tough-minded political and social re-education with an uncompromising insistence that the mandated batterer toe the line of treatment or face expulsion from the program. (Wylie, 1996, p. 60)

The typical program, which lasts about 8 months, begins with a series of informational sessions in the form of videos and discussions about the causes of abuse. These meetings are followed with group sessions for abusers and abused, both separate and together. Members of various ethnic groups who have successfully completed the program act as cultural consultants and sponsors for each participant throughout the program.

A different approach—a wellness model—is suggested for counselors working with battered women in shelters. Counselors aim at helping residents not only develop survivor skills but also become empowered. In this model efforts are made to develop the social, occupational, physical, intellectual, emotional, and spiritual growth of these women (Donaghy, 1995). Staff counselor Donaghy (1995) suggests, for example: "Shelter staff can encourage women and assist them in enrollment in training programs, if desired. Staff can also offer women instruction in writing resumes and conducting employment interviews" (p. 9). Staff also provide some counseling and, when needed, refer clients to outside counseling services.

Grief Counseling

Coping with death and dying, facing the loss of a loved one, and working through the grief process are discussed in chapter 15 because these experiences are more imminent and occur more often with older adults. However, the trauma of terminal illness, the loss of a loved one, and the need to grieve occur at all stages of life. The dying and death of an individual affects family, friends, and sometimes the whole community.

When persons die early in life or in the prime of life, "before their time," their deaths are generally more traumatic for their loved ones than is the loss of an elderly person. Most distressing is a parent's loss of a young child, a child's loss of a parent, or the loss of a spouse early in marriage. Terminal illness resulting from cancer, AIDS, or other diseases at whatever age causes emotional trauma for the dying person, the family, and close friends of both. Suicide or accidental or unexpected death also creates emotional trauma.

Taking the time to work through grief is crucial. Moreover, grief work, according to O'Malley (1998), should preferably be carried out and shared in the community, rather than in a therapist's office. But because community support for those mourning the death of a loved one has generally been unavailable and not even customary in our society, counselors and therapists, he says, need to fill the gap. They can do so by offering grief counseling, developing grief workshops, and encouraging and developing community efforts to attend to grieving persons.

A treatment plan depends on the individual's cultural background, particular circumstances, and developmental stage. The grief process for children, for instance, is different from that for adults because children are unable cognitively to process the loss of, say, a parent on their own (Golden, 1998). A case described by counselor Patrick O'Malley in

Case Studies in Child and Adolescent Counseling (Golden, 1998) concerns his work with a 9-year-old boy whose father committed suicide. According to O'Malley, the boy needed to work through grief throughout this crucial developmental period of his life. Grief counseling treatment carried him through 7 years, through most of adolescence. O'Malley describes how he helped the boy work through depression, acting-out behaviors, and difficulty in expressing his grief. O'Malley used brief, intermittent counseling with an eclectic approach based on psychodynamic therapy combined with behavioral, solution-focused, and psychoeducational techniques.

In accordance with O'Malley's (1998) emphasis on the importance of community support of families in mourning, some churches in the Seattle area sponsor grief workshops. Such workshops are helpful at Christmastime, a time that is especially difficult for individuals and families who have lost loved ones. These workshops are led by pastoral counselors or other mental health professionals who accompany church services of remembrance. In one church different grief groups are offered for children, teenagers, and parents (Iwasaki, 1998).

SPIRITUAL COUNSELING: SEARCHING FOR MEANING

Although many members of the counseling profession have considered the spiritual concerns of individuals an important part of counseling, the counseling profession as a whole has generally ignored the significance of the spiritual dimension to a client's well-being (Bart, 1998; Burke & Mirante, 1995). Increasing numbers of counselors and therapists, however, are acknowledging the importance of spiritual matters. The *DSM-IV-TR* (American Psychiatric Association, 2000), for example, added a section indicating that religious and spiritual malaise warrants treatment. "Examples include distressing experiences that involve loss in questioning of faith, problems associated with conversion to a new faith, or questioning of other spiritual values that may not necessarily be related to an organized church religious institution" (Burke & Miranti, 1995, p. 2).

The various ways in which spiritual concerns of individuals are being addressed in the mental health field are presented in a book of readings by Burke and Miranti called *Counseling: The Spiritual Dimension* (1995). One of its contributors, Ingersoll (1995), discusses how counselors can enhance the counseling process with those clients who have strong religious beliefs different from their own: "First, affirm the importance of the clients' spirituality in their lives. Second, attempt to enter client worldviews with congruent vocabulary and imagery . . . Last, counselors need to be willing to consult with other 'healers' in clients' lives" (p. 14).

Additional guidelines for counselors working with clients from different cultures with varying spiritual beliefs have been developed by Bishop (1995). He presents seven guidelines that are summarized here: Counselors must (a) assure each client that her or his religious beliefs are an important part of the process; thus, religious values become part of resolving the problem. To be effective, counselors need to (b) educate themselves about different cultures and religious values and (c) integrate them into their practice. Counselors must also (d) interact with diverse individuals and groups in the community, (e) explore and articulate their own religious beliefs, (f) be cognizant of any resistance to religious issues that clients bring up, and (g) speak in a straightforward manner regarding their own beliefs and the beliefs of clients.

Counselor educators led by Burke and Miranti (1995) have developed a set of spiritual competencies to be used in counselor training. The Council for Accreditation of Counseling and Related Education Programs (CACREP) has shown interest in incorporating these ideas into counselor training standards (Bart, 1998).

Pastoral counseling institutes have been forming liaisons with university training centers. Graduate interns in pastoral counseling now work in pastoral counseling clinics in the community under supervision. The Danielson Pastoral Counseling Institute in Boston, for example, supports an outpatient mental health clinic and is affiliated with Boston University in a teaching and training program for doctoral and postdoctoral students of pastoral counseling and ministry, clinical psychology, and counseling education. The institute's training program and clinics are accredited by the Americans Association of Pastoral Counselors (AAPC) as well as by the APA and are licensed by the Department of Public Health as a mental health clinic (Danielsen, 2003).

Most major religious groups in Seattle, Washington, offer counseling services, which focus primarily on the normal concerns of individuals and families—Jewish, Catholic, Presbyterian, Lutheran, Methodist, Baptist, Episcopalian, and Unitarian (see chap. 1). Although sponsored by specific religious faiths or denominations, these counseling centers are generally open to all faiths in terms of counseling staff and clients served. In an effort to network services, directors of those counseling centers sponsored by mainline Protestant churches meet monthly to share cases and to discuss mutual problems.

The Presbyterian Counseling Service in Seattle provides services throughout the city for the normal concerns of individuals, groups, and families (D. Anderson, personal communication, May 21, 1993; see also chap. 1). These counseling centers, which employ 24 professionals, include counselors, social workers, marriage and family counselors, pastoral counselors, and psychologists with master's or doctoral degrees. All are licensed or certified by the state of Washington and/or by appropriate professional associations. Therapists on the staff have a wide range of psychological theoretical backgrounds. About 25% of clients are Presbyterian, and 25% have no religious affiliation.

AAPC-certified counselors in religious-sponsored services such as these are ethically bound not to persuade or proselytize clients in any way. However, all are expected to respond to clients' spiritual concerns. Although certified pastoral counselors hold to the AAPC ethical standards (see chap. 1), not all pastoral counselors are certified. At some places of worship, pastoral counseling may be available only to members of the congregation, or counselors may try to evangelize or try to convert persons to their particular faith.

Ethnic Counselors and Spirituality

Many major ethnic groups consider spiritual and religious matters a very important part of their lives. Increasing numbers of ethnic counselors and therapists in the past decade—particularly Hispanic, Native American, and African American—have maintained strong spiritual values and close identification with family and community, thereby affecting the counseling profession by acknowledging that spiritual values are integral to life.

At a meeting of the Washington Association for Spiritual Ethical and Religious Values in Counseling in the autumn of 1992, for example, most participants were of ethnic background. Panel members represented a broad spectrum of religious and cultural backgrounds from the local community: Talulah Pinkham, a Yakima Indian and supervisor of Indian Health Services; the Reverend Mitch Weary, a Black Baptist pastor; Paula Mead, a counselor at the Westside Christian Counseling Center; and Carlos Carillos, born and raised in Mexico, now with a master's degree in counseling and working with local farm workers. The Yakima Valley includes the largest Indian reservation in the state and perhaps the state's largest group of Hispanic farm laborers. Their topic was "How Does Religiosity Help or Hinder the Counseling Process?"

Although they debated at length whether *religiosity* or *spirituality* was a better term, all concurred that issues of religiosity or spirituality help the counseling process. In some Black, Hispanic, and Native American communities, they pointed out, spirituality is often the only avenue to reach troubled persons because a negative stigma is attached to secular therapy in many of these communities (see also chap. 14).

Spiritual Retreats

Innumerable retreats for spiritual guidance or reawakening have sprung up around the country, sponsored by counselors, creative arts therapists, teams of artists and therapists, and various spiritual and religious leaders and healing specialists. Many private institutes, such as Hollyhock Farm on remote Cortes Island in British Columbia, schedule ongoing May-to-October holistic and spiritual workshops and retreats.

The Women of Wisdom Foundation of Seattle sponsors an annual 10-day conference in the city, featuring a variety of multicultural spiritual leaders. Its February 1999 conference included Starhawk, Luisah Teish, Jeanne Achterberg, Elena Avila, and Sandra Ingerman. At this conference seven on-site professional counselors were available free of charge or by donation. All were experienced, master's-level counselors.

For some people the personal experience of spiritual transformation and communal bonding does not last once they return home and go back to work; they may feel let down and vaguely disgruntled. Persons who united so closely at retreats may never see each other again. On-site counselors, such as those who were available at the Women of Wisdom conference, can serve as a means for participants to make the transition back to ordinary life.

Clinical psychologist and Tibetan Buddhist monk Jack Kornfield (1993) acknowledges the difficult transition from spiritual wilderness retreat back to frenetic urban lifestyle and offers helpful suggestions to ease the painful shift: "It requires patience. We must recognize that transitions can be long processes" (p. 180). In this process first one should acknowledge the loss and learn to let go; second, one should set aside regular periods of time alone for meditation; and third, one should arrange to meet regularly with others who have been to similar retreats. He also encourages individuals to use the pain of return as a learning experience: "When we return from a quiet contemplative period, we will often see the pain of the world, our own and others', in a more clear and undeniable way. This is actually part of our spiritual path, to see clearly and open our hearts to it all" (p. 181).

As Kornfield suggests, many persons who have been to similar retreats are arranging to meet regularly back in their hometowns. Community counselors who have been at these workshops and retreats and who understand what goes on can help participants integrate their experiences into community counseling services and workshops. The national magazine *Wingspan,* which focuses on the mythopoetic men's movement, offers guidelines on organizing and developing groups in communities.

SOCIAL, CULTURAL, AND POLITICAL TRANSITIONS

The numerous mental health services that are now focusing on the social, cultural, and political concerns of a person's life have added a new perspective to counseling and related mental health services. Such services have broadened the profession's outlook to include an awareness of one's psychosocial relationship with the community. Numerous issues are being raised and addressed that link an individual's personal and interpersonal concerns with external difficulties, such as loss of job or home; death of a loved one; social, economic, or cultural barriers; and political upheavals and traumas. As a result, many individual and group counseling services specifically related to social-cultural transitions are developing in communities and neighborhoods throughout the country.

Career Development and Work Adjustment

Many counselors have emphasized for many years that an individual's work-related concerns continue throughout life and that complex social and environmental factors affect job performance and satisfaction (Entine, 1976; Heddesheimer, 1976; Nugent, 1981; Rappoport, 1976). These are essential issues that both career counselors and other counselors need to address.

According to Hershenson (1996), most career counselors tend to focus only on career choice and give little attention to issues of job adjustment. To encourage counselors to work with these much-needed issues, Hershenson has developed a therapeutic model in which he delineates the highly complex personal and social factors that affect one's work adjustment. His model includes three components: work personality, work competencies, and work goals. He also describes how environmental and contextual factors—such as family, training, and cultural and social relationships—affect an individual's work progress.

"The first task for the counselor is one of comprehensive assessment; and the first part of that assessment is to determine whether the work adjustment problem is primarily one of work role behavior, task performance, worker satisfaction, or some combination of the three" (Hershenson, 1996, p. 443). Once the assessment is made, the counselor can decide what treatment is best: If it is a personality problem, then one-to-one counseling is suggested; if it is a matter of developing competency skills, then educational skill development is in order; if the problem is with the boss, then perhaps assertiveness training would be effective. In each case the counselor must also look into what impact the client's family life, training, and social relationships have on the problem. Family values and attitudes, for example, are taken into consideration to assess the degree to which they may be barriers to client effectiveness and, further, the likelihood that such barriers can be changed or resolved (Hershenson, 1996).

Life Skills Development

Life skills development is an important component of effective career development; it involves helping clients learn skills to maintain and enhance their feeling of well-being in all aspects of life. Group work, both group counseling and group instruction, is a particularly useful way to help individuals learn effective life skills. Group counseling is offered in areas such as stress management, empowerment, problem solving, anger control, coping with career transitions, sleep problems, and weight loss. These groups tend to be problem-specific with relatively homogeneous groups, in which persons share emotions and experiences and receive support. Counselors often use cognitive-behavioral techniques, relaxation exercises, and assertiveness training.

Life skills development centers offer classes and workshops on body awareness, nutrition, relaxation, assertion, yoga, tai chi, and transcendental meditation. Holistic and wellness programs are popular and lend themselves to courses teaching self-improvement techniques. Courses may be taught by mental health counselors, holistic counselors, psychologists, social workers, or persons specially trained in a certain discipline.

Rehabilitation Counseling

The Center for Comprehensive Care in Seattle is an association of rehabilitation and preventive health care services on First Hill Medical Campus, the location of the city's major hospitals and medical facilities. Geared primarily to rehabilitation, the center is a federation of several association groups, including the Northwest Counseling Associates. Here, a wide variety of services assist and retrain patients to reenter the workforce and to resume normal life functions. Besides physical therapies, chronic care programs, and alternative therapies such as biofeedback, massage, and acupuncture, the center provides psychosocial and occupational services, including individual, group, and family counseling; counseling related to physical health, work adjustment, or disability; social and family issues counseling; varied specialized counseling, including career planning and adjustment issues involving legal and financial issues; stress, pain, and addictions management; and coping with trauma, including personal injury, death of a loved one, and posttraumatic stress disorder.

Multicultural Issues

Most ethnic individuals tend to be closely tied to their cultural roots, their families of origin, extended families, religion, and community. These social-cultural ties have significantly influenced the approach of most ethnic counselors to their practice. The strong sense of community that many, if not most, ethnic counselors have, which extends their connections beyond self and family, is a good model for all community counselors and their clients.

Family therapist Ramon Rojano's Hispanic background, for example, has strongly influenced his professional practice. As director of the Department of Social and Health Services (DSHS) in Hartford, Connecticut, Rojano and his staff of 300 employees work with the hard-core inner-city poor who are primarily of mixed ethnic backgrounds. Formerly a practicing psychiatrist and family therapist from Colombia, Rojano makes family systems therapy work in the slums by broadening the concept of family to include the community as a whole. Calling it *community family therapy,* he focuses on empowerment strategies and thus helps clients learn how to govern their own lives within their community. "His goal is to use his understanding of helping systems to reconnect his clients to their community" (Markowitz, 1997, p. 32). "Therapists too often ignore the rest of the world outside their offices—the schools, courts, public assistance programs, prisons and all other systems that shape the everyday lives of poor clients" (Markowitz, 1997, p. 29).

Rojano has also changed the image of the DSHS in Hartford. Welfare agencies have gained a bad reputation: Taxpayers are disillusioned that welfare money, instead of helping people out of the ghetto, seems instead to perpetuate their remaining there, dependent and helpless (Markowitz, 1997). Rojano's answer "is to turn the large dehumanizing bureaucratic systems that can make people feel small and helpless into a kind of village that rehumanizes the helping process and ultimately makes it obsolete" (Markowitz, 1997, p. 32).

As DSHS director, Rojano incorporates the family therapy model into his community family therapy, which helps individuals become empowered within their community system, rather than trying to find ways to remove them from their community.

> The new model has to include not only finding the resources poor families need to survive, like child care, jobs, food stamps, housing, but pathways to help clients become the experts on their own lives, figuring out their own goals and developing plans to achieve them. (Markowitz, 1997, p. 29)

Rojano's convictions are based on the way he grew up within a large extended family in a close-knit community of Barranquilla, Colombia. As Markowitz (1997) points out,

> Maybe it's no coincidence that some of the most committed and passionate family therapists working in the inner cities are immigrants from Latin countries, where a person's world is first centered on family and then networked into the bonds of extended kin, neighborhoods, villages. (p. 29)

Rojano's focus on vocational training and placement seems unusual to many family therapists today; as Rojano points out, today's therapists think it odd that his primary therapeutic strategy is to get a client a job (Markovitz, 1997). They wonder why a counselor should aim at getting a person a job in the middle of a family crisis. But as Rojano says, "'Economic therapy' is one of the best remedies for family problems. With a job and the emotional support of therapy, [the client] would experience more control and direction in her life" (p. 33).

Rojano also helps parents learn how to become participants in the community by providing promising individuals with leadership training, which includes such basics as civics classes and public speaking and classes that teach how to organize and go about creating social change. "For Rojano the biggest enemy of the poor is the isolation that living in poverty can breed" (Markowitz, 1997, p. 32).

A different aspect of ethnic counseling is emerging among some African Americans. According to Jones (1998), increasing numbers of middle-class Blacks are seeking counseling largely because more Black clergy support counseling, more Black mental health professionals are available, and successful Black lifestyles have severed the link to extended families, the usual source of help.

Many concerns of both Blacks and Whites in the middle and upper classes are similar: "How do you find happiness while striving for success? How do you balance work with kids?" (Jones, 1998, p. 2A). The problems of Blacks are complicated, however, by forces related to race. Some Blacks who obtain success feel the burden of having to be exemplary representatives of their race. Others find race an impediment to getting jobs in line with their training and skills and an impediment, as well, to advance on the job:

> Blacks' struggles are made worse by the undercurrent of race, such as the feelings one must be a standard bearer for an entire group of people. Professional disappointments run deeper when skin color appears to be the only thing holding you back. (Jones, 1998, p. 2A)

Increasing numbers of well-trained Black counselors and psychologists and church-sponsored counseling services in Black communities are emerging in cities throughout the country. Thus, increasing numbers of middle-class Blacks feel more comfortable seeking help. They recognize, as well, that family love and support are often not enough to help them resolve problems, especially because many have moved away from their families of origin. In such cases, as Jones (1998) points out, they benefit from the objective service of trained professionals.

Traumas of Poverty and Political Upheaval

Because of adverse social, economic, or political conditions, entire groups of people are particularly vulnerable to serious emotional or behavioral disorders. At-risk factors discussed here are related to poverty and the trauma resulting from political upheaval. Without help crises are apt to occur, precipitating individuals into suicide, crime, or violence. Some mental health counselors, recognizing that the rising numbers of indigent people are a social issue and a civic responsibility, are drawing together with community leaders and the public to help serve and alleviate the needs of the poor.

Development of Comprehensive Neighborhood Health Centers

One of the most significant trends in recent mental health practice has been the development of comprehensive health care services for those without health insurance and those who cannot afford to pay high fees. Many of these centers combine medical health care, mental health counseling, and social services. Liaison services have also formed between universities and neighborhood communities to offer a wide variety of counseling services. Pastoral counseling centers and institutes and the community family therapy system developed in Hartford, Connecticut, discussed earlier, are examples of liaisons forming to address the needs of the poor.

Another example of a comprehensive neighborhood health clinic, the Pike Place Market Medical Clinic in Seattle, Washington, demonstrates the need for and the advantages of combining mental health services with medical and social services in one facility to serve a particular neighborhood. This clinic is open to all individuals regardless of age, race, religion, or gender, but because of its location near older adult retirement homes, over 75% who seek counseling there are older adults (Lustbader, 1990). In her discussion of this clinic, counselor Lustbader (1990) features the services to older adults because counseling services for older adults are unusual for any counseling center. A significant portion of the clinic's clients are uninsured and are charged on a sliding scale or at no fee. Private funding and grant monies are the major sources of financing.

The philosophy of this clinic is that one cannot separate emotional needs from medical and social needs. Patients are typically referred for counseling by physicians in the health clinic when they think patients need counseling help. In such cases the physician brings the counselor into the examination room and explains the value of counseling help to the patient (Lustbader, 1990; personal communication, 1998). This move is intended to reduce any fear of or stigma the elderly may have with counseling. "The realization that one does not have to be 'crazy' to see a counselor is an essential aspect of this introductory contact" (Lustbader, 1990, p. 22). The focus is on normal, age-related, situational concerns such as conflict with an adult child, loneliness, depression, marital conflicts, housing concerns, and grieving.

The counselor first attends to the immediate social needs of the client, such as housing. Next, the counselor focuses on the client's emotional concerns; if appropriate, the counselor may then refer the client to group and family counseling. Because most clients are within walking distance, counselors can carry out counseling through home visits if a client has difficulty coming to the clinic. Counselors also provide a variety of psychoeducational activities in the nearby senior center.

Yet another example of a comprehensive health care clinic established primarily for the poor and the uninsured is one developed in Bellingham, Washington, by the Interfaith Council. Composed of representatives from 40 local religious groups, the Interfaith Council has developed the Interfaith Mental Health Center in conjunction with its Family Medical and Dental Health Center. This health center draws on volunteer services from the town's physicians, dentists, and mental health practitioners. Clients are charged a $10 fee per visit, which can be waived. The Interfaith Council provides, as well, social services, such as job training, links to community resources, and assistance with family housing, clothing, and food.

The Interfaith Mental Health Center has a volunteer consulting psychiatrist and 20 volunteer licensed practitioners, mostly master's-level counselors and some PhD psychologists (D. Benjamin, personal communication, November 6, 1998). The center's unique features could well be emulated in other communities. It provides a direct link not only between medical health care and mental health services but also between mental health services and the clergy—who often are the first persons sought out by individuals experiencing emotional distress. Usually, clients are referred for counseling through their initial contact with the medical care unit, but increasing numbers are being referred directly by clergy. Rather than serving clients who are chronically mentally ill, as is typical of public community mental health agencies, the Interfaith Mental Health Center serves clients with normal developmental concerns related to family and other relationships. The counseling focus is a holistic one in which client emotional difficulties are dealt with in the context of the client's social, economic, physical, and spiritual conditions and needs.

Another innovative neighborhood center for at-risk people in low-income communities is the George Washington University (G.W.U.) Community Counseling Clinic in downtown Washington, DC, developed and operated by the G.W.U. counselor education program. The clinic serves individuals who are uninsured, unemployed, or unable to afford care (Guerra, 1998a).

> Stepping into the G.W.U. Community Clinic is to step into a world where people who desperately need help but traditionally have not been able to afford the fees, get competent mental health care costing as much as $28.00 and as little as $1.00 per session. (Guerra, 1998a, p. 24)

The G.W.U. Community Counseling Clinic closely follows the counseling model set by professional counseling associations in that it offers services that address individuals' developmental, career, personal, interpersonal, and family concerns. This clinic demonstrates the need for the development of similar clinics in other low-income neighborhood communities.

The community clinic is staffed by five counselor educators and about 25 master's and doctoral counseling interns. The interns are taught to use brief therapy and problem-focused counseling approaches appropriate for the developmental concerns of clients. Such a clinic enables counselors-in-training to work with a much wider variety of clients than is usually possible in counselor training clinics located on campus. Such a community clinic could well be emulated by counselor training programs at other universities.

The Homeless

The number of homeless people in the United States runs into the millions, and the majority of these individuals do not fit the stereotype of indigent winos sleeping it off in doorways. In the foreword to *Helping Homeless People* (Solomon & Jackson-Jobe, 1992), Jesse Jackson writes about the homeless population:

> Many were once working people—teachers, auto mechanics, veterans and construction workers. Some are highly educated. These are not just nameless and faceless people. They represent families . . . turned out because of lost jobs. Little children . . . with empty stomachs. Some are sick, physically, or mentally ill. They may be seen walking our city streets, lying under blankets on sidewalks. They are blocks from the White House. (p. v)

Cooke (1992) indicates how the helping professions can intervene to give the homeless economic, social, psychological, and institutional support. Counselors and therapists, he says, "have the skills required to empower homeless persons to take control of their environment through becoming self-aware and self-enhancing" (p. 72).

Creative arts therapist Lou Ann Nockels worked with a group of homeless people in Bellingham, Washington, in conjunction with the local chapter of the Rainbow Coalition. Using psychodrama over a period of several months, participants improvised their stories as they went along as part of the therapeutic process. Performing for the community gave them the first opportunity to express themselves about their homelessness. Their condition, when dramatized, became a social phenomenon rather than isolated, separate experiences (L. Nockels, personal communication, June 4, 1993).

Counselors also work in various community services involved in providing shelter for the homeless. The Interfaith Coalition in Bellingham, for example, has been generating housing that provides transitional shelter for those in need along with food, clothing, and counseling assistance to help get them trained to qualify for better-paying jobs and help them find affordable housing.

Victims of Political Upheaval

The 9-11 disaster prompted numerous responses from mental health professionals. According to one therapist who has worked with grief and trauma cases for many years, the 9-11 disaster completely changed her life as a therapist. "It's only in the last year that I've truly understood the vulnerability and fear so many of them walk around with every-day" (Barrett, 2002, p. 52). Other counselors who live in New York City and who came forth to provide aid to the victims said they were overwhelmed by the needs of those suffering from traumatic reactions and were learning on the spot how to respond. Since then they have created a series of workshops on new ways of working with people traumatized by disaster (Taffel, 2002).

The latest research in neuroscience indicates that brain cells are capable of restructuring and growing new cells. Thus, even though traumatic events can disrupt normal brain functioning and impair the normal balancing and integration of emotional experiencing, scientists and therapists are optimistic that within a caring atmosphere directed by a therapist skilled in neurotherapy, the brains of those suffering from posttraumatic stress disorder can be restructured to return to normal functioning (Siegal, 2002; Wylie & Simon, 2002). According to Siegal (Wylie & Simon, 2002), the brain grows and develops, not just simply biologically but also interpersonally, hence his term, *interpersonal neurobiology.*

Posttraumatic Stress Disorder. *Posttraumatic stress disorder* (PTSD) is defined in the *DSM-IV-TR* as an anxiety disorder resulting from extreme traumatic stress. Symptoms include recurring recollections or obsessive thoughts about the traumatic event, recurring nightmares, flashbacks, denial of feelings or thoughts, outbursts of rage or irritability, difficulty in relationships, and difficulty concentrating.

Groups of individuals considered at risk for PTSD because of earlier unresolved traumas are war veterans, prisoners of war, refugees, torture victims, rape victims, and adults who were abused as children. An estimated 850,000 Vietnam veterans, who brought this disorder to attention, have been affected by PTSD (Hayman, Sommers-Flanagan, & Parsons, 1987). Assessment and treatment of PTSD started with Vietnam veterans and then generalized to other populations suffering similar symptoms. The VA has only recently acknowledged that significant numbers of World War II and Korean War veterans have also experienced PTSD symptoms.

Hayman and his colleagues (1987) present a four-phase treatment for PTSD in Vietnam veterans. In the first phase, *assessment and trust building,* counselors develop a trust relationship with clients while interviewing them about their preservice, military service, and postservice history. From these interviews counselors assess the severity of client trauma. In the second phase, *stabilization,* counselors help the veterans bring troubling symptoms under control. Depression and rage, substance abuse, and flashbacks are addressed by using behavioral techniques. In the third phase, *processing the trauma,* counselors help the veterans process the trauma. In various ways veterans reexperience or relive the trauma in a protective and controlled atmosphere. Hypnosis may be used to recall the trauma vividly, or psychodrama to relive or reenact the trauma. Rap groups, in which clients talk openly and honestly with other veterans, may also be used. Other techniques used in individual psychotherapy are cognitive restructuring, desensitization, or flooding (Hayman et al., 1987). In the final stage, *reintegration,* veterans are helped to reintegrate themselves in employment, interpersonal relationships, and family life. Family counseling may then be helpful.

Prisoners of War.   The long-term impact of the traumatic experiences of prisoners of war (POWs) results in persistent symptoms of PTSD, a normal response to such severe trauma (Engdahl, Dikel, Eberly, & Blank, 1997). In a study comparing POWs with combat survivors of the Korean War, researchers determined that POWs had more severe and persistent symptoms of mental and emotional dysfunctioning than did the combat survivors (Sutker & Allain, 1996).

POWs from World War II have been active in bringing public attention to the traumas they experienced during and after imprisonment. These individuals originally returned to civilian life without an opportunity to talk through their traumatic experiences. More recently, however, veterans and POWs all over the country have been attending group therapy sessions. One such example comes from the World War II Allied airmen who were shot down during bombing raids over Germany and were captured and held captive during the war. In a personal interview (April 20, 1991), POW Lou Loevsky, a member of the U.S. 8th Air Force, attested to the therapeutic value of sharing experiences in group work. Frank Nugent relates a portion of Loevsky's story.

> An old friend of mine from grade school, Loevsky had said very little about his war experiences until he started attending these meetings. He invited me to attend a group counseling meeting for POWs at a VA psychological clinic in New Jersey. There POWs from World War II and the Korean and Vietnam wars shared their remembrances and traumas. Loevsky said that emotional problems were exacerbated for POWs because the armed services denied them the opportunity to talk through their traumatic experiences after the war.
>
> After Loevsky renewed contact with fellow POW airmen, the 8th and 15th Air Force POWs, along with POWs from the British Royal Air Force Bomber Command, made a video of their story, *Behind the Wire* (Zimmerman, 1994). It described the traumatic experiences of more than 45,000 air force POWs who were shot down in enemy territory and held in four prison camps in Germany. Using a mixture of captured German film, air combat footage, and interviews with veteran POWs themselves, filmmakers integrated the POW stories into the larger historical context of the war itself. Each man's story is a harrowing tale.
>
> As his plane was going down, Loevsky risked his life to save a crewmate trapped in the plane. At one group therapy session, when the fellow crew member told how Loevsky had saved his life, someone suggested that Loevsky deserved a medal for bravery. In 1999, 55 years after the fact, Loevsky was awarded the Distinguished Flying Cross for heroic action (personal correspondence, February 13, 1999). Now, besides giving lectures in schools about his war experiences, Loevsky has been helping other POW veterans and their families settle disability claims.

Making a dramatic replay of their experiences on video and sharing their stories with outsiders broadened personal experiences of these POWs into a larger social-political dimension. This perspective enables listeners of their stories and viewers of their video to share their suffering in the context of historical events. Their stories thus gain meaning and significance, in keeping with Victor Frankl's (1963) philosophy expressed in his book *Man's Search for Meaning* (see chap. 6).

Refugees.   Refugees differ from other immigrants in that they are displaced persons who were forced to leave their countries because of oppression or threats of abduction, torture, and death. Many of them have experienced torture, the destruction of their homes, rape, and starvation. "Leaving one's home country and the precariousness of the flight itself cause loss of family, identity, and culture; a downgrade in socioeconomic status . . . These problems have created serious mental health issues for refugees" (Bemak, Chung, & Bornemann, 1995, p. 244).

Refugees in the United States are Salvadorans, Guatemalans, Nicaraguans, Vietnamese, Cambodians, Chinese, Kurds, Bosnians, Kosovars, and many others. Their psychological symptoms include depression, anxiety, and paranoia. Difficulty in finding jobs, housing, and food contribute to feelings of hopelessness and helplessness. Brown (1987) and Leung (1991) were among the first to point out that refugees' problems are closely tied to social-political factors that contribute to and exacerbate their emotional conflicts.

To help therapists work with the special emotional needs of refugees, Bemak et al. (1995) propose a four-level counseling and psychoeducational process called the *multilevel model approach (MLM)*. "The MLM . . . comprises cognitive, affective and behavioral interventions inclusive of cultural foundations and their relation to community and social processes" (p. 256). At Level 1, *mental health education,* refugees are informed about individual, family, and group services and procedures that counselors use in these services. At Level 2, *counseling,* refugees receive individual family and group counseling. At Level 3, *cultural empowerment,* refugees are taught to use community services related to education, finances, health, employment, or other social problems. At Level 4, *integration of Western and indigenous healing,* counselors develop a partnership with healers indigenous to the refugees' culture, through which together they help the refugees express their concerns and their grief.

Torture Victims.   Many refugees are also victims of torture (Goleman, 1989, 1996; Krajik, 1986). A rehabilitation program for torture victims in the United States was first established in Minneapolis, modeled after Copenhagen's International Rehabilitation Center for Torture Victims (Holtan & Robertson, 1992). Since then, similar centers have formed in Boston, Chicago, Los Angeles, San Francisco, Tucson, and New Jersey.

Dr. Inge Genefke, originator of special treatment programs for torture victims in Copenhagen, says that torture victims have a pernicious form of PTSD. They endured unspeakable and prolonged horrors, having been isolated and silenced, and are terrified of reprisals against their loved ones (Goleman, 1996). Victims suffer from recurring nightmares, insomnia, paranoia, withdrawal, and violent outbursts. Treatment is similar to that for PTSD but is further complicated by cultural differences.

An estimated 200,000 to 400,000 torture victims now live in the United States. More than one third of refugees who seek political asylum each year in the United States are torture victims (Goleman, 1996). The numbers are expected to increase, and the need for more treatment centers "will continue to grow because the use of torture appears to be an epidemic" (Goleman, 1996, p. C3). According to Amnesty International spokesman Roger Rathman, "There is government condoned torture, or ill treatment of detainees verging on torture, in 114 countries" (Goleman, 1996, p. C3).

COUNSELING PERSONS AT RISK

Persons at risk are those suffering from emotional disorders that interfere with their psychosocial development. Major dysfunctions include depression, addictive behaviors, and attention-deficit/hyperactivity disorder.

Depression

Depression, the most common health problem in the United States, is now being treated primarily with antidepressive drugs (Yapko, 1997). Increasing numbers of counselors and therapists, however, are objecting to the overuse of medication to treat depression because, they say, drugs tend to alleviate symptoms without getting to the root of the depression. They contend that depression can best be treated by psychotherapy or counseling in which the client's social context is a foremost consideration. This view has been especially advocated by counselors Yapko (1997), Jack (1991), and family therapist Papp (1997).

Michael Yapko (1997) notes that the pharmaceutical and managed care industries have been strongly promoting the idea that depression is a disease best treated by drugs. While acknowledging that individuals who are severely or chronically depressed generally need medication along with psychotherapy, he argues that for most individuals depression is best treated with counseling or psychotherapy alone. Studies show, he says, that "cultural and social forces contribute more to the onset of depression than does biology" (p. 45). He also cites literature reviews that show "substantial evidence for the superior effectiveness of therapy" (p. 45). The type of therapy Yapko (1997) recommends for depressed people is the development of relationships and social skills and the strengthening of social connections in the face of the negative and depressing events in our world:

> Our ethos of extreme individuality and personal rights for collective responsibility and social accommodation increases the likelihood that we will be lonely and depressed, without the deep ties to family and friends that can immunize us against alienation and despair. (p. 46)

In her book *Silencing the Self: Women and Depression,* Dana Jack (1991) points out that women become depressed when their healthy needs for connection and bonding have been consistently negated in our culture (see chap. 14). She recommends that therapists and counselors can best help these women by actively listening to their concerns and validating and supporting the importance of relationships in the development of self. Her approach is to ask women directly about their feelings and to listen to their stories. In this process she looks for and corrects distorted moral themes in their stories and then uses metaphors, fairy tales, and myths to help women activate themselves and move out of depression.

In their work with couples and families, Peggy Papp (1997) and her staff at the Ackerman Institute for Family use a feminist family systems approach to help couples when either the wife or the husband is depressed. A member of the Women's Project in Family Therapy, described earlier, Papp is also director of the Ackerman Institute's Depression in Context Project. She and her staff work to "bring a systemic perspective to the treatment of depression, and to explore how issues involving gender, race, class, and sexual orientation can catalyze its onset" (p. 54).

Concurring with Jack's views about women's loss of voice, Papp (1997) and her staff encourage wives to express their feelings of loss of voice and sense of self. They also describe the influence of gender role stereotyping on the couple's expectations of each other. They explore "what effect these expectations might be having on current relationships, on their sense of power, privilege and independence" (p. 56). Consistent with their views about the influence that social context has on depressed persons, Papp and her staff also initiate discussions about the contributions of racism and sexism to negative self-image. For depressed men the staff believes that helping them develop empathy and connections with their wives helps lift their depression.

Addictions

Over the years counselors and other mental health providers have given attention to the treatment of specific addictive behaviors, such as substance abuse, eating disorders, compulsive gambling, and sex addiction. In their book *Facing Shame*, Fossum and Mason (1986) propose that addictive behaviors arise out of shame-based families. According to Fossum and Mason, counselors must go beyond treating a person's specific addiction; the family dynamics underlying the addictive behavior must be dealt with. Otherwise, a recovering alcoholic, for example, may develop a different form of addiction to replace the alcohol that was given up, or another family member may develop a new addiction to replace what was given up by the recovering alcoholic. "We have learned that the treatment of one addictive behavior does not automatically eradicate compulsivity from the system" (p. 125). Fossum and Mason (1986) include psychosocial considerations in treating addicted families, emphasizing the importance of networks of support outside the family and often including close friends and affiliates in the therapy process.

Fossum and Mason (1986) believe that it is important for clients to give up their secretive, shame-based compulsivity when they can "share their experiences openly and honestly with one another and learn from one another" (p. 124). Using AA 12-step programs, clients admit their powerlessness and receive support and acceptance from the group; a spiritual recovery takes place, "making it possible for the client to connect on an emotional and human level with other group members" (p. 125).

Also addressing the issue of addictive behaviors as a whole, Real (1997) argues that addictions, particularly in males, are defenses to cover up depression (see chap. 14).

Attention-Deficit/Hyperactivity Disorder

Until recently, mental health professionals believed that children with attention-deficit/hyperactivity disorder (ADHD) outgrew it when they reached adulthood. Experts now estimate that 30% to 50% of ADHD children continue to experience disruptive behaviors throughout their lives (Jackson & Farrugia, 1997). Attention is now focused on making appropriate diagnosis of this disorder in adults and on determining the most effective treatment.

In their review of ADHD research and practice, Jackson and Farrugia (1997) concluded that the primary characteristics of adult ADHD are similar to those of childhood ADHD: inattention, hyperactivity, and impulsivity that lead to problems on the job, substance abuse, or relationship problems. "For adults affected by ADHD, the decision to seek help is often precipitated by being fired from their job, having substance abuse problems, having their spouses ask for divorce, or some other traumatic experience" (p. 318).

Researchers believe that the most effective counseling approach is a multimodal one, educating clients about the disorder and training them in attention management skills, self-management and self-monitoring strategies, social skills and problem solving, and stress and anger management. Adult clients with ADHD need to feel a sense of empowerment and hope as they begin to use these various self-management skills (Jackson & Farrugia, 1997).

CRISIS PREVENTION AND INTERVENTION

Community counselors, like counselors in schools and colleges, must be prepared to deal with crises. They must have the knowledge, skill, and experience to know how to deal with the presenting emergency, take immediate action to help the person through the trauma, and then decide whether to refer the individual to another professional or agency. Crisis centers staffed by volunteers trained in telephone crisis intervention are available in most large communities. In some communities specialists form teams to work jointly with families in crises (Brammer, Abrego, & Shostrom, 1993).

Historically, community counselors have dealt with those who have attempted suicide, those with severe immobilizing depression or psychotic reactions, and those who have been traumatized by the sudden loss or death of loved ones. In recent years severe drug reactions have become more common, as have crises involving battered wives, rape victims, abused children, and juvenile runaways.

Suicide

Community crisis workers emphasize the importance of psychosocial factors in working with suicidal clients. Crisis counselors "focus on prevention by correcting the alienated life style that cuts off the at-risk person's connectedness with others" (James & Gilliland, 2001, p. 215). Recognizing the importance of the social context in which the client is living, crisis counselors involve family, friends, and associates of the suicidal client in prevention and support work. Counselors teach those close to the client to be aware of certain typical behaviors or feelings that suicidal persons display. They also teach family and significant others how to support suicidal persons in ways that will build their feelings of worthiness and value while making them feel accepted as fallible human beings (James & Gilliland, 2001). Crisis workers also provide clients with lists of referrals and support sources in the community. This networking not only gives suicidal clients increased feelings of security but also demonstrates to them that individuals in the community care about them. Counselors also help the friends and family of those who have committed suicide to cope with grief or excessive feelings of guilt or blame.

Regarding the training of counselors and therapists in prevention, crisis intervention, and therapy of suicidal clients, Neimeyer (2000) warns, "Despite the high frequency of suicide and its ubiquity in the caseloads of practicing psychologists . . . the training of mental health professionals in this critical area is woefully inadequate" (p. 551).

Violence

When employees witness or are victims of a traumatic experience on the job, increasing numbers of companies are calling on mental health counselors to provide help and relief (i.e., debriefing). Catastrophic and traumatic incidents—for example, mass shootings, office bombings, mine disasters, violent accidents, the deaths or suicides of fellow employees—generally cause severe emotional reactions, and if not attended to, a delayed reaction occurs in the form of PTSD. In these situations mental health counselors may be called on by EAPs, may contract with or be employed by firms that specialize in crisis intervention, or may be part of a mental health group in the community that volunteers services to crisis team intervention.

One example of a business using crisis intervention specialists occurred after the bombing of the Alfred P. Murrah Federal Building in Oklahoma City in 1995. A company located close to the bombing, Kerr-McGee Corporation, whose employees witnessed the bombing, contracted with Crisis Management International from Atlanta, Georgia, to debrief their employees. Eighteen counselors provided counseling support and informational services (Gladding, 1997). This task force set up "a command center, held group and individual counseling sessions, and established a phone tree to update information to its workers. Problems employees had . . . included grief, anger, depression, fatigue, nightmares, survivor guilt and trouble eating and concentrating" (Gladding, 1997, p. 242).

A volunteer crisis intervention team was formed recently in Whatcom and Skagit Counties in the state of Washington to debrief employees in businesses throughout the counties that have experienced job-related trauma. Called the Critical Incident Stress Management Program, the team is composed of a volunteer mental health professional and two volunteers from business and industry.

Mental health counselors may also be involved with government agencies designed to help victims of natural disasters, such as floods, hurricanes, earthquakes, or forest fires. The federal government, for example, has established the National Organization for Victim Assistance (NOVA; James & Gilliland, 2001). After a national disaster, at the request of the leaders of the community-in-crisis, NOVA sends a national crisis response team to help the community "to form local crisis response teams that are in a position to deal with the community's grief reactions, stress effects, and posttraumatic stress disorder resultant from the disaster" (James & Gilliland, 2001, p. 659).

SUMMARY

Many health care providers in the community are combining their services to offer more comprehensive treatment for clients. Groups are forming liaisons to meet the individual's and family's developmental, physical, psychological, spiritual, social-cultural, and economic needs. In some places comprehensive health care centers are emerging, which include multicultural approaches to counseling, family and career counseling, spiritual counseling and grief work, medical care, and social services.

Community counselors work with the psychosocial concerns and transitions of clients at all ages. Some community and school counselors are forming liaisons and joint services to work with at-risk schoolchildren and adolescents who live in detrimental social conditions. Young adults typically need counselor help with career planning, job adjustment, relationship issues, and raising a family. At midlife, adults have concerns about job change or job loss and changing relations with children, spouse, and aging parents. Senior centers in some places are proving to be viable places for effective counseling of older adults and for helping them carry out generative and productive activities.

Family therapists are expanding their approach in a variety of ways. Some are now acknowledging the impact of job-related issues on family dynamics. Moreover, many, particularly ethnic counselors and therapists, have extended family dynamics to include how the family is involved in the community, how the family is affected by social-cultural factors, and how the family can develop in relation to its community. Many family therapists have also expanded their perspective to attend to the aging family, focusing on intergenerational relationships that foster renewal and growth between adults and their aging parents. Many counselors are providing ways that individuals suffering the loss of loved ones can share their grief with others through grief support groups and other community-supported healing circles.

Spiritual development has been receiving increasing attention among counseling professionals. Ethnic counselors have been influential in alerting the counseling profession to the importance of spiritual concerns to personal development. Increasing numbers of religious groups, interfaith organizations, and pastoral counseling centers and institutions are providing effective and affordable counseling to the general public.

Community counselors are helping clients interact with challenging social, cultural, and political conditions and transitions, including career and work adjustment. In many cities comprehensive health care centers are emerging in poor neighborhoods to serve the needs of those who cannot afford health insurance or who are unemployed and homeless. Counseling centers are also emerging in major cities to care for those affected by political upheaval, such as war veterans and POWs with PTSD, refugees, and torture victims. Counselors also work with persons suffering from depression, addiction, and ADHD. In addition, they provide crisis prevention and intervention services for suicidal persons and victims of violence. Some counselors provide debriefing sessions for those traumatized by violence or catastrophic events.

PROJECTS AND ACTIVITIES

1. Survey your community to determine what resources are available for counseling individuals with normal developmental concerns who are not in school or in college.
2. Explore various community agencies in your vicinity from the standpoint of training. What percentage of the staff members are professionally trained counselors? How much in-service training is given? How much depen-

dence is there on volunteers? What is the specific training of other professionals?
3. Visit community counseling agencies and read their brochures and other publicizing materials. Does the information indicate that the agencies are prepared to handle the types of client concerns discussed in this chapter?
4. Interview probation officers in your community. Do they perceive any difficulty in trying

to counsel their parolees while maintaining jurisdiction over them? Do the officers have resources to whom they can refer clients?

5. What resources are available in the community for counseling elderly persons? Do these services appear satisfactory? How are they funded? What improvements would you make?

6. Survey community ethnic groups and their attitudes about and use of mental health

facilities. Are ethnic groups represented on the staffs of various agencies?

7. Visit your county or regional community mental health clinic. Ask the director whether you can obtain an organizational chart of services offered under the community comprehensive mental health program in your area. Explore which needs are being met and which are being neglected. Try to determine reasons for the selection of services.

REFERENCES

American Psychiatric Association. (2000). *Diagnostic and statistical manual of mental disorders* (4th ed., text revision). Washington, DC: Author.

Barrett, M. J. (2002). A new way of knowing. *Psychotherapy Networker, 26*(25), 52, 70.

Bart, M. (1998). Spirituality in counseling finding believers. *Counseling Today, 41,* 1, 6.

Baruth, L. G., & Manning, M. L. (1999). *Multicultural counseling and psychotherapy: A lifespan perspective* (2nd ed.). Upper Saddle River, NJ: Merrill/Prentice Hall.

Bemak, F., Chung, R. C. Y., & Bornemann, T. H. (1995). Counseling and psychotherapy with refugees. In P. B. Pedersen, J. G. Draguns, W. J. Lonner, & J. E. Trimble (Eds.), *Counseling across cultures* (4th ed., pp. 243–265). Thousand Oaks, CA: Sage.

Berry, K. (2003, July 5). Dr. Henry Giarretto, developed treatment for sex abuse victims. *Mercury News.* Retrieved from http://www.mercurynews.com

Bielski, V. (1996). Our magnificent obsession. *The Family Therapy Networker, 20,* 22–35.

Bishop, D. R. (1995). Religious values as cross-cultural issues in counseling. In M. T. Burke & J. G. Mirante (Eds.), *Counseling: The spiritual dimension* (pp. 59–72). Alexandria, VA: American Counseling Association.

Brammer, L. M., Abrego, P. J., & Shostrom, E. L. (1993). *Therapeutic counseling and psychotherapy* (6th ed.). Upper Saddle River, NJ: Prentice Hall.

Brown, F. (1987). Counseling Vietnamese refugees: The new challenge. *International Journal for the Advancement of Counseling, 10,* 259–268.

Burke, M. T., & Miranti, J. G. (1995). *Counseling: The spiritual dimension.* Alexandria, VA: American Counseling Association.

Cooke, A. L. (1992). The role of helping professionals: Developing a strategy. In C. Solomon & P. Jackson-Jobe (Eds.), *Helping homeless people: Unique challenges and solutions.* Alexandria, VA: American Counseling Association.

Danielsen. (2003). The Danielsen institute. Retrieved from http://www.bu.edu/danielsen

Donaghy, K. B. (1995). Beyond survival: Applying wellness interventions in battered women's shelters. *Journal of Mental Health Counseling, 17,* 3–17.

Dugan, W. E. (1993). *Wood Block and Toy Project: Designed for diversely-abled senior volunteers.* St. Cloud, MN: Retired Senior Volunteer Program.

Engdahl, B., Dikel, T. N., Eberly, R., & Blank, A., Jr. (1997). Posttraumatic stress disorder in a community group of former prisoners of war: A normative response to severe trauma. *American Journal of Psychiatry, 154,* 1576–1581.

Entine, A. D. (1976). Mid-life counseling: Prognosis and potential. *Personnel and Guidance Journal, 55,* 112–114.

Fossum, M. E., & Mason, M. J. (1986). *Facing shame: Families in recovery.* New York: Norton.

Frankl, V. (1963). *Man's search for meaning.* New York: Washington Square Press.

Garcia-Preto, N. (1982). Puerto Rican families. In M. McGoldrick, J. K. Pearce, & J. Giordano (Eds.), *Ethnicity and family therapy* (pp. 164–186). New York: Guilford Press.

Gladding, S. T. (1997). *Community and agency counseling.* Upper Saddle River, NJ: Merrill/Prentice Hall.

Golden, L. B. (Ed.). (1998). *Case studies in child and adolescent counseling* (2nd ed.). Upper Saddle River, NJ: Merrill/Prentice Hall.

Goleman, D. (1989, April 25). Grim specialty emerges as therapists treat victims of torture. *New York Times Magazine,* pp. C1, C12.

Goleman, D. (1996, July 9). A promising medical specialty emerges to help torture victims. *New York Times,* p. C3.

Grady, S. (1990). Senior centers: An environment in counseling. *Generations, 14,* 15–19.

Guerra, P. (1998a). Beyond the brick wall: Reaching a community in need. *Counseling Today, 41,* 24.

Guerra, P. (1998b). Innovative program addresses anger management through ice hockey. *Counseling Today, 40,* 32, 45.

Hayman, P. M., Sommers-Flanagan, R., & Parsons, J. P. (1987). Aftermath of violence: Post-traumatic stress disorder among Vietnam veterans. *Journal of Counseling & Development, 65,* 363–366.

Heddesheimer, J. (1976). Multiple motivations for mid-career changes. *Personnel and Guidance Journal, 55,* 109–111.

Hershenson, D. B. (1996). Work adjustment: A neglected area in career counseling. *Journal of Counseling & Development, 74,* 442–446.

Holtan, N., & Robertson, C. (1992). Scarcity among plenty: How to treat victims of torture in the USA without government assistance. *Torture, 2,* 11.

Ingersoll, R. E. (1995). Spirituality, religion, and counseling: Dimensions and relationships. In M. T. Burke & J. G. Mirante (Eds.), *Counseling: The spiritual dimension* (pp. 5–18). Alexandria, VA: American Counseling Association.

Iwasaki, J. (1998, December 11). Many bear a special grief during holidays. *Seattle Post Intelligencer,* pp. C1, C11.

Jack, D. (1991). *Silencing the self: Women and depression.* Cambridge, MA: Harvard University Press.

Jackson, B., & Farrugia, D. (1997). Diagnosis and treatment of adults with attention deficit hyperactivity disorder. *Journal of Counseling & Development, 75,* 312–319.

James, R. K., & Gilliland, B. E. (2001). *Crisis intervention strategies* (4th ed.). Pacific Grove, CA: Brooks/Cole.

Jones, C. (1998, August 21). More Blacks are turning to counselors for help. *USA Today,* pp. 1A–2A.

Kornfield, J. (1993). *A path with heart: A guide through the perils and promises of spiritual life.* New York: Bantam Books.

Krajik, K. (1986, November). Healing broken minds. *Psychology Today,* 66–69.

Landis, L. L., & Wyre, C. H. (1984). Group treatment for mothers of incest victims: A step-by-step approach. *Journal of Counseling & Development, 63,* 115–116.

Leung, P. (1991). Asian Americans and psychology: Unresolved issues. *Journal of Training and Practice in Professional Psychology, 4,* 3–13.

Lustbader, W. (1990). Mental health services in a community health center. *Generations, 14,* 22–23.

Markowitz, L. (1997). Ramon Rojano won't take no for an answer. *Family Therapy Networker, 21,* 24–35.

Meade, M. (2004). *Mosaic Multicultural Foundation* [Brochure]. Seattle, WA: Author.

Neimeyer, R. A. (2000, July). Suicide and hastened death: Toward a training agenda for counseling psychology. *The Counseling Psychologist, 28*(4), 551–560.

Nugent, F. A. (1981). *Professional counseling: An overview.* Pacific Grove, CA: Brooks/Cole.

O'Malley, P. (1998). Raising Martin. In L. B. Golden (Ed.), *Case studies in child and adolescent counseling* (2nd ed., pp. 92–102). Upper Saddle River, NJ: Merrill/Prentice Hall.

Papp, P. (1997). Listening to the system. *Family Therapy Networker, 21,* 52–58.

Pearson, J. E. (1988). A support group for women with relationship dependency. *Journal of Counseling & Development, 66,* 394–396.

Randolph, D. L. (1978). The counseling-community psychologist in the CMHC: Employer perceptions. *Counselor Education and Supervision, 17,* 244–253.

Rappoport, L. (1976). Adult development: "Faster horses . . . and more money." *Personnel and Guidance Journal, 55,* 106–108.

Real, T. (1997). *I don't want to talk about it.* New York: Fireside.

Real, T. (2002). The awful truth. *Psychotherapy Networker, 26,* 34–43, 58.

Sandmaier, M. (1998). Healing the family's oldest rifts. *Family Therapy Networker, 22,* 23–31, 59–60.

Scher, S. (2002, January 17). Interview with Luis Rodriguez, Seattle Station's KUOW's host of "Weekday" on NPR. Retrieved April 10, 2003, from http://www.mosaicvoices.org

Siegel, D. (2002). The brain in the palm of your hand. *Psychotherapy Networker, 26*(25), 32–33.

Simon, R. (1997). Fearless foursome: An interview with the women's project. *Family Therapy Networker, 21,* 58–68.

Solomon, C., & Jackson-Jobe, P. (Eds.). (1992). *Helping homeless people: Unique challenges and solutions.* Alexandria, VA: American Counseling Association.

Sutker, P., & Allain, A. N., Jr. (1996). Assessment of PTSD and other mental disorders in World War II and Korean Conflict POW survivors and combat veterans. *Psychological Assessment, 8,* 18–25.

Taffel, R. (2002). The many faces of trauma. *Psychotherapy Networker, 26*(25), 51–52.

Thomas, M. C., & Martin, V. (1992). Training counselors to facilitate the transitions of aging through group work. *Counselor Education and Supervision, 32,* 51–60.

Trimble, J. E., Fleming, D. M., Beauvais, F., & Jumper-Thurman, P. (1996). Essential cultural and social strategies for counseling Native American Indians. In P. B. Pedersen, J. G. Draguns, W. J. Lonner, & J. E. Trimble (Eds.), *Counseling across cultures* (4th ed., pp. 177–209). Thousand Oaks, CA: Sage.

Waters, E. B. (1984). Building on what you know: Techniques for individual and group counseling with older people. *Counseling Psychologist, 12,* 63–74.

Westefeld, J. S., Range, L. M., Rogers, J. R., Maples, M. R., Bromley, J. L., & Alcorn, J. (2000, July). Suicide: An overview. *The Counseling Psychologist, 28*(4), 445–510.

Wylie, M. S. (1992). Revising the dream. *Family Therapy Networker, 16,* 10–23.

Wylie, M. S. (1996). It's a community affair. *Family Therapy Networker, 20,* 58–65, 96.

Wylie, M. S., & Simon, R. (2002). Discoveries from the black box. *Psychotherapy Networker, 26*(25), 26–31, 33–37, 68.

Yapko, M. (1997). Stronger medicine. *Family Therapy Networker, 21,* 42–49.

Zimmerman, A. (1994). *Behind the wire: Allied airmen in German captivity* [Video]. 8th Air Force Historical Society.

APPENDIX A

ACA Code of Ethics and Standards of Practice

PREAMBLE

The American Counseling Association is an educational, scientific, and professional organization whose members are dedicated to the enhancement of human development throughout the life span. Association members recognize diversity in our society and embrace a cross-cultural approach in support of the worth, dignity, potential, and uniqueness of each individual.

The specification of a code of ethics enables the association to clarify to current and future members, and to those served by members, the nature of the ethical responsibilities held in common by its members. As the code of ethics of the association, this document establishes principles that define the ethical behavior of association members. All members of the American Counseling Association are required to adhere to the Code of Ethics and the Standards of Practice. The Code of Ethics will serve as the basis for processing ethical complaints initiated against members of the association.

As Approved by Governing Council

April 1997

Effective July 1, 1997

Note: From the American Counseling Association, 1997, Alexandria, VA: Author. Copyright 1995 by the American Counseling Association. Reprinted with permission. No further reproduction authorized without written permission of the American Counseling Association.

SECTION A:
THE COUNSELING RELATIONSHIP

A.1. CLIENT WELFARE

a. *Primary Responsibility.*

The primary responsibility of counselors is to respect the dignity and to promote the welfare of clients.

b. *Positive Growth and Development.*

Counselors encourage client growth and development in ways that foster the clients' interest and welfare; counselors avoid fostering dependent counseling relationships.

c. *Counseling Plans.*

Counselors and their clients work jointly in devising integrated, individual counseling plans that offer reasonable promise of success and are consistent with abilities and circumstances of clients. Counselors and clients regularly review counseling plans to ensure their continued viability and effectiveness respecting clients' freedom of choice. (See A.3.b.)

d. *Family Involvement.*

Counselors recognize that families are usually important in clients' lives and strive to enlist family understanding and involvement as a positive resource when appropriate.

e. *Career and Employment Needs.*

Counselors work with their clients in considering employment in jobs and circumstances that are consistent with the clients' overall abilities, vocational limitations, physical restrictions, general temperament, interest and aptitude patterns, social skills, education, general qualifications, and other relevant characteristics and needs. Counselors neither place nor participate in placing clients in positions that will result in damaging the interest and the welfare of clients, employers, or the public.

A.2. RESPECTING DIVERSITY

a. *Nondiscrimination.*

Counselors do not condone or engage in discrimination based on age, color, culture, disability, ethnic group, gender, race, religion, sexual orientation, marital status, or socioeconomic status. (See C.5.a., C.5.b., and D.1.i.)

b. *Respecting Differences.*

Counselors will actively attempt to understand the diverse cultural backgrounds of the clients with whom they work. This includes, but is not limited to, learning how the counselor's own cultural/ethnic/racial identity impacts her/his values and beliefs about the counseling process. (See E.8. and F.2.i.)

A.3. CLIENT RIGHTS

a. *Disclosure to Clients.*

When counseling is initiated, and throughout the counseling process as necessary, counselors inform clients of the purposes, goals, techniques, procedures, limitations, potential risks and benefits of services to be performed, and other pertinent information. Counselors take steps to ensure that clients understand the implications of diagnosis, the intended use of tests and reports, fees, and billing arrangements. Clients have the right to expect confidentiality and to be provided with an explanation of its limitations, including supervision and/or treatment team professionals; to obtain clear information about their case records; to participate in the ongoing counseling plans; and to refuse any recommended services and be advised of the consequences of such refusal. (See E.5.a. and G.2.)

b. *Freedom of Choice.*

Counselors offer clients the freedom to choose whether to enter into a counseling relationship and to determine which professional(s) will provide counseling. Restrictions that limit choices of clients are fully explained. (See A.1.c.)

c. *Inability to Give Consent.*

When counseling minors or persons unable to give voluntary informed consent, counselors act in these clients' best interests. (See B.3.)

A.4. CLIENTS SERVED BY OTHERS

If a client is receiving services from another mental health professional, counselors, with client consent, inform the professional persons already involved and develop clear agreements to avoid confusion and conflict for the client. (See C.6.c.)

A.5. PERSONAL NEEDS AND VALUES

a. *Personal Needs.*

In the counseling relationship, counselors are aware of the intimacy and responsibilities inherent in the counseling relationship, maintain respect for clients, and avoid actions that seek to meet their personal needs at the expense of clients.

b. *Personal Values.*

Counselors are aware of their own values, attitudes, beliefs, and behaviors and how these apply in a diverse society and avoid imposing their values on clients. (See C.5.a.)

A.6. DUAL RELATIONSHIPS

a. *Avoid When Possible.*

Counselors are aware of their influential positions with respect to clients, and they avoid exploiting the trust and dependency of clients. Counselors make every effort to avoid dual relationships with clients that could impair professional judgment or increase the risk of harm to clients. (Examples of such relationships include, but are not limited to, familial, social, financial, business, or close personal relationships with clients.) When a dual relationship cannot be avoided, counselors take appropriate professional precautions, such as informed consent, consultation, supervision, and documentation, to ensure that judgment is not impaired and no exploitation occurs. (See F.1.b.)

b. *Superior/Subordinate Relationships.*

Counselors do not accept as clients superiors or subordinates with whom they have administrative, supervisory, or evaluative relationships.

A.7. SEXUAL INTIMACIES WITH CLIENTS

a. *Current Clients.*

Counselors do not have any type of sexual intimacies with clients and do not counsel persons with whom they have had a sexual relationship.

b. *Former Clients.*

Counselors do not engage in sexual intimacies with former clients within a minimum of two years after terminating the counseling relationship. Counselors who engage in such relationship after two years following termination have the responsibility to thoroughly examine and document that such relations did not have an exploitative nature, based on factors, such as duration of counseling, amount of time since counseling, termination circumstances, client's personal history and mental status, adverse impact on the client, and actions by the counselor suggesting a plan to initiate a sexual relationship with the client after termination.

A.8. MULTIPLE CLIENTS

When counselors agree to provide counseling services to two or more persons who have a relationship (such as husband and wife, or parents and children), counselors clarify at the outset which person or persons are clients and the nature of the relationships they will have with each involved person. If it becomes apparent that counselors may be called upon to perform potentially conflicting roles, they clarify, adjust, or withdraw from roles appropriately. (See B.2. and B.4.d.)

A.9. GROUP WORK

a. *Screening.*

Counselors screen prospective group counseling/therapy participants. To the extent possible, counselors select members whose needs and goals are compatible with goals of the group, who will not impede the group process, and whose well-being will not be jeopardized by the group experience.

b. *Protecting Clients.*

In a group setting, counselors take reasonable precautions to protect clients from physical or psychological trauma.

A.10. FEES AND BARTERING

(See D.3.a. and D.3.b.)

a. *Advance Understanding.*

Counselors clearly explain to clients, prior to entering the counseling relationship, all financial arrangements related to professional services including the use of collection agencies or legal measures for nonpayment. (A.11.c.)

b. *Establishing Fees.*

In establishing fees for professional counseling services, counselors consider the financial status of clients and locality. In the event that the established fee structure is inappropriate for a client, assistance is provided in attempting to find comparable services of acceptable cost. (See A.10.d., D.3.a., and D.3.b.)

c. *Bartering Discouraged.*

Counselors ordinarily refrain from accepting goods or services from clients in return for counseling services because such arrangements create inherent potential for conflicts, exploitation, and distortion of the professional relationship. Counselors may participate in bartering only if the relationship is not exploitive, if the client requests it, if a clear written contract is established, and if such arrangements are an accepted practice among professionals in the community. (See A.6.a.)

d. *Pro Bono Service.*

Counselors contribute to society by devoting a portion of their professional activity to services for which there is little or no financial return (pro bono).

A.11. TERMINATION AND REFERRAL

a. *Abandonment Prohibited.*

Counselors do not abandon or neglect clients in counseling. Counselors assist in making appropriate arrangements for the continuation of treatment, when necessary, during interruptions, such as vacations, and following termination.

b. *Inability to Assist Clients.*

If counselors determine an inability to be of professional assistance to clients, they avoid entering or immediately terminate a counseling relationship. Counselors are knowledgeable about referral resources and suggest appropriate alternatives. If clients decline the suggested referral, counselors should discontinue the relationship.

c. *Appropriate Termination.*

Counselors terminate a counseling relationship, securing client agreement when possible, when it is reasonably clear that the client is no longer

benefiting, when services are no longer required, when counseling no longer serves the client's needs or interests, when clients do not pay fees charged, or when agency or institution limits do not allow provision of further counseling services. (See A.10.b. and C.2.g.)

A.12. COMPUTER TECHNOLOGY

a. *Use of Computers.*

When computer applications are used in counseling services, counselors ensure that (1) the client is intellectually, emotionally, and physically capable of using the computer application; (2) the computer application is appropriate for the needs of the client; (3) the client understands the purpose and operation of the computer applications; and (4) a follow-up of client use of a computer application is provided to correct possible misconceptions, discover inappropriate use, and assess subsequent needs.

b. *Explanation of Limitations.*

Counselors ensure that clients are provided information as a part of the counseling relationship that adequately explains the limitations of computer technology.

c. *Access to Computer Applications.*

Counselors provide for equal access to computer applications in counseling services. (See A.2.a.)

SECTION B: CONFIDENTIALITY

B.1. RIGHT TO PRIVACY

a. *Respect for Privacy.*

Counselors respect their clients' right to privacy and avoid illegal and unwarranted disclosures of confidential information. (See A.3.a. and B.6.a.)

b. *Client Waiver.*

The right to privacy may be waived by the client or their legally recognized representative.

c. *Exceptions.*

The general requirement that counselors keep information confidential does not apply when disclosure is required to prevent clear and imminent danger to the client or others or when legal requirements demand that confidential information be revealed. Counselors consult with other professionals when in doubt as to the validity of an exception.

d. *Contagious, Fatal Diseases.*

A counselor who receives information confirming that a client has a disease commonly known to be both communicable and fatal is justified in disclosing information to an identifiable third party, who by his or her relationship with the client is at a high risk of contracting the disease. Prior to making a disclosure the counselor should ascertain that the client has not already informed the third party

about his or her disease and that the client is not intending to inform the third party in the immediate future. (See B.1.c and B.1.f.)

e. *Court Ordered Disclosure.*

When court ordered to release confidential information without a client's permission, counselors request to the court that the disclosure not be required due to potential harm to the client or counseling relationship. (See B.1.c.)

f. *Minimal Disclosure.*

When circumstances require the disclosure of confidential information, only essential information is revealed. To the extent possible, clients are informed before confidential information is disclosed.

g. *Explanation of Limitations.*

When counseling is initiated and throughout the counseling process as necessary, counselors inform clients of the limitations of confidentiality and identify foreseeable situations in which confidentiality must be breached. (See G.2.a.)

h. *Subordinates.*

Counselors make every effort to ensure that privacy and confidentiality of clients are maintained by subordinates including employees, supervisees, clerical assistants, and volunteers. (See B.1.a.)

i. *Treatment Teams.*

If client treatment will involve a continued review by a treatment team, the client will be informed of the team's existence and composition.

B.2. GROUPS AND FAMILIES

a. *Group Work.*

In group work, counselors clearly define confidentiality and the parameters for the specific group being entered, explain its importance, and discuss the difficulties related to confidentiality involved in group work. The fact that confidentiality cannot be guaranteed is clearly communicated to group members.

b. *Family Counseling.*

In family counseling, information about one family member cannot be disclosed to another member without permission. Counselors protect the privacy rights of each family member. (See A.8., B.3., and B.4.d.)

B.3 MINOR OR INCOMPETENT CLIENTS

When counseling clients who are minors or individuals who are unable to give voluntary, informed consent, parents or guardians may be included in the counseling process as appropriate. Counselors act in the best interests of clients and take measures to safeguard confidentiality. (See A.3.c.)

B.4. RECORDS

a. *Requirement of Records.*

Counselors maintain records necessary for rendering professional services to their clients and as required by laws, regulations, or agency or institution procedures.

b. *Confidentiality of Records.*

Counselors are responsible for securing the safety and confidentiality of any counseling records they create, maintain, transfer, or destroy whether the records are written, taped, computerized, or stored in any other medium. (See B.1.a.)

c. *Permission to Record or Observe.*

Counselors obtain permission from clients prior to electronically recording or observing sessions. (See A.3.a.)

d. *Client Access.*

Counselors recognize that counseling records are kept for the benefit of clients and, therefore, provide access to records and copies of records when requested by competent clients unless the records contain information that may be misleading and detrimental to the client. In situations involving multiple clients, access to records is limited to those parts of records that do not include confidential information related to another client. (See A.8., B.1.a., and B.2.b.)

e. *Disclosure or Transfer.*

Counselors obtain written permission from clients to disclose or transfer records to legitimate third parties unless exceptions to confidentiality exist as listed in Section B.1. Steps are taken to ensure that receivers of counseling records are sensitive to their confidential nature.

B.5. RESEARCH AND TRAINING

a. *Data Disguise Required.*

Use of data derived from counseling relationships for purposes of training, research, or publication is confined to content that is disguised to ensure the anonymity of the individuals involved. (See B.1.g. and G.3.d.)

b. Agreement for Identification.

Identification of a client in a presentation or publication is permissible only when the client has reviewed the material and has agreed to its presentation or publication. (See G.3.d.)

B.6. CONSULTATION

a. *Respect for Privacy.*

Information obtained in a consulting relationship is discussed for professional purposes only with persons clearly concerned with the case. Written and oral reports present data germane to the purposes of the consultation, and every effort is made to protect client identity and avoid undue invasion of privacy.

b. *Cooperating Agencies.*

Before sharing information, counselors make efforts to ensure that there are defined policies in other agencies serving the counselor's clients that effectively protect the confidentiality of information.

SECTION C: PROFESSIONAL RESPONSIBILITY

C.1. STANDARDS KNOWLEDGE

Counselors have a responsibility to read, understand, and follow the Code of Ethics and the Standards of Practice.

C.2. PROFESSIONAL COMPETENCE

a. *Boundaries of Competence.*

Counselors practice only within the boundaries of their competence, based on their education, training, supervised experience, state and national professional credentials, and appropriate professional experience. Counselors will demonstrate a commitment to gain knowledge, personal awareness, sensitivity, and skills pertinent to working with a diverse client population.

b. *New Specialty Areas of Practice.*

Counselors practice in specialty areas new to them only after appropriate education, training, and supervised experience. While developing skills in new specialty areas, counselors take steps to ensure the competence of their work and to protect others from possible harm.

c. *Qualified for Employment.*

Counselors accept employment only for positions for which they are qualified by education, training, supervised experience, state and national professional credentials, and appropriate professional experience. Counselors hire for professional counseling positions only individuals who are qualified and competent.

d. *Monitor Effectiveness.*

Counselors continually monitor their effectiveness as professionals and take steps to improve when necessary. Counselors in private practice take reasonable steps to seek out peer supervision to evaluate their efficacy as counselors.

e. *Ethical Issues Consultation.*

Counselors take reasonable steps to consult with other counselors or related professionals when they have questions regarding their ethical obligations or professional practice. (See H.1)

f. *Continuing Education.*

Counselors recognize the need for continuing education to maintain a reasonable level of awareness of current scientific and professional information in their fields of activity. They take steps to maintain competence in the skills they use, are open to new procedures, and keep current with the diverse and/or special populations with whom they work.

g. *Impairment.*

Counselors refrain from offering or accepting professional services when their physical, mental or emotional problems are likely to harm a client or others. They are alert to the signs of impairment, seek assistance for problems, and, if necessary, limit, suspend, or terminate their professional responsibilities. (See A.11.c.)

C.3. ADVERTISING AND SOLICITING CLIENTS

a. *Accurate Advertising.*

There are no restrictions on advertising by counselors except those that can be specifically justified to protect the public from deceptive practices. Counselors advertise or represent their services to the public by identifying their credentials in an accurate manner that is not false, misleading, deceptive, or fraudulent. Counselors may only advertise the highest degree earned which is in counseling or a closely related field from a college or university that was accredited when the degree was awarded by one of the regional accrediting bodies recognized by the Council on Postsecondary Accreditation.

b. *Testimonials.*

Counselors who use testimonials do not solicit them from clients or other persons who, because of their particular circumstances, may be vulnerable to undue influence.

c. *Statements by Others.*

Counselors make reasonable efforts to ensure that statements made by others about them or the profession of counseling are accurate.

d. *Recruiting Through Employment.*

Counselors do not use their places of employment or institutional affiliation to recruit or gain clients, supervisees, or consultees for their private practices. (See C.5.e.)

e. *Products and Training Advertisements.*

Counselors who develop products related to their profession or conduct workshops or training events ensure that the advertisements concerning these products or events are accurate and disclose adequate information for consumers to make informed choices.

f. *Promoting to Those Served.*

Counselors do not use counseling, teaching, training, or supervisory relationships to promote their products or training events in a manner that is deceptive or would exert undue influence on individuals who may be vulnerable. Counselors may adopt textbooks they have authored for instruction purposes.

513

g. *Professional Association Involvement.*

Counselors actively participate in local, state, and national associations that foster the development and improvement of counseling.

C.4. CREDENTIALS

a. *Credentials Claimed.*

Counselors claim or imply only professional credentials possessed and are responsible for correcting any known misrepresentations of their credentials by others. Professional credentials include graduate degrees in counseling or closely related mental health fields, accreditation of graduate programs, national voluntary certifications, government-issued certifications or licenses, ACA professional membership, or any other credential that might indicate to the public specialized knowledge or expertise in counseling.

b. *ACA Professional Membership.*

ACA professional members may announce to the public their membership status. Regular members may not announce their ACA membership in a manner that might imply they are credentialed counselors.

c. *Credential Guidelines.*

Counselors follow the guidelines for use of credentials that have been established by the entities that issue the credentials.

d. *Misrepresentation of Credentials.*

Counselors do not attribute more to their credentials than the credentials represent and do not imply that other counselors are not qualified because they do not possess certain credentials.

e. *Doctoral Degrees From Other Fields.*

Counselors who hold a master's degree in counseling or a closely related mental health field but hold a doctoral degree from other than counseling or a closely related field do not use the title, "Dr.," in their practices and do not announce to the public in relation to their practice or status as a counselor that they hold a doctorate.

C.5. PUBLIC RESPONSIBILITY

a. *Nondiscrimination.*

Counselors do not discriminate against clients, students, or supervisees in a manner that has a negative impact based on their age, color, culture, disability, ethnic group, gender, race, religion, sexual orientation, or socioeconomic status, or for any other reason. (See A.2.a.)

b. *Sexual Harassment.*

Counselors do not engage in sexual harassment. Sexual harassment is defined as sexual solicitation, physical advances, or verbal or nonverbal conduct that is sexual in nature, that occurs in connection with professional activities or roles, and that either (1) is

unwelcome, is offensive, or creates a hostile workplace environment, and counselors know or are told this; or (2) is sufficiently severe or intense to be perceived as harassment to a reasonable person in the context. Sexual harassment can consist of a single intense or severe act or multiple persistent or pervasive acts.

c. *Reports to Third Parties.*

Counselors are accurate, honest, and unbiased in reporting their professional activities and judgments to appropriate third parties including courts, health insurance companies, those who are the recipients of evaluation reports, and others. (See B.1.g.)

d. *Media Presentations.*

When counselors provide advice or comment by means of public lectures, demonstrations, radio or television programs, prerecorded tapes, printed articles, mailed material, or other media, they take reasonable precautions to ensure that (1) the statements are based on appropriate professional counseling literature and practice; (2) the statements are otherwise consistent with the Code of Ethics and the Standards of Practice; and (3) the recipients of the information are not encouraged to infer that a professional counseling relationship has been established. (See C.6.b.)

e. *Unjustified Gains.*

Counselors do not use their professional positions to seek or receive unjustified personal gains, sexual favors, unfair advantage, or unearned goods or services. (See C.3.d.)

C.6. RESPONSIBILITY TO OTHER PROFESSIONALS

a. *Different Approaches.*

Counselors are respectful of approaches to professional counseling that differ from their own. Counselors know and take into account the traditions and practices of other professional groups with which they work.

b. *Personal Public Statements.*

When making personal statements in a public context, counselors clarify that they are speaking from their personal perspectives and that they are not speaking on behalf of all counselors or the profession. (See C.5.d.)

c. *Clients Served by Others.*

When counselors learn that their clients are in a professional relationship with another mental health professional, they request release from clients to inform the other professionals and strive to establish positive and collaborative professional relationships. (See A.4.)

SECTION D: RELATIONSHIPS WITH OTHER PROFESSIONALS

D.1. RELATIONSHIPS WITH EMPLOYERS AND EMPLOYEES

a. *Role Definition.*

Counselors define and describe for their employers and employees the parameters and levels of their professional roles.

b. *Agreements.*

Counselors establish working agreements with supervisors, colleagues, and subordinates regarding counseling or clinical relationships, confidentiality, adherence to professional standards, distinction between public and private material, maintenance and dissemination of recorded information, workload, and accountability. Working agreements in each instance are specified and made known to those concerned.

c. *Negative Conditions.*

Counselors alert their employers to conditions that may be potentially disruptive or damaging to the counselor's professional responsibilities or that may limit their effectiveness.

d. *Evaluation.*

Counselors submit regularly to professional review and evaluation by their supervisor or the appropriate representative of the employer.

e. *In-Service.*

Counselors are responsible for in-service development of self and staff.

f. *Goals.*

Counselors inform their staff of goals and programs.

g. *Practices.*

Counselors provide personnel and agency practices that respect and enhance the rights and welfare of each employee and recipient of agency services. Counselors strive to maintain the highest levels of professional services.

h. *Personnel Selection and Assignment.*

Counselors select competent staff and assign responsibilities compatible with their skills and experiences.

i. *Discrimination.*

Counselors, as either employers or employees, do not engage in or condone practices that are inhumane, illegal, or unjustifiable (such as considerations based on age, color, culture, disability, ethnic group, gender, race, religion, sexual orientation, or socioeconomic status) in hiring, promotion, or training. (See A.2.a. and C.5.b.)

j. *Professional Conduct.*

Counselors have a responsibility both to clients and to the agency or institution within which services are performed to maintain high standards of professional conduct.

k. *Exploitive Relationships.*

Counselors do not engage in exploitive relationships with individuals over whom they have supervisory, evaluative, or instructional control or authority.

l. *Employer Policies.*

The acceptance of employment in an agency or institution implies that counselors are in agreement with its general policies and principles. Counselors strive to reach agreement with employers as to acceptable standards of conduct that allow for changes in institutional policy conducive to the growth and development of clients.

D.2. CONSULTATION (See B.6.)

a. *Consultation as an Option.*

Counselors may choose to consult with any other professionally competent persons about their clients. In choosing consultants, counselors avoid placing the consultant in a conflict of interest situation that would preclude the consultant being a proper party to the counselor's efforts to help the client. Should counselors be engaged in a work setting that compromises this consultation standard, they consult with other professionals whenever possible to consider justifiable alternatives.

b. *Consultant Competency.*

Counselors are reasonably certain that they have or the organization represented has the necessary competencies and resources for giving the kind of consulting services needed and that appropriate referral resources are available.

c. *Understanding With Clients.*

When providing consultation, counselors attempt to develop with their clients a clear understanding of problem definition, goals for change, and predicted consequences of interventions selected.

d. *Consultant Goals.*

The consulting relationship is one in which client adaptability and growth toward self-direction are consistently encouraged and cultivated. (See A.1.b.)

D.3. FEES FOR REFERRAL

a. *Accepting Fees From Agency Clients.*

Counselors refuse a private fee or other remuneration for rendering services to persons who are entitled to such services through the counselor's employing agency or institution. The policies of a particular agency may make explicit provisions for agency clients to receive counseling services from members of its staff in private practice. In such instances, the clients must be informed of other options open to them should they seek private counseling services. (See A.10.a., A.11.b., and C.3.d.)

b. *Referral Fees.*

Counselors do not accept a referral fee from other professionals.

D.4. SUBCONTRACTOR ARRANGEMENTS

When counselors work as subcontractors for counseling services for a third party, they have a duty to inform clients of the limitations of confidentiality that the organization may place on counselors in providing counseling services to clients. The limits of such confidentiality ordinarily are discussed as part of the intake session. (See B.1.e. and B.1.f.)

SECTION E: EVALUATION, ASSESSMENT, AND INTERPRETATION

E.1. GENERAL

a. *Appraisal Techniques.*

The primary purpose of educational and psychological assessment is to provide measures that are objective and interpretable in either comparative or absolute terms. Counselors recognize the need to interpret the statements in this section as applying to the whole range of appraisal techniques including test and nontest data.

b. *Client Welfare.*

Counselors promote the welfare and best interests of the client in the development, publication, and utilization of educational and psychological assessment techniques. They do not misuse assessment results and interpretations and take reasonable steps to prevent others from misusing the information these techniques provide. They respect the client's right to know the results, the interpretations made, and the basis for their conclusions and recommendations.

E.2. COMPETENCE TO USE AND INTERPRET TESTS

a. *Limits of Competence.*

Counselors recognize the limits of their competence and perform only those testing and assessment services for which they have been trained. They are familiar with reliability, validity, related standardization, error of measurement, and proper application of any technique utilized. Counselors using computer-based test interpretations are trained in the construct being measured and the specific instrument being used prior to using this type of computer application. Counselors take reasonable measures to ensure the proper use of psychological assessment techniques by persons under their supervision.

b. *Appropriate Use.*

Counselors are responsible for the appropriate application, scoring, interpretation, and use of assessment instruments whether they score and interpret such tests themselves or use computerized or other services.

c. *Decisions Based on Results.*

Counselors responsible for decisions involving individuals or policies that are based on assessment results have a thorough understanding of educational and psychological measurement including validation criteria, test research, and guidelines for test development and use.

d. *Accurate Information.*

Counselors provide accurate information and avoid false claims or misconceptions when making statements about assessment instruments or techniques. Special efforts are made to avoid unwarranted connotations of such terms as IQ and grade equivalent scores. (See C.5.c.)

E.3. INFORMED CONSENT

a. *Explanation to Clients.*

Prior to assessment, counselors explain the nature and purposes of assessment and the specific use of results in language the client (or other legally authorized person on behalf of the client) can understand unless an explicit exception to this right has been agreed upon in advance. Regardless of whether scoring and interpretation are completed by counselors, by assistants, or by computer or other outside services, counselors take reasonable steps to ensure that appropriate explanations are given to the client.

b. *Recipients of Results.*

The examinee's welfare, explicit understanding, and prior agreement determine the recipients of test results. Counselors include accurate and appropriate interpretations with any release of individual or group test results. (See B.1.a. and C.5.c.)

E.4. RELEASE OF INFORMATION TO COMPETENT PROFESSIONALS

a. *Misuse of Results.*

Counselors do not misuse assessment results, including test results, and interpretations and take reasonable steps to prevent the misuse of such by others. (See C.5.c.)

b. *Release of Raw Data.*

Counselors ordinarily release data (e.g. protocols, counseling or interview notes, or questionnaires) in which the client is identified only with the consent of the client or the client's legal representative. Such data are usually released only to persons recognized by counselors as competent to interpret the data. (See B.1.a.)

E.5. PROPER DIAGNOSIS OF MENTAL DISORDERS

a. *Proper Diagnosis.*

Counselors take special care to provide proper diagnosis of mental disorders. Assessment techniques (including personal interview) used to determine client care (e.g., locus of treatment, type of treatment, or recommended follow-up) are carefully selected and appropriately used. (See A.3.a. and C.5.c.)

b. *Cultural Sensitivity.*

Counselors recognize that culture affects the manner in which clients' problems are defined. Clients' socioeconomic and cultural experience is considered when diagnosing mental disorders.

E.6. TEST SELECTION

a. *Appropriateness of Instruments.*

Counselors carefully consider the validity, reliability, psychometric limitations, and appropriateness of instruments when selecting tests for use in a given situation or with a particular client.

b. *Culturally Diverse Populations.*

Counselors are cautious when selecting tests for culturally diverse populations to avoid inappropriateness of testing that may be outside of socialized behavioral or cognitive patterns.

E.7. CONDITIONS OF TEST ADMINISTRATION

a. *Administration Conditions.*

Counselors administer tests under the same conditions that were established in their standardization. When tests are not administered under standard conditions or when unusual behavior or irregularities occur during the testing session, those conditions are noted in interpretation, and the results may be designated as invalid or of questionable validity.

b. *Computer Administration.*

Counselors are responsible for ensuring that administration programs function properly to provide clients with accurate results when a computer or other electronic methods are used for test administration. (See A.12.b.)

c. *Unsupervised Test-Taking.*

Counselors do not permit unsupervised or inadequately supervised use of tests or assessments unless the tests or assessments are designed, intended, and validated for self-administration and/or scoring.

d. *Disclosure of Favorable Conditions.*

Prior to test administration, conditions that produce most favorable test results are made known to the examinee.

E.8. DIVERSITY IN TESTING

Counselors are cautious in using assessment techniques, making evaluations, and interpreting the performance of populations not represented in the norm group on which an instrument was standardized. They recognize the effects of age, color, culture, disability, ethnic group, gender, race, religion, sexual orientation, and socioeconomic status on test administration and interpretation and place test results in proper perspective with other relevant factors. (See A.2.a.)

E.9. TEST SCORING AND INTERPRETATION

a. *Reporting Reservations.*

In reporting assessment results, counselors indicate any reservations that exist regarding validity or reliability because of the circumstances of the assessment or the inappropriateness of the norms for the person tested.

b. *Research Instruments.*

Counselors exercise caution when interpreting the results of research instruments possessing insufficient technical data to support respondent results. The specific purposes for the use of such instruments are stated explicitly to the examinee.

c. *Testing Services.*

Counselors who provide test scoring and test interpretation services to support the assessment process confirm the validity of such interpretations. They accurately describe the purpose, norms, validity, reliability, and applications of the procedures and any special qualifications applicable to their use. The public offering of an automated test interpretations service is considered a professional-to-professional consultation. The formal responsibility of the consultant is to the consultee, but the ultimate and overriding responsibility is to the client.

E.10. TEST SECURITY

Counselors maintain the integrity and security of tests and other assessment techniques consistent with legal and contractual obligations. Counselors do not appropriate, reproduce, or modify published tests or parts thereof without acknowledgment and permission from the publisher.

E.11. OBSOLETE TESTS AND OUTDATED TEST RESULTS

Counselors do not use data or test results that are obsolete or outdated for the current purpose. Counselors make every effort to prevent the misuse of obsolete measures and test data by others.

E.12. Test Construction

Counselors use established scientific procedures, relevant standards, and current professional knowledge for test design in the development, publication, and utilization of educational and psychological assessment techniques.

SECTION F: TEACHING, TRAINING, AND SUPERVISION

F.1. COUNSELOR EDUCATORS AND TRAINERS

a. *Educators as Teachers and Practitioners.*

Counselors who are responsible for developing, implementing, and supervising educational programs are skilled as teachers and practitioners. They are knowledgeable regarding the ethical, legal, and regulatory aspects of the profession, are skilled in applying that knowledge, and make students and supervisees aware of their responsibilities. Counselors conduct counselor education and training programs in an ethical manner and serve as role models for professional behavior. Counselor educators should make an effort to infuse material related to human diversity into all courses and/or workshops that are designed to promote the development of professional counselors.

b. *Relationship Boundaries With Students and Supervisees.*

Counselors clearly define and maintain ethical, professional, and social relationship boundaries with their students and supervisees. They are aware of the differential in power that exists and the student's or supervisee's possible incomprehension of that power differential. Counselors explain to students and supervisees the potential for the relationship to become exploitive.

c. *Sexual Relationships.*

Counselors do not engage in sexual relationships with students or supervisees and do not subject them to sexual harassment. (See A.6. and C.5.b.)

d. *Contributions to Research.*

Counselors give credit to students or supervisees for their contributions to research and scholarly projects. Credit is given through coauthorship, acknowledgment, footnote statement, or other appropriate means in accordance with such contributions. (See G.4.b. and G.4.c.)

e. *Close Relatives.*

Counselors do not accept close relatives as students or supervisees.

f. *Supervision Preparation.*

Counselors who offer clinical supervision services are adequately prepared in supervision methods and techniques. Counselors who are doctoral students serving as practicum or internship supervisors to master's level students are adequately prepared and supervised by the training program.

g. *Responsibility for Services to Clients.*

Counselors who supervise the counseling services of others take reasonable measures to ensure that counseling services provided to clients are professional.

h. *Endorsement.*

Counselors do not endorse students or supervisees for certification, licensure, employment, or completion of an academic or training program if they believe students or supervisees are not qualified for the endorsement. Counselors take reasonable steps to assist students or supervisees who are not qualified for endorsement to become qualified.

F.2. **COUNSELOR EDUCATION AND TRAINING PROGRAMS**

a. *Orientation.*

Prior to admission, counselors orient prospective students to the counselor education or training program's expectations including but not limited to the following: (1) the type and level of skill acquisition required for successful completion of the training, (2) subject matter to be covered, (3) basis for evaluation, (4) training components that encourage self-growth or self-disclosure as part of the training process, (5) the type of supervision settings and requirements of the sites for required clinical field experiences, (6) student and supervisee evaluation and dismissal policies and procedures, and (7) up-to-date employment prospects for graduates.

b. *Integration of Study and Practice.*

Counselors establish counselor education and training programs that integrate academic study and supervised practice.

c. *Evaluation.*

Counselors clearly state to students and supervisees, in advance of training, the levels of competency expected, appraisal methods, and timing of evaluations for both didactic and experiential components. Counselors provide students and supervisees with periodic performance appraisal and evaluation feedback throughout the training program.

d. *Teaching Ethics.*

Counselors make students and supervisees aware of the ethical responsibilities and standards of the profession and the students' and supervisees' ethical responsibilities to the profession. (See C.1. and F.3.e.)

e. *Peer Relationships.*

When students or supervisees are assigned to lead counseling groups or provide clinical supervision for their peers, counselors take steps to ensure that students and supervisees placed in these roles do not have personal or adverse relationships with peers and that they understand they have the same ethical obligations as counselor educators, trainers, and supervisors. Counselors make every effort to ensure that the rights of peers are not compromised when students or supervisees are assigned to lead counseling groups or provide clinical supervision.

f. *Varied Theoretical Positions.*

Counselors present varied theoretical positions so that students and supervisees may make comparisons and have opportunities to develop their own positions. Counselors provide information concerning the scientific basis of professional practice. (See C.6.a.)

g. *Field Placements.*

Counselors develop clear policies within their training program regarding field placement and other clinical experiences. Counselors provide clearly stated roles and responsibilities for the student or supervisee, the site supervisor, and the program supervisor. They confirm that site supervisors are qualified to provide supervision and are informed of their professional and ethical responsibilities in this role.

h. *Dual Relationships as Supervisors.*

Counselors avoid dual relationships, such as performing the role of site supervisor and training program supervisor in the student's or supervisee's training program. Counselors do not accept any form of professional services, fees, commissions, reimbursement, or remuneration from a site for student or supervisee placement.

i. *Diversity in Programs.*

Counselors are responsive to their institution's and program's recruitment and retention needs for training program administrators, faculty, and students with diverse backgrounds and special needs. (See A.2.a.)

F.3. **STUDENTS AND SUPERVISEES**

a. *Limitations.*

Counselors, through ongoing evaluation and appraisal, are aware of the academic and personal limitations of students and supervisees that might impede performance. Counselors assist students and supervisees in securing remedial assistance when needed and dismiss from the training program supervisees who are unable to provide competent service due to academic or personal limitations. Counselors seek professional consultation and document their decision to dismiss or refer students or supervisees for assistance. Counselors assure that students and supervisees have recourse to address decisions made, to require them to seek assistance, or to dismiss them.

b. *Self-Growth Experiences.*

Counselors use professional judgment when designing training experiences conducted by the counselors themselves that require student and supervisee self-growth or self-disclosure. Safeguards are provided so that students and supervisees are aware of the ramifications their self-disclosure may have on counselors whose primary role as teacher, trainer, or supervisor requires acting on ethical obligations to the profession. Evaluative components of experiential training experiences explicitly delineate predetermined academic standards that are separate and not dependent on the student's level of self-disclosure. (See A.6.)

c. *Counseling for Students and Supervisees.*

If students or supervisees request counseling, supervisors or counselor educators provide them with acceptable referrals. Supervisors or counselor educators do not serve as counselor to students or supervisees over whom they hold administrative, teaching, or evaluative roles unless this is a brief role associated with a training experience. (See A.6.b.)

d. *Clients of Students and Supervisees.*

Counselors make every effort to ensure that the clients at field placements are aware of the services rendered and the qualifications of the students and supervisees rendering those services. Clients receive professional disclosure information and are informed of the limits of confidentiality. Client permission is obtained in order for the students and supervisees to use any information concerning the counseling relationship in the training process. (See B.1.e.)

e. *Standards for Students and Supervisees.*

Students and supervisees preparing to become counselors adhere to the Code of Ethics and the Standards of Practice. Students and supervisees have the same obligations to clients as those required of counselors. (See H.1.)

SECTION G: RESEARCH AND PUBLICATION

G.1. **RESEARCH RESPONSIBILITIES**

a. *Use of Human Subjects.*

Counselors plan, design, conduct, and report research in a manner consistent with pertinent ethical principles, federal and state laws, host institutional regulations, and scientific standards governing research with human subjects. Counselors design and conduct research that reflects cultural sensitivity appropriateness.

b. *Deviation From Standard Practices.*

Counselors seek consultation and observe stringent safeguards to protect the rights of research participants when a research problem suggests a deviation from standard acceptable practices. (See B.6.)

c. *Precautions to Void Injury.*

Counselors who conduct research with human subjects are responsible for the subjects' welfare throughout the experiment and take reasonable precautions to avoid causing injurious psychological, physical, or social effects to their subjects.

d. *Principal Researcher Responsibility.*

The ultimate responsibility for ethical research practice lies with the principal researcher. All others involved in the research activities share ethical obligations and full responsibility for their own actions.

e. *Minimal Interference.*

Counselors take reasonable precautions to avoid causing disruptions in subjects' lives due to participation in research.

f. *Diversity.*

Counselors are sensitive to diversity and research issues with special populations. They seek consultation when appropriate. (See A.2.a. and B.6.)

G.2. Informed Consent

a. *Topics Disclosed.*

In obtaining informed consent for research, counselors use language that is understandable to research participants and that (1) accurately explains the purpose and procedures to be followed; (2) identifies any procedures that are experimental or relatively untried; (3) describes the attendant discomforts and risks; (4) describes the benefits or changes in individuals or organizations that might be reasonably expected; (5) discloses appropriate alternative procedures that would be advantageous for subjects; (6) offers to answer any inquiries concerning the procedures; (7) describes any limitations on confidentiality; and (8) instructs that subjects are free to withdraw their consent and to discontinue participation in the project at any time. (See B.1.f.)

b. *Deception.*

Counselors do not conduct research involving deception unless alternative procedures are not feasible and the prospective value of the research justifies the deception. When the methodological requirements of a study necessitate concealment or deception, the investigator is required to explain clearly the reasons for this action as soon as possible.

c. *Voluntary Participation.*

Participation in research is typically voluntary and without any penalty for refusal to participate. Involuntary participation is appropriate only when it can be demonstrated that participation will have no harmful effects on subjects and is essential to the investigation.

d. *Confidentiality of Information.*

Information obtained about research participants during the course of an investigation is confidential. When the possibility exists that others may obtain access to such information, ethical research practice requires that the possibility, together with the plans for protecting confidentiality, be explained to participants as a part of the procedure for obtaining informed consent. (See B.1.e.)

e. *Persons Incapable of Giving Informed Consent.*

When a person is incapable of giving informed consent, counselors provide an appropriate explanation, obtain agreement for participation and obtain appropriate consent from a legally authorized person.

f. *Commitments to Participants.*

Counselors take reasonable measures to honor all commitments to research participants.

g. *Explanations After Data Collection.*

After data are collected, counselors provide participants with full clarification of the nature of the study to remove any misconceptions. Where scientific or human values justify delaying or withholding information, counselors take reasonable measures to avoid causing harm.

h. *Agreements to Cooperate.*

Counselors who agree to cooperate with another individual in research or publication incur an obligation to cooperate as promised in terms of punctuality of performance and with regard to the completeness and accuracy of the information required.

i. *Informed Consent for Sponsors.*

In the pursuit of research, counselors give sponsors, institutions, and publication channels the same respect and opportunity for giving informed consent that they accord to individual research participants. Counselors are aware of their obligation to future research workers and ensure that host institutions are given feedback information and proper acknowledgment.

G.3. Reporting Results

a. *Information Affecting Outcome.*

When reporting research results, counselors explicitly mention all variables and conditions known to the investigator that may have affected the outcome of a study or the interpretation of data.

b. *Accurate Results.*

Counselors plan, conduct, and report research accurately and in a manner that minimizes the possibility that results will be misleading. They provide thorough discussions of the limitations of their data and alternative hypotheses. Counselors do not engage in fraudulent research, distort data, misrepresent data, or deliberately bias their results.

c. *Obligation to Report Unfavorable Results.*

Counselors communicate to other counselors the results of any research judged to be of professional value. Results that reflect unfavorably on institutions, programs, services, prevailing opinions, or vested interests are not withheld.

d. *Identity of Subjects.*

Counselors who supply data, aid in the research of another person, report research results, or make original data available take due care to disguise the identity of respective subjects in the absence of specific authorization from the subjects to do otherwise. (See B.1.g. and B.5.a.)

e. *Replication Studies.*

Counselors are obligated to make available sufficient original research data to qualified professionals who may wish to replicate the study.

G.4. Publication

a. *Recognition of Others.*

When conducting and reporting research, counselors are familiar with and give recognition to previous work on the topic, observe copyright laws, and give full credit to those to whom credit is due. (See F.1.d. and G.4.c.)

b. *Contributors.*

Counselors give credit through joint authorship, acknowledgment, footnote statements, or other appropriate means to those who have contributed significantly to research or concept development in accordance with such contributions. The principal contributor is listed first and minor technical or professional contributions are acknowledged in notes or introductory statements.

c. *Student Research.*

For an article that is substantially based on a student's dissertation or thesis, the student is listed as the principal author. (See F.1.d. and G.4.a.)

d. *Duplicate Submission.*

Counselors submit manuscripts for consideration to only one journal at a time. Manuscripts that are published in whole or in substantial part in another journal or published work are not submitted for publication without acknowledgment and permission from the previous publication.

e. *Professional Review.* Counselors who review material submitted for publication, research, or other scholarly purposes respect the confidentiality and proprietary rights of those who submitted it.

518

Section H: Resolving Ethical Issues

H.1. KNOWLEDGE OF STANDARDS

Counselors are familiar with the Code of Ethics and the Standards of Practice and other applicable ethics codes from other professional organizations of which they are member or from certification and licensure bodies. Lack of knowledge or misunderstanding of an ethical responsibility is not a defense against a charge of unethical conduct. (See F.3.e.)

H.2. SUSPECTED VIOLATIONS

a. *Ethical Behavior Expected.*

Counselors expect professional associates to adhere to Code of Ethics. When counselors possess reasonable cause that raises doubts as to whether a counselor is acting in an ethical manner, they take appropriate action. (See H.2.d. and H.2.e.)

b. *Consultation.*

When uncertain as to whether a particular situation or course of action may be in violation of Code of Ethics, counselors consult with other counselors who are knowledgeable about ethics, with colleagues, or with appropriate authorities.

c. *Organization Conflicts.*

If the demands of an organization with which counselors are affiliated pose a conflict with Code of Ethics, counselors specify the nature of such conflicts and express to their supervisors or other responsible officials their commitment to Code of Ethics. When possible, counselors work toward change within the organization to allow full adherence to Code of Ethics.

d. *Informal Resolution.*

When counselors have reasonable cause to believe that another counselor is violating an ethical standard, they attempt to first resolve the issue informally with the other counselor if feasible providing that such action does not violate confidentiality rights that may be involved.

e. *Reporting Suspected Violations.*

When an informal resolution is not appropriate or feasible, counselors, upon reasonable cause, take action, such as reporting the suspected ethical violation to state or national ethics committees, unless this action conflicts with confidentiality rights that cannot be resolved.

f. *Unwarranted Complaints.*

Counselors do not initiate, participate in, or encourage the filing of ethics complaints that are unwarranted or intend to harm a counselor rather than to protect clients or the public.

H.3. COOPERATION WITH ETHICS COMMITTEES

Counselors assist in the process of enforcing Code of Ethics. Counselors cooperate with investigations, proceedings, and requirements of the ACA Ethics Committee or ethics committees of other duly constituted associations or boards having jurisdiction over those charged with a violation. Counselors are familiar with the ACA Policies and Procedures and use it as a reference in assisting the enforcement of the Code of Ethics.

STANDARDS OF PRACTICE

All members of the American Counseling Association (ACA) are required to adhere to the Standards of Practice and the Code of Ethics. The Standards of Practice represent minimal behavioral statements of the Code of Ethics. Members should refer to the applicable section of the Code of Ethics for further interpretation and amplification of the applicable Standard of Practice.

SECTION A: THE COUNSELING RELATIONSHIP

STANDARD OF PRACTICE ONE (SP-1) NONDISCRIMINATION

Counselors respect diversity and must not discriminate against clients because of age, color, culture, disability, ethnic group, gender, race, religion, sexual orientation, marital status, or socioeconomic status. (See A.2.a.)

STANDARD OF PRACTICE TWO (SP-2) DISCLOSURE TO CLIENTS

Counselors must adequately inform clients, preferably in writing, regarding the counseling process and counseling relationship at or before the time it begins and throughout the relationship. (See A.3.a.)

STANDARD OF PRACTICE THREE (SP-3) DUAL RELATIONSHIPS

Counselors must make every effort to avoid dual relationships with clients that could impair their professional judgment or increase the risk of harm to clients. When a dual relationship cannot be avoided, counselors must take appropriate steps to ensure that judgment is not impaired and that no exploitation occurs. (See A.6.a. and A.6.b.)

STANDARD OF PRACTICE FOUR (SP-4) SEXUAL INTIMACIES WITH CLIENTS

Counselors must not engage in any type of sexual intimacies with current clients and must not engage in sexual intimacies with former clients within a minimum of two years after terminating the counseling relationship. Counselors who engage in such relationship after two years following termination have the responsibility to thoroughly examine and document that such relations did not have an exploitative nature.

STANDARD OF PRACTICE FIVE (SP-5) PROTECTING CLIENTS DURING GROUP WORK

Counselors must take steps to protect clients from physical or psychological trauma resulting from interactions during group work. (See A.9.b.)

STANDARD OF PRACTICE SIX (SP-6) ADVANCE UNDERSTANDING OF FEES

Counselors must explain to clients, prior to their entering the counseling relationship, financial arrangements related to professional services. (See A.10. a-d. and A.11.c.)

STANDARD OF PRACTICE SEVEN (SP-7) TERMINATION

Counselors must assist in making appropriate arrangements for the continuation of treatment of clients, when necessary, following termination of counseling relationships. (See A.11.a.)

STANDARD OF PRACTICE EIGHT (SP-8) INABILITY TO ASSIST CLIENTS

Counselors must avoid entering or immediately terminate a counseling relationship if it is determined that they are unable to be of professional assistance to a client. The counselor may assist in making an appropriate referral for the client. (See A.11.b.)

SECTION B: CONFIDENTIALITY

STANDARD OF PRACTICE NINE (SP-9) CONFIDENTIALITY REQUIREMENT

Counselors must keep information related to counseling services confidential unless disclosure is in the best interest of clients, is required for the welfare of others, or is required by law. When disclosure is required, only information that is essential is revealed and the client is informed of such disclosure. (See B.1. a.- f.)

Standard of Practice Ten (SP-10) Confidentiality Requirements for Subordinates

Counselors must take measures to ensure that privacy and confidentiality of clients are maintained by subordinates. (See B.1.h.)

Standard of Practice Eleven (SP-11) Confidentiality in Group Work

Counselors must clearly communicate to group members that confidentiality cannot be guaranteed in group work. (See B.2.a.)

Standard of Practice Twelve (SP-12) Confidentiality in Family Counseling

Counselors must not disclose information about one family member in counseling to another family member without prior consent. (See B.2.b.)

Standard of Practice Thirteen (SP-13) Confidentiality of Records

Counselors must maintain appropriate confidentiality in creating, storing, accessing, transferring, and disposing of counseling records. (See B.4.b.)

Standard of Practice Fourteen (SP-14) Permission to Record or Observe

Counselors must obtain prior consent from clients in order to electronically record or observe sessions. (See B.4.c.)

Standard of Practice Fifteen (SP-15) Disclosure or Transfer of Records

Counselors must obtain client consent to disclose or transfer records to third parties unless exceptions listed in SP-9 exist. (See B.4.e.)

Standard of Practice Sixteen (SP-16) Data Disguise Required

Counselors must disguise the identity of the client when using data for training, research, or publication. (See B.5.a.)

Section C: Professional Responsibility

Standard of Practice Seventeen (SP-17) Boundaries of Competence

Counselors must practice only within the boundaries of their competence. (See C.2.a.)

Standard of Practice Eighteen (SP-18) Continuing Education

Counselors must engage in continuing education to maintain their professional competence. (See C.2.f.)

Standard of Practice Nineteen (SP-19) Impairment of Professionals

Counselors must refrain from offering professional services when their personal problems or conflicts may cause harm to a client or others. (See C.2.g.)

Standard of Practice Twenty (SP-20) Accurate Advertising

Counselors must accurately represent their credentials and services when advertising. (See C.3.a.)

Standard of Practice Twenty-one (SP-21) Recruiting Through Employment

Counselors must not use their place of employment or institutional affiliation to recruit clients for their private practices. (See C.3.d.)

Standard of Practice Twenty-two (SP-22) Credentials Claimed

Counselors must claim or imply only professional credentials possessed and must correct any known misrepresentations of their credentials by others. (See C.4.a.)

Standard of Practice Twenty-three (SP-23) Sexual Harassment

Counselors must not engage in sexual harassment. (See C.5.b.)

Standard of Practice Twenty-four (SP-24) Unjustified Gains

Counselors must not use their professional positions to seek or receive unjustified personal gains, sexual favors, unfair advantage, or unearned goods or services. (See C.5.e.)

Standard of Practice Twenty-five (SP-25) Clients Served by Others

With the consent of the client, counselors must inform other mental health professionals serving the same client that a counseling relationship between the counselor and client exists. (See C.6.c.)

Standard of Practice Twenty-six (SP-26) Negative Employment Conditions

Counselors must alert their employers to institutional policy or conditions that may be potentially disruptive or damaging to the counselor's professional responsibilities or that may limit their effectiveness or deny clients' rights. (See D.1.c.)

Standard of Practice Twenty-seven (SP-27) Personnel Selection and Assignment

Counselors must select competent staff and must assign responsibilities compatible with staff skills and experiences. (See D.1.h.)

Standard of Practice Twenty-eight (SP-28) Exploitive Relationships with Subordinates

Counselors must not engage in exploitive relationships with individuals over whom they have supervisory, evaluative, or instructional control or authority. (See D.1.k.)

Section D: Relationship With Other Professionals

Standard of Practice Twenty-nine (SP-29) Accepting Fees from Agency Clients

Counselors must not accept fees or other remuneration for consultation with persons entitled to such services through the counselor's employing agency or institution. (See D.3.a.)

Standard of Practice Thirty (SP-30) Referral Fees

Counselors must not accept referral fees. (See D.3.b.)

Section E: Evaluation, Assessment, and Interpretation

Standard of Practice Thirty-one (SP-31) Limits of Competence

Counselors must perform only testing and assessment services for which they are competent. Counselors must not allow the use of psychological assessment techniques by unqualified persons under their supervision. (See E.2.a.)

Standard of Practice Thirty-two (SP-32) Appropriate Use of Assessment Instruments

Counselors must use assessment instruments in the manner for which they were intended. (See E.2.b.)

Standard of Practice Thirty-three (SP-33) Assessment Explanations to Clients

Counselors must provide explanations to clients prior to assessment about the nature and purposes of assessment and the specific uses of results. (See E.3.a.)

Standard of Practice Thirty-four (SP-34) Recipients of Test Results

Counselors must ensure that accurate and appropriate interpretations accompany any release of testing and assessment information. (See E.3.b.)

Standard of Practice Thirty-five (SP-35) Obsolete Tests and Outdated Test Results

Counselors must not base their assessment or intervention decisions or recommendations on data or test results that are obsolete or outdated for the current purpose. (See E.11.)

SECTION F: TEACHING, TRAINING, AND SUPERVISION

STANDARD OF PRACTICE THIRTY-SIX (SP-36) SEXUAL RELATIONSHIPS WITH STUDENTS OR SUPERVISEES

Counselors must not engage in sexual relationships with their students and supervisees. (See F.1.c.)

STANDARD OF PRACTICE THIRTY-SEVEN (SP-37) CREDIT FOR CONTRIBUTIONS TO RESEARCH

Counselors must give credit to students or supervisees for their contributions to research and scholarly projects. (See F.1.d.)

STANDARD OF PRACTICE THIRTY-EIGHT (SP-38) SUPERVISION PREPARATION

Counselors who offer clinical supervision services must be trained and prepared in supervision methods and techniques. (See F.1.f.)

STANDARD OF PRACTICE THIRTY-NINE (SP-39) EVALUATION INFORMATION

Counselors must clearly state to students and supervisees, in advance of training, the levels of competency expected, appraisal methods, and timing of evaluations. Counselors must provide students and supervisees with periodic performance appraisal and evaluation feedback throughout the training program. (See F.2.c.)

STANDARD OF PRACTICE FORTY (SP-40) PEER RELATIONSHIPS IN TRAINING

Counselors must make every effort to ensure that the rights of peers are not violated when students and supervisees are assigned to lead counseling groups or provide clinical supervision. (See F.2.e.)

STANDARD OF PRACTICE FORTY-ONE (SP-41) LIMITATIONS OF STUDENTS AND SUPERVISEES

Counselors must assist students and supervisees in securing remedial assistance, when needed, and must dismiss from the training program students and supervisees who are unable to provide competent service due to academic or personal limitations. (See F.3.a.)

STANDARD OF PRACTICE FORTY-TWO (SP-42) SELF-GROWTH EXPERIENCES

Counselors who conduct experiences for students or supervisees that include self-growth or self disclosure must inform participants of counselors' ethical obligations to the profession and must not grade participants based on their nonacademic performance. (See F.3.b.)

STANDARD OF PRACTICE FORTY-THREE (SP-43) STANDARDS FOR STUDENTS AND SUPERVISEES

Students and supervisees preparing to become counselors must adhere to the Code of Ethics and the Standards of Practice of counselors. (See F.3.e.)

SECTION G: RESEARCH AND PUBLICATION

STANDARD OF PRACTICE FORTY-FOUR (SP-44) PRECAUTIONS TO AVOID INJURY IN RESEARCH

Counselors must avoid causing physical, social, or psychological harm or injury to subjects in research. (See G.1.c.)

STANDARD OF PRACTICE FORTY-FIVE (SP-45) CONFIDENTIALITY OF RESEARCH INFORMATION

Counselors must keep confidential information obtained about research participants. (See G.2.d.)

STANDARD OF PRACTICE FORTY-SIX (SP-46) INFORMATION AFFECTING RESEARCH OUTCOME

Counselors must report all variables and conditions known to the investigator that may have affected research data or outcomes. (See G.3.a.)

STANDARD OF PRACTICE FORTY-SEVEN (SP-47) ACCURATE RESEARCH RESULTS

Counselors must not distort or misrepresent research data nor fabricate or intentionally bias research results. (See G.3.b.)

STANDARD OF PRACTICE FORTY-EIGHT (SP-48) PUBLICATION CONTRIBUTORS

Counselors must give appropriate credit to those who have contributed to research. (See G.4.a. and G.4.b.)

SECTION H: RESOLVING ETHICAL ISSUES

STANDARD OF PRACTICE FORTY-NINE (SP-49) ETHICAL BEHAVIOR EXPECTED

Counselors must take appropriate action when they possess reasonable cause that raises doubts as to whether counselors or other mental health professionals are acting in an ethical manner. (See H.2.a.)

STANDARD OF PRACTICE FIFTY (SP-50) UNWARRANTED COMPLAINTS

Counselors must not initiate, participate in, or encourage the filing of ethics complaints that are unwarranted or intended to harm a mental health professional rather than to protect clients or the public. (See H.2.f.)

STANDARD OF PRACTICE FIFTY-ONE (SP-51) COOPERATION WITH ETHICS COMMITTEES

Counselors must cooperate with investigations, proceedings, and requirements of the ACA Ethics Committee or ethics committees of other duly constituted associations or boards having jurisdiction over those charged with a violation. (See H.3.)

REFERENCES

The following documents are available to counselors as resources to guide them in their practices. These resources are not a part of the Code of Ethics and the Standards of Practice.

American Association for Counseling and Development/Association for Measurement and Evaluation in Counseling and Development. (1989). The responsibilities of users of standardized tests (revised). Washington, DC: Author.

American Counseling Association. (1988). American Counseling Association Ethical Standards. Alexandria, VA: Author.

American Psychological Association. (1985). Standards for educational and psychological testing (revised). Washington, DC: Author.

American Rehabilitation Counseling Association, Commission on Rehabilitation Counselor Certification, and National Rehabilitation Counseling Association. (1995). Code of professional ethics for rehabilitation counselors. Chicago, IL: Author.

American School Counselor Association. (1992). Ethical standards for school counselors. Alexandria, VA: Author.

Joint Committee on Testing Practices. (1988). Code of fair testing practices in education. Washington, DC: Author.

National Board for Certified Counselors. (1989). National Board for Certified Counselors Code of Ethics. Alexandria, VA: Author.

Prediger, D.J. (Ed.). (1993, March). Multicultural assessment standards. Alexandria, VA: Association for Assessment in Counseling.

POLICIES AND PROCEDURES FOR RESPONDING TO MEMBERS' REQUESTS FOR INTERPRETATIONS OF THE ETHICAL STANDARDS

SECTION: A
APPROPRIATE REQUESTS

1. ACA members may request that the Committee issue formal interpretations of the ACA Code of Ethics for the purpose of guiding the member's own professional behavior.

2. Requests for interpretations will not be considered in the following situations:

a. The individual requesting the interpretation is not an ACA member, or

b. The request is intended to determine whether the behavior of another mental health professional is unethical. In the event an ACA member believes the behavior of another mental health professional is unethical, the ACA member should resolve the issue directly with the professional, if possible, and should file an ethical complaint if appropriate.

SECTION B:
PROCEDURES

1. Members must send written requests for interpretations to the Committee at ACA Headquarters.

2. Questions should be submitted in the following format: "Does (counselor behavior) violate Sections _____ or any other sections of the ACA Ethical Standards?" Questions should avoid unique details, be general in nature to the extent possible, and be brief.

3. The Committee staff liaison will revise the question, if necessary, and submit it to the Committee Co-Chair for approval.

4. The question will be sent to Committee members who will be asked to respond individually.

5. The Committee Co-Chair will develop a consensus interpretation on behalf of the Committee.

6. The consensus interpretation will be sent to members of the Committee for final approval.

7. The formal interpretation will be sent to the member who submitted the inquiry.

8. The question and the formal interpretation will be published in the ACA newsletter, but the identity of the member requesting the interpretation will not be disclosed.

POLICIES AND PROCEDURES FOR PROCESSING COMPLAINTS OF ETHICAL VIOLATIONS

SECTION A
GENERAL

1. The American Counseling Association, hereafter referred to as the "Association" or "ACA," is dedicated to enhancing human development throughout the life span and promoting the counseling profession.

2. The Association, in furthering its objectives, administers the Code of Ethics and Standards of Practice developed and approved by the ACA Governing Council.

3. The purpose of this document is to facilitate the work of the ACA Ethics Committee ("Committee") by specifying the procedures for processing cases of alleged violations of the ACA Code of Ethics, codifying options for sanctioning members, and stating appeals procedures. This document is to be used as a supplement to the ACA Code of Ethics, not as a substitute. The intent of the Association is to monitor the professional conduct of its members to promote sound ethical practices. ACA does not, however, warrant the performance of any individual.

SECTION B
ETHICS COMMITTEE MEMBERS

1. The Ethics Committee, a standing committee of the Association, consists of six (6) appointed members including two (2) Co-Chairs whose terms overlap. Two members are appointed annually for three (3) year terms by the President-Elect; appointments are subject to confirmation by the ACA Governing Council. Any vacancy on the Committee will be filled by the President in the same manner, and the person appointed shall serve the unexpired term of the member whose place he or she took. Committee members may be reappointed to not more than one (1) additional consecutive term.

2. One (1) of the Committee Co-Chairs is appointed annually by the President-Elect from among the Committee members who have two (2) years of service remaining and serves as Co-Chair for two (2) years, subject to confirmation by the ACA Governing Council.

SECTION C
ROLE AND FUNCTION

1. The Ethics Committee is responsible for

a. Educating the membership as to the Association's Code of Ethics;

b. Periodically reviewing and recommending changes in the Code of Ethics of the Association, as well as Policies and Procedures for Processing Complaints of Ethical Violations;

c. Receiving and processing complaints of alleged violations of the Code of Ethics of the Association; and

d. Receiving and processing requests for interpretations.

2. The Committee shall meet in person or by telephone conference a minimum of three (3) times per year for processing complaints.

3. In processing complaints about alleged ethical misconduct, the Committee will compile an objective, factual account of the dispute in question and make the best possible recommendation for the resolution of the case. The Committee, in taking any action, shall do so only for cause, shall only take a reasonable degree of disciplinary action, shall utilize these procedures with objectivity and fairness, and in general shall act only to further the interests and objectives of the Association and its membership.

4. Of the six (6) voting members of the Committee, a vote of four (4) is necessary to conduct business. In the event a Co-Chair or any other member of the Committee has a personal interest in the case, he or she shall withdraw from reviewing the case.

5. In the event Committee members recuse themselves from a complaint and insufficient voting members are available to conduct business, the President shall appoint former ACA Committee members to decide the complaint.

Section D
Responsibilities of the Committee Members

1. The Committee members have an obligation to act in an unbiased manner, to work expeditiously, to safeguard the confidentiality of the Committee's activities, and to follow procedures established to protect the rights of all individuals involved.

Section E
Responsibilities of the Co-Chairs Administering the Complaint

1. In the event that one of the Co-Chairs administering the complaint has a conflict of interest in a particular case, the other Co-Chair shall administer the complaint. The Co-Chair administering the compliant shall not have a vote in the decision.

2. In addition to the above guidelines for members of the Committee, the Co-Chairs, with the assistance of the Headquarters staff liaison (and legal counsel where necessary), have the responsibilities of

a. Receiving, via ACA Headquarters, complaints that have been certified for membership status of the charged member;

b. Determining whether the alleged behavior(s), if true, would violate ACA's Code of Ethics and whether the Committee should review the complaint under these rules;

c. Notifying the complainant and the charged member of receipt of the case by certified mail return receipt requested;

d. Notifying the members of the Committee of the case;

e. Requesting additional information from complainants, charged members and others;

f. Presiding over the meetings of the Committee;

g. Preparing and sending, by certified mail, communications to the complainant and charged member on the recommendations and decisions of the Committee; and

h. Arranging for legal advice with assistance and financial approval of the ACA Executive Director.

Section F
Jurisdiction

1. The Committee will consider whether individuals have violated the ACA Code of Ethics if those individuals

a. Are current members of the American Counseling Association or

b. Were ACA members when the alleged violations occurred.

2. Ethics committees of divisions, branches, corporate affiliates, or other ACA entities must refer all ethical complaints involving ACA members to the Committee.

Section G
Eligibility to File Complaints

1. The Committee will receive complaints that ACA members have violated one or more sections of the ACA Code of Ethics from the following individuals:

a. Any individuals who have reason to believe that ACA members have violated the ACA Code of Ethics.

b. ACA members, or members of other helping professions, who have reason to believe that other ACA members have violated the ACA Code of Ethics.

c. The Co-Chair of the Committee on behalf of the ACA membership when the Co-Chair has reason to believe through information received by the Committee that ACA members have violated the ACA Code of Ethics.

d. Ethics committees of divisions, branches, corporate affiliates, or other ACA entities as provided for in Section F.2. above.

2. If possible, individuals should attempt to resolve complaints directly with charged members before filing ethical complaints.

Section H
Time Lines

1. The time lines in these standards are guidelines only and have been established to provide a reasonable time framework for processing complaints.

2. Complainants or charged members may request extensions of deadlines when appropriate. Extensions of deadlines will be granted by the Committee only when justified by unusual circumstance.

Section I
Nature of Communication

1. Only written communications regarding ethical complaints against members will be acceptable. If telephone inquiries are received regarding the filing of complaints, responding to complaints, or providing information regarding complaints, the individuals will be informed of the written communication requirement and asked to comply.

2. All correspondence related to an ethical complaint must be addressed to the Ethics Committee, ACA Headquarters, 5999 Stevenson Avenue, Alexandria, VA 22304 and must be marked "confidential." This process is necessary to protect the confidentiality of the complainant and the charged member.

Section J
Filing Complaints

1. Only written complaints, signed by complainants, will be considered.

2. Individuals eligible to file complaints will send a letter outlining the nature of the complaint to the Committee at the ACA Headquarters. The complaint should include, if possible, (a) the name and address of the

complainant, (b) the name and address of the charged member, (c) the names and addresses of any other persons who have knowledge of the facts involved, and (d) a brief description of the reason why the complaint is being filed.

3. The ACA staff liaison to the Committee will communicate in writing with complainants. Receipt of complaints and confirmation of membership status of charged members as defined in Section F.1 will be acknowledged to the complainant. Proposed formal complaints will be sent to complainants after receipt of complaints have been acknowledged.

4. If the complaint does not involve a member as defined in Section F.1., above, the staff liaison shall inform the complainant.

5. The ACA staff liaison shall assign the complaint to a Co-Chair to determine whether the complaint, if true, would violate one or more sections of the Code of Ethics or if the complaint could be properly decided if accepted. If not, the complaint will be forwarded to the other Co-Chair for review, as if a new complaint. If both Co-Chairs determine that a complaint would not violate one or more sections of the Code of Ethics or if the complaint could not be properly decided if accepted, then the complaint will not be accepted and the complainant shall be notified.

6. If the Committee Co-Chair administering the complaint determines that there is insufficient information to make a fair determination of whether the behavior alleged in the complaint would be cause for action by the Committee, the ACA staff liaison may request further information from the complainant or others. They shall be given thirty (30) working days from receipt of the request to respond.

7. When complaints are accepted, complainants will be informed that copies of the formal complaints plus evidence and documents submitted in support of the complaint will be provided to the charged member and that the complainant must authorize release of such information to the charged member before the complaint process may proceed.

8. The ACA staff liaison, after receiving approval of the Committee Co-Chair administering a complaint, will formulate a formal complaint which will be presented to the complainant for his or her signature.

a. The correspondence from complainants will be received, and the staff liaison and Committee Co-Chair administering the complaint will identify all ACA Code of Ethics that might have been violated if the accusations are true.

b. The formal complaint will be sent to complainants with a copy of these Policies and Procedures, a copy of the ACA Code of Ethics, a verification affidavit form and an authorization and release of information form. Complainants will be asked to sign and return the completed complaint, verification affidavit and authorization and release of information forms. It will be explained to complainants that sections of the codes that might have been violated may be added or deleted by the complainant before signing the formal statement.

c. If complainants elect to add or delete sections of the Code of Ethics in the formal complaint, the unsigned formal complaint shall be returned to ACA Headquarters with changes noted, and a revised formal complaint will be sent to the complainants for their signature.

9. When the completed formal complaint, verification affidavit form and authorization and release of information form are presented to the complainant for signature, he or she will be asked to submit all evidence and documents he or she wishes to be considered by the Committee in reviewing the complaint. The complainant shall submit all evidence and documentation in support of the claim within thirty (30) days of filing the formal complaint. The Committee may accept, at its discretion, evidence or documentation submitted late if good cause is shown.

SECTION K
NOTICE TO CHARGED MEMBERS

1. Once signed formal complaints have been received, charged members will be sent a copy of the formal complaint by U.S. mail, certified, with return-receipt requested, a copy of these Policies and Procedures, a copy of the Code of Ethics, notification of their right to request a hearing, (including the time limit within which to request the hearing, and that the failure to request a hearing within the time limit constitutes a waiver of the hearing), ACA's policy of disclosing adverse actions to its members and/or informing state and national licensure boards of a member's suspension or expulsion, and copies of all evidence and documents submitted in support of the complaint.

2. Charged members will be asked to respond to the complaint against them by addressing each section of the ACA Code of Ethics they have been accused of having violated. They will be informed that if they wish to respond they must do so in writing within sixty (60) working days.

3. Charged members will be informed that they must submit all evidence and documents they wish to be considered by the Committee in reviewing the complaint within sixty (60) working days.

4. After charged members have received notification that a complaint has been brought against them, they will be given sixty (60) working days to notify the Committee Co-Chair (via ACA Headquarters) in writing, by certified mail, if they wish to request a formal face-to-face hearing before the Committee. Charged members may waive their right to a formal hearing before the Committee and shall

sign a waiver of the right to a hearing. (See Section O: Hearings).

5. If the Committee Co-Chair determines that there is insufficient information to make a fair determination of whether the behavior alleged in the complaint would be cause for action by the Committee, the ACA staff liaison to the Committee may request further information from the charged member or others. They shall be given thirty (30) working days from receipt of the request to respond.

6. All requests for additional information from others will be accompanied by a verification affidavit form which the information provider will be asked to complete and return.

7. The Committee may, in its discretion, delay or postpone its review of the case with good cause including if the Committee wishes to obtain additional information. The charged member may request in writing that the Committee delay or postpone its review of the case for good cause.

SECTION L
DISPOSITION OF COMPLAINTS

1. After receiving the responses from charged members, Committee members will be provided copies of (a) the complaint, (b) supporting evidence and documents sent to charged members, (c) the response, and (d) supporting evidence and documents provided by charged members and others.

2. Decisions will be rendered based on the evidence and documents provided by the complainant and charged member or others.

3. The Committee Co-Chair administering a complaint will not participate in deliberations or decisions regarding that particular complaint.

4. At the next meeting of the Committee held no sooner than fifteen (15) working days after members received copies of documents related to a complaint, the Committee will discuss the complaint, response, and supporting documentation, if any, and determine the outcome of the complaint.

5. The Committee will determine whether each Code of Ethics the member has been accused of having violated was violated based on the information provided.

6. After deliberations, the Committee may decide to dismiss the complaint or to dismiss charges within the complaint.

7. In the event it is determined that any of the ACA Codes of Ethics have been violated, the Committee will impose for the entire complaint one or a combination of the possible sanctions allowed.

SECTION M
WITHDRAWAL OF COMPLAINTS

1. If the complainant and charged member

both agree to discontinue the complaint process, the Committee may, at its discretion, complete the adjudication process if available evidence indicates that this is warranted. The Co-Chair of the Committee, on behalf of the ACA membership, shall act as complainant.

SECTION N
POSSIBLE SANCTIONS

1. Remedial requirements may be stipulated by the Committee.

2. Probation for a specified period of time subject to Committee review of compliance. Remedial requirements may be imposed to be completed within a specified period of time.

3. Suspension from ACA membership for a specified period of time subject to Committee review of compliance. Remedial requirements may be imposed to be completed within a specified period of time.

4. Permanent expulsion from ACA membership. This sanction requires a unanimous vote of those voting.

5. The penalty for failing to satisfactorily fulfill a remedial requirement imposed by the Committee as a result of a probation sanction will be automatic suspension until the requirement is met unless the Committee determines that the remedial requirement should be modified based on good cause shown prior to the end of the probationary period.

6. The penalty for failing to satisfactorily fulfill a remedial requirement imposed by the Committee as a result of a suspension sanction will be automatic permanent expulsion unless the Committee determines that the remedial requirement should be modified based on good cause shown prior to the end of the suspension period.

7. Other corrective action.

SECTION O
HEARINGS

1. At the discretion of the Committee, a hearing may be conducted when the results of the Committee's preliminary determination indicate that additional information is needed.

2. When charged members, within sixty (60) working days of notification of the complaint, request a formal face-to-face or telephone conference hearing before the Committee, a hearing shall be conducted. (See Section K.6.)

3. The charged member shall bear all their expenses associated with attendance at hearings requested by the charged member.

4. The Committee Co-Chair shall schedule a formal hearing on the case at the next scheduled Committee meeting and notify both the complainant and the charged member of their right to attend the hearing in person or by telephone conference call.

5. The hearing will be held before a panel made up of the Committee and, if the charged member chooses, a representative of the charged member's primary Division. This representative will be identified by the Division President and will have voting privileges.

SECTION P
HEARING PROCEDURES

1. Purpose.

a. A hearing will be conducted to determine whether a breach of the Code of Ethics has occurred and, if so, to determine appropriate disciplinary action.

b. The Committee will be guided in its deliberations by principles of basic fairness and professionalism and will keep its deliberations as confidential as possible except as provided herein.

2. Notice.

a. The charged members shall be advised in writing by the Co-Chair administering the complaint of the time and place of the hearing, the list of any witnesses expected to testify at the hearing against the charged member (which list may not be complete), and the charges involved at least forty-five (45) working days before the hearing. A copy of the notification shall be sent to the complainant. Notice shall include a formal statement of the complaints lodged against the charged member and supporting evidence.

b. The charged member is under no duty to respond to the notice, but the Committee will not be obligated to delay or postpone its hearing unless the charged member so requests in writing with good cause received at least fifteen (15) working days in advance. In the absence of such 15-day advance notice and postponement by the Committee, if the charged member fails to appear at the hearing, the Committee shall decide the complaint on record. Failure of the charged member to appear at the hearing shall not be viewed by the Committee as sufficient grounds alone for taking disciplinary action.

3. Conduct of the Hearing.

a. Accommodations. The location of the hearing shall be determined at the discretion of the Committee. The Committee shall provide a private room to conduct the hearing, and no observers or recording devices other than a recording device used by the Committee shall be permitted.

b. Presiding Officer. The Co-Chair in charge of the case shall preside over the hearing and deliberations of the Committee. At the conclusion of the hearing and deliberations, the Co-Chair shall promptly notify the charged member and complainant of the Committee's decision in writing as provided in Section Q., Paragraphs 1 and 2, below.

c. Record. A record of the hearing shall be made and preserved, together with any documents presented in evidence, at ACA Headquarters for a period of three (3) years or until the complaint process is final, whichever is longer. The record shall consist of a summary of testimony received or a verbatim transcript at the discretion of the Committee.

d. Right to Counsel. The charged member shall be entitled to have legal counsel present to advise and represent him or her throughout the hearing. Legal counsel for ACA shall also be present at the hearing to advise the Committee and shall have the privilege of the floor.

e. Witnesses. Either party shall have the right to call witnesses to substantiate his or her version of the case.

f. The Committee shall have the right to call witnesses it believes may provide further insight into the matter. ACA shall, in its sole discretion, determine the number and identity of witnesses to be heard.

g. Witnesses shall not be present during the hearing except when testifying and shall be excused upon completion of their testimony and any cross-examination.

h. The Co-Chair administering the complaint shall allow questions of any witness by the opposition or members of the Committee if such questions and testimony are relevant to the issues in the case.

i. The Co-Chair administering the complaint will determine what questions and testimony are relevant to the case. Should the hearing be disturbed by irrelevant testimony, the Co-Chair administering the complaint may call a brief recess to restore order.

j. All expenses associated with counsel on behalf of the parties shall be borne by the respective parties. All expenses associated with witnesses on behalf of the charged member shall be borne by the charged member when the charged member requests a hearing. If the Committee requests the hearing, all expenses associated with witnesses shall be borne by ACA.

4. Presentation of Evidence

a. The staff liaison or the Co-Chair administering the complaint shall be called upon first to present the charge(s) against the charged member and to briefly describe the supporting evidence. The person presenting the charges shall also be responsible for examining and cross-examining witnesses on behalf of the complainant and for otherwise presenting the matter during the hearing.

b. The complainant or the staff liaison or the Committee Co-Chair administering the complaint shall then present the case against the charged member. Witnesses who can substantiate the case may be called upon to testify and answer questions of the charged member and the Committee.

c. If the charged member is present at the hearing, he or she shall be called upon after the case has been presented against the charged member to present any evidence which refutes the charges against him or her. This includes witnesses as in Subsection (3) above. The charged member and the complainant may submit a written statment at the close of the hearing.

d. The charged member will not be found guilty simply for refusing to testify. Once the charged member chooses to testify, however, he or she may be cross-examined by the complainant and members of the Committee.

e. The Committee will endeavor to conclude the hearing within a period of approximately three (3) hours. The parties will be requested to be considerate of this time frame in planning their testimony. If it appears that additional time will be needed to develop the issues adequately, an extension of time may be granted.

f. Testimony that is merely cumulative or repetitious may, at the discretion of the Co-Chair administering the complaint, be excluded.

g. At any time during the presentation of evidence, the presiding members of the Committee may ask pertinent questions.

5. Relevancy of Evidence.

a. The Hearing Committee is not a court of law and is not required to observe formal rules of evidence. Evidence inadmissible in a court of law may be admissible in the hearing before the Committee if it is relevant to the case. That is, if the evidence offered tends to explain, clarify, or refute any of the important facts of the case, it should be generally be considered.

b. The Committee will not consider evidence or testimony for the purpose of supporting any charge that was not set forth in the notice of the hearing or that is not relevant to the issues of the case.

6. Burden of Proof.

a. The burden of proving a violation of the Code of Ethics is on the complainant and/or the Committee. It is not up to the charged member to prove his or her innocence of any wrong-doing.

b. Although the charge(s) need not be proved "beyond a reasonable doubt," the Committee will not find the charged member guilty in the absence of substantial, objective, and believable evidence to sustain the charge(s).

7. Deliberation of the Committee.

a. After the hearing is completed, the Committee shall meet in a closed session to review the evidence presented and reach a conclusion. ACA legal counsel may attend the closed session to advise the Committee if the Committee so desires.

b. The Committee shall be the sole trier of the facts and shall weigh the evidence presented and assess the credibility of the witnesses. The act of a majority of the members of the Committee present shall be the decision of the Committee. An unanimous vote of those voting is required for permanent expulsion from ACA membership.

c. Only members of the Committee who were present throughout the entire hearing shall be eligible to vote.

8. Decision of the Committee.

a. The Committee will first resolve the issue of the guilt or innocence of the charged member on each charge. Applying the burden of proof in subsection (5) above, the Committee will vote by secret ballot unless the members of the Committee consent to an oral vote.

b. In the event a majority of the members of the Committee do not find the charged member guilty, the charges shall be dismissed. If the Committee finds the charged member has violated the Code of Ethics, it must then determine what sanctions, in accordance with Section N: Possible Sanctions, shall be imposed.

c. As provided in Section Q below, the Co-Chair administering the complaint shall notify the charged member and complainant of the Committee's decision and rights to appeal in writing.

SECTION Q
NOTIFICATION OF RESULTS

1. Charged members shall be notified of Committee decisions regarding complaints against them. Within thirty (30) days after the hearing, charged members shall be notified of the Committee's decisions and their right to appeal. The Committee's decision shall be sent by U.S. mail, certified, with return-receipt requested.

2. After the deadline for filing an appeal, or in the event an appeal is filed, after a decision on appeals has been rendered, and if a violation has been found and charged members have been suspended or expelled, counselor licensure, certification, or registry boards, other mental health licensure, certification, or registry boards, voluntary national certification boards, and appropriate professional associations will also be notified of the results. In addition, ACA divisions, state branches, the ACA Insurance Trust, and other ACA-related entities will also be notified of the results.

3. After the deadline for filing an appeal, or in the event an appeal is filed, after a decision on appeals has been rendered, and if a violation has been found and charged members have been suspended or expelled, a notice of the Committee's action that includes the sections of the ACA Code of Ethics that were found to have been violated and the sanctions imposed will be published in the ACA newsletter.

SECTION R
APPEALS

1. Decisions of the ACA Ethics Committee may be appealed by the member found to have been in violation based on one or both of the following grounds:

a. The Committee violated its policies and procedures for processing complaints of ethical violations; and/or

b. The decision of the Committee was arbitrary and capricious and was not supported by the materials provided by the complainant and charged member.

2. After members have received notification that they have been found in violation of one or more ACA Codes of Ethics, they will be given thirty (30) working days to notify the Committee in writing by certified mail that they are appealing the decision. If an appeal is not requested, the Committee shall issue its decision as the final decision as soon as the time during which an appeal may be filed expires.

3. An appeal may consist only of a letter stating one or both of the grounds of appeal listed in subsection 1 above and the reasons for the appeal. The filing of an appeal automatically stays the execution of a decision by the Committee until the appeal is completed.

4. The appealing member will be asked to identify the primary ACA division to which he or she belongs. The ACA President will appoint a three (3) person appeals panel consisting of two (2) former ACA Ethics Committee Chairs (neither of whom served on the Committee during the hearings on the matter) and the President of the identified division. The ACA attorney shall serve as legal advisor and have the privilege of the floor.

5. The three (3) member appeals panel will be given copies of the materials available to the Committee when it made its decision, a copy of the hearing record if a hearing was held, plus a copy of the letter filed by the appealing member.

6. The appeals panel will not consider evidence that was not presented to the Committee.

7. The appeals panel generally will render its decision regarding an appeal requiring a majority vote within sixty (60) working days of their receipt of the above materials.

8. The decision of the appeals panel is limited to

a. Upholding the decision of the Committee, or

b. Upholding the decision of the Committee on the finding of an ethical violation but reversing and remanding the Committee's decision on sanctions, or

c. Recommending reconsideration by the Committee of the decision providing guidance to the Committee in detail in writing for considering a new decision on remand.

9. The decision of the appeals panel need not be unanimous.

10. When a Committee decision is reversed and remanded, the complainant and charged member will be informed in writing, and addi-

tional information may be requested first from the complainant and then from the charged member. The Committee will then render another decision without a hearing.

11. Decisions of the appeals panel to uphold the Committee decision are final and binding and not subject to further hearings or appellate review.

SECTION S
SUBSTANTIAL NEW EVIDENCE

1. In the event substantial new evidence is presented in a case in which an appeal was not filed, or in a case for which a final decision has been rendered, the case may be reopened by the Committee.

2. The Committee will consider substantial new evidence and if found to be substantiated and capable of exonerating a member who was expelled, the Committee will reopen the case and go through the entire complaint process again.

SECTION T
RECORDS

1. The records of the Committee regarding complaints are confidential except as provided herein.

2. Original copies of complaint records will be maintained in locked files at ACA Headquarters or at an off-site location chosen by ACA.

3. Members of the Committee will keep copies of complaint records confidential and will destroy copies of records after a case has been closed or when they are no longer a member of the Committee.

SECTION U
LEGAL ACTIONS RELATED TO COMPLAINTS

1. Complainants and charged members are required to notify the Committee if they learn of any type of legal action (civil or criminal) being filed related to the complaint.

2. In the event any type of legal action is filed regarding an accepted complaint, all actions related to the complaint will be stayed until the legal action has been concluded. The Committee will consult with legal counsel concerning whether the processing of the complaint will be stayed if the legal action does not involve the same complainant and the same facts complained of.

3. If actions on a complaint are stayed, the complainant and charged member will be notified.

4. When actions on a complaint are continued after a legal action has been concluded, the complainant and charged member will be notified.

ACA Divisions

AACE	Association for Assessment in Counseling and Education
	Publication: *Measurement and Evaluation in Counseling & Development*
AADA	Association for Adult Development and Aging
	Publication: *AADA Newsletter, Adultspan*
ACCA	American College Counseling Association
	Publication: *Journal of College Counseling*
ACEG	Association for Counselors and Educators in Government
ACES	Association for Counselor Education & Supervision
	Publication: *Counselor Education and Supervision*
AGLBIC	Association for Gay, Lesbian and Bisexual Issues in Counseling
AMCD	Association for Multicultural Counseling and Development
	Publication: *Journal of Multicultural Counseling and Development*
AMHCA	American Mental Health Counselors Association
	Publication: *Journal of Mental Health Counseling*
ARCA	American Rehabilitation Counseling Association
	Publication: *Rehabilitation Counseling Bulletin*
ASCA	American School Counselor Association
	Publication: *Professional School Counseling*
ASERVIC	Association for Spiritual, Ethical and Religious Values in Counseling
	Publication: *Counseling and Values*
ASGW	Association for Specialists in Group Work
	Publication: *Journal for Specialists in Group Work*
C-AHEAD	Counseling Association for Humanistic Education and Development
	Publication: *Journal for Humanistic Counseling Education and Development*
CSJ	Counselors for Social Justice
IAAOC	International Association of Addictions and Offender Counselors
	Publication: *Journal of Addictions and Offender Counseling*
IAMFC	International Association of Marriage and Family Counselors
	Publication: *The Family Journal: Counseling & Therapy for Couples & Families*
NCDA	National Career Development Association
	Publication: *The Career Development Quarterly*
NECA	National Employment Counseling Association
	Publication: *Journal of Employment Counseling*

Index